HEADS

HEADS

A Biography of Psychedelic America

JESSE JARNOW

DA CAPO PRESS
A Member of the Perseus Books Group

Designed by Jeff Williams

Set in 10.5-point Guardi LT by The Perseus Books Group

Library of Congress Cataloging-in-Publication Data

Names: Jarnow, Jesse.
Title: Heads : a biography of psychedelic America / Jesse Jarnow.
Description: Philadelphia, PA : Da Capo Press, 2015. | Includes
bibliographical references and index.
Identifiers: LCCN 2015036408| ISBN 9780306822551 (hardcover : alk. paper) |
ISBN 9780306822568 (e-book : alk. paper)
Subjects: LCSH: Grateful Dead (Musical group) | Deadheads (Music
fans)—United States. | Rock music—Social aspects—United States. |
Hallucinogenic drugs—Social aspects—United States—History—20th
century. | Counterculture—United States—History—20th century.
Classification: LCC ML421.G72 J37 2015 | DDC 782.42166092/2—dc23 LC
record available at http://lccn.loc.gov/2015036408

Published by Da Capo Press

A Member of the Perseus Books Group

www.dacapopress.com

Da Capo Press books are available at special discounts for bulk purchases in the
U.S. by corporations, institutions, and other organizations. For more information,
please contact the Special Markets Department at the Perseus Books Group, 2300
Chestnut Street, Suite 200, Philadelphia, PA 19103, or call (800) 810-4145, ext.
5000, or e-mail special.markets@perseusbooks.com.

10 9 8 7 6 5 4 3 2 1

For

Jill and Al
Lois and Mel
Jeanette and Al Sr.

and

Fisher and Millet
because I promised

Contents

THE LONG RENAISSANCE

One fun activity to try at home is to declare a *psychedelic renaissance*. In the United States today, those words might conjure any number of university-funded research projects demonstrating the extraordinary power of substances like psilocybin and LSD to dissolve cluster headaches or treat posttraumatic stress disorder or provide spiritual well-being in the face of terminal illness.

Perhaps the phrase describes the spread of ayahuasca ceremonies into fashionable urban areas and the realms of cinematic satire. Maybe the words recall the annual slate of conferences and symposiums devoted to the mysteries of LSD, aya, mushrooms, ibogaine, DMT, 2C-B, and other substances, new and old. Or the annual conclaves at Burning Man and elsewhere that provide temporary physical community for a vast and learned psychonautical diaspora. Or new websites that condense the ancient and still mysterious substances into clean-seeming infographics, hashtags, and easily sharable quote-memes.

The phrase, too, is shorthand for the way the perception of psychedelics has gradually changed within American and global culture, transforming from *drugs* into *medicine*. The psychedelic renaissance comes supported by solid above-board scientists (no rogue Tim Learys here) and fashion magazines extolling the virtues of a good ayahuasca cleanse to achieve that *extra* glow, as *Elle* suggested in 2014. Indeed, when the phrase "psychedelic renaissance" is uttered, it acts (in part) as linguistic incense that might cloak the hairy, unchecked madness of the sixties. It carries the promise that *this* generation will be different.

Some no longer even use the word "psychedelic"—the term patched together by Humphry Osmond in 1957 from ancient Greek to mean "mind-manifesting"—preferring the nomenclature "entheogen," spirit manifested within. Others like just plain "sacrament."

In 2015, Thomas Roberts—the eminent professor responsible for the celebration of Bicycle Day, the anniversary of LSD inventor Albert Hofmann's first trip—outlined a four-stage model of psychedelic renaissance: medical neuroscientific, spiritual religious, intellectual artistic, and mind design. And although vast strides have been made in all those phases since the turn of the twenty-first century, few outside of the medical-neuroscientific phase have been nearly as remarkable or on as broad a scale as what happened in the half century previous.

Real renaissances (or at least the actual Renaissance) are long. By the early 1970s, psychedelics had already significantly and quantifiably transformed American spirituality, art, music, technology, countless individuals, and society as a whole. Their wide arrival was also a powerful accelerator in the century-running culture war that continues to cleave the American population. To many, the world of psychedelics remains an irresponsible fantasy. Still, the threads have danced around one another for decades, and now Roberts's four phases have started to align into unity for the first time since the drugs were made illegal in 1966.

Despite its attempt to bypass the past, the psychedelic renaissance didn't begin when the government again approved laboratory trials for psychedelics in the early twenty-first century, but the moment in the 1950s when psychedelics escaped the laboratory to begin with, ready for open minds. For more than fifty years, psychedelics have circulated through the American body controlled not by doctor or shaman or government agent but by the independent desire of the users (and the ever-gurgling black market). They have never stopped or gone away so much as just taken a while to kick in—and sometimes out.

If one wants to learn how psychedelics might change American society, it is only necessary to study the second half of the twentieth century to see how they already have. Perhaps equally fun as declaring a psychedelic renaissance at home is to set forth on a local anthropological expedition to discover a practitioner or descendent of the United States' largest psychedelic cult.

For three decades, the California band the Grateful Dead were not so much a religion as a doorway. They and their Deadhead followers provided the space that connected psychedelics to the mainstream narrative, visible evidence both of the drugs' wondrous catalytic potential and their inherent dangers. This story is a narrative carried by many people, some individual, some in groups, some for short periods, some for long, some consciously, some not, but their codes remain understood among a large segment of the population.

As multiple surveys of American LSD users discovered in the early '90s—the drug's post-1960s peak—most are white, and perhaps up to 76 percent are male. That balance is mirrored somewhat in the long arc of the substance's American history. Which isn't to say the story of the heads is exclusively male. It was psychedelic-inspired longhaired communard-utopians who began the natural childbirth movement in the United States, for example, and it sure wasn't the dudes who were responsible. Starting in the 1990s, especially as the psychedelic world came to encompass far more than LSD, the gender balance began to shift again.

Moment by moment, it is a story of how psychedelics—the actual substances—landed and circulated in the bohemian centers of San Francisco and New York, and of the complex secret society that emerged, the shadow economies that came into circulation, and the new sacred practices. And it is a story of how psychedelics—both the idea itself and the ideas they provoked—disseminated into the American consciousness long beyond the sixties, and how these ideas would eventually play out in the daily life of entire regions of the country.

Together, they make an ethnographic comic book history. Some episodes and characters overlap and directly intertwine, many don't. Exploring the territory in approximated real-time, the inner maps of psychedelia are vast and alluring, but so are the outer ones.

PART ONE

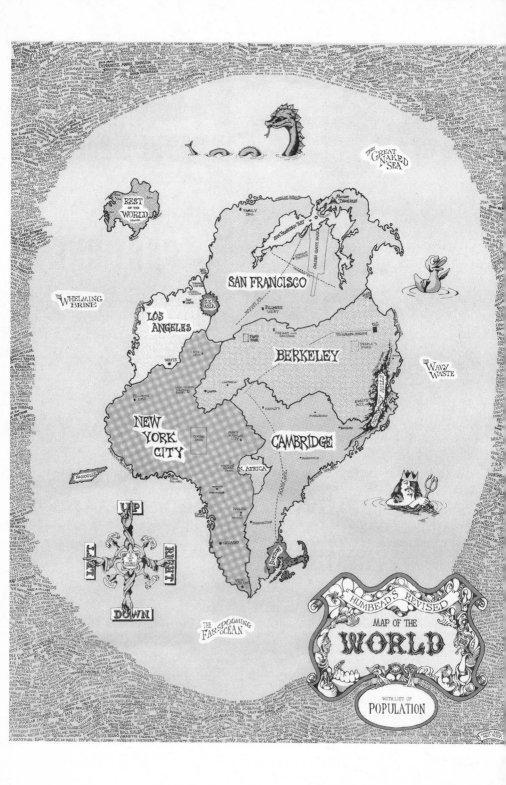

1

HUMBEAD'S REVISED MAP OF THE WORLD

The cafe is identified by the monkeys in the window and the metal shape wrapped in tin foil dangling over the Manhattan side street. People around the East Village call the place the Dollar Sign. Peter Stampfel hears that sometimes the monkeys can be seen fucking in their cage, though he never verifies this. One day in late 1959, however, the young folk musician goes inside to determine the truthfulness of the sign advertising peyote for sale.

The hallucinogenic cactus has been around the Village for a few years, though not exactly available. "The cool thing to do when I got to New York was to take peyote and go see [the Brazilian film] *Black Orpheus*," remembers Stampfel, then a fresh-faced twenty-one-year-old transplant from Wisconsin. He'd heard about the visionary plant from a classmate and soon read Allen Ginsberg's epic poem *Howl*, written partially under the influence of peyote few years earlier. But Peter Stampfel had never been able to get any for himself. It is for this reason that both he and the Dollar Sign's owner are pioneers, exemplars of two new kinds of humans: a modern psychedelic drug buyer and a modern psychedelic drug dealer. The advertised goods aren't illegal, but, for the first time, they are on the loose.

Inside the cafe, Stampfel would believe the story about the monkeys. The proprietor is a large man, burly and bearded. Despite the fact that it's November, the man is also barefoot. Stampfel remembers

3

Barron Bruchlos as "a psychotic, crazed Ayn Rand guy." Hence the tin foil–wrapped dollar sign. The owner splits a pay phone outside into three separate extensions, two for his adjacent cafes on East Sixth Street and one to his nearby basement apartment. The twenty-seven-year-old Bruchlos—a Harvard man, actually—is a true entrepreneur and right at home in Manhattan's East Village, a neighborhood of freethinkers. The poet Allen Ginsberg's place, a perpetual node on several dozen underground networks, is a few blocks away.

The hallucinogenic cactus peyote had surfaced several times in the Village since the turn of the twentieth century, usually leaving its mark in the form of one or two chaotic but isolated bohemian parties. After the gang at the San Remo bar discovered they could order it cash on delivery from a pair of companies in Laredo, Texas, it circulated semiwidely throughout the neighborhood. A legendary all-night Halloween bash ensued. It was through the San Remo crowd that Allen Ginsberg had turned on before writing *Howl.* And this is how the Dollar Sign's Barron Bruchlos gets his peyote, too, mail ordering from Laredo, grinding it up, and repackaging it for sale like the enterprising fellow he is.

From Bruchlos, Peter Stampfel purchases a bundle of the molasses-colored double-O capsules—one peyote button per cap—brings them home, and splits them with his roommate. They hang out for a while and eventually Stampfel lies down. "I hadn't really closed my eyes up to this point," he says. Then he does.

"The closed-eye hallucinations were the most beautiful shit I'd ever seen in my life. I was very fixated on the combination of blue and green, and had a long period of blue and green interactions which were of an awesome, devastating, constantly changing beauty. At a point it changed to purple and orange in a combination that I'd never really considered. It made all the great art I'd seen in my life seem second rate."

One part of Stampfel's experience is very new; another is very, very old. Peyote and its plant relatives have been in active use in North America for millennia, most recently in northeastern Mexico and the Trans-Pecos area of Texas by groups with well-established practices. Though the westward spread of European occupiers has done much to suppress indigenous settlers, a network of Native American peyote groups thrives. Across the Rio Grande, the

Mexican town of Nuevo Laredo sustains itself predominantly on its income from peyote sales, partly mail order but mostly to branches of the Native American Church. Westerners have consumed it on occasion for centuries, including Civil War prisoners who distilled it into a drink in lieu of whiskey, as well in numerous patent medicines, but none reacted the way Peter Stampfel and his friends do.

The British physiologist W. E. Dixon's 1899 account of his own unguided mescal journey, however, meshes perfectly what happens to Peter Stampfel in his East Village apartment sixty years later: "After sitting with closed eyes subjectively examining the color visions, on suddenly opening them for a brief space one seems to be a different self, as on waking from a dream we pass into a different world from that in which we have been."

The place Peter Stampfel has just returned from has been there forever, though it is not often that visitors stumble in without a guide. There is no one to tell him what he just saw. There is no one to tell him what to do. For Peter Stampfel and others like him, it is an empty shore in a seemingly unsettled place.

Just a few years earlier, the psychiatrist Humphry Osmond created the term "psychedelic"—"mind-manifesting"—from ancient Greek. Though it wasn't immediately clear, the word described a concept as old as society, a continent-skipping chronological path from the *kykeon*-gobbling Greeks of the Eleusinian mystery cult to the ayahuasca brewers in South American jungles. In these places and elsewhere, substance-induced transcendental experiences formed the center of important societal functions for generations.

By the time Peter Stampfel eats peyote and Barron Bruchlos's customers at the Dollar Sign are tripping their way through sleepy Greenwich Village, psychedelics are sprouting across the Cold War landscape like miniature Technicolor mushroom clouds. Experiments brew everywhere. In 1938, the Swiss chemist Albert Hofmann had stumbled on his own entry into the cosmos via lysergic acid diethylamide, LSD-25, which he ingested for the first time five years later. Unclear about its correct usage from the very start, pharmaceutical company Sandoz had marketed it to psychologists in hopes they might find one. From there, it leaks into the broader world.

The British philosopher Aldous Huxley had set off an interest in mind experimentation with his 1953 book *The Doors of Perception,* his own first trip report with mescaline. Word of LSD, mushrooms, and other psychedelics spread through the major media over the course of the 1950s. It is entirely possible that Barron Bruchlos learned how to get peyote in the pages of the underground publication known as *Life* magazine, circulation 5,700,000, which had published an improbable and mostly true account of the American banker R. Gordon Wasson's psilocybin escapades in Mexico.

In response to Wasson's *Life* cover story, "The Discovery of Mushrooms That Cause Strange Visions," a reader named Jane Ross writes in about the goods she, too, had acquired via mail order from Laredo. "Sirs: I've been having hallucinatory visions accompanied by space suspension and time destruction in my New York City apartment for the past three years," she writes. Another magazine discovers that, for a time, it's even possible to acquire mescaline as an over-the-counter patent medicine without a prescription at a chain drugstore in Manhattan, though there is little evidence anyone makes good on this.

But LSD, with its eight-to-twelve hours of tripping time and minuscule dose size, is a special object of interest to many. Since 1951, the rogue Captain Al Hubbard has repurposed supplies for his own use, seeding projects that use the drug to treat alcoholism and guiding hand-selected initiates through their first experiences. The CIA diddles with acid and mind control in its supersecret MKUltra program, with psychedelics shooting out to VA hospitals and irresponsible agents across the country. Not long before Peter Stampfel's first peyote excursion at the Dollar Sign, heartthrob Cary Grant appeared in *Look,* testifying to the healing power of LSD. Mind-manifestation is afoot in these United States.

Peter Stampfel's experience differs from all who came before in one crucial way: he'd sought no special pass to acquire his psychedelics. Before the Dollar Sign and its nameless Village brethren, one had to qualify in some way—by tribal affiliation, forward-thinking therapist, social network, the knowledge of that certain PO box in Laredo, or sheer determination. The peyote had simply manifested itself in Peter Stampfel's path, in his neighborhood.

All he'd done was navigate Manhattan's chilly November avenues to 306 East Sixth Street, duck into the Dollar Sign, hand a few dollars to Bruchlos, and walk out, no questions asked. He can even go back. For perhaps the first time in known human history, psychedelics are readily available to the customer who might wish to acquire them. Stampfel discovers that there's LSD around and mescaline, too.

There is a word for people like Stampfel, something that distinguishes him from the general population. It had slipped into the language in a 1952 *Time* magazine story. "I'm higher than a giraffe's toupee," an eighteen-year old Hollywood girl told police when she was arrested for smoking pot. "Everybody's a head now," she clarified for a reporter the next day. "One out of every five persons you meet on the street are heads."

"Hop heads" has been in pejorative circulation since the turn of the century. But lately the varieties multiply with a quickness. In the East Village, there are pot heads, amphetamine heads, meth heads, and relentless dabblers like Stampfel who require no prefix to describe their inclinations.

Carrying this basic initiation code, the heads connect and reconnect across a bohemian circuit of folk clubs, coffee houses, music shops, bookstores, shared apartments, and crash pads established by poets and guitar slingers before them. It sprawls from the City Lights bookstore in San Francisco's North Beach to college scenes like Dinkytown in Minneapolis and the ivy byways of Cambridge.

Peter Stampfel ping-pongs across the continent on his way to recording songs that will carry the psychedelic word to the people. He's in Los Angeles for a little while, San Francisco, New York, San Francisco again, playing the clubs wherever he goes. He recalls a joke going around to describe the closeness of the coasts: "Three beatniks get into a car in North Beach and one of them says, 'Let me sit on the outside, I'm getting off at MacDougal Street.'" The United States becomes a *Mad* magazine fold-in.

By early 1960, the Dollar Sign is in full swing. At eight dollars for one hundred buttons COD from Laredo, turned into caps and sold for sixty to eighty cents each, proprietor Barron Bruchlos clears a fantastic profit. "Do you want coffee or peyote?" he greets his customers.

It's not long before the Food and Drug Administration catches up with the Dollar Sign, sending in undercover agents to buy peyote and then raiding the place. Even though Bruchlos points out the Department of Agriculture seals of approval on his boxes, proving their legality, the agents haul away some 145 capsules and 311 pounds of peyote. No charges are filed, nor does the government make the legal basis of the seizure clear, but a story runs on the UPI wire, popping from papers around the country: "'Lay Off Peyote,' Beatniks Warned."

Word reaches the anthropologist and peyote specialist Weston La Barre at Duke University. He soon visits Bruchlos's newest coffee shop, the Dollar Sign having shut down, and interviews the peyote dealing Bruchlos in his nearby basement abode. If La Barre expects to observe the first stirrings of a colonial psychedelic culture in an East Village basement, he is disappointed—but also looking in the wrong apartment.

The objectivist coffee shop owner complains to La Barre of being ripped off by unscrupulous characters who buy his peyote capsules in bulk and resell them through classified ads in college newspapers. Before La Barre can communicate further, though, Bruchlos is found dead in his basement bedroom.

"Natural causes," the police conclude, but Bruchlos is twenty-eight, and no one quite believes that, including Bruchlos's father. Peter Stampfel hears that it was suicide and a suitably bizarre and grisly one at that, involving (ugh) pencils jammed up the nose. Like the rumors about the monkeys, Peter Stampfel could believe this, too.

But more and more catch on to the business end of psychedelics. There is obviously demand. A black market begins to thrive around college campuses. One chemical supply house in New York sells peyote-derived mescaline to students for thirty-five dollars a gram, more than four times the trade price. LSD-dosed sugar cubes turn up around Harvard Square for a dollar each. In New York, a pair of British expatriates named John Beresford and Michael Hollingshead order a supply of LSD directly from Albert Hofmann at the Sandoz laboratories where the substance was invented two decades previous, batch H-00047. Hollingshead mixes it with confectioner's sugar in a mayonnaise jar, creating a thick paste that contains about 5,000 hits.

After fifteen hours spent tripping on a Greenwich Village roof and a subsequent correspondence with Aldous Huxley, Hollingshead makes his way to Massachusetts. There, at Huxley's recommendation, he looks up the thirty-nine-year-old professor Timothy Leary, whose Harvard Psychedelic Project solidifies Cambridge's spot on the coalescing map of psychedelic America.

The previous summer in Mexico, Leary had been introduced to mushrooms and, not long after his return, initiated the project. He'd had Allen Ginsberg over for a visit, who soon burst down the stairs naked, proclaiming himself God and raving of a network of interconnected minds.

The poet plots to turn on the cream of the underground, from bebop pianists to abstract expressionists. Leary and his partners will make more credible scientific progress. Hollingshead's arrival with LSD will throw chaos into the project, but not yet.

On Good Friday 1962, the Harvard Psychedelic Project produces what becomes known as the Miracle at Marsh Chapel, a double-blind experiment to test the reliability of mushrooms as a source of spiritual ecstasy in those predisposed to religious experiences. Encouraged at first by psychedelic elder Aldous Huxley, there is a brief period of careful elitism. The well-respected, well-heeled Huxley, too, especially encourages Michael Murphy and Richard Price's Esalen Institute on the Pacific cliffs of Big Sur.

In the wild, the heads continue their own investigations. By the turn of the decade, there is evidence of small LSD cults flowering in the Pacific Northwest, using the drug similarly to peyote. "The participants do not belong to the American Indian race, and this gives rise to understandable concern and protests," reads one police report. Disconnected pockets of psychedelic users emerge and a terminology arises. "A 'good head' must always say he is ready to take the drug again, although not necessarily immediately," concludes a chapter on black market LSD users published in 1964. Reads another chapter in the same study, "Hallucinogen users are recognized as propounding special values in their drug use—values which set them apart from the common herd and which, we infer, are hardly shared by the police."

But the practices and beliefs of the American drug religion are still working themselves out. There are brief vogues for morning glory seeds (true, if one takes the right kind) and smoked banana peels (bogus) and the ever-witchy *Atropa belladonna*, better known as deadly nightshade. Recalls Peter Stampfel, "This one friend of mine took some belladonna once and he was walking down the street and he started having a conversation with a parking meter and, after a couple of sentences, the parking meter looked at him and said, 'You know too much.'"

"The only person I ever met who enjoyed belladonna was Steve Weber," Stampfel says of his drug-taking match the pair's brand-new folk duo the Holy Modal Rounders, formed in 1963. When they meet, the two play music for three days straight. In Weber's memory, they are on Benzedrex inhalers. In Stampfel's, it's crystal methedrine. They are the first band of a new breed, overtly inspired by both Harry Smith's *Anthology of American Folk Music* and drugs. Peter Stampfel becomes the first person to use the word "psychedelic" in a recorded song. Released on the Holy Modal Rounders' self-titled debut on Folkways in early 1964, their take on "Hesitation Blues" adds the word to the new musical lexicon.

"It was important to me," Stampfel says of getting the term onto an LP. "I believed, like a bunch of other people, that if Kennedy and Khrushchev took some LSD together, we'd have world peace forever."

Not long after the Holy Modal Rounders' album comes out, Stampfel and Weber are drafted into a new band that is rehearsing at the soon-to-open Peace Eye Bookstore near Tompkins Square Park. The Fugs will champion drugs and many other provocative ideas. One of the Fugs' founders, Ed Sanders, is the editor of *Fuck You / a magazine of the arts,* churned out from a Speed-O-Print mimeograph at Sanders's Secret Location on Avenue A.

"A CALL TO ACTION" reads the first page of issue #10, published in the spring of 1964, written out in Sanders's hieroglyphic-inspired calligraphy. "STOMP OUT THE MARIJUANA LAWS FOREVER."

"INTO THE OPEN!" part of the text reads. "ALL THOSE WHO SUCK UP THE BENEVOLENT NARCOTA MARIJUANA, TEEENSHUN! FORWARD, WITH MIND DIALS POINTED: *ASSAULT!* We have the facts! Cannabis is a non-addictive gentle peace drug! The Marijuana legislations were pushed through in the 1930's by the agents and goonsquads of the jansenisto-manichaean fuckhaters' Conspiracy. Certainly, after 30 years of the blight, it is time to rise up for a bleep blop bleep assault on the social screen."

The Fugs sing about LSD on their first album, too, in a song called "Couldn't Get High," but their forte is vast palette of transcendent obscenity and radicalism rendered as slop folk and poetry. Their songs are for heads by heads.

Along with Sanders, the band's other singer is Tuli Kupferberg, an old-school bohemian hero of Ginsberg's *Howl,* who (in Ginsberg's breathless descriptor) "jumped off the Brooklyn Bridge this actually happened and walked away unknown and forgotten into the ghostly daze of Chinatown."

Around the Village, the otherworldly Kupferberg is best known for his self-published book *1001 Ways to Live Without Working.* Allen Ginsberg will dub him "the world's oldest living hippie." There have *always* been heads. But now, at the Peace Eye Bookstore, in communal apartments, in the pages of Paul Krassner's zine the *Realist,* the newly launched *East Village Other,* and elsewhere, they start to shape an identity of their own, something that distinguishes them from being simply serial drug abusers. Though some of them are that, too.

NOBODY CONFESSES TO inviting Ken Kesey to speak in front of 15,000 antiwar marchers on the UC Berkeley campus in mid-October 1965. Today's words, some of the most prescient Kesey will ever utter, are not about psychedelics, except that they are, pointing the way to a new frontier. The writer has been speaking publicly about his drug use since not long after the wild success of his 1962 debut novel, *One Flew over the Cuckoo's Nest,* whose first pages were written under the influence of peyote. In 1964, while Freedom Summer voter registration drives unfolded in the South, Kesey and his Merry Pranksters had expressed their own sense of liberty, setting out cross-country in a Harvester school bus dubbed Furthur (sometimes spelled Further) and repurposed with microphones, speakers, turrets, the half-mythical amphetamine gazelle Neal Cassady (star of Jack Kerouac's *On the Road*), and a good supply of LSD.

For the Berkeley march, they arm the Bus like a military convoy and show up blasting toy guns and parading with their new friends from the Hells Angels. It's taken a few years longer for psychedelic head culture to truly take root in the American West, but—thanks to Kesey and the Pranksters—it does so deeply. They arrive at the rally tripping and one of Kesey's old friends—the one who introduced him to psychedelics—is severely disappointed and almost never speaks to the writer again.

Dressed in a World War I military helmet and Day-Glo orange coat, Kesey gets to the podium just before the march is to set forth. In between discomfiting harmonica blasts, the writer lays out a crystalline summation of what exactly the heads have been doing by making all this bluegrass and avant-garde tape music, by smoking grass, by tripping, by searching for the cool places on *all* the maps.

"They've been having wars for ten thousand years and you're not gonna stop it this way," Kesey tells the assembled crowd. He winds up to it. "There's only one thing's gonna do any good at all," he says. "And that's everybody just look at it, look at the war, and turn your backs and say . . . fuck it."

This is one of Ken Kesey's most magical moments, revealing what's there fleetingly when people turn around. It is a promised land of sorts, blurry, unformed, and perhaps only possible to see between strobe flashes, but it is the very same coastline that Peter Stampfel opened his eyes on, that all these uninstructed freaks are washing up on every day.

The split emerges in real time between those who might turn their backs and those (especially among the Berkeley tribe) who are ready to *march*. And they do, off into the Berkeley sunset while the war rages on. The Pranksters troop back to the hills outside of Palo Alto, to Kesey's pad in La Honda.

The Pranksters and many others in California and elsewhere have already turned heel in a bigger way, are already scanning enthusiastically for new horizons, and are already finding them. The back-turning might (and will) be dismissed as libertarianism or escapism or white privilege masquerading as radical politics or justification for getting really high or even a CIA plot to depoliticize American youth through psychedelics, but it is starting to take indisputable material shape as young people of all ages begin to pool their resources and discover some of Tuli Kupferberg's 1,001 ways to live without working. It helps that by mid-1965 a large supply of very high-quality LSD is making its way through California and around the country.

The social shapes and archetypes that emerge in California in late 1965 and early 1966 will echo and repeat around the country, often by literal name. Ken Kesey and the communally dwelling Merry Pranksters find a tangible form for their freak-outs in a weekly multimedia party called the Acid Test, counting the LSD-dosed human bloodstream and resultant gestalt as one of its media. Though it is the Pranksters who oversee the Tests, which begin in late November 1965, the boundaries are permeable, and the Tests become a platform for a freshly psychedelicized arts underground up and down the coast, uniting decades of evolving California spiritual and lifestyle experimentation into a veritable blueprint.

The well-spoken nonleader of the band at the noncenter of the Acid Tests is guitarist Jerry Garcia, an exemplar of head culture to parallel Peter Stampfel out on the East Coast. He'd spent Freedom Summer crisscrossing the country in search of bluegrass, but, throwing himself into his new band—the Grateful Dead—he puts down his banjo, picks up the electric guitar, and votes for the last time. He splits with his wife, who takes their young daughter and joins a parallel psychedelic collective, the Anonymous Artists of America. The charismatic autodidact Garcia and rest of the Dead and everyone else in sight belong to the new country. The Pranksters' Acid Tests continue weekly through the end of 1965 with the quintet now core to the events' existence.

In December, Ken Kesey leads a parade through North Beach with a weather balloon that reads "NOW!" decreeing a Trips Festival for the end of January, a call to the heads. It's an open beacon for all the dancers and the poets and trapeze artists and homemade synthesizer makers and light shows and rock bands and multimedia shows projected on teepees. The event will unify everyone's trips, not least the Merry Pranksters', and connect them with the vast mindspace collecting in the Bay Area. People are encouraged to bring their own gadgets. Outlets and electricity of all kinds will be provided.

Charged with organizing the three-night Trips Festival at Longshoreman's Hall on Fisherman's Wharf is a junior Prankster named Stewart Brand, who calls on Ramon Sender, director of the San Francisco Tape Music Center, an avant-garde musician-run collective in the up-and-coming Haight-Ashbury neighborhood. Grateful Dead bassist Phil Lesh had spent time hanging out there, and it was Lesh's classmate Steve Reich—with whom Lesh shared possession of a tape recorder—who first turned Ramon Sender onto peyote. It is a small circle that will soon have influence in all kinds of unexpected ways.

Electronic composer Ramon Sender and the Merry Prankster Stewart Brand are specimens of two deeply related other types of heads, here entwined as organizers of the Trips Festival, and running in close connection for years to come. After the Trips Festival, Brand will go back to the future, operating near the center of California's technology boom. Sender will go back to the earth, starting his own religion and becoming a pioneer in a new wave of California-style

DIY spirituality. At Longshoreman's Hall, where all burns white hot, there is no difference. Sender jams with the new band Big Brother and Holding Company on a Buchla box, a synthesizer built at the Tape Music Center. By Saturday night, the Trips hit full throb and the Grateful Dead play their first major San Francisco show.

Prankster-organizer Stewart Brand would say the weekend was "the beginning of the Grateful Dead and the end of everybody else," and a wave of Bay Area avant-garde does seem to crash to a close at its end. The night afterward, Ken Kesey disappears, en route to a fake suicide and an escape to Mexico in order to dodge a pot bust.

But it's not true, and especially not about Stewart Brand himself. A few weeks after the Trips Festival, he is tripping (mildly!) on the rooftop of his North Beach apartment and thinks he can see the curve of the planetary surface as the city spreads out before him.

"Why haven't we seen a picture of the whole earth?" he wonders, first in his journal and then very loudly. He prints the question on pins and sells them in Berkeley. The space program has existed for almost a decade, after all. He is sure it will change things, though he isn't sure what. He likes the phrase, *the Whole Earth*. Stewart Brand is the archetypal head futurist in a top hat with a kaleidoscope monocle, ready for his next step.

The Trips Festival does signal some endings, though. The Tape Center's Ramon Sender is ready to split and does, looking for even more alternatives and transforming himself into a head wanderer. First, he makes for the desert with surplus acid from the Trips Festival and lives in a cave near Needles, Arizona, for a while, trips, and sees God. Or, more accurately, realizes that he's been seeing God all along, because It is visible in the sky every day.

"My great epiphany in the desert is that the sun is a conscious being and I could have a very personal relationship with this being," he says. "It was so obvious that the sun is God, the creator of everything we have, and why we then had to intellectualize it and put it on another level and create all these other deities, it just went wrong as far as I could tell." It's a nice few weeks out there.

And then a pass through Socorro, New Mexico, where the ever-seeking Sender visits the peyote-taking Church of the Awakening, run by "an elderly couple, straight-looking as could be." And then finally, up to Colorado, for a destination he'd heard about at the Trips Festival. Near Trinidad, a group of geodesic domes springs from the high desert, their colorful walls made from salvaged car hoods, their ideological roots drawn from Canadian utopianist R. Buckminster Fuller. Ramon Sender has arrived in Drop City.

Drop City is more about dropping out than dropping acid, though the acid will come. Artful experimenters, the Droppers will soon construct their Theater for Electronic Psychedelics, a multimedia dome for a New Earth, hurtling toward a new future. Like psychedelics, going back to the land (or just getting away from dominant culture) isn't a new idea, but the fresh cocktail of the two in the wake of postwar American prosperity is powerful.

The Northeast had the transcendentalists and Walt Whitman in the nineteenth century. A few decades after them, the so-called Nature Boys wandered Southern California near Indio, desert-living barefoot beardo descendants of the German *Wandersvogel* and *Lebensreform* movements. But, in the present day, *dropping out* is afforded mostly to those who have enough economically to put aside. As an attempt to mask or transcend or protest class, it is a complicated maneuver but a real one. Coupled with more than a decade of the civil rights movement, the new media-ready psychedelic dropouts magnify the idea that society's lines might not be as fixed as they are made out to be, that there is a plurality of belief systems and types of people.

Ramon Sender's visit to Drop City is short and not terribly eventful. No more than an hour, probably. He asks a few questions, gets back in his car, and heads back toward California. But he gets what he needs. Ramon Sender knows he can't live in San Francisco anymore.

He makes arrangements for his San Francisco Tape Music Center compatriots to move to Mills College in Oakland. He also remembers something Lou Gottlieb, a journalist and ex-member of the folk trio the Limelighters, had told him: that Gottlieb owned undeveloped land in Sonoma.

Sender goes up for a visit with Gottlieb, Prankster-organizer Stewart Brand, their respective partners, and a pocket full of Buckwheat's Hashish Cookies, infamous in the Bay Area. It is apple blossom season, all is pink and white and fragrant, and Sender decides to stay. By the end of the year, with Gottlieb's blessing, there are a half-dozen people living on the Morning Star Ranch, the first major commune in California.

THE OLD GUARD grumbles. Aldous Huxley and Colonel Al Hubbard and the other early psychedelic luminaries had hoped to turn on the cream of society. Their former protégé Timothy Leary has run amok, fired from Harvard, but there are still plenty doing good work at the intersection of mystic experience and healing psychotherapy. Psychedelic medicine holds infinite potential, they believe. In Menlo Park, not far from Stanford, and even closer to where the Grateful Dead were coming together at the same historical moment, a former employee of the Ampex tape company named Myron Stolaroff had opened the International Foundation for Advanced Study. It charges $500 for a guided sequence of experiences that will bring one into the psychedelic light. This is where Stewart Brand had first tripped before falling in with Ken Kesey. But the flame tenders hadn't planned for LSD-25 to simply be *available*. Aldous Huxley had been severely disappointed in Timothy Leary's media-happy exuberance, and—passing away in November 1963—hadn't lived to see the full chaos set in motion by the Harvard boys. The old guard is outnumbered. The flame is no longer theirs. It's only just starting.

THE ARCHITECT OF the hip economy, the person soon most responsible for psychedelicizing the United States, makes his first moves on bulletin boards around Berkeley, where he posts a few index cards advertising the sale of "250 Heavenly Blue seeds for $1." Like the peyote-selling Barron Bruchlos at the Dollar Sign a few years before, the short, hyperactive man has ordered a still-legal substance and packaged it for resale. But Augustus Owsley Stanley III is a different kind of entrepreneur than was Barron Bruchlos. Owsley Stanley is a head. He begins to trade. He tries speed. And he finds LSD.

"The first acid I took was made by a guy who was actually a civil engineer that got interested in it," Owsley would remember to Bruce Eisner. "[He] read one of the syntheses, and performed it in his kitchen in one step." As it happens, it is some of the first acid made outside the confines of a proper laboratory and isn't very strong. But the experience piques Stanley's interest and soon thereafter he comes across a 500 microgram #4 cap, likely from either Sandoz or a state-run lab in Czechoslovakia. He splits it with his cousin and *really* discovers LSD.

"And after that I tried to get some more," Owsley would continue. "I couldn't get any, so I thought, 'Well, shit, if I can't get any, obviously there's only one other way out. Go to the library.' All the organic synthetic chemistry that I know is the stuff I picked up in a few weeks in the UC [Berkeley] library."

It helps that Owsley Stanley is a savant with an obsession for quality. He's studied Russian and alchemy and ballet. He's repaired radios in the Air Force. The disowned grandson of a Kentucky senator, he'd gone off the grid permanently around the turn of the decade. Living in Los Angeles, he'd written some bad checks and, as he recalled, "realized that I couldn't deal with the regular, commercial world of finance that allowed you to write checks, and to have credit cards and all the rest I decided after that I didn't want to deal with it, and I've never had a checking account after that, ever. Or any sort of credit card." Owsley is looking for a different value system. Like others, he leaves a family behind.

Stanley and his chemist girlfriend, Melissa Cargill, make and sell methedrine. Using the proceeds (and using lab equipment that gets confiscated and returned once en route) they work their way up to LSD. When Stanley arrives there, it is with an all-encompassing zeal. Over the next two years, he and Cargill and their associates will manufacture at least 1.25 million hits. Others will make more than they will, but no chemist will be as influential on the unfolding story of LSD in the United States as Owsley Stanley. He gives around half away. Even so, when the first batches hit the street in the spring of 1965, the money rolls in.

"All the equipment that I had to use to make it is costly, so I had to get some money back," Owsley would say. "But I never felt it was my money. None of the money that came from acid I felt was my money. I was like a custodian of it, and didn't know what to do with it. It was a real problem for me. I never bought a decent car even during this time. I certainly didn't buy any houses or anything. I just didn't believe it was mine. What I was doing was something for the community that I could. I gave a lot of the material away, gave out handfuls of the stuff in the park all the time."

His first big investment is the Grateful Dead. After the Trips Festival, the Kesey-less Pranksters decamp for a season in Los Angeles, and Owsley Stanley declares himself the Dead's patron and soundman and installs the quintet in a pink house in Watts, next door to a brothel. When they need to be discreet over public sound systems, the band take to calling their patron Bear, after a teenage nickname, sometimes with a definitive "the."

Should an anthropologist creep up the stairs into the Los Angeles house that February, she might come across the first stirrings of what will grow into the biggest psychedelic practice on the continent. Unlike peyote and its derivatives or the psilocybin mushrooms that sometimes circulate, LSD belongs to no particular tradition anywhere in world. It is there for the creating. Invented in Switzerland, it is manufactured in the United States, right in the attic of the pink house in Watts, indigenous to any region where American ingenuity might make it so. Though most head residences won't have their own acid chemist, the behavior lays out how life will be from now on for many people. There have always been heads, yes, but now they are heads together.

"A dozen or so sapient humans literally *puddled* together," sapient human bassist Phil Lesh will write of a typical scene, "draped over and around one another in completely non-sensuous and inclusive bond, seemingly as natural as breathing." Band members will speak with great earnestness about seeing through each other's eyes and hearing through one another's ears. Topping the band's reading list during their period of psychedelic discovery is Theodore Sturgeon's *More Than Human,* a science fiction novel about the emergence of a groupmind among individuals, a *blesh.* Sci-fi and its possibilities are as real as bluegrass and LSD. The LSD isn't illegal yet, but the pot they're smoking is, an added outsider mentality to keep them bonded together.

They're not the only ones, of course. In Texas, around the time the Dead were getting together as the Warlocks in '65, a group of heads from around Austin met on a peyote-gathering mission to Laredo and formed a new band (complete with an electric jug player/philosopher/dealer/lyricist) called the 13th Floor Elevators. Influenced by the Holy Modal Rounders (among other modern weirdos) the Elevators' own particular blesh leads them to the musical concept they call "the third voice," when seemingly discordant parts create a new effect that none directly intended. Their intention is to musically "play the acid" and carry the word, the flagship band of a small but influential Austin psychedelic scene.

The 13th Floor Elevators play their first show in December 1965 and nearly every one thereafter while tripping, sometimes scheduling multiple gigs per day to maximize the doses and only playing every four days in order to reset themselves before tripping again. When they make it to *American Bandstand,* Dick Clark will ask who the head of the band is. "We're all heads," electric juggist Tommy Hall replies without missing a beat. Other band-bleshes make their own discoveries, but none will carry the LSD mission as hard as the Elevators, tripping more methodically than even the Dead. Few will burn out as dramatically, either, persecuted in their home state, essentially hiding out between shows, with all three primary band members incarcerated within a decade.

The Grateful Dead succeed in part because they are enmeshed so deeply in California, already a liberal safe haven, and in part because they are reared in the safety net of the emerging psychedelic religion. It provides them with a function and a source of income.

Throughout the early spring of 1966, the Dead rehearse downstairs at the pink house in Los Angeles in a jungle of cables. They are not merely practicing but discovering a practice, the ritual combination of music and psychedelics. They don't trip at every show, but, when they do, it is with great intentionality, letting it feed back into their music. Believing there to be a symbiotic relationship between the acid and the music, Owsley Stanley donates his massive Altec Voice of the Theatre stereo speakers to the cause, lugging them to Los Angeles from Berkeley. The band might not sound like much yet, still existing on a repertoire of jug band adaptations, garage rock, and primitive originals, but they're learning. They practice all week and, if not other nights, *always* take acid on Saturdays.

Momentarily in Watts, the music of the Grateful Dead and the manufacture and sale of LSD exist in perfect alchemical and practical harmony. It is during these weeks, with the regular irregularity of the Acid Tests, dancing audiences, and a collective goal of ecstasy, that the Grateful Dead become the Grateful Dead. With the self-sufficiency of having their own acid supply, they transform into the archetypical gang of psychedelic adventurer-comrades on the open seas of American reality, soundtracking nightlong dance rituals as their music rushes to catch up with their minds.

"Back in the old days when we were taking acid and stuff, I learned some of my most important musical lessons," Jerry Garcia will observe decades later. "There were times I was so high and out there and felt so vulnerable that playing the guitar seemed like the only pathway to salvation. By taking it to that level of craziness and making it seem that important, which is obviously not the case, I learned there's no reason not to go all the way when you're playing. It's an emotional thing, and I've learned how to incorporate that somehow."

During one practice in the pink house, tripping, Owsley Stanley sees the band's notes pouring from the Voice of the Theatre's massive curved speaker cones in what he describes as "interacting waves of color." The experience sets him further down the road of sound exploration with the same zest as his LSD making, thus initiating the Grateful Dead's long and (eventually) extraordinarily influential connection to sound reproduction technology. Though not after a lot of pains in many Grateful asses.

In a further departure from consensus reality, the acid chemist lives on a protein-heavy menu of red meat and milk, a self-derived forerunner of the Paleo diet. Because Stanley is paying for the groceries, the band abides by it, too. Stanley takes over the attic, decking it with tapestries and storing the LSD.

"There's nothing wrong with Bear that a few billion less brain cells wouldn't cure," Jerry Garcia will remark of the patron/chemist/soundman. The guitarist, especially, becomes a talking buddy with Owsley. "If Garcia doesn't have a guitar in his hand, he'll rap," Bob Weir tells an interviewer. And when not talking or playing guitar, Garcia is a voracious reader and an autodidact to match the Bear.

Starting in the pink house and in the next few years, Stanley and Garcia rap out a smoke bubble fantasia that builds into what Garcia calls "hip economics," a way for the underground to operate. "You can have a small amount of money and move it around very fast," Garcia summarizes it for *Rolling Stone*. But the key to this other economy is its twin income streams: drugs and rock 'n' roll. In the same way that heads aren't merely serial drug abusers, the hip economy isn't strictly a black market but a financial arrangement guided by higher aspirations. Building a money component into psychedelics on a grand scale is another particularly American achievement, which unfolds in micro and macro across the emerging real-world map.

A glorious example of hip economics in action is found in the Dead's new temporary home in Los Angeles, in motion before the Dead even got there. One of Owsley's very first local representatives—beginning with the '65 batches—goes by the professional name Al Dente and makes up business cards advertising the Goon King Bros. Dimensional Creemo. Born Hugh Romney, the man later known as Wavy Gravy had worked as an absurdist-surrealist nightclub comedian and for a time "financed [his] free-floating lifestyle though the sale of single ounces of marijuana packaged in decorator bags and containing tiny toys." Weed slinging is a nearly stable income stream for heads, as well, and will remain so. His first brief connection to Owsley, via a mutual folk musician friend, is almost coincidental, but it's a small network.

By November 1965, Romney had been inspired to stage the Lysergic a-Go-Go at the AIAA Auditorium, a multimedia psychedelic comedic blowout that kicks off a week before the Pranksters' first proper Acid Test just up the coast. Romney's a-go-go collaborator is a psychedelicized military vet named Del Close, on his way to inventing long-form improvised comedy and influencing generations of stage actors who do for drama what the Dead will do for rock 'n' roll. When the Acid Tests come to LA, like Pigpen, Close will receive special dispensation to go undosed. He takes speed instead. A posse of friends begins to accumulate around the charismatic Romney, coming to a head with his landlord when the Dead and the Pranksters show up on their first night in town. Romney and crew find new digs that earn them a new name, and another of the early psychedelic clans is born: the Hog Farm.

It becomes a standard arrangement to use drug money to fund creative endeavors, either one's own or friends'. Austin's 13th Floor Elevators discover it, too, with electric jug player Tommy Hall making frequent trips back and forth to the West Coast to pick up LSD for local distribution. But just as psychedelics spread, so does psychedelia, a new art movement that is sometimes hard to distinguish from the drug religion itself. Around the country, musicians and filmmakers and writers and comedians and conceptualists and *everybody* work to adapt their mediums to the psychedelic vocabulary. Just as often, it seems, heads seem to adapt their psychedelic vocabularies to newly chosen mediums, often failing but sometimes unlocking deep creative channels.

Everywhere the language of psychedelia is quickly borrowed to sell whatever it is that needs to be sold. Many years later, searching newspapers from New York, Chicago, Los Angeles, and Boston, one researcher would discover that LSD was in the news every single day in the spring of 1966.

Bursting from radios and magazine covers, sucking in centuries of visual art and musical and literary movements, psychedelia becomes a viral idea that spreads more quickly than LSD itself can, and the Grateful Dead have every reason to be identified with it. Although countless musicians draw from the newly minted conceptual treasury, it is the Dead's immediate world that propagates the infrastructure on a broader scale.

When the band's benefactor runs low on cash, Owsley brings junior soundbeam handler and trainee chemist Tim Scully into the pink house's attic to get his first hands-on experience with LSD. Using a newly acquired pill press, the two convert the remainder of Owsley's crystal into some 4,000 tablets of what the chemist brands Blue Cheer. Their work coats the attic in a fine psychedelic dust. Though Owsley's products have been out on the street for almost a year, it is this batch that has the greatest impact.

They distribute the pills locally through the scene around Canter's all-night delicatessen in West Hollywood, where dealers hang out on "Capsule Corner" and in seedy apartments, playing Monopoly with real cash and shooting the breeze. Owsley's work is getting around. In early March, *Life* runs a story about an LSD epidemic in Los Angeles. A few weeks later, a *Life* photographer turns up at Capsule Corner, looking for the source of the still-legal blue-purple tabs. Panic ensues at the Dead's pink house in Watts, though Owsley's name appears nowhere in the subsequent *Life* cover story, "The Exploding Threat of the Mind Drug That Got Out of Control."

For reasons as clear to everyone as the white light of acid, the Dead and the Bear must part ways with Los Angeles and, soon enough, each other. Owsley buys the Dead some more conventional sound gear and the band makes for Olompali, a palatial spread in Marin County where they can continue their practice.

Owsley Stanley, meanwhile, establishes the modern LSD business. After the *Life* story, acid is the topic of three meetings by the Senate's Special Subcommittee on Juvenile Delinquency, and it will achieve illegality with flying colors by early fall. Timothy Leary has long claimed psychedelics to be a matter of "internal freedom," which they are, but no amount of elegant phrase making is going to make acid legal. It is clear the hip economy needs a more serious plan of operations.

"When the band asked me to stop living and traveling with them, I felt rejected," Tim Scully would recall. "For a while it had felt like an extended family." But Stanley and Scully have other work to do for now.

Calculating that it will take 72 million hits to save the world, Scully drives the Grateful Dead's now former equipment truck to Denver to scout locations for a new lab to be built in as discreet a location as possible, preferably deep in some unnoticed suburb. He and Stanley and their associates derive standard acid-making lab procedures. One discovery is that, no matter what protection they use, all attending technicians will inevitably get very, very, very high. Gloves and masks get in the way anyway, so they abandon them, work until they're tripping too hard, and take breaks when they must.

They try their hand at manufacturing DMT, which goes fine. And they try their hand at 2,5-dimethoxy-4-methylamphetamine, a.k.a. DOM, a.k.a. STP, which absolutely does not. Owsley puts a decimal point in the wrong place and sends people on three-day trips by mistake.

More successfully, Owsley Stanley gets to building a more robust pipeline. First, he establishes primary trustworthy dealers in a dozen major markets through which all product will flow. From each, he extracts a promise to resell for no more than $2 a hit. Whenever needed, a local distributor can simply hop on a plane and fly to San Francisco for some more.

"I felt that giving so much away for free kept the markup in the sale loop to a low level," Stanley reasons. "The quality stayed high and the markup stayed low, and people got it anyway. Putting it out through a sales trip allowed a wide distribution that wouldn't have happened if there had been no money in it." Keeping the price low is paramount. In San Francisco, the Hells Angels handle distribution and are able to keep order down the chain, where everybody ends up making money anyway.

The same week acid is made illegal, the *San Francisco Chronicle* calls Stanley the "LSD Millionaire," and the Dead reply with a song for their patron, "Alice D. Millionaire." Decamping to the city, the band occupy 710 Ashbury Street, a three-floor Victorian a block and a half uphill from their new neighborhood's central corner: Haight and Ashbury. They move their money around as fast as they can, supporting a small scene, keeping a steady flow of pot in and out of the house, and taking shows whenever and wherever they can, from a debutante ball down the Peninsula to the opening of the new North Face Ski Shop in North Beach.

The hip economy booms. Owsley's money is everywhere in the Haight in late 1966 as the neighborhood becomes the model for extreme self-generating urban renewal: gentrification. He helps fund the *Oracle,* a floridly designed newspaper run by one of his former dealers, Allen Cohen, that the staff sometimes scents with jasmine before distribution. Looked at one way, it's a complex tax dodge, laundering illegal profits away from government hands. Looked at another way, it's the way economies are supposed to work, with goods and services and money in fast circulation.

"Hip capitalism" becomes a buzzphrase around the Haight and in more mainstream quarters, but it's already a very different idea than hip economics, tipping the balance toward straight-world money and breaking the vacuum seal of an alternate reality. Until a head can invent something so wonderful that it transcends money, though, American currency will act on the hip economy like gravity, keeping the new alternate universe tethered to the traditional United States and reality at large. But, in the Haight, another group will attempt to tip the balance back.

Owsley donates to a group of radical street actors that take the name the Diggers, plenty conflicted about taking Owsley's supplies. More than anybody else, the Diggers provide the missing philosophical tool between Kesey's back turning and Owsley's hip economics and it is called *free.* Using comm/co, a printing press that makes its services available to the community (also funded by Owsley), the Diggers put the word out through broadsheets and missives to the press.

There is Free Food every afternoon in the Panhandle. And there is a thirteen-foot Free Frame of Reference (which lives at the Free Garage) through which one must to step to get a bowl of (free) Digger stew. There is a Free Store.

"As part of the city's campaign to stem the causes of violence the San Francisco Diggers announce a 30 day period beginning now during which all responsible citizens are asked to turn in their money," they announce calmly. "No questions will be asked."

The Dead contribute to the creation of the powerful new ethos, with a move that's one-half People's Band righteousness and one-half brilliant marketing: they play for free in the park. Many parks. In many cities, they will supplement their club debuts with free public gigs. They are no strangers to benefits, either—their very first gig as the Grateful Dead was in support of the radical Mime Troupe theater—but now they do their part more than ever. Shows for various causes dot the band's itinerary that fall, and causes are in no short supply in the Haight. Religions, diets, fashions, and spiritual teachers circulate, the economy of ideas moving no less quickly than the economy of drug cash, representatives from each inevitably ending up on the Dead's front stoop, rapping with Garcia.

After the Acid Test Graduation on Halloween 1966, which the Dead bail on anyway, the Pranksters' influence fades, and the Dead are no longer *quite* as public about their acid use. They issue a single on a local label, available at the Psychedelic Shop, the prototype head shop. The band sells their first merchandise, too: a T-shirt emblazoned with a picture of Pigpen, available for sale at the Fillmore. Also available in this extracondensed fall of '66: the first piece of fan-made merchandise. A house at the corner Stanyan and Alma, by the Panhandle, sells pins bearing the phrase "Good Ol' Grateful Dead," an awfully funny phrase to describe a band around for barely a year, but it's been a long year. If nobody is around, one can let herself in, leave some money, and take one.

WITH THEIR ASTOUNDING and wondrous medicines made illegal, the psychedelic old guard shapes their own enduring underground. The ever-welcoming Bay Area remains a center of this world, as well. One psychedelic therapist continues to quietly practice from an office in the East Bay, and he isn't alone. Under strict secrecy, Leo Zeff will train a generation of therapists in his methods, tending to a nationwide network of regular trip sessions, guided by himself or trusted associates. "If you don't know what to do and your mind wanders, listen to the music,"

Leo Zeff tells his trippers, advice the Grateful Dead's Robert Hunter will accidentally-but-not-accidentally echo in a song lyric.

Near Leo Zeff, in the Berkeley Hills, the fiercely independent ex–Dow chemist Alexander "Sasha" Shulgin forges compounds in his own backyard lab and bioassays them in his own unique body and those of his friends, evolving a system of notation and observation that will eventually become a standard for scholarly psychonauts. Between the new laws and the cutoff of official supplies and that *ghastly* Timothy Leary sloganeering about tuning into this and dropping out of that, there's not much most academic researchers can do other than build on what they've already learned or plot new studies down the Amazon. The consequences are immediate and dire.

One underground researcher is a Brooklyn man named Howard Lotsof, a head who'd experimented with a variety of substances in the early '60s. He'd become addicted to heroin, but his head-like curiosity never left him, and he accidentally discovers that the intense three-day psychedelic iboga, eaten in southeastern Africa, can serve as a withdrawal-free addiction interrupter. He initiates research. Ibogaine isn't made illegal in 1966, but Lotsof goes to jail for selling a small amount of LSD, and a serious look into the drug won't properly begin for a few more decades. In the next months, the American mainstream will go fully antipsychedelic, with a quickly circulating story about LSD and chromosome damage. The *Science* report will be debunked within months, but its negative impact on continued research is incalculable.

"If the future of LSD is to be more wholesome than its past, it must be squarely recognized that the most publicized advocates of the psychedelic are it worst enemies," bemoans Lisa Bieberman of Cambridge's Psychedelic Information Center, once an ally of Leary's. "We cannot rely on them to fight our battles for us, whether it be for religious freedom, the right to do research, or the dissemination of accurate information. Flower power is no substitute for integrity."

There is one last psychedelic conference after LSD and mushrooms are made illegal, held at San Francisco State University in January 1967, highlighted by extraordinary presentations and meetings between luminaries. R. Gordon Wasson, the first white American to experience a psilocybin ceremony, appears. So does peyote explorer and Amazonian adventurer Richard Schultes, and young Sasha Shulgin. A pair of Swedish toxicologists break new ground with their DMT snuff research. LSD inventor Albert Hofmann sends his regards.

Held in the lower Haight, just downhill from the action, the divide between the heads and rest of the psychedelic world is vast and getting vaster. Its impact seems to ripple out into other realms. In Mexico, María Sabina—the *curandera* who guided pioneering ethnomycologist R. Gordon Wasson's first trip—is despondent. "From the moment the foreigners arrived, the 'saint children' lost their purity," she says of the mushrooms, which she'd used not for divination but to cure specific maladies of her visitors. "They lost their force; the foreigners spoiled them. From now on they won't be any good. There is no remedy for it."

AS IF DRAWN by a cosmic comix artist, a procession of VW Microbuses greets the Grateful Dead at the airport on their first arrival in New York City in the early afternoon of June 1, 1967, and whisks them to the East Village. There is a welcoming parade for the visiting dignitaries, eighty hippies ambling down St. Mark's Place accompanied by a police escort and ending at Tompkins Square Park, where Pigpen is presented with a key to the city made out of white carnations. The band's two-week stay in New York will be a cartoon sequence of east-west psychedelic fusion, highlighting the differences between and unique power of the coasts and setting the stage for the world to come.

After the parade it's on to the Tompkins Square Park band shell for the Grateful Dead's Manhattan debut in front of 3,000 onlookers, yoga practitioners, and wary police officers, come to make mellow in the park only two days after a hippie/cop riot left scores injured and forty-two arrested. Park peacekeepers wear armbands. The gig is organized by Fugs leader / *Fuck You* editor Ed Sanders, who'd booked the band on behalf of the Lower East Side Civic Improvement Association.

Pigpen lays the white carnation key atop his Vox organ, Garcia dons an armband in solidarity with the peacekeepers, and the People's Band get down to business. Even with a growing hippie quorum, though, the neighborhood is tense. A framed portrait of Jesus soars from the crowd and shatters on the drums. There is something different about this band, though. Another East Coast faction taking inspiration from the Diggers will remember the afternoon as their first spontaneous smoke-in, when too many people light up at once to bust. In the tribal memory, one of the future Yippies throws joints from the stage, as if seized by some heretofore unknown energy.

During their stay, the band hangs with various Fugs and the Group Image, a local psychedelic groupmind commune-band-blesh. Via Bob Weir's old boarding school pal John Perry Barlow—who the band serendipitously connects with in New York, and who will grow into perhaps the psychedelic world's most important ambassador to the Future—the band puts in a visit to Timothy Leary at Millbrook. They hang out and listen to the brand-new *Sgt. Pepper's Lonely Hearts Club Band* but don't make a deeper connection.

"Who said we are all doing the same thing?" Garcia will say to an interviewer about the East and West Coast. "That was the difference between us and them. For me it was very profound on lots of levels. Going off into the woods and being meditative didn't cough up any-thing for me except how pretty everything is. I got my flashes from seeing other people, because I was also looking for something in this world, not out of it. I was looking for a way to get through this life, not a way to transcend it."

Before the band's June 9 show at the Cafe Au Go Go, Garcia and his girlfriend, the Merry Prankster Mountain Girl, make their way a few blocks south to the Italian restaurant Emilio's, where they meet with journalist Tom Wolfe, who interviews them for his book in prog-ress, *The Electric Kool-Aid Acid Test*. When it becomes a best seller the following year, it will help blaze the West Coast scene as psychedelia's archetype in the American consciousness.

After two weeks and fourteen shows, the Dead close their first New York visit with the Inter-Tribal Community Benefit at the Cheetah on June 12—which really just means that the Dead split the door proceeds from the $3 entry fee with the Group Image. Reporting about the gig, the *Village Voice* notes that the Grateful Dead play for "their people." It is perhaps the earliest on-the-record acknowledgment that the band's audience is different than the one other bands draw, even in the heart of hippie New York. It will never again be put more succinctly.

IN BERKELEY, A pair of heads draw a map of the New World whose shape will remain functional into the next century. The two meet in a local music store sometime in mid-1967 after they witness someone unsuccessfully trying to hitchhike from Berkeley to Kansas City. Earl Crabb observes that New York is actually far closer to California than Kansas City, and Rick Shubb's eyes light up.

A veteran picker from the Palo Alto scene, Rick Shubb is an accomplished visual artist and holds the distinction of procuring the first acid ever taken by Jerry Garcia, magenta gel tabs consumed by a houseful of friends in the late afternoon of May Day 1965. Pouring in and out of an unfurnished house, marveling at bouncing basketballs and strange street lights, almost a dozen heads find themselves on the new shores together. Many do it again a few days later, listening to live Osbourne Brothers tapes, and a day or two after that Garcia's Warlocks play their first formal show at a local pizza parlor.

When Rick Shubb and Earl Crabb connect in 1967, Crabb enthusiastically scrawls out a primitive rendition of a map. Instantly, they share a vision of coastlines and oceans and territories and retire to Crabb's nearby apartment for a multiday cartography session to chart the folkie-boho republic they envision.

The resultant Humbead's Revised Map of the World looks a lot like the Ur-continent Pangaea, filled with vaguely familiar inlets and peninsulas and spits of rocks, or a grand map out of the frontispiece to a J. R. R. Tolkien first edition. Like Pangaea (or Middle Earth) there are strange forces trembling beneath it, seemingly ready to explode with energy volcanoes and rainbow rivers.

By the time they publish the Map early in 1968, there are five major territories: San Francisco and Berkeley in the north (or "up," per the Map's compass rose), New York City and Cambridge in the south ("down"), with Los Angeles occupying a small chunk of up-leftward gold coast. Each territory is packed with tiny details and inside jokes.

There are landmarks (like the Fillmore West) and acknowledgment of far-flung territories, like Plainfield, Vermont, home to the freethinking Goddard College (on the Map, landlocked in Cambridge). The steady stream of hashish from the far side of the Atlantic is depicted by a tiny North Africa nestled in between Cambridge and New York. For similar reasons, every territory has a chunk of coast labeled "Mexican Border."

The underground population serving overseas is represented by a small territory of Southeast Asia between LA and San Francisco, frequently soldiers' last port of call before shipping to Vietnam. The Rest of the World is crunched onto a small island floating in the Whelming Brine, with Paris and Liverpool and London and Rome and Bombay and Moscow and Singapore and Copenhagen. Earl Crabb and Rick Shubb make every attempt to be complete.

The oceans include a sea serpent, a rubber duck, the isle of Nashville, and—rising from the Wavy Waste off the coast of Cambridge—with a jauntily perched crown, drooping mustache, and mighty trident—Pigpen himself. Circling the four seas is what the Map refers to as its List of Population, around a thousand names in tiny writing. Shubb and Crabb list everyone they know or think they know. As a census, it is as whimsical as the territory it illustrates—but also just as real. Though its basis is a dense social network of folkies, the list covers far more, a circumstantial coalition of Diggers and bohos and poets and rock bands and acid chemists that's lately begun to grow along with the landmass itself. The inked-in population includes predecessors, like Gypsy Boots of the protohippie California tribe of so-called Nature Boys, and logical non sequiturs, like Mickey Mantle. It lists the members of the Grateful Dead and Peter Stampfel's Holy Modal Rounders (who sometimes crash at Crabb's), plus Richard Nixon and Ronald Reagan for good measure. It's both a small world and not.

Notes Crabb, "The way the original map was designed, if you had a double-L Rapidograph, you could add your own name or any other name you thought we had missed, and nobody would notice that it was added later." (And, note to all: do keep those Rapidographs ready.) The Map is an instant hit, selling like hotcakes from head shops and music stores.

By the time Humbead's Revised Map of the World goes into circulation in early '68, though, its grand cities are already falling into ruin and its tectonic plates are starting to shift. Speed freaks have overtaken Haight Street, represented by a giant crosshairs at the top of the Map. The Dead are gone from the neighborhood now, too, dispersed to Marin County in the wake of a police raid on 710 Ashbury. Not that they abandon San Francisco. With hip economics running full tilt, Owsley and a roster of bands and their families operate the Carousel Ballroom, upstairs from a Buick dealership on a busy downtown corner.

During the same season that Shubb and Crabb create their Map, a sociologist and his assistant research a paper based on life in the Haight, "Heads and Freaks: Patterns and Meanings of Drug Use Among Hippies," published in the *Journal of Health and Social Behavior*. "While a whole penumbra of allusive imagery surrounds these terms, a 'head' essentially is thought to be someone who uses drugs—and, here, it is mainly the hallucinogens that the speaker has in mind—for purposes of mind expansion, insight, and the enhancement of personality attributes. . . . For the 'head,' therefore, the drug experience is conceived of, much as by psychiatrists and psychopharmacologists (ca. 1956–63), as a *means* for self-realization or self-fulfillment, and not as an end in itself." Though the balance will change later, early studies suggest an even use of psychedelics across gender lines.

Unlike Pangaea, however, the new Humbeadean continent doesn't split apart. Instead, it changes, the land bubbling open and expanding, new mountains shooting skyward down the middle, creating new coastlines and new territories. Ken Kesey's Mexico escape had ended in an American jail term, and, when he gets out, he makes for his family's farm in Oregon, giving the bus Furthur a new base and picking up commune-style living where the Pranksters left off a few years ago. Not that the Pacific Northwest requires Kesey or the Pranksters for headdom to root there. The dank, temperate climate and deep woods (and steady student supply from Portland) are a natural for hippies, anyway.

Psychedelic scenes are in full flower in bohemian enclaves across the globe, sprouting in Vancouver and London and Sao Paolo and the intellectual chaos of Paris, reaching Tokyo soon thereafter. There, it arrives by way of Dr. Acid Seven, Japan's chief LSD acolyte, dealer, activist, festival organizer, folk guerrilla bandleader, and hip economist. One of his larger claims to credibility is that he lived in the Haight and partied with the Dead.

But the idea of the New Earth surely propagates faster than the drugs themselves, though there are people working on that, too. In the next years, outposts will spring up near Kathmandu, on the island of Ibiza, on the banks of the French Riviera, southern Israel, Greek islands, Morocco, Kenya, and beyond. Even Saigon will get its own version of the boundary-free countercultural zone, when a group of Vietnamese longhairs jams nightly for GIs and locals at a venue known as the Fillmore Far East.

Back home, busted in December '67, Owsley is lying low on the chemistry front, but he is not inactive. Turning his attention back to the Dead's sound gear, he maintains an influence on his successors in the acid world and remains near the center of a rolling chemists' salon. The loose configuration, who sometimes gather at a cafe in the Haight, are the beginnings of what acid historian Mark McCloud identifies as the families of LSD manufacture.

Owsley's apprentice (and former Dead soundbeam assistant) Tim Scully teams with Nick Sand, the Brooklyn-reared in-house chemist for Timothy Leary, and the Millbrookers. The boyish-looking Sand had cooked DMT in his bathtub, the first independent chemist to do so. With Leary's patron Billy Hitchcock bankrolling the lysergic treasury, Scully and Sand begin manufacture of Orange Sunshine, an even bigger wave of branded LSD to follow Owsley.

Also represented at the LSD family gatherings are the manufacturers of Clear Light acid. This consortium's three primaries take on pseudonyms. Their chemist, known in some recordings of history as Pretty Boy, oversees construction of a lab on the upper two stories of a building right in the heart of North Beach. Over 1968, they observe a market-wide price drop as a glut of acid hits the streets. Because everyone is out to save the world, the competition isn't a problem. But that doesn't mean the Clear Lighters don't want to make money, so they shift production to a new kind of designer LSD. Casting the acid in tenth-of-an-inch translucent square gel tabs, the extremely powerful 250 microgram product is marketed as Windowpane.

Owsley appreciates the chemistry but is opposed to anything that might expose the acid to light. *Who keeps their acid lying around in the light?* retorts one of the Clear Lighters, Frank, a.k.a. Kelly, a.k.a. Denis, a.k.a. Denis Kelly, who also starts to pioneer the acid world practice going by many shifting names. Over the next half decade and beyond, Kelly estimates that they manufacture some 30 million hits, though accurate counts are always impossible.

There are other chemists and other distribution mechanisms connected to this core that fork over the years, but an often-obscured chain of lineage is established in San Francisco in 1968. There are also chemists not directly connected to the upcoast cabal, like the

Boston-based Tord Svenson, a Millbrook supplier busted in late '67, who will return to Europe in a few years to do even deeper work.

Down-leftward on the Map in New York, a configuration associated with the East Village's short-lived Psychedelicatessen head shop manufactures the first LSD distributed commercially on paper, specifically litmus paper, where the acid appears as a squelched blue dot. At first, the extremely strong 1,000-microgram hits even come in a Kodachrome-X 5–20 slide film package that looks almost entirely like ordinary camera film. Except down one side is a block of text clearly explaining its contents as "LSD (Lysergische säure diäthylamide)" and its strength. The text describes the drug's "Physiologic Effect," "Psychologic Effect," "Mode and Site of Action," and other details. "It is important to flow with the drug and not to resist its effects," the package suggests. "For brilliant color," it reads on the side. They switch to less traceable blotter paper quickly and help establish an industry standard. By late '68, the cult/commune/distribution operation on East Tenth Street connected to the Psychedelicatessen—the Church of the Mysterious Elation—is busted. But nothing can be stopped for long, and it'll be a few years before the Psychedelicatessen's owner is nabbed with fifteen grams of LSD crystal.

Everywhere, even for the luxury product of 250-microgram Windowpane, the price stays low, per Owsleyian decree. After realizing it could be sold in anything that might absorb it, some dealers even briefly sell LSD dipped on string. But the hip economy lurches to the next level with the arrival of the Brotherhood of Eternal Love, an ambitious and anarchistic organization who latch themselves to the Sand/Scully pipeline. A few years earlier, the group of Laguna Beach surfer-thugs had acquired their first acid by robbing a Hollywood producer at gunpoint. They soon see the clear light, meeting every week to reform themselves of their evil speed-taking ways. Taking inspiration from a pamphlet by Timothy Leary, the Brotherhood incorporate as a religion and work their way up the dealer chain.

By '68, they solidify the hash importing business, forging connections along the Old World overland route from Europe to Afghanistan, a bustling thoroughfare rapidly becoming known as the Hippie Trail. They work up a list of tricks that includes lining the interior of a car with hash and simply shipping it home by boat. They bring a similar sense of focus to the LSD smuggling game. Led by "Farmer" John

Griggs, they become the world's outlet for Orange Sunshine LSD, saturating Humbead's Map and beyond.

In San Francisco, shows at the Carousel Ballroom—*especially* Dead shows—overflow with local acid dealers like Bob Black, Luvall Bedford, Frank/Denis/Kelly/____, Super Spade, the notorious Goldfinger, and members of the Brotherhood of Eternal Love, including John Griggs. Once, at a Bay Area Dead gig, Frank/Denis/Kelly/____ takes a massive dose of Windowpane from a chalice and sits in lotus position at the center of the venue's floor until the next morning, when he is eased back to earth by the sound of the venue's staff sweeping up the debris around him. At Dead shows, especially, most of the dealers simply give their materials away. And of course there is Owsley, mixing sound and having opinions.

"Even before LSD became widely popular, there were plenty of other drugs at all of the gigs I saw," says chemist Tim Scully, who'd apprenticed to Owsley back in LA. "I'm confident that marijuana, heroin, opium, speed, and cocaine were used both backstage and front at many gigs by some people. I hoped that LSD would push away harder drugs, but that didn't happen."

The Diggers run a Free Bus from the Free Store in the Haight to the Free Land. "They'd scrape people off the sidewalk on Haight Street and ship them to us for dry-outs," says the Morning Star Commune's Ramon Sender, the fully dropped-out ex-director of the San Francisco Tape Music Center. "It was fine. There's nothing like a nature cure." Morning Star and Wheeler's Ranch, the two large communes in Sonoma, earn the collective name "the Land." The Diggers organize the communards on the Land to produce Free Food.

At Morning Star, the one-time composer Sender refines his solar religion. "I spent all my time lying on my back in the redwood groves staring at the sun through the beautiful stained glass patterns that it made through the branches, and I could do that for hours on end, and was having a wonderful time." Every once in a while he hitches a ride to the city, exchanging obscure titles at a used bookstore and returning to the redwoods. Morning Star and other communes will produce numerous DIY theologies and spin-off experiments in ecofeminism, radical bioregionalism, food co-ops, and more.

The Diggers' dream of Free grows bigger each season. As the summer of 1968 approaches, their newest plans echo the early-twentieth-century socialist theory of syndicalism, where networks of local workers become the structural basis of a nongovernment. In early May, the Diggers throw a Free City Convention at the Carousel Ballroom. Naturally, one can pay with whatever method one sees fit. When Jerry Garcia arrives, he spies a bloody lamb leg dangling from the cash register, and the chaos only escalates from there. There is open sex throughout the venue. Before the night is through, someone changes the Carousel marquee to "Free City Cuntvention" and, by dawn, simply "Free Cunt."

In a guest-edited issue of Paul Krassner's zine the *Realist*, the Diggers announce a multipoint plan that includes basic instructions on how to start one's own Free City Switchboard/Information Center, Free Food Storage and Distribution Center, Free Garage and Mechanics, Free Bank and Treasury, Free Legal Assistance, Free Housing and Work Space, Free Stores and Workshops, Free Medical Thing, Free City Hospital, Free Environmental and Design Gang, Free Schools, Free News and Communication Company, Free Festival Planning Committees, Free Co-operative Farms and Campsites, Free Scavenger Corps and Transport Gang, Free Tinkers and Gunsmiths etc., and Free Radio TV and Computer Stations.

Under the heading "Some Ideas For Liberating the Ferris Wheel," they suggest that "a certain number of records be released in plain white folders . . . saving all art and printing costs and leaving free space for local artists."

A few days after the Free City chaos, the Grateful Dead return to New York and re-enforce their People's bona fides during May 1968, the first cresting peak of American student radicalism. They smuggle themselves into the midst of the Columbia student strike for a gig on the Low Library steps.

Protestors cut off songs until Bob Weir kicks a sloganeer in the ass. In between gigs at the Electric Circus, they join the Jefferson Airplane for a massive free show at the Central Park band shell, where—in addition to the band and crew—the stage is crammed with approximately three dozen longhairs, including the Airplane, Bill Graham, someone with a smoke bomb, and the band's new second drummer, Mickey Hart.

New York gets weird as only it can. A Free Store had opened with the word "LOVE" illustrated above the door. By the end of 1967, someone crosses it out and writes "HATE." Around the same time, a young WBAI-listening radical starts calling himself Abbie Digger. He soon reverts to his last name of Hoffman and retains a flare for imaginative sloganeering and extreme self-promotion that will define the East Coast school of by-any-means-necessary psychedelic radicalism.

For heads sick of the strife, the country becomes the place to go, be it to a commune or a nice rural pad. The *East Village Other* publishes a spread of naked hippie girls and dudes wading idyllically in a pond. "WOODSTOCK '68" the headline beckons, and the article touts "the new center of Godland in seclusion." Bob Dylan's been living there for a few years and is already getting harassed. "If you're very energetic like Tall Michael from 5th Street (6'7"), you'll build your own cabin in the fall," the *Other* suggests. The next issue announces a small music festival on August 16 and 17, 1968, the third of the summer—a year to the day before its marginally more well-known sequel—this one to feature Tim Hardin, the Children of God, and others.

As the season changes, back in California, the top-hatted ex-Prankster and Trips Festival organizer Stewart Brand starts to envision the new community from an ever-bigger perspective. He assembles a six-page mimeographed packet and a plan to sell magazine subscriptions, camping gear, blueprints for houses, and "access to tools" to the communes and off-gridders spreading across the Map. He is thinking of the L. L. Bean catalog, but the results are more like Sears & Roebuck, a nearly complete guide to life on the Land: *The Whole Earth Catalog*.

In a Dodge pickup with sample items, Brand and his wife trace the shapes of the new and swelling Humbeadean territories. They buzz out to Sonoma to visit Brand's former Trips Festival compatriot Ramon Sender at Morning Star and then down to New Mexico and southwestern commune-land where geodesic dwellings pop in the Albuquerque hills near Placitas, dubbed Dome Valley. The Brands visit the self-serious Lama Foundation and the hypergoofy Hog Farm (led by auxiliary Prankster Hugh Romney) and head up to Colorado to the dazzling Bucky-dome dotted swells of Drop City. On Humbead's self-revising Map—perhaps between San Francisco and Los

Angeles—a high desert appears inland, at the foot of the new mountains, to accommodate the settlers of the New Earth.

"We are as gods," Brand suggests in the first edition of his *Whole Earth Catalog,* "we might as well get good at it." As its page count sprawls, it becomes ubiquitous around the Land. The book spawns a revolution in homemade (or homemade-seeming) publishing and plants Brand's futurist dreams in the heads of heads everywhere.

THE HELIUM-VOICED motormouthed Peter Stampfel of the Holy Modal Rounders doesn't see the Grateful Dead play until late 1969, almost exactly ten years after his first peyote trip from the Dollar Sign Cafe. Through the '60s, Stampfel's life in the underground as a working musician runs in a strange parallel to Jerry Garcia's. They trek through the same venues, playing for the same audiences. They even participate in different iterations of the same unlikely (and surprisingly successful) groupmind dream telepathy experiment run by Dr. Stanley Krippner. Soon, though, their paths will diverge, the Rounders unable to quite escape the underground, the Dead turning into something else entirely.

Given their relative proximity on Humbead's Revised Map of the World, it is almost inconceivable that the Holy Modal Rounders and the Grateful Dead don't share a bill until late September 1969 at the Cafe Au Go Go, just two blocks from MacDougal Street and the decade-old punchline about the wormhole between Map-coasts. A month earlier, the Dead played to their biggest audience yet, getting sloppy in front of 400,000 people at Woodstock and, in their own estimation, not doing much. To the naked eye, they are just a band among many, playing for a common customer base of longhairs, albeit with a slightly larger coffers to fill than most. "Our audience is like other versions of us," Jerry Garcia tells Howard Smith in 1970. "Our audience is almost always heads."

In the fall of '69, the Dead can play two nights at the 2,654-capacity Fillmore East, but—if there's a paycheck involved—will still cram into the Cafe Au Go Go, the same nook on Bleecker Street where they played their debut New York residency two years previous. Since their first trip east, they've finally figured out how to incorporate their psychedelic freedoms into their music through improvisation and modular song suites. Their repertoire seems to rewrite itself each time through town. Free shows and benefits are all well and good, but hip economics can't keep the money circulating quickly enough to prevent the Man from repossessing Pigpen's Hammond organ onstage that fall.

The Holy Modal Rounders open the middle of the three nights at the Au Go Go. They are experiencing a taste of success after the hit film *Easy Rider* employs the Stampfel-sung "Bird Song" at a peak moment and on the best-selling soundtrack. (In another convergence, Garcia's own "Bird Song" is still a year away.) The movie also marks the arrival of cocaine into the American underground matrix, made readily available a few years earlier via a nationwide network of CIA-trained Cuban insurgents selling coke to raise funds to fight Fidel Castro.

Before the Au Go Go show, Garcia introduces himself to Stampfel and tells the speedy string-bander that he enjoyed seeing him at the Fox and the Hounds in North Beach back in prehistoric times. It's a friendly interaction, but they don't completely hit it off. As a fully psychedelicized folkie, Peter Stampfel is totally on board with the Dead's concept and was ready to be blown apart by their albums, but he just isn't impressed. *How come I don't love these guys?* he thinks. *They should be in my pantheon and they're not.*

"But," Stampfel says, "when I actually saw them live, right there in this little club, my feeling was that I'd never seen, live, a group of people that more obviously and truly belonged together. Their vibe of people who had found the right people to be with, and to do their thing with, was off-the-charts powerful and something I had no anticipation of, and made me realize that there was something going on here beyond my dissatisfaction with much of what they were doing musically."

That night, the Dead play until "six in the morning, with most of the available space taken up by dancers," enthuses a young guitarist-journalist named Lenny Kaye, a few years from helping to catalyze the punk underground. "Think of New York, and think of dancers and you'll see that The Dead can perform wonders, given a time and a place." That time and place is a Tuesday night—"September 31st," as Kaye notes—a time out of place. It's what Aboriginal Australians call *alcheringa,* the space of dreaming. The Grateful Dead will it to happen, they manifest it.

Not every member of the Dead trips every night. But, between band, crew, and audience (including some cruelly dosed against their wills), there is a reliably psychedelic quorum, and the Dead remain a beacon. The week after the band plays the Cafe Au Go Go, in September 1969, a small ad appears in the *East Village Other* advertising a Prospect Park Be-In on Sunday, October 12 featuring the Grateful Dead "(supposedly)." The band is back on the West Coast by then, but—as everyone knows—they can just as easily pop from Golden Gate to Prospect Park. This time, they don't.

The head world is getting odder and, in places, darker. Over the summer, a drug-influenced minicult surrounding a terminally sketchy ex-con named Charles Manson go on a brutal killing spree in Los Angeles and introduce a blotch of especially bad vibes. The terminally sketchy Manson had lived in the Haight and experienced psychedelic crucifixion at a Dead show at the Fillmore Auditorium, naturally.

The Dead are heads, of course. But more, they're the *right* heads, and they've staked their own particular part of the new America with their ability to conjure the Humbeadean landscape. The happy apolitical psychedelic world unfolds like a patch of greenery wherever they go. Beneath it, something is churning and growing, magnetic and welcoming. The Holy Modal Rounders' latest drummer's occasional girlfriend has a particularly strong reaction one night seeing the Dead at the Fillmore East.

She scores a backstage pass from a friend. She's never been backstage at a real rock concert before. "They started playing and my imagination just went so crazy," the young poet Patti Smith tells a crowd a decade later, when her band is opening for the Dead. "The way the music was, the microphone looked so accessible that I just wandered out. . . ."

A roadie tosses her into the crowd.

2

DEAD FREAKS UNITE

The money is nice, but Chad Stickney can't even spend it. He's only fourteen—what can he really do with $53,000, anyway? In time, he'll be known by a new name and influence the course of contemporary art, but in the summer of 1970 he's just a teenager and in over his head. He brings his girlfriends for rides in horse-drawn carriages, takes them out to nice restaurants. He hides the rest from his parents and grandmother.

Not long after Woodstock, the acid-dealing Brotherhood of Eternal Love had found him and his friends near Bethesda Fountain in Central Park, by the boathouse. "They recruited us," Chad says. "It was like the CIA." They'd been watching, looking for some heads who seemed cool enough to handle the business of distributing large quantities of acid. Chad and his buddies qualify.

"They would hang out sometimes," Chad says, "but they'd more just *drop in*. They were like secret agent guys. They had short hair. When we first met them, I needed time to make sure they were who they said they were. They looked too straight. But I figured out that they're so heavy and involved in this stuff that they *can't* look like hippies. You have to be a secret agent and be so under the radar that nobody looks at you."

This is one reason Chad Stickney is who the Brotherhood are looking for: he's figured out their protocol right away and knows what's up.

Chad *is* cool. He is too street smart to be called precocious, but the cherubic longhaired teen has a sweet radiance about him that goes a long way. It's also not like they're keeping *that* secret. "Due to the great demand, freshness is practically assured," two anonymous Brotherhood evangelist-agents tell the *East Village Other* a few months before Chad is recruited. "There has never been an organized plan to run around the country selling LSD," they add. "It just happened, we assume, magically."

As nice as the Brotherhood guys are, though, Chad's increasingly less enthused. Perhaps if they'd briefed him on the hip economy, he'd figure out where to channel his new income. But he's just a teen doing teen things.

He and his buddy Todd—who the Brotherhood guys first approached—like to spend their time writing their names on walls around the neighborhood. Todd is TAZ-86. Chad just writes his name: CHAD. Lots of kids are doing it, a chattering folk network of urban teens marking territory.

Chad likes art, too. He's fond of Peter Max, whose gentle psychedelia condenses the world into cartoon shapes. Max's work had recently been displayed in an ad campaign on a certain crosstown bus that lingered just a little *too* long at the corner of Central Park West and Eighty-Sixth Street—long enough for Chad to strip it from the bus, run the other way down the block, and wrap it around three walls of his bedroom at his grandmother's place. Chad's a good kid, really, torn between split-up parents, shuffled between homes, and finding friends on the streets.

He still believes acid can save the world—that's not the problem. Chad just doesn't want to go to jail or deal with the money. With Chad and his friends as the foot soldiers for groups like the Brotherhood, alongside other sprawling operations like the Clear Light System and any number of unnamed operators, LSD circulation in the United States is growing beyond all bounds, out into the suburbs now. The Brotherhood's product, Orange Sunshine, permeates the country, at least 4.5 million pressed pills worth (so far) from its launch in 1969, the most influential brand of LSD yet. This is what Chad and his friends had been recruited to sell. Perhaps the street-smart Chad can sense that the Brotherhood are getting in over their heads, just as much as he is.

The chemist Owsley Stanley will disavow any connection to the Brotherhood, calling them a "bunch of loose cannons on a ship of fools," but they effectively take over the distribution chain after Stanley's late '67 bust. There are dozens of Brothers, including old-guard Dead freaks who once lived down the block from the band in the Haight. Many have cut their hair, shaved their beards into neat mustaches, and gone incognito.

More importantly, they have chemists to make the Orange Sunshine, idealists all around. At first, it is Tim Scully, Owsley's one-time apprentice, and the Brooklyn-born Nick Sand. The Brotherhood discover the far back end of acid manufacturing—and the truly difficult part of the equation: the problem of acquiring *ergotarmine tartrate*, LSD's precursor chemical.

This very important part of the business is no longer handled by the (usually) idealistic chemists themselves but by shadowy figures like Ronald Stark. A verifiably unverifiable international man of mystery, Stark is connected to Mafioso, African pharmaceutical scams, puppet corporations, the CIA (probably), and Arabian princes, and he draws on a host of un-Humbeadean resources and energies. It is a dark current that powers the latest and increasingly powerful batches of Orange Sunshine coming from French labs, sometimes hidden within more legit chemical operations, run by Stark himself along with in-house idealist-chemists. The latter sometimes include the British-born Richard Kemp and the American Tord Svenson, the latter busted in Cambridge in '67 and now working overseas.

But the semireformed surfer-thugs of the Brotherhood of Eternal Love have gone big with the biggest bigness they can imagine, and their imaginations are pretty well widened. At the time that teenager Chad Stickney makes his moves to retreat from dealing, the Brotherhood are in the process of putting up the money for the Weather Underground to spring Timothy Leary from jail. They continue to distribute branded LSD and relocate from California to a new spread in Hawaii.

In a few slick moves, the Brotherhood paint new territories onto Humbead's self-revising landmass. A dripping peninsula rises from the sea up-leftward of the Duck's Tail, curling (in a shape that perhaps resembles Hawaii) like a highway-connected island-chain off the end of San Francisco. There, the Brotherhood of Eternal Love dream but never quite build their Rainbow Island commune. It is the perfect destination for the Brotherhood's global drug smuggling. They sail a yacht from Mexico to Maui carrying massive amounts of pot and use it to seed Maui Wowie, among other strains. For a while around the islands, their handiwork becomes an actual currency. "Gas for Hash" signs are spotted. The Orange Sunshine dawns across the continent, beaming down on new places because of the work of countless local heads.

But, in New York, Chad Stickney decides to scale it back, and he lets his business tail off. His friends are annoyed when Chad's customers start showing up. In the summer of 1970, he convinces his grandmother to let him live on a commune a few hours north of Manhattan. He'd missed Woodstock and lays on all the charm. But his dealing friends from home track him down there, bringing with them their original secret agent friend who had recruited them into the Brotherhood and a bunch of watermelons, which they put in the stream to cool. They give Chad a stern talking to about leaving. They're smoking lots of the good Brotherhood hash, and it's so strong that Chad thinks he's tripping. But then his friend starts laughing a laugh that he only laughs when he's on acid, and Chad knows the watermelon's been dosed.

It's a long exit ceremony that weekend for Chad Stickney, but one never really leaves the Brotherhood. The guys are bummed, but there are no *real* hard feelings. His friends keep doing what they're doing. Soon enough, Chad will help carry the psychedelic culture through the '70s and beyond. But he'll have to go to a few Grateful Dead shows first.

THE DAY THEY bust St. Stephen comes not long after he and more than two hundred followers arrive in Tennessee in the sweltering summer of 1971. The Californian flock had traveled cross-country in a great thirty-two-bus Caravan to found what will be one of the country's largest, most influential, and longest-running communes, the Farm. They'd left the Haight the year before in their Prankster-style vehicles to follow the former (assistant) philosophy professor Stephen Gaskin on a lecture tour. In San Francisco, he'd regularly filled up the same ballrooms that the Grateful Dead played, and a number of his followers believe him to be the subject of the Dead's song "St. Stephen."

Owing to the steady stream of New York folk musicians traveling to Nashville, Earl Crabb and Rick Shubb had put Tennessee on Humbead's Revised Map as an island floating alone in the Whelming Brine. Mostly, though, it is uncharted territory. When St. Stephen and the future Farmers arrive, they find natives who are wary of the longhairs, but (give or take his subsequent jail term) Gaskin will talk their way onto the Land. Though he is most certainly not the subject of "St. Stephen," Gaskin is powerfully magnetic.

Like Jerry Garcia and Ken Kesey, Stephen Gaskin can rap, spinning out acid-touched parables that just make sense. "I fell in love with Ina May on DMT," Gaskin writes of his wife. "We all toked up on DMT, and I looked at her and just fell telepathically into her, and saw that we just matched up to many decimal places, and were really as telepathic as we could be. It just blew me away."

Unlike Garcia or Kesey, Gaskin has no qualms about sitting cross-legged in front of large audiences and dispensing wisdom. Some of the Farmers, including Gaskin, practice "four-marriage"—two men and two women—though they will phase the practice out as they get settled in Tennessee. Among his followers are numerous Fillmore-vintage Dead freaks, disillusioned about the Haight's collapse. En route, one of the Caravan buses even splits off and stops to hit a Dead show at the Capitol Theater in Port Chester.

The longhaired transplants of the Farm have much to learn about living on the Land, starting when Gaskin and four others get nabbed for growing pot only weeks after their summer '71 arrival. But they are absolutely committed to the task, a vast groupmind looking to take root. One traveler remembers "taking these huge group acid trips and getting into each other's heads, as it were. I learned to double clutch a school bus while driving around [San Francisco] stoned on acid with 35 other trippers on board. The air would get so thick in there that it would literally get cloudy inside if there was some sort of mental confusion going on."

By the time the Caravan gets to Tennessee, Gaskin has decreed a stop to the acid (too chemical; 'shrooms are still fine), and most of the group's prized Dead tapes are nationalized into communal supplies and erased. "The Farm had an attitude about the Dead personally," remembers a Bus traveler named John Coate, who'd once hitchhiked around the country with a copy of *Live/Dead* in his backpack (to spread the news) and, during the Caravan, accumulated a small collection of prized Dead reel-to-reels.

The Farm "was a very dope-smoking hippie thing, but it was also churchy in a certain kind of way," says Coate. Gaskin, called "Stephen" by all, is a benevolent brother-father in an overtly Judeo-Christian psychedelic family. "We were really adamant that the lyrical content of every song had to be positive in some way," says Coate.

"As storytellers, the Dead would often look at the darker side of things. It was fine with me. It didn't freak me out. But, like, 'don't murder me' on 'Dire Wolf' just didn't fly that well. People decided that the Dead weren't cool anymore because they weren't singing 'Dark Star' or something. The tapes were valued more than what was on them."

The Farmers come armed not only with copies of Stewart Brand's *Whole Earth Catalog* but at least one of the layout editors who'd put it together and had likewise worked on the best-selling instruction manual *Domebook 1*. They establish a radio station and a cross-Farm phone network, Beatnik Bell. Gaskin's got the Farm Band, too, who tour around the region with Gaskin staging hippie-jam-gospel boogie revival meetings.

They're not the only ones with their eyes on Tennessee's cheap land and history of tolerance. As historian Timothy Miller points out, "the hippies probably constituted a minority presence on the 1960s communal scene," and this extends into the '70s. Many are nonlonghair Anglo- and Asian American Christians, occasional group marriages, and other miscellaneous arrangements. The Farm achieves the trifecta of being heads, Christians, and experimenting with group marriage.

The Farm's most vital breakthrough comes via Ina May Gaskin and the group known as the Farm Wives. When the Caravan had left San Francisco, there were nine pregnant women on board. Out of sheer necessity, through painful trial and error—including an en route miscarriage by Ina May—they reinvent the practice of home birth for the Land and all of the New Earth, a simultaneously modern and ancient human technology that will filter out to the mainstream through Ina May Gaskin's book *Spiritual Midwifery*.

"The person you choose is someone you would feel all right with in life-and-death levels of tripping," she advises those picking people to help with their births. The commune offers itself as a place where pregnant women can live and have their babies, as an alternative to abortion, and stay if they'd like.

At the Farm, the midwives become the cornerstones of the community. "I had women that were helping me with my kids and with the housework and with the laundry so that I could go deliver babies," one would remember. "[We] were the first ones with the phones on the Farm. We were the first ones with transportation and people were real good to us."

Ina May's innovations will travel though the communal network alongside various Farm advances in sustainable food, but the Gaskins and crew are on their own in Tennessee, on a mission to live together. The Farm is a model. But for many heads wanting to turn their backs on the ugliness of American culture, going to the Land requires too much.

When the Grateful Dead visit nearby Nashville for a massive free show at Vanderbilt University, almost no one from the Farm can make it. Besides everything else, the food situation is starting to get dire. In Farm lore, it will go down as Wheat Berry Winter. The Farmers, except for a few strays working on a construction crew in the city, miss the band's last free outdoor concert outside of San Francisco.

IN BERKELEY IN that summer of 1971, a wild-haired, wild-bearded, wild-eyed head scribbles wildly in notebooks. He is in possession of certain information that will replicate around the world. If he can only sort it out.

His beard shoots outward, and so do his calculations, which all point toward something *big* happening, and *soon,* when *everything* will change. Terence McKenna knows that there is more research to be done. That is why he and his brother Dennis led an expedition down the Amazon earlier that year to begin with. They'd gone in search of ayahuasca. They found something else, however, which is exactly what Terence McKenna is trying to elucidate at the moment. He is not yet succeeding.

The McKennas' self-dubbed Experiment at La Chorrera involved the consumption of nineteen fresh *Psilocybe cubensis* mushrooms and the smoking of DMT. It involved (brother Dennis writing) "a set of procedures for creating, and then fixing, the mercury of my own consciousness, fused with the four-dimensionally transformed psilocybin-DNA complex of a living mushroom." It involved hexagrams, information transmission, telepathy, an extended cosmic prank designed by James Joyce, and eventually an encounter with a flying saucer.

Afterward, Dennis seemed to exist on another plane of reality for some days. When they are both back on stable ground, so to speak, both believe they are carrying data.

In his Berkeley apartment, safely back on Humbead's Map, Terence begins to chart a new theory of time based on the information and the I Ching and a sequence of dates. If his calculations are correct, there will be a great concrescence this coming November 16, 1971, a date which also happens to be his twenty-fifth birthday.

Psychedelic prophecy is in the American air that year. Timothy Leary is on the lam with the Black Panthers in Algeria, but Carlos Castaneda's second book about adventures with peyote teacher Don Juan is a smash best seller. Presented as the work of an American anthropology student, Castaneda's lingo of spirit guides and allies becomes part of the psychedelic vocabulary, like Leary's work a decade before. Many express serious doubts that Castaneda is all he says he is. Part trip report, part life manual, *A Separate Reality* will turn out to be mostly fabricated. This does not mean it is false, of course. It is popular enough to warrant satire in both the *New Yorker* and the *New York Times Magazine,* and—more significantly—it provides readers with many methods of thinking seriously about what psychedelics are and how to use them. The world is changing. But not as fast as Terence McKenna thinks it is.

In Berkeley, McKenna's calculations prove to be incorrect. He goes back to the I Ching and crunches more numbers.

IT'S COLD OUTSIDE New York's Felt Forum in December 1971 and Chad Stickney doesn't have a ticket, but he's not worried. Perhaps he can feel himself being pulled into the Grateful Dead's transformational countercultural chaos field when he spots a girl he knows from around Central Park (on the Map, of course).

"I didn't know her that well, but when you're a kid hanging out in Central Park you know 500 people second-hand," Chad says. Perhaps the sixteen-year-old ex-Brotherhood LSD dealer already knows what's going to happen—maybe it would happen anyway—but it happens like this.

"I wrote a poem to Bob Weir and I'm going to get in, so stick with me," the girl tells Chad, and Chad decides to. Fifteen minutes or so later, "this beautiful woman in a hippie dress comes out and [finds her] and says 'I loved your poem, Bob loves your poem, why don't you come on in?' and so she grabs her and is pulling her in. And she's black, by the way. And I grab her and say, 'Can I go? I'm her brother.' And she looks at me and laughs, since it's obvious I'm not her brother, and she says 'of course,' and just pulls us both in.'"

Through the door, past the cops, down an institutional corridor, over the threshold, beyond the veil, into a bunker-like backstage room, and there they are: the Grateful Dead. They're friendly, smoking joints, pulling from a nitrous tank, though Chad and his friend are afraid to talk to Pigpen, standing in overalls with his arms crossed. Dead rhythm guitarist Bobby Weir enlists Chad's help in going to the side of the stage and tossing small lit firecrackers into the audience during the opening set by the New Riders of the Purple Sage. It's a hoot of a time, and, when the Dead go on, Chad goes and watches, subsumed into the roiling crowd.

The only time Chad had seen the Dead before, in Central Park in '69, he'd stood by the mixing board and, after a friend pointed out the renowned acid chemist, watched in awe as Owsley himself did his soundbeam work. When Chad gets inside the sold-out Felt Forum in December 1971—the 5,600-capacity theater attached to Madison Square Garden—the Grateful Dead are in the active process of transforming into one of the most popular bands in the United States. Onstage, the Dead are a vision of the new California. Their speaker stacks burst in tie-dye by Courtenay Pollock, a British hippie and LSD-inspired refiner of the form who'd stumbled onto Dead guitarist Bobby Weir's ranch by way of a Vermont commune. Wherever the Dead go, they bring vibrant color. Like LSD, they bring news of tie-dye to the world.

They have an album on the charts with their self-titled new double live LP and are rapidly writing a new business model for themselves and anyone who cares to follow. In nearly each city on their fall tour—including during their five nights at the Felt Forum—the band arranges to have a complete three-hour show broadcast on a local radio station, like a free concert in the virtual park of the American airwaves.

The band's new success is captured, as well, by certain other measures. Several bootleg LPs of their music have been hits in Manhattan, selling at least five hundred copies a month over the summer, if one is to believe a heated editorial ("GRATEFUL DEAD PIG BACKLASH") in the *East Village Other* published after the band's road manager confiscated a good quantity of the illicit product outside a gig in the Bronx. It is only recently that the Dead have even become successful enough to rip off, the writer suggests in a bit of circular logic increasingly indicative of the Yippie faction using the *Other* as a platform. Until 1970, the pseudonymous Basho Katzenjammer reasons, the Dead needed the money too badly themselves. But "that was *last* year that they needed the bread," Katzenjammer huffs, allowing "and most of the year preceding as well."

The Grateful Dead maintain a complex position in the sprawling psychedelic underground as they become legitimately popular. "The Grateful Dead isn't for cranking out rock 'n' roll," Jerry Garcia explains in the band's official biography the following year. "It's for getting high." Certainly, many do that. But what is becoming clear is that many people do many things at Grateful Dead shows. As rock 'n' roll transforms into bigger business, especially following Bill Graham's closures of the Fillmores East and West earlier in 1971, Grateful Dead shows continue to remain sites of active counterculture. Besides being a place to take LSD and dance, one of the very few left, they are a place where old friends meet and where narratives spontaneously collide or brush up against one another, putting unexpected ideas into close proximity. By the next time the Dead play New York in the spring, the *East Village Other* will be out of business. Everywhere, radical storylines are coming to a close. As the '70s get going and the '60s really get to ending, a ticket to a Dead show remains a ticket to the unbroken psychedelic America.

"Regulars greeted other regulars, remembered from previous boogies, and compared this event with a downer in Boston or a fabulous night in Arizona," *Village Voice* writer Robert Christgau observes at the Felt Forum. Even if there's not enough room to *really* dance—Christgau suggests the band only play general admission venues—this is one place where ethnographers would do well to observe the new rituals and movement-shapes emerging as the Grateful Dead perform during their contractually promised five hours and attempt to conjure the dream-time.

And, dear ethnographers, do make your way down the aisle, among the dancers, to the front Garcia side of the stage where, every night at the Felt Forum, a good ol' Dead freak does what a portion of the band's fans have taken to doing and discreetly holds up a microphone to make a recording of the band with high-quality portable gear. But there are many differences between this specimen—an eighteen-year-old longhair named Marty Weinberg—and anyone else who has thought to sneak a microphone and equipment into this or any other Dead show. Perhaps Chad Stickney might notice him looking out from the stage, but that's about it.

For starters, Marty Weinberg is almost unquestionably making better recordings than anyone else in 1971, a boy genius member of the Audio Engineering Society and accelerated graduate of the prestigious Bronx High School of Science. For another, Marty veritably invented Grateful Dead audience taping a few years previous, and thus the art of audience concert taping in general: what gear to use, where to stand, how to make the best possible recording.

First seeing the band in '68, the Bronx-born Marty is the first to formulate some of the *why* of taping as well. *This doesn't sound like the album,* he thinks. If Marty doesn't tape it, he realizes, he will never hear that music again. He is both the prototypical Grateful Dead taper and, in other ways, unlike any that will follow.

Marty's thought isn't to save the music for any posterity except his own. He copies his prized recordings for a select few, enough for word to get out in New York Dead freak circles, but he keeps the bulk of his stash to himself. During most of his years taping, he never encounters another taper. None of his friends even own reel-to-reel systems, so Marty picks four of his favorite selections and presses up five hundred LPs of his own. He gives half away, sells the rest to make his money back, and winds up with an underground hit of his own. Marty makes a guest appearance on WBAI's *Radio Unnameable,* Bob Fass's all-night underground switchboard where the Yippies had formed. And a copy makes its way back to the Dead themselves. He is on his way to being a Dead freak legend: *the Legendary Marty.*

Marty Weinberg is the überhead. When not at school or Dead shows or swim team practice or working on his black belt kung fu moves or riding around late at night on the Staten Island Ferry having profound conversations with a close circle of friends, Marty is working in a midtown garage. Getting paid to rebuild racing car transmissions, Marty blasts WFMU, the new free-form radio station out of New Jersey. His idea of a profound and good time (besides a Dead show) is when he and his crew eat peyote and his dearest friend, a Jesuit priest and world-class musician, lets them into the Fordham church and improvises on the pipe organ for them. The Grateful Dead, Marty believes, are music for his people, *enlightened* people. He'd brought the father to the Capitol Theater in Port Chester one night, and the father dug it, too.

But by late 1971 Marty can feel it changing. Earlier that fall, he and some friends had driven to see the band in Atlanta and San Antonio. He remembers distinctly when the band played one of their new songs sung by guitarist Bob Weir, the self-conscious party anthem "One More Saturday Night." Marty is struck, and the thought formulates itself clearly and absolutely and permanently: *I don't like this song, I don't like the direction of these songs.*

The music critic Robert Christgau grasps where the split is going at the Felt Forum, too, writing of a "confusing combination of our fabled new community and the nightmare mob of [Spanish philosopher] Ortega y Gasset." But Marty is a head by the classic definition, a true Dead freak in the modern sense, and not sure what these new fans of the future are. They sure dance funny.

Also differentiating Marty from the other tapers is that, at the Felt Forum, Marty ends up backstage. The band has heard his LP, and Phil Lesh wants to talk. Far from being pissed, Lesh compliments Marty on both the recording quality and specific song selections. He knows Marty's not making a profit. In fact, Phil's more than cool about it. "We've dreamed about being able to play and have people get it the next day," he tells Marty, fully aware of the elusive nature of the band's live performances. It's a real talk, some forty-five minutes.

The world of the Grateful Dead remains a permeable and magical space in the early '70s, open to and influenced by heads like Marty and vibrating with a palpable energy. Backstage at the Felt Forum that week, Marty corrects Bob Weir's lyrics on Weir's cover of the country hit "El Paso," and Weir immediately corrects himself. Check the tapes. Only a few months before, the Dead's newest member—keyboardist Keith Godchaux—had been a Dead freak himself. But then his wife, Donna Jean, had approached Jerry Garcia in a club and simply informed Garcia that her husband, Keith, was the Dead's new keyboardist. There were other factors, but that is also a literal and accurate account of how Keith Godchaux joined the Dead. Even as the band's songwriting turns away from its earliest psychedelic expressions, they remain an enthusiastic blesh o' heads, powered by synchronicity, the energy of their earliest trips, and whatever is still to come. Grateful Dead shows are for getting high and connecting to whatever manifested minds are on the party line that night.

The teenage Chad Stickney understands only that he has an incredible time when he meets and sees and hears the Grateful Dead and that he needs to go back immediately. The next night. He can feel himself filling with energy and wants more of it. Coincidentally, a friend of his works for the phone company, who just happen to be on strike, and fifteen-year-old Chad borrows the full outfit, helmet and all, and melts into the front gates of the Felt Forum without a second glance from the ticket takers.

Once inside, while dodging an acid dealer friend who might blow his cover, Chad realizes he can probably just waltz backstage again, which he does. His journey is complicated and hilarious and involves bluffing his way out of a situation with a building intendant who wants him to repair the phone, but one of the Dead's British managers eventually drags him before the band in laughter. They let him stay and watch the show.

"That was the final straw to enter the world and change my name," Stickney says. "I was in the Brotherhood with the acid, but now I was with the band. I'd completed the whole LSD experience." He'd intuitively Pranked his way inside. Chad's been writing on walls for years, but now he knows what he's going to say and how he's going to say it.

LSD-OM, he thinks, *that'd be a great name to represent my people.* Soon after the Felt Forum shows, he's living in yet another divorce-dictated spot, this time with his mother up in the South Bronx, and he sets to work. On a busy stretch of the Grand Concourse near Cardinal Hays High School, a piece of graffiti appears next to a stoop in mid-1972. *LSD,* it says, in sparkling two-and-a-half-foot-high letters dotted with stars. Below it, an equally stylized rendition of the Devangari sound-symbol pronounced *om*.

"When I wrote the name, I never thought of it being me," Chad says. He is an instantly minted legend in the small, early world of graffiti in its cradle in the South Bronx. "People write things and they're like, 'That's me, I'm that guy.' With me, it was a different concept. It was more like saying, 'These are people who believe in the things I do.' I was the advertising agent for those people. That's how I looked at it. When people came up to me and said, 'Hey, LSD,' I almost wanted to say, 'It's a *people,* it's a *group,* it's a *movement.*' I never did say it, though."

He does write it on walls, though. The piece on the Grand Concourse is difficult, what with all the cars driving by at all hours. "It was a bitch to do," he says. But he gets it up there and it stays untouched for at least two years for the cars and random pedestrians and the other artists to take note. The up-front psychedelia of LSD-OM, even in its earliest incarnation, makes its way into the vocabulary of the emerging art form that is taking over the streets and subways of New York. Chad wants to make sure his people are represented in the new language.

But once that piece goes up, no more appear, at least for a little while. For now, LSD-OM disappears from the streets and walls of city because Chad Stickney gets his first serious girlfriend. Alright, Chad!

... *THUMP-THUMP-THUMP-thump-thump-thump* in downtown Manhattan. The party has been bouncing nearly every weekend since Valentine's Day 1970. While the Dead played five blocks to the north at the Fillmore East, a Timothy Leary follower named David Mancuso threw a soiree at his loft, calling the party Love Saves the Day and DJing soul and funk and rock records for his friends. As the name suggested, the punch was well zapped. Music and group zapping retains an important place in Mancuso's residence as the '70s roll on and the parties go weekly. If one can tentatively trace several major religions to psychedelics, one can confidently do the same with disco and the entire genre of dance music that follows, and pinpoint the explosion to David Mancuso's Loft, which quickly becomes capitalized.

Early on, Mancuso places a Buddha shrine between his stereo speakers, used for group psychedelic adventures as well as yoga.

Mancuso ritualizes a structure for his DJ sets based on the three bardos of Leary's translation of the *Tibetan Book of the Dead,* matching the inevitably lysergic arc of his dancers.

"The first Bardo would be very smooth, perfect calm," Mancuso tells an interviewer later. "The second Bardo would be like a circus. And the third Bardo was about reentry, so people would go back into the outside world relatively smoothly." It's an invitation-only party, and it keeps on pumping every week. As long as psychedelics circulate without rules, heads keep deriving their own non-boundaries. But the three-part trip seems to be a universal form grown from the entheogenic space and accessed by groups of people listening to rhythms together at massive volume.

Other downtown disco parties emerge where people take acid and dance to DJs spinning records, but the Loft is where the ritual is ritualized. Most won't follow the bardos at all, and not often knowingly, but they're available for anyone who knows how to get there. If people aren't labeling Mancuso's parties "disco" yet, they will soon. Other times, Mancuso blacks out the room entirely, puts on a sound effects LP of falling rain, jets up the high-powered industrial fans, and feels the dancers freak. And again: *thump-thump-thump-thump-thump-thump* . . .

SUDDENLY, IN THE spring of '72, the Bronx even gets its own hippie-named street gangs. Something is stirring under the glum concrete. Peace-loving Dead freaks notice neighbors with sawed-off shotguns. Black clubs like the Savage Skulls threaten longhairs near the Grand Concourse. Over in the mostly Italian neighborhood of Throgs Neck, in the far eastern corner of the borough, there is (like many other regions of the country) a vogue for heavy rock, and a few of the new gangs get named thusly. There are the War Pigs and the Bronx Aliens, who hang out over on Layton Avenue. And there is the Grateful Dead.

The *Post* runs an item on them: "The Counter-Coalition." "Italian gangs say they've organized against an anti-white threat." There's one of the Bronx Aliens with one of his comrades. "Grateful Dead" it says on the back of a cutoff jean jacket. The two familiar words frame a swastika. Oh *my*.

This is no sign of Humbeadia, and the members of the Grateful Dead gang aren't heads. This is just highly traditional intertribal warfare with new symbols. But the Dead's symbols have permeated the deepest Bronx. Perhaps it's the Legendary Marty's tape collection, perhaps it's Chad's LSD-OM glowing out on the Grand Concourse. The borough is getting more violent unquestionably, but between the cracks something wonderful is growing.

A local congressman gets involved and, soon thereafter, there is a rally where teenage gang members can repent. The *Daily News* runs a picture of a denim Grateful Dead jacket up in flames.

SO MANY VISIONS! So many prophecies! But at least one will generate both immediate and lasting impact, if not quite how its visioneers foresee. The message goes forth across the new republic: Mandala City shall rise on Table Mountain in Rocky Mountain National Park in Colorado over the Fourth of July weekend, 1972. *That* is the date of the great change, according to their calculations. Two men spend the summer of '71 going from commune to commune in New Mexico and Colorado and Sonoma to spread the news. It's hard to pin them down, even though they distribute a 144-page publication, part manifesto, part party invitation.

Credited to the Rainbow Family of Living Light, *The Rainbow Oracle* is even so bold as to include an illustration of a smiling prophet and a beckoning half-naked woman, below a utopian diagram of Mandala City. These Rainbows aren't exactly Christians. They just love Love, and there might be something in here about rapturous Armageddon if they achieve the task of assembling 144,000 heads on one mountaintop. It's a little hard to tell. The book is splattered with religious iconography, Whole Earth–style can-do, free Digger philosophy, and grand-scale street theater.

The return address is a post office box in Eugene, Oregon, and it is to the Northwest that the two Rainbows go when they finish their visitings. Their home is perched at the northwest corner of the fertile hippie crescent that now runs up the West Coast of the United States and bends eastward through the mountain towns and the Okanogan Valley, across the Idaho panhandle to Spokane and Missoula beyond. This emergence wreaks geological havoc on the Map, a mountain chain gently bulging upward from the middle of the incontinent continent. The towns become a trade route for gems and rocks and drugs and gossip and yoga tips and travelers and regional barter bazaars that overlap with the network of Renaissance Faires.

In traditional hippie-tribe fashion, the Rainbows are leaderless, but one of their nonleaders is the fast-talking, fast-thinking firstborn of one of the New World's oldest families. Garrick Beck is progeny to Julian Beck and Judith Molina, founders of New York's Living Theatre. Mingling with the likes of John Cage and Allen Ginsberg from the age of ten, Beck the Younger traverses the hippie highways, eventually attending Reed College in Portland, Oregon. Beck and his friends start to nail down their own variation on the American communal psychedelic tradition, one that includes neither rock 'n' roll nor the proper incantations of the Learyites.

"A lot of the time, as a clan, we went out somewhere," Beck says of the proto-Rainbow trips. "We would camp on the beach, which you could do in Oregon in those days. We would hike up to a [specific] point, sort of like a pilgrimage. At that point, we'd be looking out over the ocean, sitting there, chill. Didn't have to explain it to each other, didn't have to talk about it, just quiet. That was the high point. Then we'd come back down and dance, and have a wonderful dinner, and have fun, played with fireworks or god knows what." That moment of ritual silence is the Quaker-like absolution at the center of Mandala City. "Bring trumpets and bells to sound the silent meditation on the 4th of July," they suggest in the *Oracle*.

In practice, the first Rainbow Gathering won't run as smoothly, and it does not conjure Armageddon. But the summer 1972 event is the culmination of a lineage of participatory theater and the birth of a new nationwide psychedelic coalition. Their trip is the take-acid-and-blesh-in-the-woods variety, and their achievement will be to create a system to decide which woods to do it in and how to clean up when done. The American psychedelic ritual takes on a new form and a new destination: the annual Rainbow Gathering. It is another answer to what new rituals might emerge. With no name attractions and no electricity, the Rainbows' space is arguably the most agenda-free.

"The camp was split into tiny communities," comes one report from the first installment, "people in Biblical robes, naked people, various loners drawn together by some kind of affinity. There [are] at least five community kitchens—free food from the commune of your choice." Members of Boulder's STP Family cause some amount of chaos. The Love Kitchen emerges at the side of the lake, a vast white-tented configuration that freely feeds the freaks, operated by a tribe from eastern Washington, not to be confused with the beaming Anglo-angelic Love Family (who also operate a free kitchen) from Seattle.

The *Denver Post* estimates that the kitchens feed 15,000 during rush hour. There clearly aren't 144,000 people there, so no one really has to worry about Kosmik Armageddon suddenly coming down on their Fourth of July. They climb to the summit and sit naked, bare breasts and balls and bodies and arms linked together and *ommmmmmmmmmmmmmmmmmmmmmm,* and nothing happens, except that it does.

A *Rolling Stone* writer is there to be snarky to the Rainbows and report their words when Armageddon doesn't occur. "I can still see it," one says. "Mandala City. Over there we would have the tents of the elders, and here would be the Common Council, and on that far ridge would be tents of the tribes. . . . "

Which is almost exactly how it replicates the next summer in Wyoming and the summer after that in Utah and beyond. As Ina May Gaskin and the Farm Wives perfect childbirth, the Rainbow Gatherings perfect the portable unplugged community. Its popularity swells as it becomes a permanent summer ritual destination and a template for acoustic acid tests everywhere.

NAKED POLE GUY, ascend! In a hairy sun-stroked flash he bounds from the roof of a backstage equipment truck and scampers to a sweet perch behind the Grateful Dead while the band plays "Jack Straw" in the melting Oregon heat. At this moment in late August of 1972, more vividly than any other, the Grateful Dead's territory is completely manifest in front of them as they play for 20,000 people at a hippie-organized benefit in the northwestern countryside. It is a different America here, a wide-open and complete product of a peace-loving, postcolonial, psychedelic culture that for the past decade has staked increasing claims on portions of the tangible continent. And the day's music is the most complete rendition yet of this developing psychedelic ritual, helping to further consecrate this specific patch of land.

The Dead are already midway through the second set of the afternoon when Naked Pole Guy arrives in the frame, but it's been a magical day already. Jerry Garcia spoke of the presence of "invisible time-travelers" at Woodstock, and the Dead's gig at the Oregon Renaissance Faire Grounds has its share, too. For starters, there's the crew of tripping longhairs capturing just as much as they can on their limited film stock. Naked Pole Guy will become legend! A human freak flag boogying in the breeze while, just below, the Grateful Dead jam incandescently for the Oregon heads! Go Naked Pole Guy, go!

It's the nearby Springfield Creamery and its friendly bubble-lettered storefront sign that kicked the cosmic gear works into motion and why the Dead's performance might be seen as a symbolic pivot point for an entire way of life up there in the Northwest. The backstory reads like a psychedelic exploitation musical: small-town hippies market new-fangled organic yogurt, run afoul of the squares, need to save the family farm, call in the Dead. And that's exactly what's playing out on this insane sweltering day here in the field with all these naked tripping people.

The Springfield Creamery isn't just any creamery, though, it's the Kesey family creamery. Owned and operated by Ken Kesey's brother and sister-in-law, the creamery manufactures Nancy's Honey Yogurt, its label designed by the Merry Prankster once known as Black Maria. The hassle had come from the nearby school district, one of the creamery's long-standing contracts, perhaps a bit put off by the hippies and their new-fangled electric yogurt cultures. When it comes time to make tickets for the event, they just use leftover Nancy's Honey labels with new text.

Veneta is deep Dead country. After his jail time, brother Ken had landed in nearby Pleasant Hill, living communally on the family farm. In '69, he'd sent Ken Babbs and a Furthur-load of Pranksters to Woodstock and told him to return without most. In Babbs's memorable phrase, they wanted a community, not a commune. The Pranksters and extended family forge exactly that as they sprawl across the region, reconnecting to old roots. There are forces at work in the northwestern soil. The next year, Oregon will become the first state to decriminalize small amounts of marijuana, spurred by a campaign organized by Amorphia, a hip economy pot legalization firm based in Mill Valley that had funded itself by selling rolling papers.

It is the early '70s as well when—almost out of nowhere—a magic mushroom scene sprouts in Washington and Oregon. It's like a volcano emerging from the New Earth's Map, the vast rumbling of a million spores bulging upward against the verdant earth, ready to erupt into who knows what. The woods of coastal Oregon remain good for something else, too: absolute privacy. The Windowpane LSD manufacturers of the Clear Light System have left their North Beach warehouse for new property secreted in the deep woods of the Northwest. What nicer place to do it?

And the Oregon Renaissance Faire Grounds in Veneta aren't just any Renaissance Faire Grounds, either. Already, they deserve a Rapidographed symbol on the Map, perhaps where the new mountains meet San Francisco in the Up. The local Faire itself is three years old, a baroque outgrowth of the northwestern head scene. One suggestion for a symbol, should you pen one in, is the giant wooden light tower constructed for the Dead show, which will remain as a landmark for those who continue to use the grounds over the decades.

The American tradition of the Renaissance Faire developed in Southern California in the early '60s, a turn-your-back-and-say-dress-up outgrowth of the post-Beat/pre-rock protozoners. Owsley Stanley and his lab partners were a regular presence around the bayberry-scented Northern California incarnation, where they donned handmade Ren-finery, gobbled fresh, high-quality acid, and spoke in dialect. Two of Stanley's LSD-making assistants, Bob Thomas and Wil Spires, had gone on to found the acoustic world-folk ensemble the Golden Toad, a rolling street band collective that (by the early '70s) are making their name as the open-ended Grateful Dead of the Renaissance Faire circuit. A traveling scene of performers and craftspeople and gem dealers develops around the events. Quickly, though, the Renaissance Faires separate mostly from their countercultural roots—there's much less LSD—which only makes them more unusual.

Except in Oregon. Though it is very much a stop on the same traveling circuit of artistic practitioners, the Oregon Renaissance Faire in Veneta—the shared site of the Dead's Creamery benefit—is not like the others. Thanks in large part to the regional presence of the Merry Pranksters, it develops into its own kind of annual gathering, a classic American state fair updated for the modern traditions with built-in pathways for psychedelic passage takers. Forget costumes—it is a place for genuine wood-living freaks to come sell and, more importantly, trade their creations and be together. The Faire Grounds has a natural shape for it, too, a figure eight through the woods that makes an infinitely looping path.

Different vendors come together, called from the linked-up communes and minitribes in the region. Alongside Garrick Beck and the Gathering-organizing Rainbows (who'd helped blaze the figure eight), there is the Family of the Mystic Arts from Sunny Valley in the southern part of the state, who have it super-together and make droolingly good hand-pressed apple cider. A local commune from Veneta, the total immersion group marriage with the recursive name of the CRO Research Organization, is around, too.

Food is one place that heads have really gotten it going of late, and the Springfield Creamery rides the cutting edge. In Berkeley, the hip economy funds Alice Waters's groundbreaking Chez Panisse restaurant when drug-dealing profits from Waters's friends become some of the seed money for farm-fresh ingredients and a whole new way of looking at food. "They were the only sort of counterculture people who had money," Waters will say. "We couldn't get it from a bank, God knows."

Part of the food revolution has its roots in Menlo Park, too, a few blocks from Garcia's former hangout at Kepler's Books. Though Stewart Brand had closed down his *Whole Earth Catalog* in 1971, he continues to operate his Whole Earth Truck Store, selling the newest techno-countercultural books and becoming a locus point for communards around Northern California, especially those interested in sustainable agriculture and new technologies. Among other institutions, the Whole Earth spins off the Briarpatch Network, a coalition of Bay Area businesses. Brand's influence can be felt far and wide. At his recommendation, Random House had republished the underground hit *Living on the Earth,* a hand-drawn survival guide by Wheeler's Ranch resident Alicia Bay Laurel, and sold more than 350,000 copies. To celebrate the book's success, Bay Laurel had thrown a series of parties at the commune, including one with "homemade marzipan Easter eggs seasoned with Clear Light acid." Her book kicks off a genre of homespun lifestyle manuals published by independent houses and major presses alike. Publishers open West Coast offices to get closer to the people closest to the earth.

Though the number of upstart communes dwindles nationwide, the West Coast lifestyle now begins to stabilize. "I got a place on the edge of the group of communes around Wheeler's [in Sonoma]," says Ramon Sender, the former San Francisco tape music composer-turned-solar yogi, collaborating during the Rainbow summer of 1972 with Alicia Bay Laurel on *Being of the Sun,* a guide to starting one's own religion. "By then, there was about a square mile of friendly territory between four or five different groups," Sender says. "I could walk out of the back of my two acres nude and travel across this acreage, all friendly, except that I'd have to run across one county road real quick." For once, it holds, and no one hassles them off their part of the Land. Tracing it up around the Northwest, the head world flourishes.

And when the Grateful Dead come to Veneta, the distant reason for all the widespread heady flourishing—Augustus O. Stanley III, a.k.a. Alice D. Millionaire, a.k.a. Bear—is back on the band's soundbeam team, fresh from prison. It's been a long, strange something or other since he pressed pills upstairs from the Dead's practice space in Los Angeles. Owsley is no longer making LSD, but he still adheres to his proto–Paleo diet and is still quite active in the rock 'n' roll part of the hip economy, not to mention pioneering his own methods for excellent homegrown weed. And here he is in Veneta along with the Dead and the Pranksters and Wavy Gravy and a shit ton of LSD. Historian Nicholas Meriwether will dub the Grateful Dead's Veneta benefit "the Last Acid Test," and it is all that and so very much more, a fertile background for one of the Grateful Dead's all-time greatest artistic creations.

When the Dead come to save the Springfield Creamery, it is one of the hottest days in Lane County history, one of the highest, and surely one of the biggest traffic jams, too. Prankster Ken Babbs babbles between songs, and Wavy Gravy wanders on- and offstage in an oversized sombrero.

And there's Naked Pole Guy, bearing bare-assed witness to one of the most spectacular sights on the best of all possible galactic planes.

The sun melts over the planetary rim while the Grateful Dead unfurl their jam epic "Dark Star," thirty-one minutes of shining free-flight flowing through gentle modal waves and intricate piano runs, shifting and swelling scenes and high-speed pursuits down wormholes, all brushed in Garcia's soft-hued wah-wah guitar. It is a wondrous improvised achievement out there in the heat. At the side of the stage is the saint Betty Cantor, running the reel-to-reel recorder. Many time travelers owe her many thanks as she grabs this note-perfect interstellar fantasia, preserving text for scholars, meditation music for seekers, a great jam. This "Dark Star" is why the Grateful Dead exist, a forging of social and creative and chemical circumstances.

"We have a kind of continuity, from off the street to outer space, so to speak," Jerry Garcia tells an interviewer earlier that year about the way the band has started to structure their shows. *And then back?* "Sometimes, but then sometimes we just hang out there. It's not so organized." By the summer of 1972 the organization is creeping in, both to their business structure and their music, and very often the band returns to form on the wings of a ballad sung by Garcia. There couldn't be a more perfect denouement to the preceding pancelestial mind-journey. It is both a majestic musical trick, moving from deepest space to deepest tenderness, and a concise symbolic gesture, sewing the psychedelic arc to the American songbook.

The reformation is key. This particular "Dark Star" resolves into a pair of country songs, first Bob Weir's earnest version of Marty Robbins's "El Paso" and then Garcia's solemn gospel duet with Donna Jean Godchaux on Merle Haggard's "Sing Me Back Home."

Of all the rock documentaries of the era, the resultant *Sunshine Daydream* contains probably the most equal-opportunity nudity of all, far beyond Naked Pole Guy. Every part of the film projects an America that holds honest and weird to itself. Not only does Naked Pole Guy *not* get pummeled at any point during the day by roadies, let alone the concert's nonexistent security guards, but he returns to his spot after the band's set break in time to watch "Dark Star" and continues to freak fucking freely. Someone, perhaps Naked Pole Guy himself, has also gotten him into shorts, not visible until the print is cleaned up for proper theatrical release more than forty years later, when time-traveling theatergoers burst into applause, knowing they can rest assured that some part of Naked Pole Guy goes home slightly less sunburned than the rest.

In American reality (as the cover of the Dead's *American Beauty* reads, if looked at long enough), the yield of the $3.50 tickets falls well short of the amount needed to set the Springfield Creamery right. So the Dead invoke hip economics and simply cut a check for the difference. The Creamery gets back on its feet, and its cultures continue to spread, a staple food institution that helps set the course for the modern yogurt industry and supplies tastiness to the Northwest for decades to come.

IN THE SOUTH Bronx, Harvey Lubar had always secretly wanted to be in a gang but is too shy and nonviolent. So the skinny teenage peacenik starts a new kind of gang. And, in its own way, Harvey's nonviolent crew will end up being as influential as any of the old-guard LSD distributors, putting down the first pieces of a network that will serve perhaps millions of heads over the next decades.

On his occasional trips to the East Village, Harvey can see traces of the recent utopia as he walks past the Anderson Theater, its psychedelic paint job still visible amid the winos and bottles littering the entrance. His South Bronx home turf is getting violent, as many neighborhoods are in the early 1970s, both urban and elsewhere.

The head scene turns weird around his South Bronx home, too. The longhairs can be found partying in houses and apartments along the Grand Concourse and Pelham Parkway, doing methadone and getting sick. Not Harvey Lubar. Harvey Lubar digs meditation. It's a violent time in New York. Harvey remembers only a year before when the Weather Underground had blown up a building in Greenwich Village.

Then he discovers that there is a certain house near his in the Bronx where, every afternoon, fifteen heads cram into the living room and crank live Grateful Dead tapes at powerful volumes. It's easily the best thing going on anywhere in sight. He sees the band for the first time at the Felt Forum in December '71 and—though he likes it—can't grasp why it doesn't sound like the tapes he's heard, which turn out to be the Legendary Marty's. Harvey and Marty's mutual friend moves away and allows Harvey to make copies, but Harvey Lubar wants more. Needs more.

"People would go to Dead concerts and they were never the same," he's heard, and not inaccurately. "Or they went to a Grateful Dead concert and never went home. They would just, who knows? They would wind up in a commune somewhere." Perhaps he's heard the very true stories of the band's crew dosing unwilling people with LSD, ranging from promoter Bill Graham to actual on-duty police officers. He vaguely remembers, maybe, the nationally reported incident at Winterland in May when a thousand people drank heavily dosed apple cider. Thirty went to the hospital. "It was okay acid," ran a quote, "but I feel bad for anyone who took more than two sips."

To Harvey Lubar, who goes to see the Grateful Dead as often as he can between college classes and a job, they are already as much a myth as a real band, a generation removed from the original primal experience of the '60s. The tapes provide a show-by-show link back to the primal stew. He catches them at the Academy of Music on Fourteenth Street in early '72, but after that it's arenas and stadiums. The Grateful Dead are big time.

"DEAD FREAKS UNITE," reads the inner sleeve of the band's most recent album. "Who are you? Where are you? How are you?" it reads, plus an address for a post office box in San Rafael affixed with a new name for these fans: Dead Heads. Like the band's radio broadcasts, the newsletters that start in late 1971 are another element in the developing business model.

"Dead Heads Unite!" says their first newsletter, mostly a verbatim rap from Garcia: "If we had it really super together, if we had a lot of money, what we could have done was to organize like rough lists of members of the Grateful Dead weirdness scene or whatever or something . . . to provide a communication system of some loose sort. . . . "

Garcia continues, "Since we can't provide any way for you people to get together and since we haven't got any money to do that, everybody ought to think of ways to get together with other Dead freaks." In conclusion, the band remind their readers to "take care, have fun, and stay high." More missives follow, less a fan club than a direct news service.

It is almost immediately after this that Harvey Lubar forms his gang. "Trade tapes with the Hell's Honkies," the signs say, and they yield him a fellow Bronx-born Lehman College student named Jerry Moore, a longhaired Irishman with bottomless sarcasm and an occasionally fiery temper. To call him a serious Grateful Dead freak is to leave insufficient headroom for what he is about to become. Moore is exactly the person the word "Dead-head" quickly becomes dehyphenated to describe. Many years later, the band will trademark the phrase "Dead Head," but nobody can trademark Jerry Moore or what he is. Jerry Moore is a *Deadhead*.

The Dead themselves now provide Deadheads with a tangible access point to the psychedelic and countercultural otherworld through concerts, set lists, lyrics, jams, iconic skulls, roses, cowboys, poker games, china cats, sunflowers, and every last acid-soaked fiber of their being. The tapes and their collectors become yet another visible way that the Grateful Dead and their performances are different from the consensus reality around them. The tapes allow there to be a Grateful Dead without the Grateful Dead themselves, to bring the news wherever it needs to go, simply by documenting the day-by-day transformation of the evolving überheads in the working band known as the Grateful Dead. The tapes are powerful, the absolute capturing of the Deadheads' *alcheringa* dreaming time, and the new tape clubs become their own contribution to the hip economy. The tapes are currency, generating an energy of their own.

This is when, where, and how the Grateful Dead's music becomes the dominant psychedelic ritual in the United States. Its symbols replicate themselves via the taper network, a tool set for trippers that is richer and more American than any Egyptian pseudotranslations or slogans Timothy Leary can conjure. People can, will, and do use prized Grateful Dead recordings as trusted guides when taking acid or mushrooms or anything, really. As tapers document the gigs more frequently (to the chagrin of the band's road crew) each Dead show begins to have a guaranteed audience beyond its initial ticket buyers. For future ethnographers, every Grateful Dead concert recording might be treated as both the physical artifact of a psychedelic group-mind and directions to its nearest connection point. Find the tapes and a Deadhead isn't usually too far behind. Find one Deadhead, find many.

The Hell's Honkies, Dead Relics, and other collectors nearly all simultaneously derive rule numero uno of Grateful Dead tape trading: *FREE*. Harvey and Marty's mutual friend had stumbled off into the mists of history with the parting condition that Harvey must *never* charge for the tapes and must *always* help people start new collections. It doesn't take much for these to become informally institutionalized across the network, both the Deadhead way and the natural law of the Land, just like the Diggers decreed.

As much as the gems and crystals traded at Rainbow Gatherings, Grateful Dead tapes are talismans with their own mystic power, physical sound objects that are part map and part territory. The concert chronology of the People's Band doubles as a history of the People, a psychedelic time line that connects the musicians out on the road in the bleak early '70s with the musicians playing at the moment of pure unknown promise of the Acid Tests. Even if the collectors don't always grasp this, Dead tapes are a way of understanding what happened. The medium is the amassment.

And the amassment triggers community and entrepreneurship around the new currency. Les Kippel of Brooklyn, the ambitious proprietor of the Dead Relics Tape Exchange, prints up business cards for his club and, from then on, to be official you *have* to have business cards. The amassment triggers more demand, even competition. The Dead tape clubs all network like crazy, but there are always tapes missing. And no one can get in touch with the Legendary Marty Weinberg.

But then the Hell's Honkies score reels of two shows from July '69 at the World's Fair Pavilion, the utopian-sculptural almost-ruin in Queens. In the New York Dead freak groupmind, they are fabled afternoons, the closest many (including Marty) ever got to East Coast Trips Festivals. Marty is intrigued enough to invite the Honkies over.

Marty's place over by the NYU Bronx extension is suitably legendary, an apartment in the massive four-building complex known as the Castle. "It covered a full city block and had hundreds of apartments, turrets, and a huge medieval courtyard," Harvey Honkie remembers, still in awe. Marty's still only twenty, but hep beyond his years, sharing an exceedingly fat pad with two roommates. He brings the Honkies into his room and, with little preamble, starts DJing gems from his collection for Harvey and Mark Honkie at top volume.

Marty is nice enough to the guys, though he doesn't leave much room for talking, blasting the Dead, as one does. He seems happy to play his tapes but is in no hurry to let them go home with copies. Marty doesn't really *trade*. But Marty's in the mood to blow their minds and plays them tapes he's never played for anyone, let alone duplicated.

There's a twenty-five-minute "Dancing in the Street" from the Carousel Ballroom, a perfect soundboard of an acoustic show from San Diego, and other beautiful tapes from some undivulged source out West. He is the Legendary Marty, after all. The Honkies are too stunned to even ask where they came from.

Almost better, though, the Hell's Honkies go home with the memories of these unbelievable tapes, which get recounted over and over to their friends: oral memories of recorded music. In the hip economy, information moves the market.

Marty is cool about it, and doesn't really want to tell Harvey this, but Marty's a little weirded out by all the adulation, of himself, but of the Grateful Dead in general. Les Kippel of the Dead Relics Tape Exchange had found him recently, too, and Marty really isn't sure what to make of that guy. "The group of friends I had through the Dead were musicians, they were intellectuals," Marty says later. "I didn't use that word, but they were people into a *lot* of things, and the Dead was the soundtrack. And you *really* enjoyed the soundtrack. I must've listened to *Live/Dead* 10,000 times. I know every note of that album. It was the center of my life.

"But [for some of these tapers] it *was* their life. Their entire being from waking up to going to sleep at night. They were just surrounded by Grateful Dead stuff. I didn't dislike them, but it's not me."

Marty Weinberg might be a head and a Dead freak, but he's not a Deadhead. These Deadheads, many of them, seem powerfully un-chill. Why would anyone stand on a chair and scream *JERRRRR-RRR-RRRRRY?* The Dead's newest music since Mickey Hart left the band isn't that interesting to Marty, either, not as plainly beautiful and/or boundary destroying. All in all, Marty thinks, it's been a good run. He's got the tapes he made. And he's got the tapes he *didn't* make, the ones that are the real evidence of his coolness.

The Legendary Marty is the Legendary Marty because he doesn't get busted. Except once. It is a story he has sworn to tell no one. So he doesn't. But it goes like this:

One night at the Fillmore East, sometime in '69 or so, Marty is taping like usual, down front, second row, Garcia-side. He holds his mic at chest level, aimed upwards, someplace no one can see it. "I had it pointed midway between the PA and the instruments," Marty says. "I wanted the cymbals and the high end off the stage, I wanted [the sound] direct off the amps, I didn't want reflection from the back of the theater."

At the set break, he feels a hand on his shoulder and a voice in his ear: "Say, what do you got there?"

Oh, fuck, busted, Marty thinks. But he isn't a liar. "I'm recording the show."

As the guy comes around to face him, Marty can tell that the guy is truly angry, on the verge of losing it. Marty had never thought he was doing anything wrong by taping, but now this apoplectic man is implying that Marty is in very big trouble, indeed.

"What are you using?" the man demands, fuming, looking over Marty, following the cable from his microphone down to the floor below the seat with his eyes. Marty doesn't recognize the guy. Little dude. Bolo tie. Maybe he works for Bill Graham and spotted him from the stage somehow?

"Uher 4000L recorder and AKG D190E microphone," he tells the man.

"How do you set up the mic?"

And Marty tells him how he sets up the mic. The man is starting to get less angry.

"Wow, pretty good," the guy says after more questions and, before Marty realizes it, the man is talking to Marty like they're old pals.

The set break is coming to a close, and the inquisitive man has to get back to whatever it is that he does. "Why don't we meet afterwards," he tells Marty. "I could talk to you."

Marty figures that because the guy isn't busting him it's probably alright. "Sure," he says.

"Meet by the side of the stage after the show," the guy tells him. Marty goes there then, and, as promised, the little dude reappears. "Hey, your setup is good," he tells Marty, picking up the conversation. "I bet you have some good stuff."

"Yeah, I've got some," Marty allows.

"I have some stuff, too." Another pause. "Do you want to trade?" Marty's never even met anyone who taped. "Yeah, sure," he says. "I've never done it before. What do you have?"

"Only West Coast," the funny little man says.

"You with the band?" Marty asks, slowly (but not yet) picking up on who the fuck he's talking to.

"Yeah."

"Really?"

"Yeah."

In short order, the lean man with the bolo tie and the southwestern vibe produces a business card with a Berkeley PO box and Owsley Stanley introduces himself to Marty.

"I'm blown away," Marty says, a reader of the *Electric Kool-Aid Acid Test* and knowing good goddamn who Bear is.

"I'm blown away, too," Bear concedes and tells Marty to mail him some tapes. Only the good stuff. "You can't allow anyone to know that we're doing this, ever," Owsley tells him. "*Ever.*"

And Marty doesn't. For a while. He certainly doesn't tell the Hell's Honkies, but he's happy to destroy their minds with the music. The tapes had come from California for almost two years, direct from the first taper himself. Marty would send some of his out West, and mixes would return in the mail, light psychedelic ornamentation on the reels and the occasional but very stern warning to *not* copy the tapes. Marty holds to his word and never makes duplicates.

When Owsley disappears for a trip into the California penal system, the exchange stops. They never speak again.

ON THE RADIO as 1972 prepares to turn to 1973 at San Francisco's Winterland Arena, an otherwise sober-seeming DJ speaks of "motion-picture holograms" flickering on the venue's floor while the Dead play. The holograms are otherwise undocumented. But, as always at a Dead show, unusual visitors are present, leveraging the band as a tool to enact countercultural change.

On stage, David Crosby joins the Dead on electric twelve-string for a Planet Earth Rock and Roll Orchestra mission to Mars. A naked woman appears onstage. When promoter Bill Graham manhandles her into the wings, a group of fellow freaks strip off their own clothes in protest.

On the floor of Winterland, Doug Kiehl gets strange looks. Maybe heads can sense that he's not actually an usher, despite the badge that Bill Graham personally gave him. To nearly anybody attending the show, Kiehl's business is quite heavy, even if they can't tell what it is, and his vibrations must be tremendous, being a representative of the Bureau of Narcotics and Dangerous Drugs and all.

Kiehl has every good reason to think that spending New Year's Eve on a stakeout at a Grateful Dead show will yield the people he and the bureau seek, and they will be able to stop the pernicious flow of the LSD black market once and for all. In August, around the time the Dead played in Veneta, everything had seemed to come down on the acid distribution collective known as the Brotherhood of Eternal Love.

There'd been a massive three-state, four-location bust all along the Hippie Highway from Laguna Beach to Hawaii involving fifty-three arrests, two and a half tons of hash, thirty gallons of hash oil, and one and a half million tablets of Orange Sunshine. Tim Scully, the former Dead roadie and Owsley protégé, had left the lab years ago but is indicted along with fellow chemist Nick Sand. By New Year's, almost everyone is rounded up, either in jail, out on bail and awaiting trial, or on the run. If there's one place that Brotherhood members are sure to turn up, it's Dead shows. The previous New Year's, Brotherhood chemist Nick Sand had warranted a +5 on the band's guest list, the second most on the six-page document. Agent Kiehl has heard that sometimes the Brotherhood members get there late, come in by some backstage means, and leave early.

Between the emergence of disco in New York and the outdoor happenings of the northwestern crescent, there are options for heads everywhere, but there is nothing like a Grateful Dead show. The constant presence of LSD and its most high-level dealers keeps Dead concerts at a precious remove from consensus reality by several fundamental steps, even as other countercultural beacons start to flicker.

Inside a Dead show, it is *different* in a way the rest of the world increasingly isn't. There's a gaggle of Naked Pole Guys on stage, and only Bill Graham is probably annoyed by it. The Grateful Dead show is a zone so obviously zoned that Special Agent Kiehl isn't even shocked to spot several previously busted members of the Brotherhood, including one—John Gale, champion surfer and drug smuggler—who seems to be openly handing out LSD.

Even if the United States does have representatives there to arrest some very specific heads, there is no stopping the Zone. Does Kiehl feel overwhelmed by this? Who is to say? But, at some point during the night, Kiehl's walkie-talkie crackles. Outside, his fellow agents have nabbed Brotherhood cofounder and acting leader Michael Randall and his wife, Carol Griggs. The '60s are over, finally, and good Americans can breathe a sigh of relief. No?

3

BEYOND THE WHOLE EARTH

t's an idyllic spot for the heads to launch themselves into the future. There's a lake. There's moonlight and, in the darkness, the shapes of mountains. San Francisco twinkles in the far distance. And, perched on a hill, there's an odd semicircular structure housing a multimillion dollar research facility with a mainframe computer that is one of two dozen civilian nodes on the small system of nationally interlinked computers called the ARPANET.

The Stanford Artificial Intelligence Lab in late 1972 is just as much a product of Palo Alto as the Grateful Dead or Ken Kesey and the Merry Pranksters. And like Kesey and Robert Hunter's LSD use at local government VA hospitals, there is a complex mix of forces and funding at work at the inception of what will be a prolonged revolution. Though SAIL (as many call the Lab) is an official university facility, it feels far, far away. While many of the people who spend their time there are technically students, SAIL contains its own universe.

"These are heads," Stewart Brand declares when he visits and writes about the lab for *Rolling Stone* in 1972. "Most of them. Half or more of computer science is heads." Lots of *Lord of the Rings* fans, too, but that's not mutually exclusive.

In the lobby, there is a You Are Here–style campus map. The scientist-heads at the lab draw on their own additions, extending the pathways of the Stanford grid toward foreign galaxies. One connects to the center of the human brain. For now, this particular map is purely theoretical, but there is no question that the D. C. Power building and its residents belong on the ever-revised larger (and larger) Map.

They are up at all hours, these heads, so much so that Les Earnest, SAIL's thirty-six-year-old director, develops a system to keep track of them all. "Each day, I would go to bed one hour later and get up one hour later," he says, "which meant that every 25 days, I would intersect with everyone. It's clever, but a little stressful getting up in time for a dinner party or bicycling to work at 3 a.m. on a cold and drizzly night. That's when I gave up."

So Les Earnest invents the FINGER command for the Lab's PDP mainframe. The SAILers can leave virtual notes when they're not at their terminals. Quickly, the hackers elevate their PLAN files into forums for quotes, jokes, and other discussions. It is the world's first status update, a preview of what much of the global population will do constantly some decades hence.

"[SAIL] had the air of something between a Socratean abode and a hippie flophouse," remembers Andy Moorer, who invents arguably the world's first digital audio workstation at SAIL in 1972. It's a "big, honking machine" but one that undeniably displays sound as a waveform with a toolbar to control it.

Earlier, at MIT, Moorer had claimed the e-mail handle JAM after his initials and establishes what is perhaps the longest-running address on the net. The screen name's musical implications are hardly lost on him. He is one of many, many Grateful Dead freaks at SAIL. Perhaps fully a quarter of the hundred-person lab might count as such, not including casual fans like lab director Earnest, who sees them only two or three times a year.

A group of scientists from SAIL and the nearby (and likewise influential) Stanford Research Institute have been seeing the Dead together since the Avalon Ballroom and Fillmore West days back in '69. Pretty naturally, they start using the PDP-10's electronic mail system to organize ways to get to the shows or, as Moorer remembers, "where to meet up for a smoke-in."

SAIL is hardly a party zone on any given day at the office. But it's not *not* that. There's no dope smoking allowed in the lab, but it's California and one can pretty much always just step outside. One of the programmer-heads plants pot around the septic tank overflow area and complains to Earnest when the deer eat it. "I'm sorry, I don't think I can do much about that," his boss tells him. When the system shuts down each day for maintenance, there's an hour of volleyball. Another option is the in-lab sauna.

It's "the most bzz-bzz-busy scene I've been around since the Merry Prankster Acid Tests," Stewart Brand declares in *Rolling Stone*. Computers "are good news, maybe the best since psychedelics," he gushes. Brand is there to cover the Spacewar Olympics, a freshly made-up event where two dozen longhair programmers gather around a small glowing screen to compete at the first-ever video game.

Written at MIT a decade earlier and passed through the computer culture from lab to lab, Spacewar's code is shared and modified by programmers under the commonly understood agreement later termed "the hacker ethic." That is, free for the good of all, the People's Network made genuinely electronic.

This notion is implicit as the SAIL mindspace forms and becomes one of the most influential nodes on the emerging net. Built on distant Eisenhower-era orders to prepare communications methods in case nuclear war wiped out Ma Bell, there are only a few thousand ARPANET users in the whole country in 1972.

The e-mail system has all kinds of uses. Besides work collaborations, some organize ride shares to antiwar rallies. There are rambling internal discussions about the space program and other current events. One SAILer uses it to tabulate house accounts for his commune. With each new usage and behavior, the heads claim a little more of a stake in the future.

Along with the Stanford Research Institute, SAIL is a seething concept-hive, experimenting with impact printers, early synthesizers, eye-hand sensors, and robotics, all linked by a pulsating and externalized groupmind. It's a never-ending Trips Festival, outlets provided.

People at various labs use the new network to exchange news and opinions about science fiction. But it's the hippies who are most frequently *doing* stuff. It is the SAIL gang, for instance, that organizes the first piece of online commerce, using e-mail to coordinate a pot sale from the Stanford lab to the MIT lab.

"Cybernetic," from Norbert Wiener's notion of interconnectedness, is one of Stewart Brand's favorite concepts, and SAIL is definitely that. Burned out, Brand had shut down the *Whole Earth Catalog* after a best-selling final edition in 1971, throwing a nitrous-abetted party at San Francisco's Exploratorium, but he is already a legend around the tech scene that is multiplying along the San Francisco Peninsula. The ideas he had laid out during his earliest psychedelic days continue to propagate.

He encourages others to use the "Whole" or even "Whole Earth" prefixes for their ventures, so long as it's not a catalog. "It's free advertising," he tells his lawyer. When the Xerox PARC lab stocks its new library, they simply buy every book for sale at Brand's Whole Earth Truck Store. The *Catalog*'s logical, humanistic categorizations—understanding whole systems, shelter and land use, industry and craft, communications, community, nomadics, learning—are a Dewey Decimal System for the New Earth.

There are many heady people passing through the SAIL orbit. And then the Grateful Dead come to the Stanford campus for their first hometown show since the Palo Alto Be-In back in '67 and plant the seeds for pioneering new forms of artificial intelligence.

The Dead's crew arrives at the campus's new gym a few days early to install the latest experimental sound system, inspired by Owsley's ideas. In one memory, a team of German engineers (or are they Swiss?) in royal blue blazers run white noise tests, printing the results onto long rolls of paper. The newest sound system isn't so different from Owsley's acid: wherever it goes, it creates a new suspended reality in the space around it. His new society can be expressed as rich encoded air on the eardrums as much as a chemical release in the cerebral cortex, or (ideally) both. Deaf in one ear, the alchemy-obsessed sound freak is quite sure that stereo is elitist. In mono, all seats are equal. Some see his new system as a form of revenge. There is no more symbolic place to test out his new system and ideas than the heart of the acid-tinted Stanford research community.

The day of the show is drizzly and a little gross. In the parking lot outside, one SAIL scientist passes a few fans selling homemade Grateful Dead T-shirts, the same way—he thinks—they might on Telegraph Avenue in Berkeley. Some heads get in line early, taking turns waiting to get in while others duck into Manzanita Park to keep properly stoned.

When the doors open and they flood into the Maples Pavilion, itself new and state of the art, the Deadheads come face to face with these new soundbeam boxes that Owsley has wrought. The speaker array built by the band's in-family Alembic crew is beautiful and wooden, and hippie-crafted, head-made, high-concept, high-execution. And just, like, *wow*. Though the show is being put on by the Associated Students of Stanford, even Bill Graham is there, come to check out just what Bear and the beam-team are up to.

Out come the Dead, and they snap into "The Promised Land," Chuck Berry's ode to prosperous peacetime California, and promptly fry all the tweeters on the first note. The roadies sort it out, but the sound test is not off to a promising start.

Also, it seems that the new gym's spring-loaded floor is better suited to a few dozen guys playing basketball than a blesh of bouncing hippies. The floor bounces with them, rising and falling in visible waves a few inches high. This includes the stage, which is fine for the guitarists, who remain a constant distance from their instruments, but less so for Keith Godchaux, whose piano moves away from him like a Dixieland cartoon. The head-made speakers sway.

The Dead's usage of Stanford to experiment is more successful, debuting seven new instant favorites including "Eyes of the World" and "Here Comes Sunshine." Wavy Gravy is there onstage after the intermission, raising money for a teaching hospital in North Vietnam bombed by the United States over Christmas. "I'm told to make this announcement short and not political," he notes of the band's orders to him. "I'll make it short but political is weird. Taking a shit is a political act." He then offers one of the most beautifully contrite introductions the Grateful Dead ever receive: "And now, the rainbow makers, right?"

The Dead's newest material seems more self-aware of its back-turning than ever. The last of the Stanford debuts is called "Wave That Flag." Robert Hunter's lyrics riff through playful couplets that sound like the quips and mutterings of the Doodah Man in "Truckin'" out there on the totally-highway. It could be R. Crumb's Mr. Natural, dispensing wry advice and American colloquialisms over Gar-cee-uh's boogie. Or it could be Uncle Sam himself, as suggested when Hunter rewrites and retitles the song "U.S. Blues" the following year.

"Feed the poor, stop the war!" Garcia sings, the band's first and only statement on the still-growling skirmish in Vietnam, running concurrent to their entire existence as a musical entity. It's almost a punchline. The lyric won't stay.

The band play for more than three hours, plus set break. For the Dead, it's a good warm-up before they hit the road for a late winter tour. For Owsley, Ron Wickersham, and the rainbow-wrangling beam-team, it's back to the Alembic workshop in Marin. As the crowd files out, a beamer puts on a reel-to-reel of *Abbey Road*.

One of the newest SAIL scientists heads off to a party in the coastal hills, his brain filled with fresh ideas, on the Grateful Dead bus for good. He watches the far-off lights of Berkeley dance and hangs out until dawn.

IN THE SPRING of '73, a Supreme Court decision alters an old pillar of the counterculture. *Miller v. California* determines that different localities can decide what is and isn't obscene. As it happens, many localities use said laws to classify underground comix as obscene and many head shops now cease to stock them. The surrealistic stream of comix, kicked off when R. Crumb sold the first issue of *Zap!* from a baby carriage on Haight Street, will never cease, but it now separates from its roots. Like popular music, sequential art is a form with unlimited potential. Underground comix had always harbored close ties to the head scene. One partner at the legendary Last Gasp publishers had formerly supervised a San Francisco acid lab. And one of Last Gasp's most popular items was the Dealer McDope board game, based on a character by Dave Sheridan. After the Supreme Court decision, a small storm hits the comix industry, including a Canadian paper mill strike, and then antiparaphernalia laws. "It just slowly went down," said Spain Rodriguez, once an in-house illustrator at the *East Village Other,* which had folded in 1972. Some artists go mainstream. The amount of new titles dwindles, from 233 in 1972 to 160 in 1973. Next year, there will be even fewer.

POSTCARD FROM THE *Rest of the World:* on the other side of the Whelming Brine, the British heads are tending to their own jeweled psychedelic kingdom. The dawning is only just dawning. New Albion bulges and glows. A free festival scene starts in the UK in the summer of 1970 with Phun City ("the only British festival that isn't run by honkies") and evolves. In '71, Glastonbury Fair launches with a giant pyramid stage. They'd tried to get the Dead, but it didn't work. There is live music, but *free* runs deeper and affixes itself to the ley lines of Stonehenge and the mysterious power of Glastonbury Tor. The British travelers are very into solstices and equinoxes and sunrise meditations.

Starting in late 1971, the Central Research Establishment at Aldermaston observes a massive spike in acid seizures around Her Majesty's good lands. Specifically, British agents are seizing microdots, a new variety of tiny pills pouring right from the heart of New Albion. This LSD is made by a radical head chemist named Richard Kemp. Previously an assistant to the shadowy Ron Stark—source of ergotamine tartrate precursor for the American LSD makers—it is Kemp who discovers a new, cheaper method for yielding excellent acid.

Combined with the initial worldwide rush of Orange Sunshine, the microdots burst eastward from the United Kingdom to France and West Germany and the Netherlands, to Israel and Australia. They electrify the United Kingdom as Owsley and the Brotherhood had done earlier to the United States. The United Kingdom being much, much smaller, there's plenty left over, and a regular supply of microdots traverses the Whelming Brine and makes its way to the States.

Smaller festivals (micro)dot New Albion, sometimes extending over two or three weeks while mobile communities of several thousand form. The secretive chemist Richard Kemp channels funds to both festival organizers and Release, an organization that operates tents for people experiencing adverse reactions to the LSD.

On the towering cliffs overlooking the Bristol Channel in 1972 and 1973 and beyond, the Trentishoe Whole Earth Fayre shouts out Stewart Brand's influential *Whole Earth Catalog* and experiments with windmills and recycling and domes and alternative energy and alternative structures and free "whole food" and yoga and star chanting and childcare. Hawkwind and other bands play and the pink microdots flood the local hip marketplaces.

At the second Windsor Free Festival, in the summer of '73— a crowd of 1,500 or so—a group of heads brings a typewriter and duplicator and puts out the daily *Freek Press*. The Acid Report indexes a half-dozen varieties of microdots and consumer information when available ("White tab with a groove . . . suggest half tab for average tripper"). They request some blue microdots so they might test them personally.

A man with a briefcase approaches the stage manager and asks how he might best distribute its contents, opening it to reveal hundreds, maybe thousands, of microdots. So the stage manager makes an announcement and the British heads line up at the front of the stage and retrieve the 200-microgram pills. *Wish you were here!*

STARTING IN 1973, Steve Brown's daily commute to his job at one of the hip economy's most vanguard companies takes him up the California coast. He drives past the ruins of the Sutro Baths and the tip of Golden Gate Park, over the bridge, and through the rainbow entrance of the Waldo Tunnel into the cartoon known as Marin County. Many days, he picks up hitchhikers. The good-natured and ponytailed Brown shares joints with his passengers and plays them some freshly made Grateful Dead tapes. *Very* fresh.

Generally the hitchhikers are in a pretty good space for the day by the time Steve drops them off and gets to the office around 10 a.m. He pulls around the back and heads up the side stairs of the funky little house, smelling the French roast, and arrives at his desk, where his boss is sitting, doodling on Brown's notepad.

Jerry Garcia usually beats everyone to Grateful Dead Records head(s)quarters every morning, bopping over the hill from Stinson Beach and putting the coffee on, ready for another day pulling levers deep in the gear work of the hip economy, a happy worker-magnate with an enormous stogie-sized joint dangling from his beard as he and his comrades spit out candy-colored clouds from the rainbow factory. Among his many other tasks, Steve Brown works the phones, rolls some of the aforementioned stogie-sized joints, does radio promotion, and helps operate both Grateful Dead and Round Records. He is responsible for running in-room tapes during the Dead's studio sessions and subsequently blowing hitchhikers' morning-minds with them.

As a business and a homegrown local industry, the Dead are starting to take over a small chunk of San Rafael, an expanding Whole Earth enterprise like any other. The little office in San Rafael is part of a network of New World businesses, connected by the wave of post–Whole Earth "access catalogues" that emerge in the early '70s.

Five houses down, a company called Ice-9 handles the band's publishing, run by Garcia's Palo Alto–era brah Alan Trist. Upstairs is the Out of Town booking agency and Fly by Night Travel, handling the needs of the Dead, the New Riders, and other operations. Tie-dye innovator Courtenay Pollock makes covers for the florescent lights, and, each week, the office staff takes delivery of delicious Nancy's Honey Yogurt, fresh from the Keseys' creamery in Oregon. Nearby, Alembic and a variety of contractors handle the band's instruments and speakers. The Dead have kept their money moving quickly for years. Some iterations fail, like Kumquat Mae, a Marin Valley clothing store and head shop run by family members. But others succeed. Alembic is one of the highest-end instrument and speaker makers in the world.

The band's two-year-old mailing list has some 25,000 names. They're receiving about four hundred letters a week. Around the world, the Grateful Dead are known as the People's Band, and their public front does nothing to change this. Like Stewart Brand's *Whole Earth Catalog,* which printed expenses and profits in each issue, the Dead disclose their annual earnings in one of their periodic newsletters ($1.4 million). "What else might we do?" they ask. "Write and suggest it. Magic ideas welcome." And, lo, then the mail *really* pours in.

They get letters from the Euphoric Ice Cream Parlor in Austin, Texas, and the Quantum Geometrodynamics Task Force of the People's Library of the Department of Physics at Princeton. "If you need experienced persons to run a planetarium for you let me know," reads another postcard.

An envelope arrives from Japan on stationary: "FREE PRESS FOR FREAKS & THE FOURTH WORLD," it says. "We make underground newspaper," the letter reads in part. "In Japan . . . it is not only records [that are expensive] but also dope, acid, guitar, concert-ticket, and many things. But we have many friends and love and power. And we love Rock & Roll. Now. We think we cooperate with a Dead Heads for brothers and sisters. We love you." It is signed Mr. Dope and Miss Acid.

And it's all, you know, pretty far out. Plus (as was the goal, Steve Brown says) they accumulate more names for the ever-building mailing list. It's a double-edged banana, though. When the band announce a summer of massive stadium shows in 1973, a swarm of *supremely* angry letters buzzes into San Rafael. But what the Dead and their joint-chomping chief heads have in mind is even more radical than an open communication system with their audience.

Round Records and its many schemes are the purview of Steve Brown's *other* boss, a dude named Ron Rakow. Ron Rakow understands the hip economy, sure, sure. But he also understands the straight economy, having worked on Wall Street before dropping out. Rakow understands all *kinds* of economies. At one point in the '60s, he'd hustled a deal by which each band member received a Plymouth. All were soon repossessed, with the exception of Pigpen's, because he continued to make his payments on time. Rakow is known as the Dead's in-house scammer.

On paper, Round Records is an extraordinary business venture that taps into the countercultural world surrounding the Dead. It is the rock 'n' roll end of the hip economy worked out as theoretical math. Rakow lays it out to the band in personalized binders under the rubric "So What?": *the band will use the heads as their distribution system.*

"There's this overworked, overtaxed house in San Rafael, where fifty or sixty people come and get charged up, function, share their flashes, share their getting high," he raves in the report. Why not franchise that very concept?

He describes a local branch: A bunch of kids come in, do some work, and get paid in a stack of the latest Grateful Dead LPs. Then, they head back to their high schools, colleges, and head shops to resell the LPs and make some bread, putting money back into the hip economy as they go. "Imagine further, that same set duplicated in Rochester, N.Y., in Brooklyn, in Memphis, just outside Chicago, in Madison, Wisconsin," the report continues. "Anyplace where there's a lot of young folks, we can create little places, which when put together, form a distribution pipeline, into which products that come out of or through the house in San Rafael, go and get disseminated, all over, using every possible business method which will be adapted for this use."

It is a system that will never come to pass when it comes time to actually distribute the band's LPs, but it is just as likely that Rakow can intuit the fact that Deadheads are already building exactly the network he describes, with or without the help of Grateful Dead Records. Out in Brooklyn during the same months that Rakow is putting his first numbers together, Les Kippel and the Dead Relics Tape Exchange are acting it out to the letter.

They spend all day copying tapes, Kippel at the front of the chain of decks. *"Go!"* he calls out, and, if every head times it out right, they're all synched and they all get nice copies of whatever concert they're copying, one more generation removed from the source, only one more slight layer of hiss between the original event and the light. The shows are commodities of different values based on their scarcity and quality and source and myth. The vocabulary and good-vibed setting of the American psychedelic ritual replicate with every tape.

"We all had outboard Dolby machines," says Harvey Lubar of the Hell's Honkies, who continue their own scene in the Bronx. "We'd set our signals to the hum, and start taping, and sit around and listen for seven or eight hours. And during that time, we became friends. We started talking. We learned all about each other's families, our difficulties, our dreams, or aspirations. Every now and then we'd go 'ooh, ooh, that was a good solo he just took.'" Pause. "'So what's going on with your sister and her boyfriend?'

"I bonded with so many people like that," Harvey continues. "We were all around the same age. We weren't rich kids. We weren't poverty-stricken either. We were all lower middle class kids who had this wonderful hobby that was all-consuming and we had the same outlook on life." That outlook includes constant Grateful Dead and at least the tacit acceptance of the world that the band implies.

Ron Rakow's "So What?" papers don't fully grasp the Dead's demographic, but he's trying to quantify the energy. Rakow has all kinds of numbers, breaking down the mailing list state by state (New York is #1, with about a quarter of the fans) charted against how many gigs the Dead have played there in recent years. He hires a Dead freak cab driver in Manhattan to survey likely looking Dead freaks for their opinions about various matters including the price of LPs, people's perception of the group, and the rock world in general.

"Very much cynicism about music industry and groups themselves," the cabbie-freak reports sometimes in mid-1972. "Large contrast with three years ago when groups were looked up to for leadership. Dead sometimes excepted from cynicism, sometimes not." Rakow also proposes claiming money from the Minority Enterprise Small Business Investment Company, which is perhaps obviously a nonstarter.

A good deal of the seed money comes via Atlantic Records, which will distribute overseas, and the Bank of Boston, which provides a generous revolving line of credit after Rakow flies Garcia to the bank's office and the guitarist turns on that other hip commodity, charisma. The whole project remains a quintessentially Dead-like operation, an irrepressible and irresponsible business venture designed to get the Dead's music out and pump money into the hip economy. Not even Garcia fully understands the magic Rakow weaves with the Bank of Boston. Surely, they are doing their best to act like grownups, and perhaps a bustling office isn't the most appropriate place for a work-ingman's head to eat acid.

"Oh, sometimes the office was *totally* the appropriate place to eat acid," Steve Brown says of the days he drives up the coast to the Dead office. Psychedelic America strides toward the future as its principles start to fix themselves into forms of enterprise. They will launch this iteration of the hip economy into record stores across America by way of extra-high-quality LP pressings in the fall of '73, the words *IGNORE ALIEN ORDERS* embossed into the first pressings.

"The question is, can we do it and stay high?" Garcia ponders. "Can we make it so our organization is composed of people who are like pretty high, who are not being controlled by their gig, but who are ac-tively interested in what they're doing?" Just as one can be a head with-out being a drug user, one can stay high without drugs. But they help.

They invent a fictional record company head, one Anton Round, and joke about distributing the Dead's records via ice cream trucks and holographic pyramids. But LPs go out via the nationwide network of independent distributors in operation since the pre-Beatles days when *all* rock labels were indie. Rakow divides the business into two parts: Grateful Dead Records (owned by the band) for the Dead LPs and Round Records (owned by Garcia and Rakow) for solo trips and side projects. And away they go: a business by heads for heads.

The money moves around almost as fast as Garcia does. When the Dead aren't on the road, he gigs full time, balancing three different projects outside the Dead to fulfill different aspects of his playing. For endless chop-building R&B and jazz variations, there are regu-lar nights with Merl Saunders and John Kahn at Keystone Berkeley and locales around the Peninsula, like the Quonset hut in Palo Alto known as Homer's Warehouse. For bluegrass, there's Old and in the

Way, a new configuration, where Garcia picks up the banjo for the first time in years. For space music, there's biomusic composer Ned Lagin, now migrated to Marin and working regularly with Jerry and Phil Lesh and Mickey Hart and David Crosby on the avant-garde epic *Seastones*.

For so much of it, there's cocaine, a drug Garcia is increasingly reliant on, which marches into the head world in the early 1970s. In Marin, Garcia's just a regular ol' cartoon musician in a world of regular ol' cartoons. Some nights, when Garcia plays without the Dead, he has an audience. But he plays so often that, just as likely, he might not. It's no matter to him.

"Music is my yoga, if there is a yoga, that's it," Garcia tells *New Age Journal* in 1975, which he considers to be a "right-on" publication. "Practicing and keeping my muscles together, that is like what I would relate to a physical yoga, a certain amount of hours every day," he continues. "Life is my yoga, too, but I've been a spiritual dilettante off and on through the years, trying various things at various times, and I firmly believe that every avenue that leads to higher consciousness *does* lead to higher consciousness. If you think it does, it does. If you put energy into it on a daily basis, no matter what it is, some discipline, or whatever it is, I believe it will work. I believe that it's within the power of the mind and consciousness to do that."

There are many yogas available in this bold, fresh epoch. For the freaks back in the Bronx or the frothing heads that Steve Brown notices showing up in city after city, perhaps the Grateful Dead themselves are a form of yoga. To *New Age Journal,* Garcia muses about the Dead building their own home base, a combination performance hall and recording studio. Acid reflects its users, and that's still a regular part of Jerry Garcia's yoga, too, in 1973.

Garcia is at the forefront of the California New Age, on the verge of finding a full expression of his turn-your-back-and-say-fuckery. Living in a beautiful house with a beautiful wife and beautiful children overlooking the beautiful sparkling Pacific, he would seem to be an exemplar head. His contemporaries are those who explore the outer perimeter of art and science and esoteric crossings that no one would have thought to investigate a decade previous. Garcia's partner, the Merry Prankster named Mountain Girl, pioneers methods for harvesting potent strains of pot in the back of their house, communicating gardening tips out to a circle of women growers she knows who are setting up more serious operations in Mendocino.

At the turn of the decade, a San Francisco State University philosophy professor named Jacob Needleman had declared in his book *The New Religions* that "sooner or later we are going to have to understand California—and not simply from the motive of predicting the future for the rest of the country. . . . Something is struggling to be born here." His words echo ones that Robert Hunter will write soon in a song called "Crazy Fingers" about how "something new is waiting to be born." The Grateful Dead's entire existence is an affirmation that the higher ground is still available, an ever-present ether, no matter how battered the material world might seem in Richard Nixon's America. The Dead are pushing all the angles, trying to will consensus reality into believing their trip, and it's getting pretty close.

At Watkins Glen International Speedway, the Dead and the Allman Brothers and the Band play for 650,000 people, what will remain for several decades as the biggest rock concert of all time. There are newly designed delay towers to make the sound more righteous for people far away, as well as a pirate radio broadcast by some heads who talked themselves onto the site by claiming to be from the Canadian media. It is a concert so big that it will inspire a knockoff LP by Pickwick Records, studio musicians imitating the Dead and company with dubbed-in crowd noise.

As becomes clear, the new generation of Deadheads are perhaps quite clever, but they aren't necessarily nature equipped. Jerry Moore of the Hell's Honkies tape club devises something new for Watkins Glen: a mic stand to get the microphone up over the massive crowd and *only* pick up the PA signal. Great success! But when the temperature drops down into the thirties, though, the tapers freeze their honky asses off, burning tape-trading business cards to keep warm.

When the Dead return to Nassau Coliseum in the fall, Jerry Moore's recordings document the new technique in effect. He hits record, the lights go down, the crowd cheers, and then up with the microphone pole, the recording quality changing audibly. There is a general gasp in the vicinity when the local blesh senses what he is doing. "Come on," someone shouts, but no one follows up, perhaps realizing that Jerry Moore's innovation—the first major step forward since Marty

Weinberg—is for the good of all. The results sound extraordinary. It catches on quickly among the tapers.

In 1974, Gilbert Youth Research, a Madison Avenue marketing firm, surveys some 2,500 young people who own tape recorders and find that "a surprising number—15.4%—are smuggling their tape recorders into concerts to get their own live performances on tape." That may be so. All kinds of acts get taped in those days. Bob Dylan's been on tour with the Band all year, and just about any of those shows are around, somewhere. Led Zeppelin, sure. David Bowie. Frank Zappa. Finding the tapes, though, is much harder.

But how many of them have fans like Les Kippel and Jerry Moore? Les Kippel and the Dead Relics Tape Exchange are profiled in *Rolling Stone*—"Mr. Tapes of Brooklyn"—and then come the letters, and Les Kippel is overwhelmed with calls. A title like Mr. Tapes is hard to shake. Soon, there are Free Grateful Dead Tape Exchanges in New Jersey, San Francisco, Seattle, DeKalb, and elsewhere. The crammed apartments filled with dudes (almost always dudes) hooked to their decks is an exact real-life implementation of what Ron Rakow suggested for the Dead's music in his "So What?" papers. All that's missing is any direct exchange of money, and the Dead's music spreads and spreads.

Les Kippel might not be able to tell the difference between the Diggers and the Yippies, but he can feel that notion of *free* in his bones. It's the primary directive, really. He is the furthest thing from a Spacewar-playing Stanford visionary. But Les Kippel, who manages apartments in Bed-Stuy for the New York City Housing Authority, and Paul Martin of the Stanford Lab share a connection. Should they ever meet, they could surely find something to talk about or even some way to collaborate. Maybe.

The taper world heats up as the band's ever-surly crew notices and starts to crack down. The tapers take new and intense measures to smuggle in their equipment. One taper dresses as a businessman, puts his gear into a sealed, stamped, addressed box, telling guards that it's an important parcel for work and they are *not* to open it. At a show in a football stadium in Santa Barbara, another taper buries his equipment under the playing field a few nights before the Dead come through and bypasses security altogether, entering the venue with his friends and digging up his gear. Like many psychedelic rituals around the world, the one surrounding the Grateful Dead sometimes requires costumes and tricks.

"It was really fucking obvious that people were starting to follow the band around," says Steve Brown of Grateful Dead Records, who mans a Dead Heads booth at all of the band's shows from late 1973 and through 1974. Beneath custom tie-dyes by Courtenay Pollock, the virtual inventor of the craft, and giant signs by comix heroes Stanley Mouse and Alton Kelley, Brown doubles the band's mailing list.

"You'd see the same people," he says. "And you'd see legions of people snowballing onto that during the seasonal times of year, summertime and into early autumn. It wound up being this thing where it was obvious that a certain healthy percentage of the crowd was a repeat from the night before or the week before or the month before.

"There were some selling food, some people selling t-shirts, some people selling homemade knick-knack jewelry and stuff. In San Francisco, there are people hawking stuff on the street all the time, on Telegraph Avenue in Berkeley especially. It didn't seem unnatural for people to do the same at Dead concerts. It grew into its own thing, the folk art end of the scene. Even pirating."

That is, Deadheads begin to make new Grateful Dead items out of old images: T-shirts, tape covers, bootleg LP art, posters, and more, plus liberal dashes of their own creativity. Along with the Egyptian and European folk resonances of the band's name, each new album supplies a fresh set of iconography from their longtime crew of San Francisco poster artists, more communicable folklore. Along with the tapes, all of them circulate and create their own meanings.

There are skulls and roses and Garcia himself, first spotted caricatured on T-shirts around '71. *Bear's Choice,* released in 1973, with cover art by Owsley's former lab assistant (and *Live/Dead* artist) Bob Thomas, introduces two instantly popular new symbols. On the front cover is Thomas's Steal Your Face, a distended skull with a thirteen-point lightning bolt down the middle, designed to Owsley's specifications and previously used to identify the band's road cases. Ringing the back cover are thirty-two bears, notes Owsley, "a 36-point lead type-slug of a generic bear, a standardized figure from a printer's font of type." Strung together, it seems that they are dancing.

OWSLEY WATCHES MOST of the trial from the back of the courtroom as the shadowy world of LSD manufacture is pulled harshly into the light. He sees how they turn it into a conspiracy against acid chemists Tim Scully and Nick Sand. Scully had retired from acid making a few years back and founded Aquarius Electronics to design biofeedback and physiological monitoring instruments and systems. He picks up early assembly language programming.

Not everyone on trial is present. Michael Randall, busted at the Dead's Winterland show the previous New Year's, jumps bail and makes for distant lands. Ronald Stark had never been brought in at all. So Sand and Scully are charged with being "responsible for the psychedelic movement in California."

Out comes an ex–Hells Angel to testify, now in the witness relocation program, ditto a few members of the Brotherhood of Eternal Love. Nick Sand plans to call Timothy Leary, reincarcerated after a daring Brotherhood-assisted jailbreak in 1970. Leary doesn't make it. The day before the ex–Harvard professor is to arrive, he pre-emptively speaks with the prosecution and has further charges dropped.

Not Owsley, though, he's there nearly every day. The IRS puts together a new case against him seemingly for good measure and adds some new fines. It's just insulting at this point. It's *always* been insulting, which is perhaps why he sees fit to watch the trial. He has shows to tape and speaker systems to build. The latest version of the soundbeam machines are at Winterland for three nights that month.

The trial lasts for thirty-nine days. Tim Scully is resigned to paying his debt, sells his stocks in his tech start up, and prepares to go jail. But Nick Sand is not going gently into the penal system. He hadn't stopped making LSD as Scully had. Recently, the cherub-faced Sand had been busted in St. Louis with a massive lab and managed to walk away on a technicality. That's not going to happen this time.

When the last appeal fails, Nick Sand splits entirely, disappearing from his Sausalito houseboat and leading a car chase through the hills of Marin County. Going underground, Sand heads for Canada. Later, he will find his way into the ashram of controversial religious leader Bhagwan Shree Rajneesh in western India. Sand assumes a fresh identity while on the lam, but (as the historian Mark McCloud laughs) the Rajneesh gives him a new one anyway.

The acid won't dry up, though. There are too many faucets. In Europe and the Middle East and everywhere the cops aren't, mustachioed Ron Stark is still wheeling and dealing. Some precursor routes to Richard Kemp and Christine Bott, who've set up lab in the Welsh countryside where they raise goats and (like the Kesey family) make organic yogurt. The Clear Light System, makers of Windowpane, have big, big plans. They flush themselves of remaining stock and, in 1974, shut down their lab in coastal Oregon with designs on purchasing new land, brewing 2 billion hits and ceasing production forever. Even as Richard Nixon finally resigns and the Vietnam War sputters to a miserable end, there is no LSD shortage anywhere in the wanting world. It is even reported that there's a lab in Moscow.

A SIMPLE distribute command—dead.dis@sail—initiates one of the first asynchronous groupminds on the network sometime in 1973. The @ symbol had been put to use for e-mail only the year before and, applying it to this new purpose, a Deadhead named Paul Martin reroutes all Grateful Dead–related e-mail on the Stanford Artificial Intelligence Lab's PDP-10 through his local disk.

There have been mailing lists on the PDP-10 before for various working groups and subprojects. The human-net is a long-running internal conversation on the future of computing. Some people exchange poetry and discuss sci-fi, but the SAIL Dead list is something bigger, something newer, a way for the new network to tether to the physical world.

There are other experiments in online community brewing at various places in the country around this time, too. In Berkeley, there's the Community Memory Project, which has a few terminals at local record stores intended to be used like public bulletin boards and at least one surrealistic Dead-referencing prototroll named Dr. Benway. Out in Illinois, there is a localized community using a system called PLATO. And there's always the military-industrial groupmind, zapping bleeps with who knows what intentions. But it's the SAIL Deadheads that start using the network to connect with others like themselves.

The man most responsible for this is Paul Martin, a Woodstock veteran with long sandy hair, a beard, glasses, and a receding hairline. Arriving at SAIL in time for the Spacewar Olympics, Martin is shocked at how easygoing they are about computer access. Lab director Les Earnest tells him casually that "the main building's pretty full but the annex has some empty spaces, so pick one and get set up."

Soon, Paul moves into his own office with his own window, the equivalent of a junior faculty member anywhere else. And gets something even better. He crawls up through the attic and strings cable into the spot above his new home, drops a line down to his desk and connects his own video display to his own keyboard. Paul Martin gets a permanent interface with the PDP-10.

"Basically, I forgot all about the punchcard crap and did all my future assignments on this and started believing in the world where you just spent your day sitting in front of [a workstation] with continuous access to a computer," he says.

Paul picks his own three-letter e-mail handle—his initials, PAM—and gets some disk space on the system to use how he sees fit. And he does, creating a piece of genuine artificial intelligence. dead.dis@sail is something new: a group of people employing the net as a constant extension of their individual knowledge and abilities. The SAIL Deadheads arrange rides to shows wherever the Dead are playing around the West Coast or maybe just to a local meet-up for one of Garcia's side gigs at Homer's Warehouse, a World War II–era Quonset hut in nearby Palo Alto.

When computer chess researcher Dave Wilkins arrives in the fall of '73 and Martin is assigned as his advisor, the Deadhead game at SAIL rises to the next level. After Wilkins's first show at Winterland that season, he doesn't miss a Bay Area run for some twenty years. Dave and Paul begin to transcribe and compile the band's lyrics into a central file on Dave's disk space.

"Other people at the lab got into it, and provided some songs that we didn't know," Paul remembers. "And the main thing they provided was the ability to find recordings of tunes that we only had shabby recordings of." Tape trading comes to SAIL. Piece by piece, they transcribe the Dead songbook. Like Bob Weir, they don't get the last line of "El Paso" at first, either.

"Down on the Stanford campus in that same era, people were occasionally burning cars and stuff," Martin recalls. "There was none of that feeling at the lab." Certainly, their isolation in the hills helps, but SAIL's operation is oblique to the antiwar demonstrations and most earthly problems. With or without psychedelics, they are concerned with a far-off place.

"It was more just let's make a wonderful future and get on with it," Martin says, aligning the SAIL lab with the same find-your-own-space belief system as the Dead themselves. Like everything information-related at SAIL, there is a basic idea that information should be free. It is a deep-set belief of hackers everywhere, the idea of collaborative purpose, that a hack good for one is a hack good for all.

But "free" has an even more complex set of connotations in the rarified air of Stanford. There is no question that these Deadhead hackers are chipping at some radical new entry point to the hip economy, but they are doing so on highly specialized equipment paid for by highly specialized forces. Behind dead.dis@sail is a unique combination of the American academy, by way of their Stanford hosts, and real-world military and industrial interests, another source of funding.

It is a thoroughly complex exchange among systems, like an exotic information bazaar on the far wind-blown border of warring territories. At the middle, the SAIL Deadheads discover their sylvan oasis, both virtual and actual. Even from a historical vantage point, it is hard to tell what kind of energy transfer is under way. The SAILers' work is abstract, and they throw themselves into it, completely and fully. Many of them burrow deeper into their computers, creating whole new worlds. In 1976, a SAIL coder will transform a long-circulated text adventure game into a hacker phenomenon called Colossal Cave and, eventually, a successful commercial product called Zork.

In his 1967 poem "All Watched Over by Machines of Loving Grace," the Dead's Haight neighbor Richard Brautigan dreamed "of a cybernetic meadow / where mammals and computers / live together in mutually / programming harmony." The SAIL gang is the first to find the open green, and the Grateful Dead is the natural soundtrack to their arrival.

Dave Wilkins and Paul Martin of the SAIL lab follow the band around the West Coast in Wilkins's Microbus, the Loose Blue Caboose. They dash up to Portland and Seattle, where they witness a forty-six-minute "Playing in the Band," the longest on record, stop at home, and then down to Santa Barbara.

One night, digital audio pioneer Andy Moorer and a few senior SAIL scientists are en route to Winterland to see the Dead and marvel at the Wall of Sound when one of them spills the acid. "I guess we'll have to use the mescaline instead," a senior lab scientist says.

"I know a math graduate student who liked to sit up all night tripping and talking about math," observes Paul Martin, "but he was the exception to the rule. Generally, psychedelic stuff was recreation and not a portal to a greater understanding of how high-tech works or how your life should be." It's just part of the general energy of what's going on, the same world.

"I certainly *never* thought about work at shows," affirms computer chess researcher Dave Wilkins, who takes up juggling scarves while the band plays. The music and the psychedelics are rituals with varied relationships to practitioners' daily lives. The Grateful Dead are for dancing. Still, it is unquestionable that the worlds feed into one another.

One day, Phil Lesh himself arrives to visit SAIL. There is some warning, a flurry of e-mails, but then there's Phil in all his Phildom along with electronic composer and Dead collaborator Ned Lagin, there to visit with John Chowning and Andy Moorer to discuss various frequency-to-voltage synthesizers and quadrophonic joysticks for the Wall of Sound. Lagin and Lesh will spend much of the summer of '74 employing the Dead's speaker arrays to shoot the massive vibrations and rolling tones of Lagin's tape compositions around the bewildered Deadheads. Lagin becomes a guest user of the lab briefly.

At some point during the evening, Paul Martin approaches Phil with a printed-out copy of their lyric book. "I know this is kind of pushy to take your tunes and write them down, but we can't buy them anywhere else and we want to know the words," Paul says. "We're not really sure what the right words are, so we have different versions written down from different times."

Lesh's eyes light up as he takes the book. "Oh, what you have here is *perfectly* right," he tells an astonished Paul.

"But you haven't even looked at it!" Paul manages to stammer.

"I know," Phil replies. "But I'm going to make Bobby read this and make sure he *gets it right.*" Like a loop. If Paul's mind isn't blown already, it just shoots up into the network.

IN THE SUMMER of '74, the Gotham powers that be attempt to pull the plug on the acid-crazed *thump-thump*ing beats of New York's early gay-hippie psychedelic disco underground. Over Memorial Day, police and building inspectors descend on the Loft at 647 Broadway, where David Mancuso's ever-expanding shrine-abetted speaker set is sometimes referred to as the Wall of Sound. And pretty soon thereafter, the fire department does in the Gallery, as well. Whatever the Man is trying to accomplish, it is not going to work. As three hundred people mill on West Twenty-Second Street, DJ Nicky Siano places a box of LSD-dosed strawberries on the roof of a police car. He spreads the word, "Have the strawberries, darling, they're *fabulous.*"

THE NUDE HARVEST celebrations start happening in the early '70s around Humboldt County, five hours north of San Francisco, when the heads figure out how to farm their own weed. Soon, the region will be known as the Emerald Triangle. While the national prevalence of psychedelics begins to wane, the cultivation and spread of powerful domestic marijuana is only just beginning.

"We were looking for just enough money to survive," said one grower about the moment the Northern California heads were finally inspired to methodically harvest the seeds of all the Mexican grass they'd been smoking. Linn House had once been editor of *Innerspace,* the in-house psychedelic newspaper of the East Village's flagship Group Image commune before skipping Map-coasts to the Haight where he changed his name to Freeman and became a full-fledged Digger.

When the Haight collapsed, he'd migrated northward to homestead in Humboldt County. "We grew for three or four years, and our best year was $20,000 tops, and we managed to make land payments out of that," House would remember. "Also, it financed my ability to do positive things." He becomes a commercial salmon fisherman (listening to Dead radio broadcasts on his boat) and an ardent ecologist-activist. But it is like hitting oil, and where House stops, many prospectors start.

The new green belt widens its own happy acreage between the Santa Cruz Mountains and Oregon. In Humboldt, pot is more than just a portal to the hip economy, it is an actual economy. "You could trade it for services, having your stovepipe fixed, mechanic's services, almost any service you needed around your place, like fix your water line," remembered one resident of the Emerald Triangle.

But it is sometime in 1974 or 1975 that a simple technique for raising sinsemilla—delicious seedless pot—comes into circulation. Some remember it coming from a Vietnam vet, some recall a guy passing through town with the word to "pull all the males." It was only female pot plants that they wanted. Others remember the tip coming appropriately from Mountain Girl herself, a technique she would soon publish as an underground classic grower's guide, *Primo Plant.* However it gets there, it is a piece of information that very, very much wants to be free.

Slowly and steadily, pot vines its way into day-to-day American consciousness. If the marijuana culture is not yet recognized as an acceptable way of life, it is recognized as a way of life nonetheless. And, in the mid-1970s, to go along with the Grateful Dead's psychedelic American spiritual belief set comes a highly compatible religion (with its own musical practice) from Jamaica: *Rasta.* Jerry Garcia's on board, checking out Bob Marley at the tiny New Matrix in San Francisco in 1973 and soon incorporating reggae into his and the Dead's musical vocabularies.

The ins and outs of stonerdom act as a subtle and ongoing counterpoint that sometimes intersects directly with the psychedelic narrative. Reggae and the many genres it spawns become entries to a borderless global drug culture with its own vast roots. Rasta's sacred herb becomes another component in the practical vocabulary of the do-it-yourself mix-and-match American drug religion. Not that Americans (and especially psychedelic ones) need any encouragement to smoke pot.

In San Rafael, the small Marin town where the Dead's office is located, a group of high school students conceive of using the number 420 as code and a time to meet up for smoking, something they can say around their parents. (Sorry to blow up your secret, guys.) They call themselves the Waldos. The code zips up and down the coast as the Waldos disperse to college, and it goes directly into the Deadhead network. Some of the Waldos' fathers work in various capacities for the Dead and the New Riders of the Purple Sage, the Dead's country-rock spin-off.

The Waldos dig the Dead, but it's the New Riders they really love, who sing so wisely (and some say *knowingly*) about the weed import biz. The weed smuggler is a new class of American hero, no doubt, idolized in the underground comix like *Dealer McDope* and bands like the New Riders. And soon, the humble working-class weed smuggler gets a national platform, a new magazine aimed at countercultural and suburban readers alike.

In New York, the Yippies had spawned the Zippies, a new faction of psychedelicized pranksters led by Thomas King Forçade, a perpetual troublemaker, pot smuggler, and founder of the Underground Press Syndicate. In 1974, Forçade (born Gary Goodson) launches *High Times*, which quickly frames itself as the *Wall Street Journal* for the hip economy. Certainly, no other national publication offers anything close to their Trans-High Market Quotations listing the price of pot and psychedelics in cities around the globe. They have correspondents everywhere. One of the Hell's Honkies tape collectors feeds the magazine prices from the Bronx. Sometimes literally, the magazine offers heroic caricatures of the smugglers and their planes.

High Times caters to a whole variety of heads. Alongside more traditionally heady topics like nekkid tantric yoga and postjail Timothy Leary sci-fi manifestos and reviews of experimental LPs comes increasing coverage of cocaine and the accoutrements of its use. "Cokehead" had come into parlance at least as early as 1923 and has surfaced previously in many milieus. But in the '70s, the powder spreads from West Coast rock social circles and creates its own chain of influence and pop cultural legacy.

Mostly, *High Times* provides unity to the potheads of the United States. Humbead's Revised Map of the World had included the Mexican border on every single coastline, a sign of omnipresent linkages to south-of-the-border pot pipelines, and now *High Times* covers the dangerous air traffic in the increasingly crowded skies over Humbeadia. "Undeclared War" reads an item in the magazine's debut issue, about a series of mysterious plane crashes afflicting pot smugglers. "Marijuana: Wonder Drug," the cover of their debut issue declared. They will not run out of material any time soon.

MEANWHILE, OVER THERE: A British hippie named Wally had been involved with the Windsor Free Festival in '73 and thought it was rubbish, too much money exchanging hands between vendors. So, in '74, he and his comrades set up camp near Stonehenge before the June solstice. This British version of the Rainbow tribalists venture to Windsor again and it's no better. It's even more chaotic. One acid dealer paints his tent with the message, "I WANT TO DISTROY [*sic*] YOUR BRAIN CELLS." And it's back to Stonehenge. Not that there's any lack of completely irresponsible and horrifying acid use there. It is reported that one couple feeds their child LSD every day because "it's the religious thing to do." When the Department of the Environment comes to inspect the encampment, the squatters all identify themselves to authorities as Wally. And though the original Wally—real name: Philip Russell—is persecuted and tragically incapacitated by the state before the next Stonehenge solstice, there are now many more Wallys in New Albion. Stonehenge '75 will be legendary. The free festivals spread.

BY EARLY '75, Paul Martin patches the dead.dis@sail mailing list from the Stanford Artificial Intelligence Lab into the wide open ARPANET. It is the most efficient path yet from one side of the Map to the other. A few heads from MIT join up. He also figures out how to search the news wires and have updates on the Dead zapped right to his own little spot in the SAIL Annex. The Deadheads use their favorite band as a portal to the future.

The SAIL guys circulate their lyric file to other nodes and ask for credit. They can't help but notice that they don't always get it. Eventually, they add a bogus song to the file: "Bondi Pier," an Australian drinking round they know from somewhere. "Maybe Pigpen sang it one night, who knows?" Paul Martin reasons. It's a tracer.

When the Dead spend a year off the road in 1975, there's all kinds of information to share. Word makes into dead.dis@sail that Kingfish, Bob Weir's new side band, is booked to play a wedding at the Alpine Hills Country Club, up deeper in the hills outside Palo Alto.

What happens next is unconscious but revelatory: They hash it out over e-mail. There's a flurry of text, disseminating the information and collectively processing it. Phone trees have existed for decades, but this is a quick, open portal for conversation and plan making. The human-nets mailing list can ponder what the ARPANET is good for all they want, but the Deadheads at SAIL just use it.

The asynchronous groupmind determines to be up front about it. Some half-dozen guys from SAIL descend on the country club. "We're not exactly friends of the band, and we promise to stay away from the food and the drink," they tell the bemused hosts. "Can we stand at the back here?" It's fine.

ON A FARAWAY BEACH, another hippie sets up another tape deck. When Gil Levey gets to collecting and copying tapes, he will refine another powerful new way to disseminate the psychedelic ritual. Gil Levey is a Haight-Ashbury refugee. He left initially as a roadie for the Sons of Champlin, his own local psychedelic karass. When he returned to find the neighborhood in ruins, Levey bumped across the overland Hippie Trail from London eastward and landed in Goa, on the midwest coast of India, in 1970. He made a pass through the mainland, studied and grew further enlightened in the Himalayas, and then back to Goa where he hunkers down. He's got friends there. Soon, he is known simply by his adopted home: Goa Gil.

It's a little bohemian enclave on the beach there. Not long after the bust-up of the Brotherhood of Eternal Love in 1972, several Brothers could be spotted on the friendly Indian shores, where hash is not only legal but a sacrament. One of Goa Gil's friends is the British-born Acid Eric, last name Hodgman, once one of Owsley's dealers and an announcer at the Avalon Ballroom. Eric had skipped town when the IRS found him and now is tending the flame out near the crystal waters and white sands and blue skies where life is easy and filled with just the right kind of light.

There are naked ladies and naked dudes and dreadlocks and starry eyes. Gil's always got a supply of tapes from back home. Sometimes, he jams on the beach with some other longhairs on acoustic guitars and flutes and bongos and the tools of any ad hoc head arkestra out in the Far Reaches.

Other times, they get electricity from car batteries and bike generators, and Goa Gil starts to mix together cassettes: classic soul, the Stones, Coltrane, James Brown, and of course, the Dead. A sound system arrives in town—reportedly once belonging to the Who—and some musicians start to get it together.

Gil plays bass in the Anjuna Jam Band and organizes full moon parties. One freak returns from Hong Kong with some Stratocasters and a bass and a few amps. There's a French trio that people like to dance to. More will come, and Acid Eric makes sure everything is all good.

4

SHAKEDOWN STREET

There's a big crashing unresolved minor chord, ominous and frayed at the edges, run through an envelope filter. The chord hangs in the afternoon air like a bit of hallucinated thunder or a plane overhead as the Bethesda Fountain Band plugs in their amps at the Central Park Bandshell. It's a gorgeous afternoon in the spring of 1975 and the park is theirs, the American psychedelic tradition jumping easily toward the next generation of underground users and whole new forms of expression. But for now, just like always, jams. The longhairs in the band shell set up the twin drum kits, tune guitars, hang the tie-dye tapestry.

The band is friends with Shaky Mike, a Vietnam vet who takes care of Central Park's Naumberg Bandshell on behalf of the city of Manhattan. But he's one of them, a Parkie. The term was derogatory at first, but they make it their own. For the Bethesda Fountain Band, this is a real gig. There are posters and everything, with a perfect sun shooting beams that morph into a stained glass frame. The poster's creator, a lanky teen runaway who goes by Johnny Crunch, sometimes sleeps under the wisteria tree up behind the band shell.

There's been an ongoing party in this region of Central Park since the late '60s, originally over by the sculpted boat pond and the Bethesda Fountain, immortalized in *Hair*. By '71, though, the scene had migrated to the Naumberg Bandshell. The Bethesda Fountain

Band is proud of the park's longhaired heritage, and all the Parkies know that the Dead and the Jefferson Airplane and others had played there only a few springs earlier. Some had even been there. The scene never really died in Central Park.

On any given sunny mid-1970s weekend like this one, even without the Fountain Band, some 250 old-style New York freaks converge on the band shell from all points around the boroughs. The Fountaineers play a hard driving boogie and amped-up Bo Diddley beats, twin guitars and double drums and lead bass meshing into conversation as groupminds do.

But now observe the long, flat expanse of pavement in front of the stage, where a group of skateboarders twist and work out their moves, the first heavy crew on the East Coast, with soon-legendary names like Andy Kessler. Some will call them Dogtown East, after the SoCal skater heroes. Beyond them, on the wide stretches of city-kept greenery, another subtribe on their way to national influence and stardom: the Frisbee players, who—headbands in place—dash into the air and do tricks of their own. And it's all, like, super-groovy, right? "I've always thought the arc of a frisbee against the sky was psychedelic by itself," says Parkie artist Johnny Crunch, one of many heads wandering through the tableau, most likely tripping. The band shell is freak central.

Puerto Rican and black kids come down from the Bronx. Weirdo bohos come from the East Village. Teens pour in from Brooklyn and Queens and Long Island. With the old neighborhoods well sunk into slumdom, the park is the high ground for the New York heads, in all too many ways to count. Any day it's warm enough to be outside, there's a dependable crew by the band shell and a seemingly endless supply of pot and acid.

The Bethesda Fountain Band are racially integrated, as are almost all the Parkie bands. Their native hippie grooves slide into funk and Latin rhythms that make up the street beat of the city. Sometimes they do "China Cat Sunflower." They usually save "I Know You Rider" for the encore. As the focus of American youth culture shifts away from the heads, the heads themselves do not go anywhere. They regenerate and adapt.

Hanging out some afternoons is Adam Purple, sometimes known as Guru Adam, who dresses in purple tie-dye and maintains a sprawling community garden on the battle-scarred Lower East Side.

Occasionally, he dispenses credit card numbers liberated with tried-and-true Yippie techniques. The Park is Central, as well, to all that is left of the politico-psychedelic old guard. Every so often, the Yippies will show up from their headquarters down on Bleecker Street with an impressive array of coalition-building causes in search of funds or energy.

The crew is there most weekdays, too. Shaky Mike gives Parkies access to the outlets, or they run a wire from the phone booth, and someone almost always has a reel-to-reel or a tape deck and some awesome Dead music. That or Hot Tuna or the Airplane. Sometimes one of the bands jams. Besides the Bethesda Fountain Band, there's Sundance, who are the Parkie equivalent of the New Riders of the Purple Sage, the Dead's country-jamming sidekicks. Galactus borders into the wild blues cascades of Hot Tuna, another Parkie fave.

In 1975, these hippie street kids are developing into the newest cream of the psychedelic avant-garde, mutant freethinking lost children of the Diggers and keepers of the flame in their own equally radical way. The music of the Bethesda Fountain Band, really, is incidental. The musicians, being part of the Parkies' distribution system for acid, are not. But, for that matter, some would say the music was incidental in the Haight-Ashbury, too. To many of the Parkies, the gatherings in the park are the safest possible place to be, the best place to be.

One of the younger Parkies is a kid nicknamed Bilrock, thirteen, from the Upper West Side, not particularly happy at home, and hanging out at the band shell when he should be in junior high school. He'd instantly recognized the cool patchwork centrality of the Parkie scene, just as Park designer Frederick Law Olmsted had intended it to be used. Before finding the park, Bilrock had made trouble in various ways, nabbing the hats off subway conductors as trains exited stations and such. The park welcomes him, as it does almost anyone. He makes quick friends with the wisteria-dwelling Johnny Crunch, likewise living in the park and elsewhere to escape a home where he doesn't want to be.

The group of Parkies that Bilrock idolizes most, though, are the writers. They write everywhere. They write on the inside of subway trains in markers and lately on the outside of the trains themselves in colorful splashes of spray paint. They write on the band shell, too, an interlocking jumble code of numbers and schoolyard names. Over the past half decade, graffiti has run amok across the city's surfaces, an alpha-numeric vine.

And, in Central Park, the practice of graffiti writing is intricately connected to psychedelics, owing in large part to one Chad Stickney, LSD-OM, inspired by the Grateful Dead to take the word to the streets. Chad now leads the Rebels, one of two graffiti crews that hang around the park. Bilrock falls in with the Soul Artists, but they're generally all friends, and they all look up to Chad.

By 1975, Chad Stickney is a citywide underground hero. Chad didn't invent modern graffiti; no one did. But, as much as anyone, he was there from its late '60s start in the Bronx and a vital contributor in its evolution from schoolyard scrawl to art form. After he'd gotten his first serious girlfriend when he was fifteen, Chad had stopped writing for a while. He watched as graffiti began to spread, itching to hit the streets. And then he didn't have a girlfriend anymore and he's *back*. As a head, Chad is in the minority among the writers, many of them black and Latino, but it doesn't matter, because of what he does.

His LSD-OM tag in fat black magic marker spreads around the city, arrows and lines shooting off every which way and inspiring the writers that follow him. It is a public service announcement from and for the New York heads. More and more, Chad's been taking to the outside of the trains, too, writing "LSD" in massive cartoon letters that vibrate and buzz against the glum chrome in life-affirming cherry reds and neon pinks. Every piece is different. In one, the phrase radiates and pops. In another, fracture lines appear, the letters about to explode. He extends the fractures to other parts of the train car, an urban trompe-l'œil.

When the condensed numbers and messages of graffiti grow thick on surfaces, they are transformative, achieving majority and turning the objects into something anew, breaking reality's consensus momentarily.

"Any of the best graffiti artists that had the best styles and the best characters, great artwork, did psychedelics," Bilrock says, thirteen years old in 1975 and filling notebooks with ideas. "They did acid or, a lot of the poor kids would do the poor man's psychedelic, unfortunately, PCP. Even though it's terrible stuff, it took them to other realms. They were amazing. Some of the best graffiti artists were dusties. It ruined them, too. It's a whole different type of psychedelic. It's not LSD, it's a dissociative. It's like leaving your body. It's probably what it's like to be dead or something. It's a little scary."

Mayor John Lindsay had declared war on graffiti in the early '70s, though he left the covered trains in circulation and they only grew more covered. Abraham Beame, elected in 1974, begins to wipe the cars clean, which is when the designs *really* grow ornate, oblique, cubist, wild, beautiful, raw.

And, like the Parkies believe in LSD, they believe in the graffiti. There are codes to follow. Only public property, though exceptions might be made for surfaces in one's own territory, and never over anyone else's work. Steal your paint. Not all graffiti writers follow the nonrules, but the Parkies try to.

Once, in the New Lots yard with some friends, Chad sees his first car that's been "cleaned" by the new mayor's program and knows instantly it needs "LSD." "It was a silver and blue line train but it had acid thrown on it. Everything had been stripped off, all the remnants of graffiti and the remnants of the original paint, it looked *terrible*." Chad's been itching to do a piece for a while but unable to find a canvas. But there is no question that the car looks just *awful*. For once, Chad doesn't feel bad going over other work.

Midway through the piece, the police show up and start chasing Chad and friends through the maze of train cars and fences. Chad has a good lead and can probably get away, but he suddenly has a realization. He stops running.

"Why did you stop?" the out-of-breath cop barks at him suspiciously when he finally catches up.

"It just dawned on me: *Why am I running?* Because what I was doing was a *good thing*. That train looked *terrible*. I was trying to make it *better*," Chad tells the astonished cop firmly.

"*What?!*"

"These trains belong to the people. This is public property. That means *we* own it, and I was only trying to make it look better. You saw it."

"Yeah," the officer says, "and that's why I have to bust you." But he does so with a new amount of respect, offering Chad a cigarette before hauling him down to the station. The cops give the guys some paper to draw on while they deal with the paperwork. Chad's sentence is two

Saturdays cleaning subway stations, which is fine because it inevitably turns into a graffiti writers' convention. Chad meets tons of new people he only knows from their tags. He's never been busted before.

Chad Stickney and the Rebels, the Soul Artists, and the younger crew that look up to them, are all products of LSD fully unleashed in the wild. Together, they help create a new American psychedelic art tradition to express the modes and ideas of the other shore.

Never mind that in 1975 Chad is on the verge of retirement. He is approaching his twentieth birthday, and graffiti is for teens. As with LSD itself a half decade earlier, he feels he's done his time. It's time to move on, grow up. Though he's a high school dropout, he's studying for the GED and getting ready for college. In preparation for retirement, he steals a bunch of paint and goes on a bombing spree. Then, his father gets very sick, and Chad retires a few months earlier than planned. But he's cracked open a whole new world for others.

In discovering the Soul Artists and the Rebels, Bilrock and Johnny Crunch have found their tribe. Bilrock soon realizes that, while the hard cores hang out at the band shell, the *real* turf is the abandoned Mother Goose Playground, an elevated stronghold just behind and above the band shell, also known as Rumsey Playfield. From there, they can see people coming from any direction. Nestled on the hillside between the two is the wisteria where Crunch crashes. And it's where the dealers hang out. Bil has lots to learn.

Bilrock's been writing since '72, when he was ten. It's a natural thing to do, writing his name on the walls of his block. He was BILLY-182 at first. Then BIG CLYDE and, for a while SAGE. It's time to get serious. The first time his friend Crunch ever wrote was down in the in-construction tunnel on the southeast corner of the park, under the Central Park Zoo. It'd been there that Soul Artist leader Ali—Marc Edmonds—had declared them all to be citizens of Zoo York, the decay-twisted residents of the psychedelic city. In so many unconscious ways, Bilrock and Crunch understand that it is their job to keep Central Park and the New York subway system connected to Humbead's Map at large.

No one tells them that the head scene is dead, because it's not. The week before the spring '75 Bethesda Fountain Band show that Crunch made the poster for, Hot Tuna comes to the Academy, the Parkies' absolute favorite venue, down on Fourteenth Street. And the week after the Bethesda Fountain Band rocks the band shell, Paul Kantner and Grace Slick's Jefferson Starship lands for a gig in the park's Sheep Meadow, only a few weeks before the release of their #1 *Red Octopus* album.

More than 70,000 people flood Central Park to watch the Starship play its new songs and a good handful of the big Airplane hits, including "Somebody to Love" and "White Rabbit." Longhairs climb the backstop of the baseball field and the show has to be stopped several times to get fans out of the trees.

DICK LATVALA SPENDS his days hosing out the zoo cages in the Hawaiian sun, methodically contemplating the meaning of life and trying to suss out the next portal into the light. He knows it's around here somewhere. The sex commune had been all well and good. He'd gotten all the acid he wanted, which was (and is) a lot, but there has to be something more. He suspects maybe it's in Hawaii, and he's not wrong. Dick and his wife Carol had already lived a variety of good lives by the time they and their infant son Richie split Berkeley in '74 and make their way over the Pacific's westward horizon. They might stand in for any couple trying to find a foothold in the New Earth, off to settle a new frontier in Hawaii.

Dick, thirty-one, is on the cutting edge of a generation of California bliss-seekers, blonde-brown hair, glasses, a decently buff specimen, veteran of the International Foundation For Advanced Study and the Trips Festival, dozens of 1966–1967 era Dead shows, and a good number since. He and Carol had lived in a classic '60s commune in Berkeley, and many of the communards now migrate farther into new territory in the islands. He is a primo heads hero already and about to soar higher.

With a loan from the Farmers Home Administration, Dick and Carol are buying a house thirty miles south of town and are allowed to modify the design themselves. Dick makes absolutely *sure* it is wired for sound. While they wait for construction to finish, he and Carol and their son Richie live in an apartment in Hilo with other expats from the commune.

Dick's newest trip is audio. A friend is developing a new kind of high-powered sound system, and Dick has gotten obsessive about making compilation tapes from a constant stream of LPs, mixing jazz and gospel with his Bay Area faves. It's hard to find listeners up to his standards.

Like Jerry Garcia and others, Dick is the type of head who likes to talk and talk and talk, a font of wordplay and self-evaluation and occasional boldness. His thirty-hour-a-week zookeeper job is the perfect amount to get by, and Carol works as a waitress. Something will come, especially here in paradise.

From the zoo, he writes to Dead lyricist Robert Hunter for wisdom. And to invite Hunter (and his family) to Hawaii to listen to mixes, "be soaked in luscious beauty," and "sample the best and prettiest smoking dope in the whole wide world."

With surprising promptness, a few weeks later, Hunter responds politely, "Sponge the contentment up while you got it. Sounds like this might be the best time of your life." It might be, Dick knows, but there must be something better. It starts slowly.

At the Morehouse commune back in Berkeley, one of several outposts around town, Dick had been the resident chronicler, keeping a color-coded diary of household intrigues. Though some dismiss it as a mere for-profit Ponzi scheme, Morehouse was about hedonism, pushing human desires as far as one could want. *More*house. In Hilo, Dick extends his duty to vérité audio documentation, making stealth recordings of household groupmind conversations. To Carol's embarrassment, the former linguistics major plays them back and picks them apart. Like the San Francisco Tape Music Center, like the Merry Pranksters, like former bluegrass taper Jerry Garcia, Dick senses a power in magnetic tape, maybe not totally sure what it is. He looks for transformation everywhere. And then he finds it.

First he somehow stumbles on a copy of *Dead in Words,* the North Carolina Deadhead fanzine that had launched a year or so earlier. The first of its kind, the publication was spun from a cluster of zines dedicated to the still-thriving underground LP biz, including the Beatle-centric *Paperback Writer* and the Dylan-freaky *My Back Pages.* Soon, *Dead in Words* will receive the word of *FREE* from the evangelistic Dead Relics gang, about to launch their own zine in Brooklyn, but not before Dick Latvala borrows thirty dollars from his boss and sends it off to North Carolina for a handful of bootleg LPs.

And sometime after the bootleg Dead LPs arrive from the mainland, Dick realizes that there are more recordings out there, beyond the official releases. Many more. He'd never thought about it. He answers an ad placed in *Dead in Words* by a commune in Wisconsin, sends them some blank reels, and gets back a few East Coast shows from the early '70s. He is in shock.

Then something miraculous happens, which he notes in his still-active journal: "Swallowed peyote tar balls and listened to Dead concert tapes."

"Dick at the system all day," an entry in another hand notes almost immediately thereafter. It consumes Dick completely. When a batch of acid arrives at the house, Dick begins to stage what he calls Dead-ins, all-night tripping parties soundtracked by nothing but the finest live Grateful Dead music.

They are transformational nights. It is via practitioners like Dick and others that the Grateful Dead firmly become a psychedelic platform every bit as real as the peyote churches or any other group that might assemble a series of tools and symbols to use when they trip. The Dead themselves don't have to be there, just their music, and this is an important realization.

"My basic flash, when I took acid, was that the highest thing in life is to take acid and listen to the Grateful Dead," Dick records himself saying on one his home bootlegs from the summer of '75 at the shared apartment in Hilo. There's a special guest on this one. Dick and Carol were out somewhere, saw a guy in a Dead shirt, struck up a conversation, and invited him back to their place. The guy agrees that taking acid and listening to the Dead *is* a pretty high thing to do.

This visiting head is a perfectly lovely dude, a dope dealer (as it turns out) and a veteran of scenes in Los Angeles, New York, and San Francisco. He's a little bit jaded about the Dead by now, quite accurately observing the same shift as others have, away from the psychedelic peaks of a half decade back, and attributing it to the band's turn from LSD to cocaine.

Dick is having none of it. "I'm glad we've got this on the record before we play some stuff, man," he tells the guy, presumably gesturing at the recording reels. Dick then lays down a philosophy that many Deadheads will learn to apply in the coming decades as the Dead's music peels further from the American mainstream and even away from the broader American underground.

Continues Dick, "The feeling I always had about the Grateful Dead is that these guys were so special that it was *on me* to come to where they were to get that mind-blowing thing, and to have the attitude of 'oh, shit, they're going downhill' is to miss out on the love that they're sharing at that moment." Dick still prefers the long, extended jams, of course, but *c'mon* this is the Grateful Dead we're talking about.

"You could have every one of those shelves filled with reel-to-reel tapes without a problem," the guy says, telling Dick about some rare tapes he's heard, and Dick audibly goes googly-eyed.

"I'd just hoped things like this were really true," he tells the traveling dope dealer. Soon thereafter, Dick and Carol and Richie move to their new dream house south of Hilo, bringing along the other Morehouse friends, a little pack of familiar faces out there in the Pacific. The dope dealer declines Dick's invitation to come live with the Latvala family while he transfers a big batch of Dead reels.

The pot that Dick and Carol Latvala grow in the new neighborhood is a failure. "We had some beautiful plants in the backyard, but the neighborhood teenagers ripped us off," Carol says. Then the neighborhood kids get caught and tell their parents that they got it from the hippies down the block. Oy, poor Dick and Carol.

It's maybe not the best start on the new frontier, but both Dick and Carol are instantly likable sorts, Dick with an endless stream of chatter and wordplay, sometimes quizzical, sometimes trouble seeking, and Carol with just a bottomless sweetness. It blows over.

They make friends with other neighbors who *are* good at growing pot. Really, really good at growing, and have a little operation set up. It's a whole scene out there south of Hilo, and Dick and Carol are the neighborhood Dead freaks. Especially Dick. It is around this time, too, that Dick strikes upon new arrangements for procuring Grateful Dead music, announcing himself as a new theorist of the hip economy.

He finds a copy of the new magazine out of Brooklyn, *Dead Relix*, founded by Les Kippel and Hell's Honkie Jerry Moore to really up their taper game. *Relix*'s back page is filled with business card–like classified ads. Promptly, Dick Latvala sends a special letter to each of the tapers listed therein.

In the Bronx, Hell's Honkie Jerry Moore receives mail from Hawaii. Inside is a mindblowing joint rolled from delicious Hawaiian pot. Jerry Moore is happy to help Dick Latvala get some tapes. But that's only the tip of the bong.

A typical version runs like this: Dick bundles up ten Ampex reel-to-reel boxes and sends them off to the mainland. In nine of the boxes is blank tape, ready to be filled with the transformational vessel of Grateful Dead music, and the tenth is filled to the brim with green Hawaiian bud that the recipient can use to get very, very high.

Generally speaking, both Dick and the tapers he meets through the mail are quite pleased with the results. Grateful Dead music begins to arrive in Hawaii at an impressive clip.

Carol is not as obsessed with the Dead as Dick but also has zero problem with listening to them all day, either, and usually they do. She wakes up in the morning and wanders into the kitchen and there's coffee brewing and probably a joint going and Grateful Dead playing, and Dick sustains it all day, talking about the Dead, breathing the Dead.

If people want to come by and listen to the Dead with them, all the better. Richie, their son, is adaptable, and grows up happily among the hippies. He's got his friends, but he likes the music, too, and will hang out with the grownups while they jam out.

For Dick, it is revelatory to rediscover the *alcheringa* dreamtime zones he experienced so fleetingly almost a decade previous. He is open and enthusiastic and writes long letters to the tapers he trades with, often veering into topics of life and philosophy that have little to do with the Dead at all.

The Grateful Dead are better than Morehouse. The Grateful Dead are better than anything, just about. Dick and Carol don't have their own limo anymore, as they did at Morehouse, but the Dead tapes contain all the self-actualization Dick needs in handy, nonjudgmental form. Garcia wouldn't judge you even if he knew you. Dick dashes off an enthusiastic letter to Jerry Moore and Les Kippel at *Dead Relix*.

"I have come to discover, again, how incredibly powerful these recordings actually are," Dick writes. "I must assume that all of 'US' people, who are involved in such an adventure, have had the same kinds of incredibly joyous and 'cleansing' experiences, that I have been having with my family over here in paradise. We have . . . 'Dead-Ins' often, and these intense experiences of togetherness are the exact same as we have all repeatedly had seeing the Dead 'Live,' when we used to live in the Bay Area."

Dick invites the *Relix* gang for a visit. "If you are ever coming to Hawaii I could show you some very fantastic things. (Not to mention how much cheaper your vacation would be, if you stayed with us!)"

In another correspondence he promises a free month-long stay at his pad for anyone who was in the audience for the February 1970 shows at the Fillmore East. Seemingly any and all Dead freaks are welcome to come to Hawaii and hang out, smoke this amazing weed, and listen to the Dead all day. Maybe go to the beach, too, if they want.

Many people have found ways to express their usefulness to the New World's community through the medium of the Grateful Dead and their surrounding countercultural universe. There are tapers. There are dealers. There are growers. There are dancers. There are musicians. There are T-shirt makers and fanzine writers and graffiti artists. There are programmers. Dick Latvala invents a craft for himself that will make him one of the most important heads in the lineage that's assembling across the territories and seas and galactic planes. Dick Latvala will be a listener.

There is an art to listening to Dead tapes, like impressionist paintings for the ear, details resolving in the mind and third eye. Dick takes it very seriously and in many ways is the first person to articulate and actually understand the power of Grateful Dead tapes as a separate entity than the band itself. Out near Hilo, Hawaii, in a house designed by heads, the homebound rituals of the Deadheads' new psychedelic tradition come into form. You don't even need acid for a Dead-in, just people to listen with, and perhaps not even that.

Dick learns the names of the men (always the dudes) who make these recordings and personally invites them all to Hawaii. Dick could *never* tape a Dead show, even now that he's aware that people do it. He's got too much acid to do, too much Dead to watch. Why spend it operating a silly little box with the buttons?

Dick turns a room of the house into a tape center. It's not enough to merely dance and commune with the music, or even to accumulate and exchange the reels. One must preserve the tapes. In the tape room, he installs heating rods in the cupboards to keep the recordings from warping. And one must *listen,* really listen. To the interplay of musical voices. To Hunter's lyrics. To the quality of the individual performances.

"I used to walk four or five miles to the post office in Hawaii when I thought tapes were coming," Dick recalls years later. Carol insists they always had a car. But, to Dick, the total passion of what might be arriving in the mail is so overwhelming that even just the effort to drive to the post office could feel like an uphill walk both ways. There's also the acid and the brainfry. But Dick *breathes* the Dead. And pot smoke.

Around this time, in the visible near distance, the great volcano Mauna Loa erupts for the first time in decades. Sometimes a volcano is just a volcano. Sometimes.

Dick Latvala is awash in the cosmos, and maybe not yet sure of his own power. Like Garcia, he doesn't stop rapping until the music starts. But, when that happens, Dick quiets down completely and listens. Finally, Dick Latvala knows what he wants to do with his life and that's to be in charge of the Tapes. What tapes, Dick?

RAGUSA. FRANK RAGUSA. He'd worked his way up the LSD-dealing pipeline while in grad school at UC Berkeley, and now he turns on the jets. He travels to Europe, collecting rare books and even rarer Oriental rugs. He connects with an American jeweler in West Germany who, in turn, has a link to shadowy international martial arts–trained smugglers known as the Judo Gang. They are not hippies, they are not psychedelic, but they do provide Ragusa with a steady source of ergotamine tartrate, the extremely valuable precursor for LSD. In the summer of 1975, Ragusa and his family move to Mount Tamalpais in Marin County. Their neighbors, it is said, are all filthy rich Alice D. Millionaires, to quote the song the Dead once wrote about Owsley. It is in these twisting Marin streets that Nick Sand will elude capture in 1976 en route to an international escape. Acid chemist Frank Ragusa flies first class and shaves with a $500 gold-rimmed razor. He lives not far from where the Grateful Dead are convening daily for jams at Bob Weir's home studio, and perhaps Ragusa might even run into Steve Brown, the Dead's aide-de-camp, on a sandwich run down in Mill Valley. The arrival of Ragusa as a supply for ET is just in time, too. The Clear Light System hadn't been able to pull off their two-billion-hits-of-Windowpane-in-the-Oregon-woods-and-retire plan after all and are now on the run. Hey, someone's gotta feed the chemists.

AS IT HAPPENS, approximately when Dick Latvala first articulates the idea that he'd like to be in charge of the Tapes, there is, for the first time, a collection of the Tapes to be in charge of. Steve Brown gathers them up in early 1976 at the Grateful Dead's new storage warehouse on Front Street in San Rafael, a quick hop from the office at Fifth and Lincoln.

The band's official audio documents come in from Owsley, from sainted soundbeamers Bob Matthews and Betty Cantor-Jackson, from roadie Kidd Candelario. Up through the early '70s, the band would register a spare hotel room in the name of Mr. Nagra (the maker of their reel-to-reel of choice) in order to hang out and listen to the tapes immediately following the show. But Dick doesn't know this. Almost no one knows this. Perhaps the Tapes know this and send out a *Close Encounters*–like signal to Dick.

In Toon Town / Marin, Steve Brown indexes the reels in a marble notebook. He can't help but observe how thorough the band's record is for the years when Owsley was running sound, minus a chunk that got stolen in 1970. At the office/house, Round Records entertains the idea of spinning off Ground Records to issue live Dead sides. But, by the time Steve gets around to cataloguing the Tapes, that fantasy is long popped. There's plenty of trouble brewing without it.

The summer before, scammer-in-chief Ron Rakow had signed the company over to United Artists in order to secure a new round of funds for Garcia's *Grateful Dead Movie,* a year overdue from Round Reels. Good puns, bad vibes, and the end of the Grateful Dead's second major experiment in independent hip economics. Grateful Dead Records lasted longer than the Carousel Ballroom, but it is not the psychedelic economic model the Grateful Dead are destined to live by.

There is fallout everywhere, and one can almost feel the karmic pressure begin to build up around the Grateful Dead. The shift leaves Ned Lagin's *Seastones* in the void, an experimental quadrophonic LP on Round Records by the band's in-house boy genius and good friend. The album is recalled from stores (so it can be re-pressed by United) even as it improbably enters the *Billboard* Top 100. Lagin had virtually had become a member of the Dead during their 1975 sessions, joining them for their daily rehearsals as they developed the material that became *Blues for Allah,* playing Rhodes alongside Keith Godchaux. But (to Lagin) it had gotten worse and worse, the musicians never hanging out with one another anymore outside of scheduled band activities, as they did only a few years earlier.

Bummed and heartbroken by the mega-Dead and his friends' cavalier attitude about what he perceives to be a crashing zeppelin, Lagin splits the scene. Intact. He is a canary in the coal mine, and his departure is a quadrophonic biosquawk by the headiest head of the band's inner acid brotherhood. Lagin turns in his LSD vial, once refilled by the trusted roadie from the private stash, and takes a job at Processor Technology in Berkeley, one of the first personal computer companies. He's got other art to make, other disciplines to practice.

At the record company house in San Rafael, Steve Brown hears a lot of screaming from Ron Rakow's office. Even after the buyout, the Round machine is seizing up. The latest culprit is Mickey Hart. The percussionist is months late on his album, *Diga Rhythm Band*. It's fine to fuck around with the record company when it's Warner Brothers, it's less useful if it's half owned by your bandmate.

Rakow makes Steve talk to Mickey. Steve is friendly and on good terms with everyone. On a cartoon screen somewhere, a cartoon stock ticker spits out comically accumulating cartoon ticker tape while fictional record company mogul Anton Round's eyes bulge. One day, Steve Brown looks up from his desk at Fifth and Lincoln in San Rafael, and the eucalyptus trees on the hillside beyond the Dead's office are exploding. There's a fire on the mountain.

A BOOM BOX blasts the Grateful Dead while out behind the Central Park Bandshell, up the curving stairs, fresh-faced Bilrock and Johnny Crunch tag up the convex back with the tribal markings of the new psychedelic America. Forget the fine detail of Rapidographs, the adolescent Parkie longhairs prefer the fat black marker lines and delirious fumes of Pilots. These New York City teens in the summer of '75 could be straight off the streets of the Haight or the East Village or some college-town commune, in painter's pants (with big pockets for the Pilots) and Ike surplus jackets with extra ink.

Every day, almost, a guy comes by with a suitcase of cassettes for sale, just like a suitcase of drugs. He's got lots of Dead, but also Hot Tuna and New Riders and Allmans and a little Zeppelin. The guy charges a bit; he's no virtuous Hell's Honkie. They're pure street

slingers, all of them, and this is Central Park, where drugs and bootlegs coexist, a site of live counterculture. Sometimes, the tape dealer
accepts pot in exchange for tapes, or maybe even a little acid. Bilrock
and the guys really love Hot Tuna and the New Riders, too.

Even as Manhattan falls into debt and violent crime skyrockets,
LSD and the park scene blur boundaries. The Puerto Ricans and the
hippies share territory in bands like Santana and Malo and the later
period of the Dead's Haight/Marin compadres in Quicksilver Messen-
ger Service. *Acid,* the 1968 album by Latin percussionist Ray Barretto,
is a crossover staple.

Bilrock watches the skateboarders do their moves and does a little business. He sells some weed, some acid, pretty low level. Johnny
Crunch is showing him the ropes. A little older than Bilrock, Crunch
has been living on the streets since he was fifteen. The daily routine is
to hang out by the band shell, unless there's a show over at the Wol-
man Rink, where the action is. That's how many of the Parkies first
find each other.

Sometimes, if Crunch is off doing his thing, Bilrock takes care of
the business. He knows where the drugs are. Specifically, they're in
this one gnarled tree up the hill toward the playground. A few times,
Crunch's half brother comes by looking for him or, more to the point,
wanting some pot. Which is how Bilrock ends up hanging out a few
times with Crunch's half brother Chevy plus John and Danny and
some of the other dudes from the *Saturday Night Live* gang, freshly
moved to the City and a quick cab ride from Rockefeller Center when
they need grass. A bunch of the Parkies go up to Studio 8H and watch
the show live, though Bilrock can't make it.

"I was taught at age 13 how to sell a few joints," says Crunch, a.k.a.
John Cederquist, "and then buy a bag to make a few joints and have
my own head stash. Same thing with acid hits. I could buy a pack of
100 and sell them for a buck a pop. I worked my way up the ladder
and became a dealer."

Sometimes Crunch crashes in the abandoned IRT station at West
Ninety-First Street. The abandoned girls room at the playground is
above the heater, so it stays warm in the cold. If the weather's agree-
able, he liberates a large barricade plank from the park police's supply
and slings it atop the pergola in the wisteria grove.

A runaway from a well-to-do family, he exists entirely in the alternate Parkie economy. "We slept whenever we felt the need," Crunch would write later, sounding like an urban Huck Finn. "We'd get hummed to sleep by honey bees working the fragrant purple blooms, day and night. We didn't bother them, and they didn't bother us."

One night, Crunch and his friend J.C. grab all of Crunch's half-used spray paint from the Ninety-First Street Station, drop some rainbow blotter, and redecorate the side of the abandoned girls' bathroom in the playground. Crunch does his tag in gigantic jagged letters, rainbow stripes shooting horizontally across. He takes his sweet time, but J.C. is taking even longer to get his giant SIE-1 up. "He would lay down a few strokes, then stand back and stare at his handiwork for way too long." Crunch makes himself busy, using the still-remaining paint to decorate the rest of the wall.

J.C. is still working as the sun comes ups. Crunch is watching him, rolling torpedo joints dribbled with black hash oil, when the door to the bathroom suddenly swings open and out stumbles the alcoholic septuagenarian Parks Department attendant, sleeping off a drunk. The Parkies all call him "Hey Joe."

"I lit up, too stoned to care, and watched as he doddered up behind J.C., his mouth open in mute horror at our vandalism," Crunch remembered.

"Wake up!" Crunch calls out, and J.C. finally turns around.

Hey Joe finally speaks. "What have you done?" he says, rocking back and forth on his feet. "*What have you done?*" he repeats. Crunch offers him the joint. Hey Joe calls the cops. But it is 1975 in New York City. They don't come, though Crunch and J.C. find their boards cleared from the pergola later. The graffiti will last, at least, until the early '80s.

Even in 1975, *especially* in 1975, there is still consciousness to liberate. "We thought the more people that tripped, their minds would be expanded and we'd have peace and love," Crunch says. "I was 17. I really believed that." It is not a particularly original thought, nor is it an invalid one, but to extend that idea to public illegal art is profoundly new. If some version of the emerging American consciousness can be detected on the streets of New York in the mid-1970s between the parallel emergences of disco and punk and hip-hop, then the Parkies are part of it, too, part and parcel, working for the common good.

Tripping continues to be an essential part of Parkie life. "There was this really pure LSD going through the Park in the early '70s," says Crunch. He'd heard about the Brotherhood of Eternal Love busts, but there isn't a shortage yet. "Some of it was produced by guys right in the city, out of liquid stashes in their freezers, using micro-screens. Some of the better ones we had were the rainbow blotters, little booklets of 5,000, perforated sheets with little rainbows. As that whole thing picked up, they started to produce them in orange and black. I remember pink Windowpane came around. And the little barrels that were, at that point, still the real thing. I vividly remember seeing the Empire State Building blast off."

"The barrels all came from the Dead guys," Crunch says. He's not much of a Deadhead himself, but went along to New York–area Grateful Dead shows in the early '70s, "not so much to listen to the Dead but to back up the guys who were going there." He'd wait and watch as his friends disappeared into the backstage equipment truck void to get their business done and get the crystal goods.

And at some point, both Crunch and Bilrock come to understand that the Park's LSD connection came from the same place as its graffiti connection: Chad Stickney and his friends. LSD-OM had only briefly been a Brotherhood conduit in the park, but he was among the first and the line had been unbroken since he and his friends started dealing in 1969.

But in 1975, Crunch notices the good stuff starting to taper off, the dosages starting to get smaller, the whole of it changing. "There were purple barrels and so-called 'mesc' and bullshit," Crunch says of some of the drugs that start coming around as the bicentennial approaches. "Some of the primary sources were no longer there," he says. Perhaps the connection between the park and the source of the flame is wavering. Perhaps, in some way, Crunch is merely noticing the impact of the Grateful Dead's year off the road, writing *Blues for Allah* in Marin County.

He stops doing synthetic hallucinogens. Specifically LSD. He's quite fond of mushrooms. They're still a rarity most places, but the Parkies know where to get some. It requires a field trip. "Up in Woodstock, there was a black angus farm," Crunch says, "and the farmer used a bulldozer to shovel all the shit into the back corner of his fields. And that pile of bullshit was where these really good mushrooms would come from."

And then, in early '76, the Dead announce they're coming back, and the Parkies mobilize. The Dead experiment with a system of direct-to-fan mail-order tickets to keep shows small, the first inkling of a new hip economic model that they don't quite grasp yet. "For Dead Heads Only," the invitation says, but Bilrock doesn't get the invitation. Bilrock's never seen the Dead. But New York is his town, and if the Dead are coming to his town, he is going to see them. He's not too stressed.

A month before the Dead's June shows at the Beacon Theater, Hot Tuna play there, and Bilrock and the Parkies are right there are at the side door, sliding and sidling into the chaos. They call it the Break-in Theater. For that matter, the place is literally Johnny Crunch's home some of the time. He slips in via the roof and sleeps up in the catwalks or in the marquee.

The Parkies aren't the only people without tickets, though, and there's a near riot by that familiar side door the first night the Dead are in town. There are some shows around New York that are tough to get into, but this transcends even that. There are entire contingents from the West Coast who saw the comeback in Portland, Oregon, the week before (alongside the SAIL scientists and the Loose Blue Caboose) then hauled ass to Boston catch the eastern tour. They pour into New York.

There's Snakeman, too. A regular seeing the Garcia Band around the Bay Area, he missed his portal from one end of Humbead's Map to the other after Portland and takes the long route. He goes from Portland to Vancouver, catches a $98 flight to Montreal, and hitchhikes to Boston (via eight rides and a few hassles from the highway patrol) and makes it in time for the second set of the first night. No tickets for Snakeman, either, but he finds his way inside.

And there's the so-called Grateful Dead Bus (that is, recorded with that name in *Relix* a few months later), which trucks cross-country with a dozen occupants and not a ticket among them. They miss the first show but are there bright and early each morning thereafter (easy: parked less than a block from the theater) to scoop surplus seats at the box office. With the presence of the Grateful Dead Bus and its perhaps-lost-to-the-sands-of-time occupants (Laurie, are you out there? Gretchen? Gam?), there is now a touring vehicle parked within a close radius of wherever the band is performing. The tapers

are one thing, their mic stands abruptly sprouting into the air like me-
chanical night-growing mushrooms when the house lights go down.
But buses are bold, trundling, chrome organisms on the country's
interstates. The blocks around the Beacon Theater are still New York,
but around Johnny Crunch's marquee home, electricity crackles in
the Gotham air. The Grateful Dead perma-zone always existed inside
venues while the band played, but now it hits the streets.

The Grateful Dead are known carriers of counterculture. Following the Pacific Northwestern mushroom boom of the midseventies,
psilocybin devotees stage "guerrilla inoculations," spreading the magic
by distributing wood chips impregnated with mycelium especially at
Grateful Dead shows.

A decade and change later, a New York–born theorist who writes
under the name Hakim Bey (himself the product of a tiny psychedelic cabal called the Moorish Orthodox Church of America) will describe what he calls Temporary Autonomous Zones. In 1976, with the
fast-orbiting, rule-bending combination of touring vehicles and unauthorized concert tapers and LSD and mushroom-sprouting wood
chips, the Grateful Dead's traveling world wrenches open a TAZ
whenever it pulls into town.

Being native to the city's permanent Central Zone, Bilrock gets
in. Bilrock doesn't get caught. The Dead are still right at home in
New York, and New York freaks like Bilrock are still right at home
with the Dead. The 1976 Dead don't sound anything like the tapes
that Bilrock listens to behind the band shell. Not that he minds. The
new, new, revised Dead move more slowly than they did before with
more self-conscious gospel harmonies than ever, and there's Jerry
Garcia himself, a little detached from the People behind his tinted
glasses with a new guitar tone to match. With Mickey Hart back in the
rhythm section, the thunder sure does roll.

Bilrock has an amazing time, of course. With some Parkie buddies (and without tickets), he hits a few more of the shows in the
area—three nights in Passaic and four in Philadelphia—before the
tour heads westward for Chicago. Then reality undistorts—except for
the park, of course—and they've got a long summer ahead of them,
and some fresh *inspirado* from the Grateful Dead, exactly like their
soul brother Chad a few years earlier.

The graffiti's been getting pretty good out in the back of the band shell. Crunch keeps working at one spot. Other Parkies occasionally scale the band shell and tag up the roof, making art visible only to police helicopters. Every now and then, the city paints over everything, but nobody bothers them much.

Bilrock declares them the Rolling Thunder Writers, in the spirit of the Soul Artists and LSD-OM's Rebels. They derive their name from the hippie-revered Native American medicine man. It doesn't hurt that they're massive fans of the 1972 Mickey Hart solo album *Rolling Thunder,* with its wild lettering by Mouse and Kelley. Most importantly, what better way to describe the sound of the ever-rushing trains?

In the time-honored traditions of miscreants everywhere, the Parkies pore over underground comix, with special love for characters like Gilbert Shelton's Fabulous Furry Freak Brothers, Dave Sheridan's Dealer McDope, and the vivid dreamscapes of Victor Moscoso. Bilrock is a massive Rick Griffin fan. Crunch channels his love of the '60s artists into his poster art, which he does under his own name—John Cederquist—and looks to find a new identity for his street work.

"In graffiti, the ability to take another name and a whole other persona is very powerful," Crunch notes. The same is true of the psychedelic world, the criminal underground, and any other space of marginal or transformational culture where someone realizes he or she is someone else.

There's a whole bunch of Rolling Thunder Writers, longhairs, dreamy disaffected street-kid weirdos. There's BILROCK 161 and CRUNCH. There's ZEPHYR and REVOLT, writing partners working for a few years already and destined to influence the emerging art movement in inventive and radical ways. There's MIN-1 and SIE-1 and RASTA. There's DARK STAR. And there's DEAD, who adds a little blue-red skull and lightning bolt to his tag. They are one of many writing crews, but they will make their voices heard.

Like psychedelics, like taping, like plenty of other things, graffiti is a victimless crime. It is a bit of color and splash and joy-chaos in a fairly depressing age. It shares a characteristic with taping and drugs, too, of being beyond consensus reality, a coded connection to the invisible People's Networks. In New York, graffiti is a transmission from the city's unconscious—or at least that of its disaffected teen males of all classes and races.

Dead shows aren't the only place they're breaking into. The Rolling Thunder Writers also have something that most writers don't: keys to the city. Specifically a set of four keys that Crunch has acquired, one each for the back door and the conductors' compartments of trains in both the IND and IRT/BMT systems. One he stole from a conductors' shack in a train yard. Others he got through other nefarious means, but he has them.

"What was great was going into the conductors' booth while the train was riding and yelling over the loudspeakers," he says. "I had a friend who'd do it until they were stopping the train and the cops were coming. He'd get into an argument with the conductor over the speakers. They'd try to keep the doors closed until the cops came and I'd open the door in that car, or we'd leap off the back."

Another time, he and Bilrock are out making trouble on Central Park West and end up getting chased by a street cop. The two long-haired troublemakers rush down the stairs into a subway entrance with a locked gate at the bottom. "Shit," Bil says, but Crunch isn't worried.

"This cop slows to a walk and is, like, spinning his stick," Crunch says. "I opened the gate, let Bil through, went through, and locked it behind me." Policemen don't have keys to subway gates.

"Can you pass through a wall?" Crunch taunts the cop. "It's like magic, isn't it?" The officer grabs at the gate, beyond furious. A train comes by. "Who owns the streets?" Crunch barks at the cop and they get on and vanish.

HUMBOLDT. IS. BLOWING. UP. There might be a dope famine out East in '76, but in Northern California, the hip economy explodes outward like a head experiment gone totally awry. Actually, it's not like that at all. It *is* that. There is a head-funded arts complex in Redlands called Beginnings, with the giant multipurpose room called the Octagon. And there are reports of twenty-acre weed valleys guarded by searchlights and dudes in camo.

"Most of them were quasi-Rastafarian guys, dreadlocks and the whole thing, which was unfortunate because it gave that whole Rasta scene kind of a bad name," remembered one veteran of a pot plantation. They carry machine guns and pat people down. There is a standardized pay rate: $125 a pound to work as a trimmer. In late September every year, the hotels and motels are rented out, where they crank the heat for the freshly trimmed bud to dry.

AFTER NED LAGIN parts ways with the Grateful Dead and takes a job at an early computer company, the biomusic composer is just another psychedelicized boy genius turned adult genius in Northern California. He plays clavichord from time to time and makes other art, but that's about it. His new job at Processor Technology still makes him interface with the hippies, though, sending him down to Palo Alto to attend the regular meetings of the fledgling Homebrew Computer Club. The monthly outlet for the Peninsula's computer counterculture, there are plenty of long-haired, acid-taking tape collectors among them. A pair of obsessive Bob Dylan reel-to-reel traders both named Steve are regulars at the Homebrew meetings, sharing projects from a Los Altos garage. Eventually the Steves, Jobs and Wozniak, make their way to Processor Technology in Berkeley clutching a circuit board that they call a computer. Being longhairs, someone sends Ned Lagin down to deal with them. He talks to them for a few minutes, recognizing them from the Homebrew meetings. But he sends Steve Jobs and Steve Wozniak and their Apple prototype home. "I'm sick of helping hippies," Ned Lagin thinks.

ONE BY ONE, the Parkies work their way to the end of the subway platform at 137th Street, scan for cops and oncoming trains, and break for it into the darkness. The new psychedelic art-ritual is underway. Who's to say whether the Rolling Thunder Writers are tripping together the very first time they descend to the underground train yard together? Certainly, communal LSD eating happens on many of their subsequent journeys under Morningside Heights, as it had many of the previous afternoons in the park, so there's no reason to assume they aren't doing it the first time they go underground. They eat a lot of acid.

It's blackness down there in the tunnel with the little zig-zag hallucinations zipping out of the dark. Dissszsstortions and slight interruptions. Flickerings. If they plan ahead, they have someone who's not tripping, but they don't always plan ahead. During yonder days of '77, the Rolling Thunder guys follow this routine four or five nights a week, in various states of consciousness among the half dozen of them.

"It was very surreal by itself," says Bilrock, "very psychedelic: darkness, and the lights, and watching out for the third rail, or your enemies. Some other crew that has it out for you. It was pretty heavy. And so it doesn't help to have your mind blown on LSD or something else." And yet. A few blocks to the north, they get to their destination: an underground layup housing a supply of 1 trains, sometimes fresh and ready for modification.

Sometimes, Bilrock sketches plans for what he's going to do, but, when he hits the cars, it's mostly an improvisation, starting with his tag. If a train comes down the tracks, the Writers hit the ground and roll under the cars they're working on. When the conditions are good or the acid is right, the cars turn into collaborations between writers, their styles and tags segueing in and out of one another the same way the Dead go between songs. There is a Rolling Thunder groupmind at work.

The Rolling Thunder Writers are one of many groups in the system. Like the Dead themselves, and not at all coincidentally, the Rolling Thunder Writers stake out a neutral space in New York's deep underground, doing their best to represent the park. "My whole initial mission was to make graffiti safe to go do for Bandshell writers, for freaks, for heads, for dudes with long hair or Afros, that smoked weed and ate acid," says club founder and president Bilrock. "Because that was not the norm at the time. It was very segregated. You had the black clubs and the Puerto Rican clubs. There were a couple that mixed, and most of the whites were from so-called ethnic neighborhoods, Italian or Irish neighborhoods. It was very different. We injected the whole hippie thing for the first time, and it was like *bang*. It blew their minds."

Out go the crypto-tags of RASTA and DARK STAR and BILROCK 161 and CRUNCH and EARTH and MIN 1 and QUIK and others. Bilrock personally hits everything except the 4 and the J. Waiting for the 1, a Gothamite might come across DEAD's primitive Steal Your Face rendering. There are already hundreds of graffiti writers working throughout the boroughs in the mid-to-late '70s, and the Rolling Thunder brahs are merely one peace-loving gang among them. Their message tears through the boroughs on almost all train lines, inside or out.

Of course they're there when the Dead return to Fourteenth Street to the former Academy of Music, now known as the Palladium in the spring of '77. On the rim of the always-teeming East Village, it's funky and rundown and filled with smoke. Bilrock watches the Hells Angels pull their bikes through the open backstage door. It is absolutely the end of an era, ten springs since the Dead first arrived in New York for their hippie parade down St. Mark's Place, just a few blocks to the south. All month after the Palladium shows, there are rumors on WNEW that the Parks Department has issued a permit, even, to John Scher and Ron Delsener so that the Dead might play a giant free show in Central Park after the tour's end. But free shows have to be free for everyone, and this one ain't free for whatever reason, because it doesn't happen.

These five nights at the Palladium are the last time the Dead will play Manhattan as the reigning People's Champion of the underground, never again performing anywhere else in Manhattan besides the decidedly more legit Madison Square Garden and Radio City Music Hall. The Grateful Dead are about to undergo their strangest transformation yet.

Bilrock and a few other Parkies follow the Dead around the Northeast that spring of '77, up to New Haven and to the Boston Garden. Sometimes they take the train, sometimes someone finds a van. Everywhere he goes, Pilot at his side, Bilrock tags some walls and sells some acid.

THE T-SHIRTS are to get Keith and his girlfriend Suzy across the country to San Francisco from Pittsburgh so Keith can visit art schools in the late spring of 1977. More than the psychedelic graffiti artist LSD-OM, even, Keith's work will travel far beyond the head network from which he sprang. The T-shirts come in three different designs. One has a photo of Richard Nixon sniffing a kilo of weed and a hand-drawn logo for a fictional brand of weed named for Nixon's hometown, San Clemente Gold, and some flickering patterns around it. Another features a smiling cartoon head smoking a fat joint while its skull pops open, exploding into intricate spirals and dizzying angles that somehow seem like a rainbow even though they are inked in black and white. The last T-shirt has the Grateful Dead's Steal Your Face skull-and-lightning-bolt logo mixed with Keith's own designs, a dense field of interconnected illustrations like closed eye visuals that one can almost dive into.

Keith was a town freak back home in Berks County, tripping on LSD out in the fields, drawing in his journal. "The drawing I did during the first trip became the seed for *all* of the work that followed" and an entire worldview, he would later write. He discovered the Dead in 1975, an event he would he always consider a divine "accident." Going to school in Pittsburgh, the longhaired art student takes acid whenever he can, though he learns it's not something he can do every day. He has to space it out. Later, he will think of his acid taking as a process of "re-programming" and "finding myself."

His coconspirator in the T-shirt making is his Deadhead roommate and psychedelic soul comrade Barbara. They're both students at the Ivy School of Professional Art, and neither is happy there, both wishing to be somewhere with a more open and vibrant art scene. They find friendship in their shared love of the Dead and spend long hours together, listening to *Workingman's Dead, Blues for Allah, Steal Your Face,* and *Old & in the Way*, talking about art, working on their own pieces, sometimes collaborating.

"We used to trip all over the city," says Barbara, "wandering through neighborhoods, parks and finding places for free. Once we climbed a steep hill, then sat down overlooking Pittsburgh's north side for a long while and listened to the grass.

"I remember one time, Keith ate a whole lot more than he should have and we both looked at each other like *What's. Going. To. Happen?*"

The drawings in Keith's notebooks grow stranger but simpler, the wavy lines vibrating. On the T-shirts, which Keith and Barbara silk screen together at their place, Keith's new world is visible in interlocking tripped-out forms behind the Stealie's lightning bolt. He and Barbara are determined to do something more than "professional art" or even just have art that hangs in galleries, and that's what the T-shirts for fellow heads are, too.

Keith and Barbara don't know what they want out of life yet. "Through all the shit shines the small ray of hope that lives in the common sense of the few," Keith writes in his journal/sketchpad that year. "The music, dance, theater, and the visual arts: the forms of expression, the arts of hope. This is where I think I fit in." The journal is covered with two stickers. "There is nothing like a Grateful Dead concert!" the big one reads. The other is just a Steal Your Face lightning skull.

"The music provided a huge sense of community among other listeners and lovers of mind expression," says Barbara, of the meaning of the Grateful Dead to the young artists. Just before Keith and Suzy leave for their trip, they head to Philadelphia to see the Dead's tour opening show at the Spectrum, where they camp out to score tickets and sell some of the shirts.

"I don't remember a lot of sales," Barbara says of their T-shirt endeavors at that show. There is no parking lot scene to speak of, so they stand on the sidewalk holding up their work. "It always seemed like a triumph when we sold one," Barbara says, a fact made all the funnier because it is the first public sale of art by nineteen-year-old Keith Haring and the formal beginning of one of the twentieth century's most important art careers.

In early May 1977, Keith and Suzy hitchhike out toward Minnesota and the Minneapolis College of Art and Design. They take some acid and hang out at Interstate State Park. "I found a tree in this park that I'm gonna come back to, someday," Keith writes in his journal/sketchpad. "It stretches sideways out over the St. Croix River and I can sit on it and balance lying on it perfectly."

They meet some people who are going to see the Dead themselves the next night in St. Paul. "The Grateful Dead in Minnesota! We're going to see the Grateful Dead!" he writes, mind blown and giddy. He trades some T-shirts for acid and pot and sells others.

For all the many people who will get in buses and follow the Dead around and make stickers, there are orders of magnitude more who only pass through the band's temporary autonomous zone in brief. To them, the act of loving the Grateful Dead isn't about knowing every last version of "Dark Star" or following the band around but simply and directly taking the Grateful Dead's music to heart in a real way. Some slingshot elsewhere into the counterculture, many more carry on with their lives and fall Dead-ward every now and again to get loose. Sometimes, it's just a matter of knowing the words to a few songs. Keith Haring's passage through the Grateful Dead's world is brief but intense, and he is changed by it. More than ever, the Dead's shows are a portal to *there,* as much for the environment they provide as the music the Dead make. Keith Haring loves the Grateful Dead but had no plans to be in Minnesota when they are, but he is!

The band opens with Chuck Berry's "Promised Land," Bob Weir's perennial show starter, the two drummers locked hard on the beat, and the perfect theme song for any westward jaunt like Keith and Suzy's. The last time the band played in Minnesota, four years earlier, it had been bad vibes all around. The show ended with drummer Bill Kreutzmann tackling a security guard. This time, there are cherry bombs and bottle rockets and an audible atmospheric looseness. The news has finally spread all the way, it seems.

The group is well oiled, too, tightening up the languorous tempos of their bicentennial comeback tours. Much of the band's new pep owes to Fleetwood Mac producer Keith Olsen, hired to oversee their newest album and unamused by the collective mush. He whips the band into a round of practice sessions, especially the drummers, re-connecting limbs and minds.

None of this concerns Keith Haring or probably any audience members at the St. Paul Civic Center on May 11, 1977, except that the Dead kick ass. To many, the month of performances will become mythical for its excellence. But to Keith Haring, and to most, the Grateful Dead remain a mysterious entity out of California, always changing, riding the crest of the People's Energy. This isn't quite as true from a business standpoint anymore. After the eucalyptus trees exploded outside the Dead office the year before and the much larger United Artists swallowed the band's label, some $225,000 of the buyout money disappeared. Fictional company head Anton Round evaporated into the void, Jerry Garcia's business partner Ron Rakow vamoosed, and the Dead signed with Arista Records. It is a quiet end for one long thread of the Dead's countercultural experiment. Garcia's salary is stripped to around $50 a week in an internal remuneration that is equally symbolic and financial.

But wherever the energy is coming from, be it the People or the cocaine or whatever, the Dead sure have a lot of it in May 1977. In St. Paul that night, like most shows this tour, they play "Scarlet Begonias" into "Fire on the Mountain," the tightly wound bounce of the former resolving into the two-chord bliss of the latter over a simmering groove, like a "China Cat Sunflower" into "I Know You Rider" for the band's new era.

It's a path the band will get to know well, but that spring it glistens with newness, a joyous anchor for memorable set after memorable set. A few days before Keith and Suzy catch up with the Dead in Minnesota, the band had played it in Ithaca. The *Relix* heads had trekked up from the city, braving a snowstorm to get to Cornell University's Barton Hall. "A strong candidate for the best of the early part of the tour," they will note about Cornell.

In St. Paul, Garcia's guitar chatters with Mickey Hart's hyperactive cowbell, and they sail into the detailed rhythmic lock of "Fire on the Mountain" just as planned. It's not quite "Dark Star" as jam codes go, too insistent on groove, but there's incredible space for detail in the lava streams. This night, only "Uncle John's Band" opens in a way that pushes the consensus reality of song form, where the band step through the Stealie into Keith Haring's wavering sea of squigglies.

Garcia stays on stage by himself, a rare move. Increasingly that spring, the band's second set is anchored by a long drum duet between Mickey Hart and Bill Kreutzmann. (Borrowing from Chekhov: if you have a Mickey Hart in the first set, in the following one, it absolutely must go off.) But, in St. Paul, almost all the musicians leave. Only a spare cymbal plays while Garcia sketches in super-quiet space, and it's the most beautiful they get all night. It's great when the Grateful Dead are one giant entity encompassing the roadies and office staff and their entire collective trip, a size increasingly reflected in their sound. But it's also great when the Grateful Dead can fall away to being just one person, Jerry Garcia in the rightful spotlight at the center.

Keith Haring wouldn't know what to do with all this information even if it did drop whole into his tripping brain. That's not the function the Grateful Dead serve for Keith Haring, and that's not the function that Keith Haring serves for the Grateful Dead. Keith Haring is an energy cog, too, just like the obsessive tape collector

Dick Latvala in Hawaii, just like the zine-writing *Relix* gang in New York, or the graffiti-making Parkies in the Manhattan train tunnels. And it's through people like Keith Haring that the Dead's music seeks new vessels to stay alive.

"The Dead were great," Keith writes in his journal after the show. "We saw the people we met at the campsite, sold t-shirts, got high. The Dead even did an encore from *American Beauty*," and Keith Haring records some of the lyrics from "Brokedown Palace." It's only the second version the band has played since '74, another thing he has no way of knowing. But for Keith and Suzy, the Dead are just exactly perfect.

From the Acid Tests on out, it has always been abundantly clear that the Grateful Dead exist in the Now and that every single note they make might be considered a small miracle of human evolution and the fates of individual human specimens, a dense combination of factors. How long before those Keith Olson–tightened rhythms slip and slow again? And Garcia's voice is still an instrument of supreme sweetness, but what of the micro-cracks on "Ramble on Rose," our hero sounding the tiniest bit out of breath? Nothing lasts.

Keith and Suzy keep selling shirts and shoot off toward San Francisco by thumb, camping out at night and hitching rides from truck drivers. When they run out of money, they sell more T-shirts. A week after seeing the Dead in Minneapolis, they reach Berkeley and, a few days later, arrive in San Francisco's Castro District, where long-haired Keith Haring has a realization and begins to suspect that he might be gay. Keith and Suzy eventually make it back to Pittsburgh, living together for another year before Keith moves to New York to pursue his art career.

The Dead carry on with their tour for the rest of the month, playing the small theaters and auditoriums they'd longed for when they returned from retirement the year before. Every night of that tour, more or less, they continue minting new live albums via a second mixing board position on the side of the stage, where Betty Cantor-Jackson keeps the tapes rolling. She makes many beautiful recordings over the course of her career as an engineer for the Dead, but few will have as lasting impact as those she makes in the spring of 1977. The fall before, her husband—the veteran Dead roadie Rex Jackson—had been killed in a car accident, and Betty's pain is captured in reverse on the tapes, the Dead at their warm and healing and enduring best.

The band exists in this just-exactly-perfect form for precisely thirty shows. And then Mickey Hart rolls his car off the road and into a tree, breaking his collarbone, some ribs, an arm, and some physical part of the band's eight-limbed drum section. The beat changes again.

. . . THUMP-THUMP-thump-thump-thump. In a Chicago warehouse, there are more dancers on acid. "Everything was spiked," says one of the DJs, Craig Cannon, as the language of American dance music further transforms. "It was just crazy. [We] had marathons which lasted a couple of days. Like twenty-four hours. Kids would go home, change clothes, come back." It's not only LSD, of course, but it remains an important part of the mix. The scene in Chicago is, as it will come to be known, *poly-substance.* Club impresario Robert Williams had been through the bardos at David Mancuso's Loft in New York and brings it back with him to Chicago, a small dot on the Map but now glowing stronger. He opens his own place, the Warehouse, in '77. He lures a DJ named Frankie Knuckles back with him from New York, once employed to dose the punch and inject the fruit with LSD at the Gallery. Raised in the South Bronx, amid gangs and Hell's Honkies, Knuckles believes firmly that alcohol has no place near a dance floor. These aren't hippies in Chicago, though. This is, or was, disco. These men are black. Many are gay. Many are straight. Who cares? Just as the scene is poly-substance, just as often, a given DJ (or dancer) might not use drugs at all. Many associate the squelching beats emitted by the SP-303 sampler with acid rock, hardly thinking of the implications when a twelve-inch called "Acid Tracks" takes off. Eventually, the music will be called acid house for whatever crazy reason. *Thump-thump-thump-thump-thump . . .*

THE TIMING OF this story is hazy, but in (one of) John Perry Barlow's tellings, around the mid-to-late '70s, he and fellow Grateful Dead lyricist Robert Hunter are hanging out and getting rather drunk. It is tantamount to a meeting on some mystery mountain for the two men who provide words for Bob Weir and Jerry Garcia's songs. On this night, they make a decision that speaks for the New Earth.

"This is turning into a cult, or a religion, or something," observes Barlow about the burgeoning Deadhead scene, and one might imagine, now, the moon breaking through the clouds, church bells ringing, the cock crowing, and so on.

"Yeah," spake Hunter.

"So far it doesn't have any dogma, which makes it kind of okay as a religion, but it's got ritual, it's got iconography, it's got all these characteristics of religion; it just doesn't seem to have a belief system."

"Well, I've been thinking about that," sayeth Hunter. "If it's going to get a belief system, it's going to be because of us. We will provide it. I mean, we are the ones who are getting up in the bully pulpit and we'll give it a belief system and we could ride this sucker all the way to some dark place. But you don't want to do that and I don't want to do that."

So, up there on the magical mythical let's-pretend-it-happened-on-a-mountain, Hunter and Barlow make a pact to write lyrics that remain free of anything that might be construed as dogma. Weird wisdom, sure, but nothing that might be fixed as advice. It's what Hunter's been doing all along anyway, in the spiritual uncertainty of "Ripple" and elsewhere. Barlow's declaration is a good affirmation. It's nice to say it out loud. The church bells toll again for good measure.

IN THE AUTUMN of '77, a new psychedelic era dawns in Santa Cruz as a generation of scientists comes out of institutional hiding (or emerge from jail) for a two-day conference titled "LSD: A Generation Later." The substances may remain illegal, but that's no longer going to stop the scholars from discussing them, give or take a mushroom consortium in Washington the year before when organizers fled because of rumors of an impending bust. In Santa Cruz, there are panels and presentations and incantations. Albert Hofmann is there, and Allen Ginsberg and Timothy Leary and Baba Ram Dass and the Farm's chief communard Stephen Gaskin and others. They discuss the impurities of contemporary street acid and the relationship between psychedelics and spirituality. Many yearn for the return of proper academic research.

It is the first major conference in a decade and two weeks later and up the coast in Olympia, Washington, there is a matching symposium focusing on mushrooms. There will be many more. In Olympia, there is less nostalgia and more work. The quite active independent chemist Alexander Shulgin comes up from Berkeley. Albert Hofmann, who'd synthesized psilocybin in a lab in 1959 and subsequently trekked into Mexico to meet *curandera* María Sabina, is there, too. It is at the Olympia conference that Hofmann and R. Gordon Wasson, the bank president and ethnomycologist, make a groundbreaking historical presentation.

These modern psychedelic pioneers lay out staggering evidence that the *kykeon* potion consumed by the ancient Greek mystery cultists at Eleusis was a product of the same rye fungus needed to produce LSD. That is, Aristotle, Plato, and their brethren paid admission, took communion with the magical brew, and were transported with a combination of drugs, lights, and music, tripping together in their semisecret society. Wasson and Hofmann point out that one cultist even got in trouble for bringing the sacred *kykeon* home and consuming it for fun. They trace the use of psychedelics from the ancients up to modernity, all the way to the present. Almost.

AROUND 150,000 PEOPLE attend the Grateful Dead's massive summer-ending show at the Englishtown Raceway in New Jersey in 1977, the crowd boxed in by massive shipping containers. There are no gate crashers. The young graffiti artist Bilrock and the Parkies are there, taking the bus to New Jersey.

The event marks the emergence of a new wave of even younger Deadheads and the transformation of the band's already large-scale American psychedelic rite into something even larger and more ritualized. The Dead are pretty good, maybe not their *best*, and definitely not their most ambitious. Owing in part to Mickey Hart's healing limbs, they scrap their plans to play the complete "Terrapin Station" suite with Bob Weir on double-neck guitar. Robert Hunter pens some new lyrics for "Truckin'" during this period too, but they never make it to the stage.

Englishtown is where Bilrock meets the Wizard. Or maybe just the Wizard's assistant or undersecretary. One of those. However he ranks, Bil finally sees where all the acid is coming from: *WEST*.

Crystal LSD has been passing through the park for as long as Bilrock knows—ever since Chad/LSD-OM and his friends made the connection near the Bethesda Fountain. But now, in this portable transformational zone of a Dead show out in New Jersey, Bilrock understands how the deal goes down.

What is remarkable is that the chain is absolutely unbroken. Officially, authorities broke up the Brotherhood with their massive busts and trials in 1972 and 1973. But there was never any stopping it or "them." On the East Coast end, one Parkie passed the connection to another. On the West Coast, their equivalents continued their own lineage. There isn't necessarily a name for the organization that is now supplying LSD for sale, but that doesn't mean it doesn't exist. The Parkies' endless supply is living proof.

"The Park was just a mecca," says Johnny Crunch. "At a point in the late '70s, there were people who'd show up from the Carolinas to pick up thousands of hits."

Who knows how many American psychedelic rituals the park supply is providing for? How many other Keith Harings are out there at the far end of the distribution chain, ready for activation?

Another part of the Parkies' psychedelic art ritual is peyote, which comes from the East Village, only a few blocks north from where Baron Bruchlos's Dollar Sign used to be. There, the Native American Church has a house where the peyote arrives fresh from Texas in crates lined with lettuce, hung from wires on the ceiling to dry. The Parkies don't sell it. It's strictly for personal consumption.

One night, Bilrock shares some with his classmate at the City Alternative School out in Brooklyn, the young artist Jean-Michel Basquiat. Though Basquiat uses the street as a canvas and is already notorious for it, he is determined not to be known as a graffiti artist. Still, he knows that his classmate Bilrock hits the subway cars and is curious about it. The two of them are bombing around the Village, tripping on peyote, and Bilrock finally gives in to Jean-Michel's half-jesting plea to "take me to the trains."

What's a Parkie to do? Bil finds a pay phone and calls another Parkie. "Dude, we're fucked up on peyote, please, babysit us," he tells Zephyr. They make their way to the elevated 1-train layup at 215th Street.

"We're up there, smashed," Bilrock says. "We're writing on the inside. It's the winter. At one point, I'm standing inside the conductor's booth with my head hanging out the window, because I'm fucked up and trying to get some air or something.

"It dawns on me that I'm hearing somebody screaming at me. It didn't register at first. Finally, I focus. I look down and there was a black-and-white with four transit cops. 'You motherfuckers, stay right there, we're coming up there, don't you move.'" They move.

"We literally got chased, while tripping, on the catwalk, running, blindly running, hoping the next step wasn't going to be the last and you fall, you know, three stories," says Bilrock. "I don't know how we did it, but we got out of there."

Parkies aren't necessarily role models. But freeze on that happy image, for a moment, the longhairs and the artiste silhouetted by the wintry city glow as they haul their goofed asses down the tracks. Okay, good.

POT INCHES TOWARD federal decriminalization at the hands of Peter Bourne, the British-born advisor to President Jimmy Carter who'd been there at the start of the Haight-Ashbury Free Clinic. There's been a long, careful process of coalition building, in large part by the National Organization for the Reform of Marijuana Laws, a group with distant roots in LeMar, Legalize Marijuana, an organization founded in the East Village by Allen Ginsberg and Ed Sanders. But then there's scandal in Washington (you don't say) when Bourne is accused of doing cocaine at NORML's Christmas party with Hunter S. Thompson, *High Times* publisher Tom Forçade, and NORML's Keith Stroup. Bourne will deny the incident occurred, but by the summer of '78, after a brouhaha over a prescription written for a staff member, he is gone from the White House. Maybe next century, guys.

JERRY GARCIA, BASSIST John Kahn, and keyboardist Keith Godchaux hang out often in Godchaux's music room. They smoke a lot of pot and play a lot of music. There is a good chance they smoke other drugs, too, like the freebase cocaine and Persian heroin that are increasingly present in the Dead's scene. The trio play through the entire *Blonde on Blonde* songbook. They learn Miles Davis tunes. They do Beatles numbers. The sessions move to the Dead's storage warehouse over by the waterfront in San Rafael, where they dub themselves the Front Street Sheiks and play standards like "A Night in Tunisia."

Garcia, the enthusiastic bluegrass tape collector, operates at an astounding rate. Almost concurrently with the Dead recording *Shakedown Street,* he and Kahn start to build a new studio around themselves at the Front Street facility while working on a new Jerry Garcia Band album called *Cats Under the Stars* that features another five songs written with Robert Hunter.

"We put so much blood into that record," John Kahn would recall to Blair Jackson. "That was our major try. It was all new material and we did it all ourselves. We spent so many hours in the studio. When we were inside there we didn't know if it was day or night except for this one little crack in the ceiling that would allow you to see if it was dark or light. I remember one stretch in the studio where it changed three times before I left the studio."

Something happens out there while the light changes. The sky grows inverted and pale, and mountains grow blue with fire and then cool. An ice age spreads across Marin and recedes. And when the sun flickers on again, it's a new fork in history that Garcia and company have entered.

Keith Godchaux gets hooked pretty quickly. He fades to a nonpresence with the Dead by 1978, even nodding off onstage. One day Garcia catches the keyboardist rooting through the briefcase where Garcia keeps his stash. "He was gone right after that," John Kahn would say.

At their last show, they play for the only (known) time on stage, Miles Davis's "So What" and go on one final fantastic improv flight, Garcia and Godchaux, the shy Deadhead who popped into Garcia's life at one of these very gigs. Then Keith and Donna Godchaux are gone. Nothing lasts. You get it. Keith certainly gets it, and Jerry knows it too well.

The guitarist's finances are a mess, and he and John Kahn temporarily dissolve the Jerry Garcia Band. He joins up with an already-existing local fusion group, Reconstruction, wrapping his ever-busy chop-building ears around some complicated funk changes with Merl Saunders and, of course, bassist Kahn. Jerry Garcia no longer does much acid. Jerry Garcia has become a different kind of head.

THE TAPER HAS never met Dick Latvala before, and Dick Latvala doesn't look like the Taper expects, but he's impossible to miss. Dick and Carol greet the Taper and his wife at the Hilo airport with Hawaiian leis. It is with these connections that the Grateful Dead's music is cemented into the life of the country.

"He was kind of old and haggard, a lot of wrinkles from being out in the sun, and totally brown," taper Pat Lee remembers thinking. It's a whirlwind for Lee, who's only corresponded with Dick by mail and talked on the phone, but never seen a picture. His wife is not as keen on all of it as Pat is, but she's along for the stay at Le Grande Latvala.

At Dick's house, they walk in the front door, and "here's all these guys sitting around the front room, the living room, clipping [marijuana] buds," says Pat Lee, Dick's taper friend from the Northwest. "I'm serious, the pile of buds in the middle was at least 18 inches high, if not higher. I'd never seen so much stuff, much less seen the process of clipping buds. Immediately, someone stuck a pipe in my mouth and I was comatose."

Dick has invited so many people to visit, and they're starting to take him up on it. It's wonderful! Another taper is on the Big Island for a three-week honeymoon with his new wife, and they end up spending a lot of time over at the Latvalas. The week *also* happens to be the anniversary of the Dead's *legendary* shows at the Fillmore East in February 1970, which calls for the trio of Dead freaks to listen to *all* the recordings at absolutely top volume. Dick regales them both with stories of seeing Pigpen sing "Hey Jude" at the Fillmore West in '69. *Yeah right, Dick.*

"That was not my wife's vision of what going to Hawaii was for," Pat Lee says. So, after a day or two, they all make it out to the beach, and it turns out Dick is actually just a wonderful host. They visit the hot springs and the volcanoes. "Dick said the only time he went to the beach was when tourists came to his house and he was forced to do it," Pat Lee says, but it's all good fun.

He gets plenty of time outside, but in his tape room, Dick Latvala does what Dick Latvala does best and most significantly. He's begun to accumulate notebooks, the three-ring spiral kind. He creates a new page for each new show he acquires and tracks the genealogy of the recordings as well as his ongoing thoughts as listens. Each new meditation comes in a different color pen and is dated. In part because of the pot he mails out but mostly because he's Dick, he is now able to acquire high-quality copies of every show within weeks. But his gold will always be the early years of what he calls Primal Dead, the ferocious double-drummer peaks and dream music. Dick even sometimes erases bad shows now.

Dick creates a vital role for himself. He is an energy source. Dick feeds the Dead scene, and the Dead scene feeds the forces of positive change in the world. There is no question to Dick that he is helping the broader universe through his dedication to this music, and he's not wrong. Grateful Dead concerts in the late 1970s are rapidly becoming *the* mainstream of countercultural exchange in the United States, a dependable backbone, and Dick is his doing his best to shore that up. Massive amounts of pot flow out of Hawaii. In 1978, it becomes the state's biggest cash crop, surpassing sugar, per the Hawaiian police. The measurement doesn't take into account those, like Dick, who use it as a currency by itself.

The tape room on Hilo becomes a collection of collections. It is like one of the great private museums of nineteenth-century Europe, on happy display for those who can journey to its relics.

At the Morehouse commune back in Berkeley, Dick and Carol Latvala had learned all sorts of hexing skills. "It was a combination of Sexual Freedom League material, things they'd learned from witches, Scientology, and Buddhism," says Carol. What a waste of acid those days were. Now, Dick is spreading the Grateful Dead far and wide, sending out smiles and excellent versions of "St. Stephen" into the world. By Dick's calculations, it is the best possible position in the universe.

"One day Dick took me up to the plantation!" visiting taper Pat Lee says. "The plants were being grown by this old ancient Hawaiian guy." Dick tells Pat, "You're the only person I've even shown this field to." "I doubt that's true," Pat says, "but I felt very honored at the time."

Dick has one more request of Pat, though. Will he *please* stop asking everyone around the house what they do for a living?

IN 1979, NINETEEN and less wide eyed, graffiti writer Bilrock cuts his hair and shaves his beard into a neat mustache. Bilrock is going to be a secret agent for the Brotherhood. It's part of a tradition, and a practical one. Chad, LSD-OM, remembers the first time he met the representatives from out West, about a decade earlier. "If you saw them driving down the road, you'd think *they're alright.*"

And that's Bilrock, he's alright. He flies out to the Bay Area for the first time and meets the hookup. Once he gets to know people out there, he usually just stays with a friend in Oakland. Sometimes, he gets to see some of the sights, but he's there to do business: to pick up crystal LSD and make sure it gets back to the park.

There is a large amount of turmoil in the LSD world as the 1970s draw to a close, but with cool-headed representatives like Bilrock, there is an assurance that everything flows as it should. Like the do-nuts, the LSD must get made, and it does, finding its way into the self-reinforcing network. The manufacture and culture are native to Western shores but pop up in many places.

The late '70s see significant turnover in the deepest gear work. The West Coast precursor magnate Frank Ragusa is brutally mur-dered in his luxurious home in early 1978. In New York, the man known as the Ghost ceases production. Operating since he issued tabs in Kodachrome boxes a decade earlier, the free jazz flautist Eric Ghost had issued a private press LP in 1974, *Blues for Mr S.,* almost assuredly dedicated to a thinly veiled Southworth Swede, the pro-prietor of the East Village's Psychedelicatessen, then imprisoned for LSD.

The biggest change is across the Atlantic, where a concentrated sweep called Operation Julie nabs British chemist Richard Kemp in one of the biggest LSD busts in history, with Her Majesty's finest tracking and shutting down two parallel and mostly unconnected microdot production rings. Living frugally in a cottage in the Welsh countryside, Kemp and Christine Bott are model heads, raising goats, drilling their own well, living off their land. The press reports Kemp's investments in "head politics." Kemp prepares an 8,000-word defense statement on "my LSD philosophy" espousing the responsible use of psychedelics as a portal to thinking about ecology. The prosecution tries and fails to connect him definitively to the Brotherhood of Eter-nal Love. Kemp is put away for more than a decade.

And yet, around the time that Bilrock is properly recruited into psychedelic secret agency, LSD is starting to move at its heaviest domestic rate since the Brotherhood busts a half decade back. In 1977, the DEA's in-house anti-LSD operation, CENTAC 10 (numbers 1–9 were for other drugs), claim to eradicate the domestic acid business by busting Bio-Dyne Industries, a manufacturing front for psychedelics and "the largest clandestine drugs laboratory ever discovered." Yet, just two years later, the DEA seizes some 750,000 hits of acid in California, up 1,400 percent since 1977. "CHEMISTS REUNITE" reads London graffiti in early '78, "WE NEED ACID," but it's reported that product from California is already a-flowing back across the Whelming Brine to make sure everybody on the Map has the supplies they need.

Another major alteration comes (it is said) when the machinist responsible for maintaining the American underground's specialized pill presses dies in the late '70s. Rather than risk exposure, LSD manufacturers begin to switch even more fully to blotter paper.

Images had started appearing on blotter by 1970 (Mr. Natural, Berkeley) but only during the second half of that decade does it become the increasingly standardized distribution medium. For reasons both practical and commercial, blotters tend to contain a significantly smaller average dosage than earlier epochs, usually around 75–100 micrograms per tab by some measures, versus extraordinarily powerful "normal" hits of 250 micrograms and stronger in the Owsley and Brotherhood days.

The blotter graphics emerge into an underground art form of its own, even more outlaw than the Rolling Thunder Writers' graffiti. The two even share a fair bit of crossover in their postcomix vocabularies. In California, DEA agents seize blotter adorned with dragons and flying saucers and the ever-present Mr. Natural.

Owsley hates it, and decries blotter as an unstable method of transmission, too prone to light exposure and diminished strength. It is a topic of discussion and concern at the 1977 Santa Cruz LSD conference, with many voicing concerns (in *High Times* and elsewhere) about impurities in contemporary acid manufacture.

But LSD is starting to rumble again. San Francisco, as always, is the epicenter. For a few years, there's an underground newspaper called *Stains on Paper,* published oh so appropriately from the Haight by a guy named the Electric Buddha. Each issue previews the next month's blotter.

"Disco people like it, rock 'n' roll people like it," a Golden Gate Park–based dealer in a Dead T-shirt who calls himself Uncle Roscoe tells the *San Francisco Chronicle* in the fall of '79. "Blacks like it, gays like it." Basing himself in the Panhandle, a few blocks from the mostly wrecked Haight, Roscoe says he moves around 4,000 hits a week.

Uncle Roscoe—his Prankster pseudonym by way of Edgar Lee Masters's *Spoon River Anthology*—estimates the Bay Area to be responsible for 90 percent of it. He tells the *Chronicle* he travels cross-country—Boston, Washington, Connecticut, and New York—to deliver.

That's Bilrock's job, too. To get the bottles of crystal back to the park, he uses the US Postal Service. "I didn't have to worry about getting on a plane, or a shakedown, or that kind of shit. But some people worried about mailing ahead and were adamant about carrying. Everybody had something. A lot of times you'd use couriers, like 60-year old ladies."

Back home, "it wasn't easy, but some of the guys got their own pill presses, so they could make their own barrels," Bilrock says. "Some guys would make their own gels and their own blotters. We had the unscrupulous Arabic and Puerto Rican printing shops all over the place in those days, so they'd print up all the sheets and artwork for us."

He continues, "A lot of the guys were rooted in kung fu and the Taoism thing, because of Bruce Lee movies. So a lot of the guys were going to kung fu schools in Chinatown. Part of the uniform was Chinese jackets and Chinese shoes. So a lot of the guys in these acid dealing cliques were rooted in kung fu, too. Some of the early blotter designs were Chinese dragons, stars, yin-yangs, and stuff like that. One of the famous and most successful ones was rainbow blotter. It was like the LGBT pride flag: the whole sheet was stripes and color."

Drugs are becoming big business for both Bilrock and Johnny Crunch, who's been hanging out in Chinatown, too. Crunch has moved on to selling cocaine instead of LSD and—like Jerry Garcia—has become addicted to heroin. He says, "I snorted it until my nose gave out and then smoked it. I was taught by the Ghost-Shadows down in Chinatown—our connection for white heroin—how to chase the dragon."

Life goes dark for a while, as Crunch is able to sustain the habit at first because of the high income from coke sales. It will get better eventually, but not before it gets way worse. Many Parkies go down the same hole. Not all will come out. Life gets bleak around the park. Crunch stops writing graffiti entirely. Bilrock doesn't, down in the subway system with his normal-guy hair and mustache. But, as they pass into their twenties, they're elders now.

EVERYTHING IS FUZZYBLURRY. The sky, the stars, the distant lights, the massive auburn cliffsides, the swirl of noise, the Grateful Dead in the distance. Part of that is the acid. But a lot of it is that Dick lost his glasses somehow before the show. It's the greatest night of his life, maybe, as Dick hops a ride on the Grateful Dead express. Here is the first of several dream-come-true culminations for Dick Latvala's life in psychedelic America. Dick loves superlatives, but this really might be it, at least in part because of the near disaster at hand. Later, during the craziness, someone will take what becomes Dick's all-time favorite picture of himself.

Dick has learned about the quorum of one. He doesn't *need* anyone else to listen to the Grateful Dead. Just he and a tape will serve. The Dead can just appear there, and he can relate to them like that. In some ways, that's the best way to *listen* to the Grateful Dead, which—after all—is what Dick does. But of all the different ways one can listen to the Grateful Dead there is, of course, nothing like a Grateful Dead concert.

Carol and Dick Latvala start to make occasional trips over to the mainland for shows, including big ol' doses for the closing of Winterland on New Year's '78. Now, welp, here's Dick at Red Rocks, alone, without his glasses.

He'd flown to Colorado with a friend who had a friend with the band. But then they get to the hotel and the friend goes upstairs and *sees* something (drugs? bad vibes?) and just straight up splits. Goes back to Hawaii. Leaves Dick. Poor Dick. But Dick is resilient and, of course, has his weed at his disposal. He gets a ride from the hotel to the venue—in this case, the venue being a 9,450-seat amphitheater called Red Rocks sewn into the hills outside Morrison, Colorado. It is an ancient Indian gathering spot, a national park by day. The lights of Denver twinkle.

Dick has no tickets and is left by himself in the lobby. And then Kidd Candelario, senior roadie, comes by. He takes Dick under his wing and brings him to the show, by which point Dick is tripping way hard. In between taking care of Phil Lesh's bass gear, Candelario feeds Dick beer from the cooler and Dick watches the show from backstage. It's remarkable! Dick! Backstage! Part of the family! But Dick was always part of the family, somehow. He's been seeing the Grateful Dead, *believing* in the Grateful Dead, for thirteen years now. After that (and some shipments of Hawaiian kind) he's in.

ON THAT FARAWAY beach in Goa, at this far end of the '70s, at the far end of the Hippie Trail, there are ruptures, and it is difficult to say which is more drastic. They change the picture of global headdom. In Iran, the Ayatollah Ruhollah Khomeini rises to power, and his Revolutionary Council are a bunch of meanies, and out go the longhairs. The same year, the Soviet Union invades Afghanistan, and the civil war in hash-friendly Lebanon escalates. The centuries-old overland route, the Hippie Trail, is destroyed. There are still ways to get to Goa, but its traditional entry points from the Map are gone, and no amount of Acid Eric's magic can bring them back.

The dance-floor population grows anyway, thanks to cheaper and cheaper airfares, leaping from 17,234 visitors in 1977 to 33,430 three years later. The complexion of the revelry changes as the dancing bodies include fewer hippie backpackers and more jet-hopping Euro-partiers. One-time Haight head Goa Gil keeps it up with the Anjuna Jam Band, playing bass and throwing full moon parties at the house and on the stage at the edge of the beach, where the waves lap and everyone grooves. But he's not always so keen on this new rapture that comes with the odd electronic beats coming in from Berlin. Goa Gil likes his music crackling and alive.

THERE ARE ABOUT twenty-five people camped out in Peralta Park the night in late 1979 that Shakedown Street becomes a tangible place outside a Grateful Dead concert. It happens on a little spit of greenery in between the Oakland Auditorium and a small, southern outlet of Lake

Merritt. The Deadhead perma-zone has been on the verge of existence for a long time, but now there's no denying it, a visible slice of
psychedelic America right there *outside* the Dead show, still real when
the sun comes up the next morning. These living practitioners, driven
to some sort of visible asceticism by passion for . . . what?

Since Bill Graham closed down Winterland, the 6,400-capacity
Oakland Auditorium is the new local home for the Dead and the
heads, and everyone can make do. It's kind of an improvement over
the cavernous Winterland in a lot of ways, not the least of which is
the auditorium's spiraling outer hallways, ideal for an evening kibitz.

Graham's organization gets a permit for the tiny park because (in
the words of a rep) "we knew people would be there regardless." It's
chilly but not freezing. There's a tent of T-shirts back there belonging
to Winterland Productions, and Graham's people hire a security guard
to watch it, but he mostly just sleeps, so Bob Barsotti tells some heads
that, hey, if they watch the T-shirt tent, they're welcome to camp out.

"We've gotten to know a lot of them over the years and they're
real reasonable people who just love the Dead," Barsotti tells writer
Dennis McNally. "If you take care of them, things will go real well."

They've come from all over the country. There's Larry, who's seen
every West Coast Dead show since '77. He hitchhiked down from
Portland with his girlfriend Judy. The previous year, he'd quit his
job as a postal worker, sold his records and bike, thumbed it across
the county with Judy, and flown to Egypt to see the Dead. Another
camper, a twenty-three-year-old named Brian, is a part-time student from New Jersey, who travels with funds earned from selling
bumper stickers. Not everyone has from come from so far away. One
woman lives in Oakland but camps in the park anyway despite the
rain, because she can, and commutes to work from Peralta Park each
morning.

Like the bus dwellers out on the interstates, they are a new kind
of Deadhead, fully visible to the naked eye, no way to ignore if one
happens to walk by. "You know once we get there we won't even be
in Oakland anymore," one Deadhead says to another.

"Hell, for the next week, this isn't even in the U.S.A."

Grateful Dead shows *always* took place on Humbead's Map, but
now they conjure the Map into the visible space of the real, breathing United States. The Oakland encampment and the buses and the

twenty-four-hour hum of activity transform Peralta Park into an earthly patch of nongeospecific Humbeadia that happens to be in the Bay Area, but it doesn't have to be. It used to be the heart of town.

Bill Graham always hated the Diggers and Free This and Free That, but he *loves* these Deadheads. They are paying customers and, as on Dead New Years past, he feeds them. Graham's organization serves up some fifty gallons of minestrone and three hundred loaves of French bread to the happy hungry campers. People sell T-shirts and strum guitars, smoke pot, and lay out. Buses and vans find parking in the neighborhood and settle down for the six-night run.

Inside, the hip economy as it pertains to the Grateful Dead's business model makes multiple steps forward, too. At a press conference before the first show, the band announces that the evening will benefit the Seva Foundation, a new organization created by Larry Brilliant, once an on-call doctor for Wavy Gravy's traveling Hog Farm commune, one of two, in case the other was tripping. More lately, Brilliant has worked as a venture capitalist who'd helped with the global eradication of smallpox. As his friend Wavy Gravy so often puts it during live performances, "Let's hear it for the eradication of smallpox!" The new Seva Foundation will make cataract surgery available in India. Another early donor to Seva is Apple's Steve Jobs, who'd crossed paths with Brilliant during his own postacid trek across the subcontinent.

The Dead continue to use their money to fund an array of organizations grown from their immediate community. Around the Oakland Auditorium stage is the band's latest sound system, a composite of speaker sets from the post–Wall of Sound reality. Even the Wall is present in the form of its vocal cluster, though, brought out of retirement for occasional local performances. Owsley had heard a set of studio monitors built by a psychedelicized engineer named John Meyer and immediately worked them into the Dead's setup. Meyer had once designed the quadrophonic array for a San Rafael club called Pepperland. Meyer's new work is his best yet. Soon, Owsley is helping Meyer raise capital to manufacture a beautiful new system of tweeter arrays in custom-welded frames, all hung from scaffolding in a sleek vertical design. It's like the Wall of Sound but a whole new trip. Specifically and officially, it is Time-Aligned, which isn't as catchy, but it's rather cosmic, too, and it *is* far more portable and sounds awesome. It will become an industry standard.

Out in the crowd when the lights go down, the tapers' mic stands shoot up, some thirty sets of them, connected to many more tape decks. Give or take an occasional freak-out by soundman Dan Healy, the Dead's crew has almost come to embrace the tapers, and the circuitry out there is changing all the time. Among the recordists, one big advance is the introduction of the Sony D5, a rugged new cassette deck with super-cool VU meters that one can read in the dark without too much hassle.

On the venue's floor, the tapers hook their gear into analog-mechanical creatures that pulse with audio signal and electricity, generated by battery and groupmind alike. "There was this character that would organize everybody into insanely complex chains," says taper Pat Lee. "There'd be thirty tapers or forty, I can't even tell you how many. And he'd say, 'Okay, you stand *there,*' and there'd be this mountain of coats and you'd have to guard this little five foot square area or whatever, and then your output would go to *this* guy. At setbreak, when people would move, you'd see the area covered a good chunk of the floor in front of the soundboard."

But an even bigger force comes from outside the tapers' turf and has nothing to do with Deadheads or roadies, arriving courtesy of the Sony Corporation: the introduction of the tape-playing Walkman to American shores. Still a Japanese-only phenomenon that holiday season, the Walkman will arrive in the United States in early 1980 and transform the cassette from a niche product to an everyday component of American life.

The Grateful Dead's music is already a killer application for the medium, and the band churns out new content nightly for the taper ecosystem that's linking across the grid every which way, the taper chain on Oakland Auditorium's floor extending down the highways and through the towns. It stretches over the Atlantic to Europe, where the Dead haven't toured in five years. Beginning in the late '70s, the Dead tapers become an absolutely reliable metric. If one wants to know exactly how fast it's possible to transmit sound data from one point to another, it is only necessary to see how the Deadheads are doing it, by cassette, by mail, by hand, by radio broadcast. For now.

That first night at the Oakland Auditorium in December 1979, the band construct one of those instant must-hear tapes with a pair of breakneck twenty-minute jams before they get to the part of the set where Mickey Hart goes off like a Chekhovian gun, and he and Bill Kreutzmann get into their newly codified drum duet. The band doesn't play "Dark Star" anymore (an act as symbolic and lyrical as anything wordsmiths Robert Hunter or John Perry Barlow can conjure) but establish a safe harbor for their improvised weirdness in the blank canvas after Hart and Kreutzmann's rhythmic tromp.

For one tour—the same tour the rumor goes around that the band all took mescaline together in Rochester—there'd been an effort to get all of the musicians to join in on the new percussion section of the show. Garcia had laughed his way through steel drum jam sessions at a few gigs, but it hadn't lasted. Some tapers label it "Warp 10," some "Rhythm Devils." Lots write it as "drumz/space." Many use it to flip their tapes, many more audience members use it to visit the bathroom. A select few know it to be a renewable resource for otherworldly Grateful Dead music, a musical preserve for the real heads.

At the tail end of it almost inevitably comes the trick they'd perfected a half decade earlier: reassembling from deep space into a wrenching Jerry Garcia ballad (possibly with the interruption of a Bob Weir rock number), mirroring the redemptive late-trip reformation and integration. Tonight in Oakland, it's "Not Fade Away" and the first "Brokedown Palace" in over two years (and only the fourth since Keith Haring heard it).

"The music was an independent organism," says Steve Silberman, once a student assistant to Allen Ginsberg and a regular at Oakland shows, then beginning his own writing career. "Everybody would know when *it* came into the room and people on LSD were particularly sensitive to *it*. In a way, you lived your life in the shadow of its footsteps. Sometimes, the best shows could be the roughest. You could go through hell, but you'd often be redeemed by a song like 'Stella Blue,' and this was tied in with the drugs.

"If it was a town like Oaxaca, it'd be crawling with anthropologists because everyone would want to know how this ritual was conducted."

By 1979, with the ritualization of "drumz/space," the Dead's whole performance structure—both the music and the breaks—is now an acid trip condensed into a sequence of creative moves. It is both exquisitely conceptual and plain useful for those on psychedelics.

The dancing has grown only more tribal over the years, swirling, whirling, spastic and jumping, communicative and sympathetic, and more and more often, spinning. To outsiders, all the jelly-legged joy can seem comic. There is a self-serious solemnness to the dancers' ecstasy, arms raised, falling and rising with the music, looking for some physical expression of it. Steve Silberman loves watching people dance and sometimes spends most of his shows turned away from the stage, watching the ecstasy roll across the faces of his friends and his might-as-well-be-friends.

It looks absolutely nothing like boogie-oogey-ing as it is understood in the minidiscos in neighborhoods and malls and roller rinks throughout the country or the hip-hop block parties emerging in the Bronx. The twirling, whirling dance of Deadheads is another way to mark the territory. If they're there, you're here.

The Deadheads take over the Oakland Auditorium in a way that few other groups can take over a semipublic space, making it theirs, rules of the venue be damned. When there are already drugs involved, or sneaking D5s inside via hollowed-out books or wheelchairs, the matter of reserved seating becomes trivial. Everyone gives each other room to breathe, dancers spread out over the back of the floor and into the hallways. It doesn't matter if the shows are sold out or not, they're plenty full, and it's generally easy to score tickets.

Out in Peralta Park, it's mostly affable sorts camping out. On the day off between the shows on the 29th and 31st, Bill Graham's crew even lets some Deadheads use the backstage hot tub. The heads sell food from grills and vend crystals and incense and photos of the band and tie-dye shirts. By New Year's, there are some 150 people camping back there.

Even Bill Graham's Bluecoats will come to acknowledge what is occurring and help re-enforce subtle Deadhead order. After some show, maybe that week, they come up with a system. When the encore ends, a line starts to form for the next night. Around dawn, Graham's employees pass out numbered tickets, and the line reforms later that afternoon. Once inside, heads claim blanket space up front and the Bluecoats establish a password for each entrance point to the floor. There's room for anyone who wants to be there at a Grateful Dead show as the 1970s come to a close.

If someone else wants to be there to bear the torch, they're more than welcome. But this motley crew is welcoming, and the big, big proverbial Bus (with its many fantastic compartments and terrarium bubbles and cozy bunks) has room for Parkies and Uncle Roscoe and SAILers and even ornery Les Kippel and Jerry Moore of *Relix* magazine. The Dead's music makes a particularly good soundtrack for long highway miles as groupminds get together and keep the cosmic fire aflicker and the joints lit, because there's something coming. There's always something coming.

5

THE BURNING SHORE

And you better believe that the goddamn mountain explodes, globbing fire up into the Oregon sky while the Dead jam in Portland. Mount St. Helens had gone off in May 1980 for the first time in a hundred years, causing dramatic damage. And when the Dead arrive a few weeks later for their June 12 show at the Memorial Coliseum, the karmic vibrations from the old Pacific northwestern freaks and all these new tourheads and the band themselves . . . and, lo, there it goes again, a blast on multiple levels, aligning the worlds as the New Earth grows temporarily illuminated by the volcano's rainbow earth-fire and Jerry Garcia's guitar. If the long psychedelic renaissance has a melting point, when the spiritual technologies and methodical investigations and creative achievements and societal integrations begin to evolve and connect in postsixties harmony, it is the turn of the 1980s.

The US Geological Survey records some 54.5 million cubic centimeters of pyroclastic flows and fire domes erupting from Mount St. Helens that night in June, which sounds more impressive than 5.45 cubic meters. But at least five separate Dead tapers capture the band bopping through a pretty metallurgic version of "Scarlet Begonias" into "Fire on the Mountain" and the Deadheads come out of the Coliseum into a strange ash-rain, their cars dusted in a coating of grey, I-5 closed.

The myth enters directly into the lore: the night the Dead made Mount St. Helens blow during "Scarlet" > "Fire." Who's to say if it happened *exactly* then? But what is time relative to a Grateful Dead show, anyway, all bent and malleable and capable of moving so slow and right-on? Those in the venue are detached from the outside world and moved firmly to someplace else for a few hours while the band plays.

In the outside world, the USGS records a first flame-burp on the mountain at 7:07, just before the band's first set, and the bigger blast at 9:09.

In the outside world, night (again) seems to be falling on "the Sixties" as once-and-forever hippie antagonist Ronald Reagan rolls onto the presidential campaign trail.

But in her best-seller this year, *The Aquarian Conspiracy,* Marilyn Ferguson outlines the New Earth, a New Age, that is already here. Taking inspiration from the Esalen Institute, California-style consciousness conferences started to organize "road shows" around 1975, she pinpoints. It was "a perfect device for this national cross-fertilization," as were the "cassette tapes of conference lectures [that] were disseminated by the thousands." She connects hypnosis, "meditation of every kind" (Zen, Christian, psychosynthesis, kundalini, etc.), dream journals, biofeedback, autogenic training, seminars (est, Silva Mind Control, Lifespring, Actualizations), and draws lines between the far-out reaches of outer and inner space. She doesn't mention Deadheads, but it's not a stretch to fit their musical ecstasy in there, too.

On Humbead's Map, imagine Mount St. Helens's 1980 blasts as an explosion in the upward-center of the recent mountain range that pushes diagonally down the continent's middle. Against falling night, the volcano blasts streams of rainbow data and rainbow numbers into the dark sky, spitting rainbow cloud shapes into the ionosphere.

Jerry Garcia had always maintained that the Revolution was over as soon as the Acid Tests happened, the heads had won, and it was only a matter of word spreading. "It was over the first day, the rest of it is just a cleanup operation," he will tell Mary Eisenhart in 1987. Sometime around the turn of the decade, the rainbow blastage starts to bloom in American daily life in subtle, unpredictable ways, blown in through open windows by the volcano winds. This is one of the country's hidden, vibrating majorities.

One can travel a circuit of events like the New Earth Exposition of Appropriate Technologies, held in several cities in the late '70s. Or maybe pick up a TWA in-flight magazine and read a letter from the company prez about "the virtual revolution that has occurred in our collective social awareness." Even the US Army's early '80s meta-cosmic "be all that you can be" recruiting slogan stems from the Esalen-influenced Col. Frank Burns, who soon retires to make software for activists. Switches are flipped, connections soldered.

Perhaps the explosion became inevitable when a precocious teenage Deadhead named Gumby patched together the East Coast and West Coast contingents of computer-science Deadheads at the MIT Media Lab and the Stanford Research Institute, where the Artificial Intelligence Lab folded in the late '70s. That's when the info *really* starts spitting back and forth. There's a new port on the emerging grid called the Usenet, but the Deadheads are already way beyond that, grasping at every new Internet technology to create forms of extended, artificial intelligence to work on their behalf. They zap set lists into the net as soon as they happen and set up real-world tape trades coast to coast. Or perhaps the explosion is foreseen in the profusion of Apple II home computers across the country, the Aquarian Conspiracy envisaged in their rainbow logo, the company's founders unrepentant tape-trading ex-acidheads.

It's not merely the width of the influence; it's the depth, as well, as both acid and Deaddom make their way into the foundations of new and sub- and countercultures. The Dead are equally part of the traditions at New England boarding schools, where free tape-trading rituals subtly indoctrinate the children of the Daughters of American Revolution. Hard-partying, polo shirt-wearing, Bud-swilling frat brothers became the archetypal '80s equivalents of the hog-riding Hells Angels. The Dead's vision doesn't always translate exactly as intended, but it certainly does spread.

All are welcome at Dead shows, a turf that will grow only more open in the years to come as the society around it becomes more oppressive. As an age of extreme cultural conservatism dawns, the Grateful Dead remain a conscious and joyful bastion of powerful self-sustaining otherness.

"Why enter this closed society and make an effort to liberalize it when that's never been its function?" Jerry Garcia says to Jon Carroll in 1982. It remains a central tenet in the Book of Jerry, a direct echo and amplification of what Ken Kesey had told Berkeley demonstrators in 1965. "Why not just leave it and go somewhere else?" Garcia asks. "Why not act out your fantasies, using the positive side of your nature rather than just struggling? Just turn your back on it and split—it's easy enough to find a place where people will leave you alone." For Garcia in the first years of the 1980s, this means living in the downstairs of the house in Hepburn Heights in Marin County, below recently deposed Dead manager Rock Scully, where the guitarist spends an increasing amount of time doing Persian heroin and massive amounts of cocaine. He plays obsessively with the Jerry Garcia Band, jamming in seedy bars up and down the San Francisco Peninsula on an almost weekly basis when the Dead aren't touring. Garcia's own frailties notwithstanding, his good ol' head politics and hip economics ring clear.

Everywhere, the rainbow shoots from radios and televisions and Xerox machines and amplifiers and out into the American fabric. The news of gay liberation comes subliminally coded into the dance beats. The hip-hop network is in full swing in the Bronx and about ready to burst forth into the pop culture matrix, the new People's Music, carrying with it the graffiti subculture and operating its own equally deep and often drug-based economy. Punk is poised to overtake the suburbs, and influential Deadheads are omnipresent there, too, like Greg Ginn, Black Flag guitarist and founder of the trailblazing SST Records. Or Cris and Curt Kirkwood of the Meat Puppets, who sprinkle their band's set with sloppy-joyous nonironic covers of "China Cat Sunflower," "Scarlet Begonias," "Franklin's Tower," and others. Old countercultural notes ring semisecretly in many of the developments.

But while Deadheads *are* everywhere, more importantly, they are *elsewhere.* They've found a source, they've found the others, and they know what to do. The band and the genuinely welcoming world around them continue to serve invaluable functions for young freaks finding their way. The word never stops spreading. Each year, the Grateful Dead are slightly more popular than the previous.

IT'S HARD TO know who to trust anymore as new American psychedelic religions pop up everywhere. It is a firework show prelude to American psychedelia's almost unbelievable metamorphosis during the 1980s.

On New York's Lower East Side, one can visit the Temple of the True Inner Light, established in 1980 as an offshoot of the peyote-eating Native American Church. Visitors are (after an interview session) welcome to use the temple hookah to smoke the free DPT, dipropyltyptamine, so long as they stay for the entirety of their multihour trip to listen to some of the temple's tapes that alternate among Bible passages, ambient music, and raps about how Christ, DPT, and the Light are all one and the same.

If one needs a set of psychedelic guideposts and tools beyond the Grateful Dead, live or on tape, there's a veritable Whole Earth's worth of options in this New Age. In 1980, as well, out in Whittier, California (home of Richard Nixon), the Church of the Sunshine branches from Art Kleps's Neo-American Church.

Since the 1978 Jonestown massacre, though, mainstream America has grown only more touchy about anything that resembles a cult, let alone the demon drugs. But that doesn't seem to stop any of the new organizations, all seemingly quite sincere in their own ways.

One imagines the true American psychedelicist being, by definition, an independent American psychedelicist, capable of making up his or her own mind. Later in the 1980s, probably 1984 or 1985, the Northern Illinois University psychologist Thomas Roberts starts celebrating Bicycle Day—April 19—the 1943 event when LSD inventor Albert Hofmann first intentionally consumed his wonder drug. For good reason, Roberts is fond of the resonance between Hofmann's bicycle trip and Paul Revere's revolutionary horse ride of 1775. His celebrations offer another path for those who have used LSD as an ally, a simple and secular acknowledgment of Hofmann's discovery.

The West Coast soon has the Religion of Drugs, too, founded in Marxist peace in Santa Barbara in 1982. The Fane of the Psilocybe Mushroom, chartered in Victoria, British Columbia, in 1980 (watch that spot on the Map) seems trustworthy, though no less esoteric. It's hard to tell from a distance.

In terms of esoterica, though, no one beats the Church of the SubGenius, a mysterious organization emerging out of Texas in 1979 with a steady stream of propaganda. "The LSD did help in the methodical, reasoned chore of assembling that selfsame *Book of the SubGenius*, I must vouchsafe," Reverend Ivan Stang would later write. "But that was more in the same way coffee was a help."

By '81, J. R. "Bob" Dobbs, their mysterious pipe-smoking icon, appears on sheets of blotter acid. "Fuck 'em if they can't take a joke," reads one of the church's mottos. They might be serious, and you should definitely trust them.

THE PHONE RINGS in a home in the suburbs sometime in 1980 or so. "You've received calls from Chicago and Cleveland and Michigan," the voice on the other end says, or perhaps some equivalent cities. The Dead-head network is starting to light up on the grown-ups' switchboard, but the grown-ups don't know the half of it, let alone what's unfold-ing under their noses.

"Oh, our son was in all of those places," a poor bewildered par-ent says, telling the voice that, yes, a son or daughter was following around that *band,* the *Grateful Dead.* Then suddenly there's an agent out there on tour, tracking a group of Deadheads through the Mid-west as the heads track the Dead.

The Deadheads find all kinds of ways to survive on the road, but it's a technique borrowed from the still-active Yippies back in New York that initiates what history now records as perhaps the first coor-dinated bust operation on Grateful Dead tour since the Brotherhood of Eternal Love. And it's not for drugs.

There are about a hundred kids, mostly high school and college age, ping-ponging around the country with the band during that sum-mer of 1980. Someone discovers the current iteration of the Yippies' newspaper, *Overthrow,* with its easy-to-read chart of lightly encrypted calling card numbers for major corporations, including Shell, Chev-ron, and Johnson & Johnson. What korporate akkountant would no-tice a few extra calls on the enormous monthly ledger?

The calling card numbers go around "like candy," and the touring Deadheads use them for all their telecommunications needs, usually just calling home, which is how the phone company catches on and sends an agent out into the Midwest to figure out just what on God's green earth these heathens have gotten up to now. In Chicago, the secret phone agent man catches up with the perps, and the poor be-wildered parents have to pay a few thousand dollars in fines. Bummer.

Jay Blakesberg, a friend of the busted phone phreak, gets into a deeper line of trouble. A young hippie from New Jersey with a good eye and a Yashica 35-millimeter SLR camera, Blakesberg has been documenting life in the rose-filled Deadhead underworld since the Meadowlands in '78. He soon supports himself on the road selling 8 × 10 prints of the band, but he's also doing a good trade in his ongoing series of more artful ethnographic shots: Deadheads twirling madly in the hallways, crammed and crashed on the floors of vibed-out hotel rooms, hanging out in the backs of cars in the parking lot. The day of the Chicago phone phreaker bust, Jay takes a shot in his gang's hotel room that will wind up printed in *Rolling Stone* many years later. With his camera, Jay is a first-class time traveler, capturing the movements of the new always-mobile psychedelic community.

The young photographer keeps himself out on the road with the Dead for almost the entire year, going coast to coast. In the spring, at the Capitol Theater in Passaic, New Jersey, he meets a friendly guy who asks Jay if he'd like to dose, and Jay naturally says, "Sure." The guy rips Jay a quarter sheet of acid, divided into unperforated one-hit triangles, which Jay shares with his friends. Pretty soon, the guy becomes Jay's acid connection, one of many linkages in the new acid network solidifying around Dead shows and an archetypal way the whole operation operates, in large part, without operators.

During the first few years after the band returns to the road in 1976 and begins to regularly hit the same regions, the LSD distribution system springs to work around them. Jay lives in New Jersey, and his new LSD connection lives in San Francisco. They see one other on tour and, as needed, the connection sends Jay blotter acid—that is, acid laid into sheets of paper, usually perforated—via FedEx, 1,000–2,000 hits at a time. It is indeed a simpler era, and Jay has stumbled into the exact decentralized maw of the great and still unbroken LSD network.

The time is so simple that some blotter manufacturers even replicate their designs on the wide envelopes these use to mail out their wares, turning it into a complete visual package. Some, like the fifty samurai symbols blotter, come in their own carrying cases. Jay just receives his in plain envelopes.

The wholesale price for Jay is $50 for a hundred hits, somewhere not too far from the source, and Jay sells individual hundred-count sheets to his high school pals for $100 who, in turn, break it down into $3 individual hits. Everyone makes money, and the localized pocket of the hip economy booms.

The finely controlled price of LSD had been set long ago, by Owsley Stanley and the first generation of LSD makers, who deemed the psychedelic experience more valuable than its manufacturing costs. And so the price stays low, "101 varieties" available for $1.50–$3 a hit according to *High Times'* February 1980 Trans-High Market Quotations.

Not every town in America has Parkies who can hop on a plane to the coast to do biz or a centralized locale to ply their wares. But almost every small suburban town has a Deadhead who can act as a connection point between tour and the home front. Deadheads are like human parks, common territory, friends with punks, friends with Rastas, friends with metalheads (another branch of the head family entirely, spawned in the early '70s), friends with freaks, friends with geeks, friends with jocks. Often a Deadhead might identify as any one of these, too.

For the increasing number of non-Deadheads out there in search of psychedelics, one can often go to a local Deadhead in order to safely inquire whether they know where to get some drugs or concert tapes. It's a known quantity that Deadheads are friendly. Jay Blakesberg is friendly. Like many who have come before him, Jay believes firmly in the consciousness-manifesting power of psychedelics. He does what he feels is a good deed. He and his friends are proud of what they do, often forgetting that LSD is illegal. Jay Blakesberg and dozens—maybe hundreds, maybe thousands—of others set up informal LSD franchises in *their* towns, portals to the hip economy that might fund any number of bands or photographers or other heady start-ups.

At least until the Man catches up. The police watch Jay's connection on the West Coast, and Jay gets nabbed picking up a package back home in New Jersey in the spring of '81. He has to do a little time, which sucks pretty bad. He goes away for just over seven months, to a minimum security prison in New Jersey. The experience actually enriches his life, and it's not too bad, all things told. And when he gets out, he keeps seeing the Dead as often as he can, keeps his nose clean (lesson learned!), finishes college, and begins a storied career documenting the Dead world and plenty far beyond, clicking off into the future.

TO THE RIM of our volcano heads a man in a Hawaiian shirt. Should you chance to meet him on the road, you will find that he speaks with an immediately unforgettable voice, a high-pitched lilt, every syllable a punchline. He happily introduces himself as an explorer. It's not hard to get him to talk.

This man with grey splotches in his beard is an old-time Berkeley head and has seen the world. He studied the Tibetan language in Nepal and collected butterflies in the outer islands of Indonesia. And he's been down the Amazon. If you happen to be in a spot in your respective travels where you're waylaid together or moving in parallel for a while, he would be more than happy to tell you about *that* trip.

He's full of stories. He first smoked pot at the hands of Barry Melton, also known as the Fish, as in Country Joe and ____. This traveler doesn't *dislike* the Dead, either, perhaps similar to the way he doesn't dislike LSD. He might laugh gently at the question. They're both important *modalities,* he might say. But they're not his. He's friendly, this fellow.

He's full of opinions, too. "I see the entire New Age as a flight from the psychedelic experience," he declares once in his unmistakable voice. "People will do anything other than take a psychedelic compound. Be rebirthed, Rolfed, this, that, and the other thing. Because they instinctively sense that the psychedelic experience is real."

Terence McKenna has important business up here on the metaphoric mountain. He loves psychedelics and is operating under specific instructions. He is charismatic and likable, and—a decade after his experiment at La Chorrera involving *Psilocybe cubensis* and DMT and the transdimensional contact and the UFO encounter—his voice is starting to boom from the mountain through the networks. In the first years of the 1980s, Terence McKenna becomes suddenly ubiquitous in psychedelic circles via radio show appearances and cassette releases on labels like Dolphin Tapes and Big Sur Tapes and articles in underground journals and, especially, live appearances at conferences. In person, Terence McKenna is very convincing.

His message is simple. When he begins to publish books, he boils it down to an instructive inscription that he can write along with his signature: "Five dried grams and a silent garden."

Terence and his brother Dennis had returned from their 1971 trip down the Amazon and thrown themselves into their respective studies. Dennis takes a more traditional academic route, tackling chemistry and botany, while Terence continues to grind away at the information they'd received in South America, calculating, ever-calculating, what he calls the timewave. In 1976, the brothers had come together for their most important project.

Under the names O. T. Oss and O. N. Oeric, the McKennas published *Psilocybin: Magic Mushroom Growers Guide* and revolutionized the do-it-yourself production of psychedelic mushrooms for would-be travelers. From *High Times,* one can order mushroom spores and be well on the way to meeting the mushroom. Psilocybin had long been a rare treat for heads, available but always far more rare than the ever-plentiful LSD. With the McKennas' help, mushrooms now can (and do) sprout in any climate, at any time of year, and their impact on American culture grows to match acid's. One discovery is that, in the proper dosage, mushrooms are every bit as powerful as LSD.

The technique also allows Terence McKenna have to have a career. Through the early '80s, his work is sponsored by mushroom farming. It is later recounted that, every three weeks, McKenna can turn out seventy pounds of mushrooms. He and his wife Kat, a more scientifically grounded ethnobotanist, had been able to buy some property in Hawaii. But an acid chemist colleague gets busted. "They fucked him so terrifyingly that I saw I couldn't do this anymore," McKenna will tell Erik Davis. "I had to work something else out."

"Includes some spacey science fiction" notes one distributor's advertising brochure of the McKennas' *Guide,* referring to Terence's preface, which only scratches the soon-bluish surface of what will become a massive oeuvre. What Terence McKenna has worked out is a rap. And it will last him a long time.

In the *Guide,* readers learn that the mushroom has talked to the author of this book in the unequivocal words of an extraterrestrial voice: "I am old, older than thought in your species. . . . "

Wait, what?

Terence McKenna must think so, too, because he'd waited a few years before throwing himself fully into the task of spreading the word, waiting, writing, writing, waiting, and—by 1982—speaking. McKenna's is a clear, amiable voice, kind of pinched, kind of goofy. He drawls, he laughs, he is able to smother cynicism and project a contagious wonder. He's got chops. Jerry Garcia's a fan.

Not everybody is buying it. *High Times* had run side-by-side reviews of *The Invisible Landscape* and the *Magic Mushroom Growers Guide*, unaware that they were products of the same authors. "They have *invited* ridicule by advancing this absurd hypothesis [about mushrooms' extraterrestrial origins]," fungi scholar Jonathan Ott writes.

All along, Terence McKenna will insist that he is not a scientist but an *explorer*. He is definitely an entertainer. His eight-cassette *True Hallucinations* "talking book," complete with field recordings and jam band interludes, becomes an underground classic. By the mid-1980s, McKenna and his wife Kat establish Botanical Dimensions and start developing their property in Hawaii into an ethnobotanical reserve.

While McKenna is the most vocal, a community of psychedelic scholars begins to connect, with specialists in each field, sounding off in pages of small publications like Thomas Lyttle's *Psychozoic Press*, issued on typewritten pages from Coos Bay, Oregon, starting in 1982. They gather more and more often, fostering a world where the observations of independent psychonauts cross over into valuable scholarship. A percentage of psychedelic takers had always taken their practices quite seriously, but it is only in the early '80s that their voices begin to rise and communicate.

McKenna has his coming out in May 1983, appearing at the Psychedelics Conference in Santa Barbara alongside LSD inventor Albert Hofmann, master independent chemist Sasha Shulgin, and others. Though he is a baby boomer, McKenna's self-conscious bemusement and storytelling skills place him in a different league than most who have come before.

He finds his best outlet at the Esalen Institute, the durable institution founded in Big Sur in 1961 and home of many an idyllic navel gaze in the cliffside hot tub and hot springs. It is where the work of Albert Hofmann fully meets the theories of Carl Jung. Starting in the late '70s, Esalen becomes a forum for the cutting edge of quantum physics—the quest to prove "spooky action at a distance"—playing host to researchers from Berkeley's longhaired Fundamental Fysiks Group and others. It is under a similar rubric that McKenna makes his first Esalen appearance in December 1983, speaking at the Lilly/Goswami Conference on Consciousness and Quantum Physics. He starts dispensing aphorisms almost immediately.

"It is no great accomplishment to hear a voice in the head," McKenna tells the assembled. "The accomplishment is to make sure it's telling you the truth." It is a rapturous, passionate, endearing, enduring performance. Get the tape. "My testimony," McKenna says, "is that magic is alive in hyperspace."

THERE'S MORE HEAVINESS occurring deep in the LSD world. The onetime Windowpane manufacturer Frank/Denis/Kelly/_____ turns himself in. His life on the run had doubled as a spiritual journey, and (under an assumed name) he has been practicing, teaching, learning, and experiencing Zen, though there are insinuations of far darker underworld connections. He is well on his way to monkhood when he begins a sixteen-month jail sentence in 1980.

The Clear Light System is the first of the old acid families to crumble. Not all of the primary players do time.

There are some busts, as well, that pertain to the swelling family of acid distributors around the Grateful Dead. In reaction, perhaps even to photographer Jay Blakesberg's incarceration, they issue sheets of blotter featuring Snoopy, arms crossed, sunglasses on, a shit-eating grin on his face: a hearty strawberry blown at feds.

SARAH MATZAR IS dosed and looking up at the ceiling of the Grateful Dead's Front Street rehearsal hall in San Rafael when she figures out what she's going to do with the crystal LSD. Besides make money, that is. Sarah is in her midtwenties and no utopian, though she likes acid well enough and loves the Dead. But Sarah just wants to support her family. Desperately. She is in a fix.

By life circumstance, here she is tripping at Front Street, looking up at the fixture over the fluorescent lights with its patterned plastic bubbles undulating across the surface. And she realizes that the indentations are the perfect shape to serve as molds for LSD gel tabs.

An early '70s graduate of Pacific High, the experimental institution outside Palo Alto where students built geodesic domes and interacted with monks, Sarah is well placed in the Dead world and already has her reasons for being around Front Street in the early '80s. She asks Dead roadie and Front Street manager Kidd Candelario where he got the light fixture, acquires one, and brings it back to her new residence in Berkeley. Along with her Pacific High chemistry classes, she picks up further specialized knowledge from Melissa Cargill, Owsley's lab collaborator and LSD pioneer. Sarah and Melissa have been friends for a few years, bonding over textile design, which is Sarah's true passion.

"Melissa was like, 'You go girl!'" Sarah laughs. Cargill, out of the acid game since the '60s and working for George Lucas's Industrial Light and Magic on *Raiders of the Lost Ark* and other projects, suggests that Sarah grease the plastic bubbles with aerosol-butter Pam. It works like a charm.

Sarah Matzar isn't like other acid cooks. For starters, she is a woman, which—besides Melissa Cargill and Rhoney Stanley of Owsley's lab and scattered others in the UK—is rare in LSD chemistry circles. Sarah is 4'10" and possesses a lacerating wit. She is starting her own textile business and getting her master's in anthropology at UC Berkeley, studying Mayan art. She is not here to save the world.

"Do I believe in LSD? Yes, I do," she says, "but it's not for everybody." She is doing this for her family, lowercase. She is doing this to send money back to Guatemala, where she belongs. She'd spent part of her childhood in the States and part in Central and South America, where her mother is from. "Sometimes where you're born isn't where you're from," she notes.

"Art is my God," she says, and her God manifests in the form of intricate Guatemalan quilt making, symbols and systems colliding. "My Guatemalan color sense combined with my psychedelic color sense," she says. In her quilting she attempts to "break out of the block," the traditional division in pattern making, and does so, the fabrics continuing their conversation across rippled quilted surfaces.

She is not in the United States by choice, which is where the urgency comes from. In the late '70s, Guatemala's decades-running civil war grew too turbulent, so she and her family—her mother, brother, sister, and she—are living in a condemned house in Berkeley, near the Ashby Flea Market. One of the other squat residents is a Deadhead from New York, who has a line on grams of crystal LSD, fresh from a European chemist. And, just like that, Sarah is pulled into the upper-middle-class Grateful Dead scene she'd known during her high school years in Palo Alto. She re-establishes old connections, partially for business's sake. She always did love the Dead, though, and acid, too, but this is pure economic opportunity. In time, much of her family will return to Guatemala, but Sarah will support them.

The psychedelic world had always at least presented itself as classless. But in addition to being a woman in the LSD scene, Sarah finds herself as an outsider in the hippie-bourgie Dead scene. She uses the LSD and her not inconsiderable natural intelligence to bootstrap herself into business and, in short, into the upper echelons. In that regard, the psychedelic world becomes an access point, a place with its own social ladder with its own skills.

In the Berkeley squat, Sarah experiments with various methods before landing on the gel tabs. They're a hit, and the plastic light fixture technique becomes a standard manufacturing method in the chemical underground. There are perhaps dozens of other chemists like Sarah, picking up crystal from various sources, usually European, and converting it into marketable doses. "A lot of people learned how to do it," she says. "But a lot of people learned how to do it badly." There is one acid cook she knows who works exclusively in gas station bathrooms. He rolls up, plugs in a portable dehumidifier, lays the crystal into consumable form, and is out within an hour and a half. He is not the most precise operator, though a memorable character. They come in all stripes, as do the European chemists. The one who supplies Sarah's supply is an idealist of the old-guard Owsleyian sort.

Sarah makes all kinds of LSD besides the gels, including blotters, from unmarked squares to intricate designs she creates herself. Sometimes she works for hire, but usually she's in charge, alongside a few partners. When it gets going, about half of her vast business is with the Dead world, and about half elsewhere. She spends some time hanging out among the Talking Heads' art-punk circles in New York in the early '80s, too. She's got plenty of connections, is fun to talk to, and the product moves well.

She feels inherent sexism in plenty of interactions, customers expecting they'd be able to talk her prices down. But her resolve is strong, and fuck them, she's got a family. A group of associates forms around her, about half women, unusual in the psychedelic world, as well. The crystal LSD market in the early '80s is big on speculation, she recalls later. People will often sit on good supplies for years before converting it.

She wires money home, no more than $600 at a time, and makes $40,000 in less than a year. And though she doesn't move LSD at shows or on tour, she is absolutely part of the Grateful Dead's extended family and—since before she was in the acid game—friends with Owsley himself. "He was a total textile freak," Sarah says of their early bond. They have long conversations about how the Jacquard loom was the first computer.

Sarah estimates that there are perhaps a half-dozen heads at her level of acid manufacture moving in and out of the band's inner circle. Though cordial with most, she wouldn't characterize any as "Grateful Dead Family." Not since the days of Owsley and Goldfinger could anyone make that claim, she says. But there is Grateful Dead and there is Family and there is acid, sometimes brought back from Europe by old friends who *know*.

She travels with the band from coast to coast and goes to shows. Sometimes she sells her quilts, but rarely. Owsley shows her the ropes of the alternative business structures that are starting to thrive around the Dead. "He definitely operated in penny-ante kind of world," she says. "I would believe that he never had a real bank account." He teaches her about hip economics, even still using the exact phrase.

One time, out on tour somewhere, at a rest stop perhaps, someone offers Sarah Matzar her own acid, gels. "It's really good," she is told. Sarah declines.

JACAEBER KASTOR REMAINS acidless in New York and doesn't know about the Central Park scene, which means only that there's still room in the market. An expatriated Berkeley head, Kastor has sampled plenty of psychedelic worlds, an archetypal seeker, and always seems able to sniff out new territory. He's not far off.

He'd needed to escape California. That much was clear. "The New Age thing was *blossoming* out there in the late '70s," he says. "It was this whole New Age world. Everybody was getting healthy and *jogging*. Everybody was into these New Age and psychic pursuits. It was getting kind of upper middle class and suburbany." Not that Kastor is any stranger to New Age pursuits. He'd studied at Esalen, stayed at the San Francisco Zen Center, seriously pondered UFOs, and lived in the Haight, thinking it terribly short sighted of the so-called community to deem the neighborhood dead by 1970.

But he follows a girlfriend to New York, breaks up, and decides to stay. Some friends mail him delicious pot from the Emerald Triangle in Northern California, and FedEx him blotter when needed. But

Kastor discovers that, in a pinch, he can go up to Times Square, to one of several porn shops. "They'd have the videos and their booths, and there was a guy back in the video department. There were spots all over the City and Brooklyn where you could get pot at bodegas."

Via his ex-girlfriend, an Alvin Ailey dancer, Kastor frequents late-night discos where the crowd is predominantly (though by no means exclusively) some combination of gay, male, black, and Latino. Since the opening of Studio 54 in 1977, psychedelics had become less prevalent on the New York dance scene. "Cocaine was king," Kastor says. There is a lot of freebasing.

But then, one day, acid appears for sale at those certain porn shops on Times Square, specifically blotter, mystical symbols and Hebrew writing with the word "tetragramaton" spelled out. Kastor, always a longhair and smooth as can be, investigates and discovers its source.

"Bulk blotter acid made its way directly from the Grateful Dead people," Kastor says, "from the Grateful Dead people that only surfaced at Grateful Dead shows. They considered themselves *Grateful Dead Family*. Maybe not inner core, like their family members, but that second ring around the Dead. They were distributing."

He continues, "There was a brief turf battle that erupted on 42nd Street over LSD. Because someone ripped off the person who was delivering and it went up for sale on the other end of 42nd Street. It got straightened out. I don't think anyone got hurt."

Kastor sees the impact in the discos. Dancers discover that LSD is a cheaper and more efficient party drug than any variety of cocaine, only two dollars to stay high all night (and can be used to make a little cocaine go a long way). Of course, some dancers know this all perfectly well already.

Besides the Deadheads, Kastor observes, there is the parallel forever-young social network of art school students around the East Coast, eager for fresh inspiration. At the Pratt Institute in Brooklyn, Kastor observes, a group of students score sheets of Golden Dolphin blotter (gridded with cool blue dots), manufactured locally, and reproduce the gorgeous art on a party flyer.

Ex-Deadhead and always-vibrating graffiti-pop painter Keith Haring is well on his way to the toppermost of the art world by 1982, but he is destined to go even further. The visual vocabulary he invented on an acid trip back in Berks County will spread across the world, an instantly recognizable vision of love. Haring discovers Larry Levan's Paradise Garage in New York, where Levan DJs with samplers and minimalist cool and drum machines and occasional appearances by disco divas. The DJ blends tracks and borrows echo tricks from Jamaican dub producers. There is no booze and a killer sound system, and (in Haring's memory) "many, many people are on hallucinogenic drugs." Friday night is straight night, Saturday night is gay night.

"It's the closest thing to being at a Grateful Dead concert," Haring will say, "except that it wasn't a hippie thing, but taking place in a totally urban, contemporary setting. The whole experience was very communal, very spiritual," Haring remembers. Levan's gay night appearances are known as Saturday Mass. To doubt the veracity of the dancers' religious experiences is to miss the point of psychedelics. The drugs are a way to access and animate and contemplate the shape of the universe directly, through the medium of disco, Dead, or other. The drugs aren't necessary, strictly, so long as there is enough volume and chaos to generate freedom. Maybe some people are just dancing.

Haring eventually decorates Paradise Garage, spreading white-on-black lines up the columns of the former factory and even adorning singer Grace Jones with body paint, extensions of the public art experiments that began with his Dead bootleg shirts. Chalk one up for the Grateful Dead Family, whoever they aren't, though their work is never done.

NANCY REAGAN SEZ, "Just say no." Which seems rude.

Ken Kesey suggests, "Just say thanks." More polite.

But it's the Nancy Reagans of the universe who have the upper hand during this cold, bogus decade of the 1980s. Richard Nixon was the first to invoke the War on Drugs, but it is former movie star Ronald Reagan who transforms it from a metaphor into an actual military operation. The 1981 Department of Defense Authorization Act allows for Pentagon assistance in antidrug operations, breaking down a long-held barrier between civilian law and military enforcement.

The fan and the shit collide in California's Emerald Triangle during harvest season '83 with the launch of the Campaign Against Marijuana Planting, a coordinated twenty-seven-agency operation with helicopters and garden raids and land seizures and 128 arrests and some

64,579 plants seized, worth an estimated $130 million. But they're also barely scratching the surface. The 1978 Psychotropic Substances Act allows for government property seizures, as well, a radical change from common law precedents stretching back centuries, the grip strengthened in 1984 by the Comprehensive Crime Control Act.

Reagan's new drug policies go after marijuana growers as much as cocaine syndicates. They're not messing around and they have no sense of humor. Real reactionaries. The freewheeling traffic of powders and pills and pot and psychedelics is, for the first time, coming up against meaningful opposition. Lots of people go to jail as privacy-eroding antidrug policies, including urine tests, sweep through all levels of American culture. Sentences get harsher, surpassing punishment for violent crimes. Grown-ups get more sanctimonious. Many of them, anyway.

"To demand that a person pee in a cup whenever you wish him to, without a documented reason to suspect that he has been using an illegal drug, is intolerable in our republic," rages chemist Sasha Shulgin in a lecture he gives to his university class every year. "You are saying to him, 'I wonder if you are not behaving in a way that I approve of. Convince me that you indeed are.'

"Outrageous.

"Intolerable."

Some heads protest, but not many. A wild-eyed, wild-haired, LSD-gobbling hemp and pot legalization advocate named Jack Herer discovers that he can go to Grateful Dead parking lots and set up a table with brochures and people will listen to him. It's not over yet.

SOMETIME AROUND 1983, in a former squat in San Francisco's Mission, the Institute of Illegal Images absolutely does not incorporate, open, or at all announce its existence. Like a fiction of the Argentine writer Jorge Luis Borges—a countryman of the institute's nonfounder—the strange museum in a three-story Victorian becomes a locus for improbable activity and characters, perhaps *the* center of underground American psychedelia in the 1980s.

The collection expands and shrinks at the whims of its proprietor, a flamboyant rogue scholar on the rise named Mark McCloud, who has the tendency to sometimes eat his objects of interest. Like fine art prints, McCloud's *objets* are exceedingly rare, almost identical to lithographs, at least until the final stages of production. Unlike fine art prints, LSD blotter's natural fate is usually to be either consumed or confiscated, and certainly never collected anywhere as straightforward as a gallery or museum.

Yet, since the early '70s, give or take, Mark McCloud has attempted to make his freezer into a safe harbor for this recently developed American folk art, the antidogmatic sacrament of the emerging free religions. Sometimes Mark can't help himself, but he manages to build up a representative collection. It is art, and Mark McCloud knows art.

He'd studied at the Sorbonne in Paris under postmodern theorist Michel Foucault. "When he came into the room, we all rose and clapped," says McCloud, who (after expatriation from Argentina to San Francisco during Argentina's Black Year) became a Dead freak of the Pigpen vintage. When Mr. Pen exited the band in the early '70s, McCloud thought it all got laughable. "He kept them honest," he says. More recently, Mark has worked as an assistant to the photographer and filmmaker Robert Frank in New York.

Returning to San Francisco schooled in the art of grant writing, McCloud and his collection define themselves. He makes the commitment to frame some of the LSD and hang it on the wall, putting its blatant illegality in full sunlight and, in theory, destroying its psychedelic properties. Without eating it, though, it is hard to know for sure.

Each work, either small fragments or a whole sheet, has its own chemical and metasymbolic aura. Art! Blotter is a fertile medium, and the range of images grows only more robust over the early '80s as Mark McCloud starts to seek it out more aggressively.

Sometimes, the art comes on single tabs, like the Snoopys from '81. Other creations are far more serious. One sheet from '76, some forty-four tiny tabs each housing a piece of a cute fuzzy bunny and a mouse bearing a birthday cupcake, is a breakthrough. It is not fine art, but it is one of the first full-color perforated prints. The tetragrammaton from '77 bursts with occult signage. There are sheets awash in dizzying fields of concentric circles, like some outtake ocean from *Yellow Submarine*. There are the peace doves and dragons that spread across entire sheets. Jules Verne octopi. Ants. Unicorns. Flying saucers.

McCloud is interested in the acid art, yes, but he is an admirer of the whole culture, is *part* of the culture, and interested in how the mystical properties of the substance interact with the aesthetic value of the art, not to mention the radical political overtones of it all. McCloud's spot in the Mission becomes a psychedelic art-punk salon connecting myriad avant-gardes, like the ever-fertile, postpunk Re/Search Publications crew. A ceramicist himself, McCloud leases a massive studio in the old Viacom Studios building and breaks it into spaces for a new generation of San Francisco artists. As a collector, he becomes a generous patron to many more.

McCloud comes with the deepest psychedelic credentials and, if asked, will say he belongs to the Church of the Little Green Man, a performance-art rubric that goes bicoastal when church founder Mike Osterhout relocates from San Francisco to New York. Later in the decade, it is via the Church of the Little Green Man that McCloud becomes the first collector of works by one of the Church's East Coast parishioners, a painter named Alex Grey. Dubbing his deeply psychedelic work "visionary art," Grey spends much of the decade creating a series of twenty-one massive paintings depicting intricate cross-sections of human bodies and visualized souls that, when assembled, will create a Chapel of Sacred Mirrors.

At some point in the early '80s, Mark McCloud's three-story Victorian in San Francisco's Mission earns its nickname: the Institute of Illegal Images.

In addition to art, LSD-soaked or otherwise, Mark McCloud collects stories. Rare, precious stories of the most secret sort. Gradually, McCloud identifies the origins of the blotter and learns the workings of the business whose product opens the door to the unknown. Whisperings, really. Very few names attached. He collects tales of the shadowy Ronnie Stark, a man with complex ties to various European political undergrounds and the infamous supplier of LSD precursor ergotamine tartrate to both the Brotherhood of Eternal Love and British chemist Richard Kemp. But it is Stark's own chemist—perhaps the American-born Tord Svenson—working at labs in Europe in the late '60s and early '70s that made the best acid McCloud has ever known.

"It was like being shot out of a fucking cannon—really," McCloud would remember to Jon Hanna. "And people might say, 'Nah, that's just due to the high[er] doses [of '60s LSD].' But I don't know that I can agree in this case. There was something about that acid—five minutes after taking it you could *hear* something happening to you. . . . It was something so well finished that it just coupled to you in a way unlike anything else."

Stark had been arrested in Italy with a Bulgarian passport and, during his trial, suddenly became Khouri Ali, a radical Palestinian, answering the court in fluent Arabic. "While in jail he infiltrated the Red Brigades," McCloud will recall, "was contacted by a PLO terrorist, Italian secret service, Libyan diplomats, and American and British consulate representatives. . . .

"Stark was finally released because a judge was convinced he was a CIA agent." In his possession at the time of his arrest is a phone book with many numbers, including the Grateful Dead. Most lately, he was deported from Italy back to the United States, where in 1984 he reportedly dies in police custody. His DEA file records it as a heroin overdose. "Stark's life of criss-crossing the planet on an international scale dispensing LSD can be seen as a prank on a grand social scale," McCloud argues in *Re/Search* #11.

Another character that Mark McCloud tracks is even more elusive. There was once a character named Dealer McDope, illustrated by underground cartoonist Dave Sheridan, appearing in the pages of various titles like *Rip Off Comix* and *Mother's Oats*. McDope's exploits fell on the absurd end of the drug dealer spectrum, even by comix standards, like repurposing a fleet of World War II submarines to smuggle cocaine. Or landing on airstrips in the jungle. And there's a real guy, Mark McCloud learns, *just* like him: longhaired, bearded, stoned grin, daredevil. He's the fixer, the guy who can get it done and find the sweet ergotamine tartrate when Ron Stark is being held by the Italian authorities. He's out there, McCloud knows: Dealer McDope.

THE BIGGEST CITY in psychedelic America is a portable bopping skyline on the horizon. The little municipality moves from town to town, bringing drugs and access points to numerous alternative social networks. The hip economy drives the parallel existence of this place, and there are numerous ways to create fun and profit in the cartoon bubble outside Grateful Dead shows, opportunities at every corner of parked cars outside the coliseums and summer amphitheaters where the band plays in the early 1980s. And, everywhere the band go, they forge the type of intersections that don't occur outside performances by Van Halen or Lionel Richie or any other popular American musical acts skipping through the nation's enormo-domes, even acts with fanatical followers. It's beyond the music by now, a New Earth ready for anyone to step inside.

A rags-to-riches Grateful Dead tourhead escapade, which could happen to any white male falling in the proper demographic, but in this case happens to Eric Schwartz of Brookline, Massachusetts, then seventeen: "I'd made some tape labels in my high school printing class," Schwartz says. "They were the most rudimentary labels ever. They cost less than a penny apiece. I sold them for $1 a dozen. I'd go into a parking lot and figured there were 20,000 people there and I was going to talk to 10% of them, and 10% of *them* were going to give me a dollar bill. I was easily making 200 $1 bills a day, which was totally enough for $8 tickets and $1.20 gas. By '83, I'd graduated from campsites to Hiltons and Hyatts."

In the original computer underground sense of the word, a hack is a clever trick, and following the Grateful Dead on tour is just one hack after another. Anything to get to the next show. These are the fat years, really. There's a bust every now and again, but life as a Deadhead is still pretty under the radar for most of America—which, in some ways, is kind of remarkable. In 1982, the Grateful Dead are the #6 top-grossing live act in the country, according to *Performance* magazine.

Eric Schwartz barely misses a show in '83. Somewhere early on, he meets a slightly older bro named Chris Calise, in his midtwenties, who goes by the name Chris Goodspace, out of the semicommunal, Rainbow-affiliated vibe tribe of the same name in Philadelphia. He'd done some time rebirthing himself at Esalen in Big Sur, too. "He was the Ward Cleever," says Schwartz.

The Deadheads move in four or five car caravans, breathing and highly visible groupmind organisms zipping the interstates. Eric sells bumper stickers, too. "Wherever we go the people all complain," reads one, changing two words and turning "St. Stephen" into a metacommentary on Deadheads. One time in Boise, Eric and his friends cover a cop car in bumper stickers, including an "I Break for Hallucinations" at the rear center. Thankfully, the officer is amused.

Extra tickets are plentiful and often go for cheap or even free outside of shows. Hog Farmer Calico is on perma-tour, a liaison between backstage and the maybe one-hundred-strong Deadheads following the band in 1983. Starting around now, the number increases reliably each summer. But if one knows Calico, she'll probably be wandering around the lot right before showtime with some freebie tickets to make sure people get inside for some sunshine. And if all else fails, Eric and his friends have other techniques to get in the doors.

Out in the parking lots of the continent's middle, there is no Shakedown Street parking lot bazaar yet, but that doesn't mean there's not a massive ongoing party filled with drugs and sex and esoteric weirdos. There's much for sale, including a growing assortment of wooden pot pipes that might be found in the North American wing of some twenty-second-century history museum as exemplars of late millennial folk art.

Let's turn the floor over to the vivid stylings of Chris Goodspace, momentarily, then on the road with some of the most stunning tie-dyes on the lot, plus a few excellent T-shirts: More Kooks, Less Nukes and an *American Gothic* parody, Support Your Local Grower.

"A lot of Deadheads were hippie travelers, who were part of the much bigger hippie movement," says Goodspace of the early tour-heads. "There was a lot of crossover with the Rainbow Family. You had crystal sellers. There were a lot of Deadheads that were going to Bali and Guatemala and Indonesia and bringing back clothing to sell. They'd go down and get gemstones and do jewelry." And so begins a new hippie trade passage, an American Deadhead version of the Overland Route.

"You always had the Krishnas, they always fed people," Goodspace continues. "They had their smiley face stickers that they passed out. You had bikers. There was no nitrous scene back then. Just getting good pot was hard. You had lots of west coasters coming to make money because the east coast needed it. You had a lot of east coasters wanting to meet people from the west coast.

"You'd see 10 or 12 buses parked together, a lot of them were coming from the west coast. You also had the Rainbow buses. There was a guy Silverbear who had a great bus. It had a Volkswagen [welded] on top of it. He was friends with Kesey. It was small group, but in the late '70s it really did morph into a full-time show on the road.

"You had the different mystical groups, like the OTO [Ordo Templi Orientis], it's a western magick society. You had a lot of that on tour, especially with the San Francisco crowd," Goodspace recalls. "A lot of people into eastern mysticism, too, and this was just western magick. You had guru types on tour. Western magic, black magic, grey magic, white magic. There were people who into Christian liberal religions. There were all these splinter groups.

"You'd see dealers connected to the Mexican mafia. A guy from the Mexican mafia told my friend he couldn't get pot anymore if he didn't sell coke. Then you had the mushroom crowd. I know someone who was growing mushrooms in a bus. They would take the bus out to the woods, grow the mushrooms, park the bus when they were done, and go sell the mushrooms. Everyone had their little niches. Everyone had their soap operas."

The lore explodes. Chris Goodspace even hears thirdhand about a group of Deadhead bank robbers on tour circa '79, though he never confirms it and it could just be a mutation of the very true story of Ray "Cat" Olsen. In 1975 Olsen imitated the based-on-actual-events movie *Dog Day Afternoon* and held up a New York City bank with a shotgun and took hostages, going off script when he demanded a direct line to WNEW DJ Scott Muni so he could tell the world that he wanted "to thank Jerry Garcia. I want to thank Phil Lesh . . . they have made me high over the years. I'm psychedelic." If there *were* Deadhead bank robbers on tour, they'd add another amazing metalayer.

There is only one white dreadlocked kid on tour at this time, in Eric Schwartz's recollection, but these are the prototypes for what would become known years later, almost always in the pejorative sense, as *wookiees.* This sole white dreadie, known as Mark Dread, is also the sole vendor of marijuana edibles on tour, converting what he calls "medicinal oil" into a new culinary form known instantly as the goo ball. Perhaps it's not a new name but, on Dead tour, the green mushy concoction of granola and who knows what come in "extremely small artisanal batches," Eric says, and Mark Dread would always try to sell them to locals fresh from the stainless steel mixing bowl.

The bopping city is the anarchistic center of the Republic, a crossroads where ideas, fashions, substances, and technologies are communicated back to local communities and affiliated groups. Tie-dye had been common around the Republic since at least the early '70s, but in the late '70s and early '80s, several of the Deadhead artists get it down to a science.

Like the acid, like the music, the tie-dye saturates the country, circulating into the American wardrobe in even greater density as Deadheads transport and distribute it. The Deadhead vibe, always an amazing and delicate aesthetic negotiation between the biker/acid-taking/brainy-freak faction and the sunshine/roses/twirling/ever-twirling contingent begins to tip decisively towards the sunshine daydreamers. And so it is in the early 1980s that the drug-devouring Deadheads become cuddly, get coated in a soft blanket of bright colors and dancing bears. Borrowed from one-time acid chemist Bob Thomas's art for 1973's *Bear's Choice* LP, the bears appear on blotter paper, too, filling massive sheets with their furry leg-kicks.

Perhaps one of the truest signs of the revolution actually taking root, finally, is held at a fraternity house in Ohio. The Fijis at Miami University in Oxford organize their first annual Deadhead party and tape swap. A tape swap! That little innocuous bit of free culture, grown dimly from the Diggers and entirely from the notion that it's free because it's free because it's free because it's *freeeeeee*, making intellectual headway in the frat system! There are light years between fraternity/sorority culture and the Barter Lane and exchange circles of the Rainbow Gatherings. Or are there? How much space is really between the libertine tendencies of this outsider order and the libertine tendencies of the insider initiates of the old regimes? Each simply works with a few of the secret knots that bind the human world.

But it's less secret all the time. With each passing year that the Dead don't put out a record, there are more and more people following them around. When Garcia debuts a few new songs in the summer of 1982, the taper network gobbles them up eagerly and distributes them, like the band's very own independent record company. Weir and new keyboardist Brent Mydland have their own numbers as well. With no Dead studio album on the horizon, the only way to hear the new music—save going to a show—is to somehow make contact with the taper network and the Deadheads. A few of the songs, notably Garcia and Robert Hunter's "Touch of Grey," are instant favorites. People's Music or no, the Dead belong to the heads, the musicians essentially ceding their music distribution to their listeners.

It is during this period, as well, that a shift in the band's music becomes audible. In the early days, their chief heads were unquestionably Jerry Garcia and Phil Lesh, with Robert Hunter providing a constant soulful input. Lately, though, with chief Jer escaped into the deep end and one-time hardline taskmaster Lesh in the midst of "the Heineken years," the band's onstage punch comes from Mickey Hart's roto-toms and Bob Weir's lunges and keyboardist Brent Mydland's over-the-top blues yowl. The band gives in to nearly every impulse that made the Legendary Marty Weinberg and other first-generation heads disappear from the scene many years ago. But the victory of dragon-paraded calypso hullabaloo over the sleek Marin space cowboys doesn't bother many Deadheads. In fact, it makes many more dance and dance and spin.

Playing live was *always* the band's primary source of income. But now, inadvertently self-liberated from the cycle of recording an album every year or two—as they had since their 1967 debut—the Grateful Dead *need* the Deadheads. And they have them!

The Deadheads keep coming up with hacks. In Massachusetts, Philip Davidson publishes multiple issues of the *Deadheads Directory*. In one, he makes sure to note that the names and addresses inside are "not an open invitation for houseguests." How many heed *that* instruction?

Surely by now the perennial Deadhead joke is in circulation: "How do you know if a Deadhead stayed at your house?" Answer: "He's still there." The early 1980s are when most of modernity's impressions are born.

Not coincidentally, this period also breeds the negative stereotypes about Deadheads that give bite to the endless jokes. Groups of travelers decamp to Santa Cruz in between Dead runs. Says Eric Schwartz, "If you had three weeks off from tour between Ventura [outside Los Angeles] and Frost [on the Stanford campus], you could go there and the food stamp laws were so lax that you could walk into the food stamp office and they'd give you a bag of beans and five pound block of Reagan cheese and potatoes and carrots. They'd assign you a PO Box and a week later you'd pick up your food stamps. We'd go get our food stamps and get chips and salsa and sour cream and whatever we could buy so that it was two dollars and three cents, because they couldn't give you change for food stamps if it was under a dollar. You keep buying $2.03 purchases until you had enough for beer. You'd pay for the beer with your change and then go back to the beach."

As a life hack, it's an impressive maneuver, but, as a moral move, it carries Deadhead credos into peculiar territory. There are all kinds of reasons this is an obnoxious thing to do as a human being, an entitlement that comes with the power of pure devotion to the Dead and the idea that Deadworld is a place you can just hang out, frictionless, and surf between Hiltons and the beach. What a blinding passion that could send a groupmind awhirl enough to come up with such things! It doesn't make Eric Schwartz a bad person necessarily, though he's not on his best behavior around the Dead. Many aren't, the band always included, but their music comes to represent numerous freedoms that maybe aren't fully thought out. It is probably this kind of Deadhead that the Washington, DC, punk band the Teen Idles sing about on their *Minor Disturbance* EP, the first release on the teen-run punk label Dischord Records and the opening salvo of a punk revolution with anti-Deadness almost written into the drug-free credo known as straight edge.

Generally speaking, the Grateful Dead and their fans are not straight edge. Cocaine is absolutely prevalent on Dead tour as it is in the broader American culture in the 1980s. It's been a fixture of the Dead's inner circle since at least 1970 and—like for many others—it's been getting distinctly out of control for them. Jerry Garcia openly snorts line after line in front of one journalist from *Frets*. When Eric Schwartz meets Phil Lesh in the lobby of a hotel in Hult, Oregon, it's while his buddy is upstairs delivering coke to Garcia's room.

Dead tour is still small enough for run-ins. In Hult, Ken Kesey holds court in the hotel restaurant. Whenever Eric and his friends see Bob Weir in a lobby, they wave "Hi Brent!!" in unison. Ever thus to Pranksters. Phil laughs uproariously at the "Wherever we go . . . " bumper sticker. "I'd never put it on my car," the bassist tells them as he takes it. A few days later, en route to another show, Phil passes them on the highway, the bumper sticker affixed to his rental. He honks as he goes by.

Despite the prevalence of Peruvian marching powder, there's always acid around, too, and that remains the difference between Deadheads and any other fringe group of a similar size to which one might compare them, the difference between a subculture and a counterculture. It is what turns these rows of cars into something in the vague shape of a cityscape.

In the midsummer in the Midwest, there is the first extralarge LSD bust on tour, and one of the big network news shows covers it. By the time the entire caravan pulls into Ventura, the word has been on network news: *get yer LSD at a Grateful Dead concert.* Eric Schwartz and Chris Goodspace remember, here, a distinct shift. The streets of their city are now a little more alive with dark electricity.

If it wasn't already, it's now dangerous to drive the highways of the country flying Grateful Dead colors, an open invitation to get pulled over. Outlaws have always been part of the Dead and the heads' mythology, but now that's what Deadheads have become, en masse. It's actually not a bad business move, mystique-wise. Putting a sticker of cute-ass dancing bears on your car is actually kind of dangerous. For starters, the people that the police seek *are* actually out there.

Once, fresh-faced Eric Schwartz walks into a hotel room on Dead tour in the Midwest to see a bunch of sheets of freshly dipped blotter draped and drying over a string, freshly converted from crystal LSD. When it's time to go, the room's occupant gives Eric and his friends the recently dipped string. They gnaw on it as if it's gum and trip to the heavens during the show that night.

Near the end of the year, Eric Schwartz returns home to Massachusetts with the same amount of money that he left with. And then he goes to his grandparents' house, dries out for a while, and really thinks about what he's going to do with his life. He's not Keith Haring or anything. Eric Schwartz stays a rabid Deadhead, becoming one of the world's foremost Dead memorabilia collectors and indexers. He is quite good at it.

R. U. SIRIUS and the Lord Nose spend almost every weekend at the cove in the Marin Headlands taking acid and freaking out their friends. They know the future is around here somewhere, and they're pulling hard to make it arrive. They climb upward, thinking they can see it, and they probably can. Psychedelic futurism isn't new, but its moment has arrived. The technologies are finally ready on both sides of the equation.

There's a wooden stairway built into the cliffside, and they bring their friends up it. "If you fall, fall inland!" the Lord Nose calls out. And then there's a World War II defense bunker, from when the Japanese might be coming. And still farther up, the wooden stairs disappear and the happy futurists climb until they're tripping too hard to climb farther and they have the big view of the ocean in front of them.

They're acid-in-the-wild, California-variety, transpersonal, transhumanist brain freaks, where inner and outer worlds might align to make a beautiful tomorrow. The Lord Nose trips on acid or mushrooms three times a week, marking the days between with DMT sessions. When they lay out an advertising circular for their new zine, it's a *Sgt. Pepper's* parody with the Beatles' faces replaced by a new Rushmore of Timothy Leary, Pee-Wee Herman, Robert Anton Wilson, and Jerry Garcia. "Happy mutation" it says on the drumhead.

"The Space Age Newspaper of Psychedelics, Science, Human Potential, Irreverence, and Modern Art," *High Frontiers* promises. It's R. U. Sirius, a.k.a. Ken Goffman, who started the paper in 1984. In the first issue, he features an interview with the mushroom prophet Terence McKenna, who preaches 2012's peaceful apocalypse, the end of novelty, "the time beyond history," all predicted by his timewave.

"I think every time you take a psychedelic drug you are anticipating and experiencing this future state of electronic and pharmacological connectedness," McKenna carries on in the particular interview/lecture/oration reprinted in *High Frontiers* #1. We must *prepare*. He suggests people take copious notes on their experiences.

Ex-Merry Prankster Stewart Brand has continued to tend the flame and curate new information with his still-evolving *CoEvolution Quarterly,* and the Stanford programmers find Deadhead-appropriate hacks. But with Apple IIs flooding the land and the first generation of psychedelic hackers of the Homebrew Computer Club and beyond coming into professional maturity, the future unfolds.

It's around this time in the early '80s, too, that a veteran LSD enthusiast named Bob Wallace—the ninth employee of rising software giant Microsoft—quits his job to market his own software based on a new concept that he's helped hatch. They call it shareware.

"I think the concept came in some extent from my psychedelic experience," he will attest: give away the product, and if users like it, they pay. As it happens, his PC-Write application is a hit, as is the concept. Free and shared software becomes an integral part of the emerging Silicon Valley vocabulary—as do psychedelics.

Wallace will become one of the first to state the techno-psyche-delic party line: "I think psychedelics help you in general go beyond the normal way of doing things and to really open up your mind to more possibilities that maybe seem obvious in retrospect but you'd never think of if you were going along with the regular way of doing things."

Frank Barron and others had studied the connections between LSD and creativity as far back as the 1950s, but, for the first time, industry leaders are beginning to speak openly about their psychedelic use. In time, Wallace will become a vocal proponent of the connec-tions between psychedelics and creative work, donating his earnings to various research projects.

The psychedelic-electronic connection seems to grow stronger by the day. Utopian freedoms whiz across the wires, rainbow bits and bytes that might find one another and groove together. *High Fron-tiers* #1 offers a report on Origins, an offshoot of Communitree, one of the country's first electronic bulletin boards, online since '78 but unconnected to the broader net. Origins is . . . it's hard to say, some-thing between a new online religion and a commune, evolved from a Communitree conference into a real-life fifty-person crew with a hundred-page book of findings and vague plans to start an intentional community.

"We are avoiding organized activities at this time," the missive signs off in particularly Digger-like fashion, sounding like an acid family of yore. "To participate in Origins you must take initiative to help create it."

Well, duh, and Deadheads are a decade ahead of Origins and McKenna and utter computer newbie Tim Leary. The e-mail list started at Stanford a decade ago, now connected to MIT, has got-ten so big that it needs to be split into two: Dead-Heads, for people who *only* need to have the set lists and tour dates the moment they're posted, and Dead-Flames, also known as Jerry's Breakfast, for the people who want to talk about *everything*. They burn through memes (like the Porsche Guy and his tuna sandwich) in a way that won't be-come common to the rest of the world for almost a quarter century.

But, as always, news of the revolution still needs distributing. What does R. U. Sirius want with exchanging Dead set lists, anyway? The Lord Nose—the photographer/designer Marc Franklin—might be spotted at Dead shows from time to time, but their job is to get the word further and higher and deeper. Sirius gets *High Frontiers* to the world via Last Gasp, the venerable underground comix distributor, and at a few local bookstores around Palo Alto and the Stanford environs, including Kepler's in Menlo Park, a onetime hangout for Jerry Garcia and pals.

The drug-computer connection is becoming abundantly clear to many deep in the corners of Northern California and beyond. Recalls Sirius of the world's reaction to the first issue, "We immediately began hearing from hackers, software designers, NASA people, all saying variations on 'This is what I wanted to happen, but I was surprised that it did.'" The time is ripe. The same month, a group publishes the first issue of *2600,* a new newsletter with severe Yippie overtones that starts with phone phreaking and digs far deeper into new forms of hacking.

It's after *High Frontiers'* crudely designed first issue that the Lord Nose encounters it in a Haight Street head shop and decides R. U. Sirius requires his third eye for design. An ex–Madison Avenue art man, the Nose moves in with Sirius in Berkeley where, at least once, they pay their rent with a sheet of acid. Over the course of a year, as he assembles the next issue, *High Frontiers* transforms into a present-tense splash of New Wave cyberzest, and things really go *zip zip zap.* The second issue of *High Frontiers* is filled with popping and colorful cyberdelic design that mixes digital imagery with op-art Pranksterdom.

Sirius is invited to a party at a Palo Alto house belonging to a Silicon Valley veteran. "That was where you could actually hear the people talk about their schemes and their computer work and see that the pot was going around, that the ecstasy was going around," Sirius recalls. "There was a positive vibe around ecstasy then, when it was still legal."

MDMA was first synthesized in 1912 but takes some time to find its way to the world. Alexander "Sasha" Shulgin made the drug in the '60s but never tried it himself until a student of his synthesized a batch and cured a lifelong stutter. Since leaving Dow Chemicals, Shulgin and a close circle of friends had methodically bioassayed the various creations produced in Shulgin's cozy backyard lab. They trip together on a wide variety of substances in comfortable middle-class bonhomie, listening to classical music and drinking fruit juice. MDMA tests off their charts.

They don't believe drugs are for *everybody*, especially this MDMA, but *they* sure have fun and reflective experiences. Shulgin sometimes consumes the drug in social settings, what he calls a "low calorie martini." He introduces MDMA to a friend of his in this context, one of the pioneers of psychedelic psychology, Leo Zeff, then on the verge of retirement. By the end of the weekend, Zeff changes his mind about retirement, pioneering MDMA therapy with some 4,000 patients over the next decade under near-total anonymity. He will be known as "the Secret Chief."

Like peyote a few decades earlier, MDMA is available special delivery from Texas—specifically a company based in Dallas and Fort Worth selling pills via an 800 number, calling the drug "sassafras" after the sassafras root its precursor, safarole, comes from. During the early '80s, sassafras catches on in the Lone Star State and radiates through circles elsewhere.

Momentarily, it goes by the name "Adam" and, increasingly, "XTC," and soon enough "ecstasy," a quite unbeatable word for the drug's effect. Sasha Shulgin insists that the drug is not a psychedelic so much as "a window." "It enabled me to see out, and to see my own insides, without distortion or reservations," he writes.

On the DIY chemical exchanges of the Bay Area, MDMA is a smash. Like LSD a decade and a half earlier, and even easier to manufacture, it becomes a quite legal source of income for numerous underground organizations. But it is only one of a plethora of pills and powders being mapped, per the suggestion of Terence McKenna or some greater force.

A couple known as Gracie and Zarkov trip together in a quiet dark room on various combinations of drugs and compare results. Gracie tells *High Frontiers* that they often trip in parallel, getting "the same material at the same time, however we often get it in different forms. For instance, I'll be seeing something and Zarkov will get the dialogue." As in a really slow renaissance, it begins on the fringes, with disconnected artists and scholars working in parallel, before eventually connecting and working their way to the next level.

Elsewhere in California, *High Frontiers'* Lord Nose works through inner technologies, methodologies for tripping. They are fun, they are harrowing, they are work. He reads deeply into the developing body of literature and absorbs the off-record oral tradition by the community of psychedelic psychiatrists. One of his close friends and teachers is a shaman, "not some *Berkeley* shaman," who helps with other maps. Different combinations have different effects. The Lord Nose finds, for example, that he prefers a particular combination of DMT and 2C-B.

This is an underground serious about understanding its psychedelics, and *High Frontiers* acts like a pivot between high traditions, future kicks, and the true value of the drugs already consumed. When the second issue finally hits the streets in mid-1985, the Lord Nose jets to New York to lay the groundwork for world takeover. He goes on WBAI. *High Times* does a feature on them. The narrative of psychedelics and technology is established here and now by R. U. Sirius and his crew, soon joined by Alison Kennedy, known as Queen Mu. The magazine's graphic influence will be seen in a new generation of San Francisco designers, including the zine (and twenty-first century blog) *bOING bOING,* which will launch as a print edition in 1988.

The Lord Nose uses the term "medicines" to describe LSD, MDMA, and others. DMT, especially, is his ally. They are a life practice, a transpersonal discipline and self-therapy for people like the Nose, who has a tangled and uptight past to contend with. Sasha Shulgin's chemical recipes begin to circulate in the Berkeley networks and beyond, an accumulating assemble-at-home chemical recipe book.

Like television switching from broadcast to cable, there are suddenly many more channels for the psychedelic experience. "I knew people who made stuff, but not LSD," *High Frontiers'* R. U. Sirius recalls.

"I knew the chemists who made everything else—ecstasy, MDA, DMT," Sirius says. "And they weren't Deadheads. To a man, they were wacky, vaguely threatening people. And to a man they were all into heroin. Making psychedelics gave them too much of an edge. They were hooked into all that energy going out into the world, and they just needed to be a little less manic. They were all manic, anyway, and they all became junkies. But they were guys who would come around and go 'look into the crystals.' I never saw artists as enthusiastic about their paintings as these guys were when they created something."

There are those who find all this new home chemistry and rampant ecstasy gulping distasteful, and there are whispers among the psychedelic old guard that something should be done before the government does anything rash. The beacon goes out from the Esalen Institute about a conclave to be held there, at the former resort and perpetual New Age power spot.

The name for the new gathering is ARUPA, the Association for the Responsible Use of Psycho-Actives. The acronym is a Sanskrit word for "formless." Like all good groupminds, they have no leaders. Many are not fond of the word "psychedelic" for that matter, either, preferring the term "entheogen"—"manifesting the spirit within"—coined by a group of psychoactive elders in 1979. ARUPA convenes for the first time in 1983.

"I believe that the psychedelic experience was the light at the beginning of history," asserts Terence McKenna (who is fine with the word "psychedelic") at the 1984 gathering, which includes Albert Hofmann, Ralph Metzner, and Sasha Shulgin. "That this is actually *the* thing; that we have now reached a sufficient level of analytical sophistication to discern the force that pushed the animal mind onto the human stage."

But there is more practical business at hand. Sasha Shulgin has learned that the government fully intends to classify MDMA as a Schedule I drug—that is, made illegal for heads and psychologists alike and deemed to have no medical use, equally illegal as cocaine, heroin, marijuana, and LSD. They organize a formal response and further studies to prove its value.

Even outside the mental health community, there are those who use drugs quite responsibly, like a group out of New England called Friends and Lovers, who seek an even newer hybrid of the therapeutic and the communal. Though the healing continues in the growing therapeutic underground, none of their efforts do much good in the bigger picture. Ecstasy goes the way of LSD before it: gone but very much not gone at all.

OUT IN THE Mojave Desert in '85, the New York art-punk band Sonic Youth pulls up to the Gila Monster Jamboree, their first-ever gig in Southern California. As the sun goes down and the temperature drops, it dawns on the quartet that many of the three hundred in attendance are tripping, another one of the countless semi-under-the-radar psychedelic scenes that emerge as acid starts to grow more available in the United States. One of the Gila Monster organizers is a dealer.

"It hadn't been that long since I left my psychedelic days behind but we were just coming from a whole other place," says Sonic Youth guitarist Lee Ranaldo, a mid-1970s vintage Dead freak. Though Sonic Youth (like bands since time immemorial) enjoy grass from time to time, the sight of acid surprises them. "To find all of hipster LA coming to that gig and tripping their balls off was pretty wild. The setting was conducive for it, 100 miles from the city, no lights, make your own action. It felt like being in an irreality."

"I had forgotten acid even existed, let alone people taking it," guitarist Thurston Moore would remark later. But out in California, they are, little cliques turning on together for no good reason other than that it seems essential. The next year, the LA psychedelic art hipsters will spawn Jane's Addiction, the self-consciously transgressive band at the root of the '90s Lollapalooza festivals.

Out in the desert, Sonic Youth are awash in psychedelic imagery. The centerpiece of their Gila Monster set is "Death Valley '69," inspired by *The Family,* a Charles Manson biography by Fugs leader Ed Sanders. The guitars chime and roll and the tripping heads go wild in the desert night. The Gila Monster Jamboree is a great success.

BACK IN New York, people *are* taking acid, though. Perhaps they'd never stopped, but now the LSD finds its way into new circles that radiate fresh expressions of psychedelic radicalism. Every Tuesday in the East Village, a half block east of Tompkins Square Park, a twenty-three-year-old art critic named Carlo McCormick passes out hits of blotter at his unnamed weekly soiree at 8BC, a fashionably grotty dive between Avenues B and C.

McCormick is longhaired and angel faced and, at least on the psychedelic front, aggressively out of step with the Manhattan art establishment's prevailing notions of cool. But he's not here to save anyone, and he's not a hippie. For starters, he's sick of all the psychedelic churches. He'd been to the Temple of the True Inner Light and walked out in disgust before they could even offer their DPT.

"Because [psychedelics] offer enlightenment that people feel, in their spiritual thirst, that they have a need for, the psychedelic world ends up with a lot of seekers and a lot of false prophets," he says. He *knows* Terence McKenna is "100% full of shit, but a great talker.

"I don't mean to be a hater, but I only have enough patience for people who want to find God," McCormick says. "I thought this was to help us get over our superstitions."

On display inside 8BC, McCormick's acid vision is even more formally antidogmatic than is the Dead's. He is, after all, an art critic. Publishing regularly in the *East Village Eye,* he's working on a book titled *East Village Scene* and supporting himself by managing 8BC, working in clubland as a doorman, and selling drugs.

With the stage at street-level and the audience in a literal pit below, there are usually films blasting on all available surfaces. McCormick's girlfriend (and future wife) Tessa Hughes-Freeland is an underground filmmaker working under the banner of Cinema of Transgression. At the Whitney during one performance, she projects several dozen extreme gay porn films on saxophonist John Zorn. "We had a really intense body of violent nasty visuals going," McCormick says of the 8BC parties. Hughes-Freeland employs the multiple-projector devices of expanded cinema to project work by Richard Kern featuring brutal sexuality alongside other eyeball-poppers. The bands are often the hardest core McCormick can find, including Unsane, Cop Shoot Cop, and Black Snakes.

"All we wanted to take from [traditional] psychedelia, no more and no less, were certain strategies of representation in the post-modern sphere. Does that sound pretentious?"

Well, sure, but not unheady. "It wasn't trying to reinvent anything," McCormick asserts, "but to repurpose, to add something to the diet of the creative community, just another way of doing things." With an excellent record collection, McCormick and Hughes-Freeland's apartment becomes a crash pad for touring bands, including the Butthole Surfers, an untamed psychedelic karass from Texas who share a fondness for film projection, onstage chaos, nudity, and noise.

"I didn't want the politesse of going back-to-nature," McCormick says of his psychedelic aesthetic. And, no matter his distaste for spiritual apparati and his love for the city, he's not above heading up into the Catskills with the Church of the Little Green Man's Mike Osterhout. "We'd get 50 people up there and dose them hardcore," he says.

He observes psychedelics moving through the art world via painters like Keith Haring and Haring's roommate Kenny Scharf, and through the St. Mark's Place hangout, Club 57. He knows of the first generation of psychedelic Parkie graffiti artists and recognizes the collision of street art and hallucinogens as part of continuum stretching to the French mescaline visionaries of the '50s and further back.

"Psychedelia [can] exist as this coded bit of information that's passed along through all these other scenes that aren't evidently about that," he remarks.

He makes friends with the blotter collector Mark McCloud on his regular visits to San Francisco, crashing often at McCloud's Institute of Illegal Images. Like many, Carlo McCormick's LSD connections are in the Bay Area. But he finds stuff out East to contribute to the collection. "I was bringing in New York prints," McCormick says. "Every now and then I'd have to buy a sheet of acid at top dollar just to get it to the museum," he says. "I really believed in Mark's vision."

As the drug war is turning white hot in 1985, McCormick takes his LSD enthusiasm on the road. His critical work had drawn requests from galleries around the country to curate shows of East Village art. He comes up with an alternate plan.

In one iteration, he and nine artists caravan to Virginia. Among them are the multidisciplinary activist David Wojnarowicz, sculptor Luis Frangella, cartoonist James Romberger, painter Marguerite Van Cook, and others. They arrive for the installation, McCormick distributes the LSD, and they get to it.

"They'd have however long the acid lasted to fuck up the space, to paint the walls," says McCormick. And, listening to music on boom boxes, they do. "It would have moments of incredible genius. It was existential, cathartic spilling." McCormick, of course, is tripping, too.

"The people at the galleries and museums were generally very disappointed every time with the whole thing. They'd always feel disrespected, like, *I can't believe you took oil paint and painted all over these walls.*"

But for the New York gang, who bill themselves as the Nuclear Family at one show, this is about something larger. "We were all pretty angry," McCormick says. "People were beginning to die of AIDS and we had a President who wouldn't even say that word." Both Wojnarowicz and Frangella will succumb to the disease in the early '90s. McCormick's acid jams are conscious, active *fuck you*s to the Republican American establishment of the 1980s. In Virginia, they get out of town before *East Village Meets East Broad Street* opens. Documentation is poor.

"Everyone had their own careers, but this was its own thing," McCormick says. "In New York, there was an audience for it," drawn from the regulars at the McCormick's ongoing 8BC nights.

Theirs is not the only psychedelic response to the AIDS crisis. The other, in fact, has a home base only a few blocks to the west of McCormick's 8BC nights, at the longtime headquarters of the Yippies. Their cause for the decade is ibogaine, the Gabonese root substance that sends users on nonrecreational multiday trips to meet their ancestors and that is said to be an addiction interrupter. Building a coalition of Black Panthers, scientists, anarchists, and others, the mustachioed Yippie holdout Dana Beal works for ibogaine's legality, organizing studies to prove its efficacy. If they can stop heroin addiction, Beal argues, they can help prevent the spread of AIDS through dirty needles.

In the underground drug lore, LSD had long been touted as a way to blast people free from addiction. Back in the '60s, Bill Wilson, the founder of Alcoholics Anonymous, had touted LSD as a way to achieve the visions of the alcoholic's delirium tremens minus the bottoming out. He'd even suggested that it become part of the standard AA program, before being threatened with expulsion from the organization. More recently, Carlo McCormick had given LSD to drug-addicted friends, sometimes achieving similar results. But Dana Beal will become an indefatigable fighter for ibogaine in the next decades, trying to connect enough people to prove that the psychedelic is literally accessing stored cellular memories that take the form of seemingly real interactions (meeting the *bwiti*) that can then reprogram parts of the addicted brain. Ancient psychedelic mind-design technology.

Carlo McCormick's 8BC parties last only four or five months, slightly longer than the Acid Tests. The point is made: the first flashes of a different kind of psychedelic rebirth in avant-garde New York. "A lot of us were trying to keep ideas in the culture without it being about that," he says.

Naturally, the big-antennaed psychedelic art collector Jacaeber Kastor makes his way to one of McCormick's 8BC parties and loves it, though he won't meet McCormick until a few years later. "There was no philosophy," Kastor recalls. "There were no leaders, no speakers. There were no pretensions, but there was artsy stuff around." Another attendee is the painter Alex Grey, not yet an international brand.

"There was a level of discretion going on. It's not like I was worried about getting busted," Carlo says.

Indeed, in the summer of 1986, *High Times* puts McCormick on the cover and gives him his own column. "The Prince of Acid," it calls him. It mentions nothing of his parties or anything about him. "I'm a critic," he says. "I wasn't about to be a subject."

A SHEET OF paper circulates out in the suburbs, scorched and Xeroxed and retyped: "WARNING TO PARENTS." The authors aren't as informed as the average *High Times* reader, but they're starting to put it together, and the panic will begin anew. It notifies them of "a form of tattoo" called "Blue Star," presenting itself as an innocent rub-on transfer and appealing to the innocent youth via Mickey Mouse or some other beloved cartoon characters and oh the humanity. It's not quite accurate. In one researcher's estimation, sometime around 1980, a Seventh Day Adventist Church community misunderstood a New Jersey State Police warning about blotter acid starring Mickey Mouse in his *Sorcerer's Apprentice* costume.

The information keeps circulating and changing, variations eventually spotted as far away as Dubai and Norway. Somewhere along the line, Mickey Mouse disappears from the flyers. The parents only just partially misunderstand. The Mickey blotter *had* been legendary.

A darkness lingers around psychedelics in some places and periods of history, and not without reason. They are strange medicines, yield unexpected transformations, and can contribute to irrational behavior, by those taking them and just as often as by those fretting about them. But for all their mischaracterizations over the years, psychedelics remain a nearly mystical current.

Forget Tim Leary or Sasha Shulgin or Albert Hofmann, around Northport, New York, during the early 1980s a high school kid named Ricky Kasso holds the title of Acid King. And he is trouble city, folks, in need of help. He's a metalhead—a head, nonetheless—and dabbled in Satanism, as one does. "You gotta trust in Satan," he reportedly told his smoking buddies, a friend of the devil.

As the story (in the later-published exploitation paperback) goes, he walks into Avatar New Age Books and Records downtown one day before freshman year and buys a copy of Anton LeVey's *Satanic Bible* and gets into the rituals of it all. He's a sketchy-ass PCP and LSD dealer and, to summarize a very complex sequence of events, kills a poor kid while allegedly screaming "Say you love Satan" as they (plus two witnesses) are out in the woods high on mescaline. One of the witnesses is arraigned in a bootleg Dead tie-dye, a Steal Your Face logo filled by the au courant Cold War symbol for radioactivity. The tabloids descend.

To the popular imagination of the official grown-up United States in the 1980s, psychedelics equate more with Charles Manson and Ricky Kasso and innocent teen girls throwing their virgin bodies through fifth-story windows than they do with self-healing and world building. Which means only, maybe, that there's more world building to achieve.

By 1986, the parents at large can maybe sense something changing, too. Measured on the University of Michigan's *Monitoring the Future* report, surveying high school drug use, LSD use ticks up for the first time in several years. The previous year, just under 5 percent of twelfth graders said they'd done acid in the past twelve months. In 1986, the number is just over 5 percent. The needle on our imaginary seismograph wavers. Sometimes volcanos are invisible.

OVER THE 1986 summer solstice, the Grateful Dead are at the Greek Theatre in Berkeley, one of the two outdoor Bay Area sites where their culture comes into fullest flower. With the daylight at its longest extension, a world-over time of ritual and celebration, the Dead are playing three nights, and more pieces of the future are locking into place. Everything starts to swirl faster, all of the different psychedelic Americas starting to echo together.

Outside the show, longtime Deadhead music journalist David Gans discovers something new: an entire satellite parking lot colonized for Deadheads to sell their wares, make food, eat, germinate, and dance to the music, which is piped in live on special speakers. The ritual and its apparatus grow larger. The vending has been going on for a few years in the eucalyptus grove outside the Frost Amphitheater, on the Stanford campus, too, the Dead's other nearby home, where the Silicon Valley protoluminaries compare the latest tech and boogie down in mutual Deaddom.

There's an increasing divide between California-style Deadheads like David Gans and the ones who follow the band around and sell T-shirts and the like. But Gans has reason to cross that divide into the aromatic bazaar. With his friend and conspirator Mary Eisenhart, Gans wades through the crowd with a stack of flyers bearing the familiar words, "Dead Freaks Unite." Below them, some less familiar ones: "ELECTRONIC VILLAGE NOW FORMING."

"You don't have to be a computer person, just a person with a computer," Gans will often tell audiences on his KFOG radio show, *The Deadhead Hour*. It's genuinely hard to gauge how many people out in this Berkeley iteration of Shakedown Street have computers. But the WELL, where Gans and Eisenhart make their new electronic homes, has many unexpected residents.

Short for the Whole Earth 'Lectronic Link, the service's roots are wholly countercultural. The first seed came from Larry Brilliant, once one of two doctors with Wavy Gravy's Hog Farm buses. More lately responsible for the Seva Foundation, Brilliant recruits the *Whole Earth Catalog*'s Stewart Brand, who in turn hires a trio of former residents of the Farm, the post-Haight commune in Tennessee.

One WELL user is Ramon Sender, the former director of the San Francisco Tape Music Center, Trips Festival organizer, and Morning Star communard. Sasha Shulgin is there, too, answering queries about psychedelics. The WELL is not the first online community but it contains a coherence that few others do, a psychedelic-digital bond that begins to beam an old-world coalition one by one into the new digital age.

And when David Gans and Mary Eisenhart lead the Deadheads onto the system in early 1986, the Deadheads bring needed revenue that transforms the WELL into one of the most successful digital enterprises to date, a fully active textual hangout, albeit mostly populated by Bay Area counterculturalists. The WELL is simultaneously local and not-local. A decade hence it will be called "the world's most influential online community."

"Information wants to be free," WELL founder and former Merry Prankster Stewart Brand had said in 1984, at the inaugural Hacker's Conference, a phrase that quickly becomes part of the tech world's emerging lexicon. Like the precepts of the so-called Hacker Ethic, listed by journalist Stephen Levy that same year, Brand's coinage can and does equally apply to Deadheads and their exchange of recordings and rumors.

"Information also wants to be very expensive," Brand had noted, too, a maxim one can apply to the ever-thirsting Deadheads, too, calling the band's info hotline at all hours, sending in art-covered mail-order ticket requests, and filling all the spaces of their lives with talismans that point back toward the band. Or, for example, using a modem to dial up the WELL at all hours, as some even do long distance. It is the perfect place for Deadhead culture to flourish, as it does everywhere.

The Grateful Dead are the modern world's most articulated psychedelic ritual, an authentic mystery cult where one can go and witness the flame for oneself. An entire infrastructure exists to tend it. One can see the flame without the band or their music. One can even see the flame without psychedelics. But it's a lot easier with both.

The Dead's little empire in San Rafael is swelling, like the inner sanctum of a holy city. If the band's roadies are Deadland's true power brokers, then the band's new mail-order ticket office becomes the treasury. A Roman comedy could be written about the turns of power, court intrigues, and screwball episodes within the imperial seat there in Marin County.

The eminent mythologist Joseph Campbell, Bob Weir's next-door neighbor, attends a Dead show at the Kaiser Auditorium in Oakland, and the Deadheads blow his mind. He calls it a "real Dionysian festival" and an "antidote for the atom bomb." He will speak of it often.

Campbell will be re-evaluated by future scholars, but his blessing is assimilated into the groupminds of both the Dead and the heads. "The Joe Campbell thing gave them their metaphor," marvels Dead radio host David Gans. "I was at the party at Weir's house and got to watch Phil Lesh and Jerry Garcia sitting at Joseph Campbell's feet, just like we would sit at theirs. His description of it gave them their license to become rigid in their [musical] structure, going from order to chaos and back to order."

The Dead's Greek Theatre appearances are part of a time lapse that seems to change seasons behind the band's increasingly caricatured figures. The Greek weekends run with the first show in the dark, the second at dusk, in twilight, and the third in full afternoon brightness. The solstice itself falls in the middle of a three-night stand. Celestial navigations with 9,000 Deadheads via the Greek.

And just like the members of the Dead bleshed into one at their practice sessions so many years back, fingers on the hand, the Dead and their audience melt together in the early and mid-1980s, creating something new. Captured on the rich audience tapes of the obsessive recordists, who treat their gear with a New Age reverence, the results are no longer quite rock 'n' roll, though it's still for getting high. The Dead finally legitimize the tapers, selling seats just for them starting in 1984, though many still prefer to tape closer to the stage and refine new methods to do so. One notable recordist is named Doug Oade, who might more properly be called what the Canadian composer R. Murray Schaefer would call an "acoustic ecologist," a distant branch of the Aquarian Conspiracy. Before he'd gotten into Dead taping, Oade had spent his time hiking to quiet mountain lakes, setting up a microphone rig, and capturing the rich sonic atmosphere right down to the sound of flies humming directly through his stereo field. What Oade and others (many others) are trying to capture at Dead shows isn't music but an entire natural environment.

"The daytime is kind of harsh," a woman remarks as a front-of-board audience recording fades in on our night at the Greek Theatre in June 1986 and Phil Lesh announces that the Sunday show will be broadcast on KPFA. Around the bowl, people find places to dance or perhaps spark joints in the giant faux-Greek thrones dotting the perimeter of the floor.

This particular Greek run kicks off the band's summer touring season, a warm-up for a leg of shows out East with Bob Dylan and Tom Petty. As the band lands in Chuck Berry's "Promised Land," the drums sound a million miles away, but Garcia is right there with a torrent of ideas, responding to whatever's coming off the warm bowl of the amphitheater. He's blurry, though, the details and phrasing not quite in time with the world around him. On "Loser," Garcia peals off a quicksilver solo, and the whole band nails the entrance back into the chorus, drops out together, and gives Brent Mydland's B3 some room to breathe, plus a little space for Garcia's quiet feedback bullet points. But oh golly that *wheezing*.

Extended collective improvisation isn't on the band's groupmind tonight, though people probably still have their minds blown, meet new friends, or think through some knotty idea. At the end of the show, the Deadhead crowd-blesh bursts into the semirecent trick where it keeps clapping the Bo Diddley clave beat behind the set-closing "Not Fade Away" after the band leaves the stage and continues until the musicians return and pick up the rhythm again, restarting the song. Many years ago, perhaps accidentally, Weir (likely) had changed Buddy Holly's "you know my love not fade away" to "you know our love not fade away." It is an original lyric of sorts and the Deadheads take it to be inclusive. Sometimes, the heads pick up the rhythm from the stage like a flame and carry it out into the parking lot, into drum circles or the satellite parking lot or home to keep pulsing underneath them until the next Dead show.

The crowd disperses into the Berkeley night. And, should a head be of the correct mind to observe it, he or she could—right now—witness a Humbeadean meteorological blast akin to Mount St. Helens's rainbow explosion a few years earlier. There's a fire, a fire down by the water. All it takes is a leisurely wander south, off the campus and up into the Berkeley Hills. It'd take about an hour, this walk, but maybe you gobbled something and have some extra *energy*. It's really worth it to see this. The world is getting ready to change again.

It'd be *especially* good if the gobbling occurred at set break or maybe even after the show entirely. Maybe this is even a very specific walk to your very favorite tripping spot. Bring friends. Think of it like this in terms of the plausibility scale: one of Terence McKenna's going precepts during this period, supported (McKenna claims) by experiments at the National Institute of Mental Health in the '60s, is that mushrooms improve visual acuity in those who munch them.

Say that's going on with you and your friends as you climb your way in the one-day-short-of-being-full moonlight about halfway up

Panoramic Hill. There, you can look out over the tiny twinkling lights of Berkeley, over the Bay Bridge, to San Francisco in the distance.

And, it being a clear night and all, you can even see the Golden Gate. This is true, this is the view from this spot. And just beyond the crook of where the Golden Gate meets the San Francisco Peninsula is a spot called Baker Beach, where a thin sliver of smoke trickles upward. That's where the acuity comes in handy. Either that or just the right kind of eyes. But what's occurring on Baker Beach is something that some other hippies have dreamed up there, right at the literal edge of Humbead's Map, by the lapping water.

Larry Harvey is just a bohemian. Mostly Larry Harvey's pissed at his ex-girlfriend. So he sets an eight-foot effigy of a man to burning, and the flames lap into the pleasant San Francisco evening. There are only a dozen witnesses, maybe a few more, but there weren't that many people at the first Acid Test, either. Pencil in the Burning Man on the Map, maybe a stark stick-like figure or a three-dimensional glyph. Do it lightly at the corner of the upward coastline near where Golden Gate Park meets land. Larry Harvey and his friends will repeat it next year, and the year after, and the crowd and meanings will grow.

Finish watching the smoke from the first Burning Man and look into the immediate future. After the Berkeley shows, the Dead head eastward, and the noise starts to grow louder and bear down, as if the psychedelic decade is coming to a boil. The shows are in stadiums, the heat unbearable. Even with Dylan and Tom Petty on the bills, the Dead still play their regular two sets. Jerry Garcia is miserable. When they get back home, it grows worse, and far weirder. Mind-manifesting.

"I started feeling like the vegetable kingdom was speaking to me," Garcia will recall. "It was communicating in comic dialect in iambic pentameter. So there were these Italian accents and German accents and it got to be this vast gabbling. Potatoes and radishes and trees were all speaking to me. It was really strange. It finally just reached hysteria." Jerry Garcia collapses into a diabetic coma.

PART TWO

6

THIS EVERLASTING SPOOF

ichard Wright had an imaginary friend named Nancy when he was little, but this is different. The name lingers on somewhere inside the nineteen-year-old's head. Unheard yet, it echoes and repeats under the brutal hum of the twelve-hour bus ride that delivers the stocky, longhaired Wright from Maryland to Vermont in January 1983. Eventually it will come out and make its way out across the head networks, carrying new codes and building new bridges. But for now, the cold is surely bitter, and all he remembers is the ensuing headache.

Wright's destination—Plainfield, Vermont—was a dot on the original Humbead's Revised Map of the World, drawn fifteen years earlier by Earl Crabb and Rick Shubb. They'd made it a landlocked speck in the state of Cambridge. In real life, it's way up north but, with the shifting of the Map plates over the years, the Rainbow Mountains zig-zagging hither and tither down the continent's middle, Plainfield now sits in a cool valley in the downward foothills of the headlands.

The far Vermont north country is separated from the rest of the world by miles of treacherous road. But then, there, Richard Wright *arrives:* Vermont and rolling hills and mountains and farms and free territory. The highway billboards disappear.

Wright matriculates at Goddard College, a tiny experimental institution in tiny Plainfield, outside Montpelier. The school's freethinking roots stretch back to the Civil War era, and it was *the* Vermont stop-over for folkies and heads and bohos in the first part of the '60s, at least in the estimation of Map creators Earl Crabb and Rick Shubb. "Why would anyone go to Burlington?" Shubb asks.

In one estimation, at least 100,000 hippies marched forth to Vermont during the '60s. It was only natural. There were hills and hills and the other hills. For those opting out of society at large, it was an ideal spot for idealism. An actual psychedelic sect, the Paleo-American Church—an offshoot of the Neo-American—made their home near Waitsfield. Plus, Vermont is close to Canada.

Way, way, way up in Franklin, practically on the border, is Earth People's Park, 550 acres purchased by Wavy Gravy and the Hog Farm and handed over to communards in the summer of '71. "The last turn-off in America," Wavy says, and there's a reason for that. The park is the northernmost tip in a network of communes and socialist institutions known as Free Vermont, an underground railroad that assisted draft dodgers in escaping to Canada. The goal of the Free Vermonters was, in the words of one founder, "fucking revolution!" On the East Coast, Vermont is *the* model for how countercultural ideals play out in the life of a region. Vermont was plenty free without the hippies, but it's the longhairs who put the "fucking" in "free fucking Vermont." The next generation begins to come of age in the early '80s.

Not that young Richard Wright knows any of this, of course, when he goes north and finds himself in a friendly place for the first time in his life. He's just a sensitive but troubled head from suburban Maryland. He likes LSD and prog rock and the Beach Boys and the Beatles and Pink Floyd and Frank Zappa and heaps of psychedelic music. *Not* into the Dead. A natural-born troublemaker, he'd been expelled from high school three months short of graduation, and his uncle heard of this place up in Vermont, a design-your-own-curriculum college that might be just right for a smart but difficult lad like him. *Him?* Hmm.

Various schools had implemented design-your-own major policies, but Goddard's is one of the most do it yourself available. Its most famous alums include jailed activist Mumia Abu-Jamal and playwright David Mamet. Like some local communes, though, Goddard isn't weathering the '80s too well. The institution is committed to its course, but enrollment is down, way down, about three dozen when

Richard arrives on campus. But it as fertile a place as one can imagine for an identity-questioning young acidhead.

At first, though, Richard can't find a focus even at Goddard. It's almost too free form on the small campus with barns and valleys and snows and woods and some geodesic domes across the street. "I was just sort of lost, not really sure what to do," Wright recalls.

Home in Maryland over the summer, Richard hears something. "I was really stoned, and I had sort of a rhythm going through my head that had the name *Nancy* in it." He returns to Plainfield and perks up a little. "I did kind of like a book report," he says. "Except on an album. I did reports on albums like *In the Court of the Crimson King* by King Crimson and *Close to the Edge* by Yes."

Something opens up inside Richard Wright there in the quiet corner of all the parallel worlds where Goddard exists. "Over a period of time, I began to feel that my legal name was not my real name," Wright says. "I was starting to feel that I had a natural name, a name that my soul actually has, and I decided after a while that my name was Nancy. By wearing that name proudly, it was also like being blatant about my feminine side." He takes an insult and makes it himself.

The full name of Richard Wright's soul is, he suspects, Nancy Bitterbug Voodoo Coleslaw. At the time, in early 1985, he doesn't think any gender reassignment operations or change of pronouns are necessary, a decision he will wonder about for years. But he tells his classmates to call him by his new name. Sometimes he wears dresses. Everyone knows him as Nancy.

The psychedelic society, the deep-embedded countercultural diaspora, has staked wide geographical claims. Because of it, there are places in the world where Nancy can be at home, and Vermont is one of them. Nancy is of the first generation of LSD users almost completely removed from the '60s, and he uses it and other tools available to him to discover who he is and what he does.

He is ready for all fair-minded transmissions, and there are many out there, be they new LPs or even just the acid he's been taking regularly for a few years, every three weeks or so during 1984, wandering about the rolling bowl and little gardens of the mostly empty campus and absorbing what Goddard and Vermont have to offer. Nancy is a total product of psychedelic America in the early 1980s where it is no big deal to assume a new identity.

The college has just the infrastructure for Nancy. For a time, he hosts a literally all-night radio show on WGDR, midnight to 7 a.m. Often staying up all night anyway, he writes Patti Smith–inspired stream-of-consciousness poetry. He reads from the *Book of the Sub-Genius,* published by an odd Texas organization that seems as if they're probably a parody, but maybe not.

Name change notwithstanding, he is still looking for his particular path when WGDR acquires its own Fostex four-track in early 1985. "You could always find someplace to play and not be obnoxious and annoy people," remembers Jim Pollock, a graphic artist who signs out the Fostex on occasion. "There was barely anyone on campus, so there was tons of space." Pollock takes over an empty dorm wing and records songs like "Dear Mrs. Reagan," a woozy self-harmonized folk blues tune with topicality to spare.

One night when Nancy is tripping, Jim plays some of the recordings, and it all clicks for Nancy. He'd played with a four-track before, but now he fully understands what to do.

"After I left Jim's room and went back to my own dorm, that's when I started freaking out," he says. "That's when this spirit invaded my system. I think it was a mixture of energies." It's a classic bad trip, but one whose ramifications will ring out in other dorm rooms aplenty in the decades to come as the spirit comes to make its presence known in Nancy's body. Spirits and paranormal encounters have a long and worldwide history with psychoactive drugs of all sorts. The spirit that lodges in Nancy's body might not meet this same measurable standard, but, over the next months, it seems to have some influence on his activities.

Applying his tripping brainstorm, Nancy gets his bearing on the four-track by recording some David Byrne covers but really sinks his teeth in at the end of the semester, after he's kicked out of the dorm for the summer. He takes up residence in the campus radio station, putting himself on the air whenever another DJ isn't around, and gets to know the station gear. The first result is what he calls *Nancytronics.* One piece is fourteen minutes of layered voices called "Super-Delicious Crunchy Forest Critters," sounding like avant-garde vocalist Meredith Monk rendered via British guitarist Robert Fripp's delay loops. The spirit is a creative one.

The songs come soon thereafter, the spirit feeding Nancy's natural creativity. Their first original collaboration of sorts is called "Silver Flu," the melody repurposed from the Fugs' "Supergirl." But then comes a big one, and it arrives almost miraculously in multipart harmony, which Nancy records in seven voices on the Fostex four-track by slowing down and speeding up his singing over a skeletal rhythmic click. His father had sung barbershop, and maybe that has something to do with it.

The lyrics to "I Didn't Know" source from Patti Smith–inspired journal sessions but are far more acid bent. "Kool-Aid silver tooth broke my sunny shoe-shine," Nancy sings, "and all my plastic melon dreams are waiting for their new shine."

"The lyrics don't mean anything," he says. "They're all about how the words are constructed, how they shape the sounds of the phrasings."

The next session begins a few months later with an incessant hand-drum groove and a song that is likewise a capella but even more complex, combining fragments Nancy has been singing to himself. There is a mutated doo-wop bass line, but other than that it belongs to no particular musical tradition, both ambitious and natural in its arrangement of bridges, minichoruses, and hook after hook.

"What is the central theme of this everlasting spoof?" he asks in one of the song's many vocal parts. He combines this piece of music with another refrain he has, and the layer becomes its name: "Halley's Comet." Like its predecessor, it is an excellent song, but it is still difficult to envision the future in which arenas full of people will sing these lyrics in union, and yet this future exists, thanks directly to the power of the invisible and powerful psychedelic ley lines that Nancy sits astride.

Nancy plays the songs for his friends around campus and gives them occasional spins on his radio show. They become local hits, in a way, ricocheting over the radio free mindwaves of WGDR. The tapes are passed around campus, too. "Those were very well known songs, even around Plainfield," Jim Pollock comments.

"There's no entertainment," recalls Pollock of Plainfield. "Because of the way the mountains are there, you don't get many radio stations, and so you are broadcasting to a bunch of people. There was no cable in Vermont. Unless you're in a certain place, you're only receiving a handful of television or radio stations, so you become the only game in town." There is a certain way that time passes up there in the mountains, and Nancy's songs fill that space naturally and become hyperregional hits.

One person Nancy plays his tape for is a recent transfer student from Southern Methodist University in Texas, lately cohosting a show with Pollock on WGDR. Page McConnell is an affable guy. Nancy's seen him playing Traffic covers on the piano in the Haybarn Theater, where people hang out. McConnell plays with the R&B group Love Goat and other bands around campus, too.

Nancy likes him alright, but they don't hang out too much. They share a taste for psychedelic rock and pot and cross paths occasionally. But Page McConnell hangs out with the Deadheads, and Nancy might be a nancy, but he's no Deadhead. Nice guy, though. McConnell helps to book a big three-day spring fling.

Nancy skips it. He doesn't like loud music or crowds, particularly.

HERE'S WHAT NANCY misses: it's fairly typical malarkey. There's only enough money to rent a PA for two days. Despite being Plainfield, Vermont—or perhaps because of it—there are enough bands for three. But Sunday the PA is gone, and there are still more bands who want to play, including a local act called the Few that the organizers don't really know. They try to scrounge together some mics and speakers.

A band-filled van arrives. Page McConnell and his friend notice that the group has a PA with them. A strange-looking dude with long curly hair gets out.

"Are you The Few?" someone inquires.

"No," the curly-haired guy says. "We're Phish. The Few couldn't make it."

The quartet sets up their PA while twenty or so people mill about. In the accepted story, someone asks them whether they know any Dead covers. Phish play a few hours of Dead covers.

BY THE TIME Nancy hears Phish's music a few months later, Page McConnell is already member of the band. The keyboardist plays Nancy a tape and Nancy is impressed. To him, it sounds like Yes, complicated but airy. They are outsiders to Vermont, but not for long. Like Nancy, they will discover something substantial in the place.

When Nancy meets the band, the weekend before Halloween 1985, he is wandering the campus in a green rubber monster mask. The group is setting up to play a party in the Haybarn, and Nancy is introduced to the band's guitarist.

"Are you Nancy?" the guitarist asks him.

"Are you the guy who sounds like Frank Zappa?" Nancy inquires, remembering the wry cartoonish tinge in the guitarist's voice. Nancy *loves* Frank Zappa.

Trey Anastasio laughs. Phish has recently debuted a cover of "Dear Mrs. Reagan," by Nancy and Page's friend Jim Pollock, and Anastasio asks Nancy whether they can add "Halley's Comet" to their set, too. Naturally, Nancy is a bit flattered and, of course, doesn't mind.

Like the rest of the campus on that Saturday before Halloween, it seems, Nancy is on acid. It's certainly not that uncommon. Lately, though, he'd grown conflicted about the spirit that had entered into him during his April LSD trip.

"It felt like I had this incredible resource attached to me that I could draw from, but I felt like it was drawing something out of me," he remembers. "It just didn't feel right. It was stealing my energy, and causing me to steal energy from other people, and I just didn't like being in that position."

A week earlier, he'd formulated his radio show as a musical exorcism and recorded the broadcast so he could use the three 90-minute tapes to force the spirit from him.

Phish is taking *forever* to set up, so Nancy decides to go for it. In the green mask and green gloves, his longhaired confused-ass self trundles back to his dorm, cues up the first tape from his radio show, and gets exorcising.

The band doesn't play anyway. All except their bassist have gulped the communal LSD-spiked apple cider, a self-planned Acid Test for the young group. Of the musicians consuming, none are psychedelic virgins by any means. But it comes on too quick and too strong and, while Nancy flushes the spirit from his body across campus, Phish freak out.

LET'S LINGER IN Vermont a while, as Nancy does, as the members of Phish will. Think of all the shades of green you've known, then try to imagine one you've never previously considered, as people on peyote sometimes report. While the rest of the world charges along by some standard urgency, people in this happy verdant Humbeadean territory go about their lives as they always have, freely.

If Vermont's status as a final destination on the hippie highway could be codified into an academic institution, Goddard is it. Unlike many liberal arts schools, Goddard is at one with its surrounding community, an extension of the rolling green calmness around it, snow covered and hard scrabble in the winter.

By 1970, there was already a Plainfield Village Chorus with a repertoire of Bach cantatas, and a Word of Mouth Chorus, too, dedicated to Balkan and early music and (their favorite) Sacred Harp singing. There was a Village Gamelan, a many-piece "instrument," each with its own unique tuning, requiring many players, the traditional Indonesian version of a groupmind.

And then arrived Peter Schumann and his Bread and Puppet experimental theater troupe, from the Lower East Side via a half decade of European exile. They took up residency at Goddard for a few years, starting in '74, before settling in nearby Glover, where they sprawl into barns and the neighboring countryside, staging a huge summer festival each year in a valley that forms a natural amphitheater on their land.

When Nancy Bitterbug Voodoo Coleslaw finds himself anew in Vermont, it is one that belongs very much to the Bread and Puppet company. Like the Merry Pranksters in Oregon, the Bread and Puppet performers and their families constitute a sprawling multigeneration tribe in the upper regions of the state. Their style of high primitive surrealist puppetry and postsocialist utopian ideals permeate the arts and outlook of the entire region.

Schumann and the Puppeteers own a printing press, spewing forth posters and texts in their distinct visual/rhetorical style, some handwritten, some typed. "the WHY CHEAP ART? manifesto," from '84, is an instant hit, marshaling a surrealist revolution. "ART IS LIKE GOOD BREAD!" it reads in part. "Art is like green trees! Art is like white clouds in blue sky! ART IS CHEAP! HURRAH!" Part radical theater, part summer camp, generations of northeastern youth pass through, sometimes just for a summer soiree, sometimes for a longer visit. Many return with the visually striking manifestos to hang on their walls. Historically, the troupe isn't necessarily psychedelic, but that doesn't mean there aren't psychedelics.

Nancy attends his first Bread and Puppet festival in the summer of '84. "I found the puppets themselves interesting," he says, "but it was too politically oriented for me in general." Like the Grateful Dead, the language of Bread and Puppet is deep and ingrown, the product of a long-running conversation between Schumann and the many-headed world around him, and Nancy doesn't connect with it.

At the Bread and Puppet not-quite-commune in Glover, the bread goes in the oven every morning, even more as they're getting ready for the summer rites. "ART SINGS HALLELUJA! ART IS FOR KITCHENS! ART IS LIKE GOOD BREAD!" Peter Schumann writes in the cheap art manifesto. They take it quite literally and bake sourdough to pass out with aioli at every performance.

At their summer pageants, they set up a Free Bread Store. There's some Diggerdom at work, but it's more their common roots in transformative street theater, except Bread and Puppet now have something much bigger than a street. They have a giant green stage in the form of their valley amphitheater. As Stephen Gaskin's commune the Farm shuffles and regroups and downsizes in the early '80s, the Bread and Puppet gang are one of the last major rural hippie concerns. While neither a literal commune nor particularly psychedelic, their narrative stands with the post-1960s tribal histories from around the continent, Pranksters or Rainbows or Yippies.

Every August they gather for what they call Our Domestic Resurrection Circus, first staged at Goddard in '74. There, with Peter Schumann at the helm, Bread and Puppet unfold the latest metaphysical art response to whatever global vibes they're processing.

By the early '80s, a few thousand come each year. The campers' tents sprawl out across the camping fields around the Bread and Puppet land, a miniature settlement of families, New England youth, Rainbows, Deadheads, and others. They stay for the weekend out among the trees. There are parties and little campfires and drum circles. It's all very peaceful, like the Dead scene used to be. The roads into the tiny town clog up, and parking spreads out across adjacent farmland. Vendors line Route 122, selling food and crafts. The cars overflow with northeastern hippies, laughing, singing, ready to make a temporary economy selling tie-dyes and food. There are drugs, too, of course. Up in Vermont, everything else seems so laughable. In addition to maple syrup and cheese, Vermont has groupminds. Come up and step into one!

The puppet-caricatures take form each year all 'round at the farm while the bread bakes. They look like benevolent Easter Island heads, scattered and framed against the electric green grass and blue sky made for floating into. They are creatures ready to animate in the psilocybic night, ideas coming alive as they flicker between the fire and the stars. Bread and Puppet don't mean to be trippy, though they're happy to be beautiful. Each year, they have stages for "Social Change in Nicaragua" and "Dialogue with Guatemalan Mayan Indians" and whatnot, but the crowds flock to Glover for the giant, amazing puppets. Each takes multiple operators, a vivid groupmind come alive.

"It's a piece that shouldn't be traveled, something we want to perform where we can integrate the landscape, that we can do with real time and real rivers and mountains and animals," Peter Schumann said around the time of the inaugural circus in 1974. "It's something that is seen in the woods, up there in the hills, back here in the river. I guess it would be called an 'environment'!" The longhairs' creation up there had fused the European circus tradition with street theater power.

In the afternoon before the big pageant, members of the troupe and volunteers gather around Peter Schumann in the amphitheater for a dress rehearsal. All performances are participatory, if one arrives early. There is no amplification of any kind, just Schumann booming in his German accent. The B&Pers around the perimeter repeat the message, telephoning it outward to the audience sitting around the bowl. It's a primitive address system, a home-brewed nontechnology that's just fine for their art. It's hippie opera, telegraphing in broad gestures developed just for their conditions.

Peter Schumann is bare chested and barefoot and spry and everywhere at once before the pageant is to start. He is there taking the bread out of the oven. "Slower, slower, slower, less," he says to critique the developing puppets and choreography. It is a philosophy that is broadcast from every ounce of Bread and Puppet.

Kids play on the ground. Elsewhere, a group of bright-eyed, bushy-tailed Bread and Puppeteers stand in a ragtag line and do whistle drills, contorting their bodies more or less in line, members of an absurdist antiauthoritarian antiarmy.

There's music among them, too, but it's hardly rock 'n' roll. To-day, someone is sawing on a fiddle. Another day, there might be a stilt walker with an accordion or a trumpet. Precision is not their strong suit, nor should it be. Musically, they lean towards sloppy joyous New Orleans brass bands. "Down by the Riverside" is their all-purpose dance hymn. "Ain't gonna study war no more," they sing, a perfect replication of the Humbeadean refusal to engage in the consensus, a crossing point of networks, of Americas.

Every year, it seems, a thousand more people come to watch and, sometimes, to join. The locals start to stay away, content to see Bread and Puppet at a Fourth of July parade or a picnic or someplace else. Their politics remain avowedly humanistic, transcending party identi-fication in a way similar to that of the Grateful Dead. But that doesn't mean they don't address events out there in the world. Schumann and the troops are no hideaways.

"Our everyday language is silly and does not tell the truth," Schumann states. "When something happens in Central America or on the television with one of Mr. Reagan's foul speeches or anything like this, then the opportunity and the necessity arises to respond to that. Or if branches of the peace movement call us and ask for our participation." In 1979, they travel to New York and occupy Wall Street, stopping traffic with stilt walkers and a giant caricature puppet head in an American flag top hat.

Finally, it's time for the pageant. They stream down the green hill into the bowled amphitheater, dressed in white, bearing flags with abstract symbols and flowers. And they whoop. Strange creatures with massed legs trundle from the trees. The man in the mask with the papier-mâché bowler hat saws on a violin, as do others, creating a wild mass of American primitive folk drones, like the composer Henry Flynt dreamed, but out here in the wild.

Multistory puppets! Squonking horn combos! Face masks hooked to big-tubed '80s television sets! Giant marionette skeletons circling the bowl, operated by five prancing longhairs in white garb! A giant caricatured Furthur-style bus! Stilt walkers smashing cymbals! White birds! Ships of redemption on the rim of the bowl, coming over the horizon and into view while everybody hums and drones and chants and generally makes the tragicomic holy.

It is celebration and it is abstraction and it is meaning. The symbols are here to be manipulated under the summer moon. Some years, the puppets are gathered at the center of the bowl and set ablaze while other masked characters circle it, their silhouettes illuminated by the flames. There is an order to things.

PHISH'S ACID TEST fails during the song "Fluffhead." When it comes time for the vocals, one of their guitarists, Jeff, steps back from the microphone. "I can't sing this, this is a stupid song," he announces, and the music falls apart.

It's the first time they've played at Goddard for any appreciable audience. The nontripping bassist tries to conduct. "Jeff, just play a G chord," he suggests. It doesn't happen.

"What's a G chord?" the other guitarist asks. Nancy's excised spirit shoots around the room, silently giggling, perhaps.

The nontripping bassist takes over one of the guitars and jams with the unfazed drummer while the other musicians wander to the campus sweat lodge, where a strange man shoves burning hot coals blindly into the room's narrow opening.

A few weeks after their failed Halloween Acid Test, Phish return to Goddard for a makeup gig in a circular, hippie-designed cafeteria where whispers can be heard across the room. Some Goddard students get the band *exquisitely* stoned, and bassist Mike Gordon has an ecstatic experience, jumping up and down with the music, "at one with the buildings, wall outlets, chandeliers, and these people I loved," he says.

After the last set, Gordon accidentally stumbles into the militant feminist separatist dorm, a brief surrealist escapade to punctuate the most important night of his life. It is guitarist Trey Anastasio and drummer Jon Fishman who transfer to Goddard from the University of Vermont, though, jumping full-bore into self-directed studies.

"Goddard was an insane asylum," Anastasio would tell Richard Gehr, and it becomes the band's home. New Phish keyboardist Page McConnell receives fifty dollars a head for the recruitments. It is the perfect solution for all, motivated musicians with little tolerance for anything else. Anastasio connects with local composer Ernie Stires, but his skills are already prodigious, a developed guitar hero with original compositional and solo voices that radiate from some of the dreamy fragments of music he's been writing and sewing into suites.

Phish take over the campus's Music Building on the edge of the woods and hole up for the winter. Then another. Time keeps on passing just ever so slowly up in Vermont.

Though the band's roots in the Dead and the Allman Brothers and Frank Zappa and classic rock are clearly audible, the music transforms into something else with an intricate internal language. In the same way that the Grateful Dead's music no longer sounds like rock 'n' roll to traditional ears, neither does Phish's. Their ambitions are big, especially Anastasio's, but mostly they're just obsessive. It is not a repertoire that any expect to take on the mantle of psychedelic America, except for the fact that it is precisely Prankster logic that holds it together and the music of the Grateful Dead that bonds the musicians and the audiences. As they assemble their repertoire in the Vermont stillness, Phish's music is a new kind of psychedelic, one for individuals raised in suburban captivity and set loose in the New Earth.

Phish is a tiny little college band up in the woods. No one expects them to do anything. They're just a group of students, after all. And, yet, some weeknights when they play in Burlington, they draw 250 or more listeners. Oftentimes, Nancy is one of them, forgoing his personal rule about big crowds and loud music to see his new favorite band.

They've picked a good time to make their way to Burlington. Besides Ben & Jerry's extraordinary iced concoctions oozing their way creamily around the country from their downtown Burlington headquarters, the city's new mayor, Bernie Sanders, is one of the very few elected Socialists in the country. The same week Mike Gordon has his epiphany at Goddard, the band plays a rare acoustic show at a new spot in the basement of the Memorial Auditorium sponsored by the mayor's office, soon to become Vermont's first punk outpost. Known as 242 Main Street, it will become a stable home for hardcore punk even as crackdowns begin elsewhere and last into the next century, the longest-running all-ages substance-free venue in the country. Phish return for a benefit with a Dead cover band in the spring of '86 but are far from substance-free and leave the place for the hardcore kids.

Another way to look at the beginning of Phish's professional career in Burlington, at the far rim of psychedelic America: the members of Phish are making the most of the finest $5,400-a-year DIY education a loving parent can purchase for his or her curious, open-minded, self-motivated child. All four band members are decidedly upper middle class. Gordon's father had founded Store-24, the New England convenience market chain. McConnell's dad is a doctor who'd helped invent (and patent) Tylenol. Plenty of well-to-do children have made music for the masses.

But rock 'n' roll doesn't often reward bands that exploit the freedom to just *feel* the slower, slower lessness the way that Phish do. The rest of the world can wait while Phish practice for eight hours a day.

But the rest of the world isn't waiting.

The rest of the world doesn't care.

The rest of the world has other things to think about.

The rest of the world has MTV.

The rest of the world has college rock.

The rest of the world has heavy metal.

The rest of the world has hip-hop.

The rest of the world has old-guard networks.

The rest of the world has bands that can do their thing in forty-five minutes.

The rest of the world has U2.

The rest of the world can look at its watch.

The rest of the world can wait.

"It was . . . quiet," Trey Anastasio will tell an interviewer later of his visits to Bread and Puppet's Resurrection Circuses. Like his bandmates, he becomes a summer regular at the Glover spectacle.

"Everyone would sit in silence and the pageant would come over the hill," Anastasio will remember. "It would have a theme. And it took, I don't know, 15 minutes for that gigantic puppet show. And it was so moving and memorable and emotional. And it's those minutes where time becomes kind of irrelevant because of the beauty of this thing that's coming slowly over the hillside. You can see the billowing of the puppets' fabrics and it's a different delivery of experience, where time slows down."

In Vermont, Phish make perfect sense, their music spiraling into the deepest, most intricate detail, hashed out over endless practice sessions, a collaboration between Anastasio's voice and his band-mates' idiosyncratic musical personalities. Barely five feet, drummer Jon Fishman is all beard and tangled hair. If the LSD chromosome scare had any validity, which it thankfully doesn't, Fish (as everyone calls him) is in trouble.

"For me, from a pretty young age up until about 21 years old hallu-cinogenics had a huge place in my life," Fish will tell a journalist later. "There was a year where pretty much I woke up at 5am, you know, set my alarm for 5am, dropped a couple of tabs of acid and went back to sleep. It would wake me up at 7:30 and I'd go to school. I got my best grades that year and I had a good time. For me, it was like a sense of humor kinda thing. When Phish started, for the first two years that we were together, I pretty much tripped for all our gigs. We didn't have that many gigs, granted. We mostly spent our time practicing. I was never high for band practice. I never really did smoke much pot."

Just as Anastasio lays off the Dead, the rigorous drummer lays off the LSD as the band clicks into gear. But, he insists some twenty years later, "I still play with the feeling I got from those experiences, trying to generate wind and fire." He loves heroic doses but doesn't hear Terence McKenna's name until Anastasio bring it up.

"I loved learning multiple rhythms that moved my body in abnor-mal ways that quickly became normal," he says. It is Fishman that makes Phish's music sound weird from the ground up.

Almost immediately after transferring to Goddard in 1986, they stop playing Grateful Dead tunes altogether. The band absorb their lessons, though, as well as everything around them, from their covers of Jim Pollock's "Dear Mrs. Reagan" and Nancy's "Halley's Comet" to nonsense poetry borrowed from Anastasio's high school friends and even the band's recently departed second guitarist. Though Anasta-sio's scored-out songs and the band's fondness for play have far more to do with Frank Zappa than Jerry Garcia, the Grateful Dead's culture is as much a part of Phish as country music is to a young musician growing up in Nashville.

The lyrics to "Fluffhead" that had triggered the Acid Test melt-down came from a poem by a friend of Anastasio's about seeing a cancer patient at a Dead show, dancing down on the venue floor, bald head covered in cotton balls. They do have an instrumental called "Jerry's Beard," an odd bit of composed atonality, but the

Dead's influence will emerge in dozens of ways. Around Goddard, they quickly become stars.

On the earliest known Phish recording of Nancy's "Halley's Comet," taped at an early October 1986 show in the Haybarn, there is an audible cheer as the song begins: already a hit. They'd debuted it a few months earlier and usually Nancy himself joins in, coming onstage to hand-deliver all the couplets about "Cadillac rainbows and lots of spaghetti and I love meatballs so you better get ready."

But, on this night, Nancy isn't there. The band arrange Nancy's layered vocals for themselves, Gordon singing and playing two separate bass lines. Phish absorb new skills as they learn to play it, and the song's inherent strangeness—a perfect musical expression of its author—re-enforces the band's growing identity as a product of deepest, weirdest Vermont.

"When I was looking at colleges, I visited 12 of them with my dad, and none of them were like [Goddard]," bassist Mike Gordon remembers, the only member of Phish who doesn't transfer in, though he commutes to Plainfield a few times a week. "It was like being part of a secret society or something, culturally off the grid. Everyone there was self-structuring their educations, and into unique stuff. There was Bruce Burgess, who was doing poetry, and who could only speak in poetry and not in English, as far as I was concerned."

Fishman befriends a metalhead named J. Willis Pratt, another divergent personality with a singular musical voice that might sound grinding and odd to many. The numbers on the campus start to swell. There is something happening out there in the woods, something born of the New Earth, and Phish tap into it.

And there's Nancy. By that time, Nancy Bitterbug Voodoo Coleslaw is no longer a Goddard student. "I'd gotten to a point where I didn't trust any of the faculty or staff at Goddard, so I wouldn't talk to any of them. I didn't care if I got college credit or not, I just wanted to be there and use the resources they had there. And they were like, 'you can't be here if you don't care about college credit.'" He pretty much sticks around anyway.

Nancy sees Phish whenever he can around Goddard and Burlington, which is plenty, and keeps recording whenever he can, too. He remains a figure around campus, his influence fully accepted into Phish's music alongside Frank Zappa and Jerry Garcia and others.

And, unlike the Dead songs, Nancy's music will stay in Phish's repertoire more or less permanently. When Phish leave Vermont and grow in popularity, as they will, it is Nancy's songs that most communicate the place they come from.

"I sang ['I Didn't Know'] with them once, while tripping on mushrooms," Nancy says. "It didn't work out so well, so from then on they either did without me or with me on drums." He never gets totally comfortable on stage. He'd sung in choirs in high school, as well as with his friend's cover band. But that was it for his live performances. He wouldn't make a compelling live performer, anyway, he thought. How could he possibly recreate his multipart vocals? Or synth-feedback epics like "The Formidable Poseur"?

Not long after Phish debuts "Halley's Comet," Nancy—somewhat audaciously, no doubt—composes and records a new song for Phish to perform titled "Snootable Snunshine." Over twelve minutes of woozy keyboards, complex drum fills, and nonsense lyrics, the song contains a surprisingly innate sense of the Trey Anastasio's compositional whimsy. Anastasio and Fishman break into hysterics upon hearing it, Nancy's most epic creation yet.

One of Phish's new songs, the mushroom-inspired "Divided Sky," includes a long palindrome with the band playing in odd times backward and then forward (or is it the other way around?) culminating in Gordon and Anastasio jumping up and down in 4/4 counter to the band. But with its hyperspeed time and section changes, Nancy's "Snootable Snunshine" is even more unlearnable, let alone playable.

Still, not long thereafter, Phish add Nancy's "I Didn't Know" to the repertoire, too, their first foray into barbershop. "I always thought the interesting cast of characters—there in Plainfield and others in Burlington—gave [Phish] its flavor," Mike Gordon says. At early shows in Burlington, their friends from the UVM radio station bring six giant speakers and mix sound effects throughout the basement of the environmentalist dorm.

Vermont seeps into Phish's music in every way, their oddness as much as the majestic sweep Anastasio conjures with his guitar, a soaring jam-happy variation on Robert Fripp's sunshine bursts from Brian Eno's *Another Green World*.

The gigs keep coming, and Anastasio makes sure the band is always on to something new. They play house parties and Burlington bars (especially Nectar's) and the occasional commune. One night, they load up Gordon's hatchback with miniamps and show up unannounced at University of Vermont frats and perform in their kitchens.

Nancy accompanies the group on a road trip for a show that will go down in band lore as the "Sex Farm" gig, in reference to the Spinal Tap song, though Nancy remembers only the room's "dry acoustics."

"Sex farm" is probably not how the members of the Quarry Hill Creative Center, founded in 1946, would describe their life, but it's another place that Phish pass through. The band's Deadheadness, in some ways, allows them access to this other Vermont.

Before the band break for the summer of '87, they celebrate Mike Gordon's graduation from UVM with a party at their friends' place in Shelburne. They set up in the backyard underneath a tent, in front of tie-dye tapestries while their friends sprawl out on the lawn. Others watch from the roof. Dogs wander about. Mike Gordon's parents had financed a PA for one of his high school bands, and he puts it to good use with Phish. There are monitors. Even the drums have microphones.

With their own PA and light show and soundman (who doubles as a luthier and guitar repair guy) and audience of Vermont hippies and Deadheads—plus families to fall back on if their career fails—Phish are fully independent. Their situation and particular crossroads in American culture are unique. Because of so many unrepeatable factors, they begin to carry forward various threads of the countercultural narrative, half accidentally and perhaps without understanding it entirely.

There are some people dancing at this backyard party, not a lot. It could be the vibe of the afternoon, but probably Anastasio wishes there were more. Those who dance do so like they might be at a Dead show. They boogie. Phish don't look like the kind of guys who might go out dancing. Or even throw down too hard to the Dead. But dance music is what they're after, it seems. That's Anastasio's goal, and it seems no less audacious or surreal than his fugues and atonality and charted compositions and mushroom tea jam sessions.

He rents a cabin up in the Northeast Kingdom for the summer, moving in with his golden retriever, Marley, and sets a goal of writing music that is both harmonically and rhythmically strange but still danceable. Trey Anastasio has a very specific idea about what makes audiences dance. He already has an audience. Though he's sworn off listening to his onetime hero, Jerry Garcia, Phish find themselves with a completely natural fan base of Deadheads in Vermont. It's not *only* Deadheads who see Phish, but they're the ones that tend to dance the most and bring their friends.

Anastasio isn't thinking about these Deadheads figuratively or abstractly when writing the next wave of dance music that will carry Phish and the Northeast Kingdom itself into unimagined territory. He is thinking about them practically and literally. He can't help it.

A FEW TOWNS over from Anastasio's cabin is a commune. This particular gaggle of transplanted Tennessee communards has been up in Vermont almost a decade now. The Northeast Kingdom is fairly hospitable to their beliefs, give or take an ugly court battle a few years earlier. But that's over, and no one was convicted, and they're back to life in the green greenery. They believe in unity. Multiplying is all well and good, but they need more people. That's also one of their beliefs. Then someone new pipes up and suggests that Grateful Dead shows might be a good place to find new members.

They go by different names, these communards in Vermont—the Light Brigade, the Church of God, the Island Pond of Northeast Kingdom—but they don't do drugs, and they definitely don't listen to rock music. Fundamentally, they love the Lord. But they love you, too, probably. They love a lot. They know a lot about love, but the Island Ponders know very little of this Grateful Dead of which their newest brother speaks. But he's been out there and he knows what it's like. He knows there are lost souls, lots of them. And he knows that they should get a bus to go collect them. In the coming years, Vermont will come to the country in many ways.

They bisect a century-old barn, park an old Greyhound inside, and seal it in. While Trey Anastasio writes songs in his cabin a few miles away, these Island Ponders spend the summer in the barn, and on into the cold fall, coldest winter, and impossible Vermont spring, its creators forsaking their families for the work they know they must do.

THERE'S NO COVER at the door of Nectar's, and John Paluska can't believe what he's walked into on this night in March 1988. Almost randomly, he is there to witness one of the last major pieces of Phish locking into place before they begin to bring their music beyond Vermont and bring their Vermont to the world. Even without knowing this, and John Paluska doesn't, it's still an impressive sight.

Paluska digs the Dead and understands the scene instantly, down to the tapers. "There was an intensity and engagement that you wouldn't ordinarily see in a club that wasn't even charging a cover," Paluska says.

On this particular night at Nectar's, he watches in astonishment when the band takes the stage for their second set with a version of Charles Mingus's "Jump Monk" before Trey Anastasio begins to narrate and the band launches into the guitarist's senior Goddard thesis, "The Man Who Stepped into Yesterday." It's campy and slightly corny, but Anastasio is convincing. Built around the prophet Icculus and his Helping Friendly Book, the Orwellian fairy tale later known to Phish fans as Gamehendge is more musical theater than rock opera.

It shows yet another side of Phish. For his decisive interest in composing music that pushes boundaries, Anastasio is also enamored with Broadway-style engagement and the most traditional of academic romantic composition. Phish are so far out that they're *normal*. The musical theater especially becomes another strategy to layer jokes, another way to play. Phish *plays* music, the notes and the signs and symbols around it, a freedom of permeable reality they can improvise with, allowed by their time among female-presenting acidheads and Dead shows and giant puppet processionals in green valley amphitheaters.

Though pieces of Anastasio's senior thesis stay in the band's repertoire, it will be years before the band plays the full musical again. It is almost a formality to perform the whole piece live from beginning to end anyway, and the single song fragments create a kind of unknowable mythology unless one can find a tape of the whole. Almost immediately, John Paluska invites Phish to play one of the psychedelic full moon parties at the Zoo, the co-op he lives in at Amherst. Within months, he will be one of the band's managers. Though the band don't follow the Grateful Dead's ritualistic set structure, it is quickly obvious that their multihour, multiset performances, long instrumental passages, and goofy sensibilities are a new platform for the psychedelic ritual, if audience members are so inclined. And many are.

Phish record some studio demos, but mostly they keep working at finding new hooks and assembling a language. Some is musical, some isn't. Most shows now, drummer Jon Fishman takes center stage in a housedress to sing covers by acid casualty Syd Barrett and others while Anastasio mans the drums. Fishman acquires a trombone, too, and adds this to his shtick. The brass instrument, which the drummer never quite masters, most frequently comes out for a break in the middle of the band's otherwise a cappella arrangement of Nancy's "I Didn't Know," literally show-stopping weirdness, the drums disappearing with a whoosh.

Such is the state of Phish when they plan their first departure from the Northeast, for a tour booked by a promoter in Colorado. It's been nearly five years since Anastasio, Gordon, and Fishman first convened to jam in a UVM dorm, and their identity is now almost completely in place, a product of the *slower slower* place they occupy.

"For me, it was just this feeling of going to Goddard," reflects Mike Gordon about listening to the tapes that Nancy made. It is a spirit that Phish now carries in their music in the summer of 1988 as Anastasio and McConnell prepare for their graduations. Fishman is still enrolled, too, and continues his practice routines. But, as he discovers, he doesn't really need Goddard for that, and the band has migrated out of Plainfield for Burlington and the surrounding area.

"It was just really special," Gordon says. "You're just nestled away from the normal institutional life of a big college or all the other institutions in our lives. I liked to play Nancy's tape for people in that same sort of context, where there's not usually too much to do, maybe at some sort of tucked away place in the middle of the night. I thought compared to that experience, our version of ['Halley's Comet'] didn't really do it justice. But whether we did it justice or not, I think our version stemmed from an emotion, not really of the comet itself, or the songwriter, or even the people playing, in a sense."

The central question of "Halley's Comet"—"what is the central theme to this everlasting spoof?" as sung by Anastasio—becomes a meta-acknowledgment from the stage that they, the ostensible storytellers, have no answers either. It isn't quite as tender or wise as

Robert Hunter's "if I knew the way, I would take you home," but sometimes a wink is as good as a nod to a head.

"I think it's a lot subtler than the Grateful Dead coming from the whole psychedelic era, or Fela Kuti coming from the political turmoil of Nigeria and having a little mecca in all of the killing," says Mike Gordon of Vermont's influence on Phish. "This was a lot subtler, but I think it was important—this Nancy tape, the way he acted, the way that he looked, kind of created this emotional backdrop and cultural backdrop that we borrowed from. It made the band what it is."

A week before their departure for Colorado, Gordon is finally able to get the promoter on the phone, and the promoter admits that he has hasn't booked a tour at all. He offers them $1,000 to come play at his bar in Telluride, though. The band has already rented a U-Haul.

They play the second night of a three-night stand at Nectar's, de-volving into deeper silliness by the end of the evening, if such a thing is possible from Phish. A few years later, this particular silliness will find its way, unexplained and misdated, onto a major label release of their first studio recordings, *Junta,* adorned with cryptic cartoons by Goddard buddy Jim Pollock.

After the set, they decide to go. Telluride isn't quite a national tour, but—like Burlington—it *is* a hippie town. Their friends in Ninja Cus-todian agree to sub for them the next night. Phish, along with a sound guy and a light dude, load into the windowless box van—mattress foam on the floor, turkey-ham, white privilege, cheese, and apple-but-ter between them—and set out into the Vermont highway night.

7

DAY OF THE DEAD

There's static, the stretch of video tape, and then an MTV VJ with sideways hair and gigantic hoop earrings and, in an always-trendy British accent, she's presenting a special *Day of the Dead* report. It's the summer of '87, and everything's gone upside-down as the secret codes of psychedelic America go shooting forth from televisions and radios everywhere. Above the VJ's enormous padded left shoulder floats the ever-popular skull and roses, first pulled from Edmund J. Sullivan's 1913 illustrations and colorized by the highly psychedelicized Mouse and Kelley to advertise an Avalon Ballroom show in 1966. The skull that graced tens of thousands of parking lot shirts beams into households cross-country, beckoning to teens like a mostly benevolent poltergeist.

Following Jerry Garcia's miraculous return to vitality after his diabetic coma the previous year, MTV take up the Dead and the band's debut video, "Touch of Grey." The focal point of the cable station's affair with the Dead is concentrated into this July afternoon when it sends a pair of VJs to the Giants Stadium parking lot while inserting Dead videos and interview clips throughout their normal day. The live-in-the-studio VJ oozes nothingness [interrupt frame with Tuli Kupferberg droning the Fugs' existential hymn "Nothing": "Monday nothing, Tuesday nothing . . . "] from the monitor.

Eventually, they cut to the parking lot. MTV's reporters, like news anchors from the straight world, interview a mustachioed and seemingly tripping Deadhead who has maybe just gotten married? In the background, Deadheads pour in and out of a bus.

Everything is blown up. The real world is miles away. Not even these Deadheads seem real. The band's new album *In the Dark* is #6, the five-year-old "Touch of Grey" is at #9 on the Hot 100, their first Top 10 hit. What's big for the Dead is big for psychedelic America, and the Deadhead population has just swollen beyond belief.

Off camera, the parking lot extends beyond the horizon. It bends with the curvature of the planet, like an R. Crumb projection of the San Francisco cityscape, but instead of Victorians it's endless cars and buses and portable kitchens and tie-dyed blankets and flags, twisting in the summer sun.

The Grateful Dead are their own clearly defined territory on all Maps, a flag for cops, a party invitation to all comers in flowing archaic script; at least it looks like that's what the lettering says. The band spend the summer playing stadiums in the familiar regions, backing Bob Dylan for a set each show, too. The media are loving Garcia's resurrection and loving the heads, too, sending cameras and their human operators into parking lots to see what comes back. There are tour veterans, of course, weekend warriors, students, old heads, secret acid cabals, frat boys and sorority sisters, onlookers, everything, everybody. The Grateful Dead are *everybody's* band, an inclusive tent, a stronghold in the Reagan '80s.

"This is our conception of what it's like to be the Grateful Dead now, in 1987," Jerry tells MTV about their new album. "I think it's 1987."

If a young almost-turned-on freak comes across "Touch of Grey" on the radio and doesn't pay attention to the lyrics, it might sound like a bunch of bouncing synthesizers and a bopping chorus, at least until the first guitar break. Then, there's about forty-five seconds of Garcia, a signal cutting through the noise with upper register ruminating, piercing even the mushiest of drum arrangements and radio static. There's no fancy flourish or big peak, and it doesn't even particularly *go* anywhere as it just instantly *is* somewhere—a cosmic news break from Jerry Garcia, the Walter Cronkite of the postverbal galactic set. [Tuli Kupferberg and the Fugs interrupt with another dronechorus of "Nothing."]

Inside the Meadowlands, the Dead take the stage. MTV has packed up and gone home, if they were ever there at all. There are just seas of people on a vast array of substances: psychedelics, uppers, some downers, beer and booze, a thousand grades and shades of grass, ecstasy. . . .

The Dead open with "Hell in a Bucket" and Bob Weir shout-sings, the drums explode and cascade. When Garcia takes "West L.A. Fadeaway," the band calms down again and, on a front-of-board field recording, the crowd depth sounds infinite, just a low rush of audience noise receding toward the far stereo horizon. A distant section erupts and it never stops, just cheer-rushes from random spots around the bowl, groupminds connecting like frogs gurgling across a pond, energy balls bouncing, the intricate whisper of starlings midmurmuration. It is a swarming natural force, and it's still building.

ALSO ON THE airwaves that spring and summer of 1987 is a bit of cross-over catchiness, regrettably memorable. Metalheads and hip-hop crews will make fun of it, skate punks and East Village postbeatnik avant-gardeners and Deadheads alike will be infuriated by it. It's a new ad campaign by the Keye/Donna/Pearlstein agency of Los Angeles that announces a new higher stakes phase of the drug war. A man fries an egg in a pan and looks at the camera. "This is your brain on drugs, any questions?" he "asks."

No doubt, drugs cause serious problems in many communities around the country. A new type of head has taken over the South Bronx turf that once belonged to graffiti-making LSD-OM and the tape-trading Hell's Honkies. Crack hits the streets in '84 and fires through many drug networks, predominantly ones in inner cities. It appears in the Grateful Dead parking lot, too, though not as often as heroin.

But this ad campaign, a public service announcement produced by Partnership for a Drug-Free America (and underwritten by beer and cigarette companies), equates *all* drugs with damaging brain-fry. As it does so, a new change in the law circulates in legal journals to mirror this illogic. Actually, it's an abandoned old law revived, the Boggs Act of 1951, which assigns mandatory minimum jail sentences to first time drug offenders based on the total weight of their special mixture or substance, not merely the amount of drug contained therein.

The new old sentencing procedures click into place in '86, just in time for the Dead world to go into overdrive after the success of "Touch of Grey." The LSD families fire even harder to meet demand and then some. For the first time in a while—maybe since the Brotherhood bust-up in '72—the going price of crystal LSD begins to drop, from its early '80s high of around $10,000 a gram edging down towards about half that, or even less.

Sarah Matzar, the Guatemalan quilter, LSD cook, and anthropology student, reports the bottom falling out of the market as early as 1984 or 1985. The street is flooded with LSD—not all of it high quality—just before the Grateful Dead explode back into the public eye. It is as if some mysterious hand organized a massive pre-release campaign for *In the Dark*. When Matzar had gotten into the crystal LSD market at the turn of the decade, it operated more like a stock investment. Cooks would sit on particularly good batches for years before converting them to usable form. Now, it's a buyer's world.

At this moment, too, the Drug Enforcement Administration is beginning to seriously wake up to LSD for the first time since the '70s. In July of 1987, the DEA's private internal journal, *Micrograms,* publishes a forty-four-page LSD Blotter Index, cataloging several hundred varieties of confiscated acid along with test results. The government captures a vast folk iconography of elves and heptagons, flying saucers, Donald Ducks, dancing bears, and so much more. The confiscated LSD, from between 1976 and 1986—picking up where the Pharm-Chem results left off in '74—almost exclusively falls far beneath the 250-microgram doses of the Owsley era. The Flower Design, spotted in California in '81, gets up to around 220, but almost everything else averages out in the 50 microgram per dose range. The price of acid stays low, yes, but dosage is also way down.

No matter, acid is more available than it has been probably since the early '70s, and so are a lot of other drugs, and that's what Sarah Matzar is having a hard time with. A byproduct of her lab work is getting very, very high. And, like others in her profession, she takes to using heroin to come down. She develops a habit and the world goes grey for a few years.

Opiates and cocaine ravage the Dead world, both backstage and elsewhere. It's just awful and Sarah needs to get away. She stays with friends in Mendocino, goes cold turkey, and shakes herself free. Though her studies have fallen off, she's never stopped sending money home, securing a large industrial machine for her textile business a few years previous, and she soon gets it together to buy land in Panajachel. Clean of heroin, she returns to quilting and her art-god with a new intensity. And in 1987, she becomes an adoptive mother for the first time. Soon, she returns home to Guatemala for good.

NOT LONG AFTER Jacaeber Kastor opens the Psychedelic Solution, his Manhattan art gallery on West Eighth Street across from Electric Ladyland studios, he adds a written clause into his agreements with certain employees, including his bookkeeper: they *will* take their vacation days when the Grateful Dead are east of the Mississippi. Because, if not, they'll be gone anyway.

Launching on Halloween 1986, Kastor's gallery becomes the City's first major psychedelic outpost in a decade or more, an East Coast home of independent psychedelia to match Mark McCloud's more informal Institute of Illegal Images in San Francisco. With the ease of the head he is, Kastor opens up a doorway into the secret vault of American psychedelic art, both folk and fine. And, the Psychedelic Solution is fully open to the public, becoming a well-spoken torchbearer for psychedelic culture in the country's media capital.

Kastor is one of the first to seriously show the original San Francisco underground artists, including flying eyeball channeler and *Aoxomoxoa* letterer Rick Griffin as well as the *Zap!* comix gang, who earn lines down the block. It is the Psychedelic Solution's shows that, in some ways, solidify the market for the so-called Big Five psychedelicized poster creators: Griffin, Stanley Mouse, Alton Kelley, Wes Wilson, and Victor Moscoso.

"In addition to doing all these things which are not just the Big Five or the *Zap!* artists, he was also doing newer stuff and understanding the bigger picture," says Carlo McCormick, organizer of the 8BC LSD Tuesdays a few years earlier, now writing regularly for both *Paper* and *High Times*. At the latter, he pens a High Art column, mostly a small bit of text and big representative work from one artist per issue, providing eyeball kicks for a generation of young stoners. "I thought the Psychedelic Solution was very vital and that we were very fortunate to have it in New York," he says. Within less than a year, the gallery's mailing list swells to 50,000 names.

Kastor shows the new waves of psychedelic art, including the deeply psychonautical painters Alex and Allyson Grey. He displays the work of the dark German futurist H. R. Giger. And second-generation *Fabulous Furry Freak Brother* cartoonist Paul Mavrides, one of the founding schemers behind the Church of the SubGenius. Devo's Mark Mothersbaugh, too. Kastor sweeps up the nitrous cartridges after that opening.

And there is his friendship with Mark McCloud. He helps the West Coast blotter collector stage his East Coast debut at Psychedelic Solution, following a massive coming-out for the Institute of Illegal Images with a pair of well-received San Francisco shows in 1987. Even the FBI had shown up. "Can we photograph this?" an agent asked McCloud.

"Sure," McCloud had told them, "this is for you guys, more so than anyone else." The show is a hit in New York, too. Kastor's openings become regular salons for the luminescent cognoscenti.

The public arrival of Mark McCloud and the opening of the Psychedelic Solution mark a new degree of historical self-awareness in psychedelia. A pair of new books begins to pin down the murky history of the midcentury American psychedelic pioneers, as well. In 1985, Martin A. Lee and Bruce Shlain's *Acid Dreams: The CIA, LSD and the Sixties Rebellion* had provided the first history of the government's long-concealed psychedelic control program, Project MKUltra, which Lee had been chasing since the first document releases a decade previous. And, in 1987, Jay Stevens's *Storming Heaven: LSD and the American Dream* traces the midcentury upsurge. But, as the University of Michigan's *Monitoring the Future* report statistics bears out, there is a new swell at hand. Every year, high school seniors report that acid is more available than the previous. The psychedelic culture has never ceased to mutate, and now it has a gallery to reveal itself.

Unsurprisingly, the Psychedelic Solution becomes a regular stopover for urban trippers. "There was lots of visual stimulation," Kastor says. "They'd come into the gallery and they'd plunk down on the floor. Sometimes, we'd have to kind of plead with them that we had to go home. If there was a black light show, we had people practically living in there." If visitors are caught smoking pot in the gallery, they are politely directed to the ventilated rear bathroom.

"Sometimes we'd get somebody who was really tripping out heavy and we'd have to help them get a grip," Kastor says, another unusual job skill learned by his staff of a half dozen. "We didn't want to be mean to people, because we knew we were like a beacon," Kastor says. But, as LSD continues to spread, "that was a problem with psychedelics creeping into the mainstream. You got a lot of not-very-educated people that weren't very deep, taking stuff and really getting lost, not having any tools to help themselves. They couldn't even center. They didn't know even rudimentary stuff like breathing, or drinking water. These were tough people to work with. They weren't using it to explore the universe. They were, like, hanging on a thread and saying sort of Yogi Berra-isms, but weren't quite on his level."

Nonetheless, the Psychedelic Solution establishes itself quickly and firmly. And when the Dead are in town, the place is out of control, even more so without its regular employees. Though Kastor is a happy tripper, especially at the gallery openings, he makes sure that none of his employees are selling anything besides the posters that keep them in business. He is quite sure the gallery's phone is tapped, and he receives various visits from various authorities through the years. Later, he'll find out that some employees disregard his requests during their cigarette breaks.

Sometime in the Psychedelic Solution's first year or so of existence, MTV discovers them, too. Having finished their brief flirtation with the Dead, who aren't going to fill up much time in the daily *MTV News* cycle, the channel's producers send a crew down to cover nearly every Psychedelic Solution event. Then it really gets hectic.

JOHN PERRY BARLOW will make a suitably weird statesman and an excellent representative for the greater psychedelic karass. He hasn't launched himself into the future yet but, when he does, songs on a Top 10 album will seem like small beans. But though he is groomed for it, statesmanhood no longer seems like an open career path for John Perry Barlow in 1987. One of his songs is on MTV in a video costarring Bob Weir and a duck. But Barlow is electrified and looking for his next outlet.

Bob Weir's songwriting partner is about to turn forty and has recently become what he will describe as "the first historically recorded male from either side of [the] family not to pass his whole career in agriculture."

Like many in his generation, Barlow zigzagged between coasts in the '60s. An ambassador from the words "go! go! go!" he'd been Bob Weir's boarding school conspirator in the early '60s and one of few fully accepted diplomats between the standoffish original East and West Coast LSD cults, equally comfortable at the Dead's Haight-Ashbury abode or at the Millbrook estate with his onetime guru Timothy Leary.

Charming to the nth degree, John Perry Barlow had also been a comparative religion major and student body president at Wesleyan, at least until the university tossed him in a sanitarium. After graduation, he accepted an advance for a novel, wrote it, went to India, destroyed the novel, dealt coke in New York briefly, then headed to Hollywood for a scriptwriting job.

It was en route that he stopped in Pinedale to visit and tend to his ailing father, a state senator. The elder Barlow did not get better, and John Perry went to ground at Bar Cross Ranch. He surfaces as often as he can to make trouble at Dead shows, but mostly he can be found out on the range. By the time the Bar Cross Ranch implodes and the lyricist is forced to sell the place in the late '80s, Barlow is fully formed in the mold of a classic American politician loaded with ten tons of earthy stories.

To wit: When he was young, he *did* ride three miles on horseback through deep winter snow to get to a one-room schoolhouse. For quite a few years, he'd done business with Darrell Winfield, the real-life rancher depicted in cigarette advertisements as the Marlboro Man.

Barlow had recently missed nomination for a seat in the state senate by only one vote, a seat his father and grandfather had both held. Like Norman Barlow and maternal grandfather Perry Jenkins, John Perry Barlow is a Republican. But that's a narrow label. Barlow is the son of Mormon ranchers, not allowed to watch television until the sixth grade, and only then to absorb televangelists. He'd escaped Mormonism easily, Republicanism less so.

But his politics are entirely psychedelic, a back-to-the-universe libertarianism built with space dust and the easy logic of the white light. Still, in '78, he was the western campaign coordinator on Dick

Cheney's successful congressional run. But now he's just a guy in a house in Wyoming with a family and a recently dashed political career and a few songs on a Top 10 album.

Though life has been getting bleak backstage for a while, Barlow adores what he finds out in the parking lots. "I started looking around for what might replace those little agricultural towns like Pinedale, the first thing I saw was the mysterious mobile community of Deadheads," he will say.

He watches them, transfixed, studying the movements of the world's most articulated psychedelic practitioners whenever he has a chance to cross from Cora, Wyoming, to the thick of the Humbeadean empire by way Dead tour. He never renounces his insider status but passes into the Deadhead world without a care, a perfectly smooth connection point to the heads at large. Besides, Barlow can party with the best of them. "I've been in redneck bars wearing shoulder-length curls, [and in] police custody while high on acid," is a classic Barlowism.

Barlow doesn't have much of a plan. He is the author of a few unshot TV pilots. But somewhere around then, Barlow recalls, "I was informed by Weir one day that we were supposed to go down to Apple and give a lecture on songwriting with the Macintosh. Which was poppycock, because neither of us used a Macintosh. I got in front of this audience at Apple, and I realize that these people are all Deadheads—and you can't actually lie to a Deadhead, if you're in my position, or you shouldn't anyway. They're much too credulous. They'll believe anything you tell 'em."

As always, the anecdote is as smooth as a gemstone, especially with its conclusion: Barlow cops to not having a computer and Apple gives him one, which he takes home to Wyoming for his kids to play with.

Not long thereafter, the Dead-loving journalist, radio host, and ambassador in his own right David Gans sets up Barlow with an account on the WELL, the Bay Area electronic bulletin board that had become a hub for counterculturalists from California and elsewhere. Gans tells Barlow that the beloved Deadhead community had figured out how to surf the mindwaves when they aren't at shows. The lyricist-farmer finally gets the modem rigged to make a long-distance call to the server in Sausalito, and then John Perry Barlow isn't in Pinedale anymore.

THE YELLOW BALLOONS appear on the West Coast for the first time a week after the Harmonic Convergence in the late summer of '87. It is as if they are an apparition of grace and mercy from beyond the veil, sent from the type of loving groupmind that has started to emerge in the thick air of Grateful Dead shows. It is perhaps the psychedelic cult's most unlikely product yet, but the band's new popularity almost dictates it. Dead tour takes on a crucible-like quality, establishing new forms for the ages.

Out East, the bushels of yellow balloons have been showing up since spring, first attached to the car of a woman named Laura and within months become a fixture inside the shows themselves. It's estimated that more than a hundred people find their way to the balloons at set break in Philadelphia. In the rapidly expanding free territory of Grateful Dead concerts, the yellow balloons claim a new, beautiful, calm space.

Like the tapers two decades earlier, the idea emerges in a half-dozen places at once. They have trouble finding each other at first until the idea of the yellow balloons comes around, and they're an instant fixture: sober Deadheads.

At first, they simply operate by the precepts of the classic leaderless Twelve Step recovery programs of Alcoholics and Narcotics Anonymous. For all intents, that's all they are, a regular NA/AA meeting taking place within the time-scape of a Grateful Dead set break, whenever and wherever that happens to fall. "It only takes two to have a meeting," runs one of AA's many sayings, and Deadhead enthusiasm ensures attendance. The name emerges naturally: the Wharf Rats. They are the Friends of August W., narrator of the 1971 Garcia/Hunter tune about a bottoming-out drunk nearing his delirium tremens and the redemptive bliss that happens, it is said, with acceptance of powerlessness.

The decentralized nonhierarchical self-organizing recovery group model turn out to be a perfect fit for the antiauthoritarian, self-organizing tendencies of Deadheads. The Wharf Rats come to life over the course of 1987, a bright column of yellow in what is becoming a more and more regularized show-map at the heart of the Grateful Dead's bopping cartoon metropolis. The most basic anchor in the show landscape are the Dead themselves, human compasses: Jerry-side to the right, the Phil Zone to the left. And, as Jerry has come to resemble Santa Claus, Phil Lesh has come to resemble Dad. He's stopped the drinking and the cocaine, too. He hasn't stopped tucking in his T-shirts or wearing giant dorky wristbands, though.

There's the Wharf Rats meeting and the tapers' section and the Greenpeace table and people carrying other balloons and signs. The Grateful Dead are an enormously popular rock band and their shows are collisions of age groups and professions. Perhaps you'll see someone you haven't seen in years, or never would've dreamed of seeing to begin with.

There is no way to overestimate the impact of "Touch of Grey" and MTV's *Day of the Dead* have on the New, New Triple-Revised Map. It's as if the lava from the rainbow volcano finally lands, melting and shaping new lands and valleys and forests and deserts and coastal islands and undiscovered hamlets. A new and unfettered flow of souls arrive on the hippie highway, not to mention a rainbow bridge-and-tunnel set that drop by casually via some portal in the sky, now as seemingly permanent as the Golden Gate.

Jerry Garcia transforms into a Ben & Jerry's flavor, made of cherry ice cream and cherries and delicious fudge flakes. He doesn't care. He likes the ice cream and it's not motor oil he says, but the Dead's attorney convinces him to ask for a cut. The iconography of Garcia, so captivating to the underground press and T-shirt makers since the early 1970s, makes the jump to freezers around the country, an icon transmogrified into something else entirely. The band sells some 450,000 tickets directly to their fans that year. All in all, the summer tour grosses $18 million. But that's merely seismic data.

Coursing through the veins of the broader counterculture that summer, as well, is the Harmonic Convergence: the end of nine hell cycles on the Mayan calendar that begin when Harnán Cortés (the Killer) made landfall in Mexico on April 22, 1519. Heavy stuff to a head. "There were a lot of people on that whole tour that were very into the Harmonic Convergence," remembers WELL-being Mary Eisenhart, who makes the trip out to Colorado for the shows at Red Rocks and Telluride. "It was making people loony."

When the Grateful Dead's summer tour passes through Telluride in August 1987, downtown is sealed off for the throngs of Deadheads. In the town park, Nigerian percussionist Babatunde Olatunji leads a convergence ceremony / drum circle with Dead drummer Mickey Hart.

But like the Mount St. Helens blast, something *has* happened. The median age of Grateful Dead fans drops even further, from roughly twenty-seven to eighteen in the ticket office's estimate, remarkable for a band that's been around for nearly a quarter century. That summer, there's a sociologist out on tour named Rebecca Adams, beginning the first serious look at the band's audience. When she distributes her preliminary study, she receives a response rate of higher than 100 percent, more responders than questionnaires sent. Her work will suggest that Deadheads have nearly exactly the same makeup as psychedelic users: white, nearly three-quarters male, from comfortable backgrounds, in their late teens and early twenties.

Forget taking acid, even just *going* to a Dead show becomes an American rite of passage to a large segment of the country's youth. And with the acid Dead shows become the nearly official template for a late twentieth-century spiritual initiation.

More new coagulations blossom in what Garcia calls "the Grateful Dead outback." Hearing-impaired Deafheads colonize a corner of venue floors to feel the bass vibrations through the skins of balloons and watch sign interpretations of Hunter and Barlow lyrics. In the gay-oriented *Bay Area Sentinel,* a young science writer, Buddhist, and onetime assistant to Allen Ginsberg named Steve Silberman writes an article titled "Gay and Lesbian Deadheads Unite!" and includes a new PO box. They merge with the Radical Faeries, a group of gay men who "center their spiritual lives around various and sundry pagan doctrines." The Dead scene is an interconnected incubator, facilitating old-line underground connections and fostering new ones.

One person who finds his platform at the crossroads of Grateful Dead parking lots is the acid-fueled pro-pot activist named Jack Herer. It's at a summer 1987 Dead show that Herer meets Rick Pfrommer. The two soon form the Cannabis Action Network, a group as responsible as any for marijuana legalization some quarter-century later, and they build a network on Dead tour.

The Deadheads are on the front end of many technologies, even beyond the emergent Internet. A glassblower named Bob Snodgrass accidentally invents a silver fuming process that creates stunning multicolored glass pot pipes and, by the early '90s, will be selling them on Shakedown Street. The technique jumps far beyond the Deadhead wall. The beautiful glass bowls replace boring old wood and metal around the globe, and a new art-craft is born.

In the parking lot, the Deadheads are getting outright serious about this actual, verifiable, living, breathing, shitting folktale in front of them. They're discovering their own history, beyond simple measures of tap-ing. Building a Deadhead manuscript tradition that includes an array of parking lot publications as well as privately collected documents, a trio of Deadheads self-publish the first edition of *DeadBase* in 1987. The chronological list of Grateful Dead performances and set lists creates a definitive geography for the Grateful Dead timewave, a map up the San Francisco Peninsula to the Fillmore Auditorium, Golden Gate Park, New York, Springfield Creamery, Winterland, and so on. That's part of the myth, too: that it's all there, recorded, those far-away nights where those strange people did these strange things and were transformed along with their audience. The conspiracy grows.

Johnny Dwork, the founder of Hampshire College's Grateful Dead Historical Society and proprietor of *Dupree's Diamond News,* the on-tour newssheet turned quarterly magazine, unpacks increasingly deep spiritual meanings in the Dead's recordings. Under the auspices of the Phurst Church of Phun, their very own Prankster troupe, Dwork and his badillions use the August 27, 1972, "Dark Star" as a sacred guide, playing it for more than a thousand listeners over the years to elicit the visionary states suggested by transpersonal researcher Stan Grof. With it, "they can access a holographic dimension that contains all of the archetypal energies, mythological images, and evolutionary history of the universe." This "Dark Star" is for "healing soul work."

To close out the summer of '87 in Deadland, Wavy Gravy calls. The Hog Farm commune is establishing a permanent camp up in the Emerald Triangle, just south of Humboldt, and Wavy asks for Gar-cia's help in acquiring the land. Though the Dead themselves don't play, it's the closest thing the new era has to the legendary '72 benefit for the Kesey family creamery, the countercultural machinations of the hip economy still operating as designed.

For those who navigate the two hundred miles north from San Francisco, it is bliss. The territory is invisible to both the mainstream of American pop and the emerging indie-punk circuit alike. Like Ver-mont, like certain nestled valleys in Colorado, it is a place that is sweet and mostly untouched. While naked hippies frolic on the bank of the Eel River, Garcia brings his new old acoustic band, including 1964 road-trip buddy Sandy Rothman and early tripping/picking comrade David Nelson.

Garcia plays three sets, one with the acoustic band, and two with his long-running electric bar combo, having introduced a whole cluster of new songs in the months after his miraculous coma recovery. He's been singing gospel tunes for perhaps two decades but now seems to occupy their grace. Both bands will soon make the jump to theaters, but for this afternoon in the sunshine, Garcia is there at the crook of the Eel River.

There in Laytonville, life is still pretty alright. Hold onto it my sweet little heads. The Man is bearing down even more on the pot business, too, though Triangle residents continue to work their angles. The hip economy gains a radio station when the growers' money funds KMUD into life at 91.1 on the FM dial. There are astrology-themed weather reports and up-to-the-minute warnings about the doings and whereabouts of the government's CAMP task force. A joke goes around the task force that, if they're lost deep in the underbrush of the Emerald Triangle, they can just turn on KMUD and find out where they are.

PSYCHEDELICS DON'T ALWAYS turn one into a *correct* prophet, but they certainly get the imagination firing. During the extended psychedelic swelling that starts in the late '80s, as since the '60s, lots of white men prognosticate about the universe.

Timothy Leary wouldn't be complete without a vision of the future. "In 20 years there will be hundreds of neurotransmitters that will allow you to boot up and activate your brain and change mental performance," he foretells in '87. "There are going to be what I call brain radios—hearing aids you put in your ear—that will pick up and communicate with the electricity in your brain. You will be able to tune in any brain aspect, like sex, that you want. You will speed up or slow down your thinking. Anything you can do with chemicals you can do with brain waves and they are so much healthier." Sure Tim, sure.

Terence McKenna, still up there at the rim of the rainbow volcano with his Hawaiian shirt and benevolent nasal voice, has a much better rap. He digs the future, but he's into the *past*. The way, far back past. He calls it an archaic revival.

"Whether the mushrooms came from outer space or not, the presence of psychedelic substances in the diet of early human beings created a number of changes in our evolutionary situation," McKenna asserts. "When a person takes small amounts of psilocybin their visual acuity improves. They can actually see slightly better, and this means that animals allowing psilocybin into their food chain would have increased hunting success, which means increased food supply, which means increased reproductive success, which is the name of the game in evolution. It is the organism that manages to propagate itself numerically that is successful. The presence of psilocybin in the diet of early pack-hunting primates caused the individuals that were ingesting the psilocybin to have increased visual acuity."

It is wonderful "psychedelic blarney," as *High Frontiers* layout visionary (and McKenna associate) the Lord Nose puts it, but it belies an accurate understanding of evolution. And, as writer Brian Akers and others point out much later, it misrepresents Fischer and Hill and team's original study regarding mushrooms and visual acuity.

McKenna will present a full-formed version of the vision a few years later in a 1992 book called *Food of the Gods: The Search for the Original Tree of Knowledge, a Radical History of Plants, Drugs, and Human Evolution*. He might overstate his case about mushrooms and evolution, but it doesn't mean psychedelics didn't and don't play a significant role in the development of human culture, arguably providing the more quantifiable seed for multiple major world religions.

Here's how Garcia put it in the early '70s and widely circulated in *A Signpost to New Space*, a book-length interview with Jerry published by *Rolling Stone*: "To get really high is to forget yourself, and to forget yourself is to see everything else, and to see everything else is to become an understanding molecule in evolution, a conscious tool of the universe. And I think every human being should be a conscious tool of the universe. That's why I think it's important to get high."

It's an ancient tradition, this getting high business, Terence McKenna asserts, and it's all the same mystery. On that front, McKenna's got solid historical support from the other quarters of the psychedelic world. Albert Hofmann, first synthesizer of acid, and Gordon Wasson, mycological pioneer, coauthored *The Road to Eleusis*, proposing that the *kykeon* potion of the ancient Greek mystery cults was the same as the ergot fungus that made LSD.

McKenna advocates what he sometimes calls "heroic" doses of mushrooms, the *third* toke of DMT, that extra push into hyperspace. Specifically, McKenna reports the "interiorized linguistic phenomenon" beginning to appear at somewhere around the consumption of 9.5 grams of dried mushrooms, a bit more than a quarter ounce. He deems it to be a manifestation of the Logos, the communicative voice between earthly humans and the Other Side.

"Few people are in a position to judge its extraterrestrial potential because few people in the orthodox sciences have ever experienced the full spectrum of the psychedelic effects that is unleashed," McKenna points out. "One cannot find out whether or not there's an extraterrestrial intelligence inside the mushroom unless one is willing to take the mushroom." It's a bit of a beautiful logical loop, that.

Or consider this as an extension of McKenna's stoned ape theory: it's entirely possible that Deadheads are helping the human race move forward by experimenting with psychedelics and jumping onto their computers and collecting tapes and dreaming whatever dream they're all dreaming together.

Some Deadheads have *heard* of Terence McKenna, but he's hardly that kind of prophet. Why isn't *Relix* putting him on the front cover? Jerry Garcia's on board.

As above, so below, though. Most Deadheads no longer represent the experimental edge of the entheogenic bell curve. The psychedelic illuminati do drop in on Dead shows from time to time but they've got their own cliques, mostly along the traditional lines: Sasha and Ann Shulgin in Berkeley, Esalen in Big Sur, the new Multidisciplinary Association for Psychedelic Studies, soon relocated to Cambridge. They are getting serious about psychedelics, *all* psychedelics. Many are academics of the hard sciences. Most, generally speaking, are not interested in the Grateful Dead or what the Deadheads are doing, besides maybe a passing enjoyment of their music. Dead shows are crude and gaudy, like a psychedelic Disneyland.

And, generally speaking, Deadheads are rarely interested in the new cognoscenti either. As a historical entity, though, just as the Deadheads branched off from the counterculture as a whole, they now represent their own distinct path in the psychedelic world. There, however, they still constitute something more like a geographical feature than a population.

Rick Doblin, MAPS founder, counts himself as a Dead fan. "Psychedelic use at Dead shows was a sustaining use through the '70s and '80s," he says. "I thought it was an important and valuable way to keep the culture alive."

But now Deadheads *are* the screaming masses. Whenever a member of the Dead plays with other musicians, inevitably the Deadheads follow, doing what Deadheads do: boogying, taping, smoking grass at various levels of discretion, maybe hooting or hollering or talking or just treating the venue as an extension of Dead-conquered territory.

The Grateful Dead are enormously popular, and their newly acquired Top 10 status is their final alchemical transformation from a heads-only phenomenon into an exploding technicolor static of white-ish humanity: young, old, straight, gay, other, male, female, empowered, disenfranchised, psychonautical, sober, college educated, fully dropped out, frat boys and sorority sisters, many Jews, future civic leaders, computer geeks, and lots of people that don't fall under any particular category.

The Grateful Dead world has gone absolutely beyond critical mass into some white-hot improbability zone. "At this point the Deadheads and the Grateful Dead have to get serious," Garcia told Blair Jackson *before* "Touch of Grey" came out. "We have to invent where we can go from here, because there is no place. . . . Bigger venues isn't going to get it. When you're at the stadium, that's it, that's the top end, and that's already not that great."

"It's bigger than a drive-in movie, ooo-eee," John Perry Barlow will write in 1989's "Picasso Moon," eventually one of Bob Weir's favored set openers. It is an image too big for even the biggest blockbuster. Too much information, too much exploding at once. The culture has matured.

The Dead have hijacked, borrowed, or accidentally ended up as stewards of the mainstream of psychedelic America. It is known at high schools and college campuses and everywhere, across all lands: if you want LSD, you go a Grateful Dead show or find a Deadhead.

Grateful Dead tour is *the* distribution network for LSD in the United States because their audience remains its number-one consumer. Dead shows, with their rubbed-smooth, calypso-scented Dionysian portals, remain how many people are initiated to the psychedelic experience. What happens after that is between them and the Logos.

CLICK. CLICK. CLICKCLICKCLICK. Whole new psychedelic/entheogenic vocabularies emerge around the therapeutic community over the '70s and the '80s, and the Lord Nose—Marc Franklin—grows an art form he calls transpersonal portraiture. It has Jungian rigor and psychedelic time compression rolled into one and is quite serious as a craft. Transpersonal portraiture is created with high-resolution photography, capturing a moment between photographer and subject down to the pores. The Lord Nose is an excellent photographer.

There are all kinds of ways to interpret and translate the psychedelic experience, Spinners or Noses or beyond. The Lord Nose can see this and wants to honor the elders at the start of this particular fork in history. In 1988, the Nose acquires wings in the form of a plane ticket. Off he goes to Europe to begin his Pioneers series, transpersonal portraits of the psychedelic luminaries, beginning in Switzerland with Albert Hofmann himself. *Clickclickclickclicklclick.*

DANIEL KOTTKE IS a regular among familiar eucalyptus groves outside Stanford University's Frost Amphitheater, seeing the Dead there whenever he gets the chance. Into the '80s, the venue remains a picnic ground for Stanford research scientists and Silicon Valley characters old and new, conspiring on various levels of future building.

A computer industry veteran himself, at one show in the late '80s, Daniel Kottke runs into an old friend who is visiting Deadland with a new lady. Daniel and his friend have been on the outs for years. The band is playing and they don't have much time to talk, but their interaction is cordial.

Spontaneously, Daniel offers his old friend a few hits of Windowpane he has in his pocket. "An old-times gesture," Daniel says. They used to do a lot of acid together in the meditation room they built in the attic of their college home. They'd hung out at a commune and picked apples. They'd gone to India together, started a company together. They were bros, at least until Steve freaked out and/or went straight and/or met his psychedelic destiny as the creator of user-friendly personal computers. Apple founder Steve Jobs accepts the acid from Daniel Kottke, and they go their separate ways.

Later, Daniel hears that Jobs tells his girlfriend, "Oh, I can't take this, it's probably poison."

"I just feel bad for Steve if that's what he thought," says Kottke, the first of Apple's many Deadhead employees. (Though, to be fair to the late Steve Jobs, sometimes if one doesn't want to commit to a half-dozen hours in the Beyond, the first excuse is sometimes the snarkiest.)

Even without Steve Jobs tripping at the Frost, the linkage between the rainbow underground and the burgeoning computer culture grows more robust and high-speed by the day. Kottke remains active on the circuit of Deadhead cybergeeks going strong since (and still including) the SAILers and MIT Media Labbers of a decade ago.

The Internet is a far-off unsettled place in the '80s, more a collection of various text-based technologies that don't add up to much in most places. But, yet, here are these Deadheads, new kinds of citizens.

Take, for example, Gumby. Gumby is an appropriately heady figure among the early Deadhead digerati. "He basically bounced between MIT and the AI lab at Stanford," remembers dead.dis@sail mailing list founder Paul Martin. "He was just a good hacker who hadn't actually had any training in any of the AI stuff, but would really work hard at swinging code and making something work."

Gumby is connected and on the go, reaching for a new form of digital harmony. "Gumby was the kind of person who was back and forth, you couldn't just call him on the phone," Paul Martin says. "You just had no idea where he was going to be that week, and e-mail was a way around that problem." Once, when working in Austin in the mid-1980s, Gumby departs for Dead tour, the *whole* tour.

In each city, Gumby connects with a head at a local computer lab. Never a partier, Gumby's postshow routine involves going immediately to a terminal and posting a set list. The tour happens to end in Austin, where he's living at the time, and he *happens* to go into work that day, where he encounters his boss.

"We haven't seen you much," the boss man says.

"Well, I've been thinking," he half bluffs.

"Thinking about what?" and Gumby spells it out on the white-board. Without really working at it, he'd untangled the whole problem in his head over the previous weeks, following the Dead, listening to the Dead, breathing the Dead. The Dead's long jams, either experienced live or on tape, are good for thinking, Garcia's solos unfolding with crystal themes and unexpected variations.

"There was a culture of people that believed in sharing," Gumby says of the computing world he finds himself helping to define in the mid-1980s. "It's always been around. It's just the people doing the cool stuff. It's how the network happened. We all passed patches around, different ideas. There weren't clear boundaries in my life between being a Deadhead, going to shows, working on computers. We'd arrange consulting jobs around the tour."

There is something new afoot in the computer industry, the deep merging of the New Age and the new economics. Observed David Byrne, via actor Spalding Grey, in 1986's *True Stories,* "They don't work for money anymore, or to earn a place in heaven, which was a big motivating factor once upon a time, believe you me. They're working and inventing because they *like it.* Economics has become a *spiritual* thing. I must admit it frightens me a little bit. They don't see the difference between working and not working. It's all become a part of one's life . . . there's no concept of weekends anymore!"

That's not all. In 1989, D. V. (Gumby) Henkel-Wallace, as his e-mail reply-to sometimes reads, cofounds a new Palo Alto venture: Cygnus Solutions. It is the world's first free software company, building on the shareware/freeware concepts that have been circulating for some time. Free. Free! Free, free, *free!* It's built on GNU, the world's first free operating system. John Gilmore, another founding Cygnus partner, is an equally libertarian Silicon Valley Dead freak and employee #5 at Sun Microsystems. He comes with his own legendary maxims: "The Net interprets censorship as damage and routes around it." It's not that trading Dead tapes (or eating acid) inspired Cygnus, but the shared idea of *FREE* birthed from the American alchemical ooze.

At first, it merely seems like they've collectively hit rainbow oil. The Merry Prankster and Whole Earth founder Stewart Brand is one of the first to notice. He quietly establishes the Global Business Network (not as catchy as "Whole Earth") and, over the next years, stages learning conferences at the Esalen Institute in Big Sur and Biosphere 2 out in the Arizona desert. Every month, subscribers receive books handpicked by Brand. It feels much like Whole Earth endeavors of the past, but this venture is underwritten by Shell, AT&T, and Volvo, with clients like Xerox, IBM, Bellsouth, Arco, Texaco, and—by the Clinton years—the Joint Chiefs of Staff and the Defense Department. Its subscription fee is much higher than the *Whole Earth Quarterly*.

Something is being built, a massive modern work, both intellectual and physical, and many people have many different kinds of stakes in it. No one is quite sure what it looks like, but there's no question that the San Francisco Peninsula is once again the locus. "There were Deadheads everywhere," says Gumby of Silicon Valley in the late 1980s.

"Megatest was full of Deadheads," he says. "They made semi-conductor equipment. Lots of pot was smoked. There were tons of Deadheads there all through the organization. You'd see the guys from Cisco and Apple and Sun and Stanford at Frost [Amphitheater] and the Greek [Theatre], just around, at shows." And, built into the Grateful Dead's psychedelic two-set, street-to-space framework is another handy feature: a set break, perfect for a good schmooze.

At a show at the Greek Theatre in Berkeley, early Apple employee Daniel Kottke is summoned backstage. "Barlow wants to see you," someone tells him and hands him a laminate to go see the Grateful Dead lyricist.

"I was thrilled, I had no idea why," Kottke says. "So I got backstage, first time ever for me, and I was a little starstruck. I didn't even know what Barlow looked like. But I found him, and he wanted to thank me."

Recently, Kottke had been the recipient of a massive file of Grateful Dead lyrics, a descendent of the original lyric collection created by Stanford's Dave Wilkins and Paul Martin back in 1973, passed from server to server until Kottke had split them into 120 searchable Microsoft Word documents on three Macintosh floppy discs that somehow made it to John Perry Barlow. It is the first time Barlow has ever held a complete compendium of his own work.

One part of that transaction's magic is the achievement of sharing useful content through the network. But another even more astonishing fact is the resilience of the data, that it held from machine to machine with some kind of life force of its own. Something inside of it made it self-replicating and alive, something begging to be copied and shared and listened to and sung.

Barlow and Kottke become pals, one more bit of Deadhead networking, at which Barlow is as adept as anyone. Established as a user on the WELL, the San Francisco dial-up message board, John Perry Barlow jumps full force into the new digital universe and uncorks a public personality previously unseen anywhere in the network, either offline or online. Eloquent and funny, Barlow emerges as a star on the WELL amid a community of tech journalists, science fiction writers, programmers, and Deadheads, the social and economic glue of the entire system.

There are regular WELL gatherings at the network's home office in Sausalito next to the houseboats that bob in the pleasant Marin weather. It is networking par excellence, the rich community of WELL beings. But John Perry Barlow keeps climbing.

AND, OH SHIT, here come the bad trips.

There've been bummers before, but the reaper has arrived in Grateful Deadland, and the karmic Hells Angels are pushing their way to the front of the stage. There are too many people around the Dead, and bad stuff is starting to happen.

The Dead come through Hartford, Connecticut, in '88, where eighteen-year-old Timothy Tyler is a busboy. He has never heard of the Grateful Dead. His girlfriend's sister tells him about the people who are camped downtown, on the lawn of the governor's mansion. Tim goes down there. There is someone passing out LSD and Tim takes some. He wanders around all night, just looking at the sights and the strangeness. He sees people selling nitrous, and the massive crowds curling towards the tank-hiss transform into cartoonish dollar signs in Tim Tyler's already troubled teenaged mind.

When he finally *sees* a Dead show, a few days and some five states later in Illinois, someone gives him acid again. "I began to really love the feeling and energy that was at this concert," Tyler will write years later. "The music felt and sounded better than any I had ever heard. I decided right there that I would be seeing this band whenever I can. The show ended and I went outside. I walked up to the first person that I saw and asked him if he knew where I could get some LSD. I was steered in the right direction and I bought 200 hits for $99."

And, ugh, do we really have to go on? No good is going to come by learning the specifics of the story of Timothy Tyler right now, but that is one way that bad stories can start. He is not the type of person who should be doing acid, let alone in those quantities.

There's another guy, too, who gets nabbed in June 1988 with 11,751 hits of blotter during the Dead's run at Alpine Valley in Wisconsin. Because the hits are on paper, heavy when weighed, the new mandatory minimum sentences kick in and he's sentenced to twenty years in jail. It's ugly. Real ugly. He's not even a big player, just a mid-level kid dealing acid on paper who gets nabbed. The word around the parking lot is that two federal agents had come into the show and pulled him out.

OUT IN THE Whelming Brine floats the Rest of the World and, there, 1988 sees an unexpected development: the rise of acid house in the UK. The Chicago club music—whose progenitor Frankie Knuckles had been responsible for the psychedelic punch at the influential Manhattan disco the Gallery—had made its way to London by way of Ibiza. The music hadn't been really druggy until it'd gotten to Spain. Then the ecstasy hits. Someone declares it a second Summer of Love. In London, there are clubs with names like Shoom and Phuture and the Trip and a #1 hit, "We Call It Aceeeid." And while some of these pogoing, hand-waving Brits are on LSD, most of them are on ecstasy. No matter what drugs they're on, it's enough for a public scare. Bright yellow happy faces are ubiquitous. Like disco before it, much of the new music doesn't seem psychedelic at all, but it marks a turn in a wild international dialogue and a gathering cultural force of its own. The British free festival scene had only been broken up in 1985. There are heads waiting.

ALONG WITH THE American LSD market rise in the late '80s comes an almost unthinkably massive injection of currency into the taper network: a cache of pristine Grateful Dead concert recordings made between

1971 and 1980 by Betty Cantor-Jackson, onetime Dead soundwoman. Along with the LSD network, the tapers' alternative music distribution is among the Grateful Dead world's massive contributions to the underground infrastructure, an accidental public project as vast as the Roman aqueducts.

The private release of the so-called Betty Boards quantifies thousands of memories, perhaps millions, and their spread makes the network stronger. The new old tapes are a further energy source driving the present-day Grateful Dead, as if they had released several dozen new albums simultaneously.

Psychedelics and taping continue to travel together in a graceful yin-yang formation, the magnetic recordings communicating the alchemical truth of the Dead's flights with a surprising accuracy. By contrast with the dread LSD, the magnetic tapes are safe and benevolent. Or are they? In the Deadhead religion, the tapers are the keepers of the relics, the protectors and promoters who keep the hip economy churning and the Diggers' idea of *free* spreading into frat houses and high schools and head shops. The tapes are powerful vessels, worth following because of the force with which they travel and the ways they map new courses for information.

And then there's Dick! Dick! Acid-loving, sweet, and frenzied tape-collecting Grateful Dead freak Dick Latvala! A few years earlier, he'd been hanging at Dead's office in San Rafael, playing a mix of his favorite primal Dead for a friend when bassist Phil Lesh came up behind him, probably hearing him scream, *"it's better than Beethoven!"* or some variation. Dick sits Phil down, makes him listen to some '68 jammage, and soon Dick has a job as the band's tape archivist.

He reports to work dutifully each day at the Dead's Front Street tape vault for his miraculous job, probably fortified by bong hits or a joint or something or other, maybe naively hoping that he won't be sabotaged in some way by a roadie or psychedelic bureaucracy. Life is sometimes hell for Dick, our conflicted archetype for what the long haul can look like in psychedelic America.

Even at a historical distance, one wants to give the guy a hug and talk about anything but the Grateful Dead. Maybe Philip K. Dick or the gospel music Dick saw in Oakland in the early '60s. Dick and his wife Carol divorced in the early '80s, around the time they both moved back to California from Hawaii. But, like some self-achieving

The original lineup of The Fugs, East Village's psychedelic folk-punk poets, 1965, including serious heads Peter Stampfel and Steve Weber also of the Holy Modal Rounders. L–R: Steve Weber, Ken Weaver, Peter Stampfel (standing), Tuli Kupferburg (sitting), Ed Sanders. *Photograph by David Gahr/Getty Images*

Inventor of high-fidelity Grateful Dead concert taping Marty Weinberg, 1970. *Courtesy of Marty Weinberg*

Chad Stickney, the pioneering graffiti artist known as LSD-OM, in front of his first major piece, made in 1972 on the Grand Concourse in the Bronx and documented in 1974. In the late 1960s, Chad and his friends were Central Park's first connection to the LSD-distributing Brotherhood of Eternal Love. *Photograph by Flint Gennari*

The Grateful Dead with Ken Babbs (Merry Pranksters) and Naked Pole Guy (unaffiliated) at the August 27, 1972, benefit for the Springfield Creamery at the Old Renaissance Faire Grounds in Veneta, Oregon. An unrepeatable American psychedelic tableau. *Courtesy of Sam Field*

The light tower constructed for the Springfield Creamery benefit in 1972 would become an Oregon Country Fair landmark as the site grew into one of the Northwestern heads' most beloved summer destinations.

Courtesy of Sam Field

Jerry Moore and Harvey Lubar of the Bronx-based Hell's Honkies tape club pose with the Uher reel-to-reel once belonging to legendary Grateful Dead taper Marty Weinberg, 1975. *Courtesy of Harvey Lubar*

David Wilkins and Paul Martin of the Stanford Artificial Intelligence Lab following the Grateful Dead, 1974. *Courtesy of David Wilkins*

Paul Martin, founder of early Deadhead e-mail list dead.dis@SAIL, at the Stanford Artificial Intelligence Lab, 1974. *Courtesy of David Wilkins*

Early Deadhead fan art ironed onto a hotel hand towel, circa 1973. *Courtesy of Steve Brown*

Steve Brown of Grateful Dead Records in the Deadheads booth, collecting signatures for the all-important mailing list, 1974. *Courtesy of Steve Brown*

Dick Latvala in his tape room outside Hilo, Hawaii, mid-1970s, holding one of his annotated tape notebooks. *Courtesy of Carol Latvala*

MAY 8, 1977

PLACE: BARTON HALL - CORNELL UNIV., ITHICA, N.Y.

TAPE HISTORY: RECEIVED FROM JERRY MOORE (7-5-77) ON MAXELL (UD)
REEL AT 3¾ IPS. SECOND GENERATION, DOLBYIZED, AUDIENCE TAPE,
LASTING ABOUT 2½ HRS.

(2ND SET)

★ NEW NEW MINGLEWOOD BLUES   ✗ SCARLET BEGONIAS →
★ LOSER   → FIRE ON THE MOUNTAIN →
  EL PASO   → SCARLET BEGONIAS
★ THEY LOVE EACH OTHER   ESTIMATED PROPHET
★ JACK STRAW   ✗ ST. STEPHEN →
  DEAL   → NOT FADE AWAY →
★ LAZY LIGHTNING → SUPPLICATION   → ST. STEPHEN →
★ BROWN-EYED WOMAN   → MORNING DEW
★ MAMA TRIED   (ENCORE)
  ROW JIMMY   SATURDAY NIGHT
 ★ DANCING IN THE STREETS

COMMENTS

7/14/77 - AFTER A FEW HEARINGS I REMAIN PRETTY CONVINCED THAT
THIS IS THE BEST SHOW I'VE YET HEARD FROM THE 1977 TOUR.
OF COURSE, THERE ARE SHOWS WHERE THEY EXCELL ON SOME OF THE
ABOVE TUNES, BUT OVER-ALL, I HAVEN'T HEARD A FINER SHOW.
EVERY SONG IS DONE WELL & WHAT IS ESPECIALLY NICE, IS
THAT THEY PUT EXTRA CHARGE INTO SOME OF THEIR AGE-OLD
STANDARDS, THAT USUALLY ALWAYS SOUND THE SAME. THE JAM
THAT ENDS THE 2ND SET IS OUTSTANDING. IT HAS TO BE ONE OF THE
BEST "NOT FADE AWAY'S" I'VE EVER HEARD. THE QUALITY IS VERY EXCELLENT;
IT "SPARKLES" WITH CLARITY. I ALMOST FORGOT TO MENTION THAT
"MORNING DEW" WAS POSSIBLY THE BEST VERSION YET, WITH
A BURNING FINISH, IN MANY WAYS SIMILAR TO THE ENDING
RUSH OF "CASEY JONES"
4/24/83 - ENOUGH CAN'T BE SAID ABOUT THIS SUPERB SHOW. THE
"MORNING DEW" IS WITHOUT ANY DOUBT, THE MOST ROUSING &
THRILLING ONE EVER. THE QUALITY IS EXCELLENT, REGARD -
LESS WHAT ROB BERTRANDO MAY SAY.

Excerpt from Dick Latvala notebook.
Courtesy of Carol Latvala

Bilrock, founder of the Rolling Thunder
Writers, in Rumsey Playfield, Central
Park, 1976. *Courtesy of Bilrock*

Bilrock in front of Bilrock & Revolt subway car, 1979. *Courtesy of Bilrock*

Early Bilrock graffiti (as "Sage"), 1976. *Courtesy of Bilrock*

Central Park LSD dealer and graffiti artist Johnny Crunch with nunchaku in the abandoned 91st Street train station on Broadway, 1977. *Photo by Ali. Courtesy of Johnny Crunch*

Bathroom at the Mother Goose Playground—now Central Park's Summerstage–tagged up one night circa 1975 by Johnny Crunch and SIE-1 with remaining art supplies and rainbow blotter. *Courtesy of Johnny Crunch*

Graffiti artist Bilrock, around the time he cut his hair and became an East Coast/ West Coast connection for LSD crystal between the Bay Area and Central Park, late 1979. *Courtesy of Bilrock*

Steal Your Face silkscreen by Keith Haring, 1977, used to make bootleg T-shirts. The first artwork sold publicly by the world-renowned artist. *Courtesy of Barbara Clarke. Keith Haring artwork © Keith Haring Foundation*

Stanford Artificial
Intelligence Lab programmer
David Wilkins juggling at
Red Rocks, 1978. *Courtesy of
David Wilkins*

A Deadhead tour book covered in bootleg stickers by Eric Schwartz, early 1980
(with Built To Last promo added later).

Deadhead photographer and teenage acid networker Jay Blakesberg, early 1980s, long before an illustrious professional photography career. *Courtesy of Jay Blakesberg*

An early incarnation of the Deadheads' portable Shakedown Street vending community outside Oakland Auditorium, early 1980s. *Photo by Jay Blakesberg*

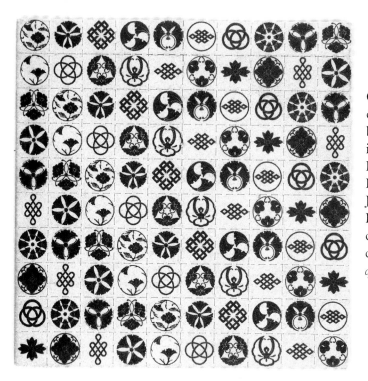

One of the earliest complete pieces of blotter art archived in Mark McCloud's Institute of Illegal Images known as the Japanese Seals, 1976. Part of the "iso" series of paper that has been dipped in LSD. *Courtesy of Mark McCloud*

Blotter art featuring J. R. "Bob" Dobbs, 1980. Clip-art figure-head of the Church of the SubGenius, a psychedelic art-prankster collective originating in Texas in the early 1980s, Dobbs appeared on LSD even before the widespread publication of the *Book of the SubGenius* in 1983. *Courtesy of Mark McCloud*

An undated piece of full-sheet blotter acid containing 250 hits of LSD that depict a wide range of imagery borrowed from the Beatles, avant-garde band the Residents, the movie *Airplane*, Disney and Warner Brothers, cartoonist R. Crumb, and much more. *Courtesy of Mark McCloud*

The "Gorby [blotter] that brought the Berlin Wall down," in the words of collector Mark McCloud, depicting Russian president Mikhail Gorbachev, 1988. Popular on Grateful Dead tour and across Europe alike. *Courtesy of Mark McCloud*

LSD art moves into the1990s with a modification of Mike Judge's Beavis and Butt-head.
Courtesy of Mark McCloud

The front cover of pioneering tech/psychedelic magazine *High Frontiers* #2, edited by R. U. Sirius, designed by The Lord Nose, 1984.
Courtesy of Marc Franklin

The Bread and Puppet Theater's Our Domestic Resurrection Circus summer pageant in Glover, Vermont, 1982. *Photo by Walter S. Wantman/Creative Commons*

Joseph and the Spinners, the Deadhead sub-cult that created a theology based on ecstatic sufi-like spinning and Grateful Dead music, Kaiser Auditorium, mid-1980s. *Photo by Jay Blakesberg*

Larry Bloch (right), founder of New York's Wetlands Preserve, who funneled club profits into a radical environmental action center, 1989. The headlamp of the club's VW Microbus (housing environmental literature) is visible at right.
Courtesy of Laura Bloch Bourque

September 1989 Wetlands Preserve calendar by Laura Bloch, 1989.
Courtesy of Laura Bloch Bourque

Jacaeber Kastor, owner of New York's Psychedelic Solution gallery, in Wirikuta, Mexico, 1990. In Mexico to meet the Huichol ~arn artist Cristobal Gonzalez, Kastor was afforded a rare visit to the sacred ~ace where the peyote grows. *Courtesy of Jacaeber Kastor*

Cigarette in hand, New York art critic Carlo McCormick rides a horse for the first time in Wirikuta, Mexico, 1990. McCormick (who'd thrown LSD-fueled parties in Manhattan's East Village in the '80s) would end up in a Mexican prison on trumped-up charges, a pawn in an international drug war. *Courtesy of Jacaeber Kastor*

Karen Horning, mid-1990s, in federal prison following her arrest for selling LSD crystal to a DEA informant. *Courtesy of Last Gasp*

Artifacts left on the Jerry Garcia memorial altar in Golden Gate Park following his death in August 1995 and preserved in the Grateful Dead Archive. Unpreserved in the archive were not-insignificant amounts of marijuana and LSD. *Photographs by Scott Carlson. Courtesy of Grateful Dead Archive, McHenry Library, UC Santa Cruz*

THE FOLLOWING IMAGES, EXCLUDING THE LAST ONE, ARE EXCERPTS FROM
THE PIONEERS SERIES, AN ONGOING SERIES OF TRANSPERSONAL PORTRAITS
OF PSYCHEDELIC PIONEERS BY MARC FRANKLIN, TAKEN 1988-2015.

Albert Hofmann, discoverer of LSD. *Photograph by Marc Franklin*

Allen Ginsberg, poet and psychedelic networker. *Photograph by Marc Franklin*

Jerry Garcia, Grateful Dead guitarist. *Photograph by Marc Franklin*

Nick Sand, underground psychedelic chemist of Orange Sunshine LSD and beyo

Photograph by Marc Franklin

n Scully, underground LSD chemist trained by Owsley Stanley and one-time
ateful Dead sound assistant. *Photograph by Marc Franklin*

Dennis McKenna, ethnobotanist. *Photograph by Marc Franklin*

Terence McKenna, author and psychedelic advocate. *Photograph by Marc Franklin*

Alexander "Sasha" Shulgin, independent psychedelic chemist whose scholarly pursuits set the course for a new generation. *Photograph by Marc Franklin*

Ann Shulgin, independent psychedelic researcher and writer.
Photograph by Marc Franklin

Mark McCloud, artist and founder of the Institute of Illegal Images in San Francisco, collecting LSD blotter art. *Photograph by Marc Franklin*

Sarah Matzar, Mayan quilter and underground LSD chemist.
Photograph by Marc Franklin

Xochi Speaks poster by Marc Franklin, minus detailed informational text depicting psychoactive compounds. L–R: DOB, THC, DMT, 5-Meo-DMT LSD, Mescaline, Psilocybin, MDA, 2C-B, Harmaline, MDMA, Ketamine.

Courtesy of Marc Franklin

hex from Morehouse, the commune-cult Dick and Carol Latvala once belonged to, they both wind up working for the Grateful Dead, Dick in the vault, Carol at the ticket office. They stay friends, too. But the truth is that Dick drinks a lot now, and that's really a bummer. He's as committed to LSD as he ever was, of course, as well as the Grateful Dead. He has an *Aoxomoxoa* tapestry hanging in his bedroom, still.

They're not *always* mean to him, the roadies. Sometimes, he and veteran crew taper Kidd Candalerio go up to Kidd's house on the Russian River, turn the speakers toward the water, and blast tapes at top volume to figure out what's on them. And Dick gets paid for this! In no way is this something Dick ever forgets. He's become friends with Dead lyricist Robert Hunter, of all people. They hang out at Front Street and other times have winding phone conversations about arcane corners of philosophy and their views on life. Just friends.

ALL OF THIS is the psychedelic America that Phish sees when they open the back door of their rented white box truck at the Colorado border in late July 1988. They take pictures next to the Welcome to Colorful Colorado sign and pull into Telluride to discover that they've been royally screwed by the promoter. Reluctantly, he agrees to let them play at his downtown basement venue, Roma. As bleak as it might seem, they've arrived at a fertile place to begin their career on the road, and a test case for many bands to follow.

A few blocks from where Babatunde Olatunji and Mickey Hart had welcomed the Harmonic Convergence the summer before, Phish set up in their odd configuration—all four at the front of the stage, drummer in a dress—and play for six nights. One evening their drummer takes too much acid and gets lost on the mountain, so their guitarist takes over behind the kit for a set of jazz standards and they play anyway. The band brings word of Nancy to Colorado.

And a tape trader named Michael Lynch pops cassettes in the soundboard and documents as many of the sets as he can, sometimes recording over other cassettes. The band sputter back East in the box truck, their profits stolen before they cross the Colorado state line. But the tapes stay behind, at least until Michael Lynch starts feverishly copying and sharing them.

ɌT ɌLPINE VɌLLEY in the summer of '88, 40,000 people watch the Dead inside the venue and another 20,000 stay in the parking lot and party.
Timothy Tyler's rampage continues, the bad trips here to stay. He
starts off selling fruit smoothies.

"My friend gave me a sheet of LSD to walk around with," he writes
later. "I found someone who was willing to trade some opium for what
I had. I had never tried opium before so I traded."

This part of the story ends with Timothy Tyler walking down the
side of the highway a few states away. When the cops arrive and ask
where he's going, he tells them a Dead concert. Feeling the opium, he
tells them he is Jesus. "They ended up beating me up as I was telling
them that I loved them," he will write.

Timothy Tyler is probably not an aficionado of Frank Zappa's
hippie-mocking "Who Needs the Peace Corps," with its narrator
who "love[s] the police as they kick the shit out of me on the street,"
but Frank Zappa would recognize Timothy Tyler. Timothy Tyler is
personifying a long-deferred darkness in the Grateful Dead world at
large, ponging around the outer periphery, a signal, a dark ink in the
stream. Timothy Tyler is not a bad person. Timothy Tyler needs help.

8

WETLANDS PRESERVE

The mural is hideous and yet the mural will become a portal. It wraps around the interior of the new Manhattan club at the command of its owner, a thirty-six-year-old longhair named Larry Bloch. Larry has never owned a nightclub before 1989. Larry had barely ever *been* to a nightclub before his vision for an ecosaloon. But here he is about to conjure something up for real, an important new transfer station for psychedelic America. The name had come along with the vision: the Wetlands Preserve.

A bar for environmentalists and community organizers, that's what Larry Bloch thinks he's opening. In New York City. DJs and dancing. Maybe some acoustic music. Food. Higher consciousness. Larry's wife Laura thinks it's fairly batty but goes along with it. By the time they're getting ready to open in late 1988, she does most of the translating with the contractors who are helping to build what Larry has in his stonydreamymoody mind. Even if Larry Bloch can't always communicate it, he can absolutely visualize it.

The contractors install the beautiful wooden shingles around the kitchen and hang the handcrafted light fixtures, paste the wall with several thousand dollars' worth of posters from Jacaeber Kastor's Psychedelic Solution in the Village. Laura does much of the craftwork herself and designs the club's logo. Downstairs, there will be a second bar and a room filled with low comfortable couches for people to sit and talk and, if they want, get stoned.

From a technical perspective, the wraparound mural is quite well executed. It's by an artist named Breck Morgan. The realist nature painting begins behind the small platform where the cafe tables are going to go, depicting a literal wetlands of reeds and birds. But then the image opens up and wraps around the dance floor in front of the DJ booth and shows a pastoral hippie scene replete with beatific children ring dancing in the center, a utopian pre-Rainbow Ur-gathering in a lush meadow.

Larry Bloch could melt right into the mural. No longer sporting a beard, he resembles a gangly overgrown elf with a slight hardening around the eyes. As Larry and Laura were investigating nightclubs, a real estate broker got them on several guest lists around town, where the Blochs were the complete unhip opposite of the normal clientele. Laura was also seven months pregnant. "They looked right through you, like you weren't there," Laura says, getting turned away at the Heartbreak, despite being on the guest list. Finally they'd made their way inside the Limelight, the crème de la crème of New York nightlife in the late '80s.

And the Blochs think it's bullshit, the lines and the judging and the bad vibrations. Larry wants raw space. Larry wants nooks. He wants to foster interaction. He wants patrons to feel like they're hanging out in his living room. He wants someplace people can feel comfortable tripping. He wants a bar and a separate hang-out spot. He wants someplace where he can DJ his Dead tapes at proper volume. Go, Larry!

He also wants to save the planet. Larry and a French-born environmentalist named Remy Chevalier design a financial structure for the club. While the bar remains for profit, a portion of the proceeds will always go toward a full-time and mostly independent activism center. That's central to the whole scheme, the breathing reason at the center, the idea that welds Wetlands to theoretical hip economics. Even in the 1980s, Larry Bloch suggests, there are new ways to channel the money streams.

Says Larry, "The idea [was to have] an organization, an enterprise—in this case, a nightclub, but it could be any kind of enterprise—that would devote its resources, its energies, its support, its vision, to an in-house group of people that worked for the enterprise running—with guidance—a full-time environmental and social justice organization. . . . It's just like paying the rent."

There are all kinds of different hip economic models, and Larry Bloch is working out a new combination of factors. Larry Bloch also has at least one other ace in his pocket. Bedsack.

His father, Ephraim Bloch, invented the Bedsack. It is a sack that goes over a bed. Larry is heir to a bedware fortune. "He completely changed the character of the industry in 1976 when he invented Bedsack Bedclothing," one of Ephraim's friends would later remember. It is another truth of hip economics. If each town doesn't have its own Owsley to fund its Free Press and its rock band and its communes, then perhaps it at least has a couple of righteous people who have family money they're willing to spread among friends and the universe at large. Gazillionaire Billy Hitchcock kept Timothy Leary and others afloat for years. Many fine bands and communes and cults and publications have launched as such. If one has money to spare, it seems like a more proactive way to contribute to the universe than simply donating it to charity.

Priced out of Chelsea, the realtors politely push Larry to a spot south of Canal Street, just north of the World Trade Center, in the once-industrial southern Manhattan neighborhood soon known as TriBeCa. "It was quiet, to say the least," Larry says. "Most of the buildings down here were not even in use, in terms of the commercial buildings. Not that many people living down here, not that many tall buildings. It was really kind of cool.

"I fell in love with the neighborhood right away. It was out of the way, but it was a different type of place that was being built, anyway. It wasn't meant to be in the middle of the tourist district. There was open space. The Holland Tunnel was right there." Indeed it is, an open maw to suburban New Jersey and the entire country beyond.

It doesn't take long for Larry to notice that Wetlands' new home is at the cross of Hudson and Laight, a pleasant rhyme with that famous San Francisco street on the other side of the Holland Tunnel and down 3,000 miles of treacherous road, with a few safe stops along the way. If only there was a better way to fly.

Wetlands' finishing touch is the Microbus. Only a '66 or '67 will do. Those mythic times of Drop City and the *Modern Utopian* and the

Haight are the only era that Volkswagen produced the iconic vehicle with doors that opened from the side, and Larry Bloch absolutely needs his to open from the side so he can park it permanently inside Wetlands and distribute activist literature. They find a long-deceased '66 in a field in New Hampshire.

After Laura's dad helps refurbish the exterior, they haul the Microbus into Wetlands, just about done. The wrap-around mural, which continues over by the bus, is corny in the context of any nightclub, but it does the uncanny and not only isolates Wetlands from the smug-smog indigenous to Manhattan but actually provides transportation. When the garage door is welded shut behind the Microbus, the vehicle's side doors open up into the alternate psychedelic America. Its parking spot becomes a fresh-painted dot on Humbead's New, New Revised Unchecked Annotated Map of the World (fourth edition): the Wetlands Preserve at 161 Hudson Street.

There are several opening nights. The first evening the place is open to the public, a Virginia band named New Potato Caboose cram onto the tiny cafe platform to play Dead covers and their own originals. The band bring in their own sound system, too, which is good, because that's something Larry hasn't foreseen: bands.

He's just opening a bar to fund activism center, plain and simple, plus a solid system to play LPs and tapes. Larry and Remy had been sending press releases to various environmental organizations and causes for months. This band stuff is pretty different, but people seem to like it.

All their friends come and the place is packed. Remy meets Bedsack king Ephraim Bloch for the first and last time. "It wasn't exactly the A-list," Remy notes. The next night, there is nobody there. "I guess we're going to have to have bands," shrugs Remy.

KAREN HORNING WATCHES through binoculars. She watches from wherever she can on Grateful Dead tour. She wants to know what's going on. There is an incredible amount occurring out there on the road, especially Karen's mobile, psychedelic corner of it. Too much to know. There's a motel overlooking the Nassau Coliseum parking lot on Long Island that provides a good vantage point. Other times, she climbs to the top of a bus, either hers or her friends'. She's lost track of all the different vehicles she's traveled in by now.

She's from Maine, saw shows throughout New England, and started slinging acid around her hometown, bringing it back from Dead tour. She's just nineteen in 1989 and already a veteran of the mobile economy. She and a friend sell clothing sometimes. She sews velvet hats. He makes shirts.

"Andy was one of the first who could fold out a Steal Your Face with a space in the middle," Karen says about her partner's considerable tie-dye skills. "There were a lot of head shops across the country and you could set up accounts and sell things there," she says, and they would stop by as the Dead passed through various towns to settle accounts.

"I used to sell food. We would sell chicken and beer. Down at Irvine Meadows, I made several grand selling beer. I was one of the first to sell the imports. Everybody else was selling Budweiser. I didn't drink Budweiser, I wasn't going to sell Budweiser."

She feels the same way about acid. There's stuff going around on tour called Tornado Juice, and, Karen knows this much, it is not acid. As far as she knows, it's ALD-52, a psychedelic analogue that certainly is capable of blasting through to the other side but is not actually the classic combo.

"*Zippy zippy zing-zing, zippy zippy zing-zing,*" is how Karen describes the juice. "It's heavy trails, like being in a pinball machine. *Zingzingzing.*"

The stuff she's starting to sell is the real stuff, extra clean, actual honest-to-Owsley LSD-25. "Easy on, easy off," she says. "You can take a nap.

"We used to have friends who were having trouble because people would think they were getting ripped off," she says. "But it took an hour to ease yourself in. My friend got jumped in the park by someone who thought he was being ripped off, but it was like, 'your girlfriend's over there talking to a tree. She's at one with this tree, and you're swearing that you got ripped off?'"

Karen is also young and smart and vivacious and organized, almost manically so. She knows the touring scene inside and out. There are a lot of people in the lot these days, but not that many. If you watch.

The band themselves estimate that there are about 5,000 people on the road in the summer of '89—roughly the population of a small-to-medium-sized college campus. Karen Horning gets to know the faces. From a distance, she can tell who the undercovers are, watches them haul away low-level dealers, and knows that the undercovers are locals. The undercovers always stick out like sore thumbs and never show up anywhere else on tour. She doesn't carry drugs around the lot anyway, give or take for personal use. She's past that, and going further.

On tour, she's almost always the driver. She trips a lot, which keeps her awake. That's a key to safe tour driving. Staying awake. Too many Deadheads get hurt by nodding off at the wheel during a long haul.

Soon it will be showtime. Karen always goes in. Jerry-side. Sometimes, she dances. Sometimes, she's just too high. The important thing is to be there, to be with the music. She watches, she waits, and she works, and the real stuff will come to her.

ONE DAY IN the spring of '89, John Perry Barlow wrangles a +1 to visit the trendiest groupmind in the West and brings along Jerry Garcia. The acidheads have really done it this time. They'll be mocked soon enough, but Barlow and Garcia are getting to peek at something that is legitimately a quarter century ahead of its time, which in Garcia's case is especially wondrous.

Lately, Barlow had used the WELL, the Bay Area online service, to kick-start a burgeoning and reluctant tech journalism career, applying his acidhead cattle-rancher libertarian mysticism to profiles and general pontification. Via *MicroTimes* editor and Deadhead WELL-being Mary Eisenhart, Barlow scores assignments interviewing Steve Jobs and other players. Barlow still dresses the part of statesman with an ascot atop his western wear, replacing it with a bandana in situations of appropriate ruggedness.

For the trip to AutoDesk, Barlow rouses Garcia, who is more open to getting out since his miraculous postcoma recovery. When Barlow and Garcia visit AutoDesk's San Rafael headquarters, not far from the Dead office, the tech firm is the fifth biggest in the industry and one of the headiest. The money maker is AutoCAD, rendering software for architects and engineers, but founder John Walker has higher aspirations. They've got a big office complex with room to plug away at various future problems. Deep in the bowels is none other than Tim Scully, Owsley's onetime protégé and long-retired chemist for the Brotherhood of Eternal Love. Scully had jumped into engineering even before his late '70s prison sentence, and at AutoDesk he's just another qualified employee. In-house dreamers also include cyberdelic sci-fi novelist Rudy Rucker and Ted Nelson, author of '70s Silicon Valley classic *Computer Lib*.

But the most buzzed-about corner of AutoDesk, where John Perry Barlow has already been once, and the one that gets Jerry Garcia out of the house, the one that everyone else is going totally gaga for, may sound a bit laughable when it pops into your brain in T-minus one word, go: *virtual reality*. Or it might not. What year is this?

Barlow and Garcia visit with the team, strap the stereoscopic goggles over their faces, and transport themselves to the extended horizon-grid that the heads at AutoDesk have willed into being. They play with the geometric representations of their hands, pointing to move around. They look keenly to the distance of this new landscape, maybe not so different from other alternate landscapes Garcia and Barlow have shared in the past (or the ones Garcia has enjoyed during his recent scuba-diving expeditions).

"Technology is the new drugs," the nine-fingered guitarist crows. It's not a terribly original sentiment but that doesn't mean it's wrong. "They outlawed LSD. It'll be interesting to see what they do with this." Barlow, especially, is transfixed.

Virtual reality project leader Jaron Lanier is not pleased with the comparison of virtual reality to psychedelics. Jaron Lanier does not do psychedelics. But, it is also said, Jaron Lanier is one of those humans who just *is* psychedelic. With a solidly countercultural upbringing, he'd spent his teenage years in a geodesic dome that he helped design, plays many varieties of odd instruments, and sports massive dreadlocks.

"With a saxophone you'll be able to play cities and dancing lights, and you'll be able to play the herding of buffalos made of crystal," he proclaims to the *Whole Earth Review*. "And you'll be able to play your own body and chance yourself as you play the saxophone. You could become a comet in the sky one moment and then gradually unfold into a spider that's bigger than the planet that looks down at all your friends from high above."

But, besides Lanier, "to a man and a woman, the people behind [virtual reality] were acidheads," Mark Pesce would recall, himself a veteran psychonaut and key engineer at the cosmically named Shiva Corporation, who developed early dial-up modem technology. In a few years, Pesce will help originate virtual reality modeling language, VRML, for use by the coders of the future. AutoDesk hires Timothy Leary to be a talking head in a new promotional video.

It's like getting high without the drugs, of course. In the always-crowning New Age, something new is still waiting to be born. AutoDesk aren't only in it for the utopia. They can also make a ton of money. But what's not utopian about that? They've already licensed some of the basic technology to Power Glove, a Nintendo controller available by Christmas of '89.

AutoDesk's guest list doesn't do much to discourage the drug comparisons. Mushroom champion Terence McKenna drops by for a spin. "It seems highly unlikely that the development of VR will be treated as the spread of a new drug," he writes in New Age staple *Magical Blend*. "Rather, it is now seen as a new frontier for marketing and product development. . . . My hope is that virtual reality at its best may be the perfect mind space in which to experimentally explore and entrain the higher forms of visual linguistic processing that accompany tryptamine intoxication." For now, it will be neither. But not forever.

John Perry Barlow stays in the thick of the shtick. As if making up for lost time on the ranch in Wyoming, Barlow throws himself into all known territories, meeting and greeting and writing and dancing and becoming. He's too much of a troublemaker to be a politician, anyway.

He visits his onetime guru Timothy Leary for the first time in more than two decades. "Our brains are learning how to exhale as well as inhale in the data-sphere," the former Harvard professor tells him. For the first time in a while, Barlow admits that Timothy Leary sounds reasonable.

AT THE OAKLAND Coliseum, 1988 is turning into 1989 and twenty-three-year-old Chris Doyon talks to a pair of Deadheads who are getting married at the show. For a few years now, he's been so committed to various aspects of the psychedelic cause that he'd been skimping on some of his cosmic duties. Namely going to see the Grateful Dead. He's a very busy man. "They told me how they had spent the last year following [the band] and made it in every night," he remembers later. "That actually made me feel guilty for all the shows I neglected to even try to get in. I made a New Year's resolution to get to get *into* every show for the next year until I was back at the Coliseum." So he does. It all blurs together. "I was continuously tripping 24/7 for the better part of four years," he states, perhaps exaggerating only slightly.

For the longhaired redhead from New England, LSD had come first, soon thereafter (when he was fourteen) the Grateful Dead, and then radicalization. "In my opinion," he writes, "psychedelics have the power to strip away calcified, internalized, and trained learning foisted upon us by society. And if you happen to live (as we do) in a sick, demented, and dysfunctional society, then that is the truth that will be revealed to you—among others, such as metaphysical [ones]. It would be logical that if your mind survives that stripping, that you would act on that new truth and try and work to correct that society by whatever means available to you."

Initially drawn into the world of activism via the antiapartheid movement, Doyon's sense of injustice runs deep. Between Dead tours, Doyon spends time "releasing minks for the Animal Liberation Front in Oregon, burning shit in Colorado and California for the Earth Liberation Front, protesting on nearly every campus on the east coast [against] apartheid. I lived wherever there was either a show or an action, essentially." An avowed loner, he'd hitchhiked and taken Greyhounds, at least until there was money involved.

A wide reader and a natural drifter, Doyon had run away from home not long after his first Dead show in Augusta, Maine, in 1979 and ended up on Cambridge, ye olde quadrant on Humbead's Map and home to the very active Artificial Intelligence Lab at the Massachusetts Institute of Technology. Led by Richard Stallman, who, in his own estimate, followed the Dead for around five years, the lab was as bustling as any lab of futurists anywhere.

What Chris Doyon finds on Dead tour is different. He finds nourishment. The music plays and the ideas germinate. There are many people germinating on Dead tour, most of them not a fraction as radical as Chris Doyon. One who rivals him, though for nearly completely opposite reasons, is a woman who's been seeing the Grateful Dead since the early 1980s. Though there will remain some dispute about when she was born and she won't recall her first show, Ann Coulter comes of Deadhead age during the '80s when, during the experimental space segments, the law clerk and future right-wing columnist will ignore the music and "go to the bathroom, get a hot dog." When she starts collecting tapes, Ann Coulter edits the space segments out altogether. Ann Coulter is proactively unheady. "No one who was not on drugs [liked space]," she will assert. Let's not talk about Ann Coulter. She might be a Deadhead, but she is no head.

Like LSD, Grateful Dead shows can work with only the material they receive. And when they receive Christopher Doyon of Maine, they help to turn him into Commander X, a cofounder of the Peoples Liberation Front, a group of protohackers who base themselves in Cambridge. Most of them are punks, except X, and this is a key difference, because it means X has access to LSD. And not just any LSD, but high-grade, straight-from-the-source, Grateful Dead tour LSD. His paths into the equally radical worlds of hardcore transgressive activism and high-level psychedelic distribution are exactly parallel. Importing the LSD back to Cambridge as so many Deadheads had imported LSD home before, the Peoples Liberation Front find themselves with a new source of funds.

"I don't recall it as being a specific conspiracy, per se," says X/ Doyon, another in a long line of heads to change a name to suit a new place. "It was more a matter of a sort of holistic circle of need. As hackers we always viewed LSD—and its distribution—as one of the ultimate hacks. A hack of people's minds, their beliefs and worldview. As such, we always felt compelled to distribute as much LSD as we possibly could. And while we saw it through that particular technological lens, the rest of the 'Acid Family' also saw it that way, but with a more 'spiritual' sort of focus."

As a radical organization, the Peoples Liberation Front finds many specific uses for their hip economic stream to hopefully effect change. They buy a van and outfit it with techno-protest gear for short-range FM stations sized to fit in backpacks. They generate their own 800 numbers and sell "chingers," phreaky boxes that yield free calls from payphones. In 1990, they begin the Prankster-like Operation CIA, setting out to spook the spooks away from recruiting on New England college campuses. And as the PLF activities begin to take off, the Dead shows become even more special for the Commander, "a chance to escape the world of the PLF without completely abandoning it," he writes. "A chance to get some space and think." At Dead shows, he is just Chris again.

"Tour was tour," Chris says. "It was all about the Dead and the music. We never mixed the two worlds, really. But we often took people off tour with us to actions, thus radicalizing them. My political activities didn't really revolve around 'protesting' per se. I was involved with groups like Animal Liberation Front and Earth Liberation Front and other 'domestic terrorist' organizations. You don't exactly stand around handing out flyers for shit like that. You mostly wait until a likely prospect expresses interest and then you poke into their background, and if they seem safe and useful you present them with an opportunity to join an action."

And tour is great. Doyon moves into higher and higher circles, learning the inside dope of the LSD trade, and there is a lot. One trick he picks up is "double dipping," a term that will enter the folklore with *extra special* connotations, like ice cream, but it's not that at all. "Sometimes if you had shit tons of paper and it took a really long time to get rid of it, or if you were careless about storage, the quality degraded," he explains. "So rather than discount it or trash it, you would make a weak solution, perhaps one-quarter strength or less, and dip it again. Thus, double-dipped. As for triple-dipped, yeah, that's a scam. If you are fucked enough to let acid go bad twice in a row, you should be selling [grilled] cheese, not LSD."

He moves into the liminal zones between the backstage and the outer reaches of Shakedown Street, the mysterious alleyways where worlds connect. There are bikers and old-world Prankster connections and even a mobile LSD lab. "It was like a big-ass Winnebago-type thing," Doyon says. "Relatively new, no stickers, well kept. My understanding is that it stayed well out of sight, tooling around the wilderness of Oregon and Northern California. It is in that setting that I encountered it several times during my Dead tour days."

Except, Doyon says, that one time when the Dead played Laguna Seca Raceway in Monterrey and it shows up backstage. "Backstage" at a Grateful Dead concert is a vast territory, a place band members only venture peripherally, as part of their commute to the stage itself, where they virtually live in their private tent-nooks. Backstage, inside its maze of equipment trucks and production trailers, other rules exist. Doyon speaks of being there at Laguna Seca, where he assists the Family and Ken Kesey himself in the dipping of blotter of Stanley Mouse and Alton Kelley album covers, famous hits. Maybe he did.

"While we all reveled in making shit tons of cash and living high, we also felt a strong impulse to get as much 'product' out there as cheaply as we could, sometimes for free," he says.

"As for using LSD distribution as a funding mechanism, there was no one moment when we said, 'hey, let's do this,' it just sort of happened. We made money at it, and as with anything made money at, it went straight into hacker gear and travel expenses for activism. After awhile it simply became a habit. One that happened to land my sorry ass in prison for five years."

Commander X goes back to being Chris Doyon, or more likely an inmate number, busted for selling three hundred hits of blotter to an undercover in Indiana. Meanwhile, the Peoples Liberation Front keep on liberating, getting more and more electronic, another band of psychedelic futurists not waiting for the future.

A HALF-DOZEN teenagers, male and female, meet at noon in a brownstone on 113th Street in New York City. In another, more real way, the children are our future. These children. These well-placed children. Some might know each other casually, but just as likely not. One by one, they are brought into the steam-filled bathroom of the brownstone and told of a Red Angel and a Blue Devil. Then given a dose of LSD.

Once tripping, guides bring the Neophytes into the city. The path is different each time this ritual is enacted. The first stop might be a church, where a little person in holy robes greets them with a suitcase and instructions to deliver it to a certain terminal at the airport, and off they go on what they now know to be their Odyssey.

The Neophytes tumble across surreal New York. Men in tuxedos greet them in Times Square and bring them to rooftop bars, perhaps. Their guides disappear, replaced by people they've never met. Outside the Stock Exchange, tour guides narrate visions of hell while leading them to the gallery over the trading floor.

Every six hours, the Neophytes get more acid, maybe some mushrooms, while trying to piece together what's happening. There is a party scene, likely, at a bar with a prechosen band, and then out to deepest scary Brooklyn for a very late-night stroll through Prospect Park for more encounters. Dawn passes, and by noon they're back at the brownstone on 113th Street where they began and where the Neophytes are allowed to fall into comfortable, warm sleeps.

When they wake, they are welcomed formally into their new home with a giant feast in the basement featuring many of the characters from their Odyssey. To all outside authorities, the brownstone is just another frat on Frat Row at the edge of the Columbia University campus in Morningside Heights, Manhattan. They pay their dues with the annual organization and all, but Alpha has a secret. Part of the secret is psychedelic, but the deeper secret is New York real estate.

As the story is passed down, it was in the mid-1980s that a group of Columbia heads infiltrated a dying fraternity to take over their sweet four-floor brownstone. They immediately dispensed with the many aspects of traditional frat life, going co-ed almost immediately. And while they don't practice Greek life as most college students understand it in the 1980s, Alpha Delta Phi are connecting themselves to a more ancient and authentic Greek culture: the mystery cults at Eleusis, brotherhood of Plato and Socrates and many others who drank the *kykeon,* made (in Albert Hofmann's estimation) from the same fungus as LSD.

The Delta Phis' groupmind-brain trust are smart. After all, they're Columbia students with Western civilization history requirements in the college's renowned core curriculum. Most Odyssey participants have actually read the *Odyssey.* But they have no idea of their connection to the ancient psychedelic practice, only that they have found themselves in the midst of their own ritual. Given a blank slate, this is their creation.

Another psychedelic ritual that the fraternity organizes is Reality Fest, an annual all-campus party at the student center, paid for with university budgets. It's bad form to say it out loud, but Reality Fest is a giant Trips Festival, with bands playing throughout the building, which also houses other vibey environments with sitar players and soul records and whatnot. (Wesleyan, too, has its own twice-a-year psychedelic equivalents, too, Uncle Duke Day and Zonker Harris Day. Who knows how many other well-heeled colleges indirectly funded psychedelic rituals?)

Not everyone at Reality Fest is on acid, of course, but not everyone needs to be. It's well known in the lore that a critical mass of trippers creates an altered atmosphere for all. For that matter, not everyone who lives at the frat participates in the Odyssey, nor does everyone who participates in an Odyssey wind up living at the brownstone.

In early 1989, a young Princeton band called Blues Traveler show up to play a party at the frat. A few months later, their friends' band, the Spin Doctors, will play their first show anywhere in the house basement. Driven by lightning harmonica and metaloid blues hammer shreddage, Blues Traveler's music wraps itself into the contours of late '80s Deadland. Both bands will find their way to Larry Bloch's Wetlands Preserve and the rest of the country soon.

There is an entire nation bred on *In the Dark*–era Grateful Dead, waiting for the next "Touch of Grey," ready to dance to music that's made by their own. Everywhere there are Odysseys. Odysseys need music. Everywhere there are Blues Travelers.

IN THE 1988 edition of the *Journal of Drug Issues,* available at a medical library near you, *Psychedelic Monographs and Essays* editor Thomas Lyttle catalogues drug-based religions and contemporary drug taking. By "drugs," Lyttle means psychedelics and leaves out, for example, the Rasta. He charts minihistories of Manhattan's DPT-smoking Temple of the True Inner Light and others, including the recently christened New American Church of Albany, New York, whose ritual LSD-taking "tube parties" feature blaring hypercut videos. "SYNCHRONIC-ITY FOR DIVINATION," their literature reads.

"Drug-based religions collectively fall into two broad philosoph-ical/ethical categories," Lyttle writes, "these being the deterministic/ iconic and the situational. The deterministic/iconic offers sacrament or communion (in drug-based form) contingent upon a central deity and usually with some corresponding liturgy and secularization so far as initiation, indoctrination, and other activities are concerned. The situational stance also involves an agreement so far as there being a connection between certain drugs and spirit. Conversely, however, the situational examples offer sacramental exposure without consistent catechism or theistic goals beyond what occurs spontaneously within each drug user's spirit."

Lyttle doesn't cover the Deadheads, or the portable liturgical structure provided by the Dead's two-sets-with-*jams* format, but nearly all of the *deterministic* applies to them, especially the ongoing secularization of the ritual, given the many thousands who regularly step into the Dead's temporary autonomous zone and *don't* trip. Nor does Lyttle make any mention of ayahuasca, the South American brew that is arriving on American shores almost exclusively in the form of academic citations, lab samples, and (of course) the unceasing raps of Terence McKenna.

"The ayahuasca cult still has not percolated down to recreational druggie circles in California," reports *Reality Hackers*, the latest iteration of *High Frontiers*, the tech/drug zine from Berkeley. Their pad in Berkeley is a thriving nexus as the magazine spits out the latest futurist sky writings from the Bay Area and beyond. If a psychoactive drug is trending, it'll show up at their place.

Psychedelics and tech continue to live side by side at *Reality Hackers*, especially as John Perry Barlow comes on board as a *Reality Hackers* writer, by now a one-man historical combustion of the magazine's two themes. Like Neal Cassady connecting the Beats to the Merry Pranksters and the Dead, John Perry Barlow now stands as a conscious bridge between the old counterculture and the new.

The *Hackers* gang raise money for yet another transformation, into a newer magazine called *Mondo 2000*. One Dutch investor, a mild-mannered tech entrepreneur, tries acid for the first time at a Hackers Conference and soon moves to the Bay Area, has "some amazing mystical experiences," visits Esalen, and begins "to see computers in a much wider and more spiritual context." He opens a small store to sell brain-machines, smart drugs, and other new tech. In the thrall of it all, he co-pens a manifesto of Silicon brotherhood. He and the newly christened *Mondo 2000* gang are what Thomas Lyttle would call "situational" trippers. Their sacramental icon is the future and the future is always.

RICK DOBLIN STARTS sending out newsletters for the Multidisciplinary Association for Psychedelic Studies from his new quarters in Cambridge. Working on a master's in public policy at Harvard, Doblin's MAPS becomes an umbrella for the newly emerging class of respectable psychedelic society. Like many big-dreaming psychedelic takers, their plans are audacious, but Doblin thinks they can do it. MAPS wants nothing less than a return to formal scientific research on psychedelics and other psychoactive substances.

MDMA can become a legal medicine used for therapy, Doblin had emphasized in his first modest newsletter. His second, sent out in the summer of 1989, reports some progress. In Switzerland, ever-neutral birthplace of LSD, scientists are again working with acid, along with MDMA, DMT, mescaline, and 2C-B. In the States, the National Institute on Drug Abuse research is getting under way, and Doblin's newsletter makes a call for volunteers for an all-expense paid trip to Johns Hopkins in Baltimore to take part in risk assessment studies.

Doblin doesn't report on it yet, but in New Mexico a doctor named Rick Strassman is working tirelessly to design a formal study of DMT, a drug that he will theorize as "the spirit molecule." But he is having a hell of a time. The alien mindscapes produced by the drug are a much harder sell than MDMA therapy. After initially finding support among potential psychedelic researchers in the academic world, all jump ship when the project is miraculously ready to get going. They give a variety of reasons to Strassman, but most of it boils down to the fact that psychedelics are simply still too controversial. The threads of the long psychedelic renaissance continue to move around one another, not ready for unity. There is still too much chaos to be clear headed about it. For now, the drugs still belong to the heads.

MAPS estimates 400,000 ecstasy tablets are in circulation every month domestically on the black market in 1989. There are many differences between ecstasy and LSD, both pharmacologically and economically, but the parallels are strong as well.

The following year, an exchange at the New Music Seminar in Manhattan will highlight just how it works during the UK's so-called Summer(s) of Love in 1988 and '89. Happy Mondays, the scene's flagship band, "became the E dealers in Manchester," their manager will tell a room of semiscandalized music industry insiders, provocatively but not entirely inaccurately. "First it was the drugs, and then through drugs they found music."

ONE OF THE new buses on Grateful Dead tour in the summer of 1989 carries twenty-one students, two course assistants, and sociologist Rebecca Adams (with husband and daughter), leading her charges into the thriving hive of Grateful Dead culture, as big as it's ever been. And getting bigger. It's a wonder there aren't even more academics in this field. Grateful Dead shows present the ultimate multidisciplinary learning ground, encompassing music, spirituality, economics, pop culture, and so much more. Students and scholars can and will find ways to bend the Grateful Dead to nearly every area of study. The Grateful Dead offer something for any course level, from those content to listen to a greatest hits album to those who might want to approach the matter more experientially.

The formal name of Rebecca Adams's course is Field Research Methods and Applied Social Theory. Everybody just calls it Deadhead Sociology. Adams trains them in the work and methods of German neo-Kantian Georg Simmel. They travel by coach bus. The sociology professor strikes up a friendship with Dennis McNally, the onetime Kerouac biographer turned Dead publicist/liaison. The Grateful Dead are under a great deal of pressure from this strange and alien outside world by now, and Adams's class makes good press.

In fact, though, life on Grateful Dead tour is now starting to get out of control in an undeniable way. That spring, near riots at a Pittsburgh show made the national news feed. Eventually, local newspapers had come to the Dead's defense, and the mayor reversed her disinvitation to the band, but the tide is rising. The sociologist and her class are here to amass some of the first hard data about the phenomenon.

In a hotel in Virginia, waiting for her students, Rebecca Adams encounters Owsley. When the Dead tour, he magically reappears, selling his handcrafted jewelry at the Greenpeace table, bartering, and just generally hanging out.

"Bear found out who I was and he immediately tried to recruit me to be the sociologist who would help plan the community on the property he had purchased in Australia for after the Big Flood," Rebecca says. "His bigger plan was always to be in Australia when storm season hit because that was one of the only places where there was going to be anything left.

"He said something like, 'from the very beginning [of the Dead], we've always been looking for people who could fill certain roles,' and that they always needed a tribal sociologist." It's going to take more than a sociologist to make sense of all of this, anyway, to get down to the weird and beautiful and dangerous center of it all. There are many angles. Enter the anthropologist from stage right.

The anthropologist, whose name is Jenny Hartley, is not part of Rebecca Adams's class, but she finds them quickly enough and makes friends. She goes to an Ivy League school and is drawn immediately to the mystical spinners at the back of the venues' floors, the dancers who take over the available empty space and paint it with motion. Among them, she discovers a developing theology and a leader named Joseph.

The anthropologist takes up pretty naturally with the Spinners, a small tribe of ecstatic dancers that stakes the widest available territory to spin and spin and spin and spin and find bliss to the Dead. At first, she just hitches rides from show to show with friends but soon is just traveling with the Spinners themselves. She and Rebecca Adams have a joke: *sociologists sleep in hotels and anthropologists sleep under the bus.*

"She definitely went a lot more native than I did," Adams observes. "But she was also so young. I had a husband and daughter on tour." The Spinners are a few dozen strong by the time the anthropologist joins them for another Dead tour through the most goddamn gigantic venues throughout the Northeast. It's all stadiums. The idea of playing anything smaller is terrifying from a management point of view.

Dressing all in white, the Spinner women in long homemade or hand-tailored dresses, they call themselves the Family. The Spinners are bound to a long family tree of the Families. Joseph wheels, Joseph deals, Joseph keeps "20 or 30 people on tour who otherwise might not've been able to be on tour because of the logistics," says Luther

Delaney, a sometime ski patroller who travels with the Spinners but never fully surrenders himself.

"They ate *a lot* of psychedelics, even by my rather expansive standards," observes the acid Family dealer Chris Doyon / Commander X, who'd crossed paths with the Spinners out around Shakedown Street. "I never had any problem with them personally. I would never get into any vehicle driven by any of them though!"

The leader Joseph is able to whisk the Spinners from crash spot to crash spot. He is able to get them into shows. He is able to materialize their rituals in the outer industrial zones of ugly American cities, to find a place to be blissful, to dress in white, and to chant and to spin. The Spinners have what no other hippie cult before them had: the music of the Grateful Dead. They trip often, too, but it's the music that is paramount and they go where Garcia is.

On days when the Dead or the Jerry Garcia Band are playing, they eat only fruit and drink only juice, a purification. They need to be light. They don't want heavy stomachs while spinning. It is an act of reverence to fast; it is an act of devotion to spin.

Spinning is their meditation. The lyrics of Robert Hunter, as passed through the soul of Garcia, are their texts. But even more fundamental is Garcia's guitar playing, his note-clusters direct translations of the Logos, as valuable and real as what Terence McKenna speaks of when describing his DMT experiences. It's Jerry, the Spinners know.

And, what's more, the Spinners know, completely and perfectly, is that it is *not* Bobby. In the Spinners' mythology, there is the sacred and there is the profane, and Jerry Garcia is sacred and Bobby Weir is profane. "Bobby is seen as worldly and self-absorbed," observes the anthropologist, "both because of the songs he writes (with some notable exceptions) and his stage presence, while Jerry is frequently described as 'humble.'" And when it's finally possible to get close enough to Joseph the Spinner to realize that his basic rap is *Jerry: good, Bobby: silly,* one might pause to admire the dude's wisdom.

The anthropologist joins them. Tentatively, she starts to spin, as well, worrying that she's getting too close to her subject. She keeps a journal of her findings. She takes pictures.

During the set breaks, the Spinners sit and smoke pot and share fruit and talk about the first set. The Spinners don't worry about

good or bad, or how "China Cat Sunflower" stacked up to a '70s
version, or complain that they don't do the "Feelin' Groovy" tran-
sition anymore. No, the Spinners talk about what they *learned,* what
they *felt,* how particular lyrics resonated, what Jerry might've meant,
what the river looked like at this particular point in the stream. It is
this personal and spiritual analysis of the Grateful Dead's music that
makes the Spinners special. They possess a complete and thorough
understanding of an artist's repertoire and body of work and choose
to decode it in this way. There are several more recognized religious
groups on the Dead tour now, searching for followers, though none
are Deadheads.

There are Hare Krishnas out on Shakedown Street, visible
through the crowd with the shaved heads and robes. And one of the
Spinners can't help but notice the "meticulous burgundy bus with
all the woodwork on the inside" that has started to turn up at shows,
as well. It houses a first aid operation that treats a variety of parking
lot maladies including (per sociologist Rebecca Adams's field notes)
"acid overdoses, nitrous oxide drops, dog bites, sunburns, cut feet,
a woman who had ingested an entire bag of heroin, a man who fell
into a barbed wire fence, a woman with a rash from a jellyfish sting
that was spreading, and even a man who 'was having relations' with
the highway and ended up with a 'road rash.'"

Every so often, the bus-tenders emerge and perform on me-
dieval-looking acoustic instruments, dressed in ancient-seeming
garb. They don't go into the shows; they don't listen to the Dead.
Though they won't say it directly, the bus residents—coming from
the Island Pond community, near where Phish's Trey Anastasio
spent the summer of 1987 writing music—are here to *save* people
from having to go into shows, to save them in the name of the
Lord. Oy.

There are the rows of buses out in the lot, forming temporary
geographies. There's a school bus with the top of VW affixed to it
that's been there since the early '80s. Another bus has a terrarium.
One double-decker is known as the Burrito Bus. People have pets
and bunks and kitchens. There's a guy who sells spare parts for VW
bugs and buses. It's the Whole Earth honking down the highway on
gypsy wheels.

Whatever one imagines is going on in the parking lot is probably going on in the parking lot, a temporary autonomous zone filled with teenage runaways and radicals and grad students and professors and people who never quite got out of their hometowns until the Dead vacuumed them up. There are scores of high school kids and local thugs looking to make a buck and some stray straight-edge punk rockers and trustifarians and drug dealers and Hog Farmers and Wharf Rats and the gay and lesbian heads and too many others to name. It's the Grateful Dead; there's a space and place for everyone.

The crowd inside Dead shows is an enormous, constant rumble. "There's something like 70 to 90 db just of crowd," Phil Lesh remarks. "That's the noise floor when we're playing, comparable to driving a car with the windows down at 55 miles per hour." The crowd sings along to every song in ecstasy. In places of the arena, the Deadheads sing louder than the band.

It is growing too much for the band to handle. In the fall of 1989, the band officially ban vending and camping. But it doesn't stop many, especially the Spinners. They make new tickets out of old stubs and get everyone in for free, on the logic that they're just *extra* people in the show. Between tours, they go to Guatemala and import fashions back to the parking lot.

"[There] was a type of top that Guatemalan women all weave in the same basic pattern within the same village," remembers the sometime-Spinner Luther Delaney. "You'll have the same sort of color coordination within a village, and then you go to a different village and it's completely different." The Spinners decide that it's the latest thing. "Even the guys would wear them," Luther says. "We'd go down to Guatemala and we'd be wearing these tops and the [Guatemalan] guys would look at us funny because we were wearing women's mini ponchos." The former LSD chemist Sarah Matzar, now back at home in Panajachel, hears about the Spinners' appropriations and simply laughs.

But on the familiar American byways of Dead tour, all the Spinners' systems are working. They sweep into towns, stay with one of their Family's many friends, sardined onto some strange floor before the next leg. And soon there will be more Jerry.

IN LATE 1989, Karen Horning stands at one of the most dangerous crossroads in America, living in San Francisco in between Grateful Dead
tours, sometimes making money shipping acid home to New England. Doors are starting to open for her in the secret reaches of psychedelic America. It is a singular criminal vocation, and Karen will
make a choice. Most of the time she works as a babysitter, usually for
an editor at the liberal magazine *Mother Jones*. Karen gets a place in
the Mission with her friend the tie-dyer and helps him make jewelry.

During a recent run of shows, she'd been handed an issue of *Deadheads Behind Bars,* a new zine published by a federal prisoner in Wisconsin named Pam Fisher. A onetime hardcore tourhead, Fisher had
recently began serving a twenty-one-month sentence.

"By some small miracle, another not so lucky friend who got ten
years ended up in the same prison," she writes. "Right next door is another jail and just the other day we noticed another deadhead friend of
ours there. We stood in our recreation yard waving at him . . . so nice
to see family . . . wait a minute, something is definitely wrong with this
picture. Maybe it's the dual razor wire fences." Elsewhere in the issue,
they get to the meat of the matter: carrier weight laws.

As part of the War on Drugs, the Drug Free America Act of 1986
had reinstated the Boggs Act of 1951, mandatory minimum prison
sentences for first-time drug offenders. It was a legal move mostly
directed at crack users, but it plays out on low-level LSD dealers: pun-
ishments are levied based on the weight on the whole drug, including
its carrier substance, blotter paper, sugar cube, Windowpane, gel tab,
whatever.

All that beautiful art is becoming increasingly dangerous. It's only
been getting more beautiful over the years, too. Hits depicting Soviet
president Mikhail Gorbachev ("the Gorby blots") are a smash in the
Dead parking lot, originating (it is revealed later) from Acid Eric, the
psychedelic guru of Goa, India, who aims to bring down the Berlin
Wall. One of the lushest and most heavily dosed runs of the past few
years depicts a series of twelve album covers by Stanley Mouse and
Alton Kelley, including the Dead's *American Beauty,* Bob Weir's *Ace,*
Mickey Hart's *Rolling Thunder,* and others. The acid in the sheets is
linked to a lab in Mountain View, near Shoreline Amphitheater, the
heart of Dead country, the heart of Silicon Valley. The dipping of at
least one set of the sheets is connected (via Chris Doyon) to the Dead

Family, its profits seeping out into the far reaches of activism. It's all the same, and the characters and goods and money and ideas now flow between spaces with increased urgency. The scene is set for a clash out on the highway of American reality.

Another detail that rising LSD dealer Karen Horning (and all other *Deadheads Behind Bars* readers) learns is that prisoners aren't allowed to correspond with one another, only the unincarcerated. The zine publishes a list of a few dozen Deadhead prisoners and includes their addresses, a practice that long-running Dead fanzine *Relix* takes up. That Christmas, Karen mails out Christmas cards to them all and maintains correspondences with anyone who writes back.

"This problem started coming up about the carrier weight," she remembers. "'I'm doing 20 years,' 'I'm doing 30 years.' I just kept writing. I wasn't asking people why they were there. Some would just say, 'I got this much time.' This would go on and on. Some would ask if I'd write to a certain person. I started gathering information. One of them was Stanley Marshall, who had received 20 years for almost nothing."

Karen is establishing herself in a growing industry built around the LSD market in the late 1980s. There are many opportunities for advancement, and her friends will later testify that they are worried about her, but Karen has a career to launch. She makes friends around the flea market in the parking lot of the Ashby BART station in Berkeley. There are grams of crystal LSD floating around there, if one has the right connections. It's an epicenter for the same scene that Guatemalan chemist Sarah Matzar was once connected to; she and others had used locations within a several-block radius to convert crystal acid to product.

One of Karen's friends, Waverly, is moving grams. A black Vietnam vet turned New York City cop, he'd grown sick of the violence and made for California where he drives a cab and mines for crystals, which he sells at flea markets. He moves into the acid game, more for the hippie girls than the money.

"We were thicker than thieves, Waverly and me," Karen says. But she doesn't do biz with Waverly. Karen makes her own inroads. She meets people who know people who are people, and before long Karen is getting LSD in crystal form, fresh from the lab, before it's laid into blotter or pressed into pills. It is just pure, raw powder. For some of the people at this level of LSD dealing, this is the form it will be consumed in, as well. Many high-up LSD movers speak of taking concentrated LSD at levels unthinkable to the average tripper let alone anybody who has never taken psychedelics.

They dip their fingers in the crystal and away they go. "I remember the first time I did a finger, I went running through the Park, crossing through the Panhandle," Karen says. She doesn't remember the babbling, and her friends tease her about that, waking up everybody in the apartment as she looks for her missing friend.

"I was like, 'Wake up, wake up! I think he's under the couch!' and checking. I tried to move the furniture around and was babbling all night. It's fat soluble so you're not gonna die. Off you go and down." That is, one goes comatose, out into the far reaches.

"It's almost like you're in a nod, because you have to re-acclimate," Karen Horning describes. "It's almost like being too stoned on grass. And you're coming back up and every now and then it's like *jabberjabberjabber.*"

JOHN PERRY BARLOW loves it here in this place made of text, loves the magical sensation of the new mind-manifested vistas built of conversation and improbable global nodes. It is a world of synchronicity. And, being who he is, the Grateful Dead lyricist finds the future's new underbelly and promptly makes history.

He winds up in a kerfuffle in an open forum with a pair of teenage computer jockeys calling themselves Acid Phreak and Phiber Optik who, after escalation, promptly post Barlow's credit information. In lingo that won't be common for a quarter century, John Perry Barlow is perhaps the first person on the emergent Internet to be doxxed.

Barlow challenges one of the hackers to call him at home. Wrote Barlow, "I told him I wouldn't insult his skills by giving him my phone number and, with the assurance conveyed by that challenge, I settled back and waited for the phone to ring. Which, directly, it did."

The situation cools, but not the new sensation rattled free in Barlow's head. What he/we are looking at is bigger than anyone has posited yet. It is a mystical place beyond the phone lines, like the mind-body problem rephrased for the collective, someplace new: *cyberspace.*

Barlow borrows the term from science fiction author William Gibson who wrote (in 1984's *Neuromancer*) of the "consensual hallucination experienced daily by billions of legitimate operators, in every nation." Or, as the Jefferson Airplane's Paul Kantner put it (in a song the Dead modified into a favorite jamming theme): "the mind has left the body."

There is a rich linking of the word "cyberspace" to the hippies who came before, especially via the *Whole Earth Catalog*'s frequent call-outs to Norbert Wiener's theory of cybernetics. There is resonance, too, with the wild present-future of Terence McKenna's beloved "hyperspace." "Cyberspace" is open and blank and it has a whiff of danger.

For now, human access to cyberspace is extraordinarily limited, and it is mediated almost completely by words. John Perry Barlow is very much a man of means in that regard. In the way that the forefathers of the American republic were rich landowners, Barlow is an obvious ambassador from an earlier generation and several tribes of already-settled mindspace. Barlow's *Mondo 2000* dispatches broadcast his tone with effortless charm.

Via an encounter with another hacker, Barlow winds up with a hapless FBI agent in his Wyoming living room. And, after posting about it on the WELL, Barlow finds himself with yet another visitor to Pinedale. Mitch Kapor, founder of computer company Lotus, calls Barlow from his jet and asks whether he can drop by to compare notes about a similar disconcerting and comical visit from the FBI.

Barlow picks up Kapor from a nearby airfield and, in Barlow's kitchen as it snows outside, they hatch plans for a civil liberties organization for the new territory that they both see. It is territory that they were both somehow trained to see.

Kapor will remember, "We also had a common set of experiences in the '60s—involving what I, when I speak to straight business audiences, charitably refer to as recreational chemicals—that really I think contributed to a fundamental outlook."

The Computer Liberty Foundation. Maybe something like that?

ONE WAY TO get to the Inner Sanctum of the Wetlands Preserve in New York City is to wake up there. And if one does wake up there in late 1989, it might seem like virtual reality, except not virtual at all. It is a place where psychedelic America isn't imaginary. What a wonderful invention, this Wetlands. The Inner Sanctum is the club's architectural masterstroke, down the stairs and a blacklit hallway covered in rock posters, into the basement bar, down farther into the dim lounge, and then—in the back—the Sanctum, with its comfortable couches and implicit invitation for heads to make themselves at home and light up.

It is not at all unusual to see someone curled up down there, lulled to sleep by the weed or the throb of the drum circles that sometimes sprout during the new weekly Grateful Dead night. Without asking, Larry Bloch's staff had simply bolted down the custom modular stage upstairs. As is the standard at many New York clubs, Wetlands is open to anyone eighteen and up.

Some Sunday afternoons, Larry Bloch opens up the Wetlands for the Wharf Rats, the Deadhead sobriety group, who host all-ages shows featuring primo Dead cover band Crazy Fingers and a nonalcoholic juice bar only. These gatherings are announced far and wide, in the nationwide *Mississippi 12-Step* newsletter and *Dupree's Diamond News* tour broadsheet alike.

How many bars open themselves to sobriety groups? How many sobriety groups have any reason to go to a bar? But Wetlands isn't a bar; Wetlands is a place. In the pages of *Mississippi 12-Step,* a newsletter whose title puns on the 1972 Garcia/Hunter song, the sober heads offer enthusiastic alternative answers to the snarky joke, *What did the Deadhead say when the drugs wore off?* At Wetlands they can have their own space, too. Like it or not, that hokum nature mural that wraps around the club does the trick.

By the first summer Wetlands is in business, the portal is wide open. Besides Dead cover bands and reggae night and a rotating cast of early jammers, they have a slide show for Burma and a Tibetan dance troupe. There are Yippie storyteller nights, a presentation by the New York City chapter of the United States Psychotronics Association, sitarists, satirists, Tuli Kupferberg of the Fugs, Peter Stampfel of the Holy Modal Rounders, Country Joe, a Celtic hootenanny, an Andean folklore ensemble, and the "triumphant New York return" of Anguillan reggae hero Banki Banx.

Though the Deadheads might sign some petitions, they're not showing up in droves for the activist meetings. "Even the guys who did the tie-dyed shirts, you tried talking to them about organic cotton and they looked at you like you were nuts," Wetlands activism director Remy Chevalier groans. But that's okay, too. The Sunday night Eco-Saloon is still the club's first priority, when the representatives from the environmentalist tribes come together for presentations, networking, and some light consciousness raising. Some, including Earth First, use the club as a local mailing address.

Jacaeber Kastor and the Psychedelic Solution gang are semiregulars too, selling tickets to Wetlands events from their gallery in the West Village. "Larry loved us," Kastor says. "We all had carte blanche at Wetlands." Kastor's friend, the art critic Carlo McCormick dismisses Wetlands as "a theme park," but there's nowhere else like it, in New York or anywhere.

Larry Bloch's decrees define the place, from the biodegradable cocktail straws to his insistence that bands play multiple sets. Late-night shows are the norm in Gotham, but this gives Wetlands a distinct character. On a three-band bill, the first act starts at 10, the second at 11, and the headliner playing (at least) two sets starting at midnight.

"There's something extraordinarily magical about a band playing two sets," Larry says. "Many times a band is even better in second set—it's looser once that first set is out of the way. But also, for audience members, the time spent interacting between sets is really a magical time." The decision invites time for tripping, too, especially during the Psychedelic Psaturdays, boldly advertised on Laura Bloch's hand-drawn monthly calendars.

Wavy Gravy comes. So does Timothy Leary, demanding cash payment in advance. And Allen Ginsberg, reading to eight hundred people—four hundred inside, four hundred outside—at a memorial for Abbie Hoffman, following the Yippie's suicide. The people of the subcontinent have a new home.

July 1989 is particularly busy. One Sunday includes a presentation by Bat Conservation International and their video *Bats: Myth vs Reality* by Dr. Merlin Tuttle, a talk on vegetarianism, and—following the Dead's show at Giants Stadium out in the wilds on the other side of the Holland Tunnel—a full two-set show by the Dead cover band the Zen Tricksters. The regular Dead Center that week is going to start late, too. In the early evening, environmental director Remy Chevalier has scored a coup for the activism center: an invitation-only fund-raiser for mayoral candidate David Dinkins.

"Out of Wetlands came an organization called Environment '89," Chevalier says, a coalition, "and they supported Dinkins. So Dinkins came to the club and Wetlands pretty much gave every single environmental group in New York City, on a platter, to Dinkins." When Dinkins is elected, Chevalier believes, "I think he had an unwritten thank you to Wetlands to leave the place alone. All these clubs were getting shut down everywhere and Wetlands kept going unscathed, which was a miracle."

And when the Dinkins fundraiser is done, in comes Johnny Dwork's Speed of Light Show (representatives of the 8/27/72-loving Phurst Church of Phun) to illuminate the next few shows, including the next evening's three-band bill. The middle act are making their Wetlands debut, trying to work their way into the club's lineups. Little brothers to Blues Traveler (Larry Bloch's favorites), the Spin Doctors' achievement is reduction, a boogie backbeat tightened to a modern snap, cosmic silliness turned into pun-filled blues-pop with elongated solos. They play almost every evening around Manhattan, multiple sets a night, and will hit MTV and the charts in a few years.

The term "jam band" has been in usage since at least the late '70s, notably Goa Gil and Anjuna Jam Band, a group of hippie expatriates (horns! grooves!) playing on the Goa beaches in the loose coterie around local LSD hub Acid Eric. As the '80s become the '90s, the two words contract, *smoosh*, "jamband." It is naturally generic and, after Wetlands is open a bit, comes to mean certain kind of dance-ready jamming in a proscribed range of novelty-happy tempos, frequencies, approximated genres, and arrangements.

From Vermont, Phish haul ass around New England with their own PA and light show and custom instruments by their own soundman. Phish are very much doing it themselves. Word is getting out.

They have their own studio-recorded tape now. They're accustomed to being laughed at or rejected by record companies and venues, often resorting to renting places and selling them out on their own. In Burlington, they move to larger bars, and Nancy—their songwriting weirdo sibling from the Goddard campus—can't handle it anymore.

Nancy had never liked loud music or crowds to begin with, and even seeing the band in a full bar could be tough. He has a meltdown onstage with them one night doing "Halley's Comet." It's not an evil spirit or anything, he just can't take it. It's the last time Nancy ever appears on stage with them. They stop playing the song for a while.

Nancy is very confused. He attends a few Rainbow Gatherings. Later, he visits a psychic who tells him that "Nancy" is just the name of a lover he had in a past life. He goes by other pseudonyms for his music—MantaRay, Dick FaceBat—but in real life goes by Richard Wright, and keeps making tapes.

9

THROUGH THE LOOKING GLASS

new age of psychedelic discovery (and all its metaphors) has begun. It's called the '90s. "It's too early for a science. What we need now are the diaries of explorers," mushroom champion Terence McKenna tells *Revision*. "We need many diaries of many explorers so we can begin to get a feel for the territory." In this decade, the mysterious substances and their complex legacy will have their widest and most chaotic impacts yet, and the territory—as McKenna knows it—will transform entirely.

"Psychedelics are to psychology what telescopes in the sixteenth century were to astronomy," is another Terence McKennaism. "If a person is not willing to look through the telescope he cannot call himself an astronomer." The hero of the brewing entheogenic revolution, now in residence at the Esalen Institute in Big Sur most summers, remains a source of pliant symbolism. In the new decade, many are acquiring telescopes.

Into the '90s, some of the best and most consistent astronomer-explorers in the broader American psychedelic world remain the visual artists. Arguably more than musicians or writers, they have brought back the most convincing and accessible reports from the psychedelic shores, translating the signal of the light-spirit into instantly understandable form. On that note, the psychedelic '90s begin on a supremely sad note, with the February 1990 HIV-related death of Keith

Haring, the proudly gay, psychedelic, Dead-loving, disco-dancing artist whose work is now iconic around the world. Even selling in galleries or marketed on T-shirts, the thick primal lines of Haring's LSD-inspired vision resonate with the power of street art, communicating Haring's joyous being. His work only grows more universal, and the world does seem to become more accepting in its wake. Bye, Keith.

But the psychedelic art thread remains strong. There's an Acid Show at Max Fish on New York's Lower East Side in the first month of the decade, featuring some of the same conspirators who'd taken part in the psychedelic protest-art installations with curator Carlo McCormick a few years earlier.

And it is in 1990, as well, that the painter Alex Grey assembles his work into the retrospective volume *Sacred Mirrors: The Visionary Art of Alex Grey*. The book announces him as an instinctive cartographer of the first order, launching a new generation of entheogenic-minded (if sometimes rather somber) "visionary" artists. It is a genre name that is almost comically highfalutin when self-applied, but Grey's style possesses an intricate and intimate mathematics designed to express the spiritual magnitude of hyperspace.

Like psychedelic figures before him, Grey reveals ambition, announcing his dream of establishing a permanent Chapel of Sacred Mirrors for his work. Not unfairly, either. At full size, Grey's paintings can be revelatory. Shrunk down, they make their way onto postcards and lo-fi head shop–ready posters, showing up diminished in dorm rooms everywhere. And though Grey is a baby boomer too, his work defines a new psychedelic aesthetic that separates itself from the earlier generations.

Grey will trigger waves of imitators, becoming part of the visual language that adorns flyers for both jambands and the ecstasy-fueled dance music circuit. Embodied in the oversized *Sacred Mirrors* book (with introduction by Carlo McCormick), Grey's sacred geometries, mysteries, and mirrors join "Dark Star" and other tools and tableaus for explorers. Like *Live/Dead,* it is also large enough to roll joints on. "It takes a 'head' to recognize a 'head,'" Grey will tell Jon Hanna of his audience.

The artist himself, however, is the type of tripper who advocates for what Terence McKenna calls "the silent garden." In 1990, too, Grey begins selling an invention of his own design, the Mindfold, a gentle eye mask attached to light earplugs, to aid the sensory deprivation of a head in the midst of whatever silent travel is on the itinerary. For the new astronomers, it is a way of blocking out the city lights of the mind to see the full night sky.

Grey's creations, too, are a brisk seller at the Psychedelic Solution in New York, the first outlet to distribute his postcards and posters (initially alongside a show of original work). The gallery hits a peak of operation around the turn of the decade, too. Says owner Jacaeber Kastor, "We were sponsoring parties, doing openings, doing after-parties, loaning stuff to museums, getting articles [written about us], documentary stuff going on, sales of work, putting out lists, doing reference material work, repping for certain people, trying to handle different artists. There were lots of entertaining odd little things going on." The gallery's staff swells to about a dozen.

Along with the business, Psychedelic Solution's influence swells, too. "I'm probably exaggerating, but it seemed like one of every ten people in that place was an art director," says Jacaeber. "And they ranged from art directors for theater, art directors for film, art directors for television, art directors for fashion, art directors for book publishing. I just started seeing the influence of classic psychedelic art work from the '60s, west coast, LA and San Francisco primarily. You name it, we saw it: lighting effects, print advertising, fashion, film, set design."

The Psychedelic Solution does an exhibit featuring Stanley Mouse's early hot rod work and, presto whammo, Jacaeber sees hot rod art turn up in Absolut vodka ads and elsewhere.

Psychedelia had survived the twentieth anniversary of the Summer of Love and even its nonpsychedelic British sequel. It is alive and well. The scales begin to tip. In the mainstream culture, psychedelia slowly begins to signify something far more than simply the sixties, an ongoing world. Within psychedelia, the space age has arrived.

Terence McKenna and his associates continue to refine newer versions of Timewave Zero software that proves (he claims) a definite *change* will be coming in late 2012. McKenna is not the only one building a reputation on this notion. The author José Argüelles is onto it as well. The same man who'd spread the idea of the Harmonic Convergence in 1987, Argüelles had begun his travels creating an open-source Whole Earth Festival in 1970.

But Terence McKenna rises to new heights of popularity, openly engaging with enthused fringe millennialism. Much later, there will be rumors of a bad mushroom experience that causes McKenna to take psychedelics far less frequently than he once did. McKenna himself will never mention it. His brother Dennis will call him out for not "walking his talk," and it becomes a point of tension between the siblings. Brother Terence's avocation of the psychedelic modes grows more amplified and articulate, even if Dennis (pursuing a more scholarly path) will think Terence's mind is more worthwhile when expounding on anything *but* psychedelics.

The timewave is only a slightly harder sell than the talking mushrooms, but the joy of Terence McKenna is in the performance of his ideas. He tours an endless circuit of conferences, conclaves, festivals, universities, alongside the occasional appearance at Wetlands in New York. He's a friendly guy, Terence. If one hangs with him a little bit, it's possible he can arrange to pass along some concentrated ayahuasca brew in a brown bottle. For many years, McKenna and his wife, the esteemed ethnobotanist Kat Harrison, had operated Botanical Dimensions. Out in the rich Hawaiian soil, they aim to preserve and study examples of the major psychedelic substances.

People trade tapes of his lectures, but this is no longer unusual. An unmeasurable amount of sub- and countercultures around the world are now powered by cassettes.

Partially in reaction to the new(est) age of exploration that is so clearly upon them, the veteran chemist Alexander "Sasha" Shulgin and his wife Anne publish the milestone *PIHKAL: A Chemical Love Story* in 1991. The 978-page book provides the serious astronomy behind McKenna and Grey's star gazing.

Besides a lightly veiled account of their courtship, the Shulgins present decades of work detailing more than two hundred different chemical combinations and their effects at various levels on them and a close circle of friends. It is the definitive psychedelic work, more doctor, less gonzo, serious to the last decimal, and equally filled with compassion. It also presents their long-standing system for trip reports, from baseline up to +5 ("A rare and precious transcendental state"). With the drug war battlefronts heating up, the Shulgins worry that Sasha's lab could be raided with little pretense, his notes destroyed. They decide it is best for this information to be free.

Alexander Shulgin is a strange but not-strange figure in the pantheon. A regular at gatherings of the high-powered men's club known as Bohemian Grove along the idyllic Russian River in Sonoma County, his head politics can't easily be contained by the psychedelic libertarianism on view elsewhere. Shulgin is no Owsleyian and probably closer in disposition to the playful old-world enlightenment of Albert Hofmann.

The great doctor Sasha works from a shed in his backyard filled with beakers and burners and vials, bearing paperwork of approval from the Drug Enforcement Administration. With white beard and twinkling eyes, he is as close as the psychedelic Map gets to a state-acknowledged wizard, and he is on duty.

THE LAND THAT the Spinners spin themselves onto in mid-1990 is a blessing. They are the first group to formally proclaim a religious faith discovered through the Grateful Dead, and they are up in classic commune territory a few hours north of San Francisco to figure out how their new church is going to work.

Even from the start, the Land is capitalized when it is said out loud, and it has a blessed history, or at least a countercultural one. Luther Delaney, a well-to-do sometime Spinner and always Deadhead loans the group $108,000 for the purchase. "108,000 at 1.08% for 108 periods or something," he remembers. "It was all 108 because 108 is a Hindu mystical number, because that's how many beads there are on the meditation bead necklace. It went from there, before it went downhill from there." But not yet.

The Land "got freaky in the '60s," Luther remembers. It belonged to a longhaired holistic healer, "a lesbian cult," then the Berkeley Krishna temple, and, somehow, the Spinners, except they're not the Spinners anymore. Joseph and the inner core have given them a new name, incorporated under that name, even. They are the Church of Unlimited Devotion, echoing "The Golden Road (to Unlimited Devotion)," the Dead's Haight-era sunshine pop single and a phrase with a lingual heritage stretching across dozens of English-speaking faiths. Don't let anyone mistake these Spinners for non-Deadheads, though.

They've been on the road now for almost a half decade, the Spinners. They take vows of chastity and wear white. The Land is the next step. They'd made up with the anthropologist fairly quickly, though the Spinner leaders don't let anyone else in the group read her thesis. She keeps spinning for a time. The Spinners go through all kinds of changes. "The Church is not a cult," the leader Joseph will explain. "What we're doing isn't new. We see the unity of all bona fide world faiths." And, indeed, that's just how the Dead fit into the picture. In the Spinners' theology, the Grateful Dead are one of many available conduits. By the end of the year Joseph is saying that while the church use only the Dead's music for purposes of meditation, but it could be *any* music, really. He has a point. Still, the Church of Unlimited Devotion becomes the first incorporated religion sprung from the Grateful Dead.

Despite Robert Hunter and John Perry Barlow's keen attempt to keep their lyrics dogma-free, spirituality is a different story. It is never far from the surface in Deadland, like the endless skull-and-roses variations in the iconography. Its unknowingness hovers just beyond the veil of many of the band's songs and their whole existence.

Do-it-yourself and alternative approaches to spirituality have surrounded the Grateful Dead since before there was a Grateful Dead. Lyricist Robert Hunter and pals forayed into Los Angeles to study Scientology in 1964, a thread picked up by keyboardist Tom Constanten and (briefly) Bob Weir later in the decade. The Dead even played a benefit for L. Ron Hubbard's quack scientific tribe at Winterland in '69. The band did a "Krishna Consciousness Comes West" dance at the Avalon Ballroom in '67, too, a belief set that proves to have a far more lasting impact on the counterculture than Scientology.

The constant flow of psychedelics around the Dead ensures an endless stream of curious and turned-on youth open to the universe's wonders, sometimes to the point of excess but perhaps just as frequently to the point of authentic religious discovery. It's been that way since the '60s, and there's no reason it's going to change now.

Later in the '90s, the Buddhist quarterly *Tricycle* will conduct a reader survey and discover that 83 percent of respondents report arriving at Buddhism via psychedelics. This number probably doesn't include those conflicted about their pasts, such as those who— encountered by DMT researcher Rick Strassman during the course of his research—ostracize him from the New Mexico monastery where he practices. The debate about the proper place of psychedelics in contemporary spiritual practice will continue well into the next century in texts like Allan Bediner's Zig Zag Zen, on Dead lot, at Burning Man, and elsewhere.

There are many people passing through many portals in Deadland, and the Spinners are merely one group. Also in the Dead lot, beginning in the late '80s, is the Peacemaker bus, piloted by the mega-Christian Island Pond community, also known as the Twelve Tribes. "We know the way, we will bring you home," they paint on the back of the Peacemaker, a perverted inversion of the tender and wondrous uncertainty expressed by Robert Hunter in the Grateful Dead's "Ripple." The Twelve Tribes use the bus (built in Vermont, near where Phish's Trey Anastasio was writing songs) to carry lost souls back to their longhaired but quite conservative commune.

On the whole, the Spinners' place up in Mendocino is pretty benevolent. The 170-acre grounds contain a main building, which they call the Redwood House, and a 25 × 40-foot structure where they set up a stereo, the Spinning Hall. There's also a cluster of genuine Buckminster Fuller–style geodesic domes, remnants of futures passed. "They were all ratty," Luther Delaney observes. "I don't think Bucky would've been proud or impressed, necessarily."

Luther doesn't live on the Land, but he keeps rolling with the gang. "I never really was up there much, because of the whole surrendering thing," he admits. "I had some cash, I was living pretty good. I had my truck. I didn't want to give up my truck. I didn't want to give up my money. I was always a little suspicious. I wanted to keep my own space, and they said that was fine and that I could always go there and, you know, park my trailer or whatever and have a place to live. They said, 'surrender or not, you're a brother and you're helping us out.' It was really enchanting." The truth is that Luther is completely in love with one of the Spinner women and wants to do right by her, whatever that takes.

The church stays in motion, going to shows, and traveling down to the city when the Jerry Garcia Band takes up its semimonthly residencies at the Warfield Theater when the Dead aren't on the road. They work whatever schemes they can to get everyone in the door. In the room with Jerry is *the* place to be, and the Warfield Theater in San Francisco is *the* church for the Church of Unlimited Devotion and other more casual sects, Garcia's eternal musical home at the edge of San Francisco's ever-seedy Tenderloin.

Luther Delaney savors these nights with Jerry at the Warfield. Luther still spins sometimes, but the Jerry Band is a wholly different version of the American psychedelic ritual, and, especially at the Warfield, Garcia's song choices increasingly veer into gospel music. Luther has his own even more personal reading, though, that represents yet another extreme of psychedelicized Deadhead religion.

"I took those songs literally," Luther remembers, "like he was really talking to me. Like in 'How Sweet It Is (to Be Loved by You),' he's not talking about everyone, he's talking about *me* and all this knowledge that I need to take personally. When I started to do that, my whole vision of the world started to change and my vision of The Family started to change, and my vision of myself started to change and I realized that they were either hypocritical or there was some darkness involved. I was following my heart and following Jerry and following Jerry's heart. And that really changed things.

Luther says, "There wasn't a whole lot of talk about Jerry being a guru, besides the idea of Jerry as a pure channel, like he was channeling a divine energy through his music, through his guitar. And that really stuck and held validity for me. I realized that I can relate."

There's a sweetness to Luther's version, and he keeps playing with those ideas when and wherever Garcia plays. Even more than the Spinners' articulated doctrine, Luther Delaney's interpretation of the Dead's music represents an absolute, complete, played-to-the-end extension of one way to deeply appreciate music, as a literal text to live by. In the case of Garcia, though, the vast majority of that literal text is what comes through his guitar playing.

"I didn't feel like my arm was twisted or I was doing something outrageous," Luther says. "All of a sudden life is exciting and everything is opening up for me."

The vast majority of Dead listeners surely don't subscribe to Luther's way of listening to the Dead exactly, but many probably feel small variations on it, the feeling of life perpetually opening up. It's a reason to return.

Most people at a given Grateful Dead show simply love the Grateful Dead for whatever reasons most people love the Grateful Dead. And there are so many millions of reasons to love the Grateful Dead with all-burning, life-enveloping enthusiasm. Everywhere the band plays is like a constant fireworks show of beautiful love manifestations, people dressing up and dancing and making stuff and meeting each other.

"There were literally individuals that I saw for 25 years," says Bay Area–based Deadhead journalist Steve Silberman. "I would see them as cute teenagers, I would have crushes on them. I would see them in the first flush of love, I would see them get married, I would see them when they became fathers, I would see them when they got gray hair. I would see the whole human lifecycle, and not in some abstract sense. I would see it literally in front of my eyes when I went to see my favorite band, and there was no other experience like that, and there never will be."

The same holds true for Garcia Band shows, and those Jerry shows at the Warfield are central for core chunks of Bay Area Deadheads. In the 2,300-capacity theater, they all mix: young, old, Spinners, stealth tapers, inner core LSD intelligentsia, and countless hometown Deadhead families, like the one based around Regan McMahon and Blair Jackson's beloved *Golden Road* fanzine.

Everyone works through their own versions of the Church of Jerry. Outside, where it's not Sunday, it's a turbulent time in the Dead scene, following the July 1990 overdose death of keyboardist Brent Mydland.

The fiery promoter Bill Graham catches onto the Spinners' ticket scheme one night at the Warfield during a Garcia Band show. They'd acquired a roll of re-entry tickets from the same vendor that Graham uses. Lead Spinner Joseph is dragged before Graham himself and bawled out, a San Francisco tradition that legitimizes the church's existence in its own way. This particular jig is up. One of the Spinner girls is led away in handcuffs. "I guess we're not getting into the show tonight," Luther observes.

WITH A NAME like Psychedelic Solution, a location near the still-hep crossroads of West Eighth Street and Sixth Avenue in Manhattan, and a sizzling neon sign glowing in the window, Jacaeber Kastor's second-floor gallery gets its share of travelers. The early 1990s is an extraordinary time to be an American head. It is still an age of shadowy information and rumors, an oral network unverified by the Internet to come. It is in the 1990s that the American heads finally begin to make full contact with other psychedelic cultures, though the outcome will surprise even Jacaeber Kastor.

"Leo was one of hundreds to thousands of people who would pop through because we were like a lighthouse on the route," says Kastor of Leo Mercado, the newest enthusiastic arrival at Psychedelic Solution. Young, longhaired, and Mexican American, Mercado is actively involved with the long-running Peyote Way Church of God, raising funds, campaigning, making art, and growing peyote. Jacaeber sells some of Leo's pottery on consignment, though he doesn't really deal in that. But then Leo shows Jacaeber the traditional Huichol yarn paintings of a Mexican artist named Cristobal Gonzalez, peyote visions depicted in vivid colors.

"I decided that it would make a great art show, as opposed to doing more of the '60s artists," Kastor says, "and the opportunity to get somebody who's a member of a tribe who works in a traditional manner."

Quickly it becomes obvious that Jacaeber will have to travel to Mexico to figure out how to make the show happen, to pay Gonzalez, and hopefully return to New York with the art itself. He tells his friend Carlo McCormick, *Art Forum* critic and psychedelic enthusiastic and, before Kastor can finish, McCormick is on board. Carlo takes a week off from the bars where he works, and, in the spring of 1990, the two New York heads travel to Tepic, Mexico, to meet up with Leo Mercado and crew.

When they reach the artist Cristobal Gonzalez's house, Kastor discovers that the yarn painter is in no way prepared for his New York debut. Rather than press the issue, an alternate solution is presented: Kastor and McCormick will extend their visit and travel with some Huichol on one of their regular visits to Wirikute, the site of creation, where the peyote grows.

As it happens, one of the Huichol is married to an American-born man and he's along for the ride along with a few others. They take a long bus ride to a long train ride to another long train ride and are dropped at the tiny depot nearest the spot whose secret has been closely guarded for centuries. The residents of the town are not Huichol but have agreements going back generations and watch over a small tool shed near the train depot.

The group gets a ride out into the desert in the back of a pickup truck. There are many psychedelic adventures left to be had in this world, and the two longhairs from New York are just at the start of theirs.

"It was dusty dirt road out into nothingness in the desert," says Jacaeber. "There was lots of mesquite bush and terrain and stuff, but no trees. But then finally there was one tree. And maybe one smaller tree next to it. And it was apparently that same exact spot where this one group of Huichols goes every time. They dropped us off and said they'd be back in three days to pick everybody up.

"The tree was definitely needed because there was no shade or anything. We set up camp around the base of this tree."

Everyone's ready to go hunt for peyote, but there are ceremonies first. Jacaeber has no idea what peyote looks like in the ground. Finally, someone spots some. "I swear you could walk right up to it and not see it, they don't come up above ground level there," says Kastor. Then there's another ceremony, some items are burned, and the Americans are taught how to properly remove peyote from the ground without severing its root.

Jacaeber continues, "They showed us several ways of preparing it, but the simple way they did it was to cut the outside skin off and core the center like you might core an apple. Then they slice it, like an orange into maybe six slices. They tell you don't chew and don't swallow it, just suck on it. We were surprised to find it doesn't taste awful. It has an edge to it, like aloe vera, a metallic edge, but it wasn't bad at all. It's not necessary to get it past your palette and throw it up."

Within the hour, all turns sparkling. Suddenly, the peyote is not only easy to find; it's everywhere, veritably glowing like some strange seabed creature. It's a splendid night in the desert, and whenever Jacaeber feels the need, he cuts himself another slice of peyote and keeps on a-suckin'. Wonders occur. At one point, Jacaeber leans back and watches the sky as the stars communicate with each other, shooting zaps from one light-point to another, until all of a sudden one zaps earthward and hits Jacaeber Kastor in the head. He feels it move down his spine and there it throbs.

"It was like having a muscle I never knew I had, and it started spasming, not at all unpleasant," he says. "And then all this energy came broiling up through my spine and I think came right through my head. I don't know what happened. It was a pretty remarkable physical experience. It sounds like a kundalini experience, is the closest thing I found to what happened. I had some kind of obviously telepathic communications with these *entities,* or whatever part of myself I was talking to. Whichever way you want to look at it, it was very fucking amazing."

He spends hours on the bluff overlooking the campsite, watching the emptiness of a desert. A pack of wild horses ride up to within thirty feet of the camp, check out the humans, and disappear back into the desert. He watches a light blink on and off in the distant mountains; later, he discovers it's a molybdenum mine, there being an odd relationship between sacred plants and rare earth–type materials. And, near dawn, a stranger rides quietly into camp on a horse. Jacaeber watches frozen as the man dismounts. But nothing seems to happen and he rides off.

In the morning, Jacaeber sees that the man has left two giant bags of enormous peyote buttons. The man is the land's caretaker, not a Huichol but very much in sympathy with them. He always leaves peyote. Their days by the lone tree out in the desert remain magical, give or take some sunburn. Someone picks a beautiful peyote button bouquet for the yarn painter Cristobal Gonzalez. The New York art critic Carlo McCormick rides a horse for the first time.

As promised, the pickup truck returns and delivers them to the train. Bedraggled and dirty, they trek back to Tepic with the Huichol community's peyote supply, taking a train to a train to a bus, and disembarking in the middle of the night in the Tepic bus station.

Jacaeber and Carlo trail behind the main group, wondering over the adventure they've just completed. And then they are stopped. And searched. Carlo has his hair down and is wearing a T-shirt featuring some kind of cartoon disembodied zombie head. Jacaeber is certain this contributes to what follows. In Carlo's bag, their searchers discover the peyote bouquet picked for Cristobal Gonzalez, placed there somewhat arbitrarily. Those in the party who haven't dispersed yet are called back from the curb, including the Huichol, and they are all summarily thrown in jail.

ELECTRONIC FRONTIER FOUNDATION! That's it, that's exactly it. Among others, Grateful Dead lyricist John Perry Barlow, Whole Earth cataloguer Stewart Brand, virtual reality dreamer Jaron Lanier, free software pioneer John Gilmore—a conclave of the new digerati—come up with the name one night over dinner in San Francisco in the late spring of 1990. Declaring cyberspace to be a "frontier" is a straight-up Digger move, akin to yawping "it's free because it's yours." Lanier backs out quickly, worried about the glamorization and empowerment of hackers.

It is completely presumptuous, of course, in the way that organizations founded by privileged white men are often completely presumptuous. The Electronic Frontier Foundation's existence is an assertion that the network is more than the sum of its nodes. It is also a reflection of them and their experience, in California, on psychedelics, here on this New Earth.

Members of rock 'n' roll families often refer to their respective bands with the hilarious road manager–esque "we," as if he (usually he) is one of the musicians on stage. But in the Grateful Dead it's more valid than in most places, and especially for Barlow. And what John Perry Barlow is doing in 1990 is the absolute cream of the Grateful Dead, light years beyond the musicians' experiments with new MIDI technology.

The Electronic Frontier Foundation hire Steve Jobs's former publicist, throw fundraisers in San Francisco, and put forth the two-fisted notion that the terrain beyond the computered wall is intended for all human imaginations and that they are there to respect and protect its wildness. Over the summer they go public and quickly John Perry Barlow is receiving more than one hundred e-mails a day.

It fits right in line with everything the Grateful Dead ever meant, just another tribe in a sea of Bay Area Whole Earthers, Diggers, Farm residents, acid monks, Krishnas, and poets, and here's Barlow making good. John Gilmore finds their first intern, an enthusiastic Deadhead.

Barlow is as elegant about his turf as Terence McKenna is about hyperspace. "Sometimes it seems as if all of humanity is engaged in a Great Work," Barlow says, "which I imagine to be the hard-wiring of human consciousness. It is as if we must literally connect ourselves electronically before we can appreciate the connections which have always existed."

THE AMERICAN HEADS' attempt to connect with their Mexican brethren is failing. Jacaeber Kastor and Carlo McCormick and most of their party
are thrown into a 12 × 12-foot cell. It's packed. The latrine is a hole
in the corner. There are no explanations to be had in either English
or Spanish. Night turns to day turns to night and beyond. Jacaeber
talks to the *heffe* a little each day in his half-functional Spanish and receives no firm answers. "You know we didn't do anything," he says in
a hundred iterations. Eventually, at the American prisoner's request,
the *heffe* retrieves a book from Jacaeber's backpack, so he can have
something to read.

In the binding of this book are a few hits of blotter that Carlo had
smuggled down and given to Jacaeber without knowing about their
impending peyote adventure in the desert. Now, in a tiny Mexican jail
cell, Carlo is all too happy to dispose of them. "I tripped to the shit
stains around the hole in the floor," he laughs. "It wasn't the best trip,
but it was an interesting way to adjust to the new reality on hyper-
extremest terms." It is the fullest realization of the demented
anti-flower-power aesthetic the art critic had championed at his Lower
East Side parties: tripping in a crammed Mexican prison.

Finally, they are all dragged into the prison's open courtyard where
they spy the two giant bags of peyote from the desert. They also see
a table filled with many items that were assuredly not theirs, drugs
of almost every kind, including a brick of weed, cocaine, and more.
There is a film crew. Jacaeber feels the sun literally burning on his
small bald spot.

The *heffe* pulls Jacaeber from the line and puts him in the shade to
watch as Carlo and the others are taped for broadcast on the national
news, held up as examples of international drug smugglers. That day,
Jacaeber is set free, but the rapture of Carlo McCormick has only just
begun.

Everyone else is released, and Carlo McCormick is sentenced to
twenty-five years in Mexican federal prison as Jacaeber Kastor struggles to figure out what the *fuck* is happening and get his friend out of
jail. As he learns once he's sprung, this isn't about Carlo but about
revenge. The men who'd searched their bag weren't even government
officials. The drug war has been heating up at the Texas/Mexico border, and it seems a group of American mercenaries had enacted an

embarrassing raid in a border town, and various forces at work are *muy* pissed.

Jacaeber has to fly back to New York without his friend, and soon there's a tangle of lawyers and Carlo's wife and the consulate trying to spring him. It's first worldism in action, of course, but he really *hadn't* done anything that warranted this.

Going into federal prison, where Carlo McCormick is grouped with anyone serving twenty-five years or more, the New York art critic is *terrified*. But everyone in the prison stays far away from him at first. It takes time, but he learns that, beyond merely being a drug smuggler, the Mexican news has reported that Carlo McCormick is some sort of Satanist cult leader, too. It was his zombie head T-shirt. And the lifers are a bit freaked.

It allows the American head a buffer as he settles into the prison routine, surrendering to it. "Incarceration and being sentenced to 25 years is a kind of monumental ego death," he says. "I can compare it to things I know, like a death of a parent, to things I don't, like a near-death experience or the horrors of war. But it felt substantial in that way. It so fundamentally changed me.

"I gave up pretty immediately," he says. "My mother and my wife were fighting it, [while] I was, like, trying to make a new life and telling them to move on. Somehow, being such an abject quitter spared me some misery." There is a whole culture among the long-haul prisoners, even a fairly peaceful one. Carlo attempts to blend into it.

Back in New York, a "Free Carlo" benefit is organized at Irving Plaza with the Psychedelic Furs and others. Miraculously, Carlo is able to attend, freed via the many machinations of lawyers and government representatives. It's surreal. A new supermodel-columnist for *Paper* takes him out to lunch. He is barred from entering Mexico for ten years.

Carlo hadn't made the Cristobal Gonzalez opening at the Psychedelic Solution, though. The show received nice notices and did well, but Jacaeber Kastor is thoroughly disillusioned by how everything had transpired, let down by how the seemingly holy Huichol had disconnected themselves and treated the government's actions as simply the fates of the universe.

"You can find your spirituality in your own backyard," Jacaeber concludes. "You can find it with your own friends, in your own area. It's not that the truths are hidden away here and are available there."

A half decade later, when he is able to return to the country, Carlo McCormick enacts his revenge. He puts on an art show, *Unmade in the USA*, at La Panadería, an artist-run gallery in a rough and soon-gentrified neighborhood in Mexico City. He includes many of his favorites, like the late and always-controversial David Wojnarowicz, who'd participated in Carlo's tripping installations a decade earlier. Carlo also includes a few stamps of quite electric Mark McCloud–designed blotter. When the news cameras come, he guides them to the acid, though doesn't explain what it is. As he suspects will happen, a few pieces of the art—including some of the live blotter—get stolen. As the psychedelic '90s continue, the global psychedelic trails will reawaken.

AT AN ANTIDRUG summit, the Colombian president asks the American president about all the marijuana coming out of Northern California. The American president, a former CIA chief, is embarrassed. The drug war ignites fully on the home front and the shitfire *really* comes down on Humboldt's pot farmers: two hundred soldiers, National Guardsmen, federal agents, including members of the same infantry division that deposed Manuel Noriega. But the grass keeps on growing, *High Times* keeps on publishing, lush bud of the month centerfolds featuring strains like Sharkey's Garden and Freedom Fighter keep falling into the hands of innocent high schoolers everywhere.

At the urging of Secretary of Defense Dick Cheney, the activities of the federal government's drug war becomes increasingly militarized. Operations in North and South America get increasingly terrifying names like Green Sweep, Green Merchant, Ghost Dancer, Ghost Zone, Wipeout, Badge, and Blast Furnace. Fuck you, Cheney.

Some programs, such as the Operation Grizzly in California, are designed specifically to show South American governments that the American drug warlords are serious about stopping drug use (that's what they're doing, right?) within the consensus reality borders of the United States. The agents earn patches for their achievements, both locally and federally, a kind of folk art within the law enforcement community. One, for the DEA's Dangerous Drugs Intelligence Unit, is an appropriation of some Stanley Mouse art for the Dead. In the original, Mouse's top-hatted, sun-glassed skeleton raises a toast with a bubbly martini glass, olives trailing off to the cosmic horizon. In the DEA version, some sicko has replaced the martini with a syringe.

What with the new computers and all, there increasingly really *is* a permanent record. At some blurry time, the government's TIPSTER application evolves into NADDIS, the Narcotics and Dangerous Drugs Information System. All agencies consolidate their information into the highly secretive database, cross-referencing reports from DEA agents in the field. Once information is in the system, it neither gets out nor is acknowledged by anyone outside the law enforcement establishment. Heads need to be extra careful. There are eyes everywhere. There's got to be some new unwatched territory around here somewhere.

Get out your Humbead Map and Rapidograph yet again, friends. Find an upwardly spot on the mountain range that spirals inland, maybe somewhere above Boulder, somewhere remote. And there, you might illustrate Vancouver and, most especially, Kootenay and the remote Gulf Islands. Communes communized in the '60s cultivated their own tradition of pot farming. It keeps growing there, too, up on the metaphoric mountaintop plateaus of British Columbia, a little volcano of its own, about ready to blow.

THE GROUP OF eighty or a hundred or so gather at dusk at Golden Gate Park at the start of Labor Day weekend 1990, the last night of August. New territory is on the itinerary, and the place they find will thrive. There are a bunch of cars and at least one Ryder truck, already overstuffed with people and bags and gear and supplies and costumes and sculptures. One woman brings only a massage table. The first Burning Man in the desert will be a learning experience for all. They'd outgrown San Francisco's Baker Beach, and it's time for new climes.

Among the luggage, surely one of these adventurers has the September issue of *Rough Draft* with the original invitation to the gathering. Printed on an extralong green sheet, the announcement instructs participants to pack for a weekend in the desert, to bring "something of strong symbolic value" for the Zone-crossing ceremony, and some favorite CDs for a formal cocktail party.

"We are the Merry Pranksters of the 90's," *Rough Draft* declares. The Cacophony Society been operating since '86, but it has much deeper roots in the San Francisco beatnik ooze. The group traces its origins to a distant Prankster-style subtribe that dubbed itself the Suicide Club, which had *its* roots in the city's '60s free university system. The Suicide commandos specialized in post-Digger street theater, which included naked cable-car riding and the infiltration of the American Nazi Party. Another still-operating wing is the Billboard Liberation Front, which will infamously block out letters on a sign outside the Hillsdale Mall in California to read "LSD."

On this Labor Day weekend of 1990, the Cacophony Society's destination is not only over state lines but further. Furthur, genuinely, though none would be so gauche as to spell it out in such a manner. They call it a Zone Trip, their inspiration coming from Russian filmmaker Andrei Tarkovsky's haunting mind epic, *Stalker*.

It's an all-night drive, four hours to the northwest and another three hours up local roads. They get to Gerlach, Nevada, at dawn and pull en masse into the town's only cafe. It's the last spot before the desert starts, an ocean of blankness, a vast dried-up lakebed. Gerlach is a tiny town, but there's some amount of underground culture established there already.

The chain of autos pulls out of the cafe and chugs six or seven miles more down the road before, as by cosmic signal, they pull off the blacktop en masse, drive a hundred feet, and stop. This has all been decreed in advance, in the *Rough Draft* newsletter, which promises an "en-route ceremony of the caravan crossing into the Zone boundary." The mountains are off in the distance.

The instruction to bring something of symbolic value has surely been uttered before, but this time it works, it *really* works. A Cacophonist named Michael Mikel (part of the vague coterie partying with the cyberdelic *Mondo 2000* magazine) etches a Zone gateway in the rough desert floor. And then they get back in their cars and the Ryder truck and drive over it, into the new place.

They know a little bit about the physicality of the Zone, though not a lot. Windstorms blow over the first encampments almost instantly. Once established, many head for the hot springs. Others build an oven to bake bread, perhaps a genetic memory of Bread and Puppet's fire pageant stirring atavistically in Humbeadean blood out there on the playa. "The women baked small goddess-shaped boxes of bread to balance out the male energy in camp," Mikel will recall.

Then up goes the Burning Man, an avant-barn-raising with a hundred-foot long rope, ready for torching. "Dawn worshippers can easily watch as the sun rises and passes through the statue, illuminating in turn, each of his chakra points," one Burner remembers. "Eventually the sun pauses to cast a beatific halo around his head before continuing on its daily arc to mark the day."

They spend the rest of the weekend in awe of and in play with the blank space. Someone sets up a drum set and drops beats into the vast emptiness, decaying across the desert. On the final night, they torch the giant Man while the drums play, a new combination of signals trailing up into the free air of the republic. To celebrate the burn—or as it will very quickly come to be known, the Burn—there is a cocktail party, an act more prescient than even the most psychonautical Cacophonist could envision.

The territory they mark there, infinite miles from nowhere, is brand new, which was their intent. Imagined on Humbead's Map, Burning Man lives in the Great Naked Waste up-rightward of San Francisco, like a jetsam island that emerges once a year from an underwater volcano.

From the diamond sky above the diamond sea, Burning Man might seem like an island. Perhaps just a whirlpool. And it might resemble a giant belly button in the desert spitting white-hot rainbow flames toward the stars.

KAREN HORNING CHANGES her name a few times. Mainly, she goes by Karen Hoffman—two *F*s, one *N*, as in Abbie, not Albert. The stakes are rising for the people who are trying to keep America psychedelic, and Karen's path is symbolic. She'd been busted on the road once before and made it back for one probation but not a second. She and her crew switch from Furthur-style Deadhead school buses to more discreet RVs. Soon, they get Canadian plates, so they can fly undercover when they're out there between Dead shows, in those long unfriendly stretches where they fall off the Map, where names disappear, trusting in themselves and Jerry to get them and their cargo to the next city unharmed.

It's very, very dangerous out there for Deadheads carrying massive amounts of LSD from show to show. In many ways, Karen Hoffman and her friends are seriously unwanted. "I think we're being followed by professional drug dealers," Bob Weir tells *Rolling Stone*. "I don't know if they're Mob related or if it's bathtub acid of questionable quality. But if we come to town and there's LSD choking the schools for the next three months, I can see how people get upset—especially if it's bad acid." But Weir is the only Dead member willing to talk about it all.

The Dead have nothing against LSD, but they'd be quite happy if people would just figure out other places to get it. They issue statements in the parking lot, reprinted in tour newsletters like *Terrapin Flyer* and elsewhere. "Please don't buy or sell drugs at any of our shows," one reads.

But because of forces set into motion many years before, Karen Hoffman is destined to exist. Karen and her crew transport their material however they can, because they believe they must.

"Sometimes, I'd break it down into a liquor and carry it in a liquor bottle," Karen says. "Sometimes, you'd fly with it. Sometimes, you'd drive with it. Sometimes we'd do both, because we had so much. One time, the flask vaporizer broke, so it came out liquid and it was all black, so obviously that went in liquor bottles."

The most important hack the network continues to employ, though, is the names and the lack thereof. "While you may meet someone and he might call himself Frank, when he introduces himself to me, he might call himself Ted," says Karen. "That's the name of the game. It's all secrecy. That's survival. It has to be that way. For the most part, you will never meet the person who is actually doing it. You're going to meet the next one down or the next one down."

She might not know the names, but it is absolutely clear to Karen that the *they* on the other end of the line are the people who've been responsible all along, the distant descendants of the Brotherhood of Eternal Love, the light-wielding surf-gangsters from Laguna Beach. It is absolutely an unbroken chain. "This person here, they walk away, the next one walks in and picks it up, and they pass it off," Karen says.

The War on Drugs runs at full tilt and so far isn't doing much statistical damage. The 1990 National Institute on Drug Abuse survey concludes that drug abuse rates among eighteen- to twenty-five-year-olds hasn't changed drastically since 1982. Dope smoking is down from 27 percent to 22 percent, cocaine use is up from 7 percent to 8 percent. By other measures, though, more colorful effects are occurring. According to the *Monitoring the Future* report, more than 40 percent of high school seniors now say LSD is fairly or very easy to get, easier each year than the last. Still, only around 6 percent of the seniors will say they've used it in the past year. But that will go up soon, too.

Such a tiny, teeny number to represent so many burgeoning teenage heads. And a whole goodly number of the people responsible for that tiny percentile are lingering around the Grateful Dead. The co-ed Alpha Delta Phi society at Columbia have started to evolve past the jam world, growing more multicultural while maintaining their devotion to acid. But it's the Grateful Dead scene they go to when they need their special chemicals.

Statistics from a variety of surveys in 1990 and 1991, including *Monitoring the Future,* NIDA, and others, confirm the average demographic of LSD users: white, late teens or early twenties, more affluent than other drug users, and predominantly male. Perhaps more telling is the teens' perception of how hard it is to get LSD. In 1986, the year before the Grateful Dead's "comeback," *Monitoring the Future* measured an all-time low of high school seniors reporting that it would be "fairly easy or very easy to get," at 26 percent. By 1992, the Grateful Dead bigger and bigger each year, the number will hit 45 percent, matching the report's all-time high.

The DEA and the parents and all bearers of consensus reality maybe *do* have reason to be worried. The price of acid is always low, per Owsley's decree. But it's getting even cheaper. One of Karen Hoffman's older friends tells her that it went for $10,000 a gram in the early '80s. A decade later, Karen is picking it up for around $2,000 per gram, or 20 cents per 100 microgram hit, as is the standard in Karen's branch of the acid family. The dosage has gone down over the years, from an average of 250 micrograms a hit in the early Orange Sunshine days. There are plenty of levels of wisdom behind this, as well as just how much acid one should be taking to begin with. Many estimate that ego death happens around 150.

The real problem, though, is neither the ego death nor potentially unprepared humans, but the black market reality that makes it almost impossible for most customers to ever know what or how much LSD they are getting. Many contend that the acid itself has gotten weaker over the years, though others (including Karen and Mark McCloud) insist it is simply a matter of evolving underground ideas of proper dosage. The Man isn't making it any easier, though.

The legal debate over the LSD carrier weight laws makes its way all the way to the Supreme Court in the spring of 1991, where the court affirms the government's case by a 7–2 majority, that acid is sold by dose, not weight, and therefore the carrier weight is the correct measurement, merely reflecting the relative value of the drugs.

The situation seems terribly, terribly hopeless. The case that embodies this decision is against Richard Chapman, a Deadhead arrested in a Madison, Wisconsin, bar for selling a thousand hits (at about 57 cents a pop) to an undercover police officer. But the blotter paper weighed more than four grams, so Richard Chapman is screwed.

The chemists are up in arms, as Karen discovers when she meets some. "This is obviously of great concern to them, because it's hurting others. They're not touching paper, they're just touching crystal. To them, it's like spitting in their face. You can have an ounce of crystal and someone else has a fifth of a gram, and [someone with blotter paper] is going to get a heavier sentence. So this bothered them. They were going to fight it in their own way. They were hysterical.

"They were trying to use the lightest paper possible. They started trying to put it down in tiny little pieces that were like confetti so that if you got caught, you could blow it to the air. I was like, 'Well, that's fantastic, but how am I going to count out 1,000?!' Then there was the problem of trying to bring back the gels. Yes, you can spit on them real quick and they'll dissolve, but if you get caught with them, they're five times as heavy. Plus, there's nothing worse than putting the gels in the wrong place and having them melt on you, anyway. Keep away from heat when traveling! Oh dear God almighty."

On a business level, Karen says, the LSD business is "unlike anything else. You don't have competition. You're all allies. They did one thing, I did another. We were running in parallel with one another," Karen says of her big-moving comrades on Dead tour and in the acid world.

She remembers the darkness really creeping in around late 1991. "Looking back, that was when the whole thing clicked," she says. There had been a memorial gathering for Bill Graham at the Mark

Hopkins Hotel in San Francisco in early November 1991 after the long concert at the Polo Fields when the Dead jammed with Neil Young, Credence Clearwater Revival's John Fogarty, and Blues Traveler's John Popper.

"None of these people knew who I was," Karen says, but she and her competition/allies are there. Bill Graham was one of Karen's idols, especially for how he'd pioneered concert access for the handicapped. The world around the Dead mourns after his sudden death in a helicopter crash.

In comes a kid who wants ten grams. "It was a phenomenal amount for 1991. We were in a recession then. I'm shaking my head [at my friend], but she agreed to do it anyways. But that was the magic number: 10. She had been selling to him for a long time. The kid didn't even know he was being set up."

The kid ends up in jail, and eventually Karen's friends get nailed with more than thirteen kilos of LSD, the single biggest bust so far. The case explodes like a chain of firecrackers, each one potentially setting off more.

Karen is making plenty of money, and she throws her time and resources into the battle. She puts up money for various friends' lawyers. It's the hip economy principle continuing to operate. She gets involved with the Committee for Unjust Sentencing and spends her time canvassing in the parking lot at shows.

"My friends were getting hysterical," she recalls. "Saying, 'No, we don't want you on the front line, passing out this information.' Well, somebody's got to do it, and I do it very well. I'd pass out flyers and get signatures and do petitions about trying to change the LSD carrier weight laws. I'd have dummy letters to different representatives."

She connects with John Beresford, source of the original LSD that made its way to Timothy Leary's bemushroomed posse in Cambridge. The doctor had recently resurfaced as an on-call expert witness for the Committee for Unjust Sentencing, ready to evoke images of his childhood in Nazi Germany in the senseless War on Drugs. "He felt responsible," Karen says.

Another organization that gets involved is Families Against Mandatory Minimums, founded by Julie Stewart in 1991. "I always sort of felt like it was a body count when the band left town," Stewart says of the Dead. "You'd find the string of Deadheads that would be in the local jail who'd been busted by the authorities while they were in the parking lot at a Dead concert. It was very common that we'd get LSD cases sent to us, or that we'd hear from parents or from the defendant themselves."

The DEA has a new head of LSD enforcement, a veteran lawman named Gene Haislip, widely credited with stopping the flow of Quaaludes in the early '80s, who afterward turned his attention to crystal meth. He'd appeared as a panel of MDMA experts on *Donahue* in 1985, looking dapper in rectangular glasses. But here it is, 1992 and he's only just recently discovered the existence of the Grateful Dead. Some drug expert he is.

But a n00b with power. "We've opened a vein here," he crows about the Deadheads, a positively crackling cackle that cuts like lightning. "We're going to mine it until this whole thing turns around."

By the end of 1993, an estimated 1,500–2,000 Deadheads will be imprisoned, up from about a hundred only a few years before. Word goes around on tour that the DEA are working a program called Operation Dead End, specifically targeted at Deadheads. The truth is even more prosaic.

It is actually Operation Looking Glass. A 1992 *Los Angeles Times* article is one of the few places its existence is confirmed.

"We don't have any specific intent or operation that is targeted at the followers of the Grateful Dead," DEA administrator Robert Bonner says in an interview. "It is true that we have had some investigations that have led us to some Grateful Dead concerts."

Via their charitable Rex Foundation, the Dead donate some $10,000 to Families Against Mandatory Minimums, an angel grant that shows up at FAMM's office one day. It's the Rex's standard MO: laying surprise money on a diverse and heady array of recipients.

In 1992, the year the Rex Foundation first gives money to FAMM, they donate over a half-million dollars to sixty-five different causes, ranging from old standbys like the Haight-Ashbury Free Clinic and the San Francisco Mime Troupe to jazz musicians like Pharaoh Sanders and local programs including the Marin Ballet, as well as Prison Bible Studies, the Southern Humboldt Senior Center, and elsewhere.

But many believe that, given the Dead's position, $10,000 to FAMM is a cop-out and the Dead have a bigger responsibility toward the psychedelic culture they've been entwined with for decades. Conspiracy theories and paranoia abound. *Dupree's Diamond News* receives letters that claim that band members "are being forced, with the threat of their own incarceration, to keep touring, so the Feds can keep filling their bust quotas."

"That's something we are working on," Phil Lesh will say in 1994, when the *New Republic* publishes an editorial titled "Box of Pain" that argues the band's nonconfrontational stance is causing more harm than help. "But we're not working on it because this guy says we should. We're working on it because we think it's wrong. We just haven't quite figured out exactly what we should try to do about it. It's the kind of thing we all have to agree on."

The band never really does figure out how to respond to the DEA's presence on Dead tour or the mandatory minimums. The ticket office Xeroxes copies of a 1992 *USA Today* article titled "Attack on Deadheads Is No Hallucination" and includes it with all mail order tickets.

"We've seen a marked pattern of LSD distribution at Grateful Dead concerts," it quotes the DEA's Gene Haislip. "That has something to do with why so many [Deadheads] are arrested." In a sidebar, the article notes that, in some prison systems, such as Colorado, to be Deadhead is to be labeled as "gang affiliated," subject to the kind of prison treatment designed for Crips, Bloods, and members of the Aryan Nation.

There's nothing the Dead *can* do really. Their job has only ever been to make music for their people. But, among their people, something profound is amiss. It's not just the DEA, and it's not just Jerry Garcia, dabbling dangerously with opiates again after a few wonderful and productive and creative and (basically) clean years since his coma.

And it's not just the nitrous dealers and the ticketless miracle-seeking hordes who waggle their pointer fingers in the air outside venues, looking for free admission. Nor is it solely the Deadheads who've evolved into a breathing species of their own, spending their ascetic days pursuing the Dead life, panhandling and living at the margins of society. At their best, which is rare, these Deadheads imply a lower caste grace. At their worst, which is equally rare, they really do pose a problem worthy of lawmakers' consideration. It's not just any of these people. But there is something in the air, like the darkness of *Shakedown Street* has doubled.

In Karen Hoffman's hidden but powerful corner of psychedelic America, life is vicious. "People were stealing, killing," she says. "There was violence. Heavy heroin.

"There were a lot of drug overdoses. A lot of people who sold crystal [LSD] did heroin to come down. That was bad. They did [lines of] the crystal and [they'd] get so high sometimes that they couldn't handle it, so they'd do heroin to come down and the heroin would become a habit." That, thankfully, is a road that Karen never goes down. She's too busy.

Not that she doesn't snort crystal LSD. Karen Hoffman snorts crystal LSD. Karen Hoffman is someone who *shouldn't* exist. One of the few medical reports on the subject, published in 1974 in the *Western Journal of Medicine,* reported that eight San Franciscans, ages nineteen to thirty-nine, accidentally snorted crystal LSD thinking it was cocaine. "Within five minutes they experienced anxiety, restlessness, generalized paresthesias and muscle discomfort, vomiting and physical collapse," reports. Really, really *not* recommended.

"You always have to have something in your stomach, same thing if you take mushrooms," Karen says about her crystal trips. Also required, surely, is a long and progressive history of constant, escalating LSD use and tolerance. Sometimes there's nausea or worse. "One friend, I gave a plastic bag that had an ounce in it, and he touched it, and he got so high that he peed himself." The medical journal reports diarrhea.

What a waste, thinks the retired Guatemalan acid cook Sarah Matzar when she hears of the crystal snorters. And not particularly good for anybody's mental state, Karen included.

There's a lot of money flowing around, too, with all kinds of odd ramifications. "None of them have jobs, never want jobs," one government investigator will say. "They don't think of things like getting a house and a family and a car. . . . I invest in assets, in money and gold jewelry. LSD dealers could care less . . . none of them, they don't have credit cards, they don't have jewelry. It's just a . . . free lifestyle."

The agent is wrong about the jewelry, for starters. Out on Shakedown Street, Karen gains a familiar mentor: Owsley himself. Karen had started buying jewelry and pendants from Owsley "Bear" Stanley at the Greenpeace table. Recently, the original head chemist had legally dropped the Augustus. Karen thinks of her purchases as investments. She talks to and befriends Stanley, as obdurate as ever.

"I would go backstage with Owsley," she says. "My other friends had laminates. It wasn't cool to get me a laminate, because I had too much stuff. Owsley, when he was back [from Australia], I could go anywhere in the country and he'd walk me into a show." Bear is as filled with practical esoterica as ever. He instructs her in the sly ways of the game. He'll pretty much instruct anybody if they buy enough of his handcrafted jewelry.

"You've got to take it to the side," she recounts of his financial advice. "You've got to keep it moving. That's why I was buying his art. That's why he brought me over to Jerry's art show to buy Jerry's art." Garcia, the onetime art student, had begun to display his paintings at the gallery of one Roberta Weir (no relation) in San Francisco, and Karen buys a dozen pieces. She begins to accumulate a collection of poster art. "It was Owsley who was trying to tell me that I should save for a rainy day, but at the same time I'd also be turning around and dropping $50,000 or $60,000 on other people's attorneys.

"As he learned, when shit hits the fan, when he got busted, who's going to get you out? They did keep it flowing. But when he got in trouble, then what?"

Imagine the forthcoming trouble as grainy point-of-view camera footage rushing through myriad incongruous American landscapes, as if from the vantage of some cosmic head-chomping tremor-worm. The images start to look more and more familiar, a flash of tie-dye here and there, but you are unable to ever see the grotesque Thing itself. It's coming.

Oakland motel rooms are a central point for the sketchiness, whether the Dead are performing at the nearby Coliseum or not. It's a permanent Shakedown Street out there, crystal getting laid to blotter, or whatever else needs doing on the down-low. "My rule was no smoking weed," Karen says. Seems sensible.

A crew Karen knows is making too much noise and a cop arrives. "He walks into the room and he sees the powder on the table and assumes it's coke," she hears. The representative of the good people of the United States does the classic cheesy cop move and dips his finger triumphantly in the pile of crystal and wipes it on his teeth.

"You could see the look on his face and he knew it wasn't cocaine," Karen reports the story. A line of crystal directly on the gums would explode in the brain in *1 . . . 2 . . . 3 . . . someone get the gun.* "They took the gun off the cop so he wouldn't hurt himself," Karen says. As the poor guy soars towards some unknown transpersonal fate, the crystal crew clears out, taking the gun with them. As the story goes, the cop is found wandering naked on a bridge, but then they're *always* found wandering naked on a bridge, aren't they?

THE DESIGNATED GENERATIONAL signifier pulls on one of his signature handmade T-shirts. It's time for the backlash against the Grateful Dead to go mainstream, but something even deeper is at hand, a profound trans-formation in the American counterculture. And right now it's Kurt Cobain's turn to be on the cover of the *Rolling Stone,* and, shit, what year is it? (1992) What continent am I on? (Australia.) What color is my hair today? (Orange-pink.) Shredded jeans or dress? (Shredded jeans.) The shirt has a punk rock duck with a pink mohawk. The duck is also flipping the bird. Above, the designated generational signifier has scrawled his own special message for *Rolling Stone* readers: "KILL THE GRATEFUL DEAD."

!!!!

Why would anyone *say* such a thing? But Nirvana's Kurt Cobain says what he wants, man, that's what makes him Kurt Cobain, and having a virulent hatred for the Dead is an important stance for many young punks in the early 1990s. The shot doesn't get used on the cover, though it gets out there and makes its point. "I wouldn't wear a tie-dyed tee-shirt unless it was dyed with the urine of Phil Collins and the blood of Jerry Garcia," the Nirvana bandleader sneers into an interviewer's microphone sometime.

Deadheads are longhaired freaks to feel sorry for. So much mis-placed promise, so close to finding the path but getting sidetracked into shadow play and psychedelic mumbo jumbo. Cobain and his lit-tle tribe are grown from a distant branch of the counterculture with firm and consistent parallels to the Dead going all the way back to and below the root: the two 1965-era bands called the Warlocks.

Both the California and New York Warlocks dug R&B and Dylan and the Stones. One turned into the Grateful Dead. One flipped into the Velvet Underground. The Velvets even had their own legendary tapers who helped build a message-carrying network of their own. Where Dead tapes broadcast the shape of the Dead's psychedelic ritual, the small cache of Velvet Underground bootlegs became secret passwords in places of deep subterranean cool.

"The Dead seemed more like a group of ex-folkies just dabbling in distortion (as their albums eventually bore out)," critic Lester Bangs wrote in *Creem* in 1970, stating the protopunk party line. "It seems likely that the Velvet Underground were definitely eclipsing the Dead from the start when it came to a new experimental music." It was an early branching point in how rock developed after the '60s, a series of parallel regional scenes exploding from the time of Lou Reed's last stand with the Velvets in August 1970.

The Dead, at some point, simply became a stand-in for all that's bogus about the always-smoldering remains of '60s baby boomer rock—perhaps because the Dead are still out there touring every season. Even the well-sold-out ex-Eagle Don Henley uses a line about a Dead bumper sticker on an expensive Cadillac as a symbol of generational sellout. Hating the Dead has little to do with the Dead's music much of the time.

"I think the Dead are weird because a lot of people who say they don't like them haven't actually heard them," says Dylan Carlson, the guitarist in an underground Seattle doom/sludge/drone-rock band called Earth and a rabid Dead fan. He is also Kurt Cobain's best friend and heroin buddy. "Unfortunately, Kurt was not one I was ever able to turn [on]," Carlson sighs about the times he played the Dead for the Nirvana leader. He does get the Screaming Trees into "Mountains of the Moon," though.

Nearly every white American musical scene, it seems, no matter how punk or country or electronic or classical, will eventually include a Deadhead; and if the scene reaches any kind of critical mass whatsoever, an invisible contingency. But any notion of a unified counterculture has long since disappeared, a figment of an outmoded imagination, now a beautiful array of different fronts, from empowering riot grrl yawps to throbbing tribal dance scenes to massive hip-hop parties and metalhead bacchanals. Anything antiauthoritarian that reconfigures consensus reality via music and art has value. The Dead and the Deadheads float in the cloud of a vast slow explosion, ongoing since the '60s, the elders and tenders to the early golden light of a cultural universe that coalesces into planets and atmospheres and fixed points and continues to expand.

After Nirvana explodes into popularity, the record companies don't know who to sign or where to throw their money. The same Soundscan technology that crowns Nirvana as pop gods also reveals the true marketplace primacy of hip-hop and country, a vast audience of record buyers beyond the rock narrative. Madison Avenue grows reinverted with the new advertising of authenticity. The marketplace has room for everyone. It's bigger than tents. It's the biggest tent. Its underside is the color of the sky.

As in the '60s, many undergrounds suddenly become flush with record company money. The Vermont quartet Phish are well on their way to getting signed by a major label anyway, but the unlikely success of Nirvana suddenly turns the pop marketplace into a briefly reasonable place for bands with any kind of experimental pop aspirations. Phish releases their major label debut, *A Picture of Nectar*—named for a Burlington club owner—in early 1992. But everybody knows that to *really* hear Phish's music, even if you think it sucks, it's necessary to see them live or find the tapes.

The '90s pop confusion recalls the upheavals of the '60s in its sudden inclusiveness. But people compare every decade to the '60s. There is change afoot in the cultural pathways, though, not the least of which is the final mainstreaming of punk in part due to accidental designated generational signifier Kurt Cobain. Plus, there's that 2012 date that's only two decades away. A character in the cult TV series *Twin Peaks* is based on Terence McKenna. Even just the existence of *Twin Peaks* seems to radiate like a signal of strange change. It's beautiful. It's too real now to confine to a rainbow.

LUTHER DELANEY MEETS the Spinners in Indiana for a showdown at the start of the Grateful Dead's 1991 summer tour. Even the inevitable collapse of the Dead-influenced spiritual sect reveals something fundamental about the personality of the Deadhead-variety American psychedelic ritualist.

Luther, the Spinners' onetime benefactor, rents a car in Indianapolis and cuts down sweltering midwestern highways toward the improbable location of a parking lot in Noblesville. The prefab summer concert amphitheater known as Deer Creek has become a popular destination with Deadheads for the precise reason that it's in the middle of nowhere. Locals have taken to the Deadheads, realizing the annual arrival of the portable psychedelic ritual-horde is a boon to the economy. Like a sacrifice, the Noblesvillians offer their fields for camping.

The Dead and their hordes require vast tracts of space to fully unfurl their Humbeadean carpet across the landscape and take their substances and dance and congregate. So that's where the well-to-do ex-Spinner Luther Delaney points himself. Lately, he's gotten into wearing military fatigues and a beret. It's never hard to find the Spinners. And he finds them and their portable storefront easily.

The situation had come to a boil. He'd told the Spinner woman that he was in love with her and received the sad-eyed reply, "But . . . I'm a nun."

Not long after that, the Spinners had physically barred Luther from visiting the Land he'd helped them purchase. That doesn't sit well.

At Deer Creek, "I had my full bagpipes or whatever and played them and walked up to their spread," Luther says. When he gets into a space, he really goes for it. The Scottish war drones echo across Shakedown Street as Luther approaches the makeshift Spinner encampment. "They sent all these nuns out, and they tried to push me off the spread. Next thing I know, I see this golf cart with a sheriff in it and a couple of nuns hanging off the back."

Oh, friends, it all spins out from here, and all Luther wants is to see their deal through on its original terms and for the sweet Spinner nun to be happy. But now, after some legal wrangles and rehab, Luther just sits back and waits for the Spinners to implode, which, by the spring of 1992, they do.

And what's remarkable about the subsequent implosion of the Spinners is that nobody really gets hurt. The details of the collapse are pretty mundane: The bearded leader is caught sleeping with several nuns when they were all supposed to be celibate. There are allegations of emotional abuse and possibly more, which is bad, but neither long term nor systemic. It's complicated but personal and almost instantly the leader is ejected from the blessed Land and goes back to his parents' house with his tail between his legs. There's some newspaper coverage of it, because the Spinners always make good copy.

The Spinners are the closest the Grateful Dead ever get to a genuine cult grown ostensibly from the ideals of the band's lyrics. Sure, there'd been Ray "Cat" Olsen, the Deadhead bank robber. Yes, Charles Manson passed through a Dead gig or two, and the band's crew had a hand in the planning of Altamont. There's weird historical juju, dark vibrations, and vampires everywhere in the Dead's time-track, including a recent spate of horrible police brutality in the parking lot. But for a cult, the Spinners are more or less benign. Sure, the leader turns out to be a creepy womanizing sketchball with his own motivations, but the enterprise as a whole—Spinning as bliss, worked out with footnotes and texts—why not?

The Spinners' demise is a testament to the antiauthoritarian, antidogmatic common sense implanted at the deepest level of the Deadhead mind. Joseph is hardly messianic, despite his beard and long hair and strictures and whatnot. He's just a louse, and the Spinner ladies aren't going to stand for it once they know what's up.

"They kept it going for another five or six months," Luther says. "And then they started not paying off the note, and then I called the sheriff and implemented foreclosure and all that."

As a group, the Spinners dissipate. Luther Delaney takes over the Land and plants some pot and drifts off into the hippie mists and out of the text, always a Deadhead. The others head into different spheres. The anthropologist becomes a physician, eventually helping to organize and administer a Doctors Without Borders–like nonprofit. And people keep on spinning at shows, always spinning, rarely with a capital *S*. Maybe someday somebody will again get the urge to go deeper, to spin, spin, spin someplace new. Bye now, Spinners.

GOA GIL IS called Goa Gil even in Goa, but it's even more obvious when he starts coming back to the States in the late '80s to visit his mother and gets DJ gigs around San Francisco. He is not the originator of electronic dance music, but Gil becomes an unexpected connection point as psychedelic Americas begin to link up in the early 1990s. He is a big-bearded, super-chill, dreadlocked oddity in garish psych-wear from Anjuna Beach, spinning music from DAT tapes. He doesn't match beats so much as vibes.

Like the Grateful Dead, Goa Gil carries with him an almost fully formed and idealized psychedelic ritual. Unlike the Dead and the Acid Tests, Anjuna Beach had been able to sustain its primally psychedelic full moon parties for decades. The music that developed there, Goa trance, seemed to wash ashore from the Arabian Sea like an evolving luminescent bioform over the course of the '80s.

Gil is a tape trader, too. He'd been DJing cassettes on the beach since the mid-1970s. When the new beats started arriving from Europe—"wave music," it was called—Gil got so excited that he sold his whole previously accumulated collection, and he and his friends get to transforming it. "There was a lot of records that had really great music, but then it would have some singing, or something that was really horrible—many records like that," he will remember in 1997.

The records, though, might have "these really radical synthesizers and drum machines. In those days, we used to record just the good parts of the record to a cassette. And then with two Walkman Professionals, I used to make another tape with stop and start, and arrange the good parts in different sequences, and make my own mixes with a lot of cutup." Gil uses the idea to build long, narrative-like sets, not beat matching so much as arc building.

Unlike even the jammiest rock band, Goa Gil and his beat-happy ilk *do* actually go all night, leaving wide open spaces for new psychedelic rituals and MDMA love-ins, for surprises, for holy dance-floor portals. Goa Gil sometimes DJs for literally twenty-four hours, a Port-O-Let installed just behind his DJ rig in case he has any earthly needs.

Gil discovers the same bardo-flow that David Mancuso had found at the Loft in the lower Manhattan in the early '70s, organizing his DJ sets around the three stages of an acid trip as represented in Timothy Leary's *Tibetan Book of the Dead*. "I always said a Goa party was not just a disco under the coconut trees, it's an initiation," Gil says. "So we would create a story that touched on all things of the whole story of man at this point. The Crossroads of Humanity."

There will be plenty who maintain that the Goa scene passed its peak sometime in the '80s and everyone else is just a tourist. And plenty more who find the whole affair a center for new-world kitsch.

Undoubtedly, though, it remains a home for global psychedelia, part real, part caricature. After serving out his jail sentence, idealistic British microdot chemist Richard Kemp is spotted there.

When the SF-Raves e-mail list strikes up a groupmind on a Berkeley campus server in 1992, the listers discover the Bay Area's prodigal trance DJ playing frequently around town. As always, Goa Gil—a teenage member of the Family Dog collective in the '60s—carries the ethic of the People's Music, always eager to spin. One evening, an SF-Raver posts, surprised, "Goa Gil called _me_ today" asking to get on a bill.

Gil is a relatively small player in the bigger American rave wave that crashes onto many dance floors, just as disco had two decades earlier, including Dead shows. The SF-Raves list has its share of Deadheads. "I noticed that going to raves has affected my rock-spacy dancing style," posts one. "I'm incorporating the rave blade-hand wave-jab arm motions into my repertoire of dance moves."

Around now, at Oakland Dead shows, a party bus run by the Atomic Dog Collective wedges open the connection between the Shakedown Street *carnaval* in the Dead parking lot and the new global party that's sweeping across beaches and grotty British warehouses and tropical climes and SF-Raves and a spring break near you. "It just feels so right," one of the Atomic Dogs tells a British journalist outside Oakland Coliseum. "Here's this huge parking lot in this totally industrial part of town, with all these people hanging out. There's absolutely no reason not to do it."

"The task that rave organisers face now is to learn from the hippies and to further fuse the two traditions," the British journalist will conclude after a Shakedown Street visit. The cross-pollination is beginning. Sometimes, the house kids go into the shows, even. They're out in the parking lot, skateboarding between discarded beer bottles and stray dogs and fireworks and departing cars, the wheels on cement adding to the ambient sound picture along with the ever-present hiss of nitrous balloons.

In San Francisco, the fusion of hippies and dance music feels natural and begins to speed up, a connection of archetypes that will radiate across the country during the next two decades. Even in the Bay Area, there are still plenty of connections to be made. Like Dead shows, SF-Raves—and the Bay Area dance scene in general—becomes a connecting point for techheads, old and new, from pioneer phone phreaker John Draper (who'd inspired Steve Jobs) to future free software pioneer Brian Behlendorf, who will also be involved in one of the online world's first psychedelic info repositories.

Someone on SF-Raves inquires about Burning Man, and a user from the WELL registers that the event "is _very_ newage oriented. Last year, the women baked bread, while the men did some kind of manly task, as part of the ritual. I'm kind of surprised to hear they're having djs."

For the first time in 1992, there will be ritual dance beats out in the desert. And, naturally, one of them is Goa Gil. "The Burning Man organizers made us go like a mile away in the desert and set it up there because they wanted to sleep at night," chuckles Gil. "There were less than a thousand people at Burning Man; it was actually really sweet."

ONE TUESDAY AT Wetlands in 1992, there's Brian Eno–championed New Age zither-strummer Laaraji Venus at an event billed as "White Light Cafe," hosted by someone named Peyote Bird. Even more than the touring Lollapalooza festival that begins that summer, Wetlands and its mural become an actual place where the different electric tribes collide.

Most weeks though, Tuesdays now holds the Eco-Saloon activism meetings on the same free night as Dead Center. Out go the environmentalists and in come the cover bands and drum circles and spontaneous chant-ins by the local Rainbow Family, who (on at least one occasion) storm the stage when the Dead cover band happens to be on.

That year, too, there's spoken word by former Black Flag singer Henry Rollins (a sometime Dead fan) and riot grrl art-punk by Bikini Kill. There's the Black Rock Coalition, headed by Living Colour, in numerous variations. Hip-hop act Cypress Hill blow out a Cannabis Action Network benefit.

It's the Deadhead clubhouse of all of our dreams and all are welcome, all types and trends and signifiers and countercultural survivors.

Come Daevid Allen of Franco-British prog-psych legends Gong! Come sloppy, ecstatic, LSD gobbling Arizonian punk brothers, the Meat Puppets! Come original P-Funk guitarist Eddie Hazel! Please welcome, from Kingston, Jamaica, the Wailers! Those who might raise money for presidential candidate Jerry Brown, do come in! Come, Mighty Mighty Bosstones and fill the room with skanking, pogoing straight-edge rude boys and girls in checkered finery, a new punk subculture from the 'burbs! Come old-wave ska figureheads like Desmond Dekker!

And gluing them all together, those new kinds of jammy bands, those new kinds of jammy fans. They'll listen to almost all of it. Club owner Larry Bloch employs a rotating crew of DJs every night of the week to cater to whatever crowd might be in the room. Pearl Jam and Ani DiFranco and Oasis and many others have or will make their Manhattan debuts on the weird sideways stage.

One non-Deadhead DJ and new staff member at the club is shocked to find fans dancing barefoot among broken glass at a Spin Doctors show, their last at the club, en route to MTV success in 1993. But the staffer is more shocked later when he goes downstairs to the Inner Sanctum in the comfortably appointed basement one Tuesday evening while the environmentalists are meeting upstairs.

"I saw these guys, older guys," he says. "They're lining up. Some of them have hoodies. There were all these [other] guys lining up, like five or six guys . . . it didn't seem like the typical Tuesday volunteer staff. Some guy had a little desk thing."

The staffer asks the volunteer coordinator, "Is there is something going on [down] there?" After some cajoling, the coordinator admits that it's a medicinal marijuana exchange. It is one of the earliest in New York outside the Yippies.

"It was a lot of AIDS patients there were coming down and getting the stuff. We were all worried about it. It was too risky. But then, fuck it: we're Wetlands, we've got a responsibility." Wetlands founder Larry Bloch raises his staffers well.

THE BLOTTER ACID collector Mark McCloud has long referred to his dwelling as the Institute of Illegal Images, so it shouldn't be *too* much of a surprise when the FBI give him the "black kiss," accusing him of being someone called the Cadillac Man. Even with nu-liberal baby boomer Bill Clinton in the White House, federal agencies continue their aggressive pursuit of LSD cases, and Mark McCloud *will* be used to make an example. Pulled close to the mouth of the tremor worm, McCloud gets a look at the secret apparatus the government is using to fight LSD distribution.

Mark McCloud might admit to collecting LSD, but that's not the same as being involved in a conspiracy to deal it, which is what he is charged with in Houston in 1992. The judge dismisses the case without even waiting for the defense to present McCloud's side.

For several years, Deadheads have whispered of being targeted by a federal program called Operation Dead End. Mark McCloud uncovers the true spook rubric of Operation Looking Glass. "No one knew about Operation Looking Glass on the people's side of the thing because it was kept secret by [the government]," he says. "They don't mention it very openly, it's hard to see in a report. In their braggadocio, when they brag about the bust, they often mention it."

In 1992, in denying the existence of Operation Dead End, a DEA administrator confirms the existence of the agency's LSD-oriented Looking Glass, though he says it is not targeted at Deadheads in specific. Many, including Mark McCloud, believe otherwise.

Some years later, Mark will hear about another consequence of his 1992 Houston bust. He'd finally tracked down the mysterious Dealer McDope, the old-world psychedelic figure who remains one of the increasingly few steady suppliers for extremely rare LSD precursor chemicals. McDope and McCloud become shadow colleagues in the secretive acid world where truth becomes parable and parable becomes cartoon.

"My first arresting officer, the agent that tried to kill me back in '92 in Houston, Texas," McCloud says, "my buddy gave him the [acid-dosed] *handshake* and he ended up in the hospital, after my trial. I certainly never asked for anything like that. That's just because he was who he was.

"McDope was that way with his crew, too. If he thought anything needed checking in with, he'd dose you. He had a group that was getting into crack, so he put a chemist to work on it, and he came up with a thing called the Space Base. It was crack with acid that didn't lose its potency when heated. So he fixed them good. The next Monday, they were all on time, dressed up, and clean shaven." McCloud cackles when he tells the parable-cartoon-exactly-as-it-happened truth.

McCloud is sure to note that the agent who ends up in the hospital, dosed with the crystal LSD handshake, is Gene Haislip, scourge
of Deadheads everywhere.

THE MOTORCADE WHIRLS up to the Saint Francis Hotel in San Francisco with
blaring police sirens and full regalia. Though the drug war rages on
in the Clinton years, other parts of psychedelic America careen into
the consensus reality of high-ranking government officials, both sides
perhaps changing from the transaction. At the Saint Francis in 1993,
the Secret Service case the scene, and a moment later the vice president and his entourage emerge and enter the lobby.

They make for the check-in, and the vice president's assistant
scans the room. The assistant spots his man and glances back at the
vice president and then again at the man in the baseball cap. The vice
president's assistant signals. The man in the baseball cap shakes his
head. The assistant signals again. And the man shakes his head again.

Finally, the vice president and his entourage disappear into the elevators. Shortly, the assistant reappears in the lobby. His posture is different. He walks over to where the man in the baseball cap is sitting in
a chair, smoking cigarettes, and waiting. And since that man is Grateful Dead tape freak Dick Latvala, there's also, say, a 50/50 chance
that he's tripping. And if he's not, Dick is absolutely having his mind
blown anyway. Oh, Dick, it's been too long. Sorry to ignore you!

The vice president's assistant, Dennis Alpert, approaches Dick,
and the two sit in the lobby bar, while a newly semisober Dick Latvala
drinks sodas and chain smokes.

"I just wanted to see you and observe you in your natural element,"
Dick tells Alpert, a cousin of Ram Dass. "I didn't want to be a bother.
I didn't want to be a part of it, because if I was a part of it, I wouldn't
be able to appreciate it as much as I just did."

The performance is vintage Dick, as weird and sage as ever, marveling over the strange reality that he, the ex-Morehouse hex slinger,
the Hawaiian pot farmer, the king Grateful Dead tape collector, could
even be invited to greet Air Force Two at the airport and join the motorcade as it swept toward the city. What a life! But Dick would rather
watch from afar. He is more curious about Dennis Alpert than he is
about the vice president. With good reason, too. Likely, Dick spies a

new archetype that Dennis Alpert embodies, a Deadhead who has not turned his back on mainstream society at all but assimilated into the very fabric of government.

Alpert, a twenty-something Deadhead from New England, holds the appropriate title of Al Gore's trip director, a decidedly unpsychedelic task except in the most figurative sense. On the campaign trail, Gore had told Alpert how, in Vietnam, he'd listened to his eight-track of *Workingman's Dead* over and over to remind him of home. When Alpert moved into the White House at the start of the Clinton administration, his own personal first act was to invite the Dead to stop by when they were in town. Dennis McNally, the Dead's press liaison, hung up on him at least once before Alpert had a White House operator call the Dead's office to prove his veracity.

Eventually, the band come through and Alpert hosts Garcia and Phil Lesh and Mountain Girl and Mickey Hart and more, and they meet the vice president. It's not the hugest of surprises, in some ways, the Grateful Dead at the White House. Willie Nelson as well as various presidential offspring had smoked pot there, but the Dead represent a different class of outlaw.

"They became older, as we all do, and they became more active in political issues and social issues," says Dennis Alpert of the band's changing apolitical priorities. "Bobby [Weir] became more active in environmental causes." The whole band had embraced earth-saving via the Rex Foundation, which Alpert himself will eventually join as a board member.

But Jerry Garcia still hadn't voted for Bill Clinton. As usual, Jerry Garcia hadn't voted at all. Alpert, however, comes away from the Dead's White House visit with the feeling that Garcia will surely cast himself for the Democrats in the next election. The communards are still out there, the pot farmers up in the Emerald Triangle continue to harvest their delicious marijuana, the Deadheads continue to follow the Dead around. To be a head is no longer to be strictly counter-American. It's true. Communes and heads are fully part of Al Gore's and Bill Clinton's realities. As a young reporter for the *Tennessean,* Gore had even written a thoughtful story about a visit to Stephen Gaskin and the Farm.

But to relegate the counterculture to just another constituency in Bill Clinton's America is to diminish the utopian stateless/leaderless dream of a natural psychedelic order. And if that dream is increasingly untenable, it will remain useful and even practical in places, often directly proportional to its dreamers' youth. There is a sadness in watching psychedelic America age in the '90s, as well, when the drug war still looms over the culture's every act of celebration. But that's also where the Grateful Dead fit in. Dick Latvala goes and sees them frequently and enthusiastically—after all, that's part of his job—but it's the tapes and community that provide the renewable solace and joy that Dick and so many other people require.

Dick Latvala has split from his new wife. She stopped smoking grass and he won't, so he moves up to Petaluma to a subdivided bungalow with a roommate, heartbroken in a lot of ways. His house abuts his ex-wife Carol's place. They're still great friends, Carol working down at the Dead's ticket office, and the two abodes make up a little minicommunity of ex-Morehousers, Deadheads, and the usual motley array of friends. In the neighborhood is Harvey Lubar, the Bronx-born cofounder of the seminal Hell's Honkies tape club, who becomes a Latvala pal, too. Dick can be grumpy, but he's a true head for whatever he has to put up with at work. At home, he makes no attempt to hide his rampant Deadheaddom. "Better than Beethoven!" he'll still bellow.

"He was used to people ignoring him or thinking of him as low status in the scene," says journalist Steve Silberman, "but I actually thought of him as one of the secret buddhas that protected the music, a benevolent deity. He was very beautiful in a weird way, even though by the time I met him he was an old man and you could tell he'd been addicted to various bad things, but you could tell by his physical presence. We used to talk several times a week for hours. We talked about the Dead, but we also talked a lot *not* about the Dead. He was completely aware in Zen fashion that his work was the ultimate gift and the ultimate curse. He had to suffer because the collective ethos of the backstage scene was very bruising and masculine. He was in part a stand-in for all Deadheads, for whom [the band's roadies] had contempt. Though I also thought the crew were great, for all the ill one hears being spoken about them."

Dick Latvala's job in the virtual treasury of the hip economy isn't so bad some of the time, but he's still mainly the sandwich getter. Phil Lesh's involves avocado, onions, and rye bread. The benefits are excellent. No, really. At one point, it's decided that Dick is drinking too much, and he probably is, and needs to go to rehab. So—on the Dead's dime—he cleans up, give or take the acid and the pot. For a while, the drinking and other drugging goes by the wayside.

For all his struggles, Dick is guardian of the increasingly valuable crypto-currency that Grateful Dead tapes have become, chairman of the Humbeadean Federal Reserve in a sense. To control inflation, Dick just keeps on clandestinely releasing the Tapes. It's beautiful, sometimes. But the Tapes retain a dark power when they're scarce. They remain the flip side of the band's acid trips in every way, the absolute historical preservation of ephemeral alchemical wanderings, and they carry gravity and meaning that some Deadheads will lie, cheat, and steal to acquire. Tapers tangle themselves in knotted trust hierarchies. In one case, Dick lends out a batch of tapes to a friend, who departs for his honeymoon, only to have the tapes secretly copied by a house watcher.

Occasionally, Dick angers when the tapes he makes for friends escape into the world. One time, a pal makes copies for another, and Dick blows his top and doesn't talk to the guy for two years. Other times, Dick is totally unfazed when he hears about it. He knows the power of the Tapes as well as anyone, but there is something compulsive about Dick's sharing. He simply can't stop making copies.

In that sense, Dick Latvala *is* doing his job. Even as the Grateful Dead enter another creative fallow period while Jerry Garcia struggles with addiction, Dick releases unheard material into the ever-present taper network. Representing the absolute mainstream of Deadheads, the taper network is an important cog in keeping the Dead's American psychedelic ritual in demand throughout the country.

The notion of free tape exchanges grows more popular. A few years earlier, a fellow San Rafael–based band, Metallica, had instituted a taper's section at its shows, borrowing the legal text directly from the Grateful Dead's taper tickets. Many bands will come to see it as a boon.

The Grateful Dead's notion of communal service through transcendence and transcendence through boogie seemingly belongs to a quaint aesthetic backwater. But powered by in-the-moment improvisation, it remains all powerful, keeping listeners pumping money back into the hip economy, buying tickets and T-shirts or making

purchases of drugs and food and sundries in the parking lot and keeping it all spinning at top speed.

This is the ship that Dick and Carol Latvala sail with, along with
perhaps hundreds of other professional colleagues who work in San
Rafael and the neighboring towns. Though divested into a number of
operations, the Grateful Dead are a vast California corporation, even
if they don't resemble or behave like most.

Dick Latvala sends tapes to Dennis Alpert at the White House,
perhaps even leaked ones, and Dennis Alpert sends Dick postcards,
and Dick continues to marvel at it all. The new economic boom years
have just begun in the United States, and the Grateful Dead's psychedelic republic now seems fully reconnected.

Finally, the Dead (and specifically Phil Lesh) approve the first *Dick's
Picks* CDs to go out into the world, a two-disc set. Lesh edits out a
bass solo, and Dick has to arrange some other bits to make it fit. The
December 1973 show from Miami maybe isn't Dick's *first* choice, but
it's a legit great night. Donna Jean Godchaux is home on maternity
leave, and it's just the guys' voices again, like it was in the early days,
and the second set has a supreme meltdown after "The Other One"
that resolves into a tender "Stella Blue." And there's Dick's name on
the front cover. On future editions, his silhouette will be added to the
CD art. Dick's going to be a star, and he just can't stop sharing.

One of his old taper friends comes for a visit, and Dick loads him
up with tapes, some of them probably ones he shouldn't be giving
away, and Grateful Dead merchandise, too. He gives his buddy a
Grateful Dead keychain. Later, as his friend pulls away, Dick comes
running out of the house and across the lawn.

"Thinking I had forgotten something, I stopped the car," the taper
remembers. "Dick had found two little flashlights and decided that
my friend and I needed these tiny little flashlights and he had to pass
them on before we left. No Grateful Dead insignias, just flashlights."
Thanks, Dick!

THE CHINESE DRAGON parade happens while the Dead drift into the ritual
psychedelic drumz/space portion of a late January 1993 show at the
Oakland Coliseum. It's that little portal that the musicians force open

every time they perform in their traditional two-set manner, the clearest genetic connection to the Acid Tests. The Grateful Dead and their followers have created so much freedom for themselves that sometimes the freedom itself seems to disappear, confined into a painted corner by various realities.

On this night, the nearest convenient song for the big jam is "Terrapin Station," and the band unfold into open-ended territory and stay there for more than a full half-hour of straight improvisation. Carlos Santana joins on guitar while the joyous dragon parade procession wends across the floor.

The whole night is chaotic and high stakes. LSD dealer Karen Hoffman is high, high, high, as usual. The parade only accentuates the usual *carnaval*-esque intrigues of a Dead show, a backdrop for dramas of everyday ecstasy, and all other functions the music has come to serve. And out into the parking lot, the carnival rolls on, continuous and carnivorous and slithering and serpentine and threatening to open up. Karen Hoffman has to watch herself. Despite the freedoms that come with being a money-making drug dealer, the amount of places she can now go is tiny.

Out on Shakedown Street after the show, the sensory input rages. There's a bus pumping dance music, where members of the Atomic Dog collective spin house jams and the world is a whirl. Karen Hoffman absorbs the ambience but takes in few of the specific details in the white noise of the postshow parking lot scene. She doesn't have a lot of time for the parking lot anymore.

And this night she is arrested in a big multimotel postshow bust in the broken hinterlands of Oakland. There's a decent amount of LSD involved, some 60,000 hits—"double-strength," the *San Francisco Chronicle* claims—and eight heads arrested, including Karen, her name reported in the paper as Hoffman. She gets out, though.

She'd been busted before, in Vermont, and had shed one of her identities. And Louisiana. And Iowa. Karen gets out. Karen detours. Karen has to move.

"I got my hair cut," she says. There are multiple IDs. "I used to always have hair to my waist. I chopped it, dyed it mouse-brown. I would dress in Ralph Lauren, all the rage. Polo. The whole thing." When it's short, her hair gets frizzy, and she needs a supply of product to keep it tamped down. Karen goes undercover in the mainstream, still always watching. She keeps on following the Dead on their rounds, making her moves, keeping the acid a-flow.

It is during these days of flight that Karen herself first hears the phrase Grateful Dead Family applied to a certain sect of LSD dealers in the vicinity of the Grateful Dead. The term "Family" had long circulated around the dealers, but, in the words of the then-incarcerated Commander X, the term was meant to be "anarchistic, ad hoc, holistic and spontaneous. No rituals, secret shakes, or any of that nonsense. And it was in constant flux as people met each other, came and went from the scene, changed allegiances," and more. But now, this Grateful Dead Family begins to acquire a folklore. Central to their legend is the consumption of crystal LSD.

Karen Hoffman laughs at the term "Family," especially with the bad vibes that are getting even worse in the ranks of high-level LSD dealers. All is far from right in early 1993. In the acid chain, people plead and beg and snitch. It's how the biscuit explodes. Karen lays off sales for a month or so, but then she's back in the game and seriously on the lam, holing up in hotel rooms for months at a time under false identities, plus spring tour, where she can melt into the familiar Deadhead zone. Some months, she sells upward of a hundred grams of crystal acid, just shy of a quarter pound. She loses track.

Once lit, one of those snitch-fuses crackles back toward Karen. It was a non-Deadhead couple that'd gotten busted. The girl breaks down in tears and tells the Man how Karen collects art and pays for people's lawyers, and then Karen's time is up, *kapow*. The DEA had been planning to follow her on fall tour. Now, there is no need. They make arrangements swiftly and rent three hotel rooms in San Francisco, one for the setup and two adjacent rooms for agents to document the encounter.

It goes down after a Jerry Garcia Band show at Shoreline. "He wanted an ounce," Karen says of her snitch. "He forgot that he owed me money, so I didn't bring what he wanted." The whole transaction is videotaped and painful.

The woman is pregnant and it's a crappy situation all around. "You better come to our wedding," they tell Karen.

Karen tells them about the numbers she's moved. Exaggerated, she says later. They talk about prices. They have a long conversation about the state of the local dealing biz, who has rolled on who, who's running, who's left to go on tour. It's high paranoia, and for good goddamn reason.

At the end of the conversation, the DEA crashes through the door, guns drawn. They arrest Karen with five grams of crystal LSD in a Rainforest Crunch candy tin.

And, exactly as the system is designed, the buck stops there. *Just don't tell them that you know me,* as the Dead sang, and Karen can't anyway. Karen Horning *doesn't* know the names of the people above her. Karen Horning is through the looking glass.

10

THE TOUR FROM HELL

The closest the Grateful Dead come to commemorating the fiftieth anniversary of LSD's 1943 discovery happens a week early, when Jerry Garcia, Bob Weir, and Vince Welnick sing the "Star Spangled Banner" on opening day of the 1993 baseball season at San Francisco's Candlestick Park. It's a fine symbol of the band's American integration, even as the rest of psychedelic America builds toward its most frenzied transformation yet. The last time the Dead had sung the "Star Spangled Banner" into open microphones was when the cops were shutting down the Fillmore Acid Test in 1966.

Around the emergent psychedelic world, tributes to Albert Hofmann's April 1943 discovery are more aware. There's a small symposium in Switzerland. In the States, the Multidisciplinary Association for Psychedelic Studies celebrate the chemist's lysergic bike ride with a gathering that features video contributions from the likes of Hoffman and Humphry Osmond, seventy-six, who'd coined the word "psychedelic" itself, plus greetings from Merry Pranksters Ken Kesey and Ken Babbs.

MAPS founder Rick Doblin also marks LSD's fiftieth by encouraging a Raves for Research project in Manhattan. On the nearest adjacent weekend in 1993, organizers survey more than seven hundred dancers at events at Roseland Ballroom and a party hosted by a future-happy party-tribe called NASA at the Shelter, the resilient

dance loft next door to Wetlands Preserve in TriBeCa. Some 75 percent of survey respondents say they've used LSD at a rave event, ditto
MDMA. Pot is slightly less evident, and there's a steep drop off before
everything else. NASA sells only smart drinks, no beer or booze. With
the always psychedelic Wetlands next door, the two clubs make for a
chaotic nexus in lower Manhattan. The American popular ritual of
psychedelic dance is alive and well at the corner of Hudson and Laight
in New York City.

But, fifty years after the discovery of LSD, psychedelic culture at
large is mutating in the United States and worldwide. The rich chemical
combinations introduced by Alexander Shulgin proliferate. Soon, reports will come that South African shamans are using 2C-B, a drug first
concocted by Shulgin. And while the emergent World Wide Web begins to connect people everywhere through its seemingly infinite supply of esoteric texts and low-resolution graphics, the recently launched
print-only *Entheogen Review* becomes the de facto home for the broader
community dialogue of the turned-on psychonautical intelligentsia.

There are trip reports and extraction tips for a variety of substances,
updates on various legal fronts, and lively debates about the difference
between the spirit-manifesting "entheogenic" and the mind-manifesting "psychedelic." To some, the correct definition changes with
the substance user's intent. The journal's five-page debut is devoted
entirely to ayahuasca, and subsequent issues feature readers swapping recipes and admixture recommendations for the South American
brew alongside thoughtful pieces on the meaning of "shamanism" in
modern Western usage.

Ayahuasca—the brew that had terrified and enchanted William
S. Burroughs and Allen Ginsberg, the brew that initially eluded the
McKenna brothers—is now beginning to appear on American shores
with regularity. Aya-inspired travel (with varying degrees of intent) has
been a staple of the head underground since at least 1971, when writer
Paul Krassner signed up with an expedition leaving from Berkeley under the rubric South American Wilderness Adventures. Globe-trot-
ting folk rocker Paul Simon had alluded to drinking "the herbal brew"
on his 1990 hit *Rhythm of the Saints* album, and the sacred concoction
arrives in the American pop imagination. But, now, aya is coming to
the United States.

Unlike most other substances loose in psychedelic America, though, aya nearly always comes with caretakers on the material plane. In this way, it seems to resist the antiauthoritarian Americanization and repurposing of peyote and mushrooms and even DMT, made from the same South American vine as ayahuasca brew. For this reason, aya will occupy a different place in the drug culture than the "traditional" North American psychedelics.

"To get it, you had to go with these guide guys," reports the ever-antennaed Jacaeber Kastor of the Psychedelic Solution gallery, clearly disappointed. He'd noticed the brew first arriving not long after his brief stint in Mexican prison in 1990. "There were a couple of people who had access, but you weren't able to just get some for yourself," Kastor grumbles.

Jacaeber Kastor is a head. Ayahuasca, in shaman-guided form, is not necessarily for heads, at least the same way other psychedelics sometimes appear to be. In this way, the meaning of psychedelics in the United States begins to subtly shift, making a first attempt at harmony with other psychedelic cultures. The drug makes further inroads via a popular collection of paintings by Pablo Amaringo, a former shaman, with text that translates the imagery.

One of the new American wave who squarely prefers the term "entheogen" to "psychedelic" is Bob Jesse, a vice president at Oracle, the enormous California software company. In 1993, Jesse takes a sabbatical and founds what he names the Council on Spiritual Practices.

Where Rick Doblin and MAPS pursue clinical psychedelic research in the hopes that it might be integrated into the therapeutic repertoire, Jesse believes that LSD and MDMA and other substances aren't only for therapy. Guides and structure and integration are needed, but Jesse thinks Schedule I drugs are capable of making well people even better. They are tools for spirituality and creativity and other things that can't be described, and Jesse thinks it high time for people to start acting like grown-ups about it.

That year, a biochemist named Kary Mullis wins a Nobel Prize for his work on the polymerase chain reaction, which will change the study of modern biology. "I was down there with the molecules when I discovered it and I wasn't stoned on LSD, but my mind by then had learned to get down there," he will tell the BBC. "If I had not taken

LSD ever would I have still been in PCR? I don't know, I doubt it, I seriously doubt it."

THE NEXT POT volcano comes from British Columbia, a rich green vein in the earth exploding from Kootenay and the Gulf Islands and the heart of Vancouver. Draw it onto the Map. Like the weed-producing Emerald Triangle in California, the region pumps even more marijuana into the American networks, filling all the cracks. In the early 1990s, the weed trade transforms the Canadian city. Plain brick houses are taken over by illegal gardeners and converted into massive pot-growing operations, the walls covered in light-blocking sheets.

But it's not hippies running the show anymore. Pot in Vancouver is big business and getting bigger, and it's just straight-up organized crime by this point. In the Vancouver police's estimation, there are about 10,000 grow houses throughout the city, each growing an estimated $1 million worth of grass every year. They bust about three hundred operations per annum. They're not holding it back. They're not even stopping it in any notable way. The marijuana industry provides a vital material to psychedelic America and regular citizens both.

The lava shoots forth from Vancouver in a million crossfading shades of green, blasting forth toward every corner of North American society, heady and straight, black and white, Humbeadia, Squaresville, and all places between.

ANOTHER UNCONSCIOUS fiftieth-anniversary tribute to Albert Hofmann's wondrous compound comes in 1993 when the graffiti writer once known as LSD-OM decides he wants to tag up some trains again. Psychedelic America is always filled with surprise openings and closings as its participants age, get real jobs, have kids, and apply their learning in various ways. But sometimes they get cravings to send their messages out by the old channels, and Chad Stickney is nearing forty.

"I was realizing I was getting old and I wouldn't always be able to do shit like this," he says. An unheralded innovator in the psychedelic and art worlds, Chad Stickney remains quiet and unassuming. He calls a friend who is still active in the graffiti scene.

"I was living in Washington Heights, on 177th and Broadway," Chad says. "And my friend said that on the next block there was an emergency [underground] layup, right here, under Broadway, for the B-train. So we did that."

As luck would have it, there's a nor'easter that year, and the MTA doesn't clean the trains for five whole days. "LSD-OM" shoots out into the boroughs once more. "It made it to Brooklyn and friends saw it," Chad reports. "I was getting calls like, 'Dude, you're *back?*'"

He is, briefly. For a year or so. The New York scenes bubble along in new and different permutations. At some point in the '80s, the Parkies had migrated from the Central Park Bandshell over to the vast open space of the Sheep Meadow. "That was a very nice peaceful scene, people playing frisbee," says Johnny Crunch of the vibe there. "Guys selling LSD, but they would hide it in the grass, they'd turn up a piece of turf, and have it buried. There were various ways." Old graffiti writers and Parkies pass in and out of the scene.

Bilrock, who'd been Central Park's Brotherhood connection for a few years alongside other clandestine jobs, meets his future wife while hanging out at the Sheep Meadow. Soon, a friend gets Bilrock a paralegal job investigating police brutality cases and sends the graffiti writer on a course for maybe the most bizarre straight job for a Parkie: wearing a badge as a sworn peace officer at several city agencies, including the internal Department of Investigation. He loves his work.

It is during this period, too, that Chad Stickney / LSD-OM—the onetime teenage Brotherhood dealer—unexpectedly encounters the original secret-agent Brotherhood of Eternal Love representative who'd recruited him and his friends into business in 1969 and begun Central Park's long association with LSD. Chad sees the ex-Brotherhood guy at a wedding and greets his old friend warmly.

The ex–secret agent hushes Chad. He has been on the run for many years and has a new name. It's all a bit awkward, Chad remembers, but not every twist of psychedelic America will resolve.

THE GUATEMALAN QUILT maker Sarah Matzar gets only three days' warning to prepare her family before she is suddenly thrown in jail in 1993 at the behest of the American government. The American legal system rips apart friends and families as it tries to stop LSD distribution. It is seemingly part of government's prime directive, an American reactionary force as unable to stop as the psychedelics themselves and perhaps even more dangerous.

Sarah Matzar is a half decade retired from the acid game and living back in her home country with seven children, some adopted, all hers, plus an enormous family. She operates her business quite successfully, teaching and employing the women of Panajachel to create in her style of postpsychedelic, outside-the-square Mayan textiles. But a snitch-bomb explodes up North.

The American newspapers will describe Sarah, now in her late thirties, as the head of a major LSD distribution ring. That is what several of her ex-associates (and associates of associates) accuse her of being. It is the biggest LSD bust in the States since the Brotherhood of Eternal Love days, some forty grams seized, capable of making 400,000 honest hits at the current industry standard of 100 micrograms each. The group of bad-doers is responsible for a million doses a month, according to the DEA.

The accusations against Sarah aren't precisely true and definitely not up to date. But there's a lot that has to happen before that can be said in a court of law, and until then Sarah is in Guatemalan jail to await extradition. It is not brutal there. It is humane. Her youngest child is allowed to live with her there for much of the time, where the thirty-seven-year-old Sarah is a model prisoner. It is there that she resumes her anthropology studies, preparing to complete the master's she'd abandoned a decade previous, decoding the ancient graphic slang of Mayan textiles. Several academics with a standing interest in Sarah's deep graphic knowledge facilitate the work, paying for her legal fund in return for some academic ghostwriting.

And it is a month and change after Sarah's arrest, as she's settling into life in the Guatemalan prison, that Karen Hoffman is arrested in California. Except by (perhaps) a distant connection here or there, Sarah's and Karen's cases are unrelated. But, as specimens of the American legal system's persecution of the American psychedelic practices in the 1990s, they're not unrelated at all. And, with the newspaper accounts connecting Sarah's ex-associates to the Grateful Dead, it's entirely probable that her and Karen's cases are exactly linked at the deepest departmental levels.

Each case finds the government hammering away at the liberty of individuals to punish nonviolent crimes that have caused no provable harm. As Karen begins her own tumble through the looking glass and into the cold, unwondering claw of the legal system up in California, her alternate identities fall away and she's just Karen Horning again.

Karen blasts through attorneys. The first quits when Karen runs out of money. There is a legit conflict of interest with the second, who is working on another LSD case. And then come the court-ordered representatives. She is held without bail, put into lockdown for twenty-three hours a day.

"Like a person at death's door, memories of days past would come back to me, people and places I'd been, things I'd done or wished I'd done," she will write. "I was alive yet as close to death as I'd ever come. I might as well have been dead. I was dead to the world outside. No contact with anyone I used to know."

If there is a Grateful Dead Family, they do not save or even recognize Karen Horning. Perhaps she is simply not connected to them. She feels no warmth from that rose-filled world.

And the court records show, clearly and unequivocally, that Karen Horning does not roll on anyone. "She has a belief that she cannot possibly trust anybody working for the government, which includes any attorneys or anybody else that the attorney hires," the court-appointed psychologist tells the judge.

"She talked to me as if I and her attorney were enemies and representitives [sic] of the government having no right to intrude into her private life," the psychologist writes in his report. "She seemed to be aware of the consequences of her actions but for some reason behaved as if cooperating with the government was not an option for her."

The report continues, "She also appears to have accepted a 'deadhead' (a current group of 'Grateful Dead' fans) or hippy philosophy that the government or the establishment is repressive, that getting high is a human right and all those working for [the government] cannot be trusted."

She has, the psychologist believes, a "severe mental disorder." Putting Karen Horning's countercultural assertions aside, there is something misfiring. "Her hands attracted my attention and on questioning it was discovered that she was suffering from rheumatoid arthritis which made the knuckles of both hands swollen and stiff," the psychologist observes. The prison dosage of the necessary medicine is too weak. Karen is very sick and very angry, the psychologist says when he testifies.

"Let's back up," the judge says. "She was essentially set up by a friend."

"That's what she told me, yes," the psychologist says.

"So it doesn't surprise me then that she doesn't trust people," the judge says.

"No. It certainly doesn't surprise me, either," the psychologist admits.

The snitch-bombs have done their work. Through a series of court confusions, Karen Horning is deemed fit for trial and waives her right to an attorney. The drug war rages onward. In a jail in California, Karen Horning keeps fighting. In a jail in Guatemala, Sarah Matzar keeps fighting. The LSD supply does not stop.

THE MYTHICAL ELLIPTICAL Zippy tour lands on the American Hippie Highway in spring 1994. The world is primed for some fresh techno-hippie utopianism, and this crew from the United Kingdom could be it. They have fresh technologies and platforms at their disposal, and seem to promise a full collision of the old psychedelic customs and the modern ones. The garish new magazine *Wired* fuels them with a cover story that spring.

Published out of San Francisco, *Wired* draws from the energies and talent pools of the WELL, including John Perry Barlow, Stewart Brand, and others. In their 1993 debut, the magazine's editor, Louis Rossetto—once associated with the Radical Libertarian Alliance—had predicted "social changes so profound their only parallel is the discovery of fire." And that was before the brand-new World Wide Web had begun to glow from computer screens the same month that the first issue of *Wired* was rolling off the press. *Wired* is here to tell us of the present future and make mainstream advertising dollars while doing so. As *Mondo 2000* cofounder R. U. Sirius knows from trying to keep various cyberdelic magazines afloat, "acid dealers don't advertise." *Wired* keeps the counterculture more and more at arm's length. The future transforms again. Welcome, Zippies! *Wired*'s rooting for you!

The pack of British pranksters drop from the Manhattan skies like some Peter Max–inspired trick in *Yellow Submarine*. The Zippies, in *Wired*'s hype, are "a product of UK dance-scene hedonism, cyber street tech, pagan spirituality, postpunk anarchism, and go-for-it entrepreneurism."

Sounds familiar, except the beats they zip to are different from their jammier American equivalents, a collision of electronica, German Krautrock repetitiveness, New Age glow, stoned Jamaican echoes, and post–Pink Floyd bardo drama. The Zippies and their music are the product of an entirely parallel head history that's been going on since the '60s, as tangled as its American equivalent, though condensed onto a much smaller landmass.

The Zippies are also presumably unaware of the New York psychedelic political group of the same name, sprouted from the Yippies in the early '70s by future *High Times* founder Tom Forçade. But Forçade is long gone. When the new model Zippies make landfall in Manhattan, a little over a dozen of them, mostly British and Irish, they announce themselves with a press conference in Central Park's Sheep Meadow, where the remnants of the park's band shell scene drift had drifted and regenerated over the course of the '80s. The Zippies' leader, Fraser Clark, stands on a rock and addresses some thirty journalists.

While hippiedom became massively unfashionable in the UK between glam and punk, the festival craze had never died in the jolly ol' kingdom, tent and teepee seas spreading around Stonehenge and the mystical countryside through the mid-1980s. Ecstasy arrived on British shores in 1988, kicking off the isle's own Summer of Love. While the first wave of acid house was psychedelic in name only, in 1992, the ecstasyheads partying out beyond London's M25 highway had collided with the festival survivors, and some critical mass emerged.

The *Independent* estimates that there are roughly 60,000 squatters about the country, and—come summer—some 40,000 heads wandering down Britain's highways and the ancient ley lines near Stonehenge. During mushroom season, some head for Wales, where a regular low-key psilocybe festival in the late '70s had nurtured the UK heads' fungus obsession. Throughout the '80s and '90s, they remain available through British head shops and mail order, along with the usual array of spore-print kits.

In London, lead Zip (and ex-editor of the magazine *Encyclopaedia Psychedelica*) Fraser Clark runs the more recently launched semifloating party called Megatripolis. There, Clark convenes a Parallel University with lecturers and philosophers and esoteric experts of all stripes. DJs sample Terence McKenna's lectures, and McKenna's voice becomes a hit on the dance floor.

"Thatcher did us a favor," one of the Zippies tells *Wired*. "There's been a rejection of the control structure at the same time that the technology has appeared for us to remain totally independent. Fulfillment now comes not from political adherence but by not voting, in fact by having nothing to do with the system." It is yet another direct echo of Ken Kesey's "turn your back and say 'fuck it.'"

After Central Park, the Zippies' first proper American stop is downtown at the Wetlands Preserve, who apparently don't know much about what's coming, the advance monthly schedule mentioning little more than the musical talent. But the night turns into a complete welcoming party, where representatives from various tribes gather into Larry Bloch's pristinely crafted basement lounge for a full-on summit in the form of one of the Zippies' Parallel University sessions.

One of the psychedelic Americans there to welcome them is Terence McKenna. "None of us are consciously choosing this moment to try and direct the energies of youth culture," McKenna tells the crowd. "The moment has chosen us." With his dulcet speaking tones, McKenna is the perfect candidate for sampling by the new music producers, turning up on tracks by new trance producers like Shpongle and Entheogenic and Alien Dreamtime and others, as this corner of dance culture begins to shift even more psychedelic. Like Timothy Leary before him, McKenna is also apt to hop on with many of those who invite him, bending with the novelty of the universe.

"The emphasis in house music and rave culture on physiologically compatible rhythms and this sort of thing, is really the rediscovery of the art of natural magic with sound," McKenna says on one recording. "That sounds, properly understood, especially percussive sound, can actually change neurological states, and large groups of people getting together in the presence of this kind of music are creating a telepathic community, a bonding, that hopefully will be strong enough to carry the vision out into the mainstream of society."

At Wetlands, there are members of the Rainbow Family, who plan to reconvene with the Zippies later in the summer. And from the Electronic Frontier Foundation, the WELL, and the Grateful Dead is John Perry Barlow, who picks up Fraser Clark's zipped-up term "pronoia," the idea that universe is conspiring in one's favor. He finds it a complete fit with his experiences among Deadheads and the general population of groupminds to which he belongs. Being a generally white middle/upper-middle-class population, life certainly sometimes might feel pronoic for the heads. It is a useful life slogan, though, even if it borders dangerously near the comic "best of all possible worlds" rationalizations of Voltaire's *Candide*.

From the Wetlands, the Zippies hit the Highway and transport themselves along the familiar Map, as if they were using it as a tour planner, even. They make plans to stop at the Oregon Country Fair in Veneta, and they turn up in Colorado (by way of a week in British Columbia) where they throw a party in Boulder in conjunction with Allen Ginsberg, the Naropa Institute for Disembodied Poetics, and the Merry Pranksters.

The meeting goes coldly, and, at the end of the night, they confront Ken Kesey, trying to scoop him into joining them for the Rainbow Gathering in Wyoming. "Will you come along peacefully to this tribal summit?" asks one in a *bOING bOING* shirt. The long-retired chief Prankster, ready to drive off in his white Cadillac convertible and surely knowing full well what the Rainbows are about, glares at them.

"I've bitten the ankle of the beast," he says. "Don't ask me to bite where you want to bite."

"What about inspiring the next generation?" the Zippoid asks, not in the mood for parable.

"Son," sez Keez, "I've done that movie, now it's your turn." Bye, bye Chief. Good luck Zippos.

They have some fun at the Rainbow Gathering and make for the Bay Area where there's already a fledgling American rave scene up in the Oakland warehouses, and Haight expatriate and new psy-trance forerunner Goa Gil is going to DJ some DATs at a party for them. But by the time the Zippies make it to San Francisco, they disintegrate into the Humbeadean atmosphere.

So maybe the Zippies aren't the future. Except they kind of are: a short-lived idea skipping through the Zones, going where the energy is and supplementing it with some of their own. Even if the world doesn't bend to Zipdom, Fraser Clark is right on the money about the next generation of kids who might want to take drugs and dance.

That same summer of 1994, while the Zippies are zagging, a fresh psychedelic ritual is beginning to take definite shape out on the American continent as the new rhythmic consciousness emerges. In Milwaukee, some young dance-music promoters have been reading Tom Wolfe's *Electric Kool-Aid Acid Test*.

"At that point we were over doing E and were taking acid instead," one of the Drop Bass Network promoters would recall to Michaelangelo Matos. "This book was all about these people doing this every day. I was like, 'Holy shit, we're thinking on 'ten,' but we're only on 'five' or 'six'—these guys have it turned all the way up to eleven. We're not doing this right. We need to kick this into high gear. What is the next level?"

The answer is camping. They launch an outdoor festival up there in Wisconsin and call it "Furthur." It's not a new spot on the Map so much that the Map is starting to curl and peel back from the surface of reality such that it resembles the United States as a whole. The lysergic British beat experimenter Aphex Twin headlines. There's acid everywhere. The festival even gets its own Naked Pole Guy when one of the organizers strips and climbs a speaker stack.

In the Zippies, in "Furthur," in yet-to-be-discovered iterations, domestic heads can now dance (in body and mind) in ways that aren't boogying or spinning or obsessive Deadhead noodle shaking, though elements of those can be seen. Where there is an indigenous form of dance, it has been said, there is a culture. There are many cultures. It is not a youth movement, exactly, though many youth are involved. The ravers, as the press will call them, are the self-conscious front of the new New Age, dancing to the first beats of a long end of the world party.

THOUGH IT IS hard to measure exactly, it is probably 1994 when the acid dealers and full-on touring culture hits critical mass around Phish while the Grateful Dead aren't (and are) on the road. The borders blur, the first wedge of an oncoming future appearing in the present.

At first glance, it looks familiar. But first glances can be deceiving. Shakedown Street has been a common sight at Phish shows for a few summers, and the nitrous tanks have been hissing regularly. Their audience has been getting bigger and bigger. The band sell out Madison Square Garden once and are booked for two nights to ring in 1996. Phish are for real.

But the Grateful Dead are hyperreal, and there's no sign of abeyance. When the band play three shows at the Silver Bowl in Las Vegas in May 1995, they bring somewhere between $17 and $28 million of fresh money into the city. Looked at another way, it is extremely wasteful. Beyond the environmental cost of tens of thousands of Deadheads descending on the Nevada desert oasis by car and plane, that's millions hissing from the hip economy and countercultural pursuits into a karmically questionable place with no real head scene. It's getting harder for the Grateful Dead to find cities that are enthusiastic about hosting them, but Las Vegas is certainly one.

The decade-long echo of the Dead's hit song "Touch of Grey" keeps building into something more ominous and irreversible, years of darkness coming, compasses spinning. There are perhaps up to 2,000 Deadheads already in prison for various drug-related charges. In 1994, the Families Against Mandatory Minimums work on a successful bill to introduce a judge's discretion into sentencing, but that doesn't help the Deadheads already incarcerated. Their numbers are small compared to other groups, but real enough to keep a permanent bad shiver ricocheting through the groupmind like a silvery pinball of doom. And what happens in the Grateful Dead world as spring 1995 turns to summer carries supernatural overtones that are almost impossible to ignore, like the enormous and obvious pull of an impending cataclysm.

But summer's here, and the time is right for the Dead to be back on the road, doing what they do, soundtracking beautiful life experiences, creating ecstasy for dancers and spinners and trippers and you and me, providing a portable home for this community made up of infinite factions. Or maybe they're just feeding the out-of-control ouroboros their band has become, a serpent chomping on its own tail. The acid families are ready to get the doses out into the distribution chain for the coming school year, with or without foot soldiers like Karen Horning.

It should never be forgotten that no matter what the band sound like or what's happening in the parking lot, Grateful Dead performances are still making many thousands of people gloriously happy. Right through the end, as the band's music breaks apart on stage, audience members have life-changing moments at Dead shows, with or without psychedelics or giant bowls of pot.

But to many, it is obvious that Jerry Garcia needs a long break. He is a very sick man. But that break cannot happen. History and the Grateful Dead's touring schedule will not allow it.

The eastern leg of the tour begins in the friendly green terrain of Vermont, where the Dead had performed the summer before in one of the groovier scenes in recent memory. The old heads came out from the commune-dotted hills, and some 60,000 showed up to camp and boogie in the fashion of the good ol' Grateful Dead.

But this time, an estimated 20,000 are without tickets. Then, malarkey at the gates, a poorly managed entry point, a bottleneck, and a massive gatecrash. The final attendance is more than 100,000, and there's a report of Deadheads breaking down a local woman's fence for firewood. A few shows later in Albany, fifty are arrested and three police officers hurt, but those are just standard casualties when the Dead come through town at this point.

Intrepid tapers figure out how to capture the low-frequency FM signals the band uses for their new in-ear monitors, each musician with his own mix. The recordings reveal the band's geosynchronous, telepathic blesh falling apart. Every player listens to Garcia, almost none to keyboardist Vince Welnick, with various combos in between. For every show the Grateful Dead perform during the summer of 1995, there are dozens of people preserving it. They're in the tapers' section and in coveted front-of-board spots down front. They're in the parking lot with their FM receivers to pluck the band's in-ear monitors onto DAT, and they're working for the band to make the official recordings to ship back to Dick Latvala in California.

The music on these tapes is now to a large degree unlistenable, the sound of Jerry Garcia approaching his end in uncomfortably high fidelity. He is using heroin again, and his playing—that endless nonverbal rap from the innermost part of his consciousness—is turning inaudible and incoherent.

The first truly ominous external sign comes on June 25 outside RFK Stadium in Washington, DC, when three fans are struck by lightning during a summer storm. One Deadhead's heart stops entirely, saved by an off-duty EMT hanging out in the parking lot with an oxygen tank in his car. It's a freak accident—that one-in-however-many chance—but that makes everything a freak accident.

In Pittsburgh in a rainstorm several fans fall from the upper levels of Three Rivers Stadium, as if tossed by seismic jolts in the local karmasphere looking for an outlet. One breaks his back. A few days later at Deer Creek, there's a death threat on Garcia, and the band plays the show with the houselights turned up, all the better to see some 5,000 fans scrambling over the rear wall of the venue. They cancel the next night and issue a letter.

"Want to end the touring life of the Grateful Dead?" they ask. "Allow bottle-throwing gate-crashers to keep on thinking they're cool anarchists instead of the creeps they are." It's sternly worded, and the show cancellation does a lot to back it up, but they've been issuing letters like this for seven years now.

Two days after the cancelled Deer Creek show, there's another vicious rain storm, and one hundred Deadheads clamor for cover on the porch at a Missouri campground, the porch collapses, and people get way mangled. Even before it's over, many will call it the Tour from Hell. It's as if the skywork machinery over Deadland can't hold the stars in place anymore.

Back home, after the tour's end in Chicago, Garcia records a cover of "Blue Yodel #9" with David Grisman, a mandolin buddy he'd met during his first exploratory cross-country tour with a friend and a tape deck, some thirty-one music-filled summers previous. He does a short stay at the Betty Ford Clinic in Palm Springs, checking out days later, far short of completing any kind of program. In early August 1995, Garcia signs in at Serenity Knolls, a residential rehab clinic in Marin—in the old green hills of Humbead's Revised Map of the World—and dies that night. Good-bye, Jerry, and thanks, man.

Here, a giant void-dot goes into the timetrack, a period at the end of a multidecade sentence. It's been decades since Garcia retreated almost exclusively into Deadland, but Jerry Garcia was a head, and the heads are going to miss him. He was one of them, one who did more to keep the flame lit than most, and that bohemian thread isn't going anywhere.

"There's no way to measure his greatness or magnitude as a person or as a player," Bob Dylan says in a statement. "There are a lot of spaces and advances between the Carter family, Buddy Holly and, say, Ornette Coleman, a lot of universes, but he filled them all without being a member of any school."

At the Polo Fields in Golden Gate Park—site of the Human Be-In, in view of where Jerry was busted in a parked car in 1985—the crew from Bill Graham Presents erects a full stage, as if for a concert. But there is no concert. There is a full concert PA, and Dick Latvala and David Gans play Dead music. The Polo Fields fills with mourning Deadheads. Just as the Dead and the heads improvised an American psychedelic ritual, the stage becomes an altar in the improvised tenets of their faith.

They leave beaded necklaces and objects found in their pockets. They leave handwritten notes and cards from children. They leave shells, rocks, bones, small animal skulls, gems, crystals. There are photographs of Jerry, drawings of Jerry, letters to Jerry, and many beautiful bouquets. There are ticket stubs and bumper stickers, poetry, pinwheels, a guitar covered in writing, an elaborate decorated egg, pot paraphernalia, and almost two dozen sobriety chips from various twelve-step programs. There is a heaping amount of marijuana left on the altar, and some psychedelics, too.

THE DAY JERRY GARCIA dies in August 1995 is the same day that a California company called Netscape goes public. At the Stock Exchange in New York, demand is so high that trading can't start for two hours. It marks the first echoing rumble of the dot-com boom. The global economy changes, and its ground zero is Netscape, the company that distributes Mosaic, first real browser for the World Wide Web.

Based in Mountain View, home to Shoreline Amphitheater and the heart of Dead country, the sixteen-month-old Netscape distributes a piece of software developed by the same programmers who'd more or less invented the World Wide Web itself while working for the National Computer Supercomputing Agency. Like the early days of the net, the web remains a powerful and unresolved collision of high technology, government funds, and counterculture energy.

As the online population grows, so do the stakes. Since even before the arrival of the web, the Electronic Frontier Foundation's John Perry Barlow has taken a passionate interest in digital privacy, the shielding of data by encryption. It makes good sense within the intellectual continuum of hackers and tape traders and dope dealers and acid makers and heads and communards and anyone else who feels like living under the radar, managing their own personal filters for how, where, and when to deal with consensus reality. The web is a vast trick in that regard, literally connecting counterculture ideals to the digital apparatus of the grid. There has been drug info and Dead set lists on the net for decades, thanks to the scientists at the Stanford Artificial Intelligence Lab in the early '70s. But now everybody wants a piece of the net.

It is a vast exchange of energies, a torch passed at some secret party out in the Peninsula hills. Perhaps the most amazing part of Netscape's launch isn't merely that they are already a formidably profitless company but that their main product is and will remain available for nothing. It is free.

The same month as Jerry Garcia's death and Netscape's public sale, British theorists Richard Barbrook and Andy Cameron publish "The Californian Ideology," a long critique of the neoliberalism suggested by Louis Rossetto's *Wired*.

"This new faith has emerged from a bizarre fusion of the cultural bohemianism of San Francisco with the hi-tech industries of Silicon Valley," they write. "Promoted in magazines, books, tv programmes, Web sites, newsgroups and Net conferences, the Californian Ideology promiscuously combines the free-wheeling spirit of the hippies and the entrepreneurial zeal of the yuppies."

And, in many ways, John Perry Barlow might be seen as a poster boy. "Nature itself is a free market system," he writes in the mid-1990s. "A rain forest is an unplanned economy, as is a coral reef. The difference between an economy that sorts the information and energy in photons and one that sorts the information and energy in dollars is a slight one in my mind. Economy *is* ecology."

Maybe so, but, transported to places besides Grateful Dead shows and tech labs and the psychedelic underground, the Californian Ideology might sometimes act as an invasive species, disrupting local economies as much as providing opportunities. And, as the twentieth century ticks down, the idea of *free* bursts from the tech-hippie underground into the mainstream, though it often comes with a pair of quotation marks around it as its usage feeds commercial interests, hip capitalism supplanting hip economics. Everything starts to flip. The sky becomes yellow, the sun blue, and so on. Even John Perry Barlow might agree that coral reefs need protection.

Separate from any economic positions, the Grateful Dead lyricist's aim is to protect all sides. The Electronic Frontier Foundation comes from a desire not to be left alone but to create dogma-free infrastructures that can support human endeavors. It is a scalable society-wide application of what Barlow and Robert Hunter had decided twenty years earlier to do in their Grateful Dead lyrics, now transmuted into a late twentieth-century political ideology.

Soon comes the Telecommunications Act of 1996, and Barlow peers at it. In Davos, Switzerland, the corporeal Barlow is present for that year's World Economic Forum, already a sign of the Electronic Frontier Foundation's growing stature, even if the organization's stint in Washington, DC, hadn't worked. But now Barlow lobs his own manifesto into the networks.

"Governments of the Industrial World, you weary giants of flesh and steel, I come from Cyberspace, the new home of Mind," he writes in an essay modestly titled "A Declaration of the Independence of Cyberspace."

"On behalf of the future, I ask you of the past to leave us alone. You are not welcome among us." It's all worth reading in any future. "We will create a civilization of the Mind in Cyberspace. May it be more humane and fair than the world just governments have made before."

To manifest a society of the mind is an almost literally psychedelic task, in the original Greek sense from which Humphry Osmond derived the word.

Libertarian though Barlow might be, his beliefs aren't meant to protect the inalienable free-market rights of businesses in the gleaming new cybersphere. They are part of the old world, too. Barlow's declaration is to protect the rights of the mind-manifesters who have gathered to build the future in the new blank terrain.

Barlow sends his declaration to fifty people and it circulates from there, quickly becoming the biggest hit of his solo career and one of the net's biggest viral sensations yet. Almost immediately, he is receiving three hundred e-mails a day. He likes the ego stroke of the nice ones, but he acknowledges the best written are usually from the cranks. "We are about as much a community, they claim, as are all the people with electricity in their homes," is how Barlow summarizes their arguments. Three decades of experience in groupmind telepathy, with and without computers, tell him otherwise.

ON THE FAR side of the looking glass, life goes from bad to worse for Karen Horning. Convicted at the end of 1994, she fights ceaselessly. As her arthritis worsens, she remains an unhappy and unwilling symbol of the portion of psychedelic America that is locked away. She'd been unable to prepare a proper defense, unable to grip books during her limited hours in the prison library.

On appeal, she finds a new argument that is worth making in court. Karen tells the judge that the Grateful Dead and psychedelics are her religion, and that the government's Operation Looking Glass is a form of persecution.

She sees that her court documents are cross-referenced with the code GFAN-91–8008, which she takes to mean Grateful Dead fan (there's also GD-91–0167 and some others). "And that most definately [sic] does not stand for George Michael," she writes.

A decade and change later, the Freedom of Information Act will yield one of the few records from the DEA's secretive NADDIS meta-database: Owsley Stanley's. It likewise bears the esoteric spook code GFAN-91–8008. Though other cross-references will suggest the GFAN lettering is perhaps a coincidence, they are unquestionably all linked in the government's own network.

The court dismisses her argument on several grounds, mostly that she made it on appeal, partly that she was arrested for sale of psychedelics, not personal usage. No further supporting evidence is presented or requested, nor is any information surrendered on NADDIS. Back to her cell Karen goes.

A month after Karen Horning's appeal fails in one San Francisco courtroom, Sarah Matzar's trial finally concludes in another. The Guatemalan quilt maker had been in prison in the United States for a little more than a year, separated from her family. She says, "American prison really sucked. In my country, at least they treat you like a human."

While Sarah is incarcerated in the States, another woman comes through who is involved with an LSD case. The woman—a Deadhead, Sarah remembers—had gotten caught in a chain of snitches. She is from a reasonably well-off family and absolutely cannot handle prison. Within days, she is ready to start naming names and make a deal.

Sarah's case takes a few comic turns when it becomes clear that the government can't actually pinpoint the source of the acid. It's coming out of Bolinas, the enclave in deep Marin County, out past Stinson Beach. But, even after months of work, that's as much as they know. "Bolinas was a very difficult place to establish surveillance," a DEA agent tells the judge. "On several occasions, which were documented, surveillance agents were approached by people in Bolinas and challenged as to who they were."

When Sarah had left the LSD business in the late 1980s, a group Sarah knew, mostly women, took over most of the operations. By the time the DEA came looking, Sarah really was long gone and had done her best to extricate herself fully, absorbed in her life with her family, running her quilting business. Another complication, though, is that Sarah's successors had continued to use code word "quilts" to describe LSD.

Sarah cooperates with the government, though not as far as telling them the who and where of acid manufacture. But she admits to the sales of which she's been accused, two grams plus 2,000 hits. That relatively small amount, really just a favor to a friend, is an afterthought to her LSD career.

Because of Sarah's obvious retirement, the government dismisses the charge of conspiracy to distribute acid and, under recent safety valve sentencing guidelines, decides that the thirty-seven months she has already served is commensurate to the crime. She is needed at home with her family. Sarah is free.

Karen Horning is not free. Karen Horning's condition worsens as her body begins to shut down, reflecting her physical incapacitation and her mental incapacitation. Her arthritis turns out to be a symptom of Lyme disease, another ailment that the hospital prison system is woefully unprepared to treat. Karen Horning is nobody's symbol. She receives almost no correspondence from Deadhead acquaintances, even as she helps organize *The Tallahassee Project,* a book documenting the experiences of nonviolent female drug offenders. The Anarchist Black Cross, an organization dedicated to helping political prisoners, takes up her cause and saves her life.

11

FESTIVAL SEASON

With the Grateful Dead gone, many—and not just Deadheads—are very curious about what's going to happen next. There is a vast amount of displaced energy in the psychedelic American countercultures, multiple generations of heads discovering that the punctuation at the end of the Grateful Dead's career turns out to be a question mark. To others with the right kind of saucer eyes, this is the secret that's been obvious all along: the universe is just question marks all the way down. Gigantic, wondrous question marks, with question-mark-shaped holes and more question marks inside.

The Dead's tour dates provided a constant reassuring seasonal timeline for a nation of Deadheads. What now? Some other jamband? Phish? Raves? Burning Man? Rainbow Gatherings? The remaining Dead members' new combos? Local cover acts? New rituals? Straight lives? New drugs? The mainstream of psychedelic America flickers like a janky hologram.

What's more, the LSD market takes a nearly immediate hit. In *Monitoring the Future,* American high school seniors report that it is slightly harder to get acid than the year before. With the exception of a slight tick in 1990, this is the first time the seniors have reported a drop in LSD availability since the Grateful Dead's popularity was exploding in the mid-1980s. In 1993, it blows past the previous record, set in 1976 during the first year the survey measured it.

In 1995, the year of Jerry Garcia's death, 53.8 percent of high school seniors say that, sure, no problem, acid is around. And then the number goes down. The decline is not steep yet, but it will continue.

But LSD dealers aren't the only financial entities in the hip economy. In addition to the Deadhead hearts and minds, there are also the Deadhead wallets. With the diaspora of souls, a gold ring appears in the sky over the expanded Humbeadia—a fire wheel, the promise of riches, or both. The millennium (and 2012) signals as many heads find themselves having to define themselves for the first time in their adult lives. There are still plenty of psychedelics to go around.

The Map becomes a jumble of only semidisconnected events and activity. That first Memorial Day after Jerry Garcia's death, in 1996, Terrapin Tapes—the Deadhead-run blank cassette supplier—throws a three-day festival with jam acts and Dead cover bands that they call "Deadhead Heaven: A Gathering of the Tribe." More than 7,000 attend. And that same weekend out in Wisconsin, a month before the surviving Dead members launch their *own* Furthur Festival, the Drop Bass Network stage the third iteration of their seriously lysergic electronic dance music campout, this time billed as Even Furthur.

The Even Furthur flyer advertises a Techno Campout / Electric Festival in psychedelic lettering below a friendly picture of the Pranksters' bus. Now in its third year in 1996, one of its organizers is lately spending time hanging with Timothy Leary. Alongside new dance heroes like Frankie Bones and Scott Hardkiss comes the first US performance by the American-influenced French electronic duo called Daft Punk, not yet hiding in the robot costumes for which they will be known.

The drug use has only dialed up since previous Furthurs. People identifying themselves as some branch of the vast and quarter-century-old Rainbow Family are dealing acid. Other revelers are eyeballed as post-Jerry wanderers, looking for the next party. People candyflip, the relatively recent trend of combining LSD and MDMA. It's a poly-substance scene. There is chaos. Some stay up all night, crashing about the campgrounds looking for more. Festival season has begun.

IT IS IN 1996, as well, that Terence McKenna experiences the classic combination of a postdivorce midlife funk coupled with a literal dismantling of one's theory of the universe. Maybe all this psychedelic mumbo jumbo has gone on long enough and the heads should find better things to do.

A young mathematician approaches McKenna at the annual Entheobotany Seminar in Palenque, Mexico, and presents substantial proof that McKenna's timewave mathematics are essentially bogus. The young mathematician is polite about it, of course, but his formal work says otherwise, and McKenna admits that some of the timewave calculations "have no basis in rational thought." He suggests the title for Matthew Watkins's subsequent paper: "Autopsy of a Mathematical Hallucination." Perhaps charitably, Watkins adds a question mark.

Over the course of the year, McKenna and company hammer at it on the Novelty List, the e-mail distribution chain devoted to the timewave. In his brother Dennis's later estimation, McKenna grows depressed. "He was active on the lecture circuit promoting psychedelics but taking them only rarely," Dennis will write, "just at a point when I thought he should be taking them to facilitate insight and self-reflection. He disagreed and resented my efforts to engage him on it."

But just because Matthew Watkins disproves the timewave doesn't mean that 2012 isn't coming. Awareness of the date and its significance seems to multiply as a matter of folk knowledge. One of McKenna's perennial favorite quips comes from the British enzymologist J. B. S. Haldane: "Not only is the universe stranger than we suppose, it's stranger than we *can* suppose."

If anything, McKenna's idiosyncratic timewave was only an attempt to make sense of the world's strangeness and hold tight as it flips toward what no one *ever* can suppose. Terence McKenna was able to hold on for some two decades, but the world has grown stranger still.

On the familiar Pacific cliffsides of the Esalen Institute in Big Sur, psychedelic America takes its first step back toward integration. At nearly the same time that Watkins had confronted McKenna in Palenque, the Oracle software executive Bob Jesse convened a meeting at Esalen under the auspices of his new Council on Spiritual Practices. More than a dozen psychedelic old-guarders attend, including pioneers of long-underground, LSD-influenced transpersonal psychology. It is an attempt to determine the next step in the broader psychedelic project.

The council determines—as Jesse will describe to Michael Pollan—"to get aboveboard, unassailable research done, at an institution beyond reproach" with no therapy-oriented results because the idea is that, while guides are good, therapists are not needed. As a result of the council's connection-fostering, Dr. Roland R. Griffiths at the Johns Hopkins School of Medicine in Maryland begins to construct the first clinical psychedelic research in the United States in many years, studying mystical experiences produced by mushrooms.

If Terence McKenna's timewave was symbolic of his called-for Age of Exploration, then its debunking signifies the start of a legitimate psychedelic Age of Discovery, where the landmasses come into view and the sea monsters are erased from the oceans. To many, it might seem as if the time for listening to the mushroom's communiques has passed.

But in 1996, as well, a California psychiatrist named Horace Beach publishes a doctoral thesis with the curiouser and curiouser title of "Listening for the Logos: A Study of Reports of Audible Voices at High Doses of Psilocybin." In it, Beach goes a long way toward proving the consistency of the mushroom voice over many trips by many people.

Terence McKenna had first experienced the voice during his South American adventures with *Psilocybe cubensis* in 1971, and it was first reported elsewhere in 1973. McKenna had experimented with his heroic doses over the years, enough to get where the voice dwelled, and bring back ideas that he insisted were not his own. Building his study on interviews with 128 mushroom users, Horace Beach determines that the mushroom voice's specific kind of alien information *is* somewhat universal.

Nearly every culture that consumes mushrooms reports it, in some variation. As Terence McKenna and others have suggested, it has most likely always been in the mushrooms. The mushroom never gives *orders;* it simply presents what it wants to present.

THE OLD-TIME Bread and Puppet people have a name for the new wave of hard-partying attendees at their long-running Vermont gathering, and it's not necessarily a flattering one: Breadheads. And during the first psychedelic summer post-Garcia, in 1996, these old-guard avant-garde street theater puppeteers up in Vermont can *feel* that something has changed. There is a presidential election going on, but the economy is booming and Bill Clinton will win handily.

They know Deadheads, sure, but they associate these Breadheads with Phish, the band that sprouted from the same northern Vermont soil where the puppet troupe has deep roots. The Breadheads have been trickling in for years, but this summer it borders on real chaos.

The theme for the 1996 installment of Bread and Puppet's Domestic Resurrection Circus is the American Sleep (and Wake-Up Service). The hand-pressed posters feature a winged skeleton in an American flag top hat, inviting all to the green rolling amphitheater of their art commune up in Glover, Vermont. The Bread and Puppet farm in Glover now even appears as a red dot on the official Vermont state map.

A vast percentage of the audience is from out of town now. The locals haven't abandoned the puppets but are content to get their fix of transcendent absurdist politics at smaller town fairs and Fourth of July parties. The pageant crowd is swelling toward 30,000, packed around the big green bowl with room only for the performers to get through.

Festivalgoers had been camping and partying on a neighboring farm for years, but recently the town had purchased the property between the two and made it public. Most of the vending rushes to the footpath in the shady grove, a liminal zone within a liminal zone. Now, the drug dealers have a place to hang out, weaving their way among those selling pizza, falafel, hemp clothing, tie dyes, rocks, crystals, and whatever else is hot on Shakedown Street at the moment.

Present, too, are representatives from the Twelve Tribes religious community, selling delicious food at reasonable prices from a mobile cafe operated by their unpaid devotees. The Bread and Puppet chaos field recalls a northeastern version of the barter festivals that dot the West Coast, closest, perhaps, to the Oregon Country Fair, minus the live music.

And the Breadheads are more plentiful than ever this summer, thanks to a new development: Phish's own summer pageant, held nearby the weekend before. The spillover is tremendous. Phish's version is called the Clifford Ball, staged on a decommissioned Air Force base across Lake Champlain from Burlington, in New York. And so it is that 70,000 attendees attempt at least temporary respite from American reality and cross fully into Phish's world.

As the tourheads and the Twelve Tribes' Peacemaker bus and college students and everyone roll onto the tarmac of the Plattsburgh Air Force Base, something new comes into shape out beyond the Ferris wheel and the official food vendors. There'd been regular camping in the vicinity of Dead shows since the late '70s. For a few years out West, there'd been the multiband and winkingly acronymed Laguna Seca Daze. But, like Burning Man, this new Zone on this ex–Air Force base comes into being specifically because it is in the middle of nowhere. Those who arrived the night before (assuming they slept) awake in a new place. Tent City is alive.

Tent City is the new instinctual portable community, more portable than Deadheads themselves, even. In this case, it assembles for Phish, but all it takes is a critical mass of heads, more than (say) 20,000 camping in one place. There've been smaller big campouts on the West Coast for years, like High Sierra (10,000) or Laguna Seca (12,000), as well as national touring endeavors like Lollapalooza and the more jam-friendly H.O.R.D.E., but Phish's Clifford Ball initiates the season of overnight megagatherings.

The soiree's sensibility lifts fondly from Bread and Puppet's moves. When Phishheads line up at the gate to get to the front row, they are met by a small, ragtag marching band. A stilt walker! A beardo stomping forward playing an electric bass through a battery-powered amplifier strapped to his back! The bandleader is a longtime Bread and Puppet comrade, and the festival's numerous installations, visual design, and general architecture are engineered by Russ Bennett, another veteran of the troupe.

The Clifford Ball and what follows are different from what happened in Grateful Dead parking lots for a new de-emphasis on auto culture and temporary realignment around foot traffic, just like a real city. Multiple teeming Shakedown Streets emerge as the central geographical feature. The Phish festivals especially get excellent official food vendors, but that doesn't stop the hawkers of grilled cheese and bootleg T-shirts and bumper stickers and glass pipes. Nor does it stop people wandering the pathways with baskets filled with ganja goo balls, perhaps packed with M&Ms and raisins and cookie dough and drizzled in honey or sugar. Sometimes they are bunk. Sometimes they blast buyers off the runway. Psychedelics are readily available. The nitrous tanks hiss like badly dubbed cassettes.

Says Phish manager John Paluska, "What we got basically was the dregs of the Dead's parking lot scene, who immediately went looking for the next biggest scene to hawk their wares and follow around. We ended up with a ton of headaches. That was a very stressful period after Jerry Garcia died, because our security needs exploded and the complexity of our parking lot scene got much greater. But our ticket sales didn't see much of a spike at all, if you look back at our overall growth pattern. We thought maybe we'd have all these people coming."

To assume that Deadheads were just going to give their hearts to Phish "was kind of insulting to Grateful Dead fans," says Paluska. "Give them a little more credit than that. There was something deep that took a long time to cultivate there, they're not en masse going to find some new band to follow. It doesn't happen that way. I'm sure we picked up some fans that might not've found out about Phish as quickly. The thing that bums me out is that we'd worked our asses off to that point and had really developed our own scene and a lot of people assumed that we'd been toiling fairly quietly until Jerry Garcia died and then suddenly we exploded, which is not how it happened." But Phish, who were already selling out Madison Square Garden, find themselves landlocked in Humbeadia.

Above the tarmac at the Clifford Ball, prop planes trail surreal messages. "Hopeless Has Exceptions," reads one. Phish play their six sets in front of some 70,000, doing all the Phishy things they do. Burlington ice cream magnates Ben and Jerry emerge on stage to sing a chorus of an obscure Phish tune. Within the year, the ice cream company will put Phish's faces in the freezers of grocery stores around the country in the form of Phish Food. It is not psychedelic America. It is not vegan, but neither was gelatin-made Windowpane LSD. Phish Food is sugar and milk product. But it is delicious, and a creamy gateway.

Phish's summer 1996 Clifford Ball festival is a smashing success by most standards, especially those of an independent band. But the Bread and Puppet company feel the hard ricochet of the post-Garcia shockwaves. "There was that week between the Clifford Ball and Bread and Puppet when Burlington was just crazy with Phishheads," a veteran local music writer remembers to Phish's Trey Anastasio, who in turn admits that he now sometimes grows uncomfortable going out in Burlington.

The influence of the Clifford Ball is instant. It captures the flash and imagination of the Deadhead autonomous zones in a way that the amphitheater-touring HORDE or Lollapalooza festivals never could, nor even the various post-Dead enterprises. Tent City is real. Tent City is viable. Tent City doesn't need Jerry Garcia. Tent City doesn't even need Phish, really, though Phish helps. It's better, perhaps, if the city-organism isn't reliant on any one energy source. It just needs . . . electricity.

OUT IN THE Nevada desert, Earth and Fire Erowid meet a man on a bicycle with a patch-covered coat and, hidden behind the patches like prizes on an advent calendar, drugs. Though veteran attendees will report an uptick in undercovers, Burning Man is one place that psychedelic America doesn't have to worry about its future. Celebrating its tenth anniversary and its seventh year on the playa, the anarchistic build-it-yourself art festival is experiencing its own growing pains.

Fire Erowid will later write, "[The man] traveled around the United States, buying, selling, and trading novel materials: part salesman, part information resource, and part psychedelic bard ready with McKenna quotes and campfire trip tales."

She and her partner Earth had taken on their pseudonyms the year before. There is some spirit of Pranksterdom, but more often new identities are simply known as usernames. The idea of finding, creating, and naming a new self is a long tradition in fringe under-grounds everywhere, but especially the psychedelic world. The recent college graduates had declared themselves Earth and Fire Erowid and registered a new website without quite knowing what they or it will become.

"It was an explicitly psychedelic event with a heavy 'and hard alco-hol and crazy' component," recalls Earth of his and Fire's first Burn-ing Man the year before. "It was known about by anyone using any of the major online libraries, discussion forums, and the like."

A large part of the event's reputation owes to its lawlessness. Not coincidentally, the event's size has doubled every year in the desert to date, from the 90 or so in 1990 to about 8,000 in 1996. Even when the organizers start adding numbered streets and Burning Man's population hits 20,000 a few years later, it will never be Tent City. Burning Man is a jeweled kingdom of its own.

Many freedoms are celebrated at Burning Man involving art, dance, explosions, nudity, speed, and other rites (and rights), but drugs remain a permanent and central portal to Black Rock surreality. When the Erowids return in 1996, there are dozens of substances available, a full post-Shulgin array there for the picking.

The man with the coat has the usual "classic" psychedelics, plus rarer materials like N,N-DMT. That year, too, Earth remembers, "there was one fellow wandering around with a large jug of ayahuasca he was offering up as a party drug." Camped nearby is the crew from the Lycœum, a recently launched psychedelic info website the Erowids are friendly with.

The Erowid camp evolves into an informal psychedelic crisis center, says Earth, in the sense that "people who we found or met or wandered into our zone were having trouble [and] we had the time, space, and folks to help out." One of their friends tries a drug called GHB. Enjoying it at first, he ups the dosage and accidentally takes a different concentration, becoming nauseous and unconscious. It's terrifying, but among the crew is a doctor, and they make sure everything is okay, hooking him to a blood-gas monitor and watching him.

Burning Man's collective recklessness is increasing to dangerous levels. As in previous years, organizers locate the DJs several miles into the desert, away from the main camp where the *untz-untz-untz*ers can *untz-untz* all night long without disturbing the sleep-sleep-sleepers. This is hardly a satisfactory arrangement to the dancers either, where six separate sound systems clash across the empty miles of dried lake bed. There is chaos and reports of arrests. DJ Goa Gil is bummed.

Coupled with people itching to make high-speed desert drives, it proves fatal that year when a motorcycle accident kills one of the organizers' friends, and several are seriously injured when an art car shuttling between the main camp and the techno ghetto runs over several sleeping campers. In the next years, the DJs will be folded into a Community Dance with Goa Gil and others. There will be friction and a comical scene involving a man in a fire-burping art car demanding that Gil play some Led Zeppelin. Gil just turns up the volume and that's pretty much that.

Burning Man is now a major psychedelic stopover on the expanding global dance circuit. Even more than psychedelics themselves, the bardo-shifting beats become part of the international vocabulary. Though there is a fully formed dance subculture and package tours and DIY raves and mainstream crossovers aplenty in the United States throughout the late 1990s, it will be a few years before the music makes full American landfall. As the millennium pulls closer, the new untz-democracy pings from Goa and Ibiza and Europe and back into the American dance network, recombining and soundtracking full moon parties the world over.

At Burning Man, the beats soundtrack the desert sky, the ecstatic rhythms and art-chaos wrenching open a portal to pure existence. The psychedelic pipeline between Black Rock and the lower San Francisco Peninsula's technology corridor grows strong. In 1995, an Apple employee had thrown an after-party in the Cupertino company's largest on-campus conference room, the Town Hall Theatre, to show home videos. "See couch surfers and idiots (like me) parasail over a hard, unforgiving desert floor (splat!) RAVE RAVE RAVE till dawn in the rain!" the host had posted. "Witness the mindless destruction of various computing devices which would have been valued at millions of dollars only a couple of decades ago."

The Black Rock classes of the mid-1990s also included the pseriously psychedelicized virtual reality programmer Mark Pesce. He'd hit the playa and saw nothing but the flat digital VR plane for miles in all directions. In his midthirties, Pesce is among the new wave of Silicon Valley denizens increasingly public about his psychedelic heritage. "I'd probably be some silly software engineer working in New England and bored with life, without psychedelics," he will declare. At the Shiva Corporation, he'd helped invent dial-up Internet technology.

It is clear that the psychedelic culture is spreading in dozens of new directions and reinforcing itself in old ones. After their friend's GHB overdose at Burning Man, Earth and Fire Erowid decide to push forward with a new website, the Vaults of Erowid, and shape it into the online drug information repository they believe is needed.

They are unsure about how much of themselves they want to put forward. In the fall of 1996, the couple attend the Entheobotany Conference at the Palace of Fine Arts in San Francisco, where they meet the independent psychedelic scholars Sasha and Ann Shulgin, who give them moving encouragement. In the growing middle space between science and the street, the Shulgins are *the* heroes, then embroiled in a struggle with the federal government. Without warning two years earlier, the DEA had rescinded Sasha Shulgin's right to produce Schedule I compounds in his backyard shed-laboratory, informing him of this matter in the form of a dramatic and humiliating raid by federal agents.

The Erowids' archive is far from finished, but it is another quiet and significant step in the maturity of head culture. There is, of course, a rich and ongoing academic literature on psychedelics and entheogens, though fully legal research had stopped in the United States by the mid-1960s. For the past decade, the Multidisciplinary Association for Psychedelic Studies have led the charge to reinstate psychedelic research within the academy. But while there are heads in the academy, there are many more who aren't. Along with their colleagues at the Lycœum, Erowid.org grows to become one of the common independent repositories for trustworthy information about illicit psychoactive materials.

Out there, everywhere, there is more and more psychedelic use. Even if LSD availability begins to drop, the *Monitoring the Future* report measures LSD use at an all-time high of 8.8 percent among graduating high school seniors in 1996. More than 10 percent say they've used hallucinogens within the previous twelve months. The Grateful Dead tour network may've been damaged, but it's practiced enough to reassemble. When the psychedelized co-ed fraternity kids from Columbia University need LSD for their Odyssey, they can show up at a Phish show, and there it is. When it's needed at Burning Man, someone's got some. If there's some half-spontaneous assemblage of Rainbows, it arrives. It's there for ravers and college students and Yippies and yuppies and frat boys and sorority girls and (for better or worse) 8.8 percent of high school seniors.

THE MOUNTIES WATCH the place for a while. They suspect their man might be about to pack up the warehouse and go elsewhere, so in September 1996 they make their move. They are right. Their man will not get to make his exit this time. Unlike many government moves, this one will be noticeable on year-end surveys of drug availability.

The lab they find inside the warehouse is so big that the subsequent police report states that it produced "enough acid to dose every man, woman and child in Canada" one and a half times. When the Health Canada lab tests the LSD, it somehow returns at 106 percent purity. The Mounties find $500,000 worth of cash and gold bullion.

There's DMT and ecstasy and 2C-B, too, at an estimated value of some $6.5 million. There is also a residence, as well as some weapons. The man occupying the warehouse is named David Roy Shepard. He is in his fifties and handsome, with sleepy eyes and sensitively furled lips that seem to indicate some resignation and bemusement for having to occupy the late twentieth-century cult of reality. Before the agents dismantle Shepard's lab, they use it to film a training video for future busts. But there probably won't be many future busts like this.

For two months, Shepard refuses to talk to the Canadian police. Then the FBI get back to them. The Americans have run Shepard's fingerprints and made an interesting discovery. David Roy Shepard is none other than Nick Sand, the old-guard chemist who first synthesized Orange Sunshine for the Brotherhood of Eternal Love back in the late '60s. He'd jumped bail in 1976 and his identity changed often.

Sand had split for Canada, then spent time at an ashram with Bhagwan Shree Rajneesh in western India, says LSD archivist Mark McCloud. "I was part of a team that helped supply the ashram with ecstasy 'til it went illegal," says McCloud. He figured "the whole thing must be a 24/7 party. And it was, until it went south and they couldn't come up with any safrole," the chemical precursor to ecstasy.

Sometime, Sand returned to service as a chemist, shuttling between Mexico and Canada, evading capture once with one of his many alternate identities. But this time, the Mounties have got Nick Sand for real. He is shipped back to the States and goes up against the same judge who sentenced him 1976. Sand must face his original fifteen-year sentence, with another five added for his escape.

There is a steep drop-off in the high school seniors who say they've used LSD in the previous year, from 8.4 percent to 7.6 percent between 1997 and 1998 (and down 1.2 percent since 1995). And yet the flow of LSD still doesn't stop. Sand is gone, but there are other chemists. And, when they slide away, there are others to slide into their place. But it's not the chemists that are the hard part. The hard part is—still, as ever—the ergotamine tartrate, the precious precursor. But that's still covered, thankfully, give or take the occasional drought.

After Sand goes to prison in 1997, there are stories of a conclave of acid family higher-ups out in Stinson Beach, California, the luscious land-spit in southwestern Marin County. This meeting, it is reported, even takes place in the former abode of Jerry Garcia and Mountain Girl, known as San Souci—"without cares"—overlooking the Pacific. Several odd and shady figures are said to be in attendance. If time lines are to be believed, the meeting's biggest achievement is to introduce the house's current occupant, a perpetual nogoodnik named Gordon Todd Skinner, to a man named Leonard Pickard.

Whether he is there in Stinson Beach or not, Leonard Pickard had synthesized MDA and donated to Nick Sand's defense fund in the '70s. He'd been busted making blotter in a Mountain View warehouse (right in the heart of Silicon Valley) in 1988, caught with sheets full of LSD decorated with Dead family album covers designed by San Francisco artists, including *American Beauty* (or does it say *American Reality?*), Robert Hunter's *Tiger Rose,* Bob Weir's *Ace,* Jerry Garcia's *Cats Under the Stars,* and others. He'd lived for a spell at the San Francisco Zen Center.

And according to psychedelic historian Mark McCloud, Leonard Pickard's chemistry CV extends back to the '60s when, as a member of the so-called Clear Light System, Pickard was involved with the makers of the premium-priced Windowpane LSD, rolling free time after time. And now, the acid families seem to decree that it's again his turn to get back truckin' on.

ANOTHER WAY TO transmit psychedelic America into the hearts and minds and eyeballs of the country is to go on television, which is why Dick Latvala and Big Steve Parish, Jerry Garcia's trusted roadie, are live on the QVC home shopping network to convince viewers to order the latest volume of *Dick's Picks.* But now Dick Latvala won't stare into the unblinking TV eye, looking every which way but at the camera. The Grateful Dead archivist has different ideas about how to accomplish the task of transmission, ideas that will prove more effective than going on the home shopping network in the long run. But, at this moment, he sits on a studio set that is made up to look like the Dead's warehouse.

Our taper-hero is wearing a Hawaiian-style shirt made up of recursive blue Steal Your Face logos, a baseball cap, and sunglasses. He grinds his jaw a little bit when he's not talking and begins to explain to the host *why* his latest pick, from 1972, is amazing. He doesn't get very far. Dick enjoys public appearances surrounding the albums almost less than the politicking required for their release. Some aspects of Dick don't change, however.

At a recent release party for a *Dick's Picks,* journalist Steve Silberman had come across his friend cornered by a camera crew, being queried by a snide entertainment jockey. "Mr. Latvala," the interviewer sneers, "when was the last time *you* took acid?"

Dick looks at him. "Well," he says happily, "right now!" Dick will trip for anything. Once, his ex-wife Carol reports, he leaves for the airport and returns twenty minutes later. "Forgot to dose," he says. It's just part of him. Unfortunately, so is the drinking, which ratchets up as he makes the promotional rounds.

On the home shopping network, though, he and Big Steve make for a funny combo. Dick is tripping and occasionally emits quiet wordless moans into his clip-on microphone.

Lost in the middle of the QVC sale is the music itself. That is, the Tapes, as Dick Latvala knows and loves them. They might look like CDs now, but Dick knows that packed inside each release is everything a home listener needs to create an instant Dead-in. The shows, released almost only in unedited forms, are psychedelic America in a can—the music, the language, the signs, the setting—waiting for decoding by the right heads.

The idea to go on QVC isn't a terrible one, wherever it originated. The Deadheads are still legion. Another post-Garcia lineup of the remaining band members is set to hit the road this summer o' 1998, and, in preparation, the band's management commissions the sociologist Rebecca Adams to undergo a rigorous study of the

Deadheads. She estimates, conservatively, a population of some half a million, a mean age between twenty-three and thirty-two, from middle- and upper-class families. The vast majority are at least college educated, probably bound for white-collar careers. Had Garcia lived, the band would have then been entering its thirty-third year, around for longer than nearly all of its primary fan base. It is a fan base that is not only alive but *young*. There's plenty of uniting for Dead freaks to do yet.

Of all the employees at Grateful Dead Productions, tape archivist Dick Latvala probably has among the highest job security. He started from the bottom and now he's here, on QVC, with his name right at the top of nearly all the new Grateful Dead albums. There's virtually no one else in the organization who can do what he does. In some ways, Dick Latvala *is* the Grateful Dead.

Though a deeply real person who has spent his life talking and connecting deeply with fellow Deadheads, it is the same Dick Latvala who'd only wanted to observe the vice president from close range, not actually meet him. Whatever sobriety Dick was able to practice after his stint in rehab is long gone. Many people who discovered themselves via psychedelics also struggle with other substances. Dick is one of them.

It carries over to his home life, up there in Petaluma, in a little complex of low homes, his ex-wife Carol right next door amid clusters of ex-Morehousers. Dick is a constant acid consumer, a bong hit taker, a coffee drinker, a cigarette smoker, a drinker. And, now, with all this Dead music to listen to, all these e-mails to respond to, Dick can't take acid all the time. Sometimes he resorts to other, speedier substitutes. He does his work, hops through Internet forums to see what people are talking about, and sometimes gets into trouble when he impulsively says dumb stuff. Dick is not built for mass communication.

When Napster turns the mp3 into the new People's Format in June 1999, *free* hits the American marketplace like never before. Like every user-controlled medium in the past and like every one introduced in the foreseeable future, Napster becomes a way for Deadheads to exchange recordings. Tapers inclined toward higher fidelity have figured out ways to do this before through complex file transfer protocols. Deadheads start to build a central repository of live recordings.

Dick is happy people can hear the music, but direct human interaction is a vital part of tape trading in his cosmology. Where would he be without it?

The wave of the future is here, and it's possible Dick senses the coming digital flood. It's bearing down on all frontiers, electronic and otherwise, in all its silvery deathness. It's sweeping up everything in its path, and here it comes for Dick and the Tapes, the precious Tapes. It's Dick's job to protect the Tapes.

Dick knows what he's supposed to do to keep the Tapes safe. Really safe. He makes copies of them. All of them. The whole vault.

It is probably not a single conscious decision, and it happens over the course of years. Dick loves the Grateful Dead too much and wants the word of their music to travel into every ear and mind possible. Copies of nearly everything end up with a taper and professional studio guitarist named Rob Eaton, who, in 1997, begins to play the Bob Weir role in a new Dead tribute act called the Dark Star Orchestra. Dick might well give a near-complete copy of the vault to multiple people. But who he copies it for is immaterial. He gives them to everybody, to everyone, to anyone. The official *Dick's Picks* is only a mechanism to deliver more at once. And, once Dick makes copies of a show, the recordings inevitably explode out onto DAT and burned CD, onto cassettes, and out into Napster and RealAudio and FTP sites and other online spaces. And whenever the Dead (and Dick) put out a new old recording, people buy it anyway.

It is the true arrival of the information age, everything that the data-gobbling techheads and tape collectors had understood for years. Napster and mp3s are only the start, the Diggers' power of *FREE* fully unleashed into the American economy like a trickster spirit. The weird-market rules once applied to tapes and drugs and countercultures now scale outward into legitimate American business. "Anything that can be expressed as bits will be," an Electronic Frontier Foundation fellow elucidates a decade later.

In some ways, the arrival of mp3s represents a complete corrosion of the hip economy, a sudden and violent inflation of free. Underground and mainstream value systems collide. Everything is free. But everything comes with a price, too, sometimes negative. Dials go askew, compasses spin.

And, in late summer of 1999, Dick Latvala has a heart attack and dies a week later. "Dick died August 6th, Hiroshima day," Carol Latvala observes. "Jerry died August 9th, Nagasaki." This isn't a Lincoln/Kennedy-level conspiracy, just another bittersweet historical rhyme. "They both died within a few days of their birthday on the days of the big bombs." Sometimes timetracks click together to show pictures.

The newest *Dick's Picks* is the fourteenth installment, a collection of two shows from the Boston Music Hall in late 1973, the Dead's homemade system stacked into the intimate space. "I could . . . stay in the winter of '73 forever," Dick had once remarked. Good-bye Dick, so long and thanks for all the tapes, and the pot, and for being Dick. Onward. Latvala!

THERE'S A WHOLE new batch of chemical recipes by Alexander "Sasha" Shulgin in circulation at Burning Man and elsewhere thanks to *Tryptamines I Have Known and Loved,* Sasha and Ann Shulgin's 1997 collection. But it's Dr. Sasha's biggest hit—a cover song, relatively speaking—that's blowing up even more, and the Shulgins couldn't be more aghast.

MDMA first appears on the well-established *Monitoring the Future* and relatively recent *Drug Abuse Warning Network* surveys in 1996, with just under 5 percent of high school seniors having admitted to using it in the previous year. It goes under 4 percent by 1998 but then it *rockets*, more than doubling as 2000 approaches. The DEA seizures and emergency room statistics do too.

The evidence is everywhere. It isn't a proper psychedelic, many believe, not manifesting the mind or the God-spirit as much as amplifying the soul (to say it nicely) and it's just, like, wow, I *love* you, man. Terence McKenna and Owsley Stanley, to name only two, remain deeply suspicious of the love drug.

Ecstasy cuts across classes in American society, an almost perfect party drug with almost zero chance of nail-biting cosmic wipeouts—provided it's real MDMA and one stays hydrated and doesn't take too much. It brings big ideas (or, at least, a sense of bigness) to its users. Like acid and pot before it, it provides a quick tax-free income stream for creative entrepreneurs of all platforms and ambitions. It is gentler than LSD, better suited for therapy.

The drug hits the post-Dead jam scene full force in 1997 as a new wave of bands bursts from the Wetlands and Colorado and other hippie epicenters. As the apparent heir to the Dead narrative and the mainstream of psychedelic America, the jam world takes a different course with the arrival of ecstasy. Over 1998 and 1999, MDMA overtakes LSD in annual usage by high school seniors in the annual *Monitoring the Future* report, and availability spikes. LSD continues to be an enormous seller in the jam scene, with pieces of the Dead network continuing to operate from Phish's tours.

At the start of the ecstasy age, Phish's jams widen and widen, until they are playing hour-and-a-half sets composed of four or five songs linked by wide grooves. They stop practicing. They start partying. They grow beards. They quit their traditional postshow discussion, instituting a "no analysis" rule and writing a whole new repertoire that briefly overtakes their set lists almost entirely. Soon, the drugs will take a turn. But, in the first days of ecstasy, Phish's teleological prog-rock marching orders have never been clearer. They are always reaching for the next rung, the next step.

There's a whole army of young, hungry jammers nipping at Phish's heels, each with its own charismatic lead guitarist(s), Internet-enabled fan base, and novelty-driven musical philosophy that promises access to the cosmos or at least, ahem, ecstasy. Funk grooves begin to outweigh communal space explorations as the primary jam language. In the new order, if it didn't before, dancing trumps all.

The scenes grow even more strongly regional. From Colorado, there are the conspicuously Phishy good-vibe jam-grassers String Cheese Incident. Their offshoot management firm, Madison House, soon offers a record label, travel and booking agencies, merchandise, and the all-important ticketing office. What was formless and primal and chaotic is now a business model and basis for a new class of lysergically connected professionals.

In Philadelphia, the Disco Biscuits begin life as Phish/Dead-covering frat jammers but by 1999 are going through their own changes at a fast-flickering rate. When the ecstasy hits, they become the first of the new jammers to adopt the latest waves of dance textures and beats into their already genre-bent sound. They pump out rock operas and set list acrobatics, plus a few requisite drug tunes. The quartet acquire a Roland JP-8000 synthesizer and go for it, one of the very few bands on the Wetlands roster that actually *jam*. The song structures drop away as the band learns to love disco's four-on-the-floor thump, building long improvised passages that approximate the pulses of dub, drum-n-bass, jungle, and other life-enveloping subgenres.

What's surprising is how new it is. With these gestures, jam-ready guitarists finally have access to minimalism and a whole new kind of maximalist drama. Other bands in other cities pick up on the technique or discover it for themselves, in the case of Atlanta's Sound Tribe Sector 9, who mix it with McKenna/Mayan cosmologies, or Toronto's New Deal. Finally, through a wave of newly sprouted drug-referencing electronic subgenres (psybient, psytrance), drug-referencing electronic acts (Hallucinogen, 1200 Micrograms), and drug-referencing electronic tracks ("Divine Moments of Truth"), the American hippies finally start really dancing to the European beats.

To actual ravers, though, the new bands might sound like rinky-dink hippies. But the Disco Biscuits get labeled a "traveling ecstasy circus" by a club owner, and they are exactly that. The drug envelopes nearly every jam scene, but especially theirs. Though the Disco Biscuits are still playing tiny bars throughout the country in 1999, there are already those who follow them from show to show. And, at every destination, no matter how landlocked, should anyone need ecstasy, it is there.

Perhaps it's the ecstasy, perhaps it's the millennium, perhaps it's the big market share, but the jam scenes suck in a vast amount of ambition and energy. Bands throw festivals, fans make archives, and all hurdle toward the twenty-first century. Tapers remain at the cutting edge of all new music reproduction technologies and distribution system models. They get outboard CD burners, link up their FTP sites into a network called eTree, and invent a new piece of software for exchanging large files that they call Furthurnet.

The software is new but carries tribal history, employing its code to make users do what nice tapers have done for decades: share. If someone offers up a large file and two users start to download it, the program feeds the two users different bits of the master file and forces them to exchange. The faster they share, the rounder they get. It's magic. The heads have solved the age-old dream: high-quality music can be disseminated as soon as it is recorded. And just in time for the twenty-first century.

The millennium drops as planned from every sky. New Year's Eve is the holiday that the Grateful Dead made its own psychedelic ritual, largely because of their shows through the years with Bill Graham. Around the jam world, especially, it remains a night when the music retains the possibility of unlocking whatever it's going to unlock.

In the Florida Everglades, Phish throw another festival and, along with their regular programming, play an eight-hour set that is transcendental for band and crowd alike. There is a Port-o-Let onstage, for any of the band's bodily or chemical needs. In bringing Tent City (population 80,000) into the Everglades, Phish become the largest single-act event in all of North America that night and locate a new answer to Jerry Garcia's suggestion for heads to find their own space to act out fantasies.

Phish's Bread and Puppet–influenced festival architects turn part of a swamp into a vivid miniature village complete with promenade. Driving down Alligator Alley into the central Florida swamp, Phish and their heads turn their backs, cross into Seminole Indian territory, and leave the United States entirely.

THE THREE-DECADE-running nationwide psychedelic autonomous zone starts to shut shortly after the millennium. Many events happen in quick succession, a disconnected swirl that manages to have a total effect. First, Terence McKenna dies in April 2000 of a brain cancer that advanced with dark swiftness. He says he's not scared.

Whether there is any Earth-bound math to support Terence McKenna's reveries of eating mushrooms to immanentize the eschaton (or whatever) is only partially the point. The late beloved Terence always insisted that he wasn't a scientist but an explorer, and his maps of human credulity are an invaluable legacy. In a way, his enormous imagination stood in for psychedelic America as a whole, dreaming it as it dreamed him. Overenthusiastic, he could sometimes be seen as a pitchman for novelty in the broadest sense, but always touched with a stream of skepticism. Did it come from the mushroom voice? Or did it come from the creative far reaches of a brilliant mind? Which would be more impressive? So long, Terence.

The first sign of psychedelic America's shutting is structural and seemingly small: Phish decide to stop touring. For the musicians, the partying has gotten bad. They need a break. But, when they take one, the continuous historical line of LSD distribution is broken. It had leapt from the Dead to Phish so naturally that there was no time to blink. And, besides Phish, no currently touring band comes close to the required critical mass. One can still dependably find psychedelics around the jammers, but they're no longer the pipeline. The acid world has bigger problems to worry about at the moment.

A few weeks after Phish's last show, the heat come crashing down on Leonard Pickard in Kansas. He'd been too flamboyant as an LSD chemist. His peers in the entheogenic underground hadn't failed to notice his taste for luxury. None of this would've been a problem, necessarily, were it not for Pickard's partner, Gordon Todd Skinner, who is a genuine weird person, and not in any Humbeadean sense. He is trouble city, folks, putting the psycho in the psychonaut. The DEA chase Leonard Pickard around Kansas and haul him in on Election Day 2000, as a majority of Americans don't vote for the cowboy-talkin' victor who will soon further close the frontier.

In the Kansas missile silo, the DEA find a $120,000 stereo, Persian rugs, and a giant hot tub. The stereo, at least, is understandable. It was always important for Owsley to play music during the sacred alchemical moments. Nick Sand and other chemists had dug rugs, too.

The silo scene had begun how any party scene in a missile silo might, with sex and drugs and strippers and ravers, and only then began to go a little out of control. It ended with a guy tied up in a hotel room, stuffed full of LSD, and eventually left to die. Details are fascinating but irrelevant and the hour is getting late. Leonard Pickard receives two concurrent life sentences. His associate Gordon Todd Skinner remains on the run.

The DEA claim an immediate 74 percent decline in LSD availability at the hand of their Operation White Rabbit, its deep-level sequel to the Operation Looking Glass that snagged Karen Horning and other dealers almost a decade earlier. Many of them continue to languish in prison as the dream of psychedelic America seems to slip away.

The *Entheogen Review* in 2001 publishes several of longtime fugitive acid chemist Nick Sand's letters under the pseudonym ∞Ayes in which Sand grows reflective, and unrepentant in the slightest.

"Someday, somewhere," he writes, "I will establish the University for Psychedelic Studies. There will be a department of psychedelic botany and chemistry. There will be a beautiful park and temple with lawns and ponds, peacocks, swans, and wildlife walking fearlessly. There will be pavilions for initiation. There will be a department of entheogenic worship." Sand describes a campus filled with schools for yoga and breathing and music and ecological studies and love and beauty and more. "There will be no government inspectors or policy," Sand writes. "They will not be necessary." It is still a far-off dream when Nick Sand writes these words, and then arrives the triple summer bummer of 2001.

First comes a massive LSD drought that sweeps over festival-land during the virgin years of the new century. On the *Monitoring the Future* report, there'd been a little dip in 1999, but the bottom really drops out after 2000. In 2001, 6.6 percent of high school seniors said they'd taken LSD in the previous year, dropping to 3.5 percent in 2002 and then 1.9 percent in 2003, and one can only surmise that it's not because American high school seniors no longer want to take acid. Perceived availability dips more than 10 percent while the so-called disapproval rate among the same seniors rises slightly but floats around the 80 percent line, an all-time low it hit in the mid-1990s. Put another way, 20 percent of high school students think it's fine to take acid, an opinion that holds steady even after a decade of antidrug propaganda. Certainly, the Kansas missile silo bust of Leonard Pickard doesn't help, but it is not the full or only reason real LSD becomes hard to get, even for heads, for the first time since 1965.

The real missing piece is when the man known to almost no one (except blotter collector Mark McCloud) as Dealer McDope becomes sick and falls inactive. He'd been one of the elite and mysterious characters who, for decades, was able to liberate the necessary chemicals from European supplies. But McDope is the last of his generation. Everyone else is gone. He is the source of the vast majority of ergotamine tartrate circulating among the chemists, the all-important precursor for the production of LSD-25.

"Even Pickard would work through this guy," Karen Horning says later. By then, "there was one fellow," and that was McDope. "And he supplied, basically, five main LSD labs, five main people. Pickard was one of them. There was but one source for the ergotamine. And people were swapping and trading back and forth, and around you go, because everybody was still on the same page, even though Pickard went his own way."

When Dealer McDope becomes ill, the acid doesn't disappear entirely, but its broad-scale absence is palpable across many American undergrounds. "There were other outfits still active," acid archivist Mark McCloud notes. "If you look, you see a purple ohm [blotter] appear in Europe. Some European outlets were still active at the time."

There's a British lab going for a few years run by an American expatriate named Casey Hardison who'd done some time on Dead tour. Inspired by LSD, he earns degrees in biochemistry and botany despite never having finished high school. Teaching himself to make psychedelics, he works with an unwavering faith in his and others' cognitive freedoms. He sells some of what he produces, but it's a small operation compared to the American labs of yore. By the time he gets busted in 2004, the thirty-four-year-old Hardison is testing a new method of LSD synthesis, which he contributes to the *Entheogen Review* from prison but never completes himself. The future is still always, but psychedelic America's now getting glum.

The fade of McDope, the stoppage of the Dead/Phish continuum, the ends of Nick Sand and Leonard Pickard, though, all add up to a particular pausing point. And while the LSD disappears, ecstasy is at the peak of an 800 percent increase in availability over the previous half decade and, along with ever-prevalent marijuana, does the job picking up the slack as far as most groupmind needs go, even if it lacks proper psychedelic qualities. LSD is always out there, but—in the telling of Mark McCloud—because of unfolding events, the chemists of the acid families now decide that it's best to take a breather, as well.

Mushrooms, DMT, and many others are all findable, however, as are other compounds from the Shulgin cookbooks. Among the twelfth graders of the *Monitoring the Future* report, usage of hallucinogens other than LSD surpass acid at this time, too. There is also, for that matter, plenty that purports to be acid but is some cocktail of speedy otherness.

It is entirely possible that LSD is now obsolete or, at the very least, supplanted by any number of other substances. One lesson of Terence McKenna, if nothing else, is that mushrooms are every bit as powerful as LSD in the proper dosage. But his biggest lesson will always remain the power of novelty.

Leonard Pickard's sketchy cohort Gordon Todd Skinner is picked up by the feds at Burning Man over Labor Day in 2001, and, a week later, a pair of planes soar into the World Trade Center, disrupting a gorgeous September morning in Manhattan and life around great portions of the planet. It also disrupts life within the radius of the blast site itself, including the Wetlands Preserve, twelve blocks to the north.

The club is already in the midst of its own end-of-the-world hysteria. Over the summer, the noise complaints had built to a maddening hum, the once-empty TriBeCa now fully gentrified and unamused. The rents rise. Larry Bloch had bailed a half decade back, threatening to close the club until a bright-eyed twenty-three-year-old named Pete Shapiro arrived with access to a combination of funds and nearly unlimited chutzpah. Shapiro had gone electric at a Dead show while attending Northwestern University in Evanston and hung around a local head shop casing out the whole Dead scene as he plunged in fully. He'd promised Larry Bloch that he'd take good care of Wetlands, its portal-like mural, and its hardcore environmentalists. And he does. It remains a crossroads for jammers and many other constituencies. It is home to a bigger community. The acid remains easy to find there.

But, by 2001, the headaches are throbbing, and it's not like the club is profitable, anyway. It was a good run. Pete Shapiro and his crew book a few weeks of finales. He has gotten good at conjuring big bills. Lots of bands come to say good-bye, a schedule that is set to include neighborhood favorites with connections to the '70s Central Park scene alongside members of the Grateful Dead themselves. Bob Weir, who'd played with teen wonders Hanson at the club, is going to come back. And then. And then. And then.

The realist part about Wetlands and 9/11: it is exactly the moment in local and global history that Wetlands' extended community most needs a place to gather.

The surrealist part about Wetlands and 9/11: the terrorist act itself is a perverted critique of the same cartoonish capitalism that crept over New York and choked out Wetlands and that Wetlands was founded to counter. Among other things.

September 11 "was the death of fun, unreeling right in front of us," Hunter S. Thompson writes, "unraveling, withering, collapsing, draining away in the darkness like a handful of stolen mercury." It is a moment of clarity for the good doctor, still occupying his Humbeadean compound outside Aspen. Because of this change in the global climate, Mark McCloud says, the LSD families decide to let matters cool for a while until the heads can prevail.

Pete Shapiro manages to get Wetlands Preserve open for one last night. In New York visiting his daughter, Grateful Dead lyricist Robert Hunter returns from retirement for a solo acoustic valediction. Hunter's performance is tentative, but he says later that it reconnects him with the Grateful Dead's music and he subsequently encourages the rest of the band to reconvene, which they do again the following summer.

When Hunter is done, there is a funk power jam that lasts until about five in the morning, when the last musician onstage is a dude with dreadlocks and a didgeridoo. After that, the familiar groove of the May 8, 1977, "Scarlet Begonias" rainbows out of the speakers, and Larry Bloch takes the helm for one last set, closing well after dawn. The idyllic mural-portal is soon painted over for a Scandinavian furniture store. Bye, Wetlands. See you in our dreams.

APPEARING ON THE horizon in early 2002 is a vast new metropolis, perfect and sustainable: a cartoonish Tent City on the Hill for the heads. It is built with old world hippie resources. Though the organizers of Bonnaroo will surely deny it, they are building a new destination for the mainstream of psychedelic America. Bonnaroo might look like an old-fashioned rock festival put on by hippies, but that time has passed. Bonnaroo sets the course for the future of America's festival season.

The director of visual design is the same Bread and Puppet veteran who works with Phish. Editors of *Relix,* the staple Deadhead tape-trading magazine started in the midseventies, write and edit the daily newspaper. The organizers rely on the good ol' bands for the entertainment and on the familiar networks to spread word of the vast land-tract they are providing to create a new semipermanent home for Tent City, USA. From the get-go, it is clear that the promoters have designs on repeating the event. Until now, Americans could never get it down quite as efficiently as the festival-loving British hippies of Glastonbury and elsewhere.

They launch with a "What Is Bonnaroo?" campaign. Bonnaroo is a half-Creole/half-nonsense derivative from a Dr. John song. Bonnaroo is a new music festival. Bonnaroo is whatever you want. Bonnaroo is _____. The inaugural edition sells out without any traditional advertising besides mentions in the jam sphere.

The first band to play the first Bonnaroo is from Minnesota and called the Big Wu, after a line in *Joe vs. the Volcano*. Starting as a Dead cover act, they have a strong regional following and host their own annual Big Wu Family Reunion in Wisconsin. Since Phish's Clifford Ball, many of the bands have their own festivals each summer now: the Disco Biscuits' Camp Bisco, moe.'s moe.down and Summer Camp (cohosted with Umphrey's McGee), ekoostik Hookah's Hookahville, Max Creek's Camp Creek, Yonder Mountain String Band's Northwest String Summit, String Cheese's multinight Incidents at Horning's Hideout in Oregon, and a whole slew of fill-in-the-blank stocks. Terrapin Tapes has their annual Gathering of the Vibes, too, the tape business going by the wayside as the collecting world goes digital.

There are large-scale rave events in California, especially, like the Electric Daisy Carnival and Coachella's dance fest with rock headliners, but few emphasize a camping component. If one wants to enter the zone beyond the dance floor, it's necessary to find the heads. Each of the big hippie summer jams gathers a certain tribe, and each is as magical as its participants want to make it. They are all American psychedelic ritual festivals, should one want to find the proper signposts. As it defines itself, Bonnaroo is a place for all of them.

The planners choose Tennessee for plenty of reasons, not the least of which is that it is suitably far from everywhere. Like the Phish festivals the organizers modeled it on, Bonnaroo is a journey before one even has to make camp. Tennessee had been on the original Humbead's Map, a lonely island north of the Farspooming Ocean. Stephen Gaskin and the Farm had built a rainbow bridge. But the new festival has so much more planned.

Hippie bands aside, it is a Gotham-sized undertaking with massive capital behind it. The promoters are the Knoxville-based Ashley Capps, the local talent, and the ambitious young Superfly Presents. Founded in New Orleans, Superfly reasserted New Orleans' spot on the Map by booking jam-heavy late-night Jazzfest throwdowns for the sleepless set.

The real money behind Bonnaroo, however, is Coran Capshaw, who amassed a fortune shepherding the Dave Matthews Band from his Charlottesville clubs and through the jam circuit to stadium-filling success. But Coran Capshaw is so much more than that.

Capshaw is a Deadhead. Was a Deadhead. Saw the Grateful Dead a lot. Four hundred times. That number locates him squarely among the heads. Like John Perry Barlow, Coran Capshaw is an ambassador, and he builds a skillful pipeline between the hip economy and the real world that will make them almost indistinguishable.

Being in the music management business was never Capshaw's plan, and it still isn't. First, he'd diversified, cofounding Red Light Communications, a Charlottesville-area Internet service provider, to go along with Red Light Management. But, by the late '90s, his allegedly diverse interests collide into a new online venture, MusicToday.

MusicToday folds in all the revenue streams and innovations he'd noticed in the Grateful Dead world: websites, merchandise sales, direct ticketing, the music itself. Everything is codified; everything is part of the plan. Unlike the Grateful Dead, now there *is* a plan.

And it's not that Bonnaroo is part of Coran Capshaw's plan, exactly. He didn't dream it up—that credit goes to the Superfly guys, or maybe Bonnaroo dreamt itself up—but it's the kind of event that fits into Capshaw's world. There's synergy involved, one of those New Age business words that isn't terribly different from an intellectual riff on psychedelic synchronicity mixed with hype and more money. A great codification is at work. It's not very sexy or underground or interesting or psychedelic, but that's what Coran Capshaw achieves. He rarely grants interviews.

At Bonnaroo, teenagers and twentysomethings and thirtysomethings and beyond find themselves inside the same temporary autonomous zone that the Grateful Dead helped discover. Bonnaroo organizers wager that they can conjure the place annually. There is drugs and sex and interaction. Sociologists can analyze Bonnaroo within the model of Bahktin's *carnaval,* but, more than an event, it's a place. And while its architects and original inhabitants are hippies, it does not necessarily belong to them.

The Twelve Tribes commune who'd recruited on Dead and Phish tours now build a two-story Common Ground Cafe for Bonnaroo and the rest of festival season. It requires multiple trucks for transportation and can run twenty-four hours a day, serving delicious vegetarian food at extremely reasonable prices because they don't have to pay their employees.

The handcrafted Christian-hippie-sect Cafe provides a vehicle for observation. Climb the curving staircase to the top deck, catch a cool breeze in the afternoon thickness, sit in an actual chair and look out across Tent City. Listen to the mass cheers that emerge in pockets like smoke clouds over the campgrounds for no other reason than a good groupmind yell. Follow the sounds of a drum circle, reconnect with an old friend, meet someone new, duck down an alley, find drugs, find fireworks, find beer, find dogs, find humans, find life, find love. Bonnaroo is _____.

Had the first Bonnaroovians checked a newspaper before turning their backs for the weekend, they may've noticed news stories about a new bill introduced by Delaware senator Joseph Biden on the Tuesday before the festival's kickoff. The Man is starting to get worried about all this *untz-untz-untzery* over in the dance world and, more specifically, all the pills the dancers are gobbling.

Taken literally, the RAVE Act—Reducing America's Vulnerability to Ecstasy—is a subliminally Orwellian suggestion that unbridled happiness might be damaging. The section of the bill labeled "Findings" decrees that the presence of glow sticks and chill rooms and large bottles of water and pacifiers are all evidence of drug use. Anyone knowingly running an establishment or party with these accoutrements might be held accountable to the letter of the law as a prodrug conspirator and (by extension) corrupter of the nation's youth.

Citizens rightly object to the findings, and the bill is renamed the Illicit Drug Anti-Proliferation Act and passes in April 2003. The acronym sticks, especially among those it is intended to legislate out of existence, and the effect is immediate. Dance music historian Simon Reynolds dubs the next years "the nadir" of the American dance music scene. DJs move to Berlin. Those continuing to run clubs and parties face dilemmas. The organization DanceSafe, which provides chemical testing of alleged MDMA pills, is veritably handcuffed from providing its services and will be into the next century.

But two places that provide substantive shelter for the American dance scene during the first barren years of the twenty-first century are the jam world and Burning Man. Over the next half decade, the Disco Biscuits' Camp Bisco will host electronic acts including Simon Posford and Infected Mushroom and nurture nu-psychedelic favorites of both the live and electronic variety. While, at first, the band's jam-headed fans commute back to Tent City after the Biscuits' headlining slots, it is hard not to soon notice the concert field filling with the underground dancers waiting impatiently for the band to finish.

As dance music's presence grows, Burning Man is now the de facto stomping ground for psychedelicists, including those who haven't regularly had public presences since the early '70s. Nick Sand, released from prison after just four years, becomes a regular Burner and icon at the center of an annual and ongoing desert salon. Since 1997, John Perry Barlow has been a regular, too, moving as easily on the playa as at Millbrook, in cyberspace, on Shakedown Street, or any other landscape. Even Sasha and Ann Shulgin will make it to Black Rock. Ann will estimate that a third of the people are on psychedelics, which doesn't seem like much to her. But, as Burning Man crosses the 30,000 attendance mark, that's still 10,000 people on psychedelics in one place.

With acid on the wane, 2C-B circulates as a psychedelic of choice, first bioassayed by Sasha Shulgin in 1975. "Beautifully active," he'd described the drug. There are more Burning Man busts, including the DEA's Operation Web Tryp in 2004. But the future is well on its way.

Just as Dead shows were a meeting point for early Silicon Valley denizens, many now make their spiritual home in Black Rock. "So embedded, so accepted has Burning Man become in parts of tech culture, that the event alters work rhythms, shows up on resumes, is even a sanctioned form of professional development," the *San Francisco Examiner* reports in 2000.

Burning Man founder Larry Harvey issues a set of ten principles of Burning Man as the festival begins to self-replicate and spawn regional operations. The Burning Man "gifting" economy both feeds naturally into ancient hacker and Deadhead notions of *free* and also makes a bridge to new corporate-speak. Even still, it emphasizes a new path of "decommodification" that would be alien to most Deadheads, inordinately fond of logo-encrusted tie-dyes, both official and bootleg. Not that many Burning Man attendees make decommodification part of their life philosophies, either. Burners are hardly gypsies.

Both of Google's founders are regular Burners and, in part, hire their first CEO because he is one, too. The flow between Silicon Valley and Burning Man is undeniable. Google's internal policies seem to aspire to the flexibility of the desert catharsis. It's a new space they're making, up in the sky, someplace that isn't quite John Perry Barlow's cyberspace, Terence McKenna's hyperspace, the Humbead territories, or someplace far away. It is someplace that looks like the real world transformed. It will be a few years yet before dystopia starts to set in.

The new valuations wreak havoc on traditional systems as the California ideology feeds back into the hippie world. Fly over Central Park on a September day in 2003 and watch as the new, new twice-revised economy puts all matter of hip 'n' heady ideas to work in strange ways. Below, the Dave Matthews Band are set to perform a massive free concert before an estimated 100,000 people on the lush green carpet of the Great Lawn. Hey, a free concert in the park! But this is a new kind of free concert in the park.

To gain access to this performance, one is first required to find a van operated by representatives of America Online. Some vans give away tickets with bar codes and one-in-four chances of entry. Some surrender the tickets freely, albeit by gathering marketing data on the concert goers. Many tickets enter a temporary secondary market.

It's free because it's yours, the Diggers had always proclaimed of both the music and all that one can see. *It's free because it's ours,* America Online seems to now suggest. Via voluntary donations and sponsorship, the whole event manages to be a benefit for New York City schools, and Dave Matthews' manager Coran Capshaw— that ever-hip economist—channels some of the money back to the group's hometown of Charlottesville. The accompanying commemorative album and DVD are scheduled for November release before the band even takes the stage. But that's molasses slow these days, thanks to the jam bands.

The live music business shoots into the future in 2003, helped along by Phish, who provide one more radical move to help situate the psychedelic ritual inside the new economy. Having returned from their hiatus on New Year's 2002–2003, Phish are the first to answer the conundrum posed by the early Grateful Dead freak tapers. Starting with the band's New Year's comeback in 2002, the Vermont quartet make mixed soundboard recordings available for download within hours of each show's completion.

They hire a team to spend the night clearing copyrights on any cover songs, a practice with industry-wide ramifications. Sales do not disappoint. They charge $9.95 for mp3s of a show, offer high-fidelity options, route some of the profits through charities, and start giving away free downloads with concert tickets.

When Phish go back on the road in 2003, their old songwriting friend Nancy begins to draw a semiregular paycheck for his music for the first time in his life. Nancy's been living on the low-flying bohemian fringe in Vermont, making music, poetry, and psychedelic drawings as his latest self, Dick FaceBat. His discography accrues on cassette, as he lives and works in an Internet-less apartment, just fine with his LPs. His songs, once part of Phish's secret code, are there for all. There have always been those who prefer audience recordings, too, but the visible tapers section at shows shrinks almost immediately after the introduction of LivePhish's instant concert downloads.

Most of the jam-o-sphere pick up on the practice, with the Allman Brothers, the Dead, and others all making it standard by that year. It becomes a normal income stream for many bands. Companies spring forward to handle the business.

Despite and/or in addition to this, though, the tapers become the first user base for BitTorrent, a new application built specifically for the users of the Phishhead and Deadhead FTP network known as eTree. It works on the same principle as Furthurnet: everybody has to share. Them's the rules; it's built into the code. It's the fundamental truth of BitTorrent's decentralized file distribution that further overturns the cultural economy.

The jam mechanisms professionalize and now find the most literal and expedient method by which heads can turn their backs on society at large. A few days after Phish perform New Year's 2003–2004 in Miami, the MV *Regal Empress* sets sail from Fort Lauderdale for

Caribbean horizons filled with sixteen acts, nine hundred fans paying from $500 to $1,025 per cabin (booked through String Cheese Incident's in-house travel agency), transportation to Florida not included.

There'll be no thumbing a ride on Jam Cruise. The jammers have finally found a place where they will be left alone, and at a price point of one's choosing. It turns out that, in the early twenty-first century, the American system can tailor itself to them if only they'd stop turning their backs. As a tribe, they now sail away from Humbeadia and the United States both, bound for international waters.

AMID THE POLITICAL turbulence of the George W. Bush presidency and the second Gulf War, a Phishhead from New York named Andy Bernstein comes up with a natural way through the apolitical morass of head politics. He can see clearly that, in the new psychedelic America, one shouldn't take all of the old rules for granted anymore. His cause won't violate the antidogma of lyricists Robert Hunter or John Perry Barlow, and it can also make a real difference in a national way.

"If every Deadhead in this country had voted in the last election, this country would be a different place," Andy Bernstein had heard Bob Weir say.

Bernstein, a sports journalist by day, has the answer: voter registration. It doesn't require any political philosophy. One can be a Democrat, a Republican, a Libertarian, a Commie, a Greenie, a Meadowist (a la *Bloom County*), an independent, or anything. It doesn't even require that one actually vote. It requires only an acknowledgment of the system, which actually *is* a fairly large conceptual step, but one that seems like a normal choice these days, even for heads.

It is the perfect apolitical political cause for the jam world. With his old friend Marc Brownstein, the bassist for the Disco Biscuits, Bernstein launches a hippie voter registration organization under the only possible flag such a venture could fly under: HeadCount.

"This is the time to bring political back into music in one way or another," says Bernstein, who'd coedited the *Pharmer's Almanac,* a set list–filled guide to Phish. The new organization arranges for Rock the Vote–style tables on various tours, including Phish, the Dead, the Dave Matthews Band, and String Cheese Incident. But unlike Rock

the Vote, which simply aimed for youth, HeadCount has a more co-
herent base of unregistered potential voters to sign up, and they might
not necessarily be young.

"It's not gonna be Country Joe and the Fish," Bernstein says. "It's
not going to be blatant songs about protest. It's going to be about
our community having a voice, and our community being part of
the system and impacting the system. It's not quite a counterculture
anymore."

Bernstein believes that any help they provide will weigh on the
positive side of the election and aims to get 100,000 more voters on
the rolls. Naturally, HeadCount spins into a sequence of videos and
benefits and reasons to jam. Especially, it brings together bands that
once seemed to be opposing forces on the jam circuit. Festival season
is a never-ending montage of super-sessions and meaningful solos. By
now former LSD dealer and sharp-eyed photographer Jay Blakesberg
is down front (or even onstage) to capture it all, part of a postlysergic
professional class that tends to the flame full time.

"Don't forget to vote hippie," reads a sign held aloft by a Phishhead
outside a show in the Midwest that summer. It is unclear whether
there should be a comma in between "vote" and "hippie," if the sign
bearer is reminding heads to vote or suggesting that they vote for the
hippie party line.

Phish even agree to film a PSA for HeadCount, a stunning con-
cession from them. Since their return to the road the year before, the
Phishheads had hopped right back on the road. But both the drugs
and the tapes are turning against Phish, a hip economy turned grotesque and spiteful. The Vermont band isn't in a good way.

Nearly every jam musician pays lip service to the ability to fail onstage, but the advent of downloading services allows for instant dissemination of those failures with the artist's official approval. After
guitarist Trey Anastasio downloads official high-fidelity recordings of
his band's spring 2004 performances in Las Vegas and listens, he calls
a meeting to dissolve his group.

Phish had already announced a festival with the curiously unfun
name of Coventry, to be held in Vermont's Northeast Kingdom, near
where Anastasio had spent the summer of 1987 writing music and
the Twelve Tribes had first fused together the Peacemaker bus to save

souls on Dead tour. Nearby the Earth People's Park had shepherded humans across an imaginary line and into the draft-free safety of Canada. Now, Coventry becomes a funeral rite, a self-immolation, and wake all in one.

It rains and it rains and it rains and, at first, Phish are ordered to cancel the festival altogether. Bassist Mike Gordon gets on the band's onsite freeform radio station and announces that no more vehicles are to be let in. The message comes on between every other song, nearly. Instead, vehicles park by the side of the highway and their occupants walk as many as fifteen miles to get in. Let's not talk about Coventry, please. Something secret is buried in the Vermont mud.

12

HOW JERRY GOT HIP (AGAIN)

t's hard to say which is cruder, the illustration or the headline, but together they conjure a new beginning for psychedelic America. The illustration is a childlike line drawing of a longhaired bearded man with glasses and a guitar. The headline is "Uncle Skullfucker's Band," and it promises to decode the "discreet charms of the Grateful Dead." What it really does is create a blank slate.

Launched in Los Angeles in 2002, the oversized *Arthur* magazine is named for George Harrison's haircut in *A Hard Day's Night*. Its motto, "we found the others," is a turn on Timothy Leary's instructional phrase. In form and content, *Arthur* feels like a mythical underground magazine of yore. But the "others" that *Arthur* connects are a new generation of heads whose tastes and temperament recall the early residents of New York's Lower East Side and San Francisco's Haight-Ashbury. *Arthur* features pages of comix, dispatches describing the latest far-out sounds, and reports on all manner of esoteric and vaguely taboo topics, like living off the grid in Hawaii or the British mushroom revival or listening to the Dead.

The blank slate that *Arthur* promises cuts out all the hippie lameness and repurposes what is most useful. Daniel Chamberlin's July 2004 *Arthur* salvo, "Uncle Skullfucker's Band" acts an opening gong and tentative reintroduction of the Dead to the new generation of freaks. The rebirth of the Dead starts now.

"The May 14, 1974 'Dark Star' performed in Missoula, Montana sounds like *In A Silent Way* as interpreted by Sonic Youth but nearly every performance of 'Lazy Lightnin'' sounds like coke-snorting yuppies getting funky in tie-dyed Izods," Chamberlin declares to the open-eared underground.

Arthur positions itself in the center of what some will call a new shamanic resurgence. A New York writer named Daniel Pinchbeck—interviewed in *Arthur* #1 and soon with a column of his own—kicks off the new phase with his best-selling *Breaking Open the Head,* a multi-threat memoir and historical narrative about psychedelic transformation and New Age rebirth.

Something out there churns again, a power that's hard to place, sometimes overlapping with the new explorers, but just as often not.

The same season of Chamberlin's missive in *Arthur,* Shout Factory issues a DVD of a semiforgotten one-season sitcom called *Freaks & Geeks* by a director named Judd Apatow. It was far from a hit on television, but it builds a second life in release, owing in part to its young stars' blooming Hollywood careers. Chronicling the lives of high school outsiders in suburban Michigan circa 1980, the show concludes when its protagonist, Lindsay Weir, has a revelatory moment listening to *American Beauty*'s opening cut and (SPOILER ALERT!) hops in a Microbus and heads off on Dead tour.

There is something that Chamberlin and Apatow share in their usage. Among others, they share it with Animal Collective, a Baltimore-reared Brooklyn-based art-noise-dance band that sport Steal Your Face stickers on their gear, let their songs melt into one another, and occasionally end shows (or even start songs) with a cresting electro-tribal arrangement of "We Bid You Goodnight," the a cappella gospel song the '69 Dead famously used to punctuate feedback-laden sets.

In a 2003 essay titled "Who Is Dionysus and Why Does He Keep Following Me Everywhere?," philosopher Stan Spector posited that "Deadhead life" meant "saying yes to all that life offers, from mediocre veggie burritos in the parking lot to sublime moments of communal, musical joy, even to bad trips or to [Bob] Weir's closing a show with a 'profane' 'Good Lovin'' after the band had played a 'sacred' 'Morning Dew.'"

This is what Deadheads do. This is not what Judd Apatow or Daniel Chamberlin or Animal Collective do. They aren't Deadheads at all. One of the central tensions of Apatow's *Freaks & Geeks* is whether the protagonist is a freak or a geek. And, it turns out, she's a freak, a god-damn good ol' Grateful Dead freak, perhaps on her way to becoming a Deadhead, perhaps not. With all the years combined, it turns out that distinction can still stand: one can fully love the Dead without accepting every last bit of them.

The new-wave Dead freak is in no way bound to Bob Weir's versions of "Good Lovin'." Irked by Brent Mydland's blues-yowl? It never happened! Not into hearing Garcia destroy his voice year by year? Don't! The generation of jammers that distilled the Dead's anarchy into "grassroots marketing" and a demographic to be targeted with key chains and branded rolling papers? Merely an illusion!

In some ways, it is as though the Grateful Dead are just some obscure band rediscovered from the far-back mists. And, in a way, they are. It's just what publications like *Arthur* specialize in, connecting the present to the long chain of old and deep heads from the past.

But there are all kinds of lost space-crooners and guitar heroes to find, and, even in the twenty-first century, the Grateful Dead are something more. The Grateful Dead remain a permanent beachhead into the psychedelic world. The same way that Che Guevara's visage means revolution or Bob Marley's means weed, the Steal Your Face logo or Garcia's face or the goddamn dancing bears or any of the Grateful Dead's iconography is an *instantly* understood visual shorthand for psychedelics the world over. Whenever the LSD resurfaces, Dead-themed blotter is usually nearby, as in a 2012 bust in Philadelphia.

"I owe a lot of who I am and what I've done to the beatniks from the '50s and to the poetry and art and music I've come in contact with," Jerry Garcia told *Rolling Stone* in 1991, aware of himself as just one head in a chain. "I feel like I'm part of a continuous line of a certain thing in American culture, of a root," he mused.

In the United Kingdom, a mushroom revival flourishes for a few years, starting in 2002, when British heads discover a legal loophole that allows them to grow and sell magic mushrooms. Coupled with the tiny liberty caps that sprout naturally across the fields of New Albion, Her Majesty's lands are fully bemushroomed at the dawn of the new century, connecting the users to centuries of strange folk music and the cosmic mysteries of Stonehenge and Glastonbury Tor.

In the United States, there is the Grateful Dead. To find the Dead is to find something old and strange and pure, a sure and true connection to an authentic mystical and spiritual and ever-questioning America. It is a connection both to the '60s and to whatever eternal current the Dead themselves were plugged into.

Beyond the psychedelics, there are seemingly infinite tendrils to pick up, from Robert Hunter's lyrics to Ned Lagin's protogenerative *Seastones* LP, from the high hopes of the do-it-yourself Round Records to the spiritual spaces carved by the music and the rhythms, from Garcia's forays into deep American music to Owsley's soundbeam philosophies. The Dead have *always* been cool, if not quite fashionable, and so many of their creative ventures trace back to the world and ambitions opened by psychedelics.

And, in the twenty-first century, without Deadheads' seasonal migrations through the interstate system like North American mammals, it is easier than ever to appreciate the Grateful Dead's music and universe for what it was, and is.

"The world of Dead shows online allows me to explore the Grateful Dead on my own terms," *Arthur*'s Chamberlin writes, and what could be more free-loving than wanting to listen to the Dead on one's own terms? In Chamberlin's cosmology, Deadheads and their lore have become that most dreaded of things in Garcia's own hipster lingo: cops. "Most Deadheads only kill the buzz, their interpretation being a far cry from the fantasy world [the Dead] represent for me," Chamberlin writes.

Via archive.org, hosting many of Dick Latvala's leaked recordings, the music spirals into new hands everywhere. With no central Grateful Dead, the music seems more mysterious than ever, remnants of a ritual expressing some nearly captured truth.

The post-Garcia Dead world resembles early Christianity, splintering into dozens and then hundreds and then infinite interpretations. On one side of the spectrum, for proper Deadheads, there is the Dark Star Orchestra, conservative literalists who replicate exact set lists and era-specific equipment configurations. But there are also an increasing number of jammers—like Brooklyn's Oneida and Akron/Family—seeking for the same improv-blesh that the Dead sought, winking at the Dead's moves but maybe sounding like them only when one squints a third ear.

The British music magazine the *Wire* dubs the *Arthur*-championed beardos as "the new, weird America," playing off Greil Marcus's

Kenneth Rexroth–inspired phrase in his book *Invisible Republic: Bob Dylan's Basement Tapes*. But no matter how freak minded the new musicians might get, the real new, weird America is so much weirder than all that, filled with super-sized post-9/11 gas crises and reality shows and shrinking news cycles and housing booms and millennial lingoes and new gadgets. The Grateful Dead are not that. The Grateful Dead are never that.

As Jerry Garcia once noted, "It's not my fault if you watch TV, man." Even with no Grateful Dead, there remains nothing like a Grateful Dead concert.

IN A HALF-CENTURY-OLD building in the ancient Swiss city of Basel, the paintings turn into Disney characters, and Mark McCloud sees sparks shooting from Sasha and Ann Shulgin's eyes. There are plenty of no-calorie cocktails consumed as the psychedelic elite assemble in January 2006 to celebrate the one hundredth birthday of the still-living inventor of LSD-25, Albert Hofmann. Here Mark McCloud finds himself, tripping, hanging with his hero for the first time, at a small private gathering a few days before a massive international symposium in honor of Hofmann's centennial.

"We've been in constant telepathic communication since December 9th, 1971," McCloud tells the chemist, the date of McCloud's most important trip. "He covered my hands in his and said 'Absolutely,'" McCloud smiles.

Mark spends a chunk of the night hanging out with Albert's wife, Anita. "She was cool as shit and nobody was paying any attention to her," he says.

There are many reasons Mark McCloud almost didn't make it to Basel. A few years previous he'd only barely escaped another brush with the feds, even more serious than his first.

"They ruined his life," the art critic Carlo McCormick says. "Mark won, but he lost." The Man had come down (again) in early 2000, descending on the Institute of Illegal Images in San Francisco with hazmat suits. The government finds lots of blotter paper but only small amounts of LSD. On the premise that some blotter associated with Mark was found near a Kansas City school, a year later, Mark McCloud is tried for conspiracy to distribute in Missouri. Indicted along with him is Nick Sand, who Mark has never even met (but always wanted to), then already in jail.

"It was horrible," Carlo McCormick says. "In the end, his family stepped up." McCormick helps, too. Called in as a witness, "I inherited an angry jury," he says. "They wanted to kill Mark, but within a half-hour, they were laughing at the DA. He was so arrogant and so angry, asking me questions where he didn't know the answers, and then had the temerity to have a fight about art with an art critic."

And, after eight days of trial and ten and a half hours of deliberation, Mark McCloud is set free. "I want every LSD prisoner let go," he says a few days later, "whether they were a snitch or not. I want their property returned and a public apology from these people who took our right to consciousness without permission."

There are so many familiar faces around the futuristic convention center in Basel, Switzerland, that the whole gathering might seem imaginary. The event begins at 8:15 sharp on this January morning with a half-hour Tune-In, where "starting from the primeval sound of the earthly year, a C sharp with 136.10 hertz, we glide into the LSD-25 molecule's octave analogous field of frequency." Everything is unreal in the rarified Alpine air during Albert Hofmann's one hundredth birthday party and symposium.

The scattered psychedelic tribe elders gather and reunite, many meeting for the first time on the earthly plane. The advertising had started in the autumn equinox issue of the *Entheogen Review*, the de facto journal for the psychoactive set. The bill looks like a slightly more adult version of the giant text-block announcements that the summer music festivals are starting to use.

Hofmann, the accidental psychedelic hero, is the headliner, of course, and spry for a centenarian. The birthday boy is omnipresent around the convention center, surrounded by a benevolent bubble of guards and translators. Wandering the halls are old-world pre-Owsleyites like Myron Stolaroff and John Beresford. There are Millbrook veterans and unaffiliated chemists. There is a contingent from the Multidisciplinary Association for Psychedelic Studies and rogue historians and visionary artists and plenty of Burning Man regulars. Recently sprung Brotherhood of Eternal Love chemist Nick Sand is in attendance. The Dead's closest official ambassador is Dr. Stanley

Krippner, he of the dream telepathy experiments awith the Dead and the Holy Modal Rounders in '71. And there's Karen Horning.

Karen Horning had to be wheeled out of jail when she was released in early 2002. The Deadhead acid dealer had spent her last incarcerated years in a Lyme disease haze at the FMC Carswell Hospital in Fort Worth, Texas, the only women's facility in the federal prison system. She is eventually released into a halfway house in the Tenderloin, across the street from the Warfield Theater's stage door. She is in Basel in the company of John Beresford, the British expatriate whose LSD order (with Michael Hollingshead) was the source of Timothy Leary's first LSD in 1961.

Some 2,000 people mill through the Basel convention center, peering at displays of old blacklight posters, letters from the CIA, a display of Mark McCloud's blotter, and other psychedelia. One vendor sells sealed glass ampoules filled with ergot, like Sandoz might've used to derive LSD-25. Registration is $350 for three days, not to mention the other attendant costs of getting to and staying in Switzerland. This is no Jam Cruise. They are in a sacred place and treat it with reverence. Especially Mark McCloud, who will defend his psychedelic America when and where he has to, even in the esoteric conversations of Swiss psychedelic conferences.

Tensions are on the rise in the emerging twenty-first century psychedelic/entheogenic culture as governments slowly start to grant permission for formal research into the substances to pick up again, the continued illegality of the materials sometimes making it difficult for individual humans to do their work. Some scientists must now choose their affiliation between the alchemical substrata and the buttoned-down world of proper research that is now starting to emerge in universities and labs. As Mark McCloud knows, and isn't afraid to say, a head is only affiliated with the universe.

Besides Mark McCloud's ebullience, most presentations run like Swiss clockwork. In the main hall, there are headphones where one can hear simultaneous translations in German or English, when needed. There are papers on the structure of consciousness and the demystification of Teonanácatl to the global research on psychoactive mushroom species. Earth and Fire Erowid speak on the current state of LSD-25. Psychedelic therapists present their latest findings, and

Mark McCloud provides a slideshow tour of one hundred greatest hits from his blotter archive with accompanying stories.

At age one hundred, Albert Hofmann remains conflicted about acid's role in the development of Western civilization. "In the end I thank the LSD," he says in his closing remarks in Basel. He'd long called LSD his "problem child," but this conference, he said, turned LSD into a "wonder child." He beams with joy that the people in the room are going to carry the message forth, the message the LSD had so clearly articulated to him.

"Albert had this whole guilt thing going on where he thought he had decimated the European churches," McCloud says. "He thought that his LSD had awakened the people to the point where they'd lost interest in church and that's why they were so poorly attended. To help him out, we grabbed him and took him to a rave on the Rhine on a big houseboat."

DJing is Goa Gil, in the second day of a three-day set. "It was two-story houseboat with a chill room on the first floor. And when you went down into the hull, this most beautiful black light temple, far out psychedelic dance floor you've ever seen in your life. We showed Albert that we've moved it from the Church to the music."

As they arrive, a flailing naked man is being carried out. "This must be the place," Albert Hofmann declares to Mark McCloud in his bemused accented English.

AT FIRST, BONNAROO 2009 seems like any other Bonnaroo to Andy Bernstein, the onetime *Pharmer's Almanac* coeditor and, lately, founder of Head-Count, the jam world voter registration group. There is a calm routine in heading to the Tennessee megafestival for tourhead-turned-industry veterans like Andy: the flight to Nashville, rambles through Centeroo and Tent City and the vast backstage social space, as petri dish–like as Shakedown Street. Some, both backstage and in the sprawling VIP sections, get RVs for minitribe bunkhouses.

In 2007, the festival organizers purchased the land from its owner, all 530 acres of it, and began to erect a permanent festival infrastructure with whimsical names borrowed directly from the geography of Bread and Puppet's decade-gone summer pageants: Which Stage, What Stage, This Tent, and That Tent. Some enterprising w00ks, the twenty-first-century descendants of the 1980s tour rats, might sneak into Bonnaroo from time to time, but there's no danger of it spontaneously transmogrifying into a free festival.

One way in which this Bonnaroo is different in 2009 is that Phish are back and are performing there. They're clean and sober and happy now, playing their songbook with a fresh love for it. Guitarist Trey Anastasio had gotten busted in late 2006 with a car full of sketchy drugs, including heroin. After several nonstarts during Phish's earlier incarnations, Anastasio now takes his sobriety seriously, and it shows.

What's more, they're integrating with the rest of the world for the first time, sometimes playing festivals like Bonnaroo instead of staging their own. More significantly, they've signed on with Coran Capshaw's Red Light Management instead of restarting their independent Dionysian Productions.

But HeadCount's Andy Bernstein notices something afoot. "At the HeadCount table that year, we did a trivia game, music and political trivia," Bernstein remembers. "I watched it for a while and nobody was getting the jam band questions right. Phish was the headliner that year! 'Name an Umphrey's McGee guitar player' was the hardest question we had and not a single person got it right the whole weekend. There were people walking around in Phish shirts, but for the most part, there were no jam band fans at this festival that Phish was headlining, even though everybody looks like a hippie at Bonnaroo."

A few years into Bonnaroo's history—2006 to be exact—the promoters made a shift in their booking policy, slotting Radiohead and Beck to headline one of the nights, neo-classic rocker Tom Petty on another. Each year, the balance tilts away from jam. Bonnaroo, the template for American's surging festival season, becomes a musical megalopolis, its Tent City crossed by multiple grand Shakedown Street promenades, aromatic bazaars, and sketchy alleyways filled with all kinds of creeping darkness.

Bonnaroo 2009 is also its first edition that doesn't feature a single member of the Grateful Dead. There are festivals within festivals within Bonnaroo, with the jammers now only one stripe of citizenry in a legitimately rich cross section of American music. Attendees choose their own paths, with ample pickings for followers of post–Dave Matthews country-pop like the Zac Brown Band, the new wave of Dead-digging indie rock (including Animal Collective, My Morning

Jacket, and Bon Iver), people who want to dance, people who want to vibe, people who want to get righteous with Ani DiFranco, ominous with Nine Inch Nails, or narcissistic with of Montreal.

The latter, an indie-pop band from Athens, starts covering the Dead's "Shakedown Street" at festival appearances. "[It's] sort of a scenester's defense of his hood," singer Kevin Barnes observes. "It's an unconventional subject to sing about. It's a positive song but it has a little swagger to it." Leave it to the cool kids to defend the Dead on the Dead's own turf.

The Grateful Dead were able to mimic the psychedelic experience and provide a template ritual because the Dead were extraordinary. Phish could do it because they were born into it. But for many live music fans, the festival itself and its multitude of pleasure channels supplant individual acts.

The biggest transformation in festival-land, psychedelic America, and all of the United States is the near-complete presence of cell phones. Where attending a concert or a festival was once tantamount to entering a hermetically sealed box for the duration of the event, participants now share space in the great mind-manifested present, texting, posting, tweeting, and—most significantly—knowing what's going on outside. Except at Burning Man, still removed from cell phone range, sustained Zone-crossings become that much more difficult. Just as mp3s changed the value of music, social media alters the value of the event experience, splattering and diffusing its energies in real time across the networks.

With so many Americans now practicing the summer rites, with or without psychedelics (but almost definitely with other substances), the festival economy enters a bubble. Several of Bonnaroo's imitators fall apart in their second year or before, and an older circuit of regional soirees struggles to compete. The Rainbow Gatherings continue unabated, give or take various spates of federal harassment and a perpetual supply of fringe visioneers.

But when summertime comes, there are options aplenty for heads. And out in the festival territories, it is said, there exist groups calling themselves the Grateful Dead Family who claim allegiance to a line of acid distribution stretching back to Owsley. They have new rituals, an elaborate system of winged Steal Your Faces pins and other secret codes. And, drought or no, it seems they still know where to get LSD.

It's hard to say for sure who is who and what is what, but, in the informal observations of sociologist Rebecca Adams, a touring culture begins to develop around the Dark Star Orchestra, the meticulous Dead tribute band.

The promoter Bill Graham had long complained that popular images of Woodstock transformed concertgoing from dance events to packed-like-sardines hero worship. But now the smaller festival gatherings provide a reliable alternative for more local-minded bands and heads: a source of intimate fun, lots of dancing space, and perhaps even a lower threshold for transcendence.

Under the slightly new package of electronic dance music, rave culture begins to swell into American mainstream. It is at the smaller jam festivals especially that the hippie/dance fusion takes hold, the two cultures becoming virtually indistinguishable.

Up in Michigan, one of the failed Bonnaroo megaimitations, Rothbury, rebrands itself as Electric Forest. Anchored by String Cheese Incident, the festival is overseen by the Colorado band's minicorp, Madison House. The bill alternates humans jamming on old-fashioned instruments and acts that trade in the soaring crystalline New Agey bliss and life-enveloping bass thump of post-Bisco headtronica. Electric Forest, with its perfect and vivid name, spawns its own sylvan Tent City, a specific interfaith crossroads. In the middle comes a whole new realm of godheads, like Bassnectar and Shpongle and Pretty Lights.

LSD might not always be available, but there's almost always MDMA (real or fake), probably mushrooms, 2C-B, DMT (deemsters, brah), and more. Plus, of course, the ecstatic trance dance, a perfectly fine drugless Zone entrance point by itself. The less hassle, for many, the better. It's worth remembering that it wasn't Woodstock where the Brotherhood of Eternal Love dropped hits of fresh Orange Sunshine from a plane, but the Laguna Beach Christmas Happening with a roster of bands that almost no one remembers and a bootleg LP that fetches thousands of dollars on the private market.

It is an age of unceasing celebration, of festival after festival after festival, of music everywhere, an age of miracle and wonder. New technologies appear in the jammy hinterlands and migrate to the general population. There's money involved in all this research. One crew of Disco Biscuits fans conceives a new way to communicate while out seeing the band. They invent a group-chat iPhone app and, within a year, flip GroupMe to Skype for a guaranteed $43 million plus riches (maybe) to come. Holy *cannoli*.

Burning Man remains tech-psychedelia's energy source in the sacred desert. It is where the art-freaks and dancers and psychonauts and naked people and serious techheads meet, or perhaps get to be all at once. By now, there is a gilded pipeline between Black Rock and Silicon Valley, always in the process of transforming California's new, new, new economy. In San Francisco, in between Burns, the network of DJs and promoters and artists move about in a scene of warehouse parties, workshops, clubs, and communal bike rides. The rainbow rivers still stream from the old places.

Imagine a young smart girl growing up somewhere she doesn't want to be. She discovers String Cheese Incident or Bassnectar, goes to Michigan, gets Electrified in the Forest, joins a tribe or two, finds her way to Black Rock out in the desert, and discovers a new universe.

Forget the Ivy League and test prep, parents, get your kids on a track to Burning Man. Tickets become harder to get each year.

THE OCCUPATION OF Wall Street that begins on September 17, 2011, is conjured not from thin air but thick, rich with Wi-Fi and cell signals, hashtags and live streams. The simple status update that Les Earnest had invented in the early '70s to keep track of the heads at the Stanford AI Lab breaks loose and becomes a tool of revolution. In Zucotti Park in Manhattan, protesters create a new form of Zone making *without* back turning. Occupy encampments sprout across the country, an act of countercultural imagination and reclamation of public space. It is a movement for everybody, but the heads know a Zone when they see one.

Within weeks, the Twelve Tribes' Peacemaker bus is on site in New York, recruiting from stray idealists. John Perry Barlow shows up and speaks. A street action puppet company materializes and familiar faces from the still-kicking Wetlands Activism Collective wend through the crowds as drum circles pound. For a moment, the network becomes visible.

One city that doesn't need much encouragement to Occupy is Santa Cruz, where a not-entirely-successful three-month-long Peace

Camp had already protested antivagrancy laws the year before. In December 2011, a semifamiliar face makes his way to the Occupy encampment in Santa Cruz: the ex–acid dealing tourhead Chris Doyon, the once and future Commander X of the Peoples Liberation Front who'd helped funnel LSD profits into radical causes ranging from phone phreaking to animal liberation in the '80s. While X was in prison, sprung just in time for the Jerry Garcia memorial at Golden Gate Park, the Peoples Liberation Front had gone high tech. From Occupy Santa Cruz, he makes his way to Occupy San Francisco. And, from there, Commander X steps into the People's Underground, disappearing dramatically into the new mists.

In the past half decade, X had grown involved with Anonymous, the decentralized cabal of politicized chaos makers and hackers. X is a polarizing figure but an undeniable force, a direct link from the acid-dealing Dead families to the justice-making Anons. From Coffee to the People in Haight-Ashbury along with journalist Barrett Brown, he'd helped coordinate #OpTunisia and #OpEgypt, channeling digital resources and encryption tools (and occasionally firing distributed denial-of-service attacks) toward the Middle East.

"If you agree with those pundits who credit Anonymous with the Arab Spring which led to Occupy, etc., then that all can be traced back to one burned out Deadhead with a computer sitting in a coffee house on Haight Street," X says by e-mail several years later, after he has escaped to Canada, wanted for several digital crimes.

Up in Canada, as he works on a hybrid AI/VR project, Commander X will help draw the American eye towards Ferguson, Missouri, and the shooting of a young black man named Michael Brown, the first outside ear to pick up the call (via Twitter) and transmit it to the world. He will post an edit of subsequent news footage set triumphantly to the Jefferson Airplane's "Volunteers." Though it's too sad for him to listen to the Dead themselves, he remains divisive, remains active, remains an acid-sparked Deadhead radical.

As 2011 ticks toward 2012, the world's novelty and synchronicity pump at unheard levels. Out in the cyberwilds comes something just as bold as Occupy: an alternative currency called BitCoin. As Commander X settles into exile in Canada, it is this encrypted and borderless form of money that helps fund his survival. Generating value based on scarcity and creating a new class of instant millionaires (should they cash out to US dollars), BitCoin solves a problem that has fascinated perhaps millions of kooks over many hundreds of centuries, including the great Owsley Stanley: alchemy.

BitCoin transmutes the info-rich nothingness of cyberspace into value via the power of mind-manifestation. Owsley would be impressed, maybe, had he not perished sadly in a car crash in early 2011, still keeping to that proto-Paleo diet. (G'bye, Bear, and so many thanks.) BitCoin's miraculousness owes much to classic head values. That is, the first application people figure out for the new encrypted money, the transaction that makes it useful for tangible real world goods: buying and selling drugs.

With special software one can access special websites with special URLs. The new online drug bazaar called the Silk Road is just hitting its stride at the time of Commander X's escape in 2011. It looks and operates like eBay, albeit filled with blotter acid and 2C-B and MDMA and heroin and much more (including, it seems, hit men). Acid shortage? What acid shortage? Just get cleared, surf the Silk Road, enter your encrypted particulars, route your money however you route it, and have your special product delivered to your door, perhaps by FedEx.

As always, people sell phony acid. But, for the first time, secure as they can be under encryption, a group calling itself the LSD Avengers establishes itself. They post consumer reviews of the acid hawkers. "Extremely friendly and personable customer service with consistent product and regular stock" reads one for a Czech seller named Haizenberg. "Currently selling: Hofmann, Dancing Bears and Strawberrys (advertising 110ug). Trip Test Hofmann: ~100ug."

There's lots of good stuff, but also lots of scary new bogus material, too. The latest substance to pass itself off as acid is the NBOMe series, usually 2C-I, sometimes referred to as "synthetic LSD." They can trigger "eye candy" in the right amount but often get sold on blotter in the wrong dosage, which can cause vasoconstrictions. The NBOMe series leaves a trail of emergency room visits in its wake. Neither the Silk Road nor the LSD Avengers survive in their original incarnations, as high-profile busts ensue and various participants move along, but neither idea disappears. In the UK, the battle of novel psychoactive substances rages onward, with the heads of New Albion circa 2015 favoring the still-legal compound 1P-LSD, often sold online, which by some reports is as good as the real thing. The hip economy will continue to manifest itself in fresh ways. A group of scholars posits the dark-nets as a form of "constructive activism" in which the dealers create a new form of reality, but it takes on more traditional shapes, too, such as when one mushroom seller donates profits to Doctors Without Borders. The ever-shifting dark-net markets become one way to supplant music-related events as a workable wholesale distribution method.

By the time December 21, 2012, hits, psychedelics are a barely coded undercurrent in multiple mainstreams. Legalized pot transforms the economies of Colorado and Washington and elsewhere as the booming weed business comes into the open market and blooms. Some heads adapt new portable vaporizers into handy DMT roasters, blasting off with ease. Perhaps a bigger sign of psychedelic America in the twenty-first century is the widespread use of emoji, a spot-on techno-hieroglyphic iteration of the "visual language" Terence McKenna had spoken of in *The Archaic Revival*.

The entheogenic revolution flourishes in the revitalized and rapidly gentrifying cities, but especially the old-world head centers in New York and San Francisco and Colorado, sometimes with the uncomfortable surreality of a bad trip. Ayahuasca ceremonies become so common that magazines like *Elle* cover them as health and fitness trends. One publication compares a meeting with the spirit-mind to a juice cleanse. There's also the 2009 aya-loving 3D mega-blockbuster *Avatar*, with a side of psychedelic virtual reality (which is making a comeback, too, as a new product known as Occulus Rift). Ayahuasca experiences become status symbols in Hollywood, sounding much like Cary Grant's psychedelic therapy in the 1950s. And LSD makes its way into mainstream music again, as well, through former teen-pop idol Miley Cyrus, Harlem-born rapper A$AP Rocky, and others.

The work of Robert Jesse's Council on Spiritual Practices and Rick Doblin's MAPS comes to great fruition in psychedelic research projects at New York University and Johns Hopkins in Maryland. Over the course of the early twenty-first century, new psychedelic research starts to come out of the academy to match the astounding leaps and connections made in independent psychedelic disciplines, like ethnobotany and transpersonal psychology. Some dub it a psychedelic renaissance, though the expression dates back to at least the late '80s.

Thomas Roberts will suggest four phases of this renaissance: medical-neuroscientific, spiritual-religious, intellectual-artistic, mind design. But its real measure might come only with perhaps the most important tool in the entire psychedelic kit, championed by transpersonal psychologists and old-time heads alike: integration. For years, there has been a near-total divide between those Americans who consume psychedelics in clinical settings, those who do so in traditional holy practices, and the heads who do so because they want to. The American psychedelic renaissance can blossom only when it is acknowledged that psychedelic America already exists.

Considered in the big picture, the Renaissance itself lasted some three hundred years. While Terence McKenna's 2012 eschaton is perhaps too obvious a date to go by, the years following his December 21st date seemingly find the millennial psychedelic culture reaching for maturity. Perhaps one paradoxical way to measure its success is to note that, according to the *Monitoring the Future* report, hallucinogen use among high school seniors is actually at an all-time nadir, especially LSD, down from an 8.8 percent high in 1996 (the year after Jerry Garcia's death) to an all-time low of 1.7 percent in 2006. One way to interpret this number is to say that there are less psychedelics available, which is almost definitely true.

But another way to interpret this number is to wonder, perhaps, whether the average age of consumption hasn't simply gone up. Perhaps, simply, the psychedelic world is becoming what Aldous Huxley and Humphry Osmond had once envisioned: a rarified place for rarified people, a place for heads, operating as the turned-on secret society it always has been someplace in the world since the dawn of civilization.

"Wouldn't you like to see a *positive* LSD story on the news?" the late comedian Bill Hicks once asked at the peak of one of his routines. "To base your decision on information rather than scare tactics and superstition? Perhaps? Wouldn't that be interesting? Just for once?" Hicks adopted a newsman voice: "*Today, a young man on acid realized that all matter is merely energy condensed to a slow vibration—that we are all one consciousness experiencing itself subjectively, there's no such thing as death, life is only a dream, and we're the imagination of ourselves. Here's Tom with the weather.*"

And, for the first time, positive LSD stories *do* start turning up on the news. "Day Tripping: Benefits Seen in Psychedelics," a *Newsweek* story reads in 2015. "Want to Quit Smoking? Eat a Magic Mushroom, New Study Says," reads another headline via *Time*, just like the '50s all over again.

The Grateful Dead's fiftieth anniversary shows arrive and are treated with incredible reverence, too. Organized by former Wetlands Preserve owner Pete Shapiro and costarring Phish's Trey Anastasio in the role of Jerry, the band is as underrehearsed and frequently inspired as only the authentic Grateful Dead can be. All reports indicate that Deadland reassembles itself quite naturally for the two weekends, w00ks and all. The shows break all records for live online streaming, and jam fans continue to pioneer new methods of bootlegging (getting chased around by security guards while broadcasting the soundcheck from a phone) and private encrypted communications that bypass the phone network entirely (via a head-made app that operates on Bluetooth). Besides when Chicago police shut down a section of downtown a few days after the shows due to suspicious objects that turn out to be nitrous tanks, the Deadheads successfully reintegrate, a more acceptable part of the landscape than they have been since perhaps the early '70s. Word is that there's good LSD around on the Phish tour that follows.

There isn't a psychedelic university yet, as Nick Sand envisions, but there is a firm and holding middle ground between the controlled psychedelic usage and the woolly experimentation of the Dead's peak touring years. For those who think psychedelics are right for them, the information is there, dogma-free, on the Internet. Perhaps the time of large-scale rituals has passed, too. One new trend among mature adults is microdosing, given a vote of confidence by pioneer psychedelic psychologist James Fadiman among others: taking imperceptible amounts of LSD, as few as 10 micrograms, to lightly crack open the doorways. Acquiring the material is perhaps slightly more difficult than it was for previous generations, but maybe that's also a decent safeguard in the strange age.

In the early summer of 2013, a former National Security Agency contractor named Edward Snowden reveals the government's vast and continued Internet surveillance programs. Almost a year to the day after the great unveiling, Snowden appears live from Russia in a presentation titled "Surveillance and Its Discontents, a Conversation Across Cyberspace" with his recent pal John Perry Barlow. The Dead lyricist and Electronic Frontier Foundation metaphor maker has befriended Snowden during the former government contractor's exile, and the two have a smart and easy rapport.

"We need to create a better system that says security is not the only value that Americans treasure," Snowden declares.

"In fact, my motto has always been safety third," quoth Barlow, ready with head wisdom.

"You've taken some risks in your day," Snowden acknowledges, LSD hovering over their one-liners like a Technicolor specter haunting the world stage.

The idea of privacy becomes a cosmic joke, all the more reason to quest for true inner freedom, away from cyberspace's panopticon of searchlights. Dystopia is here in full, but only for those who want it. For those who don't, psychedelics grow from the earth, can be conjured from the Internet, prescribed by a doctor (depending what year this is being read), or tracked down (whatever year it is) by looking for a Steal Your Face or some other arcane symbol dangling above a side street storefront in the nearest friendly temporary autonomous zone.

Sources

The source of my first LSD was an older relative who gave me some as a gift. I never took it. The acid was presented as art, two hits of Beavis and Butt-head blotter on a pin with, I believe, Beavis mid-headbang. I knew what it was and contemplated breaking open the pin's backing but didn't. I wasn't ready and, by the time I went searching for it again, it had disappeared, uneaten. Though some of my most life-shaping experiences have involved psychedelics and I allowed them to inform my identity, I have never been a psychonaut so much as both fascinated by and somehow part of the world they seemed to create. When I started recording Grateful Dead concerts off WBAI's *Morning Dew* show as a teenager, I fell down a rabbit hole into American psychedelia, and the psychedelics themselves came later. While it all seemed exciting and sometimes scary, it rarely seemed foreign.

My parents were heads, to varying degrees; both of their careers involved handmade art, and I grew up at least always half aware of the psychedelic America somewhere nearby, accessed by the *Whole Earth Catalog* or *Zap!* comix on the shelf. My much-removed cousin, the Lord Nose, would occasionally materialize in our house from the mysterious West with stacks of *High Frontiers* (which he'd designed) or stacks of a poster (which he'd made) of psychedelic molecules that he thought should be sold at the children's museum on Long Island that my parents had helped found. You can view some of his photography at the center of this book.

Which is to say, I often wander near the story's narrative in all eras, influencing it in both direct and indirect ways and slathering on a thick coat of intentional and accidental bias. Having grown up sort of inside it, I see traces of countercultural psychedelia everywhere. But all books have perspectives, and these are (some of) the sources of mine. A bit of the information presented in the later chapters likewise comes from firsthand experiences, which I can't source other than to say that I was there. I look forward to reading any and all future histories of psychedelic America unclouded by my point of view.

The story of the North American heads is big and weird and perhaps unknowable for reasons of size or secret keeping. It is tellable in dozens (if not hundreds) of ways. Stories are often misty and mis-remembered, and I did my best to verify everything I could. Many psychedelic Americans did their best to go undocumented—and not unfairly—so it's entirely possible that there are entire cabals and philosophies absent from this account. There are certainly paths un-explored. Perhaps the CIA really *did* push LSD into the counterculture to destabilize a rapidly politicizing youth (as Carl Oglesby suggested), or maybe mass psychedelia was just all just so dreadfully *banal* anyway (as Joan Didion dismissed it). But based on the excellent volumes on other aspects of psychedelic America, as well as what I've experienced myself, my vote is with the heads.

Besides my own experiences, the source of my faith comes in the fundamental historical work done by Jay Stevens's *Storming Heaven: Psychedelics and the American Dream,* Martin Lee and Bruce Shlain's *Acid Dreams: The Complete Social History of LSD: The CIA, the Sixties, and Beyond,* Michael Kramer's *The People's Republic of Rock: Music and Citizenship in the Sixties Counterculture,* Andy Letcher's *Shroom: A Cultural History of the Magic Mushroom,* Andy Roberts's *Albion Dreaming: A Popular History of LSD in Britain,* the late Patrick Lundborg's *Psychedelia: An Ancient Culture, a Modern Way of Life,* and many others in the bibliography.

For the most part, however, *Heads* is based on a combination of original interviews, primary source research, and intensive key mashing. Firsthand interviews are used both as direct quotes and as background information. Every effort has been made to create as full a citation as possible for all other sources and to verify any information that existed only as fragments, such as undated newspaper clippings. For dead websites, the Wayback Machine at archive.org was used to verify original postings. If information within a short range of text is drawn from one source, it is cited only once.

All friendly correspondence welcome.

Interviews

All interviews 2013–2015 unless otherwise noted, most including written communication in addition to face-to-face or phone interview(s) or both.

* Written communication only.

Rebecca Adams
Dennis Alpert
Kevin Barnes (2008)*
Allen Baum
Garrick Beck
Andy Bernstein
Jay Blakesberg
Jennifer Bleyer
Laura Bloch
Larry Bloch (2001)
Steve Brown
Chris Calise, a.k.a. Chris Goodspace
Dylan Carlson (2008)
John Cederquist, a.k.a. Johnny Crunch
Remy Chevalier
Barbara Clarke
John Coate
Earl Crabb
Luther Delaney
Rick Doblin
Chris Doyon, a.k.a. Commander X*
Les Earnest
Mary Eisenhart
Earth Erowid*
Fire Erowid*
Cliff Figallo
Marc Franklin, a.k.a. the Lord Nose
David Gans
Richard Gehr*
Donna Jean Godchaux-Mackay
Ken Goffman, a.k.a. R. U. Sirius
Mike Gordon
Bill Harmon, a.k.a. Bilrock
David Henkl-Wallace, a.k.a. Gumby
Scott Herrick
Karen Horning
Bobby Hornsby
Blair Jackson
Harvey Kaslow
Jacaeber Kastor
Les Kippel
Dan Kottke
Ned Lagin

Gary Lambert
Carol Latvala
Pat Lee
Gil Levey, a.k.a. Goa Gil
Harvey Lubar
Bill Maginnis
Charly Mann
Paul Martin
Jeff Mattson (2001)
Sarah Matzar
Mark McCloud
Matthew McClure
Carlo McCormick
Dennis McNally
Andy Moorer
Doug Oade
John Paluska
Jim Pollock (2012)
Lee Ranaldo
Neil Rosenberg
Sandy Rothman
Ed Sanders (2009)
Eric Schwartz
Tim Scully*
Ramon Sender
Pete Shapiro
Gordon Sharpless
Rick Shubb
Steve Silberman
Peter Stampfel
Rhoney Stanley
Julie Stewart
Chad Stickney, a.k.a. LSD-OM
Mark Szpakowski
Eric Thompson*
Ron Turner*
Butch Waller
Marty Weinberg
David Wilkins
Mike Wren (2002)
Richard Wright, a.k.a. Nancy
Chris Zahn (2001)
John Zias

Bibliography

Books

Acton, Jay, and Alan LeMond. *Mug Shots: Who's Who in the New Earth.* New York: World, 1972.

Adams, Rebecca G. "Deadheads: Community, Spirituality, and Friendship." Unpublished manuscript.

Adams, Rebecca G., and Robert Sardiello. *Deadhead Social Science: "You Ain't Gonna Learn What You Don't Want to Know."* Walnut Creek, CA: AltaMira, 2000.

Anderson, Patrick. *High in America: The True Story Behind NORML and the Politics of Marijuana.* New York: Viking, 1981.

Azerrad, Michael. *Come as You Are: The Story of Nirvana.* New York: Doubleday, 1993.

———. *Our Band Could Be Your Life: Scenes from the American Indie Underground 1981–1991.* Boston: Little, Brown, 2002.

Badiner, Allan. *Zig Zag Zen: Buddism and Psychedelics.* Santa Fe, NM: Synergistic Press, 2015.

Bangs, Lester. *Psychotic Reactions and Carburetor Dung.* New York: Knopf: 1987.

Belasco, Warren James. *Appetite for Change: How the Counterculture Took on the Food Industry, 1966–1988.* New York: Pantheon, 1989.

Bell, John. *Puppets, Masks, and Performing Objects.* Cambridge, MA: MIT, 2001.

Bernstein, David W. *The San Francisco Tape Music Center: 1960s Counterculture and the Avant-Garde.* Berkeley: University of California, 2008.

Binkley, Sam. *Getting Loose: Lifestyle Consumption in the 1970s.* Durham, NC: Duke University, 2007.

Black, David. *Acid: The Secret History of LSD.* London: Vision, 1998.

Blum, Richard. *Utopiates: The Use & Users of LSD 25.* New York: Atherton, 1964.

Brady, Emily. *Humboldt: Life on America's Marijuana Frontier.* New York: Grant Central, 2013.

Brand, Stewart. *II Cybernetic Frontiers.* New York: Random House, 1974.

Braunstein, Peter. *Imagine Nation: The American Counterculture of the 1960s and '70s.* New York: Routledge, 2002.

Brightman, Carol. *Sweet Chaos: The Grateful Dead's American Adventure.* New York: C. Potter, 1998.

Brown, David Jay, and Rebecca McClen Novick. *Voices from the Edge.* Freedom, CA: Crossing Press, 1995.

Browne, David. *So Many Roads: The Life and Times of the Grateful Dead.* Cambridge, MA: Da Capo, 2015.

Budnick, Dean, and Josh Baron. *Ticket Masters: The Rise of the Concert Industry and How the Public Got Scalped.* Toronto: ECW, 2011.

Cavallo, Dominick. *A Fiction of the Past: The Sixties in American History.* New York: St. Martin's, 1999.

Clair, David. *Say You Love Satan.* New York: Dell, 1987.

Committee on Unjust Sentencing. *The Tallahassee Project: A Glimpse Inside the Shattered Lives of 100 Non-violent Women Prisoners of the War on Drugs.* San Francisco: Last Gasp, 2001.

Conners, Peter H. *JAMerica: The History of the Jam Band and Festival Scene.* Cambridge, MA: Da Capo, 2013.

Cope, Julian. *Japrocksampler: How the Post-war Japanese Blew Their Minds on Rock 'n' Roll.* London: Bloomsbury, 2007.

Craddock, William J. *Be Not Content: A Subterranean Journal.* San Francisco: Transreal, 2012.

Cutler, Sam. *You Can't Always Get What You Want: My Life with the Rolling Stones, the Grateful Dead and Other Wonderful Reprobates.* Toronto: ECW Press, 2010.

Davis, Erik. *Nomad Codes: Adventures in Modern Esoterica.* Portland, OR: Yeti / Verse Chorus Press, 2010.

———. *Techgnosis: Myth, Magic, and Mysticism in the Age of Information.* New York: Three Rivers Press, 1998.

Davis, Tom. *Thirty-Nine Years of Short-Term Memory Loss: The Early Years of SNL by Someone Who Was There.* New York: Grove, 2009.

DeRienzo, Paul, and Dana Beal. *Report on the Staten Island Project: The Ibogaine Story.* Brooklyn, NY: Autonomedia, 1997.

Dodd, David G., and Diana Spaulding, eds. *The Grateful Dead Reader.* New York: Oxford University Press, 2000.

Dodd, David G., and Robert G. Weiner. *The Grateful Dead and the Deadheads: An Annotated Bibliography.* Westport, CT: Greenwood, 1997.

Doherty, Brian. *Radicals for Capitalism: A Freewheeling History of the Modern American Libertarian Movement.* New York: PublicAffairs, 2007.

Drummond, Paul. *Eye Mind: The Saga of Roky Erickson and the 13th Floor Elevators, the Pioneers of Psychedelic Sound.* Los Angeles: Process, 2011.

Ebenezer, Lyn. *Operation Julie: The World's Greatest LSD Bust.* Talybont, Wales: Ylolfa, 2010.

Erven, Euge. *Radical People's Theatre.* Bloomington: Indiana University Press, 1988.

Escohotado, Antonio. *A Brief History of Drugs: From the Stone Age to the Stoned Age.* Rochester, VT: Park Street, 1996.

Estrada, Alvaro. *María Sabina: Her Life and Chants.* Santa Barbara, CA: Ross-Erikson, 1981.

Fairfield, Richard, and Timothy Miller. *The Modern Utopian: Alternative Communities of the '60s and '70s.* Los Angeles: Process, 2010.

Felton, David, and Robin Green. *Mindfuckers: A Source Book on the Rise of Acid Fascism in America, Including Material on Charles Manson, Mel Lyman, Victor Baranco, and Their Followers.* San Francisco: Straight Arrow Books, 1972.

Ferguson, Marilyn. *The Aquarian Conspiracy: Personal and Social Transformation in the 1980s.* Los Angeles: J. P. Tarcher, 1980.

Gabilliet, Jean, and Bart Beaty. *Of Comics and Men: A Cultural History of American Comic Books.* Jackson: University Press of Mississippi, 2009.

Gans, David. *Conversations with the Dead: The Grateful Dead Interview Book.* Cambridge, MA: Da Capo, 2002.

Garcia, Jerry, and Charles A. Reich. *Garcia: A Signpost to a New Space.* San Francisco: Straight Arrow, 1972.

Gaskin, Ina May. *Spiritual Midwifery.* Summertown, TN: Book Publishing, 1977.

Gaskin, Stephen. *Amazing Dope Tales.* Summertown, TN: Book Publishing, 1980.

Gehr, Richard. *The Phish Book.* New York: Villard, 1998.

Getz, Michael M., and John R. Dwork. *The Deadhead's Taping Compendium: An In-depth Guide to the Music of the Grateful Dead on Tape, 1959–1974.* New York: Henry Holt, 1998.

———. *The Deadhead's Taping Compendium: An In-depth Guide to the Music of the Grateful Dead on Tape, 1975–1985.* New York: Henry Holt, 1999.

———. *The Deadhead's Taping Compendium: An In-depth Guide to the Music of the Grateful Dead on Tape, 1986–1995.* New York: Henry Holt, 2000.

Getz, Michael M., John R. Dwork, and Brian Dyke. *The Deadhead's Taping Addendum.* San Francisco: Peppertonic, 2001.

Graham, Ben. *A Gathering of Promises: The Battle for Texas's Psychedelic Music.* Winchester, UK: Zero, 2015.

Greenfield, Robert. *Dark Star: An Oral Biography of Jerry Garcia.* New York: W. Morrow, 1996.

———. *Timothy Leary: A Biography.* New York: Harcourt, 2006.

Grey, Alex. *The Sacred Mirrors: The Visionary Art of Alex Grey.* Rochester, VT: Inner Traditions International, 1990.

Grim, Ryan. *This Is Your Country on Drugs: The Secret History of Getting High in America.* Hoboken, NJ: Wiley, 2009.

Grogan, Emmett. *Ringolevio: A Life Played for Keeps.* Boston: Little, Brown, 1972.

Gruen, John. *Keith Haring: The Authorized Biography.* New York: Prentice Hall Press, 1991.

Haring, Keith. *Keith Haring Journals.* New York: Viking, 1996.

Henderson, Leigh A., and William J. Glass. *LSD: Still with Us After All These Years.* New York: Lexington, 1994.

Hermes, Will. *Love Goes to Buildings on Fire: Five Years in New York That Changed Music Forever.* New York: Faber and Faber, 2011.

Heylin, Clinton. *Bootleg: The Secret History of the Other Recording Industry.* New York: St. Martin's, 1995.

House, Freeman. *Totem Salmon Life Lessons from Another Species.* Boston: Beacon Press, 1999.

Isaacson, Walter. *Steve Jobs.* New York: Simon & Schuster, 2011.

Jackson, Blair. *Garcia: An American Life.* New York: Viking, 1999.

———. *Goin' Down the Road: A Grateful Dead Traveling Companion.* New York: Harmony, 1992.

Jackson, Blair, and David Gans. *This Is All a Dream We Dreamed: An Oral History of the Grateful Dead.* New York: Flatiron, 2015.

Johnston, Lloyd, and Patrick M. O'Malley. *Monitoring the Future National Results on Adolescent Drug Use: Overview of Key Findings, 2000.* Bethesda, MD: National Institute on Drug Abuse, 2001.

Johnston, Lloyd, Patrick M. O'Malley, Richard A. Miech, Jerald G. Bachman, and John E. Schulenberg. *The Monitoring the Future National Survey Results on Drug Use, 1975–2014: 2014 Overview, Key Findings on Adolescent Drug Use.* Ann Arbor: University of Michigan Institute for Social Research, 2015.

Jones, Steven T. *Tribes of Burning Man: How an Experimental City in the Desert Is Shaping the New American Counterculture.* San Francisco: Consortium of Collective Consciousness, 2011.

Juno, Andrea, and V. Vale. *Pranks!* San Francisco: Re/Search, 1987.

Kaiser, David. *How the Hippies Saved Physics: Science, Counterculture, and the Quantum Revival.* New York: W.W. Norton, 2011.

Kelly, Lindais. *Deadheads: Stories from Fellow Artists, Friends, and Followers of the Grateful Dead.* Secaucus, NJ: Carol, 1995.

Kramer, Michael. *The Republic of Rock: Music and Citizenship in the Sixties Counterculture.* Oxford: Oxford University Press, 2013.

Kripal, Jeffrey J. *Esalen: America and the Religion of No Religion.* Chicago: University of Chicago, 2007.

La Barre, Weston. *The Peyote Cult.* Hamden, CT: Archon Books, 1975.

Lachman, Gary. *Turn Off Your Mind: The Mystic Sixties and the Dark Side of the Age of Aquarius.* London: Sidgwick & Jackson, 2001.

Lawrence, Tim. *Love Saves the Day: A History of American Dance Music Culture, 1970–1979*. Durham, NC: Duke University, 2003.

Lee, Martin A. *Smoke Signals: A Social History of Marijuana; Medical, Recreational,* and *Scientific*. New York: Scribner, 2012.

Lee, Martin A., and Bruce Shlain. *Acid Dreams: The Complete Social History of LSD; The CIA, the Sixties, and Beyond*. New York: Grove Weidenfeld, 1992.

Lemke-Santangelo, Gretchen. *Daughters of Aquarius: Women of the Sixties Counterculture*. Lawrence: University Press of Kansas, 2009.

Lesh, Phil. *Searching for the Sound: My Life with the Grateful Dead*. New York: Little, Brown, 2005.

Letcher, Andy. *Shroom: A Cultural History of the Magic Mushroom*. London: Faber and Faber, 2006.

Levy, Steven. *Hackers: Heroes of the Computer Revolution*. Garden City, NY: Anchor Press / Doubleday, 1984.

Lundborg, Patrick. *Psychedelia: An Ancient Culture, a Modern Way of Life*. Stockholm: Lysergia, 2012.

Lyttle, Thomas. *Psychedelics: A Collection of the Most Exciting New Material on Psychedelic Drugs*. New York: Barricade, 1994.

———. *Psychedelics Reimagined*. Brooklyn, NY: Autonomedia, 1999.

Markoff, John. *What the Dormouse Said: How the Sixties Counterculture Shaped the Personal Computer Industry*. New York: Viking, 2005.

Martell, Nevin. *Dave Matthews Band: Music for the People*. New York: Pocket Books, 1999.

Martin-Smith, Keith. *A Heart Blown Open: The Life and Practice of Zen Master Jun Po Denis Kelly Roshi*. Studio City, CA: Divine Arts, 2011.

Matos, Michaelangelo. *The Underground Is Massive: How Electronic Dance Music Conquered America*. New York: Dey Street, 2015.

McKenna, Dennis J. *The Brotherhood of the Screaming Abyss: My Life with Terence McKenna*. St. Cloud, MN: North Star, 2012.

McKenna, Terence. *The Archaic Revival: Speculations on Psychedelic Mushrooms, the Amazon, Virtual Reality, UFOs, Evolution, Shamanism, the Rebirth of the Goddess, and the End of History*. San Francisco: HarperSanFrancisco, 1991.

———. *Food of the Gods: The Search for the Original Tree of Knowledge; A Radical History of Plants, Drugs, and Human Evolution*. New York: Bantam, 1992.

———. *True Hallucinations: Being an Account of the Author's Extraordinary Adventures in the Devil's Paradise*. San Francisco: HarperSanFrancisco, 1993.

McNally, Dennis. *A Long Strange Trip: The Inside History of the Grateful Dead*. New York: Broadway, 2002.

Meriwether, Nicholas G. *Reading the Grateful Dead*. New York: Rowman & Littlefield, 2012.

Miller, Timothy. *The 60s Communes, Hippies and Beyond*. Syracuse, NY: Syracuse University, 1999.

Mockingbird Foundation. *The Phish Companion: A Guide to the Band and Their Music*. San Francisco: Miller Freeman, 2000.

Nathan, John. *Sony: The Private Life*. Boston: Houghton Mifflin, 1999.

Niman, Michael I. *People of the Rainbow: A Nomadic Utopia*. Knoxville: University of Tennessee, 2011.

Oss, O. T., and O. N. Oeric. *Psilocybin, Magic Mushroom Grower's Guide; A Handbook for Psilocybin Enthusiasts*. Berkeley, CA: And/Or Press, 1976.

Perry, Charles. *The Haight-Ashbury: A History*. New York: Random House, 1984.

Pinchbeck, Daniel. *Breaking Open the Head: A Psychedelic Journey into the Heart of Contemporary Shamanism*. New York: Broadway, 2002.

——. *2012: The Return of Quetzalcoatl*. New York: Jeremy Tarcher / Penguin, 2006.

Puterbaugh, Parke. *Phish: The Biography*. Cambridge, MA: Da Capo, 2009.

Rainbow Family of Living Light. *Rainbow Oracle*. Eugene, OR: Rainbow Family of Living Light, 1971.

Raphael, Ray. *Cash Crop: An American Dream*. Mendocino, CA: Ridge Times, 1985.

Reynolds, Simon. *Generation Ecstasy: Into the World of Techno and Rave Culture*. Boston: Little, Brown, 1998.

Roberts, Andy. *Albion Dreaming: A Popular History of LSD in Britain*. London: Marshall Cavendish, 2008.

Robson, Philip. *Forbidden Drugs*. Oxford: Oxford University, 1994.

Rodgers, Kathleen. *Welcome to Resisterville: American Dissidents in British Columbia*. Vancouver: University of British Columbia, 2014.

Rubin, Rachel. *Well Met Renaissance Faires and the American Counterculture*. New York: New York University, 2012.

St. Clair, David. *Say You Love Satan*. New York: Dell, 1987.

Sanders, Ed. *Fug You: An Informal History of the Peace Eye Bookstore, the Fuck You Press, and the Counterculture in the Lower East Side*. Cambridge, MA: Da Capo, 2011.

Saunders, Nicholas, and Rick Doblin. *Ecstasy: Dance, Trance, & Transformation*. Oakland, CA: Quick American Archives, 1996.

Schou, Nick. *Orange Sunshine: The Brotherhood of Eternal Love and Its Quest to Spread Peace, Love, and Acid to the World*. New York: Thomas Dunne, 2010.

Sender, Ramon. *A Planetary Sojourn: Stories, Articles, Essays, Letters & Four Recipes for Bliss*. San Francisco: Calm Unity, 2008.

Shenk, David, and Steve Silberman. *Skeleton Key: A Dictionary for Deadheads*. New York: Doubleday, 1994.

Shulgin, Alexander T., and Ann Shulgin. *Pihkal: A Chemical Love Story*. Berkeley, CA: Transform Press, 1991.

Siff, Stephen. *Acid Hype: American News Media and the Psychedelic Experience*. Urbana: University of Illinois Press, 2015.

Sloman, Larry. *Reefer Madness: The History of Marijuana in America*. Indianapolis, IN: Bobbs-Merrill, 1979.

Stafford, Peter G., and Jeremy Bigwood. *Psychedelics Encyclopedia*. Berkeley, CA: Ronin, 1992.

Stanley, Rhoney, and Tom Davis. *Owsley and Me: My LSD Family*. Rhinebeck, NY: Monkfish, 2012.

Stevens, Jay. *Storming Heaven: LSD and the American Dream*. New York: Atlantic Monthly, 1987.

Stolaroff, Myron J. *The Secret Chief Revealed*. Sarasota, FL: Multidisciplinary Association for Psychedelic Studies, 2004.

Strassman, Rick. *DMT: The Spirit Molecule; A Doctor's Revolutionary Research into the Biology of Near-Death and Mystical Experiences*. Rochester, VT: Park Street, 2001.

Streatfield, Dominic. *Cocaine: An Unauthorized Biography*. New York: Thomas Dunne, 2002.

Sussman, Elisabeth, and Keith Haring. *Keith Haring*. New York: Whitney Museum of American Art, 1997.

Talbot, David. *Season of the Witch: Enchantment, Terror, and Deliverance in the City of Love*. New York: Free Press, 2012.

Taylor, Astra. *The People's Platform: Taking Back Power and Culture in the Digital Age*. New York: Metropolitan, 2014.

Tendler, Stewart, and David May. *The Brotherhood of Eternal Love: From Flower Power to Hippie Mafia; The Story of the LSD Counterculture*. London: Panther, 1984.

Thompson, Hunter S. *The Kingdom of Fear: Loathsome Secrets of a Star-Crossed Child in the Final Days of the American Century*. New York: Simon & Schuster, 2003.

Torgoff, Martin. *Can't Find My Way Home: America in the Great Stoned Age, 1945–2000*. New York: Simon & Schuster, 2004.

Turner, Fred. *From Counterculture to Cyberculture: Stewart Brand, the Whole Earth Network, and the Rise of Digital Utopianism*. Chicago: University of Chicago, 2006.

Valentine, Douglas. *The Strength of the Pack: The Personalities, Politics and Espionage Intrigues That Shaped the DEA*. Walterville, OR: Trine Day, 2010.

Walsh, Roger N. *Higher Wisdom Eminent Elders Explore the Continuing Impact of Psychedelics*. New York: State University of New York, 2005.

Wasson, R. Gordon, and Albert Hofmann. *The Road to Eleusis: Unveiling the Secret of the Mysteries*. New York: Harcourt, Brace, Jovanovich, 1978.

Weiner, Rex, and Deanne Stillman. *Woodstock Census: The Nationwide Survey of the Sixties Generation*. New York: Viking Press, 1979.

Weiner, Robert G. *Perspectives on the Grateful Dead: Critical Writings*. Westport, CT: Greenwood Press, 1999.

Wolfe, Tom. *The Electric Kool-Aid Acid Test*. New York: Farrar, Straus and Giroux, 1968.

Journals, Articles, Websites, and Films

Abolafia. "Woodstock '68." *East Village Other*, August 2, 1968, 3.

"Acid Veterans Found 'Normal.'" *High Times*, May 1976, 18.

Aguirre, Abby. "The New Power Trip: Inside the World of Ayahuasca." *Marie Clare*, February 18, 2014. http://www.marieclaire.com/politics/news/a8965/ayahuasca -new-power-trip/.

Akers, Brian. "Concerning Terence McKenna's Stoned Apes." *Reality Sandwich*, 2011.

Alderson, Jeremy. "Portrait of an Artist as a Young Tripper." *Relix*, August 2008, 56.

Allen, Michael. "The Psychedelic 'Drugs Wizard' Who Ran One of England's Biggest LSD Labs." *Vice*, October 29, 2014. http://www.vice.com/read/casey-william -hardison-psychedelic-chemist-254.

"All in the Family: Courtenay Pollock." Grateful Dead YouTube channel, 2013. https://www.youtube.com/watch?v=kBAqkVC9uAg.

Alson, Robert. "Bob Weir Lets It Grow." *Relix*, May 1978, 8.

"Anastasio Avoids Jail on Drug Charges." *Billboard*, April 13, 2007. http://www .billboard.com/articles/news/1052782/anastasio-avoids-jail-on-drug-charges.

"Ann and Sasha Shulgin Speak . . . in Discussion with Earth and Fire Erowid." *Entheogen Review*, Summer Solstice 2008, 41.

"Answers." Spin Doctors Archive. http://www.spindoctors-archive.com/faq/band_ members.html.

Arnold, Corry. "October 21, 1972: Alumni Lawn, Vanderbilt University, Nashville, TN, The Grateful Dead (Last Free Concert)." *Lost Live Dead*, April 4, 2013. http:// lostlivedead.blogspot.com/2013/04/october-21-1972-alumni-lawn-vanderbilt .html.

Arnold, Jacob. "The Warehouse: The Place House Music Got Its Name." *Resident Advisor*, May 16, 2012. http://www.residentadvisor.net/feature.aspx?1597.

Arrington, Michael. "What Skype Really Paid for GroupMe." *TechCrunch*, August 23, 2011. http://techcrunch.com/2011/08/23/what-skype-really-paid-for-groupme/.

∞Ayes. "Moving into the Sacred World of DMT." *Entheogen Review*, Vernal Equinox 2001, 32.

"Bad Day at Black Rock (Zone Trip #4)." *Rough Draft,* September 1990, 1.

Bagby, John. "Boulder Rave." 1995. http://www.pronoia.net/tour/essays/colorado.html.

———. "Pronoia Tour Launch, Wetlands nightclub, Manhattan." 1994. http://www.pronoia.net/tour/essays/wetlands.html.

Barbrook, Richard, and Andy Cameron. "The Californian Ideology." *Science as Culture,* no. 6 (1996): 44.

Barlow, John Perry. "Being in Nothingness: Virtual Reality and the Pioneers of Cyberspace." *Mondo 2000,* Summer 1990, 34.

———. "Crime and Puzzlement." June 1990. https://w2.eff.org/Misc/Publications/John_Perry_Barlow/HTML/crime_and_puzzlement_1.html.

———. "A Declaration of the Independence of Cyberspace." February 8, 1996. https://projects.eff.org/~barlow/Declaration-Final.html.

———. "Declaring Independence." *Wired,* June 1996, 121.

———. "Leaving the Physical World." March 29, 1993. https://w2.eff.org/Misc/Publications/John_Perry_Barlow/HTML/leaving_the_physical_world.html.

———. "A Not Terribly Brief History of the Electronic Frontier Foundation." November 8, 1990. https://w2.eff.org/Misc/Publications/John_Perry_Barlow/HTML/not_too_brief_history.html.

Barthelmé, Donald. "The Teachings of Don B.: A Yankee Way of Knowledge." *New York Times Magazine,* February 11, 1973, 14.

Beach, Horace. "Listening for the Logos: A Study of Reports of Audible Voices at High Doses of Psilocybin." *MAPS Bulletin,* Winter 1996, 12.

Bender, L., and D. V. Siva Sankar. "Chromosome Damage Not Found in Leukocytes of Children Treated with LSD-25." *Science,* February 16, 1968, 159.

Bergquist, Laura. "The Curious Story Behind the New Cary Grant." *Look,* September 1, 1959.

"Biaggi Meets with Leaders of Bronx Street Gangs." *New York Times,* April 22, 1972, 19.

Bieberman, Lisa. "The Psychedelic Experience." *New Republic,* August 5, 1967, 17.

"Big LSD Bust in Oakland-Arrested." *San Francisco Chronicle,* January 27, 1993, A13.

Bloom, Steve. "420 or Fight." *High Times,* December 1998, 12.

"Bob Barsotti, John Meyer, Dan Healy and More." *Mix* online, October 29, 2004. http://www.mixonline.com/news/news-products/bob-barsotti-john-meyer-dan-healy-and-more/377813.

Brand, Stewart. "Fanatic Life and Symbolic Death Among the Computer Bums." *Rolling Stone,* December 7, 1972, 58.

———. Stewart Brand papers. Stanford University Library. Manuscripts Division, b. 6a.

Brautigan, Richard. *All Watched Over by Machines of Living Grace.* San Francisco: Comm/Co, April 1967.

Brown, Steve. "If I Told You All That Went Down . . . a Fond Look Back at Grateful Dead Records." *Golden Road,* Spring 1986, 21.

Burks, Edward C. "Peyote Peddler at Odds with U.S." *New York Times,* June 23, 1960, 33.

Brazil, Eric. "Drug Lord Sentenced After 20-Year Flight." *San Francisco Examiner,* January 22, 1999.

———. "Fugitive to Face LSD Charges." *San Francisco Examiner,* July 6, 1998.

Brill, Louis M. "What Is Burning Man? The First Year in the Desert." http://burningman.org/culture/history/brc-history/event-archives/1986-1991/firstyears/.

Broughton, Frank. "Deadheads: A Snapshot of the Deadhead Scene and How It Was Feeding U.S. Rave." *i-D*, February 1994.

Brown, Janelle. "Your Glow Stick Could Land You in Jail." *Salon*, April 16, 2003. http://www.salon.com/2003/04/16/rave/.

Browne, David. "The Grateful Dead's Greatest Year." *RollingStone*, July 4, 2013. http://www.rollingstone.com/music/news/the-grateful-deads-greatest-year-2013062.

Butler, Katy. "LSD Is Back—After a Long Trip." *San Francisco Chronicle*, October 26, 1979, 1.

"Cafe Owner Found Dead." *New York Times*, December 7, 1960, 43.

Cahill, Tim. "Acid Crawlback Fest: Armageddon Postponed." *Rolling Stone*, August 3, 1972, 1.

"Campus Life: Wesleyan; Student's Arrest Leads to Debate on Drug Policy." *New York Times*, November 19, 1989.

Carlson, Peter. "After Some Tough Years, the Legendary '60s Cartoonist Is Truckin' Again." *People*, June 24, 1985, 75.

Carpenter, Troy. "Jam Bands to Cruise Again." *Billboard*, July 17, 2003. http://www.billboard.com/articles/news/69956/jam-bands-to-cruise-again.

Carroll, Jon. "A Conversation with Jerry Garcia." *Playboy Guide: Electronic Entertainment*, Spring 1982.

Carter, Caitlin. "Ann Coulter Is a Dead Head, Has Large Collection of Grateful Dead Bootlegs." *SiriusXM Blog*, June 10, 2015. http://blog.siriusxm.com/2015/06/10/ann-coulter-is-a-dead-head-has-large-collection-of-grateful-dead-bootlegs/.

Cauchon, Dennis. "Attack on Deadheads Is No Hallucination." *USA Today*, December 17, 1992, A17.

Chamberlin, Daniel. "Uncle Skullfucker's Band." *Arthur*, July 2004.

Chapman v. United States, 500 U.S. 453 (1991).

Clegg, Mitch. "Deadhead Church Expels Its Founder." *San Francisco Chronicle*, April 9, 1992, A23.

Coate, John. "Life on the Bus and Farm: An Informal Recollection," 1987. http://cervisa.com/stories/farm.txt.

Cockburn, Alexander. "Busted: 'Half the World's Acid Supply.'" *Village Voice*, April 17, 1978, 1.

Cohen, Arianne. "My Journey with a Life Altering Drug: Ayahuasca." *ELLE*, November 2012. http://www.elle.com/beauty/health-fitness/advice/a14193/ayahuasca-drug/.

Collection of the Institute of Illegal Images, San Francisco, CA.

Cope, Julian. "Acid Seven." http://www.japrocksampler.com/artists/.../acid_seven/.

Cox, Joseph. "Dark Web Dealer Allegedly Donates Drug Profits to Charity." Vice.com, October 7, 2015. http://motherboard.vice.com/read/dark-web-dealer-allegedly-donates-to-charity.

Dahl, Henrik. "Struck by White Lightning: A Correspondence with Owsley Stanley." *Oak Tree Review*, April 2012. http://www.theoaktreereview.com/owsley_stanley_2.html.

Daly, Max. "Why Young Brits Are Taking So Much LSD and Ecstasy." *Vice*, July 27, 2015. http://www.vice.com/read/this-is-why-so-many-young-brits-are-taking-so-much-acid-and-ecstasy-892.

"Dave Matthews Band to Rock Central Park." *Billboard*, September 9, 2003. http://www.billboard.com/articles/news/69179/dave-matthews-band-to-rock-central-park.

Davis, Erik. "Terence McKenna's Last Trip." *Wired*, May 2000, 156.

Davis, Fred, with Laura Munoz. "Heads and Freaks: Patterns and Meanings of Drug Use Among Hippies." *Journal of Health and Social Behavior*, June 1968, 156.

Davis, Joshua Clark. "The Business of Getting High: Head Shops, Countercultural Capitalism, and the Marijuana Legalization Movement." *The Sixties: A Journal of History, Politics and Culture* 8, no.1 (2015), 1.

Dawson, Bret Maxwell. "B'gock! (or Of Omelets, WWF Wrestling, Summer Camp and What It Means to Me to Be a Disco Biscuits Fan)." *JamBands*, February 15, 2000. http://www.jambands.com/features/2000/02/15/b-gock-or-of-omelets-wwf -wrestling-summer-camp-and-what-it-means-to-me-to-be-a-disco-biscuits- fan.

"DEA Raid on Shulgin Laboratory on October 27, 1994." January 8, 2004. https:// www.erowid.org/culture/characters/shulgin_alexander/shulgin_alexander_raid. shtml.

Degenerate Art: The Art and Culture of Glass Pipes. Directed by M. Slinger, 2011.

DeKoerne, Jim. "Ayahuasca Visions: The Religions Iconography of a Peruvian Shaman." *Entheogen Review,* Vernal Equinox 1993, 10.

———. Editorial. *Entheogen Review*, Winter Solstice 1992, 1.

———. "Entheogen—What's in a Word?" *Entheogen Review,* Winter Solstice 1992, 1.

———. "On the Evolution of Psychedelic Shamanism." *Entheogen Review,* Summer Solstice 1993, 2.

The Diggers. *Realist,* August 1968, 15.

Doblin, Rick. Editorial. *MAPS Bulletin,* Summer 1988.

———. "MDMA Research in the United States." *MAPS Bulletin,* Summer 1989.

———. "The Summit Meeting Commemorating the 50th Anniversary of Albert Hofmann's Discovery of LSD." *MAPS Bulletin,* Summer 1993. http://www.maps .org/news-letters/v04n2/04252lsd.html.

Dym, Monte. "The Dead Tour: A Social Look." *Relix,* September 1976, 22.

Dym, Monte, and Bob Alson. "The Man Behind the Words, part 2." *Relix,* May 1978, 21.

Early Warnings. Green Mountain Post Films, 1980.

Ehrlich, Dimitri, and Gregor Ehrlich. "Graffiti in Its Own Words." *New York,* June 2006. http://nymag.com/guides/summer/17406/.

Eisenhart, Mary. "Jerry Garcia Interview: November 12, 1987." http://www.yoyow .com/marye/garcia.html.

Eisner, Bruce. "Cleanliness Is Next to Godheadliness," *High Times,* January 1977, 73.

———. "Interview with an Alchemist: Bear: Owsley, LSD Chemist Extraordinaire, In Conversation with Bruce Eisner." August 2004. https://web.archive.org /web/20041128235352/http://www.bruceeisner.com/writings/2004/08interview _with__2.html.

Elmer-DeWitt, Philip. "First Nation in Cyberspace." *Time,* December 6, 1993, 62.

Erowid. "2C-B Timeline." https://www.erowid.org/chemicals/2cb/2cb_timeline.php.

Erowid, Earth, and Fire Erowid. "Spotlight on NBOMe: Potent Psychedelic Issues." *Erowid Extracts,* July 2013, 2.

Erowid, Fire. "Erowid: 10 Years of History." *Erowid Extracts,* June 2005, 8.

"The Exploding Threat of the Mind Drug That Got Out of Control." *Life,* March 25, 1966, 21.

Fine, Melinda, and Jonathan Walters. "Putting a Human Face on Injustice: Reversing a Political Juggernaut." NYU Wagner School of Public Service and Ford Foundation, New York, 2003.

Fisher, Pam. "Thoughts from Prison." *Deadheads Behind Bars,* early 1990, via rec.music .gdead.

Fong-Torres, Ben. "Love Is Just a Song We Sing but a Contract Is Something Else." *Rolling Stone,* February 26, 1976, 58.

Franzosa, Edward Sykes, Charles W. Harper, and James H. Crockett. "The LSD Blotter Index." *Micrograms,* July 1987. https://www.erowid.org/chemicals/lsd/lsd_blotter_microgram_1987.pdf.

"Freedom Fighter." *High Times,* August 1990, 43.

Gandy, Sam. "Psychedelic Scientists." *Psychedelic Press UK* 2015, no. 3 (2015): 89.

Gans, David, with Ken Goffman. "Mitch Kapor and John Barlow Interview." August 5, 1990. https://w2.eff.org/Misc/Publications/John_Perry_Barlow/HTML/barlow_and_kapor_in_wired_interview.html.

Gehr, Richard. "An Interview with Jerry Garcia." *Newsday,* September 9, 1991.

Ghose, Tia. "Short Trip? More People 'Microdosing' on Psychedelic Drugs." *LiveScience,* July 8, 2015. http://www.livescience.com/51482-more-people-microdosing-psychedelic-drugs.html.

Ginsberg, Allen. "Notes Written on Finally Recording *Howl.*" *Evergreen Review* 3, no.10 (1959): 132.

Godwin, Michael. "The Ken Kesey Movie." *Rolling Stone,* March 7, 1970, 24.

Goldstein, Richard. "Scenes." *Village Voice,* June 15, 1967.

Gomez, Mitchell. "Electric Forest Shuts Down Dancesafe—but We Have a Bigger Problem to Tackle." June 30, 2015. https://dancesafe.org/dancesafe-was-shut-down/.

Goodman, Fred. "The End of the Road?" *Rolling Stone,* August 23, 1990, 21.

Gore, Albert. "Church Group Swaps Views with Gaskin's." *Tennessean,* March 13, 1972.

Gorman, Peter. "Divine Smoke and God's Flesh: Psychedelics and Religion." *High Times,* January 1990, 41.

Gracie and Zarkov. "LSD and MDA (and Little Lambs Eat Ivy)." *High Frontiers,* no. 2 (1985).

Grateful Dead. "The Book of the Dead." Distributed in London, May 1972.

Grateful Dead Archive. McHenry Library. UC Santa Cruz. Special Collections and Archives.

Gray, Rosie. "Friendly Cult Looking for Recruits at Occupy Wall Street!" *Village Voice,* November 10, 2011. http://www.villagevoice.com/news/friendly-cult-looking-for-recruits-at-occupy-wall-street-6711929.

Greenberg, Andy. "Black Market Drug Site 'Silk Road' Booming: $22 Million in Annual Sales." *Forbes,* August 6, 2012. http://www.forbes.com/sites/andygreenberg/2012/08/06/black-market-drug-site-silk-road-booming-22-million-in-annual-mostly-illegal-sales/.

Greim, Lisa. "Cognitive Dissident." *Weslayan,* 1996.

Grigoriadis, Vanessa. "Travels in the New Psychedelic Bazaar." *New York,* April 7, 2013.

Gross, Dave. "The 'Blue Star' LSD Tattoo Urban Legend Page." http://lycaeum.org/~sputnik/Tattoo/.

Gustafson, Dean. "The First Year in the Desert: A Personal Historical Account from Its First Drummer (Anecdotal Memoirs or Rather a Rant of Reveries)." https://web.archive.org/web/20070630030804/http://deangustafson.net/BlackRock90.html.

Hafner, Katie. "The Epic Saga of the Well." *Wired,* May 1997, 98.

Haggerty, Hugh. "John Perry Barlow: US out of Cyberspace." *High Times,* October 1994, 59.

Hanna, Jon. "Alex Grey Speaks. . . . " *Entheogen Review,* Winter Solstice 1998, 17.
———. "Erowid Character Vaults: Nick Sand Extended Biography." November 5, 1999. https://www.erowid.org/culture/characters/sand_nick/sand_nick_biography1.shtml.
———. "The King of Blotter Art." *Entheogen Review,* Winter Solstice 2003, 109.
———. "Reflections on Basel." *Entheogen Review,* Vernal Equinox 2006, 2.
Hardison, Casey William "Freeblood." "Novel Condensation of d-LA into d_LSD via PyPOB." *Entheogen Review,* Autumnal Equinox 2005, 94.
Harvey, Larry. "The 10 Principles of Burning Man." 2004. http://burningman.org/culture/philosophical-center/10-principles/.
Heilbrun, Adam. "An Interview with Jaron Lanier." *Whole Earth Review,* Fall 1989, 108.
Henke, James. "Jerry Garcia: The *Rolling Stone* Interview." *Rolling Stone,* October 31, 1991, 34.
Hicks, Bill. *Sane Man.* Sacred Cow Productions, 1989.
Hill, Amelia. "LSD Could Help Alcoholics Stop Drinking, AA Founder Believed." *Guardian,* August 23, 2012. http://www.theguardian.com/science/2012/aug/23/lsd-help-alcoholics-theory.
Hill, Taylor. "Deadheads Are What Liberals Claim to Be but Aren't." JamBands, June 23, 2006. http://www.jambands.com/features/2006/06/23/deadheads-are-what-liberals-claim-to-be-but-aren-t-an-interview-with-ann-coulter.
Hofmann, Albert. Closing remarks in Basel, 2006. https://www.youtube.com/watch?v=SInkOigeGno.
Hoffman, Karen. "A Plea for Help!" *November Coalition,* February 12, 2001. http://november.org/siteindex/November/goodies/thewall/thewall/horning_karen.html.
Holland, Julie. "Raves for Research or Psychedelic Researchers: The Next Generation." *MAPS Bulletin,* Summer 1993. http://www.maps.org/news-letters/v04n2/04240rav.html.
Holloway, Danny. "Dead Come Alive." *NME,* April 15, 1972.
The Holy Modal Rounders: Bound to Lose. Directed by Sam Wainwright Douglas and Paul Lovelace, 2006.
Hormilla, Natalie. "Bread and Puppet Celebrates Half a Century." *Barton Chronicle,* August 7, 2013. http://bartonchronicle.com/bread-and-puppet-celebrates-half-a-century/.
Hua, Vanessa. "Burning Man." *San Francisco Examiner,* August 20, 2000.
Hunter, John T. "Paid Notice: Bloch, Ephraim F." *New York Times,* May 23, 2000.
Ingraham, Christopher. "The Oddly Beautiful and Sometimes Disturbing Artistic Talent of the Nation's Drug Cops." *Washington Post. Wonkblog,* March 20, 2015. https://www.washingtonpost.com/news/wonkblog/wp/2015/03/20/the-oddly-beautiful-and-sometimes-disturbing-artistic-talent-of-the-nations-drug-cops/.
"An Interview with Trey Anastasio and Lars Fisk." *SuperBallIX,* June 6, 2011. https://web.archive.org/web/20110609232702/http://www.superballix.com/treylars.html.
Jackson, Blair. "Gross Facts About the Dead." *Golden Road,* Spring 1984, 30.
———. "In Phil We Trust." *Dupree's Diamond News,* Spring 1994, 12.
Jackson, Blair, and Regan McMahon. "Garcia's Longtime Ally Looks Back." *Golden Road,* Winter 1987, 26.
James, John S. "Roll-Your-Own Religion by Computer?" *High Frontiers,* no. 1 (1984): 18.
Jefferson Starship. *Live in Central Park, NYC, May 12, 1975.* Real Gone, 2012.

Jeffries, Adrienne. "The LSD Avengers, Silk Road's Self-Appointed Drug Inspectors, Announce Retirement." *Verge*, October 14, 2013. http://www.theverge.com/2013/10/14/4828448/silk-road-lsd-avengers-drug-inspectors.

Juanis, J. C. "Bay Area Bits." *Relix*, December 1987.

Kane, Jenny. "Burning Man Has Grown Beyond Founders' Dreams." *Reno Gazette-Journal*, March 3, 2015. http://www.rgj.com/story/life/2015/03/03/burning-man-grown-beyond-founders-dreams/24343027/.

Katigbak, Raf, and Victor John Penner. "A Look Inside Illegal Canadian Weed Grow Houses from the 1990s." *Vice*, December 18, 2013. http://www.vice.com/read/documenting-busted-home-grow-ops-in-1990s-vancouver.

Katzenjammer, Basho. "Grateful Dead Pig Backlash." *East Village Other*, September 5, 1971.

Kaye, Lenny. "The Year of the Dead." *Fusion*, November 14, 1969.

Kincade, Chris. "Dead Come to Life Again for Two-Day Festival." *New York Times*, June 2, 1996.

Kippel, Les. "The Making and Breaking of a Rumor." *Relix*, July 1977, 19.

Kirkman, Edward, and Henry Lee. "Raid Hippie Cult, Seize $6M Dope." *New York Daily News*, September 27, 1968, 5.

Klock, John C., Udo Boerner, and Charles E. Becker. "Coma, Hyperthermia and Bleeding Associated with Massive LSD Overdose: A Report of Eight Cases." *Western Journal of Medicine* 120, no. 3 (1974): 183.

Klug, Lisa Alcalay. "Authorities Bust Four in Nationwide LSD Distribution Ring." *Associated Press*, July 2, 1993.

Kohn, Jaakov. "Sunshine Superman!" *East Village Other*, June 11, 1969, 5.

Krassner, Paul. "High Encounters with Ecuadorian Shamans." *High Times*, March 1980, 60.

Kushner, David. "The Masked Avengers." *New Yorker*, September 8, 2014, 48.

Lashinsky, Adam. "Remembering Netscape: The Birth of the Web." *Fortune*, July 25, 2005. http://archive.fortune.com/magazines/fortune/fortune_archive/2005/07/25/8266639/index.htm.

Latvala, Dick. "Letters." *Dead Relix*, September 1975, 1.

"'Lay Off Peyote' Beatniks Warned." *United Press International*, June 30, 1960.

Logan, Casey. "Adventures in Wonderland." *Pitch*, April 19, 2001, 14.

Long, Marion. "The Seers' Catalog." *Omni*, January 1987, 36.

Lovell, Vic. "The Perry Lane Papers: A Prologue." *Free You*, June 1969, 20.

"LSD Now: A Generation Later." *High Times*, February 1978, 42.

Luke, David. "Psychoactive Substances and Paranormal Phenomena: A Comprehensive Review." *International Journal of Transpersonal Studies*, June 2012, 97.

Lyttle, Thomas. "Drug Based Religions and Contemporary Drug Taking." *Journal of Drug Issues*, Spring 1988, 271.

Maddox, Alexia, Monica J. Barratt, Matthew Allen, Simon Lenton. "Constructive Activism in the Dark Web: Cryptomarkets and Illicit Drugs in the Digital 'Demimonde.'" *Information, Communication & Society* 19, no. 1, 2016, 1.

Marshall, Jules. "Zippies!" *Wired*, May 1994, 75.

Martin, Douglas. "Humphry Osmond, 86, Who Sought Medicinal Value in Psychedelic Drugs, Dies." *New York Times*, February 22, 2004, 25.

———. "Terence McKenna, 53, Dies; Patron of Psychedelic Drugs." *New York Times*, April 9, 2000, 40.

Martin, Michael. "Love and Other Drugs." *Interview*, Fall 2010. http://www.interviewmagazine.com/culture/love-and-other-drugs/.

Mason, Michael, Chris Sandel, and Lee Ray Chapman. "Subterranean Psychonaut: The Strange and Dreadful Saga of Gordon Todd Skinner." *This Land Press,* July 28, 2013. http://thislandpress.com/2013/07/28/subterranean-psychonaut/.

McCloud, Mark. "12 Album Covers." 2007. http://www.blotterbarn.com/slideshow. html#deadalbums.

McCormick, Carlo. "The Psychedelic '90s." *High Times,* May 1990, 48.

McKenna, Terence. "Re: Evolution." On the Shamen, *Boss Drum.* One Little Indian, 1992.

Meija, Paula. "Day Tripping: Benefits Seen in Psychedelics." *Newsweek,* January 25, 2015. http://www.newsweek.com/day-tripping-benefits-seen-use-psychedelics-301847.

Melillo, Wendy. "3 Grateful Dead Concertgoers Struck by Lightning near RFK." *Washington Post,* June 26, 1995.

Mendel, William W. "Counterdrug Strategy-Illusive Victory: From Blast Furnace to Green Sweep." *Military Review,* December 1992, 74.

Milano, Brett. "Rykodisc Folds Up Its Salem Tent." *Boston Phoenix,* August 12, 1999. http://www.bostonphoenix.com/archive/music/99/08/12/rykodisc.html.

"Money Is an Unnecessary Evil" (Digger broadsheet), San Francisco: Comm/Co, 1966.

Moore, Jerry. "Spring Tour Again." *Relix,* July 1977, 16.

Morris, Bob. "Ayahuasca: A Strong Cup of Tea." *New York Times,* June 13, 2014.

Moser, Margaret. "She Lives: The Clementine Hall Interview." *Austin Chronicle,* August 20, 2004.

"Mother Is Bugged at Me." *Time,* July 7, 1952, 21.

Mulkerin, Edward F., III. "Scapegoats, Sentencing, and LSD." *Harvard Crimson,* September 20, 1993.

"NADDIS Index for Stark, Hadley Ronald (Deceased) (OIP Appeal #2010–0511)," July 24, 2010. http://www.scribd.com/doc/42274498/Ron-Stark-Naddis-Summary.

Nark, Jason, and *Daily News* staff writer. "In Philly, Keeping Tabs on LSD." *Philadelphia Daily News,* May 30, 2012.

"News." *High Times,* June 1974, 28.

Newton, Jim. "Deadheads Fight Stigma as Arrests Rise." *Los Angeles Times,* July 27, 1992.

"The 1980 eruptions of Mount. St. Helens, Washington, U.S. Geological Survey Professional Paper 1250." Washington, DC: US Department of the Interior, 1981.

Nofke, Will. "The Monkey Is Being Shed." *High Frontiers,* no. 1 (1984): 7.

Obrecht, Jas. "Jerry Garcia: The Complete 1985 'Frets' Interview." *Jas Obrecht Music Archive.* https://web.archive.org/web/20100923144558/http://jasobrecht.com /jerry-garcia-the-complete-1985-interview/.

The Other One: The Long Strange Trip of Bob Weir. Directed by Sam Fleiss, 2014.

Ott, Jonathan. "Books." *High Times,* August 1976, 93.

———. "World Conference on Hallucinogenic Mushrooms." *Head,* February 1978.

Owsley Stanley, Augustus. "Southern California Sojourn." *Relix,* August 2005. http:// www.relix.com/articles/detail/southern-california-sojourn-by-owsley-bear -stanley.

Pahnke, Walter N. "Drugs and Mysticism." *International Journal of Parapsychology,* Spring 1966, 295.

Park, Ed. "Mistaken for the Enemy." *Los Angeles Times,* April 20, 2008.

Peacock, Steve. "Jerry Garcia in London." *Rock,* July 17, 1972, 16.

Pesce, Mark. "Psychedelics and the Creation of Virtual Reality." *MAPS Bulletin,* Fall 2000, 4.

Peterson, Kim. "BitTorrent File-Sharing Program Floods the Web." *Seattle Times*, January 10, 2005. http://www.seattletimes.com/business/bittorrent-file-sharing -program-floods-the-web/.

Peterson, Victor. "Traditional Healers and Synthetic Entheogens." *Entheogen Review*, Summer Solstice 1996, 16.

Petridis, Alexis. "Frankie Knuckles: Godfather of House Music, Priest of the Dancefloor." *Guardian*, April 1, 2014. http://www.theguardian.com/music/2014/ apr/01/frankie-knuckles-house-music-dj-producer-nightclubs.

"Phun City Is Yours to Make It." *International Times*, July 17, 1970, 8.

Pickard, Leonard. "DEA's NADDIS System: A Guide for Attorneys, the Courts, and Researchers." July 2011. http://freeleonardpickard.org/NADDIS/index.html.

———. "FOIA Requests Helpful to the Defense Bar, District and Appellate Courts, and Public Interest Groups." http://www.freeleonardpickard.org/DEA-FOIA -Requests.html.

———. "International LSD Prevalence—Factors Affecting Proliferation and Control," 2008. http://freeleonardpickard.org/LSD-Prevalence.html.

Pilkington, Mark. "Re-Psychedelia Britannica." *Arthur*, January 2005, 12.

Pollan, Michael. "The Trip Treatment," *New Yorker*, February 9, 2015.

Pope Electric Yeti. "British Zippy Pronoia Tour Kicks Off in New York, a Firsthand Account." 1995. http://www.pronoia.net/tour/essays/pressconf.html.

"Psychedelic Science." *Horizon*, BBC, aired February 27, 1997.

Queen Mu. "Visual Music in the Third World." *Reality Hackers*, Winter 1988, 38.

Rapoport, Roger. "The Sunshine Murders." *New West*, April 21, 1980, 35.

Razam, Rak. "Blotter Art: The Institute of Illegal Images." *Juxtapoz*, September 6, 2009. http://www.juxtapoz.com/current/blotter-art-the-institute-of-illegal-images.

Renshaw, Michael. "Interview with Jon Fishman, July 11th 1996, Kensington, London." http://www.gadiel.com/phish/articles/fishman.html.

"Return of the Hippies." *Newsday*, June 2, 1967.

Reynolds, Simon. "How Rave Music Conquered America." *Guardian*, August 2, 2012. http://www.theguardian.com/music/2012/aug/02/how-rave-music-conquered -america.

Robbins, Paul J. "Lysergic A Go-Go as It Went." *Los Angeles Free Press*, November 26, 1965, 3.

Roberts, Andy. "Mushroom Magic at Crazy Creek: The Welsh Psilocybin Festival, 1976–1982." *Psychedelic Press UK* 2014, no. 2 (2014): 7.

Roberts, Thomas. "Four Stages of the Psychedelic Renaissance: An Op-Ed Essay." Academia.edu, May 2015. http://www.academia.edu/11144663/Four_Stages_of _the_Psychedelic_Renaissance_An_Op-ed_Essay.

———. "Why Is Bicycle Day April 19th, Not the 16th?" Academia.edu, 2015. https:// www.academia.edu/536054/Why_Bicycle_Day_is_April_19th.

Rock Influence with Bob Weir. April 1984. https://www.youtube.com/watch?v=DAC m8Lg2o2w.

Rodriguez, Daniel. "Death and Ecstasy: The Rise and Fall of Burning Man's Original Rave Ghetto." *Thump*, August 31, 2015. https://thump.vice.com/en_us/article /death-and-ecstasy-the-rise-and-fall-of-burning-mans-original-rave-ghetto.

Romero, Dennis. "Sasha Shulgin, Psychedelic Chemist." *Los Angeles Times*, September 5, 1995, 5.

Rosenkranz, Patrick. "Zap: An Unpublished Spain Rodriguez Interview." *Comics Journal*, November 24, 2014. http://www.tcj.com/unpublished-spain-rodriguez -interview/.

Rossetto, Louis. "Why Wired?" *Wired,* March 1993, 10.

St. John, Graham. "DJ Goa Gil: Kalifornian Exile, Dark Yogi and Dreaded Anomaly." *Dancecult: Journal of Electronic Dance Music Culture,* November 20, 2011, 97.

Sala, Luc. "New Edge and Mondo, Part 1-A Personal Perspective." *Acceler8or,* March 28, 2012. http://www.acceler8or.com/2012/03/new-edge-mondo-a-personal -perspective-part-1-mondo-2000-history-project-entry-8/.

Sanders, Ed. "A Biographic Appreciation of Wavy Gravy for His 70th Birthday." *Woodstock Journal,* May 15, 2006, 12.

———. "A Call to Action." *Fuck You / a magazine of the arts,* no. 10, 1964, 1.

Schwartz, Stephen. "Suspect in LSD Distribution Ring Extradited to S.F." *San Francisco Chronicle,* March 9, 1995.

"Sentencing Guidelines." *Entheogen Review,* Autumnal Equinox 1994, 17.

Sewell, R. A. J. H. Halpern, and H. G. Pope Jr. "Response of Cluster Headaches to Psilocybin and LSD." *Neurology,* June 27, 2006, 1920.

Shafer, Jack. "Acid House: The Art of LSD Blotter Paper." *San Francisco Weekly,* August 30, 1995.

"Sharkey's Garden." *High Times,* July 1990, 42.

Shroder, Tom. "The Case for Using Psychedelics to Treat PTSD, Depression." *Washington Post,* September 4, 2014.

———. "Want to Quit Smoking? Eat a Magic Mushroom, a New Study Says." *Time,* September 18, 2014. http://time.com/3399433/quit-smoking-psychedelic -drugs-acid-test/.

Shulgin, Ann, and Alexander Shulgin. Letter to Council on Spiritual Practices, February 28, 2007. http://csp.org/why/Shulgins.html.

Silberman, Steve. "Interview with Dick Latvala, 3/5/95." Posted rec.music.gdead and elsewhere, e.g., https://www.cs.cmu.edu/~./gdead/latvala.html.

———. "Who Was Cowboy Neal?" *Golden Road,* Spring 1989, 28.

Simon, Peter. "Making Music Miracles." *New Age Journal,* May 1975, 53.

Sirius, R. U. "Ted Nelson and John Perry Barlow for Mondo 2000." *Acceler8or,* May 22, 2012. http://www.acceler8or.com/2012/05/ted-nelson-john-perry-barlow -for-mondo-2000-mondo-2000-history-project-entry-17/.

Sischy, Ingrid. "Kid Haring." *Vanity Fair,* July 1997, 106.

Smart, Paul. "Closest to the Edge: Life in a Squatters' Village on the Wild Side of Maui." *Arthur,* July 2005, 15.

Smith, Andrew. "Trey Anastasio." *Good Citizen,* no. 7 (1997).

Smith, Frank. "Box of Pain." *New Republic,* March 21, 1994, 25.

Spector, Stan. "Who Is Dionysus and Why Does He Keep Following Me Everywhere?" *Dead Letters,* no. 2 (2003), 19.

Spencer, Hawes. "Resourceful: DMB Concert Answers Prayers." *Hook,* October 2, 2003.

"Spinners or Sinners?" *Worcester Telegram and Gazette,* December 9, 1991.

Stang, Ivan. "Heads Up: Terence McKenna Rant." August 6, 2003. http://www .subgenius.com/bigfist/FIST2004-1/X0671_Heads_Up-_Terence_Mc.html.

"Stanley, Owsley (aka Stanley, Augustus Owsley III) (deceased)-NADDIS Report," November 28, 2011, http://www.governmentattic.org/5docs/DEA-Owsley_2011. pdf.

State, Justice, Commerce, the Judiciary, and Related Agencies Appropriations, Fiscal Year 1978. Washington, DC: US Government Printing Office, 1977, 969.

Stuart, R. "Entheogenic Sects Religions." *MAPS Bulletin,* Spring 2002, 17.

Sunshine Daydream. Directed by John Norris, 1972. Released on Rhino, 2012.

The Sunshine Makers. Directed by Cosmo Feilding-Mellen, 2015.

"Surveillance and Its Discontents, a Conversation Across Cyberspace" (transcript). *TechPresident,* June 12, 2014. http://techpresident.com/news/25129/surveillance -and-its-discontents-conversation-across-cyberspace-edward-snowden-and -john.

Teafaerie. "How to Build a Better Spaceship." May 29, 2014. https://www.erowid.org /columns/teafaerie/2014/05/29/how-to-build-a-better-spaceship/.

Thomas, Robert McG., Jr. "Anton Rosenberg, a Hipster Ideal, Dies at 71." *New York Times,* February 22, 1998, 39.

Thompson, Derek. "1991: The Most Important Year in Pop-Music History." *Atlantic,* May 8, 2015. http://www.theatlantic.com/entertainment/archive/2015/05/1991 -the-most-important-year-in-music/392642/.

Tolles, Dan. "Burlington Punk Club 242 Main at 30." *Seven Days,* January, 28, 2015. http://www.sevendaysvt.com/vermont/burlington-punk-club-242-main-at-30 /Content?oid=2511201.

Tomkins, Calvin. "The Teachings of Joe Pye." *New Yorker,* February 3, 1973, 37.

"Trans-High Market Quotations." *High Times,* February 1980, 30.

True, Everett. "In My Head, I'm So Ugly." *Melody Maker,* July 18, 1992.

"Turning On in Moscow." *Kansas City Times,* November 13, 1972.

Tyler, Timothy. "Tim's Story." Committee on Unjust Sentencing. http://www .drugwarprisoners.org/tyler.htm.

United Press International. "1,000 at Concert Drink LSD-Spiked Cider." *Los Angeles Times,* June 1, 1971.

United States v. Carolyn Holly Fried et. al., District Court, Northern District of California, No. CR-93-0325 EFL, May 3, 1996.

United States v. Karen Horning, a.k.a. Karen Hoffman, a.k.a. Andrea Maltease. United States District Court, Northern District of California. No. CR93-0450 TEH.

United States v. Sage Appel, District Court, Northern District of California, No. CR-93-0325 EFL, February 6, 1995.

United States v. Southworth Wells Swede, 326 F. Supp. 533, No. 70, CR. 737, 1971.

Vale, V. "Mark McCloud: In Conversation with V. Vale." *SFAQ,* March 12, 2015. http://sfaq.us/2015/03/mark-mccloud-in-conversation-with-v-vale/.

Van Deusen, David. "Green Mountain Communes: The Making of a Peoples' Vermont." January 15, 2008, http://www.anarkismo.net/article/7248.

Vaughn, Chris. "Dead Fingers Talk." *Spin,* July 1987, 74.

Waddell, Ray. "Bonnaroo Organizers Purchasing Festival Site." *Billboard,* January 4, 2007.   http://www.billboard.com/articles/news/1063499/bonnaroo-organizers -purchasing-festival-site.

Wallace, Bill. "LSD Maker Gets 5 Years Added to 1976 Sentence." *San Francisco Chronicle,* January 23, 1999.

Wasson, R. Gordon. "Seeking the Magic Mushroom." *Life,* June 10, 1957, 113.

While We're Young. Directed by Noah Baumbach, 2014.

Wieners, Brad. "Hot Mess." *Outside Online,* August 24, 2012. http://www.outsideonline .com/1925281/hot-mess.

Wilkinson, Peter. "The Acid King." *Rolling Stone,* July 5, 2001, 113.

Wingfield, Larry. "A Gift from Steve Jobs Returns Home." *New York Times. Bits* (blog), November 20, 2013, http://bits.blogs.nytimes.com/2013/11/20/a-gift-from -steve-jobs-returns-home/

Wolfe, Tom. Tom Wolfe papers. New York Public Library. Manuscripts and Archives Division.

Yippie, A. "A Brief History of the NYC Cannabis Parade." https://web.archive.org /web/20140210184412/http://cannabisparade.org/history-of-the-parade/.

Zuckerman, Gabrielle. "An Interview with Steve Reich." *American Public Media,* July 2002.

Notes

Introduction: The Long Renaissance

ix   **cluster headaches:** R. A. Sewell, J. H. Halpern, and H. G. Pope Jr., "Response of Cluster Headaches to Psilocybin and LSD," *Neurology*, June 27, 2006, 1920.

ix   **posttraumatic stress disorder:** Tom Shroder, "The Case for Using Psychedelics to Treat PTSD, Depression," *Washington Post*, September 4, 2014.

ix   **terminal illness:** Michael Pollan, "The Trip Treatment," *New Yorker*, February 9, 2015.

ix   **fashionable urban areas:** Bob Morris, "Ayahuasca: A Strong Cup of Tea," *New York Times*, June 13, 2014.

ix   **cinematic satire:** *While We're Young*, directed by Noah Baumbach, 2014.

x   ***extra* glow:** Arianne Cohen, "My Journey with a Life Altering Drug: Ayahuasca," *ELLE*, November 2012, http://www.elle.com/beauty/health-fitness/advice/a14193/ayahuasca-drug/.

x   **some no longer even use:** Jim DeKoerne, editorial, *Entheogen Review*, Winter Solstice 1992, 1.

x   **four-stage model:** Thomas Roberts, "Four Stages of the Psychedelic Renaissance: An Op-Ed Essay," Academia.edu, May 2015, http://www.academia.edu/11144663/Four_Stages_of_the_Psychedelic_Renaissance_An_Op-ed_Essay.

xi   **most are white:** Leigh A. Henderson and William J. Glass, *LSD: Still with Us After All These Years* (New York: Lexington, 1994), 81–82.

Chapter One: Humbead's Revised Map of the World

   Primary interviews: Peter Stampfel, Ed Sanders, Sandy Rothman, Ramon Sender, Rhoney Stanley, Tim Scully, Mark McCloud, Earl Crabb, and Rick Shubb.

3   **around the Village:** Martin Torgoff, *Can't Find My Way Home: America in the Great Stoned Age, 1945–2000* (New York: Simon & Schuster, 2004), 61.

3   **written partially under the influence:** Allen Ginsberg, "Notes Written on Finally Recording *Howl*," *Evergreen Review* 3, no.10 (1959): 132.

4   **the owner splits:** Edward C. Burks, "Peyote Peddler at Odds with U.S.," *New York Times*, June 23, 1960, 33.

4   **San Remo crowd:** Robert McG. Thomas Jr., "Anton Rosenberg, a Hipster Ideal, Dies at 71," *New York Times*, February 22, 1998, 39.

4   **over 10,000 years:** Weston La Barre, *The Peyote Cult* (Hamden, CT: Archon Books, 1975), 258.

4   **Across the Rio Grande:** ibid., 64.

5   **Civil War prisoners:** ibid., 15.

5   **patent medicines:** Philip Robson, *Forbidden Drugs* (Oxford: Oxford University, 1994), 103.

5   **After sitting with closed eyes:** La Barre, 141.

5   **Just a few years:** Douglas Martin, "Humphry Osmond, 86, Who Sought Medicinal Value in Psychedelic Drugs, Dies," *New York Times,* February 22, 2004, 25.

5   **its correct usage:** Stephen Siff, *Acid Hype: American News Media and the Psychedelic Experience* (Urbana: University of Illinois Press, 2015), 44.

6   **circulation 5,700,000:** ibid., 68.

6   **Wasson's *Life* cover:** R. Gordon Wasson, "Seeking the Magic Mushroom," *Life,* June 10, 1957, 113.

6   **Jane Ross:** Siff, 85.

6   **Another magazine discovers:** ibid., 66.

6   **Captain Al Hubbard:** Martin A. Lee and Bruce Shlain, *Acid Dreams: The Complete Social History of LSD; The CIA, the Sixties, and Beyond* (New York: Grove Weidenfeld, 1992), 54.

6   **MKUltra:** ibid., 12.

6   **Cary Grant:** Laura Bergquist, "The Curious Story Behind the New Cary Grant," *Look,* September 1, 1959.

7   **I'm higher than:** "Mother Is Bugged at Me," *Time,* July 7, 1952, 21.

7   **Sending in undercover:** "'Lay Off Peyote' Beatniks Warned," *United Press International,* June 30, 1960.

8   **Word reaches:** La Barre, 230.

8   **Bruchlos is found dead:** "Cafe Owner Found Dead," *New York Times,* December 7, 1960, 43.

8   **One chemical supply house:** La Barre, 231.

8   **John Beresford:** Robert Greenfield, *Timothy Leary: A Biography* (New York: Harcourt, 2006), 163.

9   **Miracle at Marsh Chapel:** Walter N. Pahnke, "Drugs and Mysticism," *International Journal of Parapsychology,* Spring 1966, 295.

9   **Huxley, too, especially encourages:** Jeffrey J. Kripal, *Esalen: America and the Religion of No Religion* (Chicago: University of Chicago, 2007), 85.

9   **small LSD cults:** Antonio Escohotado, *A Brief History of Drugs: From the Stone Age to the Stoned Age* (Rochester, VT: Park Street, 1996), 117.

9   **good head:** Richard Blum, *Utopiates: The Use & Users of LSD 25* (New York: Atherton, 1964), 73.

9   **Hallucinogen users are recognized:** ibid., 231.

10   **When they meet:** *The Holy Modal Rounders: Bound to Lose,* directed by Sam Wainwright Douglas and Paul Lovelace, 2006.

10   **A CALL TO ACTION:** Ed Sanders, "A Call to Action," *Fuck You / a magazine of the arts,* no. 10, 1964, 1.

11   **Nobody confesses:** Tom Wolfe, *The Electric Kool-Aid Acid Test* (New York: Farrar Strauss Giroux, 1968), 199.

11   **They arrive at the rally:** Vic Lovell, "The Perry Lane Papers: A Prologue," *Free You,* June 1969, 20.

13   **Votes for the last time:** Dennis McNally, *A Long Strange Trip: The Inside History of the Grateful Dead* (New York: Broadway, 2002), 75.

13   **He splits with his wife:** Blair Jackson, *Garcia: An American Life* (New York: Viking, 1999), 114.

13   **with whom Lesh:** Gabrielle Zuckerman, "An Interview with Steve Reich," *American Public Media,* July 2002.

14   **beginning of the Grateful Dead:** David W. Bernstein, *The San Francisco Tape Music Center: 1960s Counterculture and the Avant-Garde* (Berkeley: University of California, 2008), 244.

14 **A few weeks after:** Fred Turner, *From Counterculture to Cyberculture: Stewart Brand, the Whole Earth Network, and the Rise of Digital Utopianism* (Chicago: University of Chicago, 2006), 69.

15 **Drop City:** ibid., 75.

15 **Nature Boys:** Patrick Lundborg, *Psychedelia: An Ancient Culture, a Modern Way of Life* (Stockholm: Lysergia, 2012), 345.

16 **The old guard grumbles:** Lee and Shlain, 88.

16 **In Menlo Park:** Turner, 61.

16 **250 Heavenly Blue seeds:** Bruce Eisner, "Interview with an Alchemist: Bear: Owsley, LSD Chemist Extraordinaire, In Conversation with Bruce Eisner," August 2004, https://web.archive.org/web/20041128235352/http://www.bruce eisner.com/writings/2004/08/interview_with__2.html.

17 **1.25 million hits:** McNally, 118.

17 **All the equipment:** Eisner, 2004.

18 **His first big investment:** McNally, 132.

18 **A dozen or so:** Phil Lesh, *Searching for the Sound: My Life with the Grateful Dead* (New York: Little, Brown, 2005), 84.

18 *More Than Human:* Nick Schou, *Orange Sunshine: The Brotherhood of Eternal Love and Its Quest to Spread Peace, Love, and Acid to the World* (New York: Thomas Dunne, 2010), 62.

18 **heads from around Austin:** Lundborg, 255.

18 **Holy Modal Rounders:** Paul Drummond, *Eye Mind: The Saga of Roky Erickson and the 13th Floor Elevators, the Pioneers of Psychedelic Sound* (Los Angeles: Process, 2011), 27.

19 **Third Voice:** Margaret Moser, "She Lives: The Clementine Hall Interview," *Austin Chronicle*, August 20, 2004.

19 **play the acid:** Ben Graham, *A Gathering of Promises: The Battle for Texas's Psychedelic Music* (Winchester, UK: Zero, 2015), 78.

19 **sometimes scheduling:** Drummond, 162.

19 *always* **take acid:** *The Other One: The Long Strange Trip of Bob Weir*, directed by Sam Fleiss, 2014.

20 **in the old days:** Blair Jackson and David Gans, *This Is All a Dream We Dreamed: An Oral History of the Grateful Dead* (New York: Flatiron, 2015), 50.

20 **interacting waves of color:** Augustus Owsley Stanley, "Southern California Sojourn," *Relix*, August 2005, http://www.relix.com/articles/detail/southern-cal ifornia-sojourn-by-owsley-bear-stanley.

20 **There's nothing wrong:** Lesh, 83.

20 **If Garcia doesn't:** Danny Holloway, "Dead Come Alive," *NME*, April 15, 1972.

20 **hip economics:** Jerry Garcia and Charles A. Reich, *Garcia: A Signpost to a New Space* (San Francisco: Straight Arrow, 1972), 35.

21 **Al Dente:** Steve Silberman, "Who Was Cowboy Neal?," *Golden Road*, Spring 1989, 28.

21 **free-floating lifestyle:** Ed Sanders, "A Biographic Appreciation of Wavy Gravy for His 70th Birthday," *Woodstock Journal*, May 15, 2006, 12.

21 **Lysergic a-Go-Go:** Paul J. Robbins, "Lysergic A Go-Go as It Went," *Los Angeles Free Press*, November 26, 1965, 3.

21 **coming to a head:** Wavy Gravy at Hampshire College, February 25, 1984.

21 **frequent trips back:** Drummond, 149.

22 **one researcher would discover:** Siff, 151.

22   **Capsule Corner:** Stewart Tendler and David May, *The Brotherhood of Eternal Love: From Flower Power to Hippie Mafia; The Story of the LSD Counterculture* (London: Panther, 1984), 75.

22   **Exploding Threat:** "The Exploding Threat of the Mind Drug That Got Out of Control," *Life,* March 25, 1966, 21.

23   **When the band:** Jackson and Gans, 57.

23   **72 million:** Tendler and May, 102.

23   **primary trustworthy dealers:** Jay Stevens, *Storming Heaven: LSD and the American Dream* (New York: Atlantic Monthly, 1987), 318.

23   **I felt that:** Eisner 2004.

24   **Owsley's money is:** Charles Perry, *The Haight-Ashbury: A History* (New York: Random House, 1984), 81.

24   **Hip capitalism:** Michael Kramer, *The Republic of Rock: Music and Citizenship in the Sixties Counterculture* (Oxford: Oxford University Press, 2013), xv.

25   **As part of the city's:** *Money Is an Unnecessary Evil* (Digger broadsheet; San Francisco: Comm/Co, 1966).

25   **They issue a single:** McNally, 153.

25   **One psychedelic therapist:** Alexander T. Shulgin and Ann Shulgin, *Pihkal: A Chemical Love Story* (Berkeley, CA: Transform Press, 1991), 72.

26   **One underground researcher:** Paul DeRienzo and Dana Beal, *Report on the Staten Island Project: The Ibogaine Story* (Brooklyn, NY: Autonomedia, 1997), 19.

26   **debunked within months:** L. Bender and D. V. Siva Sankar, "Chromosome Damage Not Found in Leukocytes of Children Treated with LSD-25," *Science,* February 16, 1968, 159.

26   **future of LSD:** Lisa Bieberman, "The Psychedelic Experience," *New Republic,* August 5, 1967, 17.

26   **psychedelic conference:** Stevens, 182.

26   **Under strict secrecy:** Myron J. Stolaroff, *The Secret Chief Revealed,* (Sarasota, FL: Multidisciplinary Association for Psychedelic Studies, 2004), 52.

26   **If you don't know:** ibid., 138.

27   **From the moment:** Alvaro Estrada, *María Sabina: Her Life and Chants* (Santa Barbara, CA: Ross-Erikson, 1981), 90.

27   **Microbuses:** Richard Gehr, "An Interview with Jerry Garcia," *Newsday,* September 9, 1991.

27   **parade:** McNally, 198

27   **3,000 onlookers:** "Return of the Hippies," *Newsday,* June 2, 1967.

27   **Another east coast:** A. Yippie, "A Brief History of the NYC Cannabis Parade," https://web.archive.org/web/20140210184412/http://cannabisparade.org/history-of-the-parade/.

28   **John Perry Barlow:** Linda Kelly, *Deadheads: Stories from Fellow Artists, Friends, and Followers of the Grateful Dead* (Secaucus, NJ: Carol, 1995), 64.

28   **Who said we are all:** Jeremy Alderson, "Portrait of an Artist as a Young Tripper," *Relix,* August 2008, 56.

28   **Emilio's:** Tom Wolfe, Tom Wolfe papers, New York Public Library, Manuscripts and Archives Division, b. 111.

28   **Inter-Tribal Community Benefit:** Rock Scully, *Lost Live Dead,* blog comment, December 16, 2009, http://lostlivedead.blogspot.com/2009/12/june-1-1967-tompkins-square-park-new.html?showComment=1260988832872#c4798606218581362167.

28   **their people:** Richard Goldstein, "Scenes," *Village Voice,* June 15, 1967.

31   **While a whole penumbra:** Fred Davis with Laura Munoz, "Heads and Freaks: Patterns and Meanings of Drug Use Among Hippies," *Journal of Health and Social Behavior,* June 1968, 156.

31   **early studies suggest:** Gretchen Lemke-Santangelo, *Daughters of Aquarius: Women of the Sixties Counterculture* (Lawrence: University Press of Kansas, 2009), 116.

31   **Japan's chief LSD acolyte:** Julian Cope, "Acid Seven," http://www.japrock sampler.com/artists/.../acid_seven/.

31   **In the next years:** Lemke-Santangelo, 132.

32   **Fillmore Far East:** Kramer, 8.

32   **Orange Sunshine:** Lee and Shlain, 242.

32   **manufacturers of Clear Light:** Keith Martin-Smith, *A Heart Blown Open: The Life and Practice of Zen Master Jun Po Denis Kelly Roshi* (Studio City, CA: Divine Arts, 2011), 109.

33   **busted in late '67:** Leonard Pickard, "FOIA Requests Helpful to the Defense Bar, District and Appellate Courts, and Public Interest Groups," http://www .freeleonardpickard.org/DEA-FOIA-Requests.html.

33   **Kodachrome-X 5–20:** Collection of the Institute of Illegal Images, San Francisco, CA.

33   **By late '68:** Edward Kirkman and Henry Lee, "Raid Hippie Cult, Seize $6M Dope," *New York Daily News,* September 27, 1968, 5.

33   **nabbed with fifteen grams:** United States v. Southworth Wells Swede, 326 F. Supp. 533, No. 70, CR. 737, 1971.

33   **LSD dipped on string:** Rak Razam, "Blotter Art: The Institute of Illegal Images," *Juxtapoz,* September 6, 2009, http://www.juxtapoz.com/current /blotter-art-the-institute-of-illegal-images.

33   **Brotherhood of Eternal Love:** Lundborg, 208. Schou, 41.

33   **hash importing business:** Schou, 88.

34   **massive dose of Windowpane:** Martin-Smith, 112.

35   **Free City Convention:** Ben Fong-Torres, "Love Is Just a Song We Sing but a Contract Is Something Else," *Rolling Stone,* February 26, 1976, 58.

35   **Free City Collective:** The Diggers, *Realist,* August 1968, 15.

36   **A Free Store had opened:** Ed Sanders, *Fug You: An Informal History of the Peace Eye Bookstore, the Fuck You Press, and the Counterculture in the Lower East Side* (Cambridge, MA: Da Capo, 2011), 74.

36   **Godland in seclusion:** Abolafia, "Woodstock '68," *East Village Other,* August 2, 1968, 3.

36   **As the season changes:** Turner, 71.

37   **We are as gods:** Stewart Brand, *Whole Earth Catalog,* 1968.

38   **arrival of cocaine:** Dominic Streatfield, *Cocaine: An Unauthorized Biography* (New York: Thomas Dunne, 2002), 197.

38   **six in the morning:** Lenny Kaye, "The Year of the Dead," *Fusion,* November 14, 1969.

39   **Prospect Park Be-In:** Advertisement, *East Village Other,* October 8, 1969.

39   **psychedelic crucifixion:** Sanders, 319.

39   **They started playing:** Patti Smith at Alumni Stadium, Amherst, MA, May 12, 1979 (opening for the Grateful Dead).

Chapter Two: Dead Freaks Unite

Primary interviews: Chad Stickney, Mark McCloud, John Coate, Cliff Figallo, Matthew McClure, Marty Weinberg, Donna Jean Godchaux Mackay, Harvey Lubar, Gary Lambert, Garrick Beck, Rhoney Stanley, Ramon Sender, Les Kippel, and Gil Levey.

42 **the great demand:** Jaakov Kohn, "Sunshine Superman!" *East Village Other*, June 11, 1969, 5.

42 **into the suburbs:** Lundborg, 212.

42 **4.5 million:** Leonard Pickard, "International LSD Prevalence—Factors Affecting Proliferation and Control," 2008, http://freeleonardpickard.org/LSD -Prevelance.html.

42 **bunch of loose cannons:** Schou, 61.

43 **cut their hair:** ibid., 81, 132.

43 **Mafioso:** Tendler and May, 172.

43 **French labs:** ibid., 182.

43 **sometimes hidden:** Lyn Ebenezer, *Operation Julie: The World's Greatest LSD Bust* (Talybont, Wales: Ylolfa, 2010), 133.

43 **Tord Svenson:** Pickard 2008.

43 **putting up the money:** Schou, 231.

43 **Rainbow Island commune:** ibid., 213.

44 **The day they bust:** Timothy Miller, *The 60s Communes, Hippies and Beyond* (Syracuse, NY: Syracuse University, 1999), 120.

45 **not the subject:** Monte Dym and Bob Alson, "The Man Behind the Words, part 2," *Relix*, May 1978, 21.

45 **I fell in love:** Stephen Gaskin, "Some DMT," *Amazing Dope Tales* (Summertown, TN: Book Publishing, 1980).

45 **blew me away:** Lemke-Santangelo, 68.

45 **taking these huge group:** John Coate, "Life on the Bus and Farm: An Informal Recollection," 1987, http://cervisa.com/stories/farm.txt.

46 **hippies probably constituted:** Miller, xiii.

47 **I had women:** Lemke-Santangelo, 108.

47 **last free outdoor concert:** Corry Arnold, "October 21, 1972: Alumni Lawn, Vanderbilt University, Nashville, TN, The Grateful Dead (Last Free Concert)," *Lost Live Dead*, April 4, 2013, http://lostlivedead.blogspot.com/2013/04/october-21-1972-alumni-lawn-vanderbilt.html.

47 **In Berkeley:** Dennis J. McKenna, *The Brotherhood of the Screaming Abyss: My Life with Terence McKenna* (St. Cloud, MN: North Star, 2012), 302.

47 **a set of procedures:** ibid., 251.

48 **satire:** Donald Barthelmé, "The Teachings of Don B.: A Yankee Way of Knowledge," *New York Times Magazine*, February 11, 1973, 14; Calvin Tomkins, "The Teachings of Joe Pye," *New Yorker*, February 3, 1973, 37.

49 **Courtenay Pollock:** "All in the Family: Courtenay Pollock," Grateful Dead YouTube channel, 2013, https://www.youtube.com/watch?v=kBAqkVC9uAg.

50 **five hundred copies:** Basho Katzenjammer, "Grateful Dead Pig Backlash," *East Village Other*, September 5, 1971.

50 **The Grateful Dead isn't:** Grateful Dead, "The Book of the Dead," distributed in London, May 1972.

50 **Regulars greeted other regulars:** Robert Christgau, "Dead Heads Pay Their Dues," in David G. Dodd and Diana Spaulding, eds., *The Grateful Dead Reader* (New York: Oxford University Press, 2000), 100.

52   **confusing combination:** Christgau in Dodd and Spaulding, 100.

53   **Check the tapes:** "greater than true loving" corrects to "cradled by two loving arms," Grateful Dead at Felt Forum, NYC, December 4–5, 1971, https://archive.org/details /gd1971-12-04.sbd.fixed.miller.110186.flac16, https://archive.org/details/gd71-12 -05.prefm.miller.3391.sbeok.shnf.

54   **The Loft:** Tim Lawrence, *Love Saves the Day: A History of American Dance Music Culture, 1970–1979* (Durham, NC: Duke University, 2003), 10.

55   **The first Bardo:** ibid., 85.

55   **Layton Avenue:** "NYC Street Gangs 1960's, 70's, & 80's Guestbook," 2005– 2006, https://web.archive.org/web/20050827201504/http://www.guestbookdepot .com/php/guestbook.php?book_id=579761.

55   **The Counter-Coalition:** "The Counter-coalition," *New York Post,* undated clipping, circa spring 1972.

56   **A local congressman:** "Biaggi Meets with Leaders of Bronx Street Gangs," *New York Times,* April 22, 1972, 19.

56   **denim Grateful Dead jacket:** "Flaming Youth Scores Big," *Daily News,* undated clipping, circa April 1972.

57   **The camp was split:** Tim Cahill, "Acid Crawlback Fest: Armageddon Postponed," *Rolling Stone,* August 3, 1972, 1.

58   **kitchens feed 15,000:** ibid.

58   **there to be snarky:** ibid.

58   **Naked Pole Guy:** *Sunshine Daydream,* directed by John Norris, 1972, released on Rhino, 2012.

59   **invisible time-travelers:** Jackson 1999, 171.

59   **The backstory reads:** Nicholas G. Meriwether, "The Field Trip, Kesey's Creamery & the Last Acid Test," *Sunshine Daydream,* Rhino, 2012, 12.

59   **he'd sent Ken Babbs:** Miller, 20.

59   **community, not a commune:** Michael Godwin, "The Ken Kesey Movie," *Rolling Stone,* March 7, 1970, 24.

59   **organized by Amorphia:** Joshua Clark Davis, "The Business of Getting High: Head Shops, Countercultural Capitalism, and the Marijuana Legalization Movement," *The Sixties: A Journal of History, Politics and Culture* 8, no.1 (2015), 1.

60   **magic mushroom scene:** Lundborg, 190.

60   **left their North Beach:** Martin-Smith, 175.

60   **open-ended Grateful Dead:** Rachel Rubin, *Well Met Renaissance Faires and the American Counterculture* (New York: New York University, 2012), 133.

61   **Chez Panisse:** Lemke-Santangelo, 91.

61   **Brand's influence:** Sam Binkley, *Getting Loose: Lifestyle Consumption in the 1970s* (Durham, NC: Duke University, 2007), 118.

61   **homemade marzipan Easter eggs:** Lemke-Santangelo, 107.

63   **kind of continuity:** Steve Peacock, "Jerry Garcia in London," *Rock,* July 17, 1972, 16.

64   **$3.50 tickets:** *Grateful Days* bonus documentary, *Sunshine Daydream* DVD, Rhino, 2012.

65   **very true stories:** Sam Cutler, *You Can't Always Get What You Want: My Life with the Rolling Stones, the Grateful Dead and Other Wonderful Reprobates* (Toronto: ECW Press, 2010), 259.

65   **It was okay acid:** United Press International, "1,000 at Concert Drink LSD-Spiked Cider," *Los Angeles Times,* June 1, 1971.

65   **If we had it:** Grateful Dead, "Dead Heads Unite!," newsletter, March 1972.

70   **On the radio:** Grateful Dead at Winterland, KSAN broadcast, December 31, 1972, https://archive.org/details/gd1972-12-31.sbd.bertha-ashley.26559.sbeok.shnf.

71   **On the floor:** Tendler and May, 235.

71   **massive three-state:** Schou, 267.

71   **The previous New Year's:** "Guest List—Winterland '71," December 31, 1971. http://www.dead.net/archives/1971/clippings/guest-list-winterland-71-6-6.

Chapter Three: Beyond the Whole Earth

Primary interviews: Les Earnest, Paul Martin, Andy Moorer, Ron Turner, Steve Brown, Les Kippel, Harvey Lubar, Ned Lagin, Pat Lee, Mark McCloud, and Dave Wilkins.

73   **It's an idyllic spot:** John Markoff, *What the Dormouse Said: How the Sixties Counterculture Shaped the Personal Computer Industry* (New York: Viking, 2005), 81.

73   **These are heads:** Stewart Brand, "Fanatic Life and Symbolic Death Among the Computer Bums," *Rolling Stone,* December 7, 1972, 58.

73   **In the lobby:** Markoff, 81.

75   **most bzz-bzz-busy:** Brand 1972.

75   **the hacker ethic:** Steven Levy, *Hackers: Heroes of the Computer Revolution* (Garden City, NY: Anchor Press/Doubleday, 1984), 39.

75   **pot sale:** Markoff, 109.

76   **nitrous-abetted party:** ibid., 195.

76   **It's free advertising:** Stewart Brand, Stewart Brand papers, Stanford University Library, Manuscripts Division, b. 6a.

76   **In one memory:** Ron Shannon, "GD at Maples Pavilion," Grateful Dead, February 9, 1973, https://archive.org/details/gd1973-02-09.sbd.ashley.12571.shnf.

78   **baby carriage on Haight:** Peter Carlson, "After Some Tough Years, the Legendary '60s Cartoonist Is Truckin' Again," *People,* June 24, 1985, 75.

78   **Canadian paper mill strike:** Jean Gabilliet and Bart Beaty, *Of Comics and Men: A Cultural History of American Comic Books* (Jackson, MA: University Press of Mississippi, 2009), 80.

78   **It just slowly:** Patrick Rosenkranz, "Zap: An Unpublished Spain Rodriguez Interview," *Comics Journal,* November 24, 2014, http://www.tcj.com/unpublished-spain-rodriguez-interview/.

78   **only British festival:** "Phun City Is Yours to Make It," *International Times,* July 17, 1970, 8.

79   **tried to get the Dead:** Andy Roberts, *Albion Dreaming: A Popular History of LSD in Britain* (London: Marshall Cavendish, 2008), 188.

79   **Starting in late 1971:** ibid., 215.

79   **new, cheaper method:** Stevens, 288.

79   **the microdots burst eastward:** Andy Roberts 2008, 189; Tendler and May, 256, 268; Martin A. Lee, *Smoke Signals: A Social History of Marijuana; Medical, Recreational, and Scientific* (New York: Scribner, 2012), 243.

79   **Richard Kemp channels funds:** Tendler and May, 250.

79   **Trentishoe Whole Earth Fayre:** "Trentishoe Whole Earth Fayre," http://www.ukrockfestivals.com/trentishoe-73.html; Andy Roberts 2008, 205.

79   **White tab:** *Windsor Freep,* August 26, 1973.

80   **man with a briefcase:** Andy Roberts 2008, 194.

81   **Nancy's Honey Yogurt:** Jackson and Gans, 235.

81   **25,000 names:** Alan Trist, "State of the Changes," in Dodd and Spaulding, 95.

81 **What else might we do?:** *Dead Heads Newsletter,* May 1973, 5.

81 **They get letters:** Grateful Dead Archive, McHenry Library, UC Santa Cruz, Special Collections and Archives, MS 332, Ser. 5, Correspondence: 1973.

82 **There's this overworked:** Grateful Dead Archive, McHenry Library, UC Santa Cruz, Special Collections and Archives, MS 332, Ser. 2, Business: 1972.

84 **Atlantic Records:** McNally, 452.

84 **The question is:** Garcia and Reich, 82.

85 **Music is my yoga:** Peter Simon, "Making Music Miracles," *New Age Journal,* May 1975, 53.

85 **Mountain Girl:** Lee, 175.

86 **pirate radio broadcast:** "JR," "The History of CFR Concert Freedom Radio," http://www.hartfordradiohistory.com/Concert_Free_Radio_-_CFR.html.

86 **when the temperature drops:** Michael M. Getz and John R. Dwork, *The Deadhead's Taping Compendium: An In-depth Guide to the Music of the Grateful Dead on Tape, 1959–1974* (New York: Henry Holt, 1998), 21.

87 **Gilbert Youth Research:** Clinton Heylin, *Bootleg: The Secret History of the Other Recording Industry* (New York: St. Martin's, 1995), 260.

87 **buries his equipment:** Jeremy Witt, "Notes," Grateful Dead, May 25, 1974. https://archive.org/details/gd1974-05-25.aud.gems.111301.flac16.

88 **36-point lead type-slug:** Owsley Stanley, "Bear Story." http://www.thebear.org/bearstory.html.

89 **Owsley watches:** Tendler and May, 243.

89 **splits entirely:** Eric Brazil, "Drug Lord Sentenced After 20-Year Flight," *San Francisco Examiner,* January 22, 1999.

89 **leading a car chase:** *The Sunshine Makers,* directed by Cosmo Feilding-Mellen, 2015.

90 **they raise goats:** Andy Roberts 2008, 231.

90 **flush themselves:** Martin-Smith, 183.

90 **lab in Moscow:** "Turning On in Moscow," *Kansas City Times,* November 13, 1972.

90 **Dr. Benway:** Levy, 178.

93 **spills the acid:** Markoff, 109.

94 **Over Memorial Day:** Will Hermes, *Love Goes to Buildings on Fire: Five Years in New York That Changed Music Forever* (New York: Faber and Faber, 2011), 66.

94 **nude harvest celebrations:** Ray Raphael, *Cash Crop: An American Dream* (Mendocino, CA: Ridge Times, 1985), 45.

94 **We were looking:** Torgoff, 286.

94 **listening to Dead radio:** Freeman House, *Totem Salmon Life Lessons from Another Species* (Boston: Beacon Press, 1999), 1.

94 **You could trade it:** Raphael, 50.

95 **pull all the males:** Emily Brady, *Humboldt: Life on America's Marijuana Frontier* (New York: Grant Central, 2013), 69.

95 **checking out Bob Marley:** Jackson 1999, 237.

95 **the Waldos:** Steve Bloom, "420 or Fight," *High Times,* December 1998, 12.

96 **Cokehead:** *Oxford English Dictionary,* June 2004.

96 **mysterious plane crashes:** "News," *High Times,* June 1974, 28.

96 **Wally:** Andy Roberts 2008, 200.

97 **I WANT TO DISTROY:** ibid., 197.

Chapter Four: Shakedown Street

Primary interviews: Bill Harmon, John Cederquist, Chad Stickney, Carol Latvala, Pat Lee, Charly Mann, Steve Brown, Ned Lagin, Mark McCloud, David Gans, Blair Jackson, and Steve Silberman.

105   **war on graffiti:** Dimitri Ehrlich and Gregor Ehrlich, "Graffiti in Its Own Words," *New York,* June 2006, http://nymag.com/guides/summer/17406/.

107   **Show has to be stopped:** Jefferson Starship, *Live in Central Park, NYC, May 12, 1975,* Real Gone, 2012.

108   **be soaked in luscious beauty:** Dick Latvala journal, May 1975 journal, courtesy Carol Latvala.

108   **Ponzi scheme:** David Felton and Robin Green, *Mindfuckers: A Source Book on the Rise of Acid Fascism in America, Including Material on Charles Manson, Mel Lyman, Victor Baranco, and Their Followers* (San Francisco: Straight Arrow Books, 1972), 18.

109   **My basic flash:** Dick Latvala audio journal, summer 1975, courtesy of Carol Latvala.

111   **I have come to discover:** Dick Latvala, "Letters," *Dead Relix,* September 1975, 1.

112   **In another correspondence:** Steve Silberman, "Primal Dead at the Fillmore East," in Dodd and Spaulding, 45.

113   **I used to walk:** Steve Silberman, "Interview with Dick Latvala, 3/5/95," posted rec.music.gdead and elsewhere, e.g., https://www.cs.cmu.edu/~./gdead/latvala.html.

113   **Ragusa:** Roger Rapoport, "The Sunshine Murders," *New West,* April 21, 1980, 35.

113   **on the run:** Martin-Smith, 191.

115   **a lot of screaming:** Steve Brown, "If I Told You All That Went Down . . . a Fond Look Back at Grateful Dead Records," *Golden Road,* Spring 1986, 21.

117   **We slept whenever:** Johnny Crunch, "West Side Stories," Facebook, April 22, 2010.

119   **direct-to-fan:** McNally, 492.

119   **There are entire contingents:** Monte Dym, "The Dead Tour: A Social Look," *Relix,* September 1976, 22.

120   **guerrilla inoculations:** Andy Letcher, *Shroom: A Cultural History of the Magic Mushroom* (London: Faber and Faber, 2006), 223.

120   **tiny psychedelic cabal:** Hakim Bey, foreword to Thomas Lyttle, *Psychedelics Reimagined* (Brooklyn, NY: Autonomedia, 1999), 9.

122   **dope famine:** Hermes, 186.

122   **head-funded arts complex:** Brady, 87.

122   **quasi-Rastafarian guys:** Raphael, 67.

123   **Bob Dylan reel-to-reel:** Walter Isaacson, *Steve Jobs* (New York: Simon & Schuster, 2011), 25.

125   **rumors on WNEW:** Les Kippel, "The Making and Breaking of a Rumor," *Relix,* July 1977, 19.

125   **the T-shirts:** John Gruen, *Keith Haring: The Authorized Biography* (New York: Prentice Hall Press, 1991), 25.

126   **Keith was a town freak:** David Frankel, "Keith Haring's American Beauty," in Sussman and Haring, 60.

126   **The drawing I did:** Haring, *Keith Haring Journals* (New York: Viking, 1996), 105.

128   **producer Keith Olsen:** Jackson 1999, 282.

128   **$50 a week:** David Browne, "The Grateful Dead's Greatest Year," *Rolling Stone,* July 4, 2013, http://www.rollingstone.com/music/news/the-grateful-deads-great est-year-2013062.

129   **A strong candidate:** Jerry Moore, "Spring Tour Again," *Relix,* July 1977, 16.

131   **Everything was spiked:** Jacob Arnold, "The Warehouse: The Place House Music Got Its Name," *Resident Advisor,* May 16, 2012, http://www.residentadvisor .net/feature.aspx?1597.

131   **dose the punch:** Simon Reynolds, *Generation Ecstasy: Into the World of Techno and Rave Culture* (Boston: Little, Brown, 1998), 25.

131   **alcohol has no place:** Alexis Petridis, "Frankie Knuckles: Godfather of House Music, Priest of the Dancefloor," *Guardian,* April 1, 2014, http://www.theguard ian.com/music/2014/apr/01/frankie-knuckles-house-music-dj-producer -nightclubs.

131   **SP-303:** Michaelangelo Matos, *The Underground Is Massive: How Electronic Dance Music Conquered America* (New York: Dey Street, 2015), 18.

132   **This is turning into:** John Perry Barlow, "Thinking About the Dead: Amateur Anthropology, the Human Comedy, and Making Good Ancestors" in Nicholas G. Meriwether, *Reading the Grateful Dead* (New York: Rowman & Littlefield, 2012), 21.

132   **new psychedelic era dawns:** "LSD Now: A Generation Later," *High Times,* February 1978, 42.

132   **mushroom consortium in Washington:** Letcher, 220.

133   **up the coast:** Jonathan Ott, "World Conference on Hallucinogenic Mushrooms," *Head,* February 1978.

133   **Around 150,000:** McNally, 505.

133   **emergence of a new wave:** Dennis McNally, foreword to Adams and Sardiello, *Deadhead Social Science: "You Ain't Gonna Learn What You Don't Want to Know"* (Walnut Creek, CA: AltaMira, 2000), iii.

133   **scrap their plans:** Robert Alson, "Bob Weir Lets It Grow," *Relix,* May 1978, 8.

133   **Robert Hunter pens:** Dym and Alson, 21.

135   **scandal in Washington:** Patrick Anderson, *High in America: The True Story Behind NORML and the Politics of Marijuana* (New York: Viking, 1981), 21.

135   **freebase:** Jackson 1999, 272.

135   **Persian:** ibid., 293.

136   **Front Street Sheiks:** Blair Jackson and Regan McMahon, "Garcia's Longtime Ally Looks Back," *Golden Road,* Winter 1987, 26.

136   **We put so much:** Jackson 1999, 290.

136   **Garcia catches the keyboardist:** ibid., 293.

138   **state's biggest cash crop:** Lee, 176.

138   **Ragusa is brutally murdered:** Rapoport, 35.

139   **raising goats:** Ebenezer, 147.

139   **head politics:** Tendler and May, 250.

139   **my LSD philosophy:** Alexander Cockburn, "Busted: 'Half the World's Acid Supply,'" *Village Voice,* April 17, 1978, 1.

140   **largest clandestine drugs laboratory:** *State, Justice, Commerce, the Judiciary, and Related Agencies Appropriations, Fiscal Year 1978* (Washington, DC: US Government Printing Office, 1977), 969.

140   **750,000 hits:** Katy Butler, "LSD Is Back—After a Long Trip," *San Francisco Chronicle,* October 26, 1979, 1.

140   **CHEMISTS REUNITE:** Andy Roberts 2008, insert.

140   **product from California:** Ebenezer, 152.

140   **voicing concerns:** Bruce Eisner, "Cleanliness Is Next to Godheadliness," *High Times,* January 1977, 73.

143   **dance-floor population:** Graham St. John, "DJ Goa Gil: Kalifornian Exile, Dark Yogi and Dreaded Anomaly," *Dancecult: Journal of Electronic Dance Music Culture,* November 20, 2011, 97.

143   **twenty-five people:** McNally, 529.

144   **we knew people:** Dennis McNally, "Meditations on the Grateful Dead," in Dodd and Spaulding, 167.

144   **There's Larry:** Blair Jackson, "Dead Heads: A Strange Tale of Love, Devotion and Surrender," in Dodd and Spaulding, 150.

145   **Another early donor:** Larry Wingfield, "A Gift from Steve Jobs Returns Home," *New York Times, Bits* (blog), November 20, 2013. http://bits.blogs .nytimes.com/2013/11/20/a-gift-from-steve-jobs-returns-home/.

145   **psychedelicized engineer:** "Bob Barsotti, John Meyer, Dan Healy and More," *Mix* online, October 29, 2004, http://www.mixonline.com/news/news -products/bob-barsotti-john-meyer-dan-healy-and-more/377813.

146   **Sony D5:** Michael M. Getz and John R. Dwork, *The Deadhead's Taping Compendium: An In-depth Guide to the Music of the Grateful Dead on Tape, 1975–1985* (New York: Henry Holt, 1999), 38.

146   **Sony Corporation:** John Nathan, *Sony: The Private Life* (Boston: Houghton Mifflin, 1999), 154.

147   **mescaline together:** Grateful Dead at Springfield Civic Center, MA, May 11, 1978, https://archive.org/details/gd78-05-11.aud.vernon.6317.sbeok.shnf.

147   **steel drum jam:** Grateful Dead at Cameron Indoor Stadium, NC, April 12, 1978, YouTube, https://www.youtube.com/watch?v=lmr3o0_92f0.

148   **Bill Graham's Bluecoats:** Adams.

Chapter Five: The Burning Shore

Primary interviews: Mark McCloud, Jay Blakesberg, Gordon Sharpless, Dan Levy, Sarah Matzar, Jacaeber Kastor, Eric Schwartz, Chris Calise, Ken Goffman, Marc Franklin, David Henkl-Wallace, Rick Doblin, Lee Ranaldo, John Coate, Matthew McClure, Cliff Figallo, and Doug Oade.

151   **Mount St. Helens:** "The 1980 eruptions of Mount. St. Helens, Washington, U.S. Geological Survey Professional Paper 1250," Washington, DC: US Department of the Interior, 1981.

152   **road shows:** Marilyn Ferguson, *The Aquarian Conspiracy: Personal and Social Transformation in the 1980s* (Los Angeles: J. P. Tarcher, 1980), 141.

152   **It was over:** Mary Eisenhart, "Jerry Garcia Interview: November 12, 1987," http://www.yoyow.com/marye/garcia.html.

153   **New Earth Exposition:** Warren James Belasco, *Appetite for Change: How the Counterculture Took on the Food Industry, 1966–1988* (New York: Pantheon, 1989), 106.

153   **virtual revolution:** Ferguson, 340.

153   **New England boarding schools:** David Shenk and Steve Silberman, *Skeleton Key: A Dictionary for Deadheads* (New York: Doubleday, 1994), 97.

153 **Why enter:** Jon Carroll, "A Conversation with Jerry Garcia," *Playboy Guide: Electronic Entertainment,* Spring 1982.

155 **Temple of the True Inner Light:** Peter Gorman, "Divine Smoke and God's Flesh: Psychedelics and Religion," *High Times,* January 1990, 41.

155 **Church of the Sunshine:** R. Stuart, "Entheogenic Sects Religions," *MAPS Bulletin,* Spring 2002, 17.

155 **probably 1984 or 1985:** Thomas Roberts, "Why Is Bicycle Day April 19th, Not the 16th?," 2015, https://www.academia.edu/536054/Why_Bicycle_Day_is_April_19th.

155 **Religion of Drugs:** Stuart.

155 **The LSD did help:** Rev. Ivan Stang, "Heads Up: Terence McKenna Rant," August 6, 2003, http://www.subgenius.com/bigfist/FIST2004-1/X0671_Heads_Up-_Terence_Mc.html.

158 **101 varieties:** "Trans-High Market Quotations," *High Times,* February 1980, 30.

159 **Barry Melton:** Douglas Martin, "Terence McKenna, 53, Dies; Patron of Psychedelic Drugs," *New York Times,* April 9, 2000, 40.

159 **the entire New Age:** Terence McKenna, *The Archaic Revival: Speculations on Psychedelic Mushrooms, the Amazon, Virtual Reality, UFOs, Evolution, Shamanism, the Rebirth of the Goddess, and the End of History* (San Francisco: HarperSanFrancisco, 1991), 12.

160 **The technique:** Erik Davis, "Terence McKenna's Last Trip," *Wired,* May 2000, 156.

160 **spacey science fiction:** Brian Akers, "Concerning Terence McKenna's Stoned Apes," *Reality Sandwich,* 2011, http://realitysandwich.com/89329/terence_mckennas_stoned_apes/.

160 **I am old:** O.T. Oss and O. N. Oeric. *Psilocybin, Magic Mushroom Grower's Guide; A Handbook for Psilocybin Enthusiasts* (Berkeley, CA: And/Or Press, 1976), 14.

160 **Garcia's a fan:** McNally, 115.

161 **They have *invited:*** Jonathan Ott, "Books," *High Times,* August 1976, 93.

161 **Botanical Dimensions:** Dennis McKenna, 412.

161 **Psychedelics Conference:** ibid., 394.

161 **playing host to researchers:** David Kaiser, *How the Hippies Saved Physics: Science, Counterculture, and the Quantum Revival* (New York: W. W. Norton, 2011), 109.

161 **no great accomplishment:** Terence McKenna 1991, 43.

162 **There's more heaviness:** Martin-Smith, 215.

162 **darker underworld connections:** Douglas Valentine, *The Strength of the Pack: The Personalities, Politics and Espionage Intrigues That Shaped the DEA* (Walterville, OR: Trine Day, 2010), 351.

167 **many, many people:** Gruen, 89.

167 **Grace Jones:** Ingrid Sischy, "Kid Haring," *Vanity Fair,* July 1997, 106.

167 **Department of Defense Authorization:** Shulgin and Shulgin, 438.

167 **harvest season '83:** Raphael, 104, 106; Torgoff, 288.

168 **To demand:** Shulgin and Shulgin, 440.

168 **wild-eyed:** Lee, 197.

170 **like being shot:** Jon Hanna, "The King of Blotter Art," *Entheogen Review,* Winter Solstice 2003, 109.

171 **Stark had been arrested:** Andrea Juno and V. Vale, *Pranks!* (San Francisco: Re/Search, 1987), 140.

171 **phone book:** David Black, *Acid: The Secret History of LSD* (London: Vision, 1998), 160.

171 **DEA file:** "NADDIS Index for Stark, Hadley Ronald (Deceased) (OIP Appeal #2010–0511)," July 24, 2010, http://www.scribd.com/doc/42274498/Ron-Stark-Naddis-Summary.

172 **top-grossing live act:** Blair Jackson, "Gross Facts About the Dead," *Golden Road,* Spring 1984, 30.

174 **Ray "Cat" Olsen:** Hermes, 148.

176 **Heineken years:** Jackson 1999, 322.

176 *Deadheads Directory:* Shenk and Silberman, 58.

177 **Jerry Garcia openly snorts:** Jas Obrecht, "Jerry Garcia: The Complete 1985 'Frets' Interview," *Jas Obrecht Music Archive,* https://web.archive.org/web/20100923144558/http://jasobrecht.com/jerry-garcia-the-complete-1985-interview/.

179 **time beyond history:** Will Nofke, "The Monkey Is Being Shed," *High Frontiers,* no. 1 (1984): 7.

179 **I think the concept:** "Psychedelic Science," *Horizon,* BBC, aired February 27, 1997.

180 **Origins:** John S. James, "Roll-Your-Own Religion by Computer?," *High Frontiers,* no. 1 (1984): 18.

182 **low calorie martini:** Shulgin and Shulgin, 73.

182 **special delivery:** Torgoff, 395.

182 **the same material:** Gracie and Zarkov, "LSD and MDA (and Little Lambs Eat Ivy)," *High Frontiers,* no. 2 (1985).

183 **the psychedelic experience:** Terence McKenna 1991, 54.

185 **I had forgotten:** Michael Azerrad, *Our Band Could Be Your Life: Scenes from the American Indie Underground 1981–1991* (Boston: Little, Brown, 2002), 253.

188 **Building a coalition:** DeRienzo and Beal, 35.

188 **Bill Wilson:** Amelia Hill, "LSD Could Help Alcoholics Stop Drinking, AA Founder Believed," *Guardian,* August 23, 2012, http://www.theguardian.com/science/2012/aug/23/lsd-help-alcoholics-theory.

189 **sheet of paper:** Dave Gross, "The 'Blue Star' LSD Tattoo Urban Legend Page," http://lycaeum.org/~sputnik/Tattoo/.

190 **Acid King:** David St. Clair, *Say You Love Satan* (New York: Dell, 1987), 138.

190 **LSD use ticks up:** Lloyd Johnston and Patrick M. O'Malley, *Monitoring the Future National Results on Adolescent Drug Use: Overview of Key Findings, 2000* (Bethesda, MD: National Institute on Drug Abuse, 2001), 13.

191 **the service's roots:** Katie Hafner, "The Epic Saga of the Well," *Wired,* May 1997, 98.

192 **Information wants to be free:** Markoff, 256.

192 **Joseph Campbell:** McNally, 387.

193 **Greek weekends:** Shenk and Silberman, 127.

193 **The daytime:** recording by Mike Grace and Annie Szvetecz, Grateful Dead at Greek Theater, June 21, 1986, https://archive.org/details/gd1986-06-21.fob.schoeps.grace-szvetecz.gems.98673.sbeok.flac16.

194 **Terence McKenna's going precepts:** Akers.

195 **Larry Harvey:** Brad Wieners, "Hot Mess," *Outside Online,* August 24, 2012, http://www.outsideonline.com/1925281/hot-mess.

195 **I started feeling:** David Jay Brown and Rebecca McClen Novick. *Voices from the Edge* (Freedom, CA: Crossing Press, 1995), 69.

Chapter Six: This Everlasting Spoof

Primary interviews: Richard Wright, Mike Gordon, Jim Pollock, Rick Shubb, Scott Herrick, and John Paluska.

200 **In one estimation:** David Van Deusen, "Green Mountain Communes: The Making of a Peoples' Vermont," January 15, 2008, http://www.anarkismo.net /article/7248.

200 **Paleo-American Church:** Stuart.

200 **last turn-off:** Wavy Gravy at Hampshire College, February 25, 1984.

200 **Free Vermont:** Van Deusen.

202 **Spirits and paranormal:** David Luke, "Psychoactive Substances and Paranormal Phenomena: A Comprehensive Review," *International Journal of Transpersonal Studies,* June 2012, 97.

204 **what Nancy misses:** "April 21, 1985: The Bowl in Center of Campus, Goddard College," 2010, http://phish.com/tours/dates/sun-1985-04-21-the-bowl-in-center -of-campus-goddard-college/.

205 **Are you Nancy?:** Mockingbird Foundation, *The Phish Companion: A Guide to the Band and Their Music* (San Francisco: Miller Freeman, 2000), 245.

206 **Plainfield Village Chorus:** John Bell, *Puppets, Masks, and Performing Objects* (Cambridge, MA: MIT, 2001), 53.

206 **WHY CHEAP ART:** "the WHY CHEAP ART? manifesto," Glover, VT, 1984.

207 **By the early '80s:** Bell, 59.

208 **It's a piece:** ibid., 54.

208 **In the afternoon:** various undated Bread and Puppet videos, circa mid-1980s, YouTube.

208 **Slower, slower, slower:** "An Interview with Trey Anastasio and Lars Fisk," SuperBallIX, June 6, 2011, https://web.archive.org/web/20110609232702/http:// www.superballix.com/treylars.html.

209 **Every year:** Bell, 58.

209 **Our everyday language:** Euge Erven, *Radical People's Theatre* (Bloomington: Indiana University Press, 1988), 58.

209 **occupy Wall Street:** *Early Warnings,* Green Mountain Post Films, 1980.

210 **at one with:** Richard Gehr, *The Phish Book* (New York: Villard, 1998), 143.

210 **an insane asylum:** ibid., 140.

211 **242 Main Street:** Dan Tolles, "Burlington Punk Club 242 Main at 30," *Seven Days,* January, 28, 2015, http://www.sevendaysvt.com/vermont/burlington -punk-club-242-main-at-30/Content?oid=2511201.

212 **$5,400-a-year:** Cass and Birnbaum, *Comparative Guide to American Colleges: For Students, Parents, and Counselors, 1987* (New York: Harper and Row, 1987), 158.

212 **It was . . . quiet:** "Interview with Trey Anastasio and Lars Fisk."

213 **For me:** Michael Renshaw, "Interview with Jon Fishman, July 11th 1996, Kensington, London," http://www.gadiel.com/phish/articles/fishman.html.

213 **multiple rhythms:** Gehr, 102.

213 **"Fluffhead":** ibid., 82.

215 **mushroom-inspired:** ibid., 63.

216 **Before the band break:** Phish at the Ranch, VT, May 20, 1987, YouTube, https://www.youtube.com/watch?v=Sh9Pws7mOjE.

217 **harmonically and rhythmically strange:** Trey Anastasio at Phish, Coventry, August 15, 2004, http://www.livephish.com/browse/music/0,347/Phish-mp3 -flac-download-8-15-2004-COVENTRY-Coventry-VT.

220 **After the set:** Gehr, 42.

Chapter Seven: Day of the Dead

Primary interviews: Sarah Matzar, Mark McCloud, Jacaeber Kastor, David Gans, Mary Eisenhart, Rebecca Adams, Marc Franklin, Rick Doblin, Daniel Kottke, Paul Martin, David Henkl-Wallace, Karen Horning, Carol Latvala, and Steve Silberman.

221 **There's static:** "Day of the Dead" fan-recorded DVD, July 1987.

223 **ad campaign:** Ryan Grim, *This Is Your Country on Drugs: The Secret History of Getting High in America* (Hoboken, NJ: Wiley, 2009), 108.

224 **private internal journal:** Edward Sykes Franzosa, Charles W. Harper, and James H. Crockett, "The LSD Blotter Index," *Micrograms,* July 1987, https://www.erowid.org/chemicals/lsd/lsd_blotter_microgram_1987.pdf.

226 **Can we photograph this?:** V. Vale, "Mark McCloud: In Conversation with V. Vale," *SFAQ,* March 12, 2015, http://sfaq.us/2015/03/mark-mccloud-in-conversation-with-v-vale/.

226 **high school seniors report:** Johnston and O'Malley, 13.

227 **first historically recorded male:** John Perry Barlow, "Leaving the Physical World," March 29, 1993, https://w2.eff.org/Misc/Publications/John_Perry_Barlow/HTML/leaving_the_physical_world.html.

228 **sanitarium:** Shenk and Silberman, 18.

228 **After graduation:** McNally, 393.

228 **three miles:** Barlow 1993.

228 **only one vote:** "Spring 1998 Fellows," Harvard University Institute of Politics, 1998, http://www.iop.harvard.edu/spring-1998-fellows.

228 **western campaign coordinator:** "PDF Conference 2010 Speakers," June 2010, https://personaldemocracy.com/pdf-conference-2010-june-3-5-new-york-city-speakers.

229 **I started looking:** Hugh Haggerty, "John Perry Barlow: US out of Cyberspace," *High Times,* October 1994, 59.

229 **in redneck bars:** John Perry Barlow, "Crime and Puzzlement," June 1990, https://w2.eff.org/Misc/Publications/John_Perry_Barlow/HTML/crime_and_puzzlement_1.html.

229 **informed by Weir:** Lisa Greim, "Cognitive Dissident," *Weslayan,* 1996.

230 **yellow balloons appear:** Shenk and Silberman, 316.

230 **Out East:** Adams.

230 **regularized show-map:** Dennis McNally, foreword to Adams and Sardiello, 5.

231 **the cocaine:** McNally, 555.

231 **Ben & Jerry's:** ibid., 463.

231 **450,000 tickets:** Shenk and Silberman, 125.

231 **$18 million:** Brad E. Lucas, "Bakhtinian Carnival, Corporate Capital, and the Last Decade of the Dead," in *Perspectives on the Grateful Dead: Critical Writings,* Robert Weiner (Westport, CT: Greenwood Press, 1999), 86.

232 **median age:** Shenk and Silberman, 290.

232 **Her work:** Adams.

232 **Grateful Dead outback:** Chris Vaughn, "Dead Fingers Talk," *Spin,* July 1987, 74.

232 **Herer meets Rick Pfrommer:** Lee, 198.

232 **build a network:** ibid., 220.

232 **Bob Snodgrass:** *Degenerate Art: The Art and Culture of Glass Pipes,* directed by M. Slinger, 2011.

233 **visionary states:** Getz and Dwork 1998, 405.
234 **While naked hippies frolic:** J. C. Juanis, "Bay Area Bits," *Relix,* December 1987.
234 **KMUD:** Brady, 178.
234 **In 20 years:** Marion Long, "The Seers' Catalog," *Omni,* January 1987, 36.
235 **Whether the mushrooms:** Terence McKenna 1991, 207.
235 **misrepresents Fischer and Hill:** Akers.
235 **to get high:** Garcia and Reich, 100.
236 **Few people:** Terence McKenna, 1991, 207.
237 **At this point:** Jackson 1999, 362.
240 **The Net interprets:** Philip Elmer-DeWitt, "First Nation in Cyberspace," *Time,* December 6, 1993, 62.
240 **Global Business Network:** Turner, 182.
242 **Barlow jumps:** ibid., 155.
242 **eighteen-year-old Timothy Tyler:** Timothy Tyler, "Tim's Story," Committee on Unjust Sentencing, http://www.drugwarprisoners.org/tyler.htm.
243 **Stanley Marshall:** United States v. Marshall, 908 F.2d 1312 (CA7 1990).
243 **Ibiza:** Matos, 24.
244 **Betty Boards:** Getz and Dwork 2000, 33.
245 **Colorado border:** Gehr, 42.
245 **Michael Lynch:** "July 28, 1988: Roma," Phish.com, 2010, http://phish.com /tours/dates/thu-1988-07-28-roma/.
246 **40,000 people watch:** McNally, 569.
246 **Timothy Tyler's rampage:** Tyler.

Chapter Eight: Wetlands Preserve

Primary interviews: Laura Bloch, Remy Chevalier, Larry Bloch, Jacaeber Kastor, Carlo McCormick, Karen Horning, Mary Eisenhart, Tim Scully, Chris Doyon, Jennifer Bleyer, Ken Goffman, Rebecca Adams, Luther Delaney, Dennis Mc-Nally, Jay Blakesberg, Sarah Matzar, and Richard Wright.

249 **Larry is heir:** John T. Hunter, "Paid Notice: Bloch, Ephraim F.," *New York Times,* May 23, 2000.
252 **5,000 people:** Adams.
252 **Barlow wrangles a +1:** John Perry Barlow, "Being in Nothingness: Virtual Reality and the Pioneers of Cyberspace," *Mondo 2000,* Summer 1990, 34.
253 **In-house dreamers:** R. U. Sirius, "Ted Nelson and John Perry Barlow for Mondo 2000," *Acceler8or,* May 22, 2012, http://www.acceler8or.com/2012/05 /ted-nelson-john-perry-barlow-for-mondo-2000-mondo-2000-history -project-entry-17/.
253 **the new drugs:** Barlow, Summer 1990, 34.
253 **With a saxophone:** Adam Heilbrun, "An Interview with Jaron Lanier," *Whole Earth Review,* Fall 1989, 108.
254 **to a man:** Grim, 228.
254 **Timothy Leary:** Turner, 163.
254 **Power Glove:** Barlow Summer 1990.
254 **McKenna drops by:** Terence McKenna 1991, 234.
254 **Our brains:** Barlow Summer 1990.
256 **go to the bathroom:** Caitlin Carter, "Ann Coulter Is a Dead Head, Has Large Collection of Grateful Dead Bootlegs," *SiriusXM Blog,* June 10, 2015, http://blog

.siriusxm.com/2015/06/10/ann-coulter-is-a-dead-head-has-large-collection
-of-grateful-dead-bootlegs/.

256 **No one who was not:** Taylor Hill, "Deadheads Are What Liberals Claim to Be but Aren't," JamBands, June 23, 2006, http://www.jambands.com/fea tures/2006/06/23/deadheads-are-what-liberals-claim-to-be-but-aren-t-an -interview-with-ann-coulter.

260 **Uncle Duke Day:** "Campus Life: Wesleyan; Student's Arrest Leads to Debate on Drug Policy," *New York Times,* November 19, 1989.

260 **first show anywhere:** "Answers," Spin Doctors Archive, http://www.spin doctors-archive.com/faq/band_members.html.

260 **He charts minihistories:** Thomas Lyttle, "Drug Based Religions and Contem-porary Drug Taking," *Journal of Drug Issues,* Spring 1988, 271.

261 **The ayahuasca cult:** Queen Mu, "Visual Music in the Third World," *Reality Hackers,* Winter 1988, 38.

261 **One Dutch investor:** Luc Sala, "New Edge and Mondo, Part 1-A Personal Per-spective," *Acceler8or,* March 28, 2012, http://www.acceler8or.com/2012/03/new -edge-mondo-a-personal-perspective-part-1-mondo-2000-history-project -entry-8/.

262 **first modest newsletter:** Rick Dublin, editorial, *MAPS Bulletin,* Summer 1988.

262 **400,000 ecstasy tablets:** Rick Doblin, "MDMA Research in the United States," *MAPS Bulletin,* Summer 1989.

263 **became the E dealers:** Matos, 47.

263 **Pittsburgh:** McNally, 572.

265 **eat only fruit:** Jennifer Hartley, "'We Were Given This Dance': Music and Meaning the Early Unlimited Devotion Family," in Adams and Sardiello, 133.

265 **lyrics of Robert Hunter:** ibid., 140.

265 **Bobby is seen:** ibid., 136.

266 **acid overdoses:** Adams.

267 **70 to 90 db:** Blair Jackson, *Goin' Down the Road: A Grateful Dead Traveling Com-panion* (New York: Harmony, 1992), 169.

268 **Right next door:** Pam Fisher, "Thoughts from Prison," *Deadheads Behind Bars,* early 1990, via rec.music.gdead.

268 **Gorby blots:** Shenk and Silberman, 116.

268 **Acid Eric:** Razam 2009.

270 **kerfuffle in an open forum:** Barlow June 1990.

271 **Via an encounter:** Turner, 171.

271 **Barlow picks up Kapor:** Barlow June 1990.

271 **common set of experiences:** David Gans with Ken Goffman, "Mitch Kapor and John Barlow Interview," August 5, 1990, https://w2.eff.org/Misc/Publications /John_Perry_Barlow/HTML/barlow_and_kapor_in_wired_interview.html.

271 **Computer Liberty Foundation:** Turner, 172.

272 **far and wide:** "Announcements," *Mississippi 12-Step,* February 1991, 1.

272 **the first summer:** Wetlands calendars, June-August 1989, author's personal collection.

274 **laughed at:** Parke Puterbaugh, *Phish: The Biography* (Cambridge, MA: Da Capo, 2009), 82.

274 **rejected by record companies:** Brett Milano, "Rykodisc Folds Up Its Salem Tent," *Boston Phoenix,* August 12, 1999, http://www.bostonphoenix.com/archive /music/99/08/12/rykodisc.html.

Chapter Nine: Through the Looking Glass

Primary interviews: Jacaeber Kastor, Carlo McCormick, Richard Gehr, Luther Delaney, Scott Herrick, Steve Silberman, Blair Jackson, Karen Horning, Ken Goffman, Jennifer Bleyer, Julie Stewart, Sarah Matzar, Dylan Carlson, Gil Levey, Jeff Mattson, Chris Zahn, Mark McCloud, Dennis Alpert, Carol Latvala, David Gans, Harvey Lubar, Pat Lee, and Chris Doyon.

277 **It's too early:** Terence McKenna 1991, 69.

277 **Psychedelics are to psychology:** ibid., 9.

278 **Acid Show:** Carlo McCormick, "The Psychedelic '90s," *High Times,* May 1990, 48.

278 **It takes a 'head':** Jon Hanna, "Alex Grey Speaks . . . ," *Entheogen Review,* Winter Solstice 1998, 17.

279 **Mindfold:** ibid.

279 **The author José Argüelles:** Daniel Pinchbeck, *2012: The Return of Quetzalcoatl* (New York: Jeremy Tarcher / Penguin, 2006), 223.

279 **Whole Earth Festival:** "About Whole Earth Festival," https://wef.ucdavis.edu/about/.

280 **walking his talk:** Dennis McKenna, 457.

280 **Terence's mind:** ibid., 453.

280 **rare and precious:** Shulgin and Shulgin, 964.

280 **the Shulgins worry:** "Ann and Sasha Shulgin Speak . . . in Discussion with Earth and Fire Erowid," *Entheogen Review,* Summer Solstice 2008, 41.

281 **Bohemian Grove:** Dennis Romero, "Sasha Shulgin, Psychedelic Chemist," *Los Angeles Times,* September 5, 1995, 5.

282 **Church is not a cult:** "Spinners or Sinners?," *Worcester Telegram and Gazette,* December 9, 1991.

282 **83 percent of respondents:** "Results from the Tricycle Poll," *Tricycle,* Fall 1996. http://www.tricycle.com/special-section/results-tricycle-poll.

282 **This number:** Rick Strassman. *DMT: The Spirit Molecule; A Doctor's Revolutionary Research into the Biology of Near-Death and Mystical Experiences* (Rochester, VT: Park Street, 2001), 304.

289 **conclave of the new:** John Perry Barlow, "A Not Terribly Brief History of the Electronic Frontier Foundation," November 8, 1990, https://w2.eff.org/Misc/Publications/John_Perry_Barlow/HTML/not_too_brief_history.html.

292 **the Columbian president:** Brady, 119.

292 **Sharkey's Garden:** "Sharkey's Garden," *High Times,* July 1990, 42.

292 **Freedom Fighter:** "Freedom Fighter," *High Times,* August 1990, 43.

292 **At the urging:** William W. Mendel, "Counterdrug Strategy-Illusive Victory: From Blast Furnace to Green Sweep," *Military Review,* December 1992, 74.

292 **agents earn patches:** Christopher Ingraham, "The Oddly Beautiful and Sometimes Disturbing Artistic Talent of the Nation's Drug Cops," *Washington Post, Wonkblog,* March 20, 2015, https://www.washingtonpost.com/news/wonkblog/wp/2015/03/20/the-oddly-beautiful-and-sometimes-disturbing-artistic-talent-of-the-nations-drug-cops/.

293 **At some blurry time:** Leonard Pickard, "DEA's NADDIS System: A Guide for Attorneys, the Courts, and Researchers," July 2011, http://freeleonardpickard.org/NADDIS/index.html.

293   **Communes communized:** Kathleen Rodgers, *Welcome to Resisterville: American Dissidents in British Columbia* (Vancouver: University of British Columbia, 2014), 85, 106.

293   **group of eighty or a hundred:** Louis M. Brill, "What Is Burning Man? The First Year in the Desert," http://burningman.org/culture/history/brc-history/event-archives/1986-1991/firstyears/.

293   **strong symbolic value:** "Bad Day at Black Rock (Zone Trip #4)," *Rough Draft,* September 1990, 1.

294   **Suicide Club:** Wieners.

294   **still-operating wing:** "Hillsdale Mall, Spring 1994, http://www.billboardliberation.com/LSD.html.

294   **all-night drive:** Brill.

295   **The women baked:** Michael Mikel, "2a222-Burning Man, 1990," flickr.com.

295   **Dawn worshippers can:** Brill.

295   **drum set:** Dean Gustafson, "The First Year in the Desert: A Personal Historical Account from Its First Drummer (Anecdotal Memoirs or Rather a Rant of Reveries)," https://web.archive.org/web/20070630030804/http://deangustafson.net/BlackRock90.html.

296   **we're being followed:** Fred Goodman, "The End of the Road?," *Rolling Stone,* August 23, 1990, 21.

296   **Please don't:** ibid.

296   **statistical damage:** Edward F. Mulkerin III, "Scapegoats, Sentencing, and LSD," *Harvard Crimson,* September 20, 1993.

297   **more than 40 percent:** Johnston and O'Malley, 13.

298   **Supreme Court:** Chapman v. United States, 500 U.S. 453 (1991).

300   **flow of Quaaludes:** Grim, 111.

300   **We've opened a vein:** Dennis Cauchon, "Attack on Deadheads Is No Hallucination," *USA Today,* December 17, 1992, A17.

300   **1,500–2,000:** "Sentencing Guidelines," *Entheogen Review,* Autumnal Equinox 1994, 17.

300   **any specific intent:** Jim Newton, "Deadheads Fight Stigma as Arrests Rise," *Los Angeles Times,* July 27, 1992.

300   **ranging from old standbys:** "1992," http://www.rexfoundation.org/1992/09/29/1992-beneficiaries/.

301   **letters that claim:** Frank Smith, "Box of Pain," *New Republic,* March 21, 1994, 25.

301   **That's something:** Blair Jackson, "In Phil We Trust," *Dupree's Diamond News,* Spring 1994, 12.

301   **marked pattern:** Cauchon, A17.

301   **dabbling dangerously:** Jackson 1999, 407.

302   **Within five minutes:** John C. Klock, Udo Boerner, and Charles E. Becker, "Coma, Hyperthermia and Bleeding Associated with Massive LSD Overdose: A Report of Eight Cases," *Western Journal of Medicine* 120, no. 3 (1974): 183.

302   **None of them:** Henderson and Glass, 110.

304   **KILL THE GRATEFUL DEAD:** Michael Azerrad, *Come as You Are: The Story of Nirvana* (New York: Doubleday, 1993), 254.

304   **I wouldn't wear:** Everett True, "In My Head, I'm So Ugly," *Melody Maker,* July 18, 1992.

305   **The Dead seemed:** Bangs, 42.

306 **Soundscan technology:** Derek Thompson, "1991: The Most Important Year in Pop-Music History," *Atlantic,* May 8, 2015, http://www.theatlantic.com/enter tainment/archive/2015/05/1991-the-most-important-year-in-music/392642/.

307 **pretty mundane:** Mitch Clegg, "Deadhead Church Expels Its Founder," *San Francisco Chronicle,* April 9, 1992, A23.

308 **horrible police brutality:** McNally, 575.

309 **a lot of records:** St. John.

310 **Kemp is spotted there:** Andy Roberts 2008, 240.

310 **Goa Gil called _me_:** Brian Behlendorf, "rave update," SF-Raves listserv, August 3, 1992, http://sfraves.org/archives/sfrlist/1992/sfr.9208.gz.

310 **I noticed that:** Larry Ching, "Mostly FMR," SF-Raves, October 11, 1992. http://sfraves.org/archives/sfrlist/1992/sfr.9210.gz.

310 **Atomic Dog Collective:** Frank Broughton, "Deadheads: A Snapshot of the Deadhead Scene and How It Was Feeding U.S. Rave," *i-D,* February 1994.

311 **pioneer phone phreaker:** John Draper, "Burning Man Question," SF-Raves, September 2, 1993, http://sfraves.org/archives/sfrlist/1993/sfr.9310.gz.

311 **first psychedelic info repositories:** Fire Erowid, "Erowid: 10 Years of History," *Erowid Extracts,* June 2005, 8.

311 **_very_ newage oriented:** The Normals, "Re: Black Rock Desert," SF-Raves, August 31, 1992, http://sfraves.org/archives/sfrlist/1992/sfr.9208.gz.

312 **black kiss:** Jack Shafer, "Acid House: The Art of LSD Blotter Paper," *San Francisco Weekly,* August 30, 1995.

315 **As a young reporter:** Albert Gore, "Church Group Swaps Views with Gaskin's," *Tennessean,* March 13, 1972.

317 **borrowing the legal text:** Dean Budnick and Josh Baron, *Ticket Masters: The Rise of the Concert Industry and How the Public Got Scalped* (Toronto: ECW, 2011), 113.

319 **multimotel postshow:** "Big LSD Bust in Oakland-Arrested," *San Francisco Chronicle,* January 27, 1993, A13.

320 **Karen lays off sales:** "Exhibit 3-Transcript of Videotaped Conversation of Karen J. Horning, CI-1, and CI-2 on 8/16/93 in Room 425 of the Cathedral Hill Hotel San Francisco, CA," United States v. Karen Horning, a.k.a. Karen Hoffman, a.k.a. Andrea Maltease, United States District Court, Northern District of California, No. CR93-0450 TEH.

Chapter Ten: The Tour from Hell

Primary interviews: Jacaebor Kastor, Chad Stickney, John Cederquist, Bill Harmon, Sarah Matzar, Karen Horning, Ken Goffman, John Paluska, Andy Bernstein, Dennis McNally, and David Gans.

323 **In the States:** Rick Doblin, "The Summit Meeting Commemorating the 50th Anniversary of Albert Hofmann's Discovery of LSD," *MAPS Bulletin,* Summer 1993, http://www.maps.org/news-letters/v04n2/04252lsd.html.

323 **nearest adjacent weekend:** Julie Holland, "Raves for Research or Psychedelic Researchers: The Next Generation," *MAPS Bulletin,* Summer 1993, http://www.maps.org/news-letters/v04n2/04240rav.html.

324 **reports will come:** Peterson, 16.

324 **lively debates:** Jim DeKoerne, "Entheogen—What's in a Word?," *Entheogen Review,* Winter Solstice 1992, 1.

324   **shamanism:** Jim DeKoerne, "On the Evolution of Psychedelic Shamanism," *Entheogen Review,* Summer Solstice 1993, 2.

324   **South American Wilderness Adventures:** Paul Krassner, "High Encounters with Ecuadorian Shamans," *High Times,* March 1980, 60.

325   **popular collection of paintings:** Jim DeKoerne, "Ayahuasca Visions: The Religions Iconography of a Peruvian Shaman," *Entheogen Review,* Vernal Equinox 1993, 10.

325   **Council on Spiritual Practices:** Shulgin and Shulgin 2007.

325   **Guides and structure:** Pollan.

325   **I was down there:** Sam Gandy, "Psychedelic Scientists," *Psychedelic Press UK* 2015, no. 3 (2015): 89.

326   **weed trade transforms:** Raf Katigbak, and Victor John Penner, "A Look Inside Illegal Canadian Weed Grow Houses from the 1990s," *Vice,* December 18, 2013. http://www.vice.com/read/documenting-busted-home-grow-ops-in-1990s -vancouver.

328   **American newspapers:** Stephen Schwartz, "Suspect in LSD Distribution Ring Extradited to S.F.," *San Francisco Chronicle,* March 9, 1995.

328   **biggest LSD bust:** Lisa Alcalay Klug, "Authorities Bust Four in Nationwide LSD Distribution Ring," *Associated Press,* July 2, 1993.

329   **She has a belief:** Vitali Rozynko, testimony, *United States v. Karen Horning,* February 22, 1994.

329   **She talked to me:** Vitali Rozynko, forensic evaluation, *United States v. Karen Horning,* September 5, 1994.

330   **Let's back up:** Vitali Rozynko, testimony.

330   **Radical Libertarian Alliance:** Brian Doherty, *Radicals for Capitalism: A Freewheeling History of the Modern American Libertarian Movement* (New York: PublicAffairs, 2007), 369.

330   **social changes:** Louis Rossetto, "Why Wired?," *Wired,* March 1993, 10.

330   **Zippies:** Jules Marshall, "Zippies!," *Wired,* May 1994, 75.

331   **UK dance-scene hedonism:** Marshall.

331   **Sheep Meadow:** Pope Electric Yeti, "British Zippy Pronoia Tour Kicks Off in New York, a Firsthand Account," 1995, http://www.pronoia.net/tour/essays/ pressconf.html.

331   **tent and teepee seas:** Andy Roberts 2008, 249.

331   **ecstasyheads partying:** Marshall.

331   **60,000 squatters:** Marshall.

331   **During mushroom season:** Andy Roberts, "Mushroom Magic at Crazy Creek: The Welsh Psilocybin Festival, 1976–1982," *Psychedelic Press UK* 2014, no. 2 (2014): 7.

332   **Wetlands:** John Bagby, "Pronoia Tour Launch, Wetlands nightclub, Manhattan," 1994, http://www.pronoia.net/tour/essays/wetlands.html.

332   **None of us:** ibid.

332   **emphasis in house music:** Terence McKenna, "Re: Evolution," on the Shamen, *Boss Drum,* One Little Indian, 1992.

333   **party in Boulder:** John Bagby, "Boulder Rave," 1995. http://www.pronoia.net /tour/essays/colorado.html.

335   **At that point:** Matos, 184.

335   **$17 and $28 million:** Adams.

335   **up to 2,000 Deadheads:** Frank Smith.

335 **successful bill:** Melinda Fine and Jonathan Walters, "Putting a Human Face on Injustice: Reversing a Political Juggernaut," NYU Wagner School of Public Service and Ford Foundation, New York, 2003.

336 **20,000 are without tickets:** McNally, 610.

336 **Intrepid tapers:** Getz and Dwork 1999, 25.

337 **struck by lightning:** Wendy Melillo, "3 Grateful Dead Concertgoers Struck by Lightning near RFK," *Washington Post,* June 26, 1995.

337 **several fans fall:** gr689, "To-feellikeastranger . . . and any others who dont know," Grateful Dead at Three Rivers Stadium, Pittsburgh, PA, June 30, 1995, https://archive.org/details/gd95-06-30.schoeps.3376.sbeok.shnf.

337 **death threat:** McNally, 610.

337 **Want to end:** ibid., 611.

337 **Back home:** Jackson 1999, 452.

337 **There's no way:** ibid., 457.

338 **At the Stock Exchange:** Adam Lashinsky, "Remembering Netscape: The Birth of the Web," *Fortune,* July 25, 2005, http://archive.fortune.com/magazines /fortune/fortune_archive/2005/07/25/8266639/index.htm.

339 **This new faith:** Richard Barbrook and Andy Cameron, "The Californian Ideology," *Science as Culture,* no. 6 (1996): 44.

339 **Nature itself:** Erik Davis, *Techgnosis: Myth, Magic, and Mysticism in the Age of Information* (New York: Three Rivers Press, 1998), 315.

340 **Governments of the Industrial World:** John Perry Barlow, "A Declaration of the Independence of Cyberspace," February 8, 1996, https://projects.eff .org/~barlow/Declaration-Final.html.

341 **three hundred e-mails:** John Perry Barlow, "Declaring Independence," *Wired,* June 1996, 121.

341 **a new argument:** Karen Horning, motion for relief pursuant to 28 U.S.C. §2255, 105 F.3d 667, *United States v. Karen Horning.*

341 **GFAN-91–8008:** "Stanley, Owsley (aka Stanley, Augustus Owsley III) (deceased)-NADDIS Report," November 28, 2011, http://www.governmentattic. org/5docs/DEA-Owsley_2011.pdf.

342 **a very difficult place:** Arthur Hubbard, testimony, United States v. Sage Appel, District Court, Northern District of California, No. CR-93-0325 EFL, February 6, 1995.

342 **government dismisses the charge:** Hon. Eugene F. Lynch, "Defendant's Sentencing Memorandum," United States v. Carolyn Holly Fried et. al., District Court, Northern District of California, No. CR-93-0325 EFL, May 3, 1996.

Chapter Eleven: Festival Season

Primary interviews: John Paluska, Scott Herrick, Earth Erowid, Fire Erowid, Gil Levey, Jessica Bleyer, Mark McCloud, Carol Latvala, Steve Silberman, Mike Wren, Karen Horning, Larry Bloch, Pete Shapiro, Scott Herrick, Richard Wright, and Andy Bernstein.

345 **slightly harder to get acid:** Lloyd Johnston, Patrick M. O'Malley, Richard A. Miech, Jerald G. Bachman, and John E. Schulenberg, *The Monitoring the Future National Survey Results on Drug Use, 1975–2014: 2014 Overview, Key Findings on Adolescent Drug Use* (Ann Arbor: University of Michigan Institute for Social Research, 2015), 450.

346 **Deadhead Heaven:** Chris Kincade, "Dead Come to Life Again for Two-Day Festival," *New York Times,* June 2, 1996.
346 **Even Furthur:** Matos, 198.
347 **young mathematician:** Dennis McKenna, 456.
347 **Bob Jesse convened:** Pollan.
348 **doctoral thesis:** Horace Beach, "Listening for the Logos: A Study of Reports of Audible Voices at High Doses of Psilocybin," *MAPS Bulletin,* Winter 1996, 12.
349 **Breadheads:** Bell, 395.
349 **state map:** ibid., 57.
349 **swelling toward 30,000:** Natalie Hormilla, "Bread and Puppet Celebrates Half a Century," *Barton Chronicle,* August 7, 2013, http://bartonchronicle.com/bread-and-puppet-celebrates-half-a-century/.
349 **property between the two:** Bell, 61.
350 **70,000 attendees:** Puterbaugh, 7.
350 **The soiree's sensibility:** "Interview with Trey Anastasio and Lars Fisk."
352 **There was that week:** Andrew Smith, "Trey Anastasio," *Good Citizen,* no. 7 (1997).
352 **buying, selling, and trading:** Fire Erowid.
353 **event's size has doubled:** Jenny Kane, "Burning Man Has Grown Beyond Founders' Dreams," *Reno Gazette-Journal,* March 3, 2015, http://www.rgj.com/story/life/2015/03/03/burning-man-grown-beyond-founders-dreams/24343027/.
353 **reports of arrests:** Daniel Rodriguez, "Death and Ecstasy: The Rise and Fall of Burning Man's Original Rave Ghetto," *Thump,* August 31, 2015, https://thump.vice.com/en_us/article/death-and-ecstasy-the-rise-and-fall-of-burning-mans-original-rave-ghetto.
354 **See couch surfers:** C. Tiberius Hill, "Mark Your Calendars!! for the Burning Man 1995 After-Party," SF-Raves, September 14, 1995, http://sfraves.org/archives/sfrlist/1995/sfr.9509.gz.
354 **I'd probably be:** Mark Pesce, "Psychedelics and the Creation of Virtual Reality," *MAPS Bulletin,* Fall 2000, 4.
355 **Entheobotany Conference:** Fire Erowid.
355 **Without warning:** "DEA Raid on Shulgin Laboratory on October 27, 1994," January 8, 2004, https://www.erowid.org/culture/characters/shulgin_alexander/shulgin_alexander_raid.shtml.
355 **all-time high:** Johnston et al., 220.
356 **The Mounties watch:** Eric Brazil, "Fugitive to Face LSD Charges," *San Francisco Examiner,* July 6, 1998.
356 **enough acid to dose:** Bill Wallace, "LSD Maker Gets 5 Years Added to 1976 Sentence," *San Francisco Chronicle,* January 23, 1999.
356 **training video:** Jon Hanna, "Erowid Character Vaults: Nick Sand Extended Biography," November 5, 1999, https://www.erowid.org/culture/characters/sand_nick/sand_nick_biography1.shtml.
356 **8.4 percent to 7.6 percent:** Johnston et al., 220.
356 **out in Stinson Beach:** Michael Mason, Chris Sandel, and Lee Ray Chapman, "Subterranean Psychonaut: The Strange and Dreadful Saga of Gordon Todd Skinner," *This Land Press,* July 28, 2013, http://thislandpress.com/2013/07/28/subterranean-psychonaut/.
357 **synthesized MDA:** Peter Wilkinson, "The Acid King," *Rolling Stone,* July 5, 2001, 113.

357   **Dead family album covers:** Mark McCloud, "12 Album Covers," 2007, http://www.blotterbarn.com/slideshow.html#deadalbums.

359   **She estimates:** Adams and Sardiello, 33.

360   **expressed as bits:** Ed Park, "Mistaken for the Enemy," *Los Angeles Times,* April 20, 2008.

361   **winter of '73:** Silberman.

361   **MDMA first appears:** Johnston et al., 221.

361   **Owsley Stanley:** Henrik Dahl, "Struck by White Lightning: A Correspondence with Owsley Stanley," *Oak Tree Review,* April 2012, http://www.theoaktreereview.com/owsley_stanley_2.html.

362   **MDMA overtakes LSD:** Johnston et al., 220, 221.

362   **no analysis:** Puterbaugh, 232.

363   **traveling ecstasy circus:** Bret Maxwell Dawson, "B'gock! (or Of Omelets, WWF Wrestling, Summer Camp and What It Means to Me to Be a Disco Biscuits Fan)," JamBands, February 15, 2000, http://www.jambands.com/features/2000/02/15/b-gock-or-of-omelets-wwf-wrestling-summer-camp-and-what-it-means-to-me-to-be-a-disco-biscuits-fan.

364   **In the Florida Everglades:** Puterbaugh, 198.

364   **he's not scared:** Erik Davis, 2000.

364   **the first sign:** Grim, 7.

365   **Pickard's partner:** Mason, Sandel, and Chapman.

365   **DEA chase:** Wilkinson.

365   **$120,000 stereo:** Vanessa Grigoriadis, "Travels in the New Psychedelic Bazaar," *New York,* April 7, 2013.

365   **Nick Sand and other chemists:** *The Sunshine Makers,* 2015.

365   **DEA claim:** Pickard 2008.

366   **bottom really drops out:** Johnston et al., 220.

366   **perceived availability:** ibid., 450.

366   **disapproval rate:** ibid., 389.

367   **British lab:** Michael Allen, "The Psychedelic 'Drugs Wizard' Who Ran One of England's Biggest LSD Labs," *Vice,* October 29, 2014, http://www.vice.com/read/casey-william-hardison-psychedelic-chemist-254.

367   **new method of LSD synthesis:** Casey William "Freeblood" Hardison, "Novel Condensation of d-LA into d_LSD via PyPOB," *Entheogen Review,* Autumnal Equinox 2005, 94.

367   **Among the twelfth graders:** Johnston et al., 221.

368   **picked up by the feds at Burning Man:** Mason, Sandel, and Chapman.

369   **death of fun:** Hunter S. Thompson. *The Kingdom of Fear: Loathsome Secrets of a Star-Crossed Child in the Final Days of the American Century* (New York: Simon & Schuster, 2003).

371   **Coran Capshaw:** Nevin Martell, *Dave Matthews Band: Music for the People* (New York: Pocket Books, 1999), 22.

371   **cofounding Red Light Communications:** Budnick and Baron, 256.

372   **RAVE Act:** Janelle Brown, "Your Glow Stick Could Land You in Jail," *Salon,* April 16, 2003, http://www.salon.com/2003/04/16/rave/.

372   **the nadir:** Simon Reynolds, "How Rave Music Conquered America," *Guardian,* August 2, 2012, http://www.theguardian.com/music/2012/aug/02/how-rave-music-conquered-america.

373   **into the next century:** Mitchell Gomez, "Electric Forest Shuts Down Dance-safe—but We Have a Bigger Problem to Tackle," June 30, 2015, https://dance safe.org/dancesafe-was-shut-down/.

373   **Camp Bisco:** Matos, 346.

373   **Nick Sand:** Hanna 1999.

373   **Ann will estimate:** Michael Martin, "Love and Other Drugs," *Interview,* Fall 2010, http://www.interviewmagazine.com/culture/love-and-other-drugs/.

373   **Beautifully active:** Erowid, "2C-B Timeline," https://www.erowid.org/chemicals /2cb/2cb_timeline.php.

373   **Operation Web Tryp:** Grim, 219.

373   **So embedded:** Vanessa Hua, "Burning Man," *San Francisco Examiner,* August 20, 2000.

373   **gifting:** Larry Harvey, "The 10 Principles of Burning Man," 2004, http://burning man.org/culture/philosophical-center/10-principles/.

374   **Both of Google's founders:** Hua.

374   **Some vans give away:** doc, "Win Tickets to Dave Matthews Band Concert in Central Park, NYC 9/24/03," September 15, 2003, http://www.flyertalk.com /forum/s-p-m/270180-win-tickets-dave-matthews-band-concert-central-park -nyc-9-24-03-a.html.

374   **channels some of the money:** Hawes Spencer, "Resourceful: DMB Concert Answers Prayers," *Hook,* October 2, 2003.

374   **commemorative album:** "Dave Matthews Band to Rock Central Park," *Billboard,* September 9, 2003, http://www.billboard.com/articles/news/69179/dave -matthews-band-to-rock-central-park.

375   **one more radical move:** Puterbaugh, 223.

375   **first user base:** Kim Peterson, "BitTorrent File-Sharing Program Floods the Web," *Seattle Times,* January 10, 2005, http://www.seattletimes.com/business /bittorrent-file-sharing-program-floods-the-web/.

376   **$500 to $1,025:** Troy Carpenter, "Jam Bands to Cruise Again," *Billboard,* July 17, 2003, http://www.billboard.com/articles/news/69956/jam-bands-to-cruise -again.

Chapter Twelve: How Jerry Got Hip Again

Primary interviews: Mark McCloud, Carlo McCormick, Karen Horning, Andy Bernstein, Rebecca Adams, and Chris Doyon.

379   **illustration or the headline:** Daniel Chamberlin, "Uncle Skullfucker's Band," *Arthur,* July 2004.

379   **off the grid in Hawaii:** Paul Smart, "Closest to the Edge: Life in a Squatters' Village on the Wild Side of Maui," *Arthur,* July 2005, 15.

379   **British mushroom revival:** Mark Pilkington, "Re-Psychedelia Britannica," *Arthur,* January 2005, 12.

380   **Deadhead life:** Stan Spector, "Who Is Dionysus and Why Does He Keep Following Me Everywhere?," *Dead Letters,* no. 2 (2003), 19.

381   **2012 bust in Philadelphia:** Jason Nark and *Daily News* staff writer, "In Philly, Keeping Tabs on LSD," *Philadelphia Daily News,* May 30, 2012.

381   **I owe a lot:** James Henke, "Jerry Garcia: The *Rolling Stone* Interview," *Rolling Stone,* October 31, 1991, 34.

381   **mushroom revival:** Letcher, 285.

382   **Dead shows online:** Chamberlin.

383 **not my fault:** Grateful Dead at McFarlin Auditorium, Dallas, TX, December 26, 1969, https://archive.org/details/gd1969-12-26.sbd.warner-evans.28448 .sbeok.flac16.

384 **every LSD prisoner:** Casey Logan, "Adventures in Wonderland," *Pitch,* April 19, 2001, 14.

384 **the primeval sound:** "Detailed Program," November 2005, http://www.lsd .info/en/detailprogramm.html.

384 **psychedelic tribe elders:** Jon Hanna, "Reflections on Basel," *Entheogen Review,* Vernal Equinox 2006, 2.

386 **In the end:** Albert Hofmann, closing remarks in Basel, 2006, https://www.you tube.com/watch?v=SInkOigeGno.

386 **festival organizers purchased:** Ray Waddell, "Bonnaroo Organizers Purchasing Festival Site," *Billboard,* January 4, 2007, http://www.billboard.com/articles /news/1063499/bonnaroo-organizers-purchasing-festival-site.

387 **busted in late 2006:** "Anastasio Avoids Jail on Drug Charges," *Billboard,* April 13, 2007, http://www.billboard.com/articles/news/1052782/anastasio-avoids-jail-on -drug-charges.

389 **long complained:** Rock Influence with Bob Weir, April 1984, https://www .youtube.com/watch?v=DACm8Lg2o2w.

389 **dropped hits of fresh:** Schou, 238.

390 **guaranteed $43 million:** Michael Arrington, "What Skype Really Paid for GroupMe," *TechCrunch,* August 23, 2011, http://techcrunch.com/2011/08/23 /what-skype-really-paid-for-groupme/.

390 **Twelve Tribes' Peacemaker:** Rosie Gray, "Friendly Cult Looking for Recruits at Occupy Wall Street!," *Village Voice,* November 10, 2011, http://www .villagevoice.com/news/friendly-cult-looking-for-recruits-at-occupy-wall -street-6711929.

391 **grown involved with Anonymous:** David Kushner, "The Masked Avengers," *New Yorker,* September 8, 2014, 48.

392 **Silk Road:** Andy Greenberg, "Black Market Drug Site 'Silk Road' Booming: $22 Million in Annual Sales," *Forbes,* August 6, 2012, http://www.forbes.com /sites/andygreenberg/2012/08/06/black-market-drug-site-silk-road-booming -22-million-in-annual-mostly-illegal-sales/.

392 **LSD Avengers:** Adrienne Jeffries, "The LSD Avengers, Silk Road's Self-Appointed Drug Inspectors, Announce Retirement," *Verge,* October 14, 2013, http://www.theverge.com/2013/10/14/4828448/silk-road-lsd-avengers-drug -inspectors.

392 **eye candy:** Earth Erowid and Fire Erowid, "Spotlight on NBOMe: Potent Psychedelic Issues," *Erowid Extracts,* July 2013, 2.

392 **1P-LSD:** Max Daly, "Why Young Brits Are Taking So Much LSD and Ecstasy," *Vice,* July 27, 2015, http://www.vice.com/read/this-is-why-so-many-young -brits-are-taking-so-much-acid-and-ecstasy-892.

393 **constructive activism:** Alexia Maddox, Monica J. Barratt, Matthew Allen, Simon Lenton, "Constructive Activism in the Dark Web: Cryptomarkets and Illicit Drugs in the Digital 'Demimonde,'" *Information, Communication & Society* 19, no. 1 (2016), 1.

393 **one mushroom seller:** Joseph Cox, "Dark Web Dealer Allegedly Donates Drug Profits to Charity," Vice.com, October 7, 2015. http://motherboard.vice .com/read/dark-web-dealer-allegedly-donates-to-charity.

393   **DMT roasters:** Teafaerie, "How to Build a Better Spaceship," May 29, 2014, https://www.erowid.org/columns/teafaerie/2014/05/29/how-to-build-a-better -spaceship/.

393   **visual language:** Erik Davis, 2000.

393   **health and fitness trends:** Cohen.

393   **juice cleanse:** Abby Aguirre, "The New Power Trip: Inside the World of Aya-huasca," *Marie Claire,* February 18, 2014, http://www.marieclaire.com/politics /news/a8965/ayahuasca-new-power-trip/.

393   **psychedelic research projects:** Pollan.

393   **the late '80s:** *Journal of the American Society for Psychical Research,* 1988, 6.

393   **four phases:** Thomas Roberts May 2015.

394   **all-time low:** Johnston et al., 220.

394   *positive* **LSD story:** Bill Hicks, *Sane Man,* Sacred Cow Productions, 1989.

394   **positive LSD stories:** Paula Meija, "Day Tripping: Benefits Seen in Psyche-delics," *Newsweek,* January 25, 2015, http://www.newsweek.com/day-tripping -benefits-seen-use-psychedelics-301847.

394   **another headline:** Tom Shroder, "Want to Quit Smoking? Eat a Magic Mush-room, a New Study Says," *Time,* September 18, 2014, http://time.com/3399433 /quit-smoking-psychedelic-drugs-acid-test/.

395   **microdosing:** Tia Ghose, "Short Trip? More People 'Microdosing' on Psy-chedelic Drugs," *LiveScience,* July 8, 2015. http://www.livescience.com/51482 -more-people-microdosing-psychedelic-drugs.html.

395   **We need to create:** "Surveillance and Its Discontents, a Conversation Across Cyberspace" (transcript), *TechPresident,* June 12, 2014, http://techpresident.com /news/25129/surveillance-and-its-discontents-conversation-across-cyberspace -edward-snowden-and-john.

Acknowledgments

First: my love, Caitlin.

My supportive family, both present and not: Al Jarnow, Jill Stamberg Jarnow, Lois Stamberg, Mel Stamberg, Jeanette Jarnow, Al Sr., Peter Stamberg, Paul Aferiat, Bea Aboff, Ruth Stamberg, all assorted Potters, Allen Farbman, and Lizzie Crowley. And even the Lord Nose, too.

My agent, Paul Bresnick, for seeing something in this idea when it was only an overexcited trend piece. Ben Schafer at Da Capo for going for it. Carolyn Sobczak for managing edits and bibliographic meltdowns.

New York heads: Bill Stites, Ariella Stok, Matt Van Brink, Gabrielle Kerson, Mark Suppes, Jack Chester (thanks for the desk space), Chris Pascerella, Jon Sumber, Tim Holmes, Frankie Pancakes, everybody at WFMU, Dan Bodah (who found the Nancy tape), Paul Lovelace and Jessica Wolfson, Kid Millions, the Tall Firs, Yo La Tengo, Alex Holden, Aaron Benor, Dan Lynch, Jonas Blank, Billy Jones, Zach Mexico, Matt Werth.

Various heady elders, who helped open doors for years both before this book existed (or I met them) and after, including (but not limited to): Dan Levy, Richard Gehr, Steve Silberman, David Gans.

Deepest extended thanks to every interview subject, most especially those who had never been interviewed before.

Nick Meriwether at the Grateful Dead Archive in Santa Cruz for genuine Southern academic hospitality and countless perspectives, as important to the archive as the collection itself. Rebecca Adams, the mother of Deadhead studies. The proprietors of the wondrous Dead historical blogs for endless help with source checking and suggestions of new paths: Corry Arnold (who introduced me to Humbead's Map), Caleb Kennedy, and Joe Jupille. Barry Barnes, Jake Cohen, Peter Richardson, Kaye Robin Alexander, Mel Backstrom, Sarah Moser, and every member of the annual Grateful Dead Scholars Caucus.

For heroic feats in transcription and special assignment scanning: Bob Trudeau, Courtney Klossner.

For thoughtful new directions in miscellaneous research: Mark McCloud, Tim Scully, Sean Howe, Tyler Wilcox, Rob Mitchum, Michaelangelo Matos, Chris Elcock, Fred Turner, Jade Dellinger, Rex Weiner, Ben Zimmer.

For tolerating miscellaneous queries: Lorren Daro, Wavy Gravy, Gilbert Shelton, Eric Thompson.

Editors of all stripes that abetted this project directly or indirectly: Maura Johnston, Judy Berman, Jillian Mapes, Chris Weingarten, Mike Greenhaus, Michael Calore, Dean Budnick, Josh Baron, Russell Kahn, J. Edward Keyes, Andrew Male, Chuck Squatriglia, Hank Shteamer, Jessica Hopper.

Mostly convincing professionals: Pete Shapiro, Amir Bar-Lev, David Lemeiux, Doran Tyson and Ivette Ramos at Rhino Records, Benjy Eisen, Jen Bernstein, Jay Blakesberg, Julia Gruen at the Keith Haring Foundation, Robert Ward.

Unrepentant and supportive Dead freaks: Blair Jackson, Gary Lambert, Eric Schwartz, Eric Taylor, Barry Barnes, Michael Parrish, Barry Smolin.

Hosts, comrades, and helpful associates: Christian Crumlish, Owen Poindexter, Rachel Terp, Andrew Fisher, Erica Lam, Allison Feinstein, Reid Spice, David Van Brink, Tory Ervin, Lisa Jane Persky, Andy Zax, Shannon Forney, Jen Strauss, Mike Rosenthal, Dave Mandl, Dominic Umile, Peter Crosman, Richard B. Simon, Tony Weiss, Michael Slaboch, Akron/Family, M. Geddes Gengras, Greg Davis, Ellie Sanders, Spacefuzz, Tom Ceraulo, Chris Harriott, @ThoughtsOnGD, Dominic Devito, Blanca Myers, the Baby, and the spirit of Hairy Mendoza.

And last: Caitlin, my love.

Index